AUBURN UNIVER
SURVEY OF WORLD HISTORY

VOLUME 1

PREHISTORY TO 1400

CUSTOM EDITION CONTAINING MATERIALS FROM

Societies and Cultures in World History
MARK KISHLANSKY
PATRICK GEARY
PATRICIA O'BRIEN
R. BIN WONG

World Civilizations: The Global Experience, **Second Edition**
PETER N. STEARNS
MICHAEL ADAS
STUART B. SCHWARTZ

Civilizations of the World: The Human Adventure, **Third Edition**
RICHARD L. GREAVES
ROBERT ZALLER
PHILIP V. CANNISTRARO
RHOADS MURPHEY

Civilization Past and Present, **Eighth Edition**
T. WALTER WALLBANK (LATE)
ALASTAIR M. TAYLOR
NELS M. BAILKEY
GEORGE F. JEWSBURY
CLYDE J. LEWIS
NEIL J. HACKETT

LONGMAN

An imprint of Addison Wesley Longman, Inc.

New York • Reading, Massachusetts • Menlo Park, California • Harlow, England
Don Mills, Ontario • Sydney • Mexico City • Madrid • Amsterdam

Auburn University Survey of World History
Volume 1: Prehistory to 1400

Auburn University Survey of World History, Volume 1: Prehistory to 1400, is a custom version of specially selected material from *Societies and Cultures in World History; World Civilizations: The Global Experience,* Second Edition; *Civilizations of the World: The Human Adventure,* Third Edition; and *Civilization Past and Present.* The source of material in this custom version is indicated by book title, chapter number, and chapter title at the bottom of each page. Selection and organization of material have been determined by the instructors at the institution for which this custom version has been created. The authors of the aforementioned works are not responsible for the selection and order of material in this custom version or for the accuracy of any material in this version that did not appear in their books.

ISBN 0-201-45658-3

1 2 3 4 5 6 7 8 9 10—ML—01 00 99 98

WORLD HISTORY AT AUBURN UNIVERSITY

The study of history that sought to place the United States' experience into a larger context than that offered by national frontiers was largely a product of World War I. Courses in "Why We Went to War" were instituted at campuses around the country at the behest of the War Department as part of a war preparedness program. University faculties, drawn from the humanities and social sciences to teach these courses, generally resorted to an expanded exposition of recent European history to explain the origins of the war and to rationalize American involvement.

Following World War I, many colleges and universities, reluctant to drop such a popular offering, recast the course as Western civilization and justified it as essential to an understanding of the twentieth-century world. The first generation of textbooks for these courses were frequently European histories supplemented with a few chapters on ancient and classical origins for background and a few more chapters expanding the modern content to include European cultural offshoots resulting from colonizing activities. Only gradually did textbooks emerge that were written from the broader perspective of the Western heritage.

The truly global dimensions of World War II caused some educators to question the adequacy of the Western civilization courses as a structure within which to analyze the contemporary world. The Cold War contest of the 1950s and 1960s encouraged the move toward a global framework to explain the struggle between the Free World (Western) and the Communist World (non-Western). Again textbooks lagged behind events. The early world histories were Western civilization texts with chapters added on the non-Western world without much effort at integration. Only in the 1980s did textbooks with a truly global perspective become available.

The emergence of global histories in the 1980s was in part a response to a curricular change. Many leading schools in the United States, recognizing that the old bipolar view of the world (that world events revolved around Washington and Moscow) was inadequate in and of itself and that the Cold War that had engendered it was passing from the scene, began to offer world history courses. The increasing recognition of the role of non-European minorities within the United States and the increasing economic and political importance of non-European areas of the world also encouraged this move to a broader and more objective perspective for the study of human historical development.

Auburn University pioneered a world history course in the late 1940s. Twenty years later, nine quarter hours of world history became part of a core program of study required of most students in the liberal arts curricula. During the 1970s, a course sequence in technology and civilization was introduced as an alternative to world history. The three-course world history/technology and civilization sequence became part of a university-wide core curriculum adopted by Auburn in 1990.

The world history core curriculum at Auburn consists of three three-quarter-hour courses (HY101, HY102, and HY103) and their honors program equivalents (HY171, HY172, HY173). HY101 is a history of world civilization from prehistory to 1400 C.E. HY102 carries the drama of human development from 1400 to 1815. HY103 completes the series, covering events from 1815 to the present. These courses may be taken in any order, though most students prefer to follow the chronological sequence presented by the HY101-HY102-HY103 arrangement.

University regulations allow substituting the history of technology and civilization sequence (HY121, HY122, and HY123) or the Human Odyssey program (U270, U271, and U272) for the world history requirement, but do not allow mixing separate courses from two or more of these three sequences. Students beginning in the world history series must complete all three courses in the world history curricula to graduate.

The objective of Auburn's world history program is to expose Auburn students to the record of human existence and, as stated in the Auburn University Bulletin, to "foster the development of educated citizens" for the "enhancement of society." From this knowledge of the human past students should develop an "appreciation for their culture and the world in which they live." This objective involves an examination of the causes and effects of the human experience in order to synthesize the various areas of human endeavor in its many and diverse cultures. These areas of endeavor include

1. Economic history—the record of human efforts to produce, distribute, and consume goods and services;
2. Political history—the record of human efforts to control, direct, and influence the leadership of a society, the actions and conduct of government, and the relationships between and among societies;
3. Social history—the record of human relationships, including the interaction of the individual or group within a society and the organization of individuals or groups within a society;
4. Cultural history—the record of human attempts to express themselves through art, architecture, literature, and music;
5. Technological history—the record of human attempts to employ tools and energy in support of human sustenance;
6. Intellectual history—the record of human thought and attempts to understand the physical and metaphysical bases for life;
7. Military history—the record of human strife;
8. Religious history—the record of human beliefs, practices, ceremonies, and worship of gods or supernatural forces and the values and morals generated by those beliefs;
9. Historiography—the writing of the human record.

This knowledge of the past should help establish a foundation for the liberal education that is necessary for every free citizen.

Contents

CHAPTER 1

The Agrarian Revolution and the Birth of Civilization

KEY TERMS

Homo sapiens	*domestication*
Paleolithic Era	*pastoralism*
hunter-gatherer people	*Jericho*
Neolithic Revolution	*Çatal Hüyük*

DISCUSSION QUESTIONS

What factors encouraged the development of agriculture?

How did agriculture change the lives of Neolithic people?

What purposes did the earliest towns serve?

Introduction

This history of human civilizations focuses on only a tiny portion—roughly 9000 years—of the more than 2.5 million years since the genus *Homo* first appeared in the savannas of eastern Africa (and perhaps contemporaneously further east in parts of Asia). Within this 9000-year time span, we will concentrate on societies that we consider civilized by virtue of their reliance on sedentary agriculture for sustenance and their ability to produce crop surpluses that support specialized elites as well as nonfarming, trading, and manufacturing groups. In most civilizations, agricultural surpluses and specialization have also given rise to concentrations of human populations in towns and cities and to complex social divisions and social stratification based on a mix of birth, sex, and occupation. The era of civilized life so defined makes up less than a quarter of the 40,000 years that our own human species, *Homo sapiens,* has inhabited the earth. But within the civilized societies that developed in this limited time span, most of human history has been lived.

Our emphasis in defining *civilizations* on the basis of the economic circumstances that give rise to them and the social patterns that characterize them makes it necessary to explore the origins of early civilizations. We need to understand why humans opted for this form of organization and path of development, and how they were able to make the transition from small-scale, nonspecialized, subsistence societies to city-states with their increasingly complex division of labor. Before studying the varying patterns of civilized life that are the focus of world history, we will examine some of the alternative modes of human organization that had evolved by the end of the transition period between the *Paleolithic* (Old Stone) *Age* and the *Neolithic* (New Stone) *Age.* In this period, from roughly 12,000 to 8000 B.C.E., changes occurred in human organization and food production that made possible the surpluses and specialization that were essential to the first stirrings of civilized life in the eighth millennium B.C.E. The economic and social patterns that developed after 8000 B.C.E. were in turn critical to the surge of invention between 4000 and 3000 B.C.E. that laid the basis for the first civilizations.

The rise of farming in the Neolithic era (between roughly 8000 and 5000 B.C.E.) is generally regarded as the source of the first truly revolutionary transformations in human history. But the thousands of years over which this process occurred suggest that it was not revolutionary in the usual sense of a rapid or abrupt change. Rather, the development of agriculture profoundly altered the relationships between human societies and their environments and between humans and other, often competing, animal species. The shift to agriculture also altered the way humans lived their daily lives.

Sedentary farming was made possible by technological breakthroughs that made the survival of the human species more secure and gave humans a much greater capacity to remake their environments to suit their needs. The most visible signs of this capacity were the spread of regularly cultivated fields and especially the development of towns, such as Jericho between 8500 and 7500 B.C.E. and Çatal Huyuk around 5500 B.C.E. Human control over other animal species was evidenced by the growing

	LATE PALEOLITHIC	TRANSITION PHASE	NEOLITHIC AGE
EASTERN HEMISPHERE	**18,000–10,000** Central Russian mammoth bone settlements **12,000** Domestication of dogs	**10,500–8000** Natufian settlements	**8500–5000** Development of farming in the Middle East **7000** Full-fledged town at Jericho **6250–5400** Çatal Huyuk at its peak **8500** Domestication of sheep **7500–6500** Domestication of pigs, goats, cattle
WESTERN HEMISPHERE			**5600** Beans domesticated
	18,000 B.C.E. **12,000** B.C.E.	**10,000** B.C.E.	**8000** B.C.E. **6000** B.C.E.

herds of domesticated goats, sheep, and cattle that became important sources of food and materials for clothing and shelter. Trade between these centers of settlement and production greatly increased contacts between different human groups, enhancing the innovation and increase of resources that were key features of the Neolithic era. Transformations of this sort occurred in all the areas of the world where civilizations emerged in the last two or three millennia B.C.E. Indeed, these transformations proved to be an essential prelude to the emergence of a variety of civilizations.

Human Life in the Era of Hunters and Gatherers

Focal Point: During the Paleolithic (Old Stone) Age, *Homo sapiens,* one of several humanlike species, had gained clear advantages over its rivals. Superior intelligence, manual dexterity, and the tool making and language development they made possible were critical to this outcome. By 10,000 B.C.E., *Homo sapiens* had spread over much of the earth. Most human groups in this era supported themselves by *hunting and gathering,* but by the end of the Paleolithic Age, many peoples were experimenting with agriculture and permanent settlements.

By the end of the Paleolithic era in 12,000 B.C.E., humans had evolved in physical appearance and mental capacity to roughly the same level as today. Our species, *Homo sapiens,* had been competing with increasing success for game and campsites with other humanlike creatures for nearly 30,000 years. *Homo sapiens'* enlarged brain, critical to the survival of all of the branches of the genus *Homo,* was virtually the same size as that of modern humans. The erect posture of Stone Age humans freed their hands. The combination of these free hands with opposable thumbs and a large brain made it possible for different human species to craft and manipulate tools and weapons of increasing sophistication. These implements helped to offset the humans' marked inferiority in body strength and speed to rival predators, such as wolves and wild cats, as well as to many of the creatures that humans themselves hunted. A more highly developed brain also allowed humans to transform cries and grunts into the patterned sounds that make up language. Language greatly enhanced the possibilities for cooperation and a sense of cohesion within the small bands that were the predominant form of human social organization in this era. By the last phase of the Paleolithic epoch, these advantages had made *Homo sapiens* a species capable of mastering the earth.

Paleolithic Culture

No matter how much *Homo sapiens* might have developed in physical appearance and brain capacity by around 12,000 B.C.E., its culture, with some exceptions, was not radically different from the cultures of rival human species such as the Neanderthals, who had died out thousands of years earlier. Fire, perhaps the most central element in the material culture of Paleolithic peoples, had been mastered nearly a half million years earlier.

METAL AGE

5000–2000 Yangshao culture in North China
c. 1766 Emergence of Shang kingdom in China
c. 3100 Rise of Egyptian civilization
3500–2350 Civilization of Sumer
2500–1500 Indus civilization in South Asia
4000–3000 Age of innovation in the Middle East: Introduction of writing, metalworking, the wheel, and the plow

5000 Domestication of maize (corn)
2000 Kotosh culture in Peru
1000–500 Olmec civilization in Mesoamerica
400 Potatoes domesticated
3500 Llama domesticated
1700–1300 Rise of village culture in Mesoamerica

4000 B.C.E. **2000** B.C.E. **1** C.E.

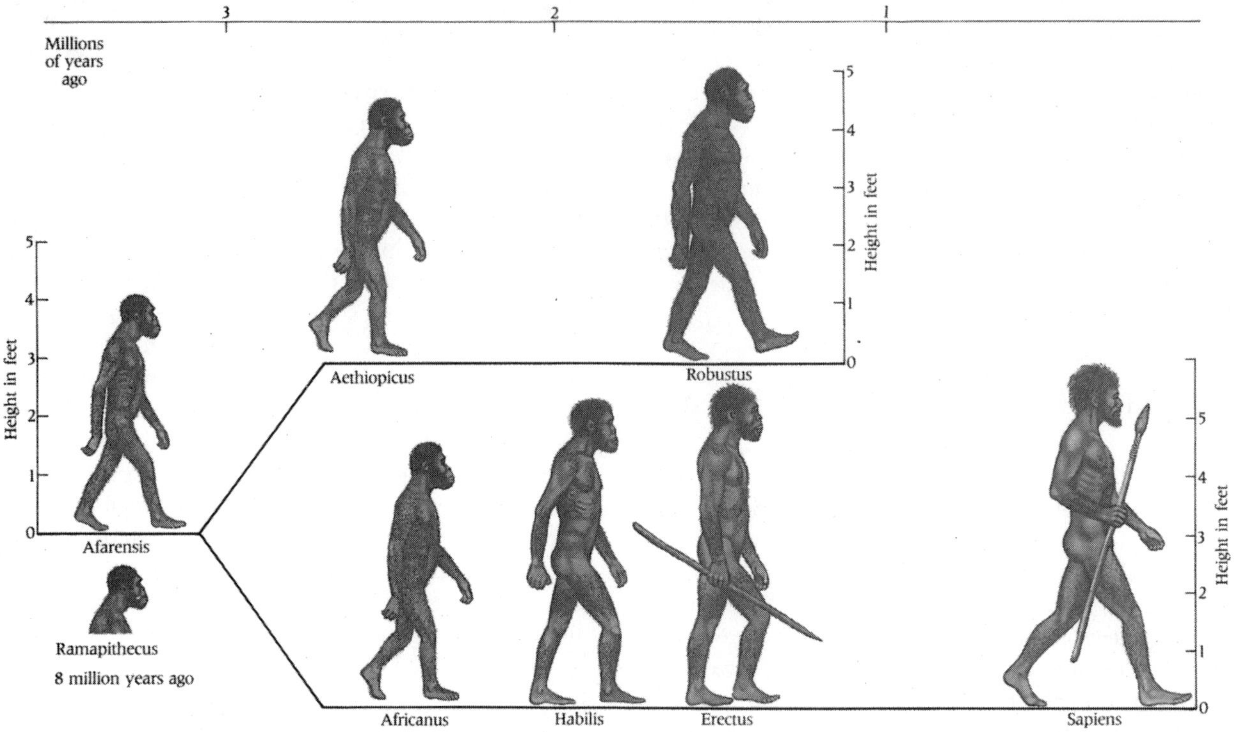

The hominoids' upright posture, which freed their hands, meant that over long periods of time Homo sapiens *could develop weapons and tools.*

Originally snatched from conflagrations caused by lightning or lava flows, fire was domesticated as humans developed techniques to preserve glowing embers and to start fires by rubbing sticks and other materials together. The control of fire led to numerous improvements in the lives of Stone Age peoples. It rendered edible a much wider range of foods, particularly animal flesh, which was virtually the only source of protein in a culture without cows, goats, or chickens and thus lacking in milk, cheese, and eggs. Cooked meat, which was easier to digest, may also have been more effectively preserved and stored, thus giving Stone Age peoples an additional buffer against the constant threat of starvation. In addition, fire was used to treat animal hides for clothing and to harden wooden weapons and tools. Its light and warmth became the focal point of human campsites.

By late Paleolithic (Old Stone) Age times, human groups survived by combining hunting and fishing with the gathering of fruits, berries, grains, and root crops that grew in the wild. They had created a considerable number of tools to assist them in these critical endeavors. Tools of wood and bone have perished; thus, surviving stone tools are our main evidence of the technology of this epoch. These tools had advanced considerably by the late Old Stone Age. Early human tools, discovered by archeologists at sites well over 2 million years old, were made by breaking off the edges of stone cores to create crude points or rough cutting surfaces. By the late Paleolithic period, humans had grown much more adept at working stone. They preferred to chip and sharpen flakes broken off the core stone. These chips could be fashioned into knife blades, arrow points, or choppers, which had a wide range of uses from hunting and warfare to skinning animal carcasses and harvesting wild plants.

Earlier human groups had produced evidence of artistic expression: small figurines and decorated implements. The late Paleolithic was a period of particularly intense creativity. Fine miniature sculpture, beads and other forms of jewelry, and carved bones were produced by Paleolithic peoples, but their most impressive artistic contributions were the cave paintings that have been discovered at sites like those in southern France and Spain. Other paintings—and in many cases small sculptures, including those found at a number of Middle Eastern sites—appear to have religious significance. They may have been intended, for example, to depict prominent

Early human groups developed a variety of stone tools. The tools shown here include weapon points (second row from the top), scrapers for peeling off animal hides or working wood (third row from the top), and a hammerstone (lower left).

deities or to promote fertility. There is also speculation that paintings at some sites may represent early counting systems or primitive calendars. Whatever their purpose, the art of the Old Stone Age era suggests quite a sophisticated level of thinking. It also indicates that humans were becoming increasingly interested in expressing themselves artistically and in leaving lasting images of their activities and concerns.

The Spread of Human Culture

The possession of fire and tools with which to make clothing and shelters made it possible for different human species to extend the range of their habitation far beyond the areas where they had originated. During the last Ice Age, which began about 2.5 million years ago and ended around 8000 B.C.E., humans first moved northward from Africa into Europe and eastward from the present-day Middle East into central Asia, India, and East Asia. Neanderthals and related peoples were found across this zone as late as 35,000 B.C.E., and some archeologists claim that by then they may also have begun to migrate across a land bridge into the continents we now call North and South America. Glaciation, which had caused a significant drop in sea levels, resulted in land bridges to the New World and Australia. By around 12,000 B.C.E., human colonies were found in North and South America and in the south and west of Australia. Thus, by the late Paleolithic period, groups of the *Homo sapiens sapiens* species had colonized all of the continents except Antarctica.

Human Society and Daily Life at the End of the Old Stone Age

Most human societies in the Old Stone Age consisted of small groups that migrated regularly in pursuit of game animals and wild plants. But recent archeological research has shown that in some places, natural conditions and human ingenuity permitted some groups to establish settlements where they lived for much of the year, and in some cases for generation after generation. These settled communities harvested wild grains that grew in abundance in many areas. After surviving for centuries in this way, some of these communities made the transition to true farming by domesticating plants and animals near their permanent village sites. Many Paleolithic peoples who established enduring settlements did not advance to domesticated agricultural production; in fact, they often reverted to a migratory hunting-and-gathering existence.

The rejection of full-fledged agriculture and the reversion to migratory lifestyles caution us against seeing farming as an inevitable stage in human development. There was no simple progression from hunting-and-gathering peoples to settled foraging societies and then to genuine farming communities. Rather, human groups experimented with different strategies for survival. Climatic changes, the availability of water for crop irrigation, dietary preferences, and patterns of procreation affected the strategy adopted by a particular group. Only those groups involved in crop and animal domestication, however, have proved capable of producing civilizations.

However successful a particular group proved to be at hunting and gathering, few could support a band larger than 20 to 30 men, women, and children. Depen-

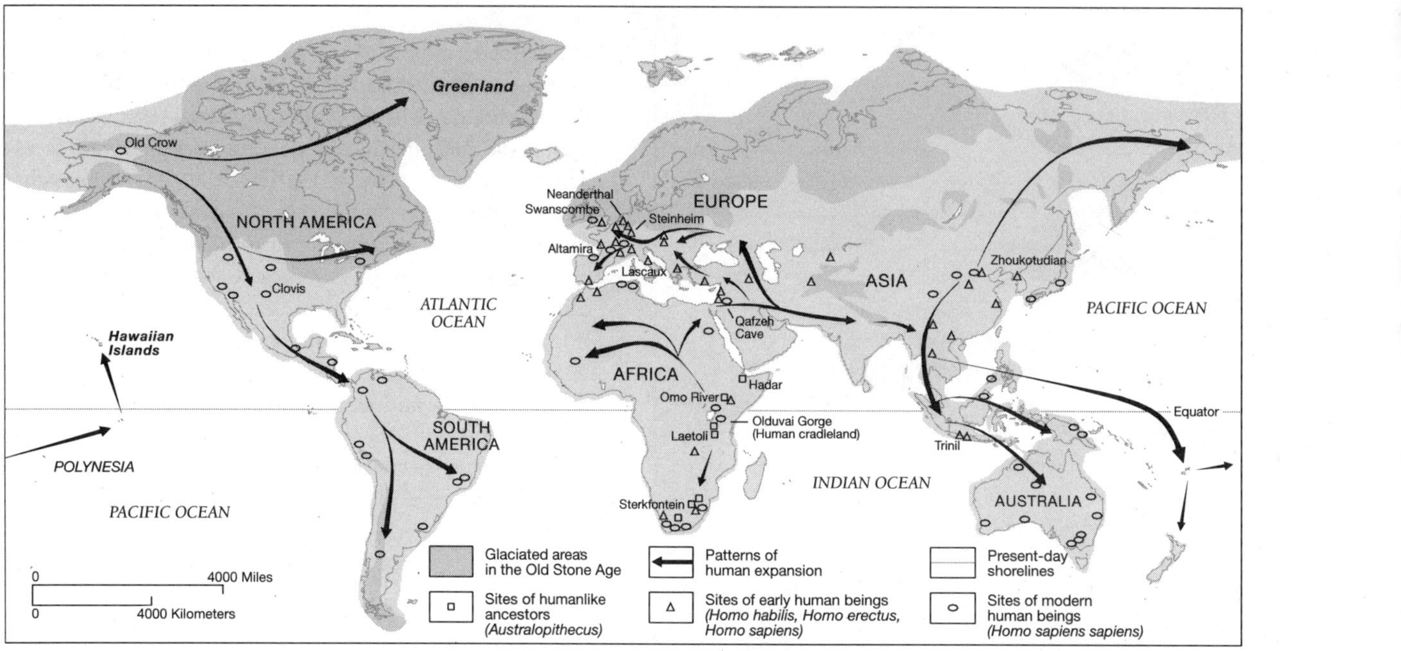

The Spread of Human Populations, About 10,000 B.C.E.

dence on migrating herds of game dictated that these bands were nomadic, though many moved back and forth between the same forest and grazing areas year after year. The migration patterns meant that small numbers of humans needed an extensive land area to support themselves, and consequently human population densities were very low.

Though we imagine Stone Age peoples living in caves, recent research suggests that most preferred to live on open ground. The migratory peoples who lived on hilltops or in forest clearings built temporary shelters of skins and leaves or grass thatching. Their flimsy campsites were readily abandoned when herd movements or threats from competing bands prompted migration. Though it is likely that bands developed a sense of territoriality, boundaries were vague, and much interhuman strife focused on rival claims to sources of game and wild foods.

Within each band, labor was divided according to gender. Men hunted and fished in riverine or coastal areas. Because they became skilled in the use of weapons in the hunt, it is also likely that men protected the band from animal predators and raids by other human groups. Though women's roles were less adventuresome and aggressive, they were arguably more critical to the survival of the band. Women gathered the foods that provided the basic subsistence of the band and permitted its survival in times when hunting parties were unsuccessful. Women also became adept in the application of medicinal plants, which were the only means that Paleolithic peoples had to ward off disease. Because life expectancy was short—20 years or less on the average—and mortality rates for women in labor and infants were very high, women had to give birth many times in order for the band to increase its numbers even slightly.

Settling Down: Dead Ends and Transitions

Though most humans lived in small hunting-and-gathering bands until well into the era of the agrarian revolution between 8000 and 5000 B.C.E., some prefarming peoples worked out a very different strategy of survival. They managed to devise more intensive hunting- and-gathering patterns that permitted them to establish semipermanent and even permanent settlements and to support larger and more complex forms of social organization. Among the most spectacular of the Paleolithic settlements are those of central Russia. Apparently there was an abundance of large but slow woolly mammoths in that region some 20,000 years ago. The hunting techniques of the local peoples produced a supply of meat that, when supplemented by wild plant foods gathered in the area, made it possible for them to live in the same place throughout much of the year. Their dependence on the mammoths is suggested by the bones found in refuse pits at the settlement sites and by the bones of the larger mammoths that were used extensively for the walls and roofing of dwellings.

The storage pits for food and the other materials found at the sites of the central Russian settlements suggest that the mammoth-bone dwellers participated in trading networks that involved groups in the Black Sea region nearly 500 miles away. Burial patterns and differing degrees of bodily decoration also indicate that there were clear status differences among the groups that inhabited the settlements. Mammoth-bone communities lasted from about 18,000 to 10,000 B.C.E., when they suddenly disappeared for reasons that are still unknown.

Even more sophisticated than the central Russian settlements were those of the *Natufian complex,* which extended over much of present-day Israel, Jordan, and Lebanon. Climate changes, which occurred between 12,000 and 11,000 B.C.E., enabled wild barley and wheat plants to spread over much of this area. When supplemented with nuts and the meat of gazelles and other game, these wild grains proved sufficient to support numerous and quite densely populated settlements on a permanent basis. Between about 10,500 and 8000 B.C.E., the Natufian culture flourished. The population at Natufian settlement sites reached as high as six to seven times that of other early Neolithic communities. The Natufians developed quite sophisticated techniques of storing grain, and they devised pestles and grinding slabs to prepare it to eat. They built circular and oval dwellings of stone that were occupied year round for centuries.

The evidence we have from housing layout, burial sites, jewelry, and other materials indicates that, like the mammoth-bone dwellers of central Russia, Natufian society was stratified. Clothing appears to have been used to distinguish a person's rank, and grand burial ceremonies marked the passing of community chieftains. There is also evidence that Natufian society was *matrilocal*—young men went to live with their wives' families—and *matrilineal*—family descent and inheritance were traced through the female line. The fact that women gathered food crops in the wild may explain the power and influence they enjoyed in Natufian settlements.

The Natufian strategy for survival did not involve the development of new tools or techniques for production. It rested primarily on the intensification of gathering wild grains and the improvement of storage techniques. The Natufians' concentration on a couple of grain staples, gazelle meat, and nuts rendered the culture vulnerable through overspecialization. After 9000 B.C.E., the climate of the region where the Natufian settlements were located grew more and more arid. The grains and game on which they had grown dependent were reduced or vanished from many locations. One thousand years later, all the Natufian sites had been abandoned. Some villagers reverted to migratory hunting and gathering in an effort to broaden the range of animals they could hunt and the foods they could harvest from the wild. Other villagers—usually those located near large and reliable sources of water—domesticated the grains they had once gathered in the woodlands.

A Precarious Existence

Until the late Old Stone Age era, about 12,000 B.C.E., advances in human technology and social organization were remarkably slow compared with the advances that have occurred since about 8000 B.C.E. Millions of years of evolution of the genus *Homo* had produced small numbers of humans mostly scattered in tiny bands across six continents. On the average, the lives of members of these bands were—to paraphrase a cynical, 17th-century English philosopher, Thomas Hobbes—violent and short. They crouched around their campfires in constant fear of animal predators and human enemies. They were at the mercy of the elements and helpless in the face of injury or disease. They had a few crude tools and weapons; their nomadic existence reflected their dependence on the feeding cycles of migrating animals.

The smaller numbers of human groups that lived in permanent settlements had better shelters, a more secure supply of food, and larger communities on which to draw in their relentless struggle for survival. But their lifestyles were precarious: their specialized hunting-and-gathering practices meant that shifts in grazing patterns or the climate could undermine their carefully developed cultures. Late Paleolithic humans had considerably improved on earlier, and by then extinct, versions of the species. But there was little to suggest that within a few thousand years they would radically transform the environments in which they lived and would dominate all other forms of life.

Agriculture and the Origins of Civilization: The Neolithic Revolution

Focal Point: In the Neolithic (New Stone) Age, between roughly 8000 and 3500 B.C.E., some human societies, in different areas over much of the globe, crossed

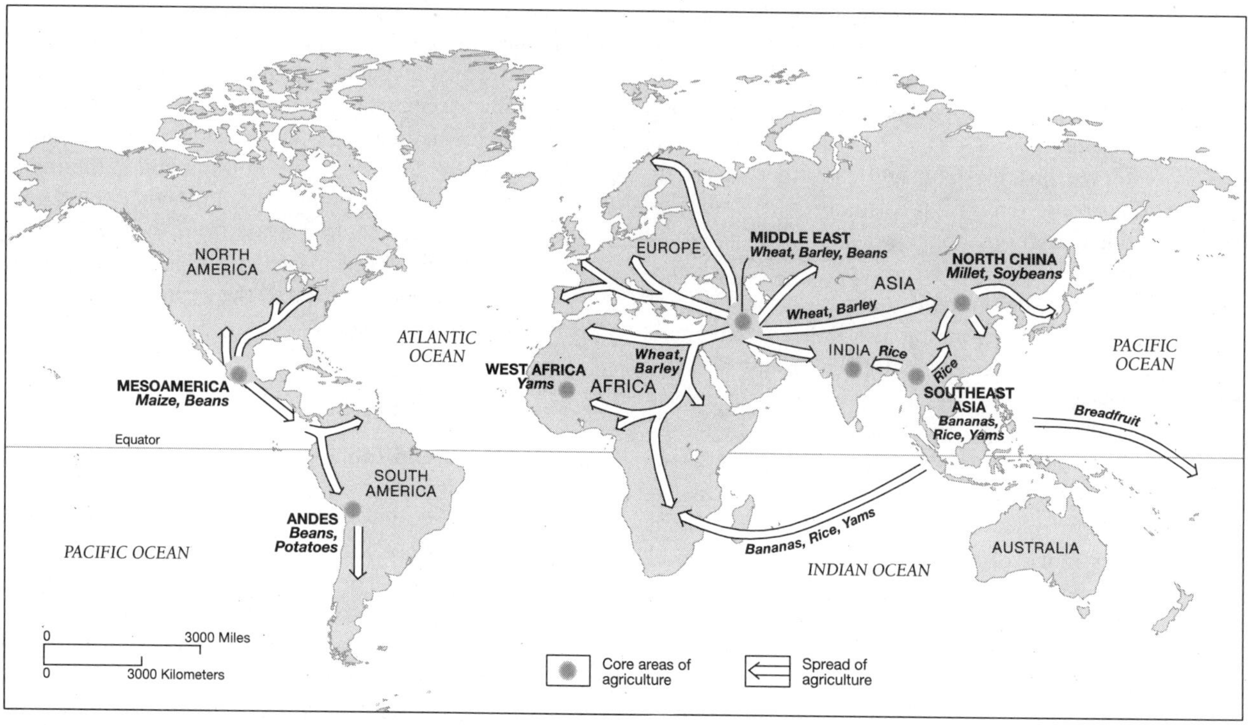

The Spread of Agriculture

one of the great watersheds in all of human history. They mastered sedentary agriculture and domesticated animals that would prove critical to human development, such as cattle, sheep and horses. These innovations produced the surpluses and rising populations that made possible the rise of genuine towns and the increasing specialization of occupations within human societies.

There was nothing natural or inevitable about the development of agriculture. Because cultivation of plants requires more labor than hunting and gathering, we can assume that Stone Age humans gave up their former ways of life reluctantly and slowly. In fact, peoples such as the Bushmen of Southwest Africa still follow them today. But between about 8000 and 3500 B.C.E., increasing numbers of humans shifted to dependence on cultivated crops and domesticated animals for their subsistence. By about 7000 B.C.E., their tools and skills had advanced sufficiently to enable cultivating peoples to support towns with over one thousand people, such as Jericho in the valley of the Jordan River and Çatal Huyuk in present-day Turkey. By 3500 B.C.E., agricultural peoples in the Middle East could support sufficient numbers of noncultivating specialists to give rise to the first civilizations. As this pattern spread to or developed independently in other centers across the globe, the character of most human lives and the history of the species as a whole were fundamentally transformed.

Because there are no written records of the transition period between 8000 and 5000 B.C.E., when many animals were first domesticated and plants were cultivated on a regular basis, we cannot be certain why and how some peoples adopted these new ways of producing food and other necessities of life. Climatic changes associated with the retreat of the glaciers at the end of the last Ice Age (about 12,000 B.C.E.), may have played an important role. These climatic shifts prompted the migration of many big game animals to new pasturelands in northern areas. They also left a dwindling supply of game for human hunters in areas such as the Middle East, where agriculture first arose and many animals were first domesticated. Climatic shifts also led to changes in the distribution and growing patterns of wild grains and other crops on which hunters and gatherers depended.

In addition, it is likely that the shift to sedentary farming was prompted in part by an increase in human populations in certain areas. This population growth may have been caused by changes in the climate and plant and animal life, forcing hunting bands to move into the territories where these shifts had been minimal. It is also pos-

Interior of Skara Brae, a prehistoric dwelling.

sible that population growth occurred within these unaffected regions because the hunting-and-gathering pattern reached higher levels of productivity. Peoples like the Natufians found that their human communities could grow significantly by intensively harvesting grains that grew in the wild. As the population grew, more and more attention was given to the grain harvest, which eventually led to the conscious and systematic cultivation of plants and thus the agrarian revolution.

The Domestication of Plants and Animals

The peoples who first cultivated cereal grains had long observed them growing in the wild and gleaned their seeds, as they gathered other plants for their leaves and roots. In late Paleolithic times, both wild barley and wheat grew over large areas in present-day Turkey, Iraq, Syria, Jordan, Lebanon, and Israel. Hunting-and-gathering bands in these areas may have consciously experimented with planting and nurturing seeds taken from the wild, or they may have accidentally discovered the principles of domestication by observing the growth of seeds dropped near their campsites.

However it began, the practice of agriculture caught on only gradually. Archeological evidence suggests that the first agriculturists retained their hunting-and-gathering activities as a hedge against the ever-present threat of starvation. But as Stone Age peoples became more adept at cultivating a growing range of crops, including various fruits, olives, and protein-rich legumes such as peas and beans, the effort they expended on activities outside agriculture diminished.

It is probable that the earliest farmers broadcast wild seeds, a practice that cut down on labor but sharply reduced the potential yield. Over the centuries, more and more care was taken to select the best grain for seed and to mix different strains in ways that improved both crop yields and resistance to plant diseases. As the time required to tend growing plants and the dependence on agricultural production for subsistence increased, some roving bands chose to settle down, while others practiced a mix of hunting and shifting cultivation that allowed them to continue to move about.

Though several animals may have been domesticated before the discovery of agriculture, the two processes combined to make up the critical transformation in human culture called the Neolithic revolution. Different animal species were tamed in different ways that reflected both their own natures and the ways in which they interacted with humans. Dogs, for example, were originally wolves that hunted humans or scavenged at their campsites. As early as 12,000 B.C.E., Stone Age peoples found that wolf pups could be tamed and trained to track and corner game. The strains of dogs that gradually developed proved adept at controlling herd animals like sheep. Relatively docile and defenseless herds of sheep could be domesticated once their leaders had been captured and tamed. Sheep, goats, and pigs (which also were scavengers at human campsites) were first domesticated in the Middle East between 8500 and 7000 B.C.E. Horned cattle, which could run faster and were better able to defend themselves than wild sheep, were not tamed until about 6500 B.C.E.

Domesticated animals such as cattle and sheep provided New Stone Age humans with additional sources of protein-rich meat, and in some cases, milk. Animal hides and wool greatly expanded the materials from which clothes, containers, shelters, and crude boats could be crafted. Animal horns and bones could be carved or used for needles and other utensils. Because plows and wheels did not come into use until the Bronze Age (c. 4000–3500 B.C.E.), most Neolithic peoples made little use of animal power for farming, transportation, or travel. There is evidence, however, that peoples in northern areas used tamed reindeer to pull sledges, and those farther south used camels for transporting goods. More importantly, Neolithic peoples used domesticated herd animals as a steady source of manure to enrich the soil and thus improve the yield of the crops that were gradually becoming the basis of their livelihood.

The Spread of the Neolithic Revolution

The greater labor involved in cultivation, and the fact that it did not at first greatly enhance the peoples' security or living standards, caused many bands to stay with long-tested subsistence strategies. Through most of the Neolithic period, sedentary agricultural communities coexisted with more numerous bands of hunters and gatherers, migratory cultivators, and hunters and fishers. Even after sedentary agriculture became the basis for the livelihood of the majority of humans, hunters and gatherers and shifting cultivators held out in many areas of the globe.

The domestication of animals also gave rise to *pastoralism,* which has proved to be the strongest competitor to sedentary agriculture as a way of life throughout most of the world. Pastoralism has thrived in semiarid areas such as central Asia, the Sudanic belt south of the Sahara desert in Africa, and the savanna zone of East and South Africa. These areas were incapable of supporting dense or large populations. The nomadic, herding way of life has tended to produce independent and hardy peoples, well versed in the military skills needed not only for their survival but also to challenge more heavily populated agrarian societies. Horse-riding nomads who herd sheep or cattle have destroyed powerful kingdoms and laid the foundations for vast empires. The camel nomads of Arabia played critical roles in the rise of Islamic civilization. The cattle-herding peoples of Central, East, and South Africa produced some of the most formidable preindustrial military organizations. Only in the rather recent period of the Industrial Revolution has the power of nomadic peoples been irreparably broken and the continuation of their cultures threatened by the steady encroachment of sedentary peoples.

In the era of the Neolithic revolution (roughly 8000–5000 B.C.E.), agriculture was far from the dominant mode of support for human societies. But those who adopted it survived and increased in numbers. They also passed on their techniques of production to other peoples. The cultivation of wheat and barley spread throughout the Middle East and eastward to India. These crops also spread northward to Europe, where oats and rye were added later. From Egypt, the cultivation of grain crops and fibers, such as flax and cotton used for clothing, spread to peoples along the Nile in the interior of Africa, along the North African coast, and across the vast savanna zone south of the Sahara desert.

Agriculture in the African rain forest zone farther south evolved independently in the 2nd millennium B.C.E. and was based on root crops such as cassava and tree crops such as bananas and palm nuts. In northern China during the Neolithic period, a millet-based agricultural system developed along the Huanghe or Yellow River basin. From this core region, it spread in the last millennium B.C.E. east toward the North China Sea and southward toward the Yangtze basin. A later but independent agricultural revolution based on rice began in mainland Southeast Asia sometime before 5000 B.C.E. and slowly spread into South China and India and to the islands of Southeast Asia. In the Americas maize- (corn-), manioc-, and sweet potato–based agrarian systems arose in Mesoamerica (Mexico and Central America today) and present-day Peru. Long before the arrival of Columbus in the Americas in 1492 C.E., these and other crops had spread through large portions of the continents of the Western Hemisphere, from the temperate woodlands of the North Atlantic coast to the rain forests of the Amazon region. Thus, varying patterns of agricultural production were disseminated on all the inhabited continents except Australia, to virtually all the regions of the globe with sufficient rainfall and suitable temperatures.

The Transformation of Material Life

With the development of agriculture, humans began to radically transform the environments in which they lived. A growing portion of humans became sedentary cultivators who cleared the lands around their settlements and controlled the plants that grew and the animals that grazed on them. The greater presence of humans was also apparent in the steadily growing size and numbers of settlements. These were found both in areas that they had long inhabited and in new regions that farming allowed them to settle. This great increase in the number of sedentary farmers is primarily responsible for the leap in human population during the Neolithic transition. For tens of thousands of years before agriculture was developed, the total number of humans had fluctuated between an estimated five and eight million persons. By 4000 B.C.E., after four or five millennia of farming, their number had risen to 60 or 70 million. Hunting-and-gathering bands managed to subsist in the zones between cultivated areas and continued to war and trade with sedentary peoples. But villages and cultivated fields became the dominant features of human habitation over much of the globe.

The growth of sedentary farming communities in the Neolithic era greatly accelerated the pace of technological and social change. The relatively sudden surge in invention and social complexity in the Neolithic era marks one of the great turning points in human history. Increased reliance on sedentary cultivation led to the development of a wide variety of agricultural implements, from digging sticks used to break up the soil and axes to clear forested areas to the introduction of the plow. Techniques of seed selection, planting, fertilization, and weeding improved steadily. By the end of the Neolithic period, human societies in several areas had devised ways of storing rainwater and rechanneling river water to irrigate plants. The reservoirs, canals, dikes, and sluices that permitted water storage and control represented another major advance in the ability of humans to remake their environment.

More and better tools and permanent settlements gave rise to larger, more elaborate, commodious housing and the construction of community ritual centers. Building materials varied greatly by region, but sun-dried bricks, wattle (interwoven branches, usually plastered with mud), and stone structures were associated with early agricultural communities. Seasonal harvests made improved techniques of food storage essential. At first, baskets and leather containers were employed. By the early Neolithic period pottery—which protected stored foods better from moisture and dust—was known to several cultures in the Middle East.

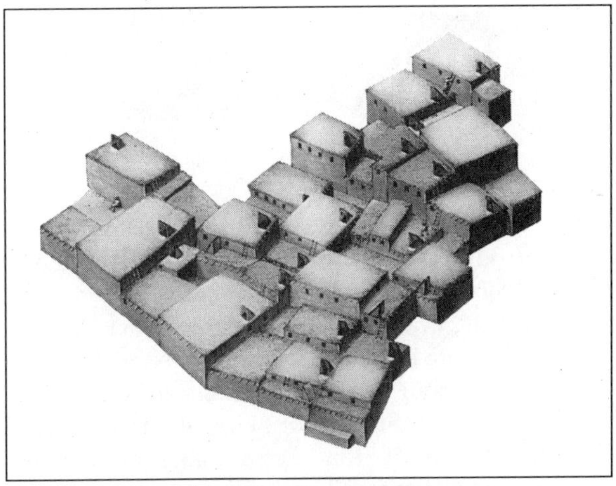

This artist's reconstruction depicts the layout of living units in the town of Çatal Huyuk. A family dwelling included an open hearth and an oven in the wall, clearly demarcated and slightly raised sleeping areas, and benches along the walls.

Houses in early agricultural settlements usually included special storage areas, and most were centered on clay or stone hearths that were ventilated by a hole in the roof. The presence of stored food in early villages made the houses tempting targets for nomadic bands or rival settlements. For that reason they were increasingly fortified. More dependable and varied food supplies, walls, and sturdy houses greatly enhanced the security and comfort of human groups. These conditions spurred higher rates of procreation and lowered mortality rates, at least in times when crop yields were high.

Social Differentiation

The surplus production that agriculture made possible was the key to the social transformations that made up another dimension of the Neolithic revolution. Surpluses meant that cultivators could exchange part of their harvest for the specialized services and products of noncultivators, such as toolmakers and weavers. Human communities became differentiated on an occupational basis. Political and religious leaders arose and eventually formed elite classes, whose members intermarried and became involved in ruling and ceremonies on a full-time basis. But in the Neolithic period, the specialized production of stone tools, weapons, and perhaps pottery was a more important consequence of the development of

DOCUMENT

Women in Early Art

The earliest writing system that we know of was not introduced until around 3500 B.C.E. in the civilization of *Sumer* in Mesopotamia (see Chapter 2). Consequently, evidence for piecing together the history of human life in the Paleolithic and Neolithic eras comes mainly from surviving artifacts from campsites and early towns. Stone tools, bits of pottery or cloth, and the remains of Stone Age dwellings can now be rather precisely dated. When combined with other material objects from the same site and time period, they provide us with a fairly good sense of the daily activities and life cycle of the peoples who created them.

As we have seen in the earlier discussion of cave paintings, of all of the material remains of the Stone Age era, none provide better insights into the social organization and thinking of early humans than works of art. Much of what we know, for example, about gender relations, or the positions of males and females and the interaction between them, has been interpreted from the study of the different forms of artistic expression of Stone Age peoples. The early appearance (c. 25,000 B.C.E.) of rock carvings, such as the wonderfully robust and very pregnant "Venus of Laussel" shown here, indicates the importance of childbearing to the survival of the small bands of hunters and gatherers that once made up the whole population of the human species.

The "Venus" was found in the remains of an early campsite at St.-Germain-en-Laye in France. Figurines or carvings of fertility symbols of this sort are among the most common artifacts of early human cultures.

agriculture than the formation of elites. Originally, each household crafted the tools and weapons it required, just as it wove its own baskets and produced its own clothing. Over time, however, families or individuals who proved particularly skilled in these tasks began to manufacture implements beyond their own needs and to exchange them for grain, milk, or meat.

Villages in certain regions specialized in the production of materials that were in demand in other areas. For example, flint, which is extremely hard, was the preferred material for the blades of axes. Axes were needed for forest clearing, which was essential to the extension of cultivation throughout much of Europe. The demand was so great that villagers who lived near flint deposits could support themselves either by mining the flint or by crafting the flint heads that were then traded, often with peoples who lived far from the sources of production. Such exchanges set precedents for regional specialization and

Such carvings and later figurines also suggest the existence of cults devoted to earth and mother goddesses. The centrality of female symbolism in early art and religion may also indicate the considerable influence that women wielded both within hunting and gathering bands and in the first cities and towns of the Neolithic era. As we have seen, the chief deity of Çatal Huyuk was a goddess, who is depicted in surviving sculptures as a young woman giving birth or nursing a small child and as an old woman accompanied by a vulture. The large number and diverse natures of the feminine figurines found at Hacilar, another early town uncovered in present-day Turkey, graphically illustrate the many roles that women played in this early town culture. Shown here in sketches made from the original baked-clay figurines, they include a mother goddess and several fertility figures.

Questions: Why do you think that women are more frequently depicted in early art forms than men? On the basis of the sample provided in these illustrations, which of women's roles in early human society were deemed the most important? Why might women have been seen as deities in these early societies, and what sort of requests might those who worshiped goddesses have made through their prayers and offerings?

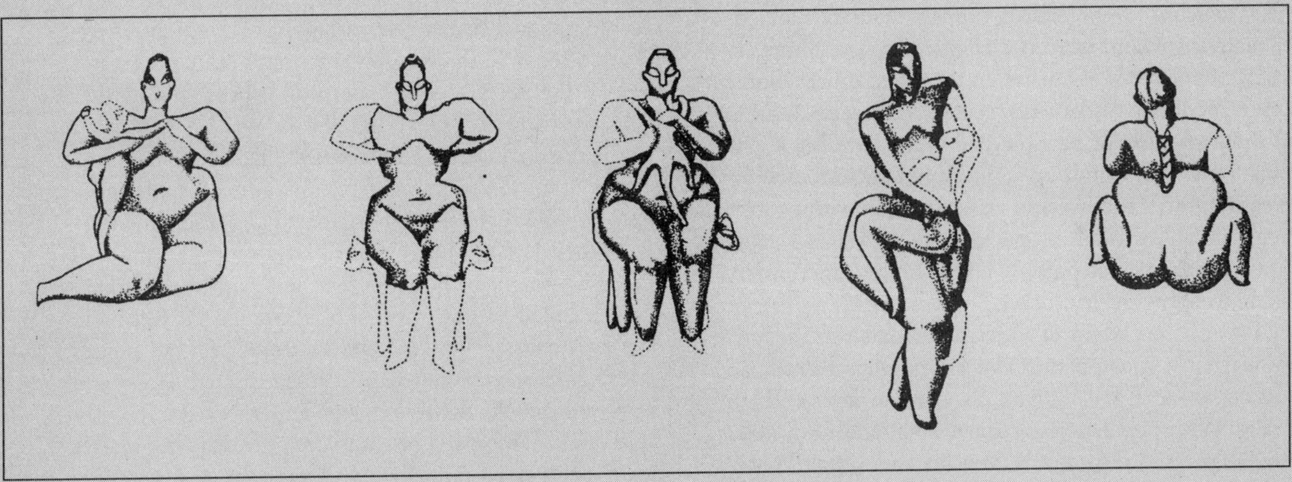

interregional trade, but the emergence of full-time merchants appears to have been associated with the rise of cities in a later period.

It is difficult to know precisely what impact the shift to agriculture had on the social structure of the communities that made the transition. Social distinctions were most likely heightened by occupational differences but well-defined social stratification, such as that which produces class identity, was nonexistent. Leadership remained largely communal, though village alliances may have existed in some areas. It is likely that property in Neolithic times was held in common by the community, or at least that all households in the community were given access to village lands and water.

By virtue of their key roles as plant gatherers in prefarming cultures, it can be surmised that women played a critical part in the domestication of plants. Nonetheless, there is evidence that their position declined in many agricultural communities. They worked the fields and have continued to work them in most cultures. But men took over tasks involving heavy labor, for example, land clearing, hoeing, and plowing. Men monopolized the new tools and weapons devised in the Neolithic era and later times, and they controlled the vital irrigation systems that developed in most of the early centers of agriculture. As far as we can tell, men also took the lead in taming, breeding, and raising the large animals associated with both farming and pastoral communities. Thus, though Neolithic art suggests that earth and fertility cults, which focused on feminine deities, retained their appeal, the social and economic position of women may have begun to decline with the shift to sedentary agriculture.

The First Towns: Seedbeds of Civilization

Focal Point: By about 7000 B.C.E., techniques of agricultural production in the Middle East had reached a level at which it was possible to support thousands of people, many of whom were not engaged in agriculture, in densely populated settlements. In these and other Middle Eastern Neolithic settlements, occupational specialization and the formation of religious and political-military elite groups advanced significantly. Trade became essential for the community's survival and was carried on with peoples at considerable distances, perhaps by specialized merchants. Crafts such as pottery, metalworking, and jewelry making were highly developed.

Two of the earliest of these settlements were at Jericho in what is today part of the autonomous Palestinian entity, and at Çatal Huyuk in present-day southern Turkey. With populations of about 2000 and from 4000 to 6000 people, respectively, Jericho and Çatal Huyuk would be seen today as little more than large villages or small towns. But in the perspective of human cultural development they represented the first stirrings of urban life.

Nonetheless, these earliest centers were quite isolated. They were merely tiny islands of sedentary cultivators and small numbers of townspeople, surrounded by vast plains and woodlands. The earliest town centers appear to have traded rather extensively but to have maintained only intermittent and limited contacts with neighboring hunting-and-gathering peoples. Though small in size and not highly specialized in comparison with the cities of Sumer and other early civilizations, the first towns played critical roles in continuing the Neolithic transformation. Their ruling elites and craft specialists contributed in major ways to the introduction in the 4th millennium B.C.E. of critical inventions—such as the wheel, the plow, writing, and the use of bronze—that secured the future of civilized life as the central pattern of human history.

Jericho

Proximity to the Jordan River and the deep and clear waters of an oasis spring account for repeated human settlement at the place where the town of *Jericho* was built. By 7000 B.C.E., over ten acres at the site were occupied by round houses of mud and brick resting on stone foundations. Most early houses had only a single room with mud plaster floors and a domed ceiling, but some houses had as many as three rooms. Entry to these windowless dwellings was provided by a single wood-framed doorway and steps down to the floor of the main room underground. Although there is no evidence that the town was fortified in the early stages of its growth, its expanding wealth made the building of walls for protection from external enemies increasingly imperative. The town was enclosed by a ditch cut into the rocky soil and a wall reaching almost twelve feet in height. The extensive excavation required for this construction is quite impressive because the peoples who undertook it possessed neither picks nor shovels. The stones for the wall were dragged from a riverbed nearly a mile away. These feats of transport and construction suggest not only a sizable labor force but one that was well organized and disciplined.

When Jericho was rebuilt in later centuries, the wall reached a height of nearly fifteen feet, and the fortifications included a stone tower at least twenty-five feet high. The area covered by the town increased. Round houses gave way to rectangular ones, entered through larger and more elaborately decorated wooden doorways. Houses were built of improved bricks, were provided with plaster hearths and stone mills for grinding grain, and were furnished with storage baskets and straw mats. In addition, small buildings have been found that were used as religious shrines during the later stages of the town's history.

Though the economy of Jericho was based primarily upon the farming of wheat and barley, there is considerable evidence of reliance on both hunting and trade. Domesticated goats provided meat and milk, while gazelles and various marsh birds were hunted for their flesh, hides, and feathers. The town was close to large supplies of salt, sulfur, and pitch. These materials, which were in great demand during this era, were traded for obsidian, a dark, glasslike volcanic rock; semiprecious stones from Anatolia, turquoise from the Sinai; and cowrie shells from the Red Sea.

The ruins excavated at Jericho indicate that the town was governed by a distinct and quite powerful ruling group, which was probably allied to the keepers of the shrine centers. There were specialized artisans and a small merchant class. In addition to fertility figurines and animal carvings like those found at many other sites, the inhabitants of Jericho sculpted life-sized, highly naturalistic human figures and heads. These sculptures, which may have been used in ancestor cults, give us vivid impressions of the physical features of the people who enjoyed the wealth and security of Jericho.

Çatal Huyuk

The first community at this site in southern Turkey was founded around 7000 B.C.E., somewhat later than the earliest settlements at Jericho. But the town that grew up at *Çatal Huyuk* was a good deal more extensive than that at Jericho and contained a larger and more diversified population. Çatal Huyuk was in fact the most advanced human center of the Neolithic period. At the peak of its power and prosperity the city occupied thirty-two acres and contained as many as 6000 people. Its rectangular buildings, which were centers of family life and community interaction, were remarkably uniform and were built of mud-dried bricks. They had windows high in their walls and were entered from holes in their flat roofs. These entryways also served as chimneys for the fireplaces within the houses. The houses were joined together to provide fortification for the town. Movement within the settlement was mainly across the roofs and terraces of the houses. Since each dwelling had a substantial storeroom, when the ladder to the roof entrance was pulled up, each became a separate fortress within the larger complex.

The standardization of housing and construction at Çatal Huyuk suggests an even more imposing ruling group than that found at Jericho. The many religious shrines at the site also indicate the existence of a powerful priesthood. The shrines were built in the same way as ordinary houses, but they contained sanctuaries surrounded by four or five rooms related to the ceremonies of the shrine's cult. The walls of these religious centers were filled with paintings of bulls and carrion eaters, especially vultures, suggesting fertility cults and rites associated with death. The surviving statuary indicates that the chief deity of the Çatal Huyuk peoples was a goddess.

The obvious importance of the cult shrines and the elaborate burial practices of the peoples of Çatal Huyuk reveal the growing role of religion in the lives of Neolithic peoples. The carefully carved sculptures associated with the sanctuaries, and the fine jewelry, mirrors, and weapons found buried with the dead, attest to the high level of material culture and artistic proficiency achieved by these town dwellers.

Excavations of the settlement also reveal an economic base that was much broader and richer than that of Jericho. Hunting remained a factor, but the breeding of goats, sheep, and cattle vastly surpassed that associated with Jericho. Çatal Huyuk's inhabitants consumed a wide range of foods, including several grains, peas, berries, berry wine, and vegetable oils made from nuts. Trade was extensive with the peoples in the surrounding hills and also in places as distant as present-day Syria and the Mediterranean region. Çatal Huyuk was also a major center of production by artisans. Its flint and obsidian weapons, jewelry, and obsidian mirrors were some of the finest produced in the Neolithic era. The remains of the town's culture leave little doubt that its inhabitants had achieved a civilized level of existence.

CONCLUSION

The Watershed of the 4th Millennium B.C.E.

Though Jericho, Çatal Huyuk, and similar settlements can best be seen as towns rather than cities, they displayed many of the characteristics that have come to be associated with urban life. Perhaps they were too small and too dependent on crops grown by their own inhabitants to be labeled cities. But they clearly set the patterns for layout, fortification, and standardization that would be found in the first cities in neighboring regions such as Sumer in Mesopotamia and Egypt, and in distant urban complexes such as Harappa in northwest India and Kush and Axum in Africa. The level of specialization and political organization these early townspeople had attained proved critical to the invention and dissemination of new tools and production techniques during the 4th millennium B.C.E. The years from 4000 to 3000 B.C.E. saw a second wave of major transformations in human culture in the Middle East and nearby regions. These shifts marked the transition from the last of the Stone Ages to the Bronze Age and succeeding epochs of metalworking.

During this transition era, the use of the plow significantly increased crop yields, and wheeled vehicles made it possible to carry a greater volume of food and other raw materials over greater distances. Both developments meant that larger noncultivating populations could be supported and concentrated in particular locales. Though copper had been used for spear and axe heads for millennia, accident and experiment revealed that when copper was mixed with other metals such as tin, it formed bronze, a harder and more durable material. The bronze tools that resulted further enhanced agricultural production. Trade-oriented, specialized, and wealthy urban peoples were also more likely than relatively isolated nomadic hunters and gatherers to acquire and manufacture bronze weapons, which were much lighter and more lethal than those made of stone. Finally, the development of writing, first in Mesopotamia and later in India, China, and other centers of agrarian production, greatly improved communications in ways that made it possible to expand trading networks and enlarge bureaucracies. Both were essential to the maintenance of large urban complexes.

The long isolation of American Indian peoples from the centers of civilization in Africa, Asia, and Europe prevented the diffusion of much of the new technology that was developed in a variety of centers at different times. This diffusion and ongoing exchange of objects and ideas between the civilized peoples of the Eastern Hemisphere had played a key role in the founding of new civilizations and the continued growth and development of those already established. Lacking these contacts, the peoples of the Americas built civilizations that were wonderfully sophisticated in many areas but were far behind those of the Old World in critical areas such as technological innovation and the harnessing of animal and machine power. Because their civilizations also developed in very different plant, animal, and disease environments from those in the Eastern Hemisphere, the peoples (and plant and animal life) of areas like the Americas, Australia, and the South Pacific proved highly vulnerable to the diseases introduced from Africa and Eurasia after 1492 C.E. These differences would eventually have catastrophic consequences for these peoples, who had long been isolated from the critical exchanges between the peoples of the Eastern Hemisphere.

FURTHER READING

A very considerable literature has developed in recent years on early humans and the critical Neolithic transformations. Sonia Cole's *The Neolithic Revolution* (1970) remains a concise and authoritative survey of this process in the Middle East and parts of Europe. For a broader overview that takes into account more recent research and includes early farming cultures in the Americas, see Robert J. Wenke's *Patterns in Prehistory* (1984). For a sense of the debates that have raged on various aspects of this process, see the sometimes quite technical essays in Stuart Streuver, ed., *Prehistoric Agriculture* (1971), which also covers the Americas extensively.

Even more lively, though often quite technical, are Donald O. Henry's *From Foraging to Agriculture* (1989) and Douglas Price and James A. Brown, eds., *Prehistoric Hunter-Gatherers: The Emergence of Cultural Complexity* (1986). M. C. and H. B. Quennell's *Everyday Life in the New Stone, Bronze and Early Iron Ages* (1955) is difficult to top for an imaginative reconstruction of life in the Neolithic epoch, though some of it is now dated. The most reliable treatment of technology in this era can still be found in volume one of C. Singer, et al., *A History of Technology* (1954). The best introduction to the earliest towns is in James Mellaart's *Earliest Civilizations of the Near East* (1965) and *The Neolithic of the Near East* (1975).

CHAPTER 2

The First Civilizations

KEY TERMS

Sahara	*monotheism*
Sudanic Zone	*David*
Bantu migrations	*Judaism*
Mesopotamia	*Assyrian Empire*
Tigris River	*Persia*
Euphrates River	*Zoroastrianism*
Uruk	*Indus River*
Epic of Gilgamesh	*Harappa*
pictograms	*Mohenjo-Daro*
cuneiform	*Aryan*
ziggurat	*Sanskrit*
Sargon	*Vedas*
Code of Hammurabi	*Shang Dynasty*
Hittites	*oracle bones*
Egypt	*Mesoamerica*
Nile River	*Olmec*
pyramids	*Teotihuacan*
Hyksos	*Maya*
Amenhotep/Akhenaten	*Andes Mountains*
Israel	

DISCUSSION QUESTIONS

Compare the influence of geography and climate on the early civilizations.

How did civilizations in the Americas develop differently from civilizations in the Old World?

Sub-Saharan Africa to 700 C.E.

In sub-Saharan Africa people shifted gradually from their earlier hunting and gathering existence to systematic stock breeding, fishing, and farming. This more settled life stood at the core of the Neolithic food-producing revolution that occurred in the Sahara/Sudanic zones. Once such changes had taken place there, Neolithic people moved into other parts of the continent, displacing or absorbing the hunters and gatherers they encountered and creating more-complex political institutions. Yet in the new process of state building one can discern patterns of a uniquely African style of history, with Africa's physical environment demanding the durability of the village and the town and ensuring the transitory nature of ruling dynasties and empires.

The Diffusion of an African Food-Producing Revolution

A change in climate some 10,000 years ago in the eastern and central parts of the Sahara/Sudanic region resulted in a sharp increase in rain. The eastern and central Sahara became a fertile grassland full of wild animals while, to the south, the Sudanic region's rivers and lakes grew ever larger. In the Sudanic zone some hunting and gathering peoples added aquatic creatures such as fish, otters, and hippopotamuses to their diet. They developed boats and rafts, harpoons and nets, bone hooks and fishing lines, and, to cook and store their food, they made pottery. Because of the richness of the environment, populations increased, with people settling down in communities of up to one hundred or so and experimenting with improved gathering of wild grains such as millet, sorghum, and rice.

With its hospitable climate, the central and eastern Sahara/Sudanic zone was also an ideal area for the spread of innovations in food production that had already occurred in southwest Asia. Except in Egypt and North Africa, Africans could not grow Asian wheat and barley because they were unsuitable for tropical conditions, but they did adopt the domesticated goats, sheep, and cattle that had been developed in Asia. By about 5000 B.C.E. these animals had spread into the eastern Saharan grasslands, and between 4000 B.C.E. and 2500 B.C.E. they provided the basis of a new pastoral way of life based on herding. In subsequent centuries, pastoralists spread southward, particularly in eastern Africa, into highland areas of Ethiopia and northern Kenya.

After about 3500 B.C.E., the climate of the Sahara/Sudanic zone began to revert to its earlier dryness, becoming progressively less hospitable. The Sudanic belt's rivers and lakes also began to shrink. As a consequence, people began to move southward in search of better living conditions in less dry climates. In the process, carriers of the new food-producing techniques expanded into areas up to then inhabited only by hunters and gatherers. In East Africa, for example, pastoralists moved southward along the interior highlands into central and southern Kenya and Tanzania. From the central Sudanic region pastoralists also moved into the environs of Lake Chad and, apparently for the first time, into the western Sudanic regions as well. While pastoralists migrated in southerly and westerly directions, people versed in the fishing technologies originally pioneered on Sudanic rivers and lakes penetrated the West African forests to take advantage of the opportunities offered by their many rivers. Sometime during this process of movement into the forests—and certainly by 2000 B.C.E. —actual agricultural production based on yams and other root crops was established as a supplement to fishing in the forest zones. In the drier areas of the savanna, people had also begun to cultivate millet, sorghum, and rice.

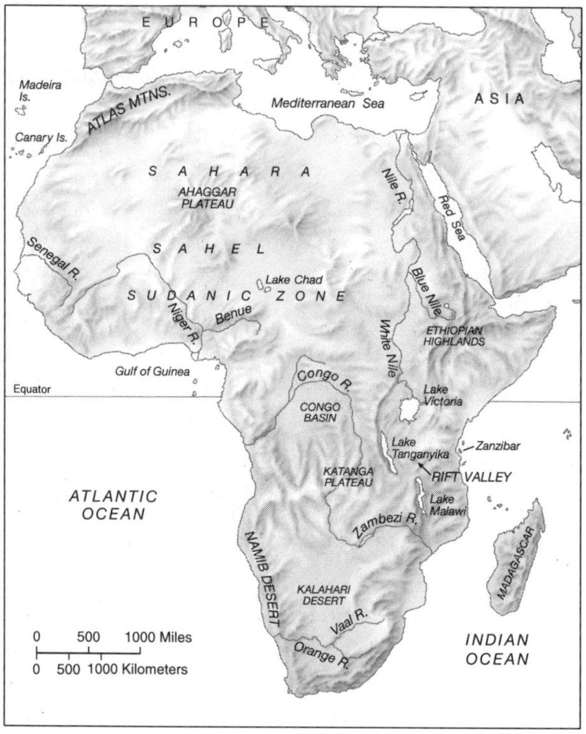

Africa

In this cave painting at Tassili in northern Africa, animal magic evokes help from the spirit world in ensuring the prosperity of the cattle herd. A similar ceremony is still performed by members of the Fulani tribes in the Sahel, on the southern fringe of the Sahara.

In effect, the wet phase that occurred in the central and eastern Sahara/Sudanic zone between about 8000 B.C.E. and around 3500 B.C.E. fostered important innovations in food production, ranging from domestication of animals to fishing and experimental agriculture, all supplemented by some continued hunting and gathering. The growing dryness of the period after 3500 B.C.E. pushed the new ways of life southward into areas of Africa still only sparsely occupied by hunters and gatherers. Virtually everywhere such movement occurred, earlier occupants were either absorbed into the new population or displaced to marginal areas, as they were too weak to mount effective resistance.

As part of this broad southerly expansion, one of the most important population movements in all human history occurred. This was the migration of speakers of a Niger-Congo language known as proto-Bantu, the ancestor of the hundreds of languages in the Bantu linguistic family that are spoken today. They moved from the forest area along the Nigeria/Cameroon border and gradually spread into almost all of Africa south of the equator. This process resulted in a gigantic area of Africa being occupied by speakers of highly similar languages. The Bantu migrations took a long time to complete and involved great complexity. They appear to have begun in the second millennium B.C.E., with people spreading in two main directions from the forested areas of the Nigeria/Cameroon borderlands. Some moved south and east, along the many rivers that crossed the Congo basin's rain forests, ultimately reaching the grassland regions of Zaire, Angola, and Zambia south of the forest. These migrants brought with them pottery and basketry, bows and arrows, domesticated goats and chickens, techniques of boating and fishing, and an agriculture based on root crops such as yams.

Others spread eastward along the northernmost fringes of the Congo forest into East Africa. As they did so, they acquired from Central Sudanic peoples whom they encountered techniques of raising sheep and cattle, information about growing grains, and, of immense importance, the knowledge of how to work iron and other metals, a discovery that rapidly spread back to West Africa. Once the Bantu speakers had reached East Africa, further migrations took place southward along two secondary routes throughout the first millennium B.C.E. One went near the coast, through Kenya,

The Nok culture flourished along the Niger River from 500 B.C.E. until about 200 C.E. Nok artists produced fine terracotta sculptures of human and animal figures. This example is hollow, with perforations for the eyes, nostrils, and mouth.

Tanzania, Mozambique, and Malawi, and it seems that migrants reached South Africa's Transvaal area by the fourth century C.E. The second was situated farther to the west, along the eastern upland fringes of the Congo basin and then into central and eastern Zambia and Zimbabwe.

Yet even after these initial migrations were completed by around 900 C.E., there were immense areas of Africa south of the equator still occupied by hunters and gatherers. Only with the passage of centuries did groups of Bantu-speaking agriculturalists grow in size, divide, and expand their internal frontiers to occupy new areas. In areas that the Bantu speakers considered undesirable, however, hunters and gatherers persisted, living on down to the present as such groups as the Mbuti people of the deep Congo rain forest and the Khoisan peoples of the southwest corner of Africa and the Kalahari Desert. By 1500 C.E. Bantu speakers occupied fully ninety per cent of the habitable land area south of the equator, having brought to it the complex material culture that had developed initially in the eastern and central Saharan/Sudanic areas, that had been enriched by the knowledge of metalworking, and that they elaborated into a myriad of new forms as they adapted to their varied new environments.

Ecology, Labor Power, and the Politics of Kinship

It is clearly impossible to make valid generalizations that apply to every part of a continent as large and diverse as Africa. Yet, while the continent had clearly been hospitable to earlier hunters and gatherers, it is fair to say that the history of Africa's agricultural and pastoral peoples has been significantly more difficult, shaped by their having to come to terms with an environment that, taken as a whole, must be considered one of the world's most difficult. This is especially true for agriculturalists, as they have had great problems in maintaining the soil's fertility.

Except for the North African coast and the area around the Cape of Good Hope, which have a temperate Mediterranean climate, all of Africa is tropical. In the tropics rains generally fall daily during four or five months of the year. This period is followed by a long dry season of up to seven or eight months. If the rains are too light or too heavy, crop yields suffer, and in a typical decade hunger is a problem in at least three years. When rains fail for two or three years in succession, famine results and people starve to death. Because African agriculture is dependent on fickle rainfall, it has always been a risky endeavor except in equatorial zones, where rains are more reliable and in certain West African river valleys, where water is perennially available.

Most of the soils of the African continent are inhospitable to agriculture. In the tropical rain forests of the Congo basin, the soil is thin and poor, with most of the nutrients locked up in living plants and animals. In cleared areas, soil nutrients are soon leached away by the heavy rains. The vast areas of grassland and savanna to the north, south, and west of the rain forests are low in fertility and have long dry seasons. Africans have managed these problems by using a system of shifting cultivation. A piece of land is cleared, used for three to five years, and then abandoned to lie fallow to recover its fertility, and a new piece of land is cleared for cultivation. This process continues with other pieces of land, until, after perhaps as long as twenty-five or thirty years, the fertility of the soil is restored to a point at which it may be used to grow crops once again for another brief period. Because most land in Africa, except for some West African areas and rare places where good volcanic soils exist such as Uganda, was used in this fashion, the carrying capacity of the soil—the number of people who could live on a unit of land—has been historically quite small. In rain forest areas, where the soils are exceptionally poor, it has been extremely low.

Finally, diseases such as endemic malaria, bilharzia, parasitical worms, and smallpox restricted productivity. Perhaps the most important disease, however, has been carried by the tsetse fly. When a tsetse bites a domesticated animal, it delivers a parasite called a trypanosome, which gradually destroys the animal's nervous system. The animal dies from sleeping sickness, or trypanosomiasis, in a matter of months. As a result, in areas where the tsetse exists it has been impossible to use draft animals for agriculture, and all agricultural work has had to be carried out by hand using only simple tools. This situation has sharply limited productivity. Ironically, the areas where tsetse flies are not found, such as in the Sudanic zone, are often those with such uncertain rainfall that pastoralism, not agriculture, is the more reliable way to survive.

With climate and problems of soil management and disease limiting the carrying capacity of its land, until the twentieth century Africa was characterized by an abundance of land and a relative shortage of labor to work it. Success in dealing with the difficult environment required effective use of available labor, especially in areas where draft animals could not be used. This fact has had a crucial impact upon the nature of politics throughout sub-Saharan Africa.

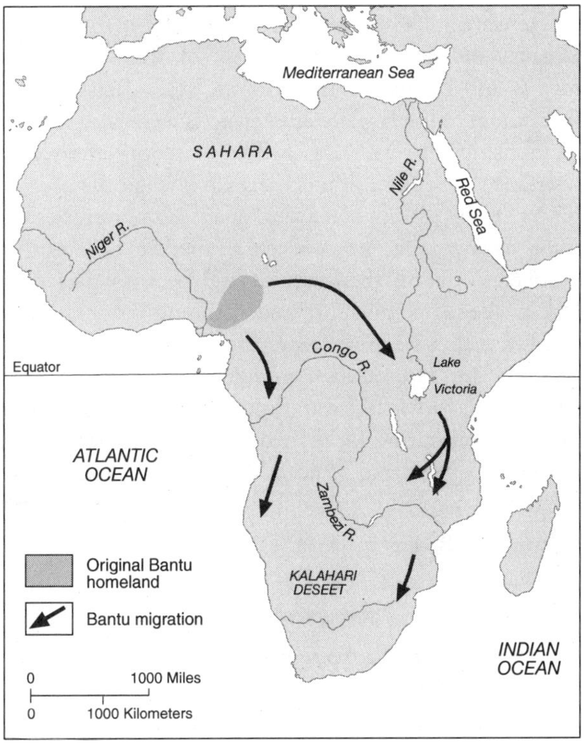

Bantu Migrations

Because of Africa's relatively sparse population, and because of difficulties of transport and communication, labor mobilization for agricultural work has historically best been done on a relatively small scale, not through the intervention of large-scale state structures. If one is to understand Africa's past, then one must break away from the assumption that the state is a necessity and imagine a situation in which there is actually little need for it for day-to-day survival. When the influence of state structures was minimal or wholly absent, relations within families served to organize virtually all African societies. They defined the roles of people and placed them in situations in which they could be mobilized as workers to ensure that the family household unit, the extended family, and, ultimately, society as a whole survived in difficult ecological conditions. The emphasis on the family was also important for a second, closely related, reason. In a situation of chronic labor shortage, family members worked without pay.

Central to this system were women. In most African societies women performed a large part of the agricultural work. The more women in a lineage, the more productive it was. Moreover, women bore the children who were crucial for the lineage's survival. When female children reached maturity, they were exchanged in marriage with other lineages. Male children remained within the lineage and attracted wives, thereby strengthening it and making it more likely to prosper and grow. In sum, then, family membership did not merely encompass existing biological relationships, but it also served as a way of ensuring that work was done at little cost. Greatest local power lay with the family head, usually a senior member, for he both shaped his family into an efficient productive unit by directing its day-to-day work and arranged marriages with other families to ensure its continuity.

"Big Men" and Political Change

Not all families were equal, however. To the extent that wealth existed in Africa, it was not usually equated with the possession of material goods. Basic wealth lay in control over people. A poor man had a wife and a child or two and, if cattle existed in the area, a cow or two. A wealthy man was one who had accumulated power over many people and, if possible, many cattle. It was to augment one's power over people—not to satisfy sexual passion—that polygyny was important in Africa. It not only

SUB-SAHARAN AFRICA TO 700 C.E.

8000–2000 B.C.E.	Wet phase in central and eastern Sahara/Sudanic zone
2000 B.C.E.	Beginning of drying phase in central and eastern Sahara/Sudanic zone
2000–1000 B.C.E.	Beginning of Bantu migrations

ensured many children to a man, but it was also a way for him to build important alliances with other families by contracting marriages for himself and his children.

Yet while it is accurate to see economic and political power as having existed primarily at the local level and as having resided with family heads, much of the history of Africa nonetheless has been the history of the growth of states, their dynasties, and the wars they have sponsored. This has been so largely because, even at the local level, there were always people who were known—as they are still today—as "big men" (in Swahili, for example, such a person was called a *bwana mkubwa*). Although women occasionally became powerful, when they did so they were usually considered socially as "men" and are hence considered as part of the overall category of "big men."

Their control over people through their families made such persons wealthy and powerful. Because of their power, poor people, weak people, or immigrants to the area also turned to them as patrons for protection and for access to food or land. In this way, even at the local level, some family heads were able to extend their powers beyond their own family's members and territory, often expressing their expanded powers in the terminology of family relationships. This situation resulted in the existence of thousands of highly localized microstates throughout Africa.

A second step toward the transformation of an embryonic microstate to a mature larger one occurred when circumstances changed in such a way that new opportunities for amassing additional power appeared. When this happened, the big men who were already powerful could take advantage of the new opportunities. When the opportunities were great enough, they could use their new power to dominate other, weaker families by force if necessary, making their states influential in regional politics.

Surveying Africa's history, one is struck by the frequency with which the catalyst for such rapid political change has been the growth of trade with outside peoples. Time and again, the creation of a market for a particular item to which local society has access—such as gold in Ghana and Zimbabwe, salt in Mali, slaves in West Africa, iron in Tanzania, or copper in Angola and Zaire—provided the opportunity for an enlargement of economic scale. The new economic activity naturally fell into the hands of those in the society with the greatest access to labor power, the big men, and the way was opened for state building. Given the opportunity and the appropriate catalyst, African societies showed a remarkable ability to change quickly, with the big men becoming chiefs, kings, and even emperors, able to pass on their power and authority to successors. Single individuals or aristocracies used their advantaged economic position to reinforce and expand their political power. Ties of kinship or clientage were reinforced by religious sanctions or coercion and, in the process, a state, dominated by a king or council of important people, emerged. Although standing armies were rare, the new state often developed military capabilities as well.

When such an increase in scale occurred, the state's demands challenged family relationships. Equally clearly, however, at the local level families remained the basic unit for mobilizing labor needed for daily survival. As a consequence, situations frequently arose in which the apparatus of the large state hovered over the villages or, in West Africa, the towns it encompassed, tapping into them from time to time for tribute or taxes, or to levy labor power, but remaining generally distant from them. Because of the persistent vitality of the villages and towns, and because their interests were often different from those of the larger state, tensions were built into the relationship between the two. These tensions often led to resistance, rebellion, or local secession when the coercive power of the distant state weakened. Moreover, because states usually relied upon access to markets beyond their borders to obtain their wealth and because they often lacked adequate transport and communications and an institutionalized bureaucracy, they tended to be at the mercy of forces beyond their rulers' immediate control. The true history of Africa, it might be argued, lies in the life of the enduring local villages and towns rather than in the often glittering achievements of states and empires ruled by successful big men who had become chiefs, kings, or emperors.

Mesopotamia: The Land Between the Two Rivers

As in Africa, geography and climate helped determine the forms of social organization in western Asia. However, in this region, which today comprises Iran and Iraq,

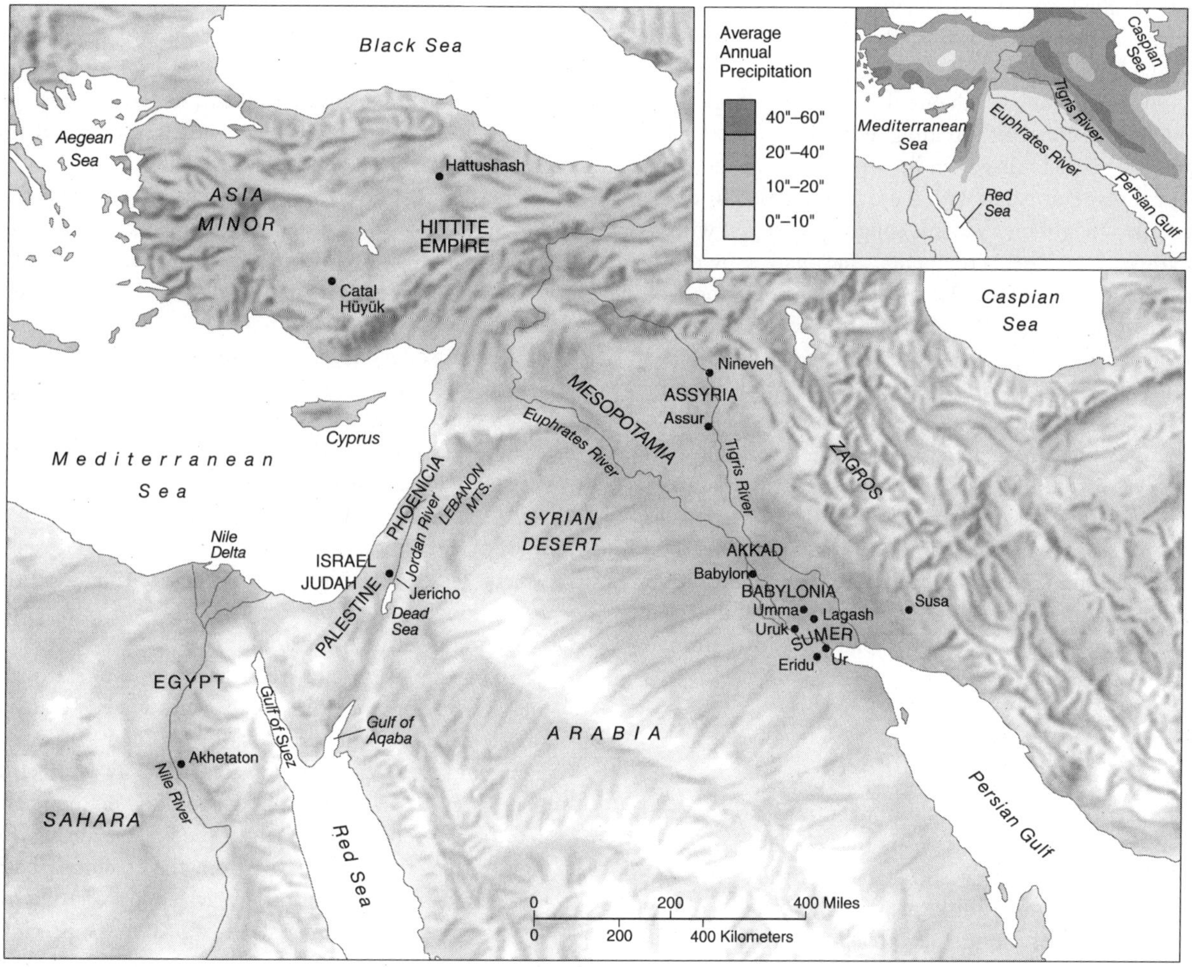

The Ancient Near East

need drove the inhabitants of Mesopotamia to create a civilization. The name *Mesopotamia* means "between the rivers," and was used for that featureless plain stretching to the marshes near the mouths of the Tigris and Euphrates rivers. Nature itself offered little for human comfort or prosperity in this harsh environment. The upland regions of the north receive most of the rainfall, but the soil is thin and poor. In the south, the soil is fertile but rainfall is almost nonexistent. There the twin rivers provide life-giving water, but also bring destructive floods that normally arrive at harvest time. Thus agriculture is impossible without irrigation. But irrigation systems, if not properly maintained, deposit harsh alkaline chemicals on the soil, gradually reducing its fertility. In addition, Mesopotamia's only natural resource is clay. It has no metals, no workable stone, no valuable minerals of use to ancient people. These very obstacles pressed the people to cooperative, innovative, and organized measures for survival. Survival in the region required planning and the mobilization of human resources possible only through centralization.

Until around 3500 B.C.E., the inhabitants of the lower Tigris and Euphrates lived in scattered villages and small towns. Then the population of the region, known as Sumer, began to increase rapidly. Small settlements became increasingly common, then towns such as Eridu and Uruk (in modern Iraq) began to grow rapidly. These towns developed in part because of the need to concentrate and organize population in order to carry on the extensive irrigation systems necessary to support Mesopotamian agriculture. In most cases, the earlier role of particular villages as important religious centers favored their growth into towns. These towns soon spread their control out to the surrounding cultivated areas, incorporating the small towns and villages of the region. They also fortified themselves against the hostile intentions of their neighbors.

Nomadic peoples inhabited the arid steppes of Mesopotamia, constantly trading with and occasionally threatening settled villages and towns. But nomads were a minor threat compared with the dangers posed by raids from settled neighbors. Victims sought protection within the ramparts of the settlements that had grown up around religious centers. As a result, the population of the towns rose along with their towering temples, largely at the expense of the countryside. Between c. 3500 and 3000 B.C.E., the population of Uruk quadrupled, from ten to forty thousand. Other Mesopotamian cities developed along the same general lines as they concentrated water supplies within their districts with artificial canals and dikes. At the same time, the number of smaller towns and villages in the vicinity decreased rapidly. The city had become the dominant force in the organization of economy and society, and the growth of the Sumerian cities established a precedent that would continue throughout history.

The Ramparts of Uruk

Cities did more than simply concentrate population. Within the walls of the city, men and women developed new technologies and new social and political structures. They created cultural traditions such as writing and literature. The pride of the first city dwellers is captured in a passage from the *Epic of Gilgamesh*, the first great heroic poem, which was composed sometime before 2000 B.C.E. In the poem, the hero Gilgamesh boasts of the mighty walls he had built to encircle his city, Uruk:

> **Go up and walk on the ramparts of Uruk**
> **Inspect the base terrace, examine the brickwork:**
> **Is not its brickwork of burnt brick?**
> **Did not the Seven Sages lay its foundations?**

Gilgamesh was justly proud of his city. In his day (c. 2700 B.C.E.) these walls were marvels of military engineering and even now their ruins remain a tribute to the age. Archaeologists have uncovered the remains of the ramparts of Uruk, which stretched over five miles and were protected by some nine hundred semicircular towers. These protective walls enclosed about two square miles of houses, palaces, workshops, and temples. For the first time, a true urban environment had appeared in western Eurasia, and Uruk was its first city. Within Uruk's walls, the peculiar circumstances of urban life changed the traditional social structure of Mesopotamia. In Neolithic times, social and economic differences within society had been minimal. Urban immigration increased the power, wealth, and status of two groups, the religious authorities responsible for the temples and the emerging military and administrative elites.

Whether they lived inside the city or on the farmland it controlled, Mesopotamians formed a highly stratified society that shared unequally in the benefits of civilization. Slaves, who did most of the unskilled labor within the city, were the primary victims of civilization. Most were prisoners of war, but some were people forced by debt to sell themselves or their children. Most of the remaining rural people were peasants who were little better than slaves. Better off were soldiers, merchants, and workers and artisans who served the temple or palace. At the next level were landowning free persons. Above all of these were the priests responsible for temple services and the rulers. Rulers included the *ensi*, or city ruler, and the *lugal*, or king, the earthly representative of the gods. Kings were powerful and feared.

Urban life also redefined the role and status of women, who in the Neolithic period had enjoyed roughly the same roles and status as men. In cities, women tended to exercise private authority over children and servants within the household, while men controlled the household and dealt in the wider world. This change in roles resulted in part from the economic basis of the first civilization. Southern Mesopotamia has no sources of metal or stone. To acquire these precious commodities, trade networks were extended into Syria, the Arabian Peninsula, and even India. The primary commodities that Mesopotamians produced for trade were textiles, and these were largely produced by women captured in wars with neighboring city-states. Some historians suggest that the disproportionate numbers of low-status women in Mesopotamian cities affected the status of women in general. Although women could own property and even appear as heads of households, by roughly 1500 B.C.E. the pattern of patriarchal households predominated. Throughout western Eurasian history, while individual women might at times exercise great power, they did so largely in the private sphere.

Changes in society brought changes in technology. The need to feed, clothe, protect, and govern growing urban populations led to major technological and conceptual discoveries. Canals and systems of dikes partially harnessed water supplies. Farmers began to work their fields with improved plows and to haul their produce to town, first on sleds and ultimately on carts. These land-transport devices, along with sailing ships, made it possible for farmers not only to produce greater agricultural surplus but also to move this surplus to distant markets. Craft workers used a refined potter's wheel to produce ceramic vessels of great beauty. Government officials and private individuals began to use cylinder seals, small stone cylinders engraved with a pattern, to mark ownership. Metalworkers fashioned gold and silver into valuable items of adornment and prestige. They also began to cast bronze, an alloy of copper and tin, which came into use for tools and weapons about 3000 B.C.E.

Perhaps the greatest invention of early cities was writing. As early as 7000 B.C.E., small clay or stone tokens with distinctive shapes or markings were being used to keep track of animals, goods, and fruits in inventories and bartering. By 3500 B.C.E., government and temple administrators were using simplified drawings, today termed *pictograms*, which were derived from these tokens, to assist them in keeping records of their transactions. Scribes used sharp reeds to impress the pictograms on clay tablets. Thousands of these tablets have survived in the ruins of Mesopotamian cities.

The first tablets were written in Sumerian, a language related to no other known tongue. Each pictogram represented a single sound, which corresponded to a single object or idea. In time, these pictograms developed into a true system of writing, called cuneiform (from the Latin *cuneus*, "wedge") after the wedge shape of the characters. Finally, scribes took a radical step. Rather than simply using pictograms to indicate single objects, they began to use cuneiform characters to represent concepts. For example, the pictogram for "foot" could also mean "to stand." Ultimately, pictograms came to represent sounds divorced from any particular meaning.

The implications of the development of cuneiform writing were revolutionary. Since symbols were liberated from meaning, they could be used to record any language. Over the next thousand years, scribes used these same symbols to write not only in Sumerian but also in the other languages of Mesopotamia, such as Akkadian, Babylonian, and Persian. Writing soon allowed those who had mastered it to achieve greater centralization and control of government, to communicate over enormous distances, to preserve and transmit information, and to express religious and cultural beliefs. Writing reinforced memory, consolidating and expanding the achievements of the first civilization and transmitting them to the future. Writing was power, and for much of subsequent history a small minority of merchants and elites and the scribes in their employ wielded this power. In Mesopotamia, this power served to increase the strength of the king, the servant of the gods.

Gods and Mortals in Mesopotamia

Uruk had begun as a village like any other. Its rise to importance resulted from its significance as a religious site. A world of many cities, Mesopotamia was also a world of many gods, and Mesopotamian cities bore the imprint of the cult of their gods.

The gods were like the people who worshiped them. They lived in a replica of human society, and each god had a particular responsibility. Every object and element from the sky to the brick or the plow had its own active god. The gods had the physical appearance and personalities of humans as well as human virtues and vices. Greater gods like Nanna and Ufu were the protectors of Ur and Sippar. Others, such as Inanna, or Ishtar, the goddess of love, fertility, and wars, and her husband Dumuzi, were worshiped throughout Mesopotamia. Finally, at the top of the pantheon were the gods of the sky, the air, and the rivers.

Mesopotamians believed that the role of mortals was to serve the gods and to feed them through sacrifice. Towns had first developed around the gods' temples for this purpose. By around 2500 B.C.E., although military lords and kings had gained political power at the expense of the temple priests, the temples still controlled a major portion of economic resources. They owned vast estates where peasants cultivated wheat and barley as well as vegetable gardens, vineyards, flocks of sheep, and herds of cattle and pigs. The produce from temple lands and flocks supported the priests, scribes, craft workers, laborers, farmers, teamsters, smiths, and weavers who operated these complex religious centers. At Lagash, for example, the temple of the goddess Bau owned over eleven thousand acres of land. The king held a quarter of this land for his own use. The priests divided the remainder into individual plots of about thirty-five acres, each to be cultivated for the support of the temple workers or rented out to free peasants. At a time when the total population was approximately forty thousand, the temple employed more than twelve hundred workers of various sorts, supervised by an administrator and an inspector appointed by the priests. The temple of Bau was only one of twenty temples in Lagash—and not the largest or most wealthy among them.

By around 2000 B.C.E., a ziggurat, or tiered tower, dedicated to the god stood near many temples. The great Ziggurat of Ur, for example, measured nearly two thou-

The southwestern side of the ruins of the Ziggurat of Ur. On top of a main platform fifty feet high, two successively smaller stages were built. The top stage was a temple containing a religious shrine. Ramplike stairways led up to the shrine from the ground.

sand square feet at its base and originally stood more than 120 feet high. It is easy to see why people of a later age thought that the people who had built the ziggurats wanted a tower that would reach to heaven—the origin of the biblical story of the Tower of Babel.

Although Mesopotamians looked to hundreds of personal divinities for assistance, they did not attempt to establish personal relationships with their great gods. However, since they assumed that the gods lived in a structured world that operated rationally, they believed that mortals could deal with them and enlist their aid by following the right rituals. Rites centered on the worship of idols. The most important care was feeding. At the temple of Uruk, the idols of the gods were offered two meals a day, each consisting of two courses served in regal quantity and style.

Through the proper rituals, a person could buy the god's protection and favor. Still, mortal life was harsh and the gods offered little solace to the great issues of human existence. This attitude is powerfully presented in the *Epic of Gilgamesh* which, while not an accurate picture of Mesopotamian religion, still conveys much of the values of this civilization. In this popular legend Gilgamesh, king of Uruk, civilizes the wild man Enkidu, who had been sent by the gods to temper the king's harshness. Gilgamesh and Enkidu become friends and undertake a series of adventures. However, even their great feats cannot overcome death. Enkidu displeases the gods and dies. Gilgamesh then sets out to find the magic plant of eternal life with which to return his friend from the somber underworld. On his journey he meets Ut-napishtim, the Mesopotamian Noah, who recounts the story of the Great Flood and tells him where to find the plant. Gilgamesh follows Ut-napishtim's advice and is successful but loses the plant on his journey home. The message is that only the gods are immortal, and the human afterlife is at best a shadowy and mournful existence.

Sargon and Mesopotamian Expansion

The temple was one center of the city; the palace was the other. As representative of the city's god, the king was the ruler and highest judge. He was responsible for the construction and maintenance of religious buildings and the complex system of canals that maintained the precarious balance between swamp and arid steppe. Finally, he commanded the army, defending his community against its neighbors and leading his forces against rival cities.

The cultural and economic developments of early Mesopotamia occurred within the context of almost constant warfare. From around 3000 B.C.E. until 2300 B.C.E., the rulers of Ur, Lagash, Uruk, and Umma fought among themselves for control of Sumer, their name for the southern region of Mesopotamia. The population was a mixture of Sumerians and Semites—peoples speaking Semitic languages related to modern Arabic or Hebrew—all jealously protective of their cities and gods and eager to extend their domination over their weaker neighbors.

The extraordinary developments in this small corner of the Middle East might have remained isolated phenomena were it not for Sargon (c. 2334–2279 B.C.E.), king of Akkad and the most important figure in Mesopotamian history. During his long reign of fifty-five years, Sargon built on the conquests and confederacies of the past to unite, transform, and expand Mesopotamian civilization. Born in obscurity, after his death he was worshiped as a god. Sargon was the son of a priestess and an unknown father. In his youth he was the cupbearer to the king of Kish. Later, he overthrew his master and conquered Uruk, Ur, Lagash, and Umma. This made him lord of Sumer. Such glory had satisfied his predecessors, but not Sargon. Instead he extended his military operations east across the Tigris, west along the Euphrates, and north into modern Syria, thus creating the Akkadian state—the first great multiethnic empire state—so named by contemporary historians for Sargon's capital at Akkad.

Sargon attempted to rule a vast and heterogeneous collection of city-states and territories by transforming the traditions of royal government. Rather than eradicating the traditions of conquered cities, he allowed them to maintain their own institutions, but replaced many of their autonomous ruling aristocracies with his own functionaries. He also reduced the economic power of local temples in favor of his supporters. At the same time, however, he tried to win the loyalty of the ancient cities of Sumer by naming his daughter high priestess of the moon god Nanna at Ur. He was thus the first in a long tradition of western Asian rulers who sought to unite his disparate conquests into a true state.

Sargon did more than just conquer cities. Although a Semite, he spread the achievements of Sumerian civilization throughout his vast state. Akkadian scribes used cuneiform to write the Semitic Akkadian language. So important did Sargon's successors deem his accomplishments that they ordered him worshiped as a god.

The Akkadian nation-state proved as ephemeral as Sargon's accomplishments were lasting. All Mesopotamian states tended to undergo a cycle of rising rapidly under a gifted military commander and then beginning to crumble under the internal stresses of dynastic disputes and regional assertions of autonomy. Thus weakened, they could then be conquered by other expanding states. First Ur, under its Sumerian king and first law-codifier, Shulgi (2094–2047 B.C.E.), and then Amoritic Babylonia, under its great ruler, Hammurabi (1792–1750 B.C.E.), assumed dominance in the land between the rivers. From about 2000 B.C.E. on, the political and economic centers of Mesopotamia were in Babylonia and in Assyria, the region to the north at the foot of the Zagros Mountains.

Hammurabi and the Old Babylonian Empire

In the tradition of Sargon, Hammurabi expanded his state through arms and diplomacy. He expanded his power south as far as Uruk and north to Assyria. In the tradition of Shulgi, he promulgated an important body of law, known as the Code of Hammurabi. In the words of its prologue, this code sought:

> **To cause justice to prevail in the country**
> **To destroy the wicked and the evil,**
> **That the strong may not oppress the weak.**

As the favored agent of the gods, the king held responsibility for regulating all aspects of Babylonian life, including dowries and contracts, agricultural prices and wages, commerce and money lending, and even professional standards for physicians, veterinarians, and architects. Hammurabi's code thus offers a view of many aspects of Babylonian life, although always from the perspective of the royal law. This law lists offenses and prescribes penalties, which vary according to the social status of the victim and the perpetrator. The code creates a picture of a prosperous society composed of three legally defined social strata: a well-to-do elite, the mass of the population, and slaves. Each group had its own rights and obligations in proportion to its status. Even slaves enjoyed some legal rights and protection, could marry free persons, and might eventually obtain freedom.

Much of the code sought to protect women and children from arbitrary and unfair treatment. Husbands ruled their households, but they did not have unlimited authority over their wives. Women could initiate their own court cases, practice various trades, and even hold public positions. Upon marriage, husbands gave their fathers-in-law a payment in silver or in furnishings. The father of the wife gave her a dowry over which she had full control. Some elite women personally controlled great wealth.

The Code of Hammurabi was less a royal attempt to restructure Babylonian society than an effort to reorganize, consolidate, and preserve previous laws in order to maintain the established social and economic order. What innovation it did show was in the extent of such punitive measures as death or mutilation. Penalties in earlier codes had been primarily compensation in silver or valuables.

DOCUMENT

Hammurabi Legislates Women's Rights

Hammurabi's code is a compilation of new laws called misharum, literally meaning "rightings." Their purpose is to right the injustices for which the old tribal customary law had no specific remedy.

If a man takes a wife and does not arrange a contract for her, that woman is not a wife.

If the wife of a man is caught lying with another man, they shall bind them and throw them into the water. If the husband of the woman wishes to spare his wife, then the king shall spare his servant.

If a man force the (betrothed) wife of another who has not known a male and is still living in her father's house, and he lie in her bosom and they catch him, that man shall be put to death and that woman shall go free.

If a man has accused his wife but she has not been caught lying with another man, she shall take an oath in the name of god and return to her house.

If a man deserts his city and flees and afterwards his wife enters into another house, if that man returns and wishes to take back his wife, the wife of the fugitive shall not return to her husband because he hated his city and fled.

If a man wishes to divorce his wife who has not borne him children, he shall give her money to the amount of her marriage price and he shall make good to her the dowry which she brought from her father's house and then he may divorce her.

If a woman hates her husband and says, "You may not possess me," the city council shall inquire into her case; and if she has been careful and without reproach and her husband has been going about and greatly belittling her, that woman has no blame. She may take her dowry and go to her father's house.

If a man has married a wife and a disease has seized her, if he is determined to marry a second wife, he shall marry her. He shall not divorce the wife whom the disease has seized. In the home they made together she shall dwell, and he shall maintain her as long as she lives.

If a man takes a wife and she does not present him with children and he sets his face to take a concubine, that man may take a concubine and bring her into his house. That concubine shall not rank with his wife.

If a man takes a wife and she gives a maidservant to her husband, and that maidservant bears children and afterwards claims equal rank with her mistress because she has borne children, her mistress may not sell her, but she may reduce her to bondage and count her among the slaves.

If a man gives to his wife a field, garden, house, or goods and delivers to her a sealed deed, after (the death of) her husband her children cannot enter a claim against her: The mother may will her estate to her son whom she loves, but to an outsider she may not.

If a man who has brought a gift to the house of his father-in-law and has paid the marriage price, looks with longing upon another woman and says to his father-in-law, I will not marry your daughter," the father of the daughter shall take to himself whatever was brought to him.

If a man takes a wife and she bears him children and that woman dies, her father may not lay claim to her dowry. Her dowry belongs to her children.

Based on the translation by Robert F. Herper, *The Code of Hammurabi* (Chicago:University of Chicago Press, 1904).

A seven-foot-high diorite stele, dating from about 1750 B.C.E., is inscribed with the law code of Hammurabi. The relief at the top shows Hammurabi standing at left in the presence of the sun-god, perhaps explaining his code of laws.

Law was not the only area in which the Old Babylonian kingdom began an important tradition. In order to handle the economics of business and government administration, Babylonians developed the most sophisticated mathematical system known prior to the fifteenth century C.E. Babylonian mathematics was based on the number sixty (we still divide hours and minutes into sixty units today). Babylonian mathematicians devised multiplication tables and tables of reciprocals. They also devised tables of squares and square roots, cubes and cube roots, and other calculations needed for computing such important figures as compound interest. Although Babylonian mathematicians were not primarily interested in theoretical problems and were seldom given to abstraction, their technical proficiency indicates the complex level of sophistication with which Hammurabi's contemporaries could tackle the problems of living in a complex society.

For all its successes, Hammurabi's state was no more successful than those of his predecessors at defending itself against internal conflicts or external enemies. Despite his efforts, the traditional organization inherited from his Sumerian and Akkadian predecessors could not ensure orderly administration of a far-flung collection of cities. Hammurabi's son lost over half of his father's kingdom to internal revolts. Weakened by internal dissension, the kingdom fell to a new and potent force—the Hittites.

The Hittites

Unlike the Hebrews and the other Semitic-speaking peoples of western Asia, the Hittites were Indo-Europeans, members of a large group of peoples who spoke a language related to Greek, Persian, Sanskrit, and Latin. The Hittites first migrated into Anatolia, probably from central Europe or the steppes of central Asia, no later than 2700 B.C.E., bringing with them horses and wheeled carts. There they intermingled with earlier inhabitants. By the middle of the second millennium B.C.E. the Hittite kings of Asia Minor were among the most powerful rulers in western Asia, equals of the monarchs of Babylon and Assyria or the Egyptian pharaohs. Yet with the fall of their empire around 1190 B.C.E., the Hittites virtually disappeared from history until they were rediscovered at the end of the nineteenth century.

The principal Hittite territory was located in what is now modern Turkey. Its capital was at Hattusas (modern Bogazkoy). From there, beginning around 1650 B.C.E., the Hittite kings embarked on aggressive military campaigns, pushing south across the Taurus Mountains into the more fertile territory of their southern and eastern neighbors. Sometime after 1600 B.C.E. they sacked Babylon with their ally, the Kassites.

Internal feuding eroded these initial successes, and the apparent obscurity of the following century may imply that the Hittites were more concerned with defending their territory against invaders than with empire building. The powerful military leader Suppiluliumas (c. 1375–c. 1335 B.C.E.) put Hittite armies once again on the attack. They conquered Syria, and even the Egyptians made peace overtures. The widow of the pharaoh (probably Tutankhamen, who had just died at the age of 18) sent a letter to Suppiluliumas begging him to send one of his sons to provide her with a new husband. Such an attractive alliance could hardly be turned down, and a Hittite prince was duly dispatched, only to be murdered en route to the Egyptian court. Suppiluliumas thus lost the opportunity to place his son on the Egyptian throne, which would have firmly linked the two empires. The career of King Hattusilis III (c. 1275–c. 1250 B.C.E.) and his queen, the priestess Puduhepa, provides a vivid picture of power and politics in the ancient world. He was an experienced military commander in his late forties when he deposed the reigning king, his nephew, in a coup. A powerful and ruthless leader, he engaged in incessant fighting to protect the kingdom's northern frontiers and negotiated with Egypt to retain control of Syria. Royal decrees were issued jointly in the names of Hattusilis and Puduhepa, and she corresponded independently with the Egyptian queen.

Hittite Society and Religion

The Hittite kingdom was basically agricultural. Many documents from the royal archives consist of land deeds, together with laws governing farming mishaps—the escape of a pig or an accidental fire in an orchard, for example. Unlike the Mesopotamians, the Hittites cultivated the vine, and wine, olive oil, and grain figure prominently in their records. In the fourteenth century B.C.E. the Hittites were one of the first peoples to discover the technique of iron smelting, but iron remained a precious metal, in short supply until about 1000 B.C.E. Hittite trading was widespread throughout western Asia, and much of the royal correspondence dealt with trade concessions and the protection of merchants traveling abroad. Egypt and Syria provided the principal markets, although the Hittites also traded with the Babylonians and were probably in commercial contact with the Mycenaeans, the chief Bronze Age people of the Greek mainland. Hittite objects sold or traded included bronze and iron vessels as well as gold and silver, and among the commodities Hittite merchants tried to buy was lapis lazuli, a precious blue stone mined in northeastern Afghanistan.

Like the Babylonians and other ancient peoples, the Hittites developed legal codes to organize their society. They made detailed provisions concerning homicide, theft, and arson, as well as regulations governing employment, property holding, and the treatment of slaves. Many provisions reflect the agricultural nature of Hittite society: rulings on crimes related to vineyards and orchards, offenses related to cattle, and accidents at river crossings.

Hittite society was patriarchal, but unlike the Semitic-speaking peoples, the Hittites did not practice polygamy. Fathers "gave away" their daughters, and the Hittites regarded marriage primarily as a financial contract. Nevertheless, young Hittite women seem to have enjoyed a little more independence than their Babylonian counterparts. The initial betrothal was accompanied by a present from the future bridegroom, but if the young woman decided to marry someone else, she could do so, with or without her parents' consent, provided that she returned the engagement present. Other regulations governed the treatment of widows and children; they included a provision that if a man died childless, it was the responsibility of his brother, father, or other male relative to marry and take care of his widow. Any children born of such a marriage took the name of the dead man and thus perpetuated his line. Although Babylonian law did not make this provision, a similar law existed in the ancient Jewish tradition, so that the dead man's name would not be "blotted out of Israel."

As might be expected among an agricultural people, the principal Hittite deity was a weather god called Teshub. In contrast to the predictability of the Mesopotamian cycle of seasons, the weather in the Taurus Mountains in southern Asia Minor is stormy and uncertain. The son of the weather god, Telipinu, an agricultural deity, who may have become the center of a cult similar to that of Osiris in Egypt, symbolized death and rebirth. As Hittite society developed, a complicated interweaving of deities, local and statewide, came into being, but the weather god remained the dominant figure, and Hittite kings claimed to rule as his deputy. The language of a treaty guaranteeing security throughout western Asia during Hattusilis III's reign describes the agreement as being between "the Sun God of Egypt and the Weather God of Hatti."

The End of the Hittite Empire

The treaty with Egypt may have secured the Hittites' eastern frontiers, but trouble soon developed in the west. Local governors there had revolted, and when the mass migrations of the Peoples of the Sea, who were repelled with such difficulty by Ramses III, swept across western Asia, the Hittites were unable to repulse the invaders. With the collapse of their capital at Hattusas around 1190 B.C.E., the population scattered. Drought, famine, and volcanic eruptions may also have contributed to the Hittite decline. Hittite culture continued in a few cities in the extreme south, in what is now Syria, but the Assyrians soon annexed them. The heirs of the Hittites in

DOCUMENT

Hittite Laws

Hittite laws were designed for reparation rather than retribution, as these examples demonstrate.

If anyone breaks a freeman's arm or leg, he pays him twenty shekels of silver and he [the plaintiff] lets him go home.

If anyone breaks the arm or leg of a male or female slave he pays ten shekels of silver and he [the plaintiff] lets him go home.

If anyone steals a plough-ox, formerly he used to give fifteen oxen, but now he gives ten oxen; he gives three oxen two years old, three yearling oxen, and four sucklings(?) and he [the plaintiff] lets him go home.

If a freeman kills a serpent and speaks the name of another [a form of sorcery], he shall give one pound of silver; if a slave does it, he shall die.

If a man puts filth into a pot or a tank, formerly he paid six shekels of silver; he who put the filth in paid three shekels of silver [to the owner?], and into the palace they used to take three shekels of silver. But now the king has remitted the share of the palace; the one who put the filth in pays three shekels of silver only and he [the plaintiff] lets him go home.

If a freeman sets a house on fire, he shall rebuild the house; but whatever perishes inside the house, be it a man, an ox, or a sheep, for these he shall not compensate.

Source: O. R. Gurney, *The Hittites* (Harmondsworth, England: Penguin Books, 1954), p. 96.

Asia Minor were the Phrygians, whose worship of Cybele, the Great Mother, became widespread in the Roman world, and the Lydians, who were probably the inventors of coinage. Hittite influence also extended, perhaps indirectly, to the Greeks and the Romans, whose conception of the pantheon of gods apparently owed much to Hittite mythology. The historical importance of the Hittites stems from their role in transmitting Mesopotamian culture to peoples of the Mediterranean.

Egypt: The Gift of the Nile

Like that of the Tigris and Euphrates valleys, the rich soil of the Nile Valley can support a dense population. There, however, the similarities end. Unlike the Mesopotamian, the Nile floodplain required little effort to make the land productive. Each year the river flooded at exactly the right moment to irrigate crops and to deposit a layer of rich, fertile silt. South of the last cataracts, the fertile region called Upper Egypt is about eight miles wide and is flanked by high desert plateaus. Near the Mediterranean in Lower Egypt, the Nile spreads across a lush, marshy delta more than a hundred miles wide. Egypt knew only two environments, the fertile Nile Valley and the vast wastes of the Sahara surrounding it. This inhospitable and largely uninhabitable region limited Egypt's contact with outside influences. Thus while trade, communication, and violent conquest characterized Mesopotamian civilization, Egypt knew self-sufficiency, an inward focus in culture and society, and stability. In its art, political structure, society, and religion, the Egyptian universe was static. Nothing was ever to change.

The earliest sedentary communities in the Nile Valley appeared on the western margin of the Delta around 4000 B.C.E. In villages, some of which had populations of around ten thousand, huts constructed of poles and adobe bricks huddled together near *wadis*, fertile riverbeds that were dry except during the rainy season. Farther south, in Upper Egypt, similar communities developed somewhat later but achieved an earlier political unity and a higher level of culture. By around 3200 B.C.E., Upper Egypt was in contact with Mesopotamia and had apparently borrowed something of that region's artistic and architectural traditions. During the same period, Upper Egypt developed a pictographic script.

These cultural achievements coincided with the political centralization of Upper Egypt under a series of kings. Probably around 3150 B.C.E., King Narmer or one of his predecessors in Upper Egypt expanded control

MESOPOTAMIA: BETWEEN THE TWO RIVERS

c. 3500 B.C.E.	Pictograms appear
c. 3000–2316 B.C.E.	War for control of Sumer
c. 2334–2279 B.C.E.	Sargon
c. 2700 B.C.E.	Gilgamesh
1792–1750 B.C.E.	Hammurabi
c. 1600 B.C.E.	Hittites destroy Old Babylonian state
c. 1286 B.C.E.	Battle of Kadesh

over the fragmented south, uniting Upper and Lower Egypt and establishing a capital at Memphis on the border between these two regions. For over twenty-five hundred years this lush corner of Africa—the Nile Valley, from the first cataract to the Mediterranean—enjoyed the most stable civilization the Western world has ever known.

Tending the Cattle of God

Historians divide the vast sweep of Egyptian history into thirty-one dynasties, regrouped in turn into four periods of political centralization: pre- and early dynastic Egypt (c. 3150–2770 B.C.E.), the Old Kingdom (c. 2770– 2200 B.C.E.), the Middle Kingdom (c. 2050–1786 B.C.E.), and the New Kingdom (c. 1560–1087 B.C.E.). The time gaps between kingdoms were periods of disruption and political confusion termed intermediate periods. While minor changes in social, political, and cultural life certainly occurred during these centuries, the changes were less significant than the astonishing stability and continuity of the civilization that developed along the banks of the Nile.

Divine kingship was the cornerstone of Egyptian life. The king lived in the royal city of Memphis in the splendor of a *Per-ao* or "great house," from which comes the word *pharaoh*, the Hebrew term for the Egyptian king. Initially, the king was regarded as the incarnation of Horus, a sky and falcon god. Later, the king was identified with the sun god Ra (subsequently known as Amen-Re, the great god), as well as with Osiris, the god of the dead. As divine incarnation, the king was obliged above all to care for his people. It was he who assured the annual flooding of the Nile, which brought water to the parched land. His commands preserved *maat*, the ideal state of the universe and society, a condition of harmony and justice. In the poetry of the Old Kingdom, the king was the divine herdsman, while the people were the cattle of god:

> ***Well tended are men, the cattle of god.***
> ***He made heaven and earth according to their desire***
> ***and repelled the demon of the waters . . .***
> ***He made for them rulers (even) in the egg,***
> ***a supporter to support the back of the disabled.***

Unlike the rulers in Mesopotamia, the kings of the Old Kingdom were not warriors but divine administrators. Protected by the Sahara, Egypt had few external enemies and no standing army. A vast bureaucracy of literate court officials and provincial administrators assisted the god-king. They wielded wide authority as religious leaders, judicial officers, and, when necessary, military leaders. A host of subordinate overseers, scribes, metalworkers, stonemasons, artisans, and tax collectors rounded out the royal administration. At the local level, governors administered provinces called *nomes*, the basic units of Egyptian local government.

Women of ancient Egypt were more independent and involved in public life than were those of Mesopotamia. Egyptian women owned property, conducted their own business, entered legal contracts, and brought lawsuits. They shared in the economic and professional life of the country at every level except one. Women were apparently excluded from formal education. The professional bureaucracy was open only to those who could read and write. As a result, the primary route to public power was closed to women, and the bureaucratic machinery remained firmly in the hands of men. The role of this bureaucracy was to administer estates, collect taxes, and channel revenues and labor toward vast public works projects. These construction projects focused on the king.

During the Old and Middle kingdoms, great pyramid temple-tomb complexes were built for the kings. Within the temples priests and servants performed rituals to serve the dead kings just as they had served the kings when they were alive. Even death did not disrupt the continuity so vital to Egyptian civilization. The cults of dead kings reinforced the monarchy, since veneration of past rulers meant veneration of the kings' ancestors. The founder of the Old Kingdom, King Zoser, who was an approximate contemporary of Gilgamesh, built the first pyramid-temple, the Step Pyramid at Sakkara.

Building and equipping the pyramids focused and transformed Egypt's material and human resources. Artists and craft workers had to be trained, engineering and transportation problems solved, quarrying and stoneworking techniques perfected, and laborers recruited. In the Old Kingdom, whose population has been estimated at perhaps 1.5 million, more than seventy

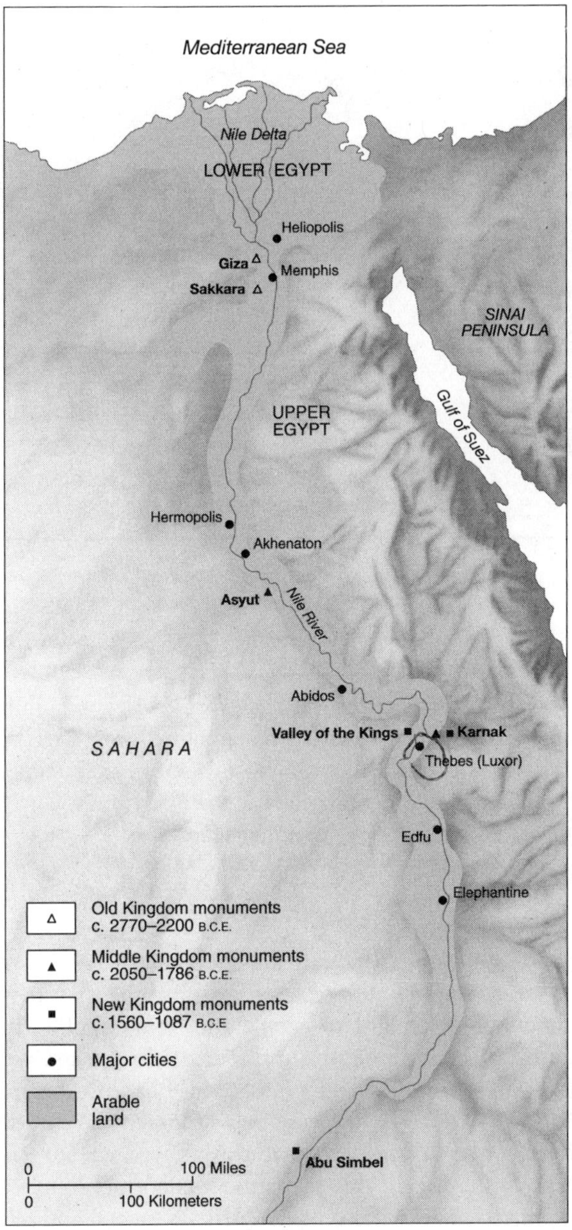

Ancient Egypt

thousand workers at a time were employed in building these great temple-tombs. The largest, the Great Pyramid of Khufu (c. 2000 B.C.E.), stood 481 feet high and contained almost 6 million tons of stone. In comparison, the great Ziggurat of Ur rose only some 120 feet above the Mesopotamian plain.

Feeding the masses of laborers absorbed most of the country's agricultural surplus. Equipping the temples and pyramids provided a constant demand for the highest-quality luxury goods, since royal tombs and temples were furnished as luxuriously as palaces. Thus the construction and maintenance of these vast complexes focused the organization and production of Egypt's economy and government.

Democratization of the Afterlife

In the Old Kingdom, future life was available only to the king or through the king. The graves of thousands of his attendants and servants surrounded his temple. All the wealth, labor, and expertise of the kingdom thus flowed into these temples, reinforcing the position of the king. Like the tip of a pyramid, the king was the summit, supported by all of society.

Gradually, however, the absolute power of the king declined. The increasing demands for consumption by the court and the cults forced agricultural expansion into areas where returns were poor, thus decreasing the flow of wealth. As bureaucrats increased their efforts to supply the voracious needs of living and dead kings and their attendants, they neglected the maintenance of the economic system that supplied these needs. The royal government was not protecting society, the "cattle of god" were not being well tended. Finally, tax-exempt religious foundations, established to ensure the perpetual cult of the dead, received donations of vast amounts of property and came to rival the power of the king. This removed an ever greater amount of the country's wealth from the control of the king and his agents. Thus the wealth and power of the kings declined at roughly the time that Sargon was expanding his Akkadian state in Mesopotamia. By around 2200 B.C.E., Egyptian royal authority collapsed entirely, leaving political and religious power in the hands of provincial governors.

After almost two hundred years of fragmentation, the governors of Thebes in Upper Egypt reestablished centralized royal traditions, but with a difference. Kings continued to build vast temples, but they did not resume the tremendous investments in pyramid complexes on the scale of the Old Kingdom. The bureaucracy was opened to all men, even sons of peasants, who could master the complex pictographic writing. Private temple-tombs proliferated and with them new pious foundations. These promised eternal care by which anyone with sufficient wealth could enjoy a comfortable afterlife.

The memory of the shortcomings of the Old Kingdom introduced a new ethical perspective expressed in the literature written by the elite. For the first time, the elite voiced the concern that justice might not always be

The pyramids at Giza, near modern Cairo. The three largest pyramids, which were built around 2600-2500 , are the tombs of the pharaohs Khufu, Khafre, and Menkure.

served and that the innocent might suffer at the hands of royal agents. In the story of Sinuhe, a popular tale from around 1900 B.C.E., an official of Amenemhet I (d. 1962 B.C.E.) flees Egypt after the death of his king. He fears that through false reports of his actions he will incur the wrath of Amenemhet's son, Senusert I. Only in his old age, after years in Syria and Palestine, does Sinuhe dare to return to his beloved Egypt. There, through the intercession of the royal children, Senusert receives him honorably and grants him the ultimate favor, his own pyramid-tomb. The moral is clear: The state system at times failed in its responsibility to safeguard *maat.*

The greater access to power and privilege in the Middle Kingdom benefited foreigners as well as Egyptians. Assimilated Semites from Palestine rose to important administrative positions. By around 1600 B.C.E., when the Hittite armies were destroying the state of Hammurabi's successors, large bands of Palestinians had settled in the eastern Delta, setting the stage for the first foreign conquest of Egypt. A series of kings referred to by Egyptian sources as "rulers of foreign lands," or *Hyksos*, overran the country and ruled the Nile Valley as far south as Memphis. These foreigners adopted the traditions of Egyptian kingship and continued the tradition of divine rule.

The Hyksos kings introduced their military technology and organization into Egypt. In particular, they brought with them the light, horse-drawn war chariot. This mobile fighting platform, manned by warriors armed with bows, bronze swords of a type previously unknown in Egypt, and lances, transformed Egyptian military tactics. These innovations remained even after the Hyksos were expelled by Ahmose I (1552–1527 B.C.E.), the Theban founder of the Eighteenth Dynasty, with whose reign the New Kingdom began.

The Egyptian Empire

Ahmose did not stop with the liberation of Egypt. He forged an empire. He and his successors used their newfound military might to extend the frontiers of Egypt south up the Nile beyond the fourth cataract and well into Nubia, solidifying Egypt's contacts with other regions of Africa. To the east they absorbed the caravan routes to the Red Sea, from which they were able to send ships to Punt (probably modern Somalia), the source of the myrrh and frankincense needed for funeral and religious rituals. Most important was the Egyptian expansion into Canaanite Palestine and Syria. Here Egyptian chariots crushed their foes as kings pressed on as far as the Euphrates. Thutmose I (1506–1494 B.C.E.) proclaimed, "I have made the boundaries of Egypt as far as that which the sun encircles."

Thutmose's immediate successors were his children, Thutmose II (1494–1490 B.C.E.) and Hatshepsut (1490–1468 B.C.E.), who married her brother. Such brother-sister marriages, although not unknown in polygamous Egyptian society, were rare. After the death of Thutmose II, Hatshepsut ruled both as regent for her

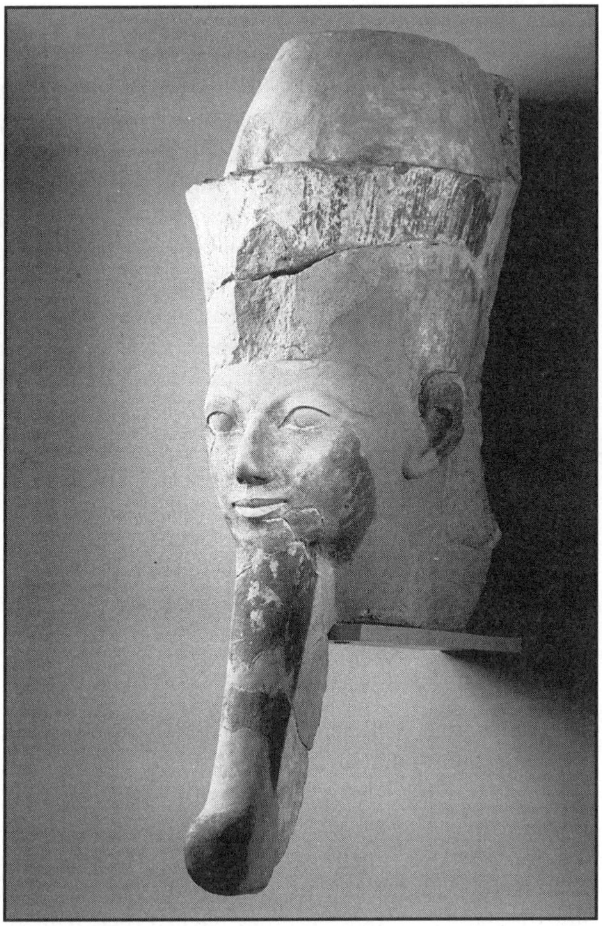

This painted limestone head of Hatshepsut was originally from a statue. She is shown wearing the crown of Egypt and the stylized "beard" that symbolized royalty and was often seen on the statues and death masks of pharaohs

stepson Thutmose III (1490–1468 B.C.E.) and as co-ruler. She was by all accounts a capable ruler, preserving stability and even personally leading the army on several occasions to protect the empire.

In spite of the efforts of Hatshepsut and her successors, the Egyptian empire was never as grand as its kings proclaimed. Many of the northern expeditions were raids rather than conquests. Still, the expanded political frontiers meant increased trade and unprecedented interaction with the rest of the ancient world. The cargo excavated from the wreck of a ship that sank off the coast of modern Turkey around 1350 B.C.E. vividly portrays the breadth of international exchange in the New Kingdom. The nationality of the ship, its origins, and its destination are unknown, but it carried a cargo of priceless and exotic merchandise from around the Mediterranean world. The lost ship was probably not a merchant vessel in the modern sense; private merchants were virtually unknown in the Egyptian empire. Instead, most precious commodities circulated through royal ventures or as gifts and tribute.

Religion was both the heart of royal power and its only limiting force. Though the king was the embodiment of the religious tradition, he was also bound by that tradition, as it was interpreted by an ancient and powerful system of priesthoods, pious foundations, and cults. The intimate relationship between royal absolutism and religious cult culminated in the reign of Amenhotep IV (1364–1347 B.C.E.), the most controversial and enigmatic ruler of the New Kingdom, who challenged the very basis of royal religious control. In a calculated break with over a thousand years of Egyptian religious custom, Amenhotep attempted to abolish the cult of Amen-Re along with all of the other traditional gods, their priesthoods, and their festivals. In their place he promoted a new divinity, the sun-disk god Aten. Amenhotep moved his capital from Thebes to a new temple city, modern Tell al-`Amarna, and changed his own name to Akhenaten ("It pleases Aten").

Akhenaten has been called the first monotheist, a reformer who sought to revitalize a religion that had decayed into superstition and magic. Yet his monotheism was not complete. The god Aten shared divine status with Akhenaten himself. Akhenaten attacked other cults, especially that of Amen-Re, to consolidate royal power and to replace the old priesthoods with his own family members and supporters.

In attempting to reestablish royal divinity, Akhenaten temporarily transformed the aesthetics of Egyptian court life. Traditional archaic language gave way to the everyday speech of the fourteenth century B.C.E. Wall paintings and statues showed people in the clothing that they actually wore rather than in stylized parade dress. This new naturalism rendered the king at once more human and more divine. It differentiated him from the long line of preceding kings, emphasizing his uniqueness and his royal power.

The strength of royal power was so great that during his reign Akhenaten could command acceptance of his radical break with Egyptian stability. However, his ambitious plan did not long survive his death. His innovations annoyed the Egyptian elite, while his abolition of traditional festivals alienated the masses. His son-in-law, Tutankhamen (1347–1337 B.C.E.), the son of Akhenaten's predecessor, was a child when he became king upon Akhenaten's death. Under the influence of his court advisors, probably inherited from his father's reign,

EGYPT: THE GIFT OF THE NILE

c. 3150–2770 B.C.E.	Predynastic and early dynastic Egypt
c. 2770–2200 B.C.E.	Old Kingdom
c. 2600 B.C.E.	Pyramid of Khufu
c. 2050–1786 B.C.E.	Middle Kingdom
c. 1560–1087 B.C.E.	New Kingdom
1552–1527 B.C.E.	Ahmose I
1506–1494 B.C.E.	Thutmose I
1494–1490 B.C.E.	Thutmose II
1490–1468 B.C.E.	Hatshepsut
1364–1347 B.C.E.	Amenhotep IV (Akhenaten)
1347–1337 B.C.E.	Tutankhamen
1289–1224 B.C.E.	Ramses II

he restored the ancient religious traditions and abandoned the new capital of Amarna for his father's palace at Thebes.

Return to the old ways meant return to the old problems. Powerful pious foundations controlled fully ten percent of the population. Dynastic continuity ended after Tutankhamen and a new military dynasty seized the throne. These internal problems provided an opportunity for the Hittite state in Asia Minor to expand south at the expense of Egypt. Ramses II (1289–1224 B.C.E.) checked the Hittite expansion at the battle of Kadesh, but the battle was actually a draw. Eventually, Ramses and the Hittite king Hattusilis III signed a peace treaty whose terms included nonaggression and mutual defense. The agreement marked the failure of both states to unify the Fertile Crescent, the region stretching from the Persian Gulf northwest through Mesopotamia and down the Mediterranean coast to Egypt.

The mutual standoff at Kadesh did not long precede the disintegration of both Egypt and the Hittite state. Within a century, states large and small along the Mediterranean coast from Anatolia to the Delta and from the Aegean Sea in the west to the Zagros Mountains in the east collapsed or were destroyed in what seems to have been a general crisis of the civilized world. The various raiders, sometimes erroneously called the "Sea Peoples," who struck Egypt, Syria, the Hittite state, and elsewhere were not the primary cause of the crisis. It was rather internal political, economic, and social strains within both of these great states that provided the opportunity for various groups—including Anatolians, Greeks, Israelites, and others—to raid the ancient centers of civilization. In the ensuing confusion, the small Semitic kingdoms of Syria and Palestine developed a precarious independence in the shadow of the great powers.

Israel: Between Two Worlds

Urban forms of civilization were an endangered species throughout antiquity. Just beyond the well-tilled fields of Mesopotamia and the fertile delta of the Nile lay the world of anticivilization—that of the Semitic tribes of seminomadic shepherds and traders. Of course, not all Semites were nonurban. Many had formed part of the heterogeneous population of the Sumerian world. Sargon's Semitic Akkadians and Hammurabi's Amorites created great Mesopotamian nation-states, adopting the ancient Sumerian cultural traditions. Along the coast of Palestine, other Semitic groups established towns modeled on those of Mesopotamia, which were involved in the trade between Egypt and the north. But the majority of Semitic peoples continued to live a life radically different from that of the floodplain civilizations. From these, one small group, the Hebrews, emerged to establish a religious and cultural tradition unique in antiquity.

A Wandering Aramaean Was My Father

Sometime after 2000 B.C.E., small Semitic bands under the leadership of patriarchal chieftains spread into what is today Syria and Palestine. These bands crisscrossed the Fertile Crescent, searching for pasture for their flocks. Occasionally they participated in the trade uniting Mesopotamia and the towns of the Mediterranean coast. For the most part, however, they pitched their tents on the outskirts of towns only briefly, moving on when their sheep and goats had exhausted the supply of pasturage. Semitic Aramaeans and Chaldeans brought with them not only their flocks and families, but Mesopotamian culture as well. Hebrew history records such Mesopotamian traditions as the story of the flood (Genesis, chapters 6–10), legal traditions strongly reminiscent of those of Hammurabi, and the worship of the gods on high places. Stories such as that of the Tower of Babel and the garden of Eden (Genesis, chapters 2–4) likewise have a Mesopotamian flavor, but with a difference. For these wandering shepherds, civilization was a curse. In the Hebrew Bible (the Christian Old Testament), the first city was built by Cain, the first murderer. The Tower of Babel, probably a ziggurat, was a symbol not of human achievement but of human pride.

At least some of these wandering Aramaeans, among them the biblical patriarch Abraham, rejected the gods of Mesopotamia. Religion among these nomadic groups focused on the specific divinity of the clan. In the case of Abraham, this was the god El. Abraham and his successors were not monotheists. They did not deny the existence of other gods. They simply believed that they had a personal pact with their own god.

In its social organization and cultural traditions, Abraham's clan was no different from its neighbors. These independent clans were ruled by a senior male (hence the Greek term *patriarch*—rule by the father). Women, whether wives, concubines, or slaves, were treated as distinctly inferior, virtually as property.

Some of Abraham's descendants must have joined the steady migration from Palestine into Egypt that took place during the Middle Kingdom and the Hyksos period. Although initially well treated, after the expulsion of the Hyksos in the sixteenth century B.C.E., many of the Semitic settlers in Egypt were reduced to slavery. Around the thirteenth century B.C.E., a small band of Semitic slaves numbering perhaps less than one thousand left Egypt for Sinai and Palestine under the leadership of Moses. The memory of this departure, known as the Exodus, became the formative experience of the descendants of those who had taken part and those who later joined them. Moses, a Semite who carried an Egyptian name and who, according to tradition, had been raised in the royal court, was the founder of the Israelite people.

During the years that they spent wandering in the desert and then slowly conquering Palestine, the Israelites forged a new identity and a new faith. From the Midianites of the Sinai Peninsula, they adopted the god Yahweh as their own. Although composed of various Semitic and even Egyptian groups, the Israelites adopted the oral traditions of the clan of Abraham as their common ancestor and identified his god, El, with Yahweh. They interpreted their extraordinary escape from Egypt as evidence of a covenant with this god, a treaty similar to those concluded between the Hittite kings and their

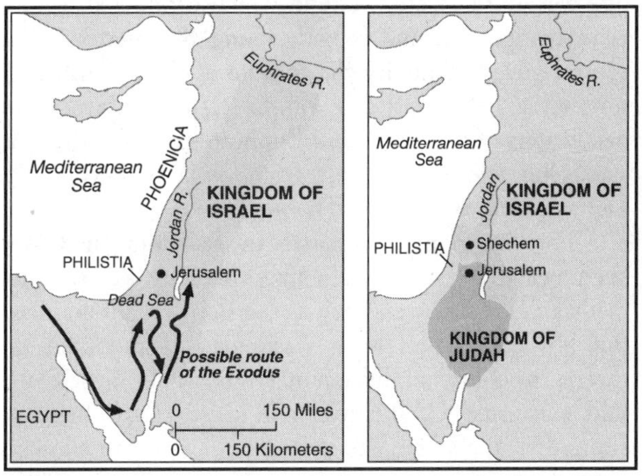

Kingdoms of Israel and Judah

dependents. Yahweh was to be the Israelites' exclusive god; they were to make no alliances with any others. They were to preserve peace among themselves, and they were obligated to serve Yahweh with arms. This covenant was embodied in the law of Moses, a series of terse, absolute commands ("Thou shall not . . .") quite unlike the conditional laws of Hammurabi. Inspired by their new identity and their new religion, the Israelites swept into Palestine. Taking advantage of the vacuum of power left by the Hittite-Egyptian standoff following the battle of Kadesh, they destroyed or captured the cities of the region.

A King Like All the Nations

During its first centuries, Israel was a loosely organized confederation of tribes whose only focal point was the religious shrine at Shiloh. This shrine, in contrast with the temples of other ancient peoples, housed no idols, but only a chest, known as the Ark of the Covenant, which contained the law of Moses and mementos of the Exodus. At times of danger temporary leaders would lead united tribal armies. The power of these leaders, called judges in the Hebrew Bible, rested solely on their personal leadership qualities. This "charisma" indicated that the spirit of Yahweh was with the leader. Yahweh alone was the ruler of the people.

By the eleventh century B.C.E., this disorganized political tradition placed the Israelites at a disadvantage in fighting their neighbors. The Philistines, who dominated the Palestinian seacoast and had expanded inland, posed the greatest threat. By 1050 B.C.E., the Philistines had defeated the Israelites, captured the Ark of the Covenant, and occupied most of their territory. Many Israelites clamored for "a king like all the nations" to lead them to victory. To consolidate their forces, the Israelite religious leaders reluctantly established a kingdom. Its first king was Saul and its second was David.

David (c. 1000–962 B.C.E.) and his son and successor, Solomon (c. 961–922 B.C.E.), brought the kingdom of Israel to its peak of power, prestige, and territorial expansion. David defeated and expelled the Philistines, subdued Israel's other enemies, and created a united state that included all of Palestine from the desert to the sea. He established Jerusalem as the political and religious capital. Solomon went still further, building a magnificent temple complex to house the Ark of the Covenant and to serve as Israel's national shrine. David and Solomon restructured Israel from a tribal to a monarchical society. The old tribal structure remained only as a religious tradition. Solomon centralized land divisions, raised taxes, and increased military service in order to strengthen the monarchy.

The cost of this transformation was high. The kingdom under David and especially under Solomon grew more tyrannical as it grew more powerful. Solomon behaved like any other king of his time. He contracted marriage alliances with neighboring princes and allowed his wives to practice their own cults. He demanded extraordinary taxes and services from his people to pay for his lavish building projects. When he was unable to pay his Phoenician creditors for supplies and craft workers, he deported Israelites to work as slaves in Phoenician mines. Not surprisingly, the united kingdom did not survive Solomon's death. The northern region broke off to become the Kingdom of Israel with its capital in Shechem. The south, the Kingdom of Judah, continued the tradition of David from his capital of Jerusalem.

Beginning in the ninth century B.C.E., a new Mesopotamian power, the Assyrians, began a campaign of conquest and unprecedented brutality throughout western Asia. The Hebrew kingdoms were among their many victims. In 722 B.C.E., the Assyrians destroyed the Kingdom of Israel and deported thousands of its people to upper Mesopotamia. In 586 B.C.E., the Kingdom of Judah was conquered by Assyria's destroyers, the New Babylonian Empire under King Nebuchadnezzar II (604–562 B.C.E.). The temple of Solomon was destroyed, Jerusalem was burned, and Judah's elite were deported to Babylon. This Babylonian captivity ended some fifty years later when the Persians, who had conquered Babylonia, allowed the people of Judah to return to their homeland.

The Law and the Prophets

The religious significance of the people of Israel is as great as their political significance is small. The faith of the Israelites is the direct source of the three great Western religions: Judaism, Christianity, and Islam. Gradually, the relationship between Yahweh and the people of Israel was transformed from one of simple exclusivity to monotheism. Particularly after the Babylonian captivity, Yahweh was not simply one god among many but rather the one universal god, creator and ruler of the universe. Yahweh was so beyond human understanding that he could not be depicted in any image.

Although beyond all earthly powers, Yahweh intervened in human history to accomplish his goals. He formed a covenant with Abraham and renewed it with Moses. The covenant promised that Israel would be Yahweh's special people, but in return for this favor he demanded not simply sacrifices but righteousness. Thus ethics was a central aspect of Israel's religion.

Religious leaders, termed *prophets*, constantly explained historical events in terms of the faithfulness of the Israelite or, later, Jewish people (the term *Jew* means a descendant of those who occupied the Kingdom of Judah) to their covenant with Yahweh. The prophets were independent of royal control and spoke out constantly against any ruler whose immorality compromised the terms of the covenant. They called upon rulers and people to reform their lives and to return to Yahweh. The prophet Jeremiah (c. 650–570 B.C.E.) boldly accused King Jehoiakim (c. 609–598 B.C.E.) of Judah of reviving the cult of Ishtar and practicing child sacrifice and warned that Yahweh would send Babylon to destroy him. In Egypt or Mesopotamia, such dissenters would have been liquidated. Even in Israel and Judah, prophets often met with persecution. Some prophets were killed. Still they persisted, establishing a tradition of religious opposition to royal absolutism, a tradition that, like monotheism itself, is an enduring legacy.

Nineveh and Babylon

The Assyrian state that destroyed Israel accomplished what no other power had ever achieved. It tied together the floodplain civilizations of Mesopotamia and Egypt. But the Assyrian state was not just larger than the nation-states that had preceded it; it differed in nature as well as in size. The nation-states of Akkadia, Babylonia, the Hittites, and even the Egyptian empire were essentially diverse collections of city-states. Each preserved its own institutions and cultural traditions while diverting its economic resources to the capital. The Assyrian Empire was an integrated state in which conquered regions were reorganized and remade along the model of the central government. By the middle of the seventh century B.C.E., the Assyrian Empire stretched from the headwaters of the Tigris and Euphrates rivers to the Persian Gulf, along the coast from Syria to beyond the Delta, and up the Nile to Thebes.

The Assyrian plain north of Babylonia had long been a small Mesopotamian state threatened by seminomads and great powers such as the Babylonians and later the Hittites. When King Assur-dan II mounted the throne in 934 B.C.E., his country was, as he himself later said, exhausted. Gradually he and his successors began to strengthen the state against its enemies and to allow its population to rebuild its agricultural and commercial base. The Assyrian army, forged by constant warfare into

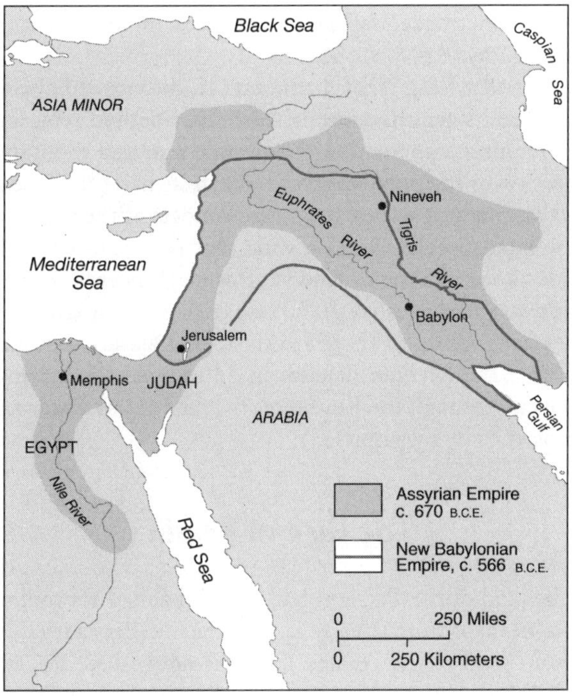

Assyrian and New Babylonian Kingdoms

a formidable military machine, began to extend the frontiers of the kingdom both toward the Mediterranean and down the twin rivers toward the Persian Gulf. However, like its predecessors, within a century this empire seemed destined for collapse.

Rapid growth and unprecedented wealth had created a new class of noble warriors, who were resented and mistrusted by the petty nobility of the old heartland of the Assyrian kingdom. The old nobility demanded a greater share in the imperial wealth and a more direct role in the administration of the empire. When the emperors ignored their demands, they began a long and bitter revolt that lasted from 827 B.C.E. until 750 B.C.E. This internal crisis put Assyria at the mercy of its external enemies, who seemed on the verge of destroying the Assyrian state. Instead, the revolt paved the way for the ascension of Tiglath-pileser III (746 B.C.E.–727 B.C.E.), the greatest empire builder of Mesopotamia since Sargon. Tiglath-pileser and his successors transformed the structure of the Assyrian state and expanded its empire. They created a model for empire that would later be copied by Persia, Macedonia, and Rome. In the sense that the Assyrians not only conquered but created an administrative system by which to rule, theirs was the first true empire.

From his capital at Nineveh, Tiglath-pileser combined all of the traditional elements of Mesopotamian statecraft with a new religious ideology and social system to create the framework for a lasting, multiethnic imperial system. This system rested on five bases: a transformed army, a new religious military ideology, a novel administrative system, a social policy involving large-scale population movements, and the calculated use of massive terror.

The heart of Tiglath-pileser's program was the most modern army the world had ever seen. In place of traditional armies of peasants and slaves supplied by great aristocrats, he raised professional armies from the conquered lands of the empire, commanded by Assyrian generals. The Assyrian army was also the first to use iron weapons on a massive scale. Assyrian armies were also well balanced, including not only infantry, cavalry, and chariots, but also engineering units for constructing the siege equipment needed to capture towns. Warfare had become a science.

In addition to the professional army, Tiglath-pileser created the most developed military-religious ideology of any ancient people. Kings had long been agents of the gods, but Ashur, the god of the Assyrians, had but one command: enlarge the empire! Thus warfare was the mission and duty of all, a sacred command paralleled through the centuries in the cries of "God wills it" of the Christian crusaders and the "God is great" of Muslims.

Tiglath-pileser restructured his empire, both at home in Assyria and abroad, so that revolts of the sort that had nearly destroyed it would be less possible. Within Assyria, he increased the number of administrative districts, thus decreasing the strength of each. This reduced the likelihood of successful rebellions launched by dissatisfied governors. Outside Assyria proper, whenever possible the king executed traditional leaders and appointed Assyrian governors, or at least assigned loyal overseers to protect his interests. Even then he did not allow governors and overseers unlimited authority or discretion; instead, he kept close contact with local administrators through a system of royal messengers.

In order to shatter regional identities, which could lead to separatist movements, Tiglath-pileser deported and resettled conquered peoples on a massive scale. He transported the Hebrews to Babylon, sent thirty thousand Syrians to the Zagros Mountains, and moved eighteen thousand Aramaeans from the Tigris to Syria. The resettled peoples, cut off from their homelands by hundreds of miles and surrounded by people speaking different languages and practicing different religions, posed no threat to the stability of the empire.

ISRAEL: BETWEEN TWO WORLDS

c. 1050 B.C.E.	Philistines defeat the Israelies
c. 1000–961 B.C.E.	David, king of Israel
c. 961–922 B.C.E.	Solomon, king of Israel
827–750 B.C.E.	Revolt of Assyrian petty nobility
746–727 B.C.E.	Tiglath-pileser III
722 B.C.E.	Assyrians destroy Kingdom of Israel
612 B.C.E.	Medes and Babylonians take Nineveh
604–562 B.C.E.	Nebuchadnezzar II
586 B.C.E.	Nebuchadnezzar II conquers Kingdom of Judah
539 B.C.E.	Cyrus II of Persia takes the city of Babylon

Finally, in the tradition of his Assyrian predecessors, Tiglath-pileser and his successors maintained control of conquered peoples through a policy of unprecedented cruelty and brutality. One, for example, boasted of once having flayed an enemy's chiefs and using their skins to cover a great pillar he erected at their city gate and on which he impaled his victims.

Ironically, while the imperial military and administrative system created by the Assyrians became in time the blueprint for future empires, its very ferocity led to its downfall. The hatred inspired by such brutality led to the destruction of the Assyrian Empire at the hands of a coalition of its subjects. In what is today Iran, Indo-European tribes coalesced around the Median dynasty. Egypt shook off its Assyrian lords under the leadership of the pharaoh Psamtik I (664 B.C.E.-610 B.C.E.). In Babylon, which had always proven difficult for the Assyrians to control, a new Aramaean dynasty began to oppose Assyrian rule. In 612 B.C.E., the Medes and Babylonians joined forces to attack and destroy Nineveh. Once more, the pattern begun by Sargon, of imperial expansion, consolidation, decay, and destruction, was repeated.

However, the lessons that the Assyrians taught the world were not forgotten by the Babylonians, who modeled their imperial system on that of their predecessors. Administration of the New Babylonian Empire, which extended roughly over the length of the Tigris and extended west into Syria and Palestine, owed much to Assyrian tradition. The Code of Hammurabi once more formed the fundamental basis for justice. Babylonian kings restored and enriched temples to the Babylonian gods, and temple lands, administered by priests appointed by the king, played an important role in Babylonian economy and culture. Babylonian priests, using the mathematical methods developed during the Old Kingdom, made important advances in mathematical astronomy.

Under King Nebuchadnezzar II, the city of Babylon reached its zenith, covering some five hundred acres and containing a population of over one hundred thousand, over twice the population of Uruk at its height. The city walls, counted among the seven wonders of the world by the later Greeks, were so wide that two chariots could ride abreast on them. And yet this magnificent fortification was never tested. In 539 B.C.E., a Persian army under King Cyrus II (c. 585B.C.E.–c. 529 B.C.E.), who had ousted the Median dynasty in 550 B.C.E., slipped into the city through the Euphrates riverbed at low water and took the city by surprise.

The Rise of Persia

The land of the Persians had been inhabited for millennia, perhaps from as early as 15,000 B.C.E. Persia itself, or Iran ("land of the Aryans"), as it is now called, lies at a crossroads between the rugged lands of western Asia, the plains of central Asia, the great steppes to the northeast, and Afghanistan and the Indus valley to the east. At the heart of Persia is a high central plateau surrounded by mountains, which separate the plains of the interior from the Caspian Sea to the north and the Persian Gulf to the south. Two extensive deserts, virtually impassable in the summer, lie in the center of the immense plateau; from time immemorial they have diverted nomads from central Asia into India to the east or the Tigris-Euphrates valley to the west. The lowlands beyond the mountains receive most of the region's precipitation and thus contrast sharply with the dry interior. The land is rich in minerals, particularly iron, copper, and brilliant blue lapis lazuli. Early in its history western Iran, known then as Elam, fell under Sumerian influence. Persia as a whole, however, was only sparsely settled by prehistoric peoples throughout the centuries of Sumerian and Babylonian rule.

Around 1000 B.C.E., as we have seen, conditions in western Asia were generally unstable. The Egyptians had begun their decline, the Assyrians had not yet established firm rule, and the mass movements of the Peoples of the Sea had created havoc, destroying the Hittites in the process. About the same time, tribes of nomadic horse-riding warriors migrated from central Asia into Iran, bringing their flocks and herds. Without horses, the prehistoric inhabitants were no match for them. Among the invading tribes were the Indo-European Medes and Persians, both of whom were related to the Aryans who settled India. The Medes and Persians were soon joined by the warlike Scythians, who had in turn been driven from the far eastern steppe, where the Huns, a people from central Asia, were at war with the Chinese.

The Medes and Persians established a number of small kingdoms, each of which was ruled by a king who was little more than a warlord supported by a band of warriors. Below this elite group, early Iranian society was comprised of free farmers, skilled artisans, peasants who owed labor to the king, and slaves. The Medes and Persians traded with other peoples in the region, particularly the Assyrians to the west, who were attracted by Iranian horses and minerals. The Medes, who had settled in northern Iran, united in the late eighth century B.C.E., after which they imposed their rule on the Persians in the south.

An alliance of Medes and Scythians, together with the help of other nomadic tribes, sacked Nineveh in 612 B.C.E., ending the Assyrian empire. Throughout these tumultuous events the Persians retained their tribal identity and through a process of intermarriage and aggression established their rule over most of Iran. In 550 B.C.E. the Medes, weakened by their struggles to the west, were resoundingly defeated by Cyrus (559–530 B.C.E.), chief of the Persian tribes. The land of the Medes became Cyrus' first province, or satrapy.

Approximately 546 B.C.E. Cyrus conquered prosperous Lydia and the Greek cities on the Anatolian coast, in what is now western Turkey. This gave him possession of the ports that marked the western terminus of the trade routes extending from the Aegean Sea deep into Asia. After securing his eastern frontiers by fighting that extended as far as Afghanistan and western India, he turned to the southwest and in 539 B.C.E. captured Babylon. That city, which had recently witnessed the splendid reign of Nebuchadnezzar, became an important symbol of Persian success. Cyrus included the title "king of Babylon" in his inscriptions and spent considerable time there. As a conqueror he distinguished himself by his appreciation of the cultures of his new subjects; local customs and religious beliefs were not suppressed.

Cyrus' son and successor, Cambyses (530–522 B.C.E.), conquered Egypt in 525 B.C.E. and tried to reach Carthage (modern Tunis), but he failed to persuade his Phoenician allies to attack their Carthaginian kinsmen. His plan to conquer Ethiopia also remained largely unfulfilled because of inadequate supplies. Cambyses was said to have been mentally unbalanced, and he was cruel enough to kill his own brother.

The accession of Darius I (522–486 B.C.E.) returned stability to the Persian Empire and inaugurated nearly two centuries of peaceful Persian rule. Among his accomplishments were the introduction of a uniform system of gold and silver coinage, standard weights and measures, a postal service, an imperial law code based on Mesopotamian principles, and a common calendar derived from the Egyptians'. Darius' reign saw further attempts to extend the empire. Around 513 or 512 B.C.E. he sent expeditions into southeastern Europe, reaching as far as the river Danube, and into India, the northwestern portion of which became the satrapy of Hindush. Darius wanted to improve communications and trade, and to that end supported an expedition that sailed from the Indus River to the northern end of the Red Sea. Darius also became embroiled with the people to the far west, the Greeks, against whom he and his successor, Xerxes, launched three unsuccessful expeditions. Despite his failure to conquer the Greeks, Darius' empire enjoyed trade relations with people as far away as India to the east and Phoenicia on the Mediterranean. The Persians planned to construct a canal from the Nile to the Red Sea; had they succeeded, Alexander the Great, with better supply lines at his disposal, might have conquered India, and fifteenth-century explorers might not have sought a passage across the Atlantic Ocean to East Asia as an alternative to sailing around the African continent.

Life and Government in the Persian Empire

At its height the Persian Empire was prosperous and cosmopolitan. Foreign artisans worked with materials that came from Greece, Lebanon, and India to decorate the royal palaces. The Persians traded widely, using their gold coin, the daric, and maintained contacts throughout western Asia. Many of the people under their control did not speak their language, and the monuments on the Royal Road, the principal highway to cross part of the empire, featured inscriptions in Babylonian and Elamite as well as Persian. Some 1,600 miles long (the distance from New York to Dallas), the Royal Road extended from Susa in western Persia to Sardis, near the port of Ephesus, a Greek city on the Aegean. It took caravans three months to travel this road, although royal couriers, using fresh horses provided at the 111 post stations along the route, could make the trip in a week.

For all the power of their ruler, the "king of kings," the Persians' view of their monarchy differed from that of the Assyrians. The king was not an object of fear but a righteous leader, elected by the gods. The empire was in general ruled with efficiency, justice, and tolerance. It was so large that it had to be divided into some 20 satrapies or provinces, each of which was administered by a governor (or satrap), aided by a military force under a separate commander. The presence of military officials, royal agents, and spies prevented the governors, who were Mede or Persian nobles, from exercising excessive power. The king was interested primarily in receiving from the satraps appropriate tribute and recruits for the military; if those demands were fulfilled, the governors enjoyed substantial autonomy.

Persian Capitals: Susa and Persepolis

The principal centers of the empire were at Susa, eastern terminus of the Royal Road; Ecbatana, the former Mede capital; and ancient Babylon. Susa, which had been inhabited since Neolithic times, was situated at the foot of the Zagros Mountains, near the bank of the river Karkheh. Beginning in 521 B.C.E. Darius made it his principal capital for most of the year, leaving only in the summer to escape the intense heat. He ordered the construction of a citadel and a sumptuous palace, as well as walls and a moat for protection. He imported workers from many lands: stonecutters from Greece and Asia Minor, goldsmiths from Egypt, brickmakers from Babylon. Their materials included cedar from Lebanon, gold from Bactria, and ivory from Ethiopia. Susa became a cosmopolitan center; the biblical Book of Esther is set there.

In 518 B.C.E. Darius began the construction of a new capital at Persepolis, a remote site in an alpine region southeast of Susa. The style of architecture and sculpture that developed at Persepolis, like that at Susa, was highly eclectic. Lacking their own architectural traditions, the Persians drew on those of others. Like the Sumerians, they employed mud brick and constructed their palaces on terraces, although they used the kind of glazed decoration found on Nebuchadnezzar's palace at Babylon. Assyrian human-headed bulls, Egyptian doorways, and Greek columns can be found at Persepolis; visiting Greek and Egyptian artists almost certainly produced some of the decorative sculpture.

The site of Persepolis was topped by a citadel. The lower slopes of the mountain on which it stands were leveled to allow construction on a terrace ranging from 14 to 41 feet above the ground. The terrace was reached by a stairway broad enough to be used by groups of riders. Upon it were monumental public buildings, each intended to reinforce the impression of splendor. The approach to the vast audience hall of the royal palace built by Darius and Xerxes between 520 and 460 B.C.E. was by an elaborate staircase lined with sculptural decoration. The reliefs showed a procession of officials, soldiers, and representatives of the peoples of the empire bringing tribute to the king. The great hall was 60 feet high and contained three dozen 40-foot columns. On a retaining wall, Darius inscribed a prayer for his subjects: "God protect this country from foe, famine, and falsehood."

Darius' successors maintained the Persian Empire until Alexander the Great conquered it between 334 and 326 B.C.E. The arrival of Alexander and his troops thrust Europe and Asia into the long period of mutual influence that has lasted, despite interruptions, to our own time.

Zoroastrianism and Mithraism

We know less about Zoroastrianism, the dominant religion of ancient and classical Persia (Iran), than about any of the others described in this chapter. Zoroaster, its founder, lived long before the advent of preserved written records in Persia, probably between 800 and 600 B.C.E., and the incomplete texts we have on the belief and practice of the religion he founded come mainly from the thirteenth century C.E., although earlier texts existed by the sixth century B.C.E. The founder's name in Persian was Zarathustra (Zoroaster was the Greek version), and his teachings are recorded and embroidered in the Avesta, but the form of the Avesta we have is only a fragmentary remnant of earlier texts and includes much later material. To the Greeks and Romans, Zoroaster was famous as the founder of the wisdom of the Magi, mythical Iranian priest-kings. In his youth he reportedly had celestial visions and conversations with divine beings, after which he became a wandering preacher. Later he interested an eastern Iranian prince in his teachings; the prince became his protector and advocate, and the new religion became a state church.

Zoroastrian Beliefs

Zoroastrianism was rooted in the old Iranian or Aryan folk religion, and there are some striking similarities between it and the religion of Vedic India. Both are polytheistic (professing many gods), and both worshiped Indra as well as natural forces, especially fire. Both believed in the supremacy of moral powers and of an eternal natural law and a creative principle. The major difference lay in the pronounced dualism of Zoroastrianism, which divided creation into the powers of good and evil, light and darkness. Vedic India called all their gods and goddesses *deva,* and although many of them had destructive aspects, in general they were seen as good. Zoroastrianism used the closely related term *daeva* in Persian to refer to evil spirits only, which are opposed and kept in check by the forces of good and light, incorporated in the supreme deity, the sexless Ahura-Mazda. In one of several striking parallels with Judeo-Christian theology, Ahura-Mazda's original twin, Ahriman, was, like Lucifer, banished from heaven to hell, where he or she reigns as the principle of evil. Earlier cults, such as that of Mithras, the god of day, survived within Zoroastrianism and later spread to the Mediterranean.

Zoroaster reportedly said that he received a commission from God to purify religion, in effect by transcending the earlier cults, introducing moral laws, and constructing a theory of the universe embodying the dualist principle. By his time Iranian society was based mainly on agriculture rather than hunting, gathering, or nomadism; had developed cities and towns; and was ready for a more sophisticated theology than nature worship alone or ritual cults. Ahura-Mazda is the personification not only of power and majesty but also of ethical principles for guidance. She or he is described in the Avesta as assisted by her or his creatures, "immortal holy ones," the forces of good sense or good principle, truth, law, order, reverence, immortality, and obedience. The history of the conflict between these good forces and the forces of evil is the history of the world. Creation is divided between these two forces, whose endless conflict has as its object the human soul. People are creations of Ahura-Mazda, but they are free to decide and to act and can be influenced by the forces of evil. All human life and activity are part of this conflict. By a true confession of faith, by good deeds, and by keeping body and soul pure, any individual can limit the power of the evil forces and strengthen the power of goodness. Evil deeds, words, and thoughts strengthen the power of evil.

After death, each person is judged in heaven, according to the Book of Life in which all deeds, thoughts, and words are recorded. Wicked actions cannot be undone but can be balanced by good works. If the balance is favorable, the person enters paradise; if unfavorable, he or she suffers the eternal pains of hell. If the account is equally balanced, a kind of limbo or intermediate stage is provided, with the final lot to be decided at the last judgment. The Avesta tells us almost nothing about ceremonial worship, but it appears from early times to have centered on a sacred fire. Later development of the religion added the doctrine of repentance, atonement, and the remission of sins, administered by priests.

Zoroaster saw himself as a prophet and believed that the end of the present world and the coming of the Kingdom of Heaven were near. For most people his doctrines were too abstract; both old and new popular deities became part of Zoroastrianism in later periods, and a priesthood developed that organized and conducted worship and laid down detailed laws for the purification of the body and soul, the conduct of good works, the giving of alms, the pursuit of agriculture, and the prohibition against either burning or burying the dead. Both soil and fire, as well as water, were considered sacred and not to be defiled by death. Bodies were to be exposed in appointed places, sometimes on an elevated platform, for consumption by vultures and wild dogs. Originally Zoroastrianism apparently had no temples, but in later periods fire altars came into use, and these evolved into temples where priests performed sacrifices and other rituals. Priests were the teachers and keepers of the religion; every young believer, after being received into the religion, was supposed to choose a spiritual guide, usually a priest. Most of the changes mentioned here seem to have come about by approximately the sixth century B.C.E. and to have begun considerably earlier.

With the rise of the Persian Empire in the sixth century B.C.E., Zoroastrianism became the state religion. Under the Achemenid dynasty and its conquests, the religion spread over most of western Asia and the Turkic republics of central Asia. After the collapse of this first empire, Zoroastrianism languished and then was restored to new vigor under the Sassanids from the third to the seventh centuries C.E., when it was again the state church; the state enforced compliance with its religious laws. The Arab conquest of Persia, complete by 637, and the persecutions that followed largely extinguished Zoroastrianism in the land of its birth. In modern Iran there remain only a very few followers, now under new pressure from the rigid fundamentalism of its Muslim rulers. The chief survivors are the Parsees of the Bombay area (the name Parsee is a corruption of *Persian*), who came originally from Persia to India about the eighth century C.E., primarily to escape Muslim persecution; they still maintain most of the doctrine and practices of classical Zoroastrianism.

Zoroastrianism, as well as the cult of Mithras, which it incorporated, had a profound influence on Eastern and Western thinking during the time of its flourishing. It has obvious similarities both with Hinduism and with Judaism and Christianity, and in part even with Islam, especially its doctrines on life after death. Its basic dualistic emphasis helped shape early Christian theology, and more than traces of what was eventually labeled the "dualistic heresy" remain even in modern Christian thought, like its pre-Christian ideas about the judgment of the dead, the relationship between faith and good works, and the role of the priesthood. Arising out of more primitive cults, especially the worship of fire and of the sun, it became through the teachings of Zoroaster and his successors a sophisticated theological, cosmological, and ethical system that was known to and admired by both Eastern and Western civilizations before or during the period when they were working out their own transition from tribal cults to mature religious thought. Although Zoroastrianism largely ceased to exist nearly 14 centuries ago, many of its ideas live on in the other great religions.

Mithraism

The worship of Mithras began as early as the fourth century B.C.E. Originally Ahura-Mazda's chief aide in the battle against the powers of darkness, Mithras became the central figure in a cult that spread rapidly throughout western Asia and into Europe, arriving in Rome in the first century B.C.E. In the years following C.E. 100 it acquired many new adherents in Italy and other parts of the Roman Empire, attracting the lower classes, slaves, and soldiers, who took their religious customs with them when they served abroad; a temple to Mithras has been discovered in the Roman remains of London. By the late third century Mithraism was vying with Christianity to replace the old paganism, though Constantine's support of the Christians caused Mithraism's rapid decline.

Mithraism's broad appeal was probably due to the fact that it combined the spirituality of its origins with humanizing detail. Unlike Ahura-Mazda, the remote god of light, Mithras, god of day, was born in human form on December 25 in a cave. When he grew up, he slaughtered a mythical sacred bull, whose blood fertilized the earth. After a time Mithras returned to heaven, where he intercedes with Ahura-Mazda on behalf of his followers.

Ceremonies in honor of Mithras were held in special temples known as Mithraea, which often took the form of underground caves in memory of his birth. Among the rites of initiation was baptism in a bull's blood, which formed one of the seven stages of induction; others included the recitation of various miracles that Mithras had performed, such as ending a drought and averting a flood. It is a measure of Mithraism's appeal that Christianity adopted a number of its external characteristics, including the symbolic date of December 25 as the birthday of Jesus; the day marks the approximate period of the winter solstice, when the sun, returning from south of the equator, is "reborn." In the end Mithraism gained no lasting hold. One reason for this may be that women were not accepted as initiates and played no part in the rituals or the myths. By contrast, many early converts to Christianity were women.

The Foundations of Indian Culture, 3000–1000 B.C.E.

The civilizations of ancient India are in some ways very similar and in other ways very different from those of ancient western Asia. As in both Africa and western Asia, geography was an important determinant of ancient Indian civilization. India can be divided into two large geographical regions: the broad plains of the Indus and Ganges rivers in the north, and the peninsular south, which is subdivided into many smaller regions by mountains, plateaus, and river valleys. The agricultural season is governed by the monsoon, seasonal rains that fall from June to October. These geographical and climatic factors have important implications for agriculture, and are important in providing a backdrop for India's regional diversity.

The earliest civilizations in ancient India arose in the Indus River valley, in what is today Pakistan. The first of these was the Harappan civilization, named after

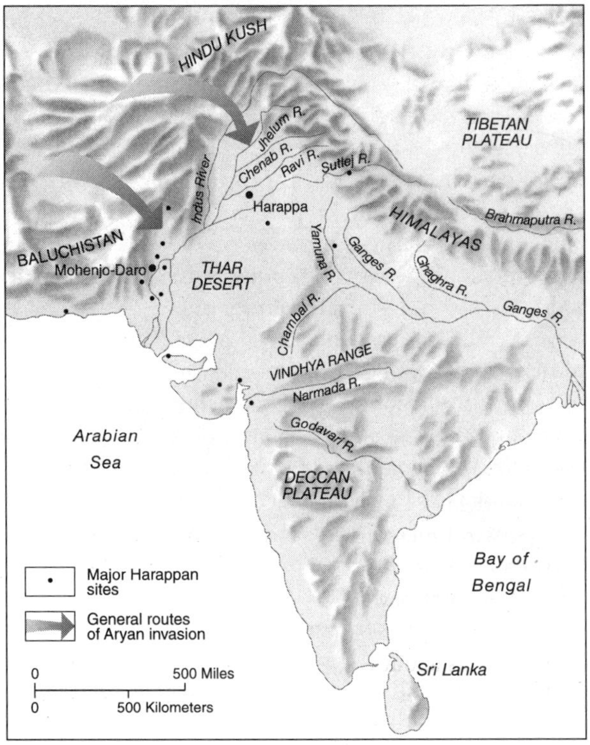

India 3000–1000 B.C.E.

Harappa, one of the most important ancient cities. The civilization comprised an area of half a million square miles, and encompassed many local cultures that maintained a degree of regional difference yet shared common features. In about 1500 B.C.E., a group of seminomadic people calling themselves Aryans invaded the Indian subcontinent from the north.

Harappa was a lost city, and its achievements and those of the civilization that bears its name were unknown to later generations of Indians. Not until archaeologists uncovered its ruins in the early twentieth century did the magnitude of the earliest civilizations in India become clear. But the culture established by the Aryans, the second civilization of ancient India, preserved in texts called Vedas, or "Books of Knowledge," has had a profound influence on subsequent Indian memory and imagination.

Seals from Mohenjo-Daro often featured mythical beasts. The writing may have identified the owner. Such seals have been found as far afield as Mesopotamia.

The Lost Civilizations of Harappa and Mohenjo-Daro

Most of our knowledge of Harappan civilization comes from archaeological excavations that began in the early 1900s and continue to the present day. Our conclusions change frequently as new finds are made, interpreted, and reinterpreted. To reconstruct the life of a people through their burial practices, their ruined cities, and fragments of their pottery or metal objects is not a precise science and lively controversy abounds. One of the liveliest controversies surrounds the deciphering of the Harappan writing system.

Sometime in the early third millennium B.C.E., Neolithic settlers from the hills of Baluchistan began to spread to the valley of the Indus River, a valley rich with silt. Farmers planted some crops, like wheat and barley, at the end of the monsoon. Those fields required neither plowing nor fertilizing, nor did the crops require additional water. Farmers planted other crops, such as cotton and sesame, at the beginning of the monsoon and harvested them at its end. To regulate the amount of water that reached these crops, farmers built embankments around fields. Thus these earliest settlers manipulated their environment to obtain a living from the soil. Although the land was fertile and the rains regular, Harappan life cannot have been easy. Analysis of human skeletons found at Harappan sites shows that the average age at death was about thirty.

The city of Harappa had a population of from thirty-five thousand to forty thousand people. A second city, Mohenjo-Daro, was somewhat smaller. In addition to several other large cities, archaeologists have found a thousand small sites. Thus, although there was an important urban component to Harappan civilization, the geographical range and the dispersal of the Harappan culture mark it as different from the city-states of western Asia.

In spite of the differences among the sites, an identifiable Harappan culture style had become dominant by the late third millennium B.C.E. The Harappan cultural style is marked by several features, including town planning, a uniform system of weights and measures, and writing. The streets of both Harappa and Mohenjo-Daro were laid out in a gridlike fashion, and the bricks used in construction are of standardized sizes. Large-scale public works, such as granaries, drainage ditches (some covered with brick slabs) and sewage facilities, also indicate a degree of centralized power and central planning. In the strata (or layers) excavated at Mohenjo-Daro, the layout of the streets is remarkably consistent from one layer to another, indicating considerable continuity. In addition, ceramics produced at various Harappan sites share common stylistic features. One of the most widespread of Harappan ceramics is small carts modeled in clay, possibly toys for the children of ancient India.

The Harappan writing system remains a tantalizing puzzle. The script bears no relationship to any surviving writing system, and has not yet been clearly deciphered. Samples of Harappan writing are preserved on small

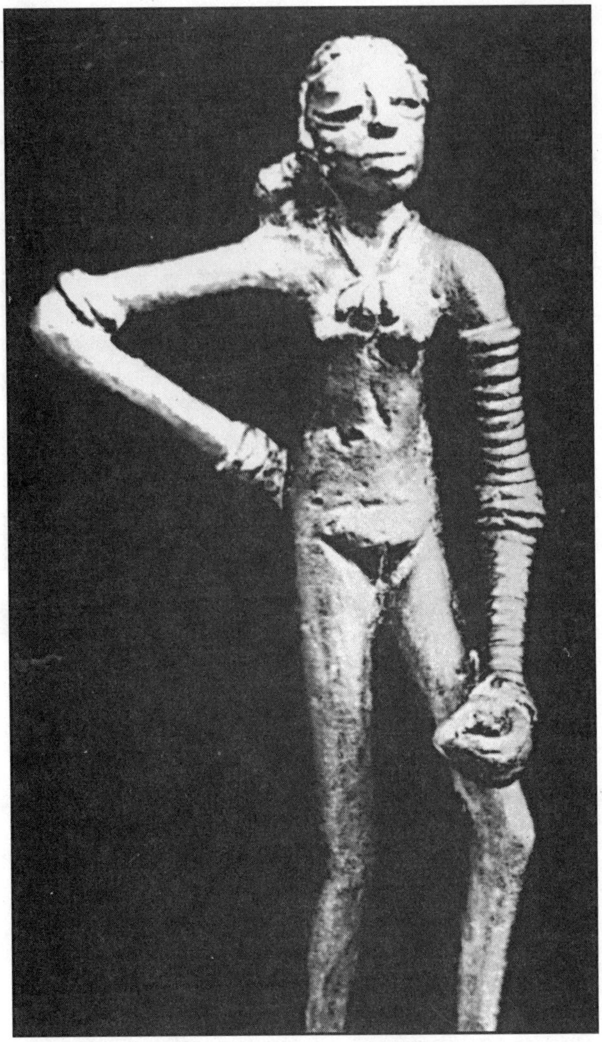

This bronze figure from Mohenjo-Daro is called the Dancing Girl.

stone and clay seals, probably used in trading. The inscriptions are short, the longest being twenty-one characters long. About four hundred symbols have been identified to date. The writing system is what linguists refer to as logo-syllabic, which means that some symbols refer to whole words and others to sounds. (Both Egyp-tian hieroglyphics and modern Japanese characters are also logo-syllabic writing systems.) The stone and clay seals may have identified goods, and the texts on them the occupation, social status, geographical location, and given name or lineage of the owner of the seal. Although much about the language remains uncertain, it appears to be related to a south Indian language family called Dravidian.

The most important economic activities concerned food production. Wheat was the most important grain, but Harappan farmers also cultivated rice. More important to the Harappan economy than agriculture was cattle breeding. Skeletal remains indicate extensive animal domestication. Indeed, these Indians were the first to domesticate the chicken, and most of today's breeds are descendants of birds first domesticated in India long ago. Exotic birds were among the products exported to Sumer.

Handicrafts were also important to the Harappan economy. Samples of dyed cloth have been found at Mohenjo-Daro. Harappans began spinning and weaving cotton about 2000 B.C.E. At Mohenjo-Daro the craftsmen's quarters seem to have been spread throughout the city, whereas at Chanhu-Daro, a much smaller city, they were clustered in the center of the city. This clustered settlement pattern may imply a system of social stratification, in which some residents had more power and prestige than others.

A careful reading of the physical remains can lead us to a variety of conclusions about the religious life of the Harappan people. A large brick tank at Mohenjo-Daro may be a pool that was used for ritualized bathing. Ritual bathing has been an important part of subsequent Indian religious practice. Hundreds of images of women with prominent breasts and hips have been discovered, suggesting that Harappans may have worshiped a mother goddess. Phallic images indicate that fertility, both of the land and of its inhabitants, was important to these early inhabitants of India.

Harappan civilization was a literate, sedentary, sophisticated culture, spread out over much of the Indus valley. About 1750 B.C.E., the civilization seems to have begun to decline, although the reasons for the decline are unclear. Thirty or so skeletons found at Mohenjo-Daro were not buried but were trapped, perhaps fleeing some catastrophe. Perhaps they were fleeing the flooding Indus River, perhaps an earthquake. Whatever the cause of the crisis, the delicate balance upon which Harappan civilization rested crumbled, and the civilization began its decline.

THE FOUNDATIONS OF INDIAN CULTURE

3000–1500 B.C.E.	Indus Valley civilizations of Harappa and Mohenjo-Daro
1750 B.C.E.	Beginning of Aryan invasions
1500–500 B.C.E.	Vedic societies

The Aryan Invasion and the Roots of Vedic Culture

Shortly after Harappan civilization fell into decline, the Aryans entered the Indian subcontinent from the northwest. The language they brought with them, an antecedent of Sanskrit, is one of the family of Indo-European languages. (One can see the relationship between the Sanskrit and Latin words for king, for example: the former is *raja*, the latter is *rex*.) They were seminomadic and illiterate. But they had superior military technology: the horse and chariot. The Aryans are but the first in a long line of examples of horse-riding invaders who conquered and transformed sedentary cultures.

The main source for the history of this period is the four collections of "Books of Knowledge," or Vedas, that were collected and preserved by priestly lineages. The oldest of these, the *Rig Veda*, consists of 1,017 Sanskrit poems and is the oldest surviving piece of Indo-European literature. According to tradition it was composed around 1500 B.C.E., though it was not written down until much later. Each priestly lineage would memorize the Vedas and pass them on orally to the next generation. Because the texts were sacred, great importance was attached to transmitting them unchanged from generation to generation.

The Vedas reveal a complex religious system and a rich pantheon of gods. Vedic religion had an important influence on later Hinduism, but it is distinct from it. Vedic religion emphasized the afterlife. The House of Clay, presided over by Varuna, the king of universal order, was the Vedic place of eternal punishment. The House of the Fathers was a place of eternal reward. The Vedas provide a rich pantheon of deities. In addition to Varuna, Aryans worshiped Indra, the thunderbolt-wielding young god of war; Rudra, the storm god; Agni, the fire god; and Ushas, the goddess of dawn.

The Vedic deities are not infallible. They are subject to emotion and error. The deities and the members of the human race each have their own specific duties. As long as god and mortal each perform these allotted duties, the cosmos is in balance. But gods and mortals are not the only inhabitants of the cosmos: there are also demons. And demons are constantly battling the gods, trying to upset the cosmic order. One of the chief ritual acts human priests perform in the Vedas is sacrifice to the gods, to obtain their favor and to restore the cosmic balance. The sacrifice was often of an animal. Central to the ritual was the consuming of soma, an intoxicating drink. The mythological origins of kingship are linked to this cosmic struggle between gods and demons. One such myth relates that during the course of a protracted battle between gods and demons, the gods selected a king to lead them in battle. Thus religion is deeply implicated in the political order.

Although the Vedas are primarily religious texts, we can derive some information on social life from them. Aryan society was firmly patrilineal and patriarchal. Fathers governed their families, and kin groups claiming descent from a common male ancestor comprised the fundamental unit of society. Earlier Vedic societies (late second to early first millennium B.C.E.) were tribal or lineage-based. The economy was largely pastoral. But by the late Vedic period (800–600 B.C.E.), the tribes and lineages had coalesced into kingdoms, typically ruled by a warrior-king. There were no regularized legal institutions: custom served as law, and its arbiters were the king and his priests.

When the Aryans arrived in India, they divided their society into three groups: the ruling warriors known as Kshatriyas; the priests, or Brahmans; and the cultivators. The non-Aryan inhabitants of India formed a fourth group. The first three groups were known as the twice-born, because males in the group underwent an initiation to adulthood. Only members of these highest three groups—both male and female—could perform Vedic sacrifices. This hierarchical way of organizing society and social interactions was the beginning of the caste system, which would be elaborated and made much more rigid in later Indian history.

In this early period, some key aspects of Indian culture were established. The Vedas would remain crucial religious texts in later eras. The language of the Vedas, Sanskrit, was to function as the classical language of later India. And the caste system was to be one of the determining aspects of Indian civilization. Regional variation is another theme we will see again in the history of the Indian subcontinent. The cultures of the Indian subcontinent are marked by a complex mixture of elements the Aryans brought with them and elements from the time before the conquest.

Cradles of Chinese Civilization, 5000–1000 B.C.E.

If Indian civilization is marked by the sharp discontinuity of the Aryan invasions and by great regional diversity, Chinese civilization reveals a remarkable level of continuity and cultural uniformity. We can see elements of this even in the earliest periods. The writing system devised during the Shang dynasty four thousand years ago

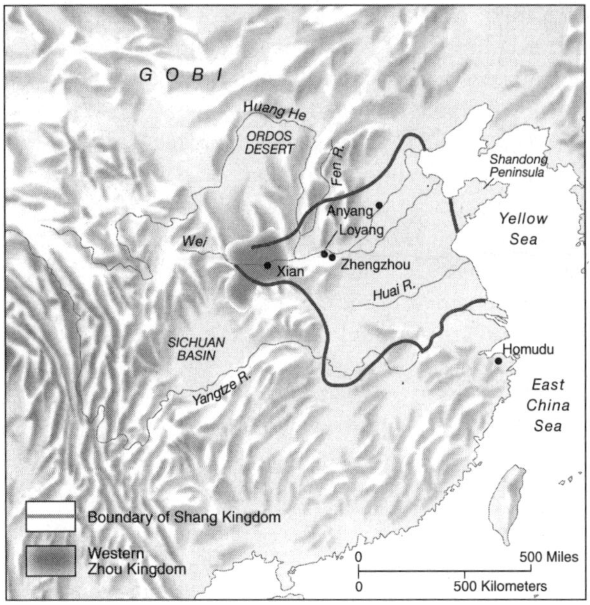

Cradles of Chinese Civilization

is clearly related to modern Chinese writing. And writing is not the only aspect of identifiably "Chinese" culture to be established in those early days. Chinese culture is not unchanging, but there is a durability to Chinese cultural forms that we rarely see elsewhere in the world.

Neolithic Villages

Chinese civilization has several cradles. Around 5000 B.C.E., when the Yangshao culture was emerging in the north, villagers farther south in Homudu (in present-day Zhejiang province) began to cultivate rice and construct complex wooden houses. In what is now Vietnam, coastal peoples developed their own distinctive agricultural and craft traditions.

The Neolithic Yangshao culture centered on small villages, frequently built on hills to avoid floods. The villagers built their houses of tamped earth with thatched roofs. They practiced slash-and-burn agriculture, a form of cultivation in which land is cleared (the growth is slashed and burned), and then cultivated. After a few years, the land is abandoned, and new land is brought into cultivation. As long as land is plentiful, this method of cultivation is reasonably productive, but it ceases to be efficient after the population reaches a certain level.

Yangshao farmers domesticated dogs and pigs. Cut silkworm cocoons found at Yangshao sites indicate that sericulture (the cultivation of silk) is as old in China as sedentary agriculture itself. Yangshao people used tools made of polished and chipped stone. Their kilns were capable of temperatures of between 1000 and 1500 degrees Fahrenheit. Yangshao painted pottery, decorated with designs of fish and birds, was elaborate and beautiful, but there is no evidence that it was cast on a potter's wheel.

The Yangshao people had elaborate burial practices that give evidence that their society was stratified. They buried the dead in special burial grounds and buried women and men separately. In some sites a high percentage of women's graves are richly endowed with grave goods, sometimes more elaborate than those of their male counterparts, raising the possibility that China in antiquity may have been a matriarchal society. In a matriarchal society, the family is the crucial social unit, and the most powerful person in the family is the mother. Later Chinese societies were strongly patriarchal.

Another north Chinese Neolithic culture, called the Longshan, followed the Yangshao. Longshan villages, also built on hills, were typically fortified with tamped-earth ramparts and surrounded by moatlike ditches. The Longshan people produced distinctive black pottery, using a potter's wheel. Potter's marks on many Longshan pots may be prototypes of numbers. Some pots bear phallic symbols and were probably objects of fertility cults. Longshan farmers domesticated the sheep and the ox, as well as the dog and the pig. Despite the importance of agriculture, hunting and fishing remained important to the economy of Longshan villages.

In addition to the northern Chinese Neolithic sites of Yangshao and Longshan, there were also important southern sites. For example, a Neolithic site at Homudu, which can be dated to about 5000 B.C.E., features rice, hand-made pottery, and distinctive wooden mortise-and-tenon architecture. Sites on the southeast coast include Bo-nam and Con Moong, in what is now Vietnam. The southeast coastal sites had a common culture, using similar pottery and stone tools. They also shared a common diet of taro, yams, and other roots. We know less about the southern Neolithic cultures because the region's high humidity destroys artifacts and the archaeological record is meager. Nonetheless the southern cultures significantly influenced the formation of what would become Chinese civilization.

Certain aspects of the Chinese Neolithic were common to Neolithic villages worldwide: villagers practiced sedentary agriculture and produced rudimentary tools and pottery. But other artifacts from Chinese villages reveal that distinctive Chinese practices were beginning to emerge: the cultivation of rice and silk, for example.

The Shang Dynasty

With the Shang dynasty, more elements of a distinctively Chinese culture emerged. The writing system, ancestor worship, and a political system characterized by both king and bureaucracy are three of the most important of these cultural traits.

The traditional Chinese written record extends about twenty-five hundred years into the past. The earliest texts describe events that happened thousands of years before their compilation. Until recently, scholars considered the first two dynasties in the written record, the Xia (2005–1784 B.C.E.) and the Shang (1784–1050 B.C.E.) to be legendary. But archaeology has radically transformed our view of China's antiquity, firmly establishing the historical existence of the Shang and suggesting that of the Xia. Ongoing archaeological research in the People's Republic of China will continue to illuminate and amplify our views of the past.

In the early twentieth century, scholars discovered Shang "texts" that are contemporary to the events they describe. These texts are called oracle bones, and are among the most remarkable aspects of Shang culture. They are the product of Shang dynasty divination practices, in which a priest inscribed a question on a turtle shell or sheep's shoulder bone (or scapula, hence the term for this kind of divination, scapulimancy). The diviner then placed the shell or bone into a fire, and interpreted the resulting cracks as the gods' or ancestors' answer to the question. A pit containing 107,000 of these bones was found at Anyang, and smaller finds have been made elsewhere. The oracle bones are an extremely important source for Shang history. They are particularly rich in information about the ruling house, about warfare, and about religion.

Inscribed bronze vessels, dating from about 2000 B.C.E., are another important source for Shang history. The vessels celebrated ceremonial occasions—succession to the throne, military victory, and so on. The inscriptions describe military exploits and political alliances.

CRADLES OF CHINESE CIVILIZATION

5000 B.C.E.	Beginnings of Yangshao and Longshan civilizations in north China
5000 B.C.E.	Beginnings of Homudu civilization in south China
2005 –1784 B.C.E.	Xia dynasty
1784 –1050 B.C.E.	Shang dynasty

This exquisite jade bird was found in the Shang dynasty tomb of lady-commander Fu Hao.

The language inscribed on the bones and bronzes is quite different from modern Chinese, but it is clearly recognizable as Chinese. The Chinese language is written with characters, rather than with an alphabet. Each character represents a word. Many, though not all, of the characters are pictographic. The forms of the characters have been modified somewhat, as have some of the fine points of grammar. But the language written by Shang diviners thousands of years ago can be deciphered by speakers of modern Chinese with a minimum of specialized training, much as native speakers of English need some training to read the Old English of *Beowulf.*

Shang civilization was urban. Excavations beginning in 1928 at Anyang revealed a walled city, since identified as the last Shang capital. And an earlier capital, one at Zhengzhou, was excavated during the 1950s. (The site of the first capital has not yet been located, though a joint Chinese-American team is currently searching for it.) The walls at Zhengzhou, built with tamped-earth construction, are massive. Archaeologists estimate that it

DOCUMENT

Early Chinese Oracle Bone

The text of the oracle bone reproduced below can be divided into four parts: a preface, a charge, a prognostication, and a verification. The text begins by giving the date according to a traditional system of reckoning. The diviner gives his name. The charge, which is here not in the form of a question, follows. It is the king who reads the cracks in the bones and interprets them. His interpretation is inscribed on the bone. Later, a verification that the king's gloom was justified was inscribed on the bone. Relations with border peoples were a constant source of anxiety for the Shang. The Tufang, who are the subject of the alarming news in this inscription, are a persistent problem.

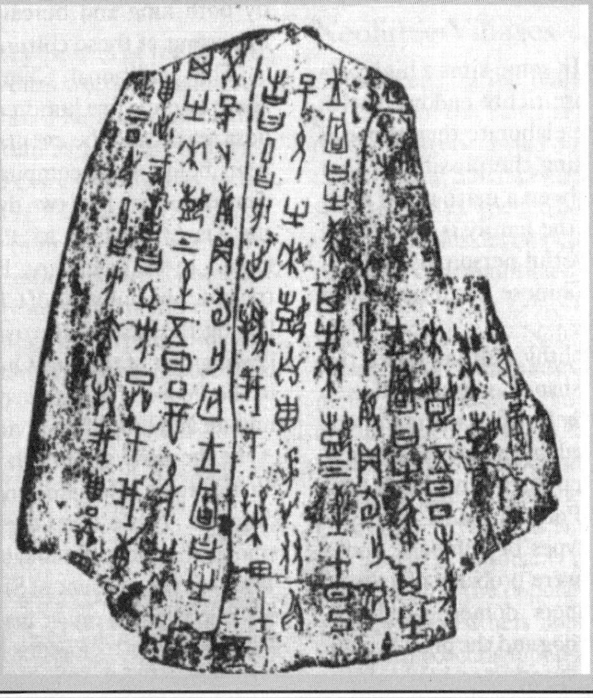

***Preface:** Crack-making on guisi day (day 30), Chue divined:*

***Charge:** "In the (next) ten days there will be no disaster."*

***Prognostication:** The king, reading the cracks, said: "There will be harm; there will perhaps be the coming of alarming news."*

***Verification:** When it came to the fifth day, dingyou, there really was the coming of alarming news from the west. Zhi Guo, reporting, said, "The Tufang are besieging in our eastern borders and have harmed two settlements. The Gongfang also raided the fields of our western borders."*

took 13 million workdays to construct them, suggesting a political power with a formidable capacity to marshal resources.

The people who built such large-scale fortifications also built elaborate royal tombs. The most spectacular of these was found in 1976 at Anyang. The grave goods were of a richness never before imagined for the Shang—two hundred bronze vessels were found in the burial chamber itself. The tomb belongs to Fu Hao, a consort of the Shang king Wu Ding. The *Book of Odes*, a text compiled between the ninth and the sixth centuries B.C.E., describes the splendor of the Shang under Wu Ding:

Even his inner domains measured a thousand leagues,
In him the people found sure support.
They opened up new lands as far as the four seas,
Men from the four seas came in homage.

It is not surprising that his consort had a splendid burial.

It is not only from Fu Hao's tomb that we know about this extraordinary woman. Her momentous achievements (she gave birth to several children and she led armies in battle) and her trivial afflictions (she was prone to toothaches) are described in oracle bones.

The data from bones, bronzes, and later textual accounts paint an interesting picture of Shang society.

The presence of walled cities, massive bronzes, and chariots implies the existence of an aristocratic class defined by its participation in sacrifices and war. Bronze metallurgy implies a stratified society not only because the technology of casting is so complex, but because of the requirements of mining. Different kinds of burial also imply a degree of social stratification, as do more puzzling finds, like caches of agricultural tools. A cache of 444 stone sickles unearthed at Anyang indicates that there might have been some centralized control of agriculture.

At the pinnacle of Shang society was a king, who had unified religious and secular duties. Under the king was a group of officials who performed specialized functions, but we have no idea how they were selected, paid, or trained. The importance of the minister, a trusted advisor to the king, perhaps one of the defining characteristics of traditional Chinese political culture, can be discerned as early as the Shang. Among the most important of the officials was a priestly class, the diviners. One hundred and twenty of these diviners have left their names on the oracle bones.

The Shang polity in no way resembled a modern state. It was more like a network of linked towns, perhaps a thousand of them. Indeed, the polity was probably defined by the personal power of the king and his officials and their kinship association rather than in terms of control of territory. Outside the core area, the Shang divided their world into friendly and nonfriendly powers. At least one hundred areas sent tribute goods to the Shang king, and these friendly areas were regarded by the king as Shang. The king did not control their territory, but allegiance was signified by the payment of tribute. But all neighbors were not friendly, and the Shang frequently engaged in warfare with peoples on their borders. We can conclude from the accounts of warfare on oracle bones and on bronzes that the king had extensive military power.

The oracle bones reveal a complicated Shang religion. The premise behind the divination practices is that the dead ancestors of the king retain an interest in as well as a power over the world of the living, who can communicate with them by divination and placate them by sacrifice. The chief Shang deity is called Di or Shang-di (the word *Shang* is written with a different Chinese character than is the word for Shang dynasty), and he is the ancestor of the ruling house. Throughout Chinese history we will see a lively interaction between the world of spirits and the human world.

By the fall of the Shang dynasty in about 1000 B.C.E., many of the characteristics we have come to think of as Chinese were established. The writing system, the importance of ancestors, and belief in a spirit world that interacts with the world of humans were all established.

Middle and South America to 700 C.E.

The first humans came to the New World over a land bridge between Siberia and Alaska in a series of migrations that probably began 40,000 years ago and ended in approximately 10,000 B.C.E., when the end of the Ice Age raised the sea level. Within a thousand years these nomads had reached southernmost South America. Although the first of these people likely originated mostly in northern China, they consisted of a mixture of Mongoloid, Caucasian, and Negroid types from all over Asia. The gradual transformation from hunting and gathering to sedentary agriculture began at roughly the same time as elsewhere in the world, between 9000 and 7000 B.C.E., when drastic alterations in climate caused large game animals to disappear, making it necessary for humans to find other sources of food.

The first civilizations arose in two areas—Mesoamerica, the region comprised of modern-day central and southern Mexico, Guatemala, Honduras, and Belize; and the central Andes, comprised of modern Peru, Bolivia, and Ecuador. These civilizations grew in two types of geographic and climatic areas: the coastal lowlands and the highland plateaus. The exchange of technology, art, and commodities between them was a crucial part of the development of their respective societies.

The principal factor in the creation of human civilization in the New World, as in the Old, was the transformation from nomadic hunting and gathering to sedentary agriculture. Sometime between 9000 and 5000 B.C.E. humans began to cultivate the avocado pear, chili pepper, amaranth (a grain), and squash. Between 3500 and 2500 B.C.E. they domesticated beans and maize, settled in villages, and started to make pottery and weave cotton in complex designs.

Because the earliest peoples left no written record and archaeological discoveries reveal only small segments of the past, there are many more unanswered than answered questions about the first civilizations of the New World. Great gaps exist in our knowledge about the rise and fall of empires, as well as everyday life and custom. Archaeologists only recently have come to understand much of the record that exists and historians must constantly revise their interpretations.

For the most part, great advancements took place later in the New World than in the Old and they evolved more gradually. The most notable lag was in the technologies of transport and agriculture, for pre-Columbian civilizations lacked the wheel and the plow. We know that Mesoamerican peoples mastered the technology of the wheel, for archaeologists have unearthed toylike artifacts with wheels, but since there were no large mammals to pull wheeled vehicles and the terrain was often too difficult for them, there was no need to adapt this technology. Relatively primitive metallurgy and the lack of large mammals to pull it also stymied the development of the plow. Moreover, the plow was not usable on terraces and *chinampas* (floating gardens), the most productive methods of agriculture. Nonetheless, the accomplishments of the great preclassic and classic civilizations of Mesoamerica and Peru in art, architecture, mathematics, astronomy, and hydraulic engineering were remarkable and in many ways surpassed those of contemporary civilizations in Europe and Asia.

Society in Mesoamerica and the central Andes evolved increasingly complex social hierarchies and states, which rose in response to the need for intense agriculture. Civilization resulted from success in producing food surpluses. Work, custom, and religion revolved around agriculture and its cycles.

The Olmecs and Teotihuacanos of Mesoamerica

Mesoamerica includes widely diverse climatic, topographic, and ecological regions. The two principal areas in which civilization arose were the central highlands and the southern lowlands. The highlands consisted of mountains, fertile valleys, and plains. The Valley of Mexico, with its network of lakes, was particularly fertile and was strategically located to dominate the area. Other important plateaus were the Oaxaca Valley and the plain of Guatemala. The lowlands, located along the Caribbean and Pacific coasts, were tropical jungle, for the most part disagreeable for human habitation, with the exception of the dry areas of the Yucatán Peninsula.

Nothing in the historical record proves any theory other than that the Americas gave birth to their own remarkable civilizations independent from the Old World. However, given what we do not yet know, and given the recent, radical changes in interpretation of the nature of these earliest peoples, the possibility of exchanges, perhaps extensive, between them is certainly not out of the question.

Archaeologists divide pre-Columbian Mesoamerican civilizations into three historical periods: the pre-Classic, or Formative (2000 B.C.E.–1 C.E.), the Classic (250–900 C.E.), and the post-Classic (900–1519 C.E.). In the Formative era villages became larger and residents built the first temple mounds and ceremonial centers, painted their first hieroglyphics, invented a special religious calendar, played a ritual ball game, and practiced human sacrifice.

The so-called "mother" civilization of Mesoamerica, the Olmec (1200 B.C.E.–200 C.E.), arose along the Caribbean in the lowlands of southern Veracruz and Tabasco, a most unlikely region, where the hot, humid climate is unsuitable for human habitation. They constructed three major centers, San Lorenzo, La Venta, and Tres Zapotes. La Venta was situated on an island in the middle of marshland. Tropical soils, cultivated by slash-and-burn agriculture of the sort practiced in much of sub-Saharan Africa and in early Asia, produced food surpluses but did not support a dense population. A total of approximately 350,000 people lived in the Olmec region.

We know little of the Olmecs' origins or rise. We do know that their society spawned a stratified social structure in which kings and, perhaps, warriors ruled where there had been clans and villages, a transformation similar to that in Mesopotamia. This centralized social and political system allowed the Olmecs to organize labor and technology to construct the earliest Mesoamerican ceremonial centers, pyramids, and palaces. San Lorenzo had an elaborate water drainage system, the first form of water control known in the New World.

Their most astounding artistic accomplishments were giant heads, sculpted from stone, weighing many tons. These enormous sculptures represent not only colossal artistic achievements but notable engineering feats as well, for the Olmecs hauled the massive stones a considerable distance to their sites. The Olmecs are also well-known for "were-jaguars," part human and part jaguar figures. These objects, made from jade in varying sizes, represent humans with flat noses, snarling mouths, and jaguar fangs. The Olmecs invented the art of writing and recording calendar dates on stone, bar and dot dates, and glyphic writing.

They initiated the crucial interchange of commodities, crafts, customs, and ideas between highland and lowland peoples. The lowlands provided the highlands with luxury and religious goods, such as precious jewels, bird feathers, jaguar skins, and cacao. The highlands sent corn and other staples.

The Olmecs also provided the first cultural unity to Mesoamerica, introducing many of the gods, myths, and rituals later found among their successors, just as the Sumerians did for subsequent civilizations in western Asia. This spread of Olmec culture is evident, but not the mechanisms by which it took place. However, since it is unlikely that the Olmec region's relatively small population could have sustained conquests of large scope, and archaeological evidence suggests that Olmecs did not live outside their central region in any significant numbers, this spread probably resulted from trade rather than conquest.

We know as little about the decline of the Olmecs as about their origins. Around 950 B.C.E. the monuments at San Lorenzo suffered mutilation and burial according to deliberate plan. Olmec influence seems to have waned thereafter, though La Venta lasted to 600 B.C.E.

The Olmec heritage of deities, large temples, rituals, glyphs, and widespread commerce was received and raised to its greatest heights in Teotihuacán (200-700 C.E.). A city with remarkable art and architecture, Teotihuacán dominated the central plateau of Mexico, reaching a size larger in area than Rome, its contemporary, and housing perhaps 200,000 inhabitants. Its spectacular architecture included two gigantic constructions, the Pyramid of the Sun and the Pyramid of the Moon along the Street of the Dead, 600 other pyramids, the temple of Quetzalcoatl, two thousand apartment compounds, and five hundred workshops. Its obsidian crafts and "thin orange" pottery (made from fine, polished orange clay) were unsurpassed. Because its excavation has been more thorough than that of any other site in Mesoamerica, our knowledge of the city is extensive. Its exquisite wall paintings reveal a city that was "austere . . . gay and graceful, and intensely religious." Teotihuacán was also an enormous economic power, which like the Olmec, seems to have spread its influence through trade, not warfare. The city's large-scale construction points to a sophisticated state apparatus and hierarchical social structure.

We do not know why Teotihuacán declined. Between 650 and 750 C.E., the main buildings were burned and wrecked and the population scattered. Possibly a combination of ecological and agricultural deterioration, such as deforestation and soil erosion, caused its downfall. Or perhaps Teotihuacán was conquered. In either case, its collapse, like the fall of other great states, "left in its wake a disordered world, whose surviving cities were like planets in orbit around an extinct sun."

The Rise and Fall of the Maya, 300–900 C.E.

More than in the case of any other early American civilization, our knowledge of the Maya has altered radically in light of recent excavations and discoveries. Whereas once we thought that their enormous achievements in mathematics, astronomy, art, and architecture were based on a sparse population and precarious agricultural base, we have learned that by means of a complicated system of canals, reservoirs, and raised fields, the Maya supported a far larger number of people than previously thought possible. We also once believed that the Maya were peaceful. Now we know from the recent translation of their hieroglyphics that scores of independent city-states, like those of Mesopotamia, lived in constant warfare. Archaeological evidence has changed the view that the Maya resided in villages and that the large, excavated sites were only ceremonial centers; new discoveries indicate that the ceremonial centers had densely populated suburbs.

Central to the reinterpretation of Maya civilization are recent archaeological excavations and the deciphering of the hieroglyphics painted on stone pillars, fig-bark paper, and ceramic vessels. Cracking the Maya code (which had no key to its code, as did the the Egyptian Rosetta Stone, to interpret it) involved three new approaches: recognition that the glyphs were phonetically based, that they are related to present-day Maya language, and that they relate not myths but actual history.

Terrain and climate—swampland and tropical rains—created the conditions for much of the Maya innovations. They had to learn to manage the great quantities of water and to use the swampland for farming. Overcoming these obstacles demanded a stratified soci-

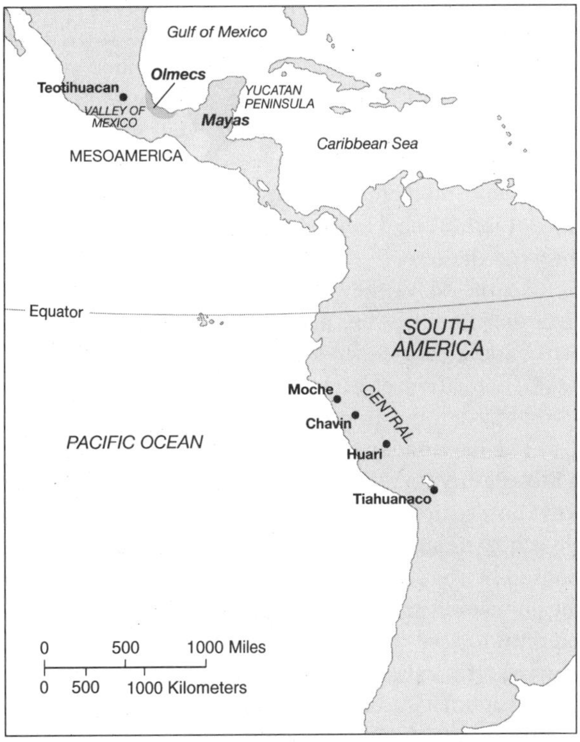

Middle and South America

ety, occupational specialization, and a ruling elite. The Maya solved these problems through enormous, complex systems of reservoirs and canals. Maya agriculture included a system of raised fields and canals constructed by excavating the swamps and piling the muck. The canals held water and fish, whose excretions provided fertilizer for the fields. The complex system was difficult to build and maintain, but produced two or three crops a year.

Maya architecture, literature, measurement of time, and mathematics were as impressive as Maya agriculture. In this, the early Maya were heavily influenced by the Olmecs and later by Teotihuacán. The first great Maya pyramids rose at Tikal and El Mirador sometime after 250 B.C.E. These pyramids were notable for their false arches, carved stone facades, ornamental roofs, and frescoes. Maya hieroglyphics are the only surviving written literature from a pre-Columbian civilization. Much of it consisted of sacred books written on bark paper, only three of which survived the conquest. In the words of one scholar, "writing was a sacred proposition that had the capacity to capture the order of the cosmos, to inform history, to give form to ritual, and to transform the profane material of everyday life into the supernatural."

The Maya calendar was more accurate than the European. There were two cycles of days. The first was ceremonial. It contained 260 days and consisted of 20 months of 13 days each. Another cycle had 365 days divided into 18 months of 20 days, with an extra 5-day month. Completion of the two cycles coincided every 52 years. The Maya also compiled an era-based calendar of 360 days known as the Long Count. They used a bar-dot system for indicating the number of years since the base date. Maya mathematics consisted of units of 1, 5, 20, the dot indicating 1, a bar 5, and positions 20. They also invented the zero.

To the Maya the world consisted of three overlapping domains, heaven, a middle world of humans and earth, and a dark underworld, all of which were interrelated. The world of earth was connected to the underworld through the king.

The lowland kingdoms of the Maya collapsed in the ninth century C.E.. We have only a few clues to explain why this occurred. In some cases the written record actually ends in mid-sentence, suggesting sudden disruptions. The root cause may have been that at some point the population grew to an extent that it overwhelmed the capacity to feed it. Because of social strife or increased warfare, the raised-field agricultural system was neglected and fell into decay. Simultaneously, the Maya evidently lost faith in their kings, whose legitimacy depended on their ability to communicate with the gods. Warfare among the kingdoms grew more intense, a result, perhaps, of pressure from a growing nobility to further its privileges. In the end the Maya gradually stopped building, ceased maintaining their agriculture, scattered into the countryside, and even abandoned literacy.

Although the civilization of the southern lowlands collapsed, this did not end Maya civilization. The kingdoms of the lowlands of the northern Yucatán Peninsula, the greatest of which was Chitzén Itzá, depended not on raised-field agriculture but on rainfall and were thus able to flourish in the ninth, tenth, and eleventh centuries. There was a final resurgence of Maya culture after 1200, lasting until 1441 under the auspices of the state of Mayapán.

The Civilizations of the Andes

Though the area is divided into highlands and lowlands, Andean geography and ecology differ substantially from those of Mesoamerica. The transformation from hunting and gathering to sedentary agriculture took place in the central Andean coastal region between 2500 and 1800 B.C.E. In the Peruvian coastal lowlands rivers traversed deserts, making irrigation necessary for agriculture. Civilizations arose first in the valleys of the north coast which were larger than those in the south. Irrigation required an organized central authority, which gave rise to state bureaucracies and stratified social structures. In the Andes, the altitude and harshly cold climate precluded the cultivation of maize, the staple crop of Mesoamerica. Potatoes were suitable for the environment and became the staple of the Andean highlands, which also supported large mammals—the llama and alpaca—which provided both meat and transportation.

In the Andes no one region dominated in the way that the Valley of Mexico dominated Mesoamerica. Thus a vast increase in food production increased population and gave rise to classic civilization and great achievements, but people lived for the most part in dispersed settlements with ceremonial centers, not in cities as in Mesoamerica. Valleys united as units to maintain their irrigation agriculture. Such dispersed communities housed large populations but did not encroach on farmland.

One of the most important features of Andean life was the colonization by one group, such as a state, community, or even family, of a number of different ecological zones. Highlanders, for example, might establish a colony on the coast to assure supplies of fish or elsewhere in the lowlands to acquire coca or other tropical plants.

The basic exchange, however, was lowland maize and cotton for highland potatoes and wool. Colonization sometimes allowed states to extend political control over large territories.

The first civilization in the Andes was the Chaín, a religious cult that probably spread through conversion rather than warfare. Around 900 B.C.E., Chaín art and architecture began to spread throughout northern Peru. Typically, these included stone carvings with mouths, eyes, and snakes intermingled, and stylized human, animal or deity figures in geometric forms. The animals were often ferocious jaguars or hawks, giving rise to theories of Olmec influence. The Chaín peoples erected pyramids which, though not as large as those in Mesoamerica, were constructed with rooms and passages. Around 300 B.C.E., the Chaín culture abruptly disappeared.

The Moche (or Mochica) culture, which peaked around 300 C.E., exemplified the great achievements of Peruvian civilization and marked the acme of Peruvian population density, art, and technology. The Mochicas are noted for exquisite art work: magnificent pottery, especially stirrup spout bottles, figure painting, and sculpture. Mochica pottery reveals a realistic view of life at the time and provides more information about its culture than exists for any other society of the region. The paintings on the pottery, often very erotic, portray scenes of everyday life, including hunting, fishing, farming, and warfare, as well as images of gods and scenes from myths. They illustrate social classes through differences in dress. The Mochicas were also highly accomplished at weaving and their metallurgy was more advanced than elsewhere in the region.

Mayan Temple I at Tikal. The huge temple-pyramids at the Tikal ceremonial center were built in the eighth century C.E.

MIDDLE AND SOUTH AMERICA

40,000 –10,000 B.C.E.	Migration across the Bering Sea
5000 B.C.E.	First agriculture in Mesoamerica
4000 B.C.E.	First agriculture in Andes
1200–200 B.C.E.	Olmec civilization in Mexico
900–300 B.C.E.	Chaín civilization in Andes
200–700 C.E.	Height of Teotihuacán civilization
300 C.E.	Height of Mochica civilization in Andes
600–800 C.E.	Tiahuanaco civilization in Andes
300–900 C.E.	Maya civilization in Yucatán
950–1150 C.E.	Toltec civilization in central Mexico

In addition to their great artistic achievements, the Mochicas were accomplished engineers. Theirs was the only great pre-Columbian state structure in the Americas that developed solely dependent on artificial irrigation. The construction and maintenance of these large irrigation systems spawned a powerful state bureaucracy, since the state owned the land and controlled the water. Irrigation thus intensified and fixed the differences between rulers and ruled. Violence accompanied this social stratification, and the era of the Mochicas also marked a time when warfare emerged as an important part of Andean life, and Mochica cities were protected with stone walls.

Of the cities built in the era before the Inca in the fourteenth century C.E., the best known is Tiahuanaco, on the southern shores of Lake Titicaca in present-day Bolivia. This ceremonial center of perhaps 10,000 inhabitants is noted for its stone statues and stelae. Tiahuanaco, along with Huari, was one of the two empires that arose around 600 C.E. and brought the first unity to Peru, a unity that lasted two centuries. We know nothing of the reasons for their decline, but by 800 B.C.E. there were no more cities in southern Peru and there would be none for nearly 700 years. Instead, the entire population lived in villages and small towns.

Regional Fragmentation and War

The end of the classic cultures in both Mesoamerica and the Andes brought a long interlude of fragmentation until the rise of the great empires of the Incas in Peru and the Aztecs in the Valley of Mexico some 600 years later. In Mesoamerica, the collapse of Teotihuacán and the decline of the Maya meant the end of significant high culture. Between 950 and 1150 the Toltecs, a grim, warlike people, dominated central Mexico from their capital of Tula northwest of present-day Mexico City. They were the predecessors of the Aztecs, the greatest warrior state of Mesoamerica. The end of classic culture in the Andes was not as catastrophic as in Mesoamerica for several reasons. First, it was not accompanied by fatal crises in food production or ecology as in the case of the Maya. Second, the Andean ruling classes were evidently not as vulnerable as their Mesoamerican contemporaries, perhaps because their position was founded not on serving as intermediaries between the gods and their people but rather on their control of vital irrigation.

The first civilizations of the Americas ultimately rose and fell on the strength of their ability to produce agricultural surpluses. Despite their sometimes precarious ecological bases, they succeeded to a remarkable extent. A complex of social classes and governmental systems developed around agriculture. Priests contended with deities, bureaucrats organized labor to build and operate irrigation works, and craft workers provided goods for trade. In Mesoamerica the environment was evidently unable to sustain great states and their achievements without cyclical catastrophes. In the Andes, geography dictated a dispersed population that for millennia precluded powerful, centralized states.

The legacy of the first three thousand years of civilization is more than a tradition of imperial conquest, exploitation, and cruelty. It goes beyond a mere catalog of discoveries, inventions, and achievements, impressive as they are. The legacy includes the basic structure of modern civilization. The floodplain civilizations and their neighbors provided the first solutions to problems of social and political organization and complex government. Pastoralists and agriculturalists in Asia, Africa, and the Americas found ways to support complex societies in spite of climatic and geographical limitations. These societies built what we now recognize to have been the first cities, city-states, nation-states, and finally, multinational empires. They attacked the problems of uneven distribution of natural resources through irrigation, long-distance trade, and communication. Their religious traditions, from polytheism to monotheism, provided patterns for subsequent world religious traditions. Mesopotamian astronomy and mathematics and Egyptian engineering and building were fundamental for future civilizations.

FURTHER READING

General Reading

Cambridge Ancient History, Vol. 1, Part 1 (Cambridge: Cambridge University Press, 1970). Contains essays on every aspect of ancient civilizations.

* A. Bernard Knapp, *The History and Culture of Ancient Western Asia and Egypt* (Chicago: Dorsey Press, 1987). A good general survey of the entire period.

* Gerda Lerner, *The Creation of Patriarchy* (New York: Oxford University Press, 1986). A study of gender and politics in antiquity by a leading feminist historian.

* Barbara Lesko, "Women of Egypt and the Ancient Near East," in Renate Bridenthal, Claudia Koonz, and Susan Stuart, eds., *Becoming Visible*, 2d ed. (Boston: Houghton Mifflin, 1987). A general survey of women in ancient civilizations.

Before Civilization

* Lewis R. Binford, *In Pursuit of the Past* (New York: Thames & Hudson, 1988). A general introduction to prehistoric archaeology, intended for a general audience by an expert.

Peter Ucko and G. W. Dimbleby, *The Domestication and Exploitation of Plants and Animals* (Chicago: Aldine, 1969). Technical essays on the origins of domestication.

Sub-Saharan Africa to 700

* Philip Curtin, Steven Feierman, Leonard Thompson, and Jan Vansina, *African History* (London: Longman, 1978). A standard text of African history that, though somewhat dated, is still useful.

* Jan Vansina, *Paths in the Rainforests* (Madison, WI: University of Wisconsin Press, 1990). A difficult but important discussion of Bantu migrations into the Congo basin.

Roland Oliver, *The African Experience* (New York: HarperCollins, 1991). A highly stimulating overview of the main themes in all African history.

Mesopotamia: The Land Between the Two Rivers

Hans J. Nissen, *The Early History of the Ancient Near East 9000-2000 B.C.* (Chicago: University of Chicago Press, 1988). An up-to-date survey of early Mesopotamia.

* A. L. Oppenheim, *Ancient Mesopotamia*, 2d ed. (Chicago: University of Chicago Press, 1977). Another general introduction by an expert.

* Georges Roux, *Ancient Iraq* (New York: Penguin Books, 1980). A very readable general introduction intended for a broad audience.

Morris Silver, *Economic Structures of the Ancient Near East* (New York: B&N Imports, 1985). A controversial analysis of ancient Near Eastern economy.

* O. Neugebauer, *The Exact Sciences in Antiquity* (New York: Dover, 1970). A series of technical essays on ancient mathematics and astronomy.

Egypt: The Gift of the Nile

H. Frankfort, *Ancient Egyptian Religion* (New York: Harper & Row, 1961). A classic study of Egyptian religion.

* B. B. G. Trigger et al., *Ancient Egypt: A Social History* (Cambridge: Cambridge University Press, 1983). A current survey of ancient Egyptian social history by a group of experts.

Israel: Between Two Worlds

John Bright, *A History of Israel*, 3d ed. (Louisville, KY: Westminster John Knox Press, 1981). A standard history of the Israelites until the middle of the second century.

A. T. Olmstead, *History of Assyria* (Chicago: University of Chicago Press, 1975). The fundamental survey of the Assyrian Empire.

H. W. F. Saggs, *Everyday Life in Babylonia and Assyria* (New York: Putnam, 1965). A readable account of Babylonian and Assyrian society.

The Foundations of Indian Culture, 3000-1000

Gregory L. Possehl, "Revolution in the Urban Revolution: The Emergence of Indus Urbanization," *Annual Reviews of Anthropology 19* (1990), pp. 261-82. A summary of recent scholarship and controversies.

Bridget and Raymond Allchin, *The Rise of Civilization in India and Pakistan* (New York: Cambridge University Press, 1982). A standard work.

Walter Fairservis, *The Harappan Civilization and Its Writing: A Model for the Decipherment of the Indus State* (Leiden: E.J. Brill, 1992). A detailed account of one approach to the deciphering of the Harappa script.

Romila Thapar, *From Lineage to State: Social Formation in the First Millennium B.C. in the Ganga Valley* (Bombay: Oxford University Press, 1984). A lucid account of state formation in early India.

Wendy Doniger O'Flaherty, *The Rig Veda* (New York: Penguin, 1982) An annotated translation of the classic text.

Cradles of Chinese Civilization, 5000-1000

Chang Kwang-chih, *The Archaeology of Ancient China*, 4th ed. (New Haven, CT: Yale University Press, 1986). The single most authoritative source on Chinese archaeology.

David N. Keightley, "Early Civilization in China: Reflections on How It Became Chinese," in Paul Ropp, ed., *Heritage of China: Contemporary Perspectives on Chinese Civilization* (Berkeley and Los Angeles: University of California Press, 1990), pp. 15-54. A stimulating article that explicitly contrasts ancient Chinese and Greek civilizations, and examines what is distinctive about each.

Chang Kwang-chih, *Shang Civilization* (New Haven: Yale University Press, 1980). A synthetic interpretation of what was known about the Shang as of 1980.

David N. Keightley, *Sources of Shang History: The Oracle Bone Inscriptions of Bronze Age China* (Berkeley and Los Angeles: University of California Press, 1978). A survey and explanation of the oracle bone documentation.

Chang Kwang-chih, *Art, Myth and Ritual: The Path to Political Authority in Ancient China* (Cambridge: Harvard University Press, 1983). A highly readable interpretation of early Chinese art and politics.

Middle and South America to 700

Richard E. W. Adams, *Prehistoric Mesoamerica.* Rev. ed. (Norman, OK: University of Oklahoma Press, 1991). Thorough overview for those interested in archaeology.

* Shirley Gorenstein, Richard G. Forbis, Paul Tolstoy, and Edward P. Lanning, *Prehispanic America* (New York: St. Martin's Press, 1974). Contains excellent essays on preconquest peoples of the Americas.

* Nigel Davies, *The Ancient Kingdoms of Mexico* (New York: Penguin Books, 1992). Lively survey of the civilizations of the Mesoamerican highlands.

* Linda Schele and David Freidel, *A Forest of Kings: the Untold Story of the Ancient Maya* (New York: William Morrow, 1990). Magnificent drawings and illustrations of architecture, sculpture, and stelae. The most up-to-date information on the radically new interpretation of Mayan history.

Friedrich Katz, *The Ancient American Civilizations* (New York: Praeger Publishers, 1972). Though the archaeological information is dated, it still provides an excellent framework for comparing Mesoamerican and Andean pre-Columbian civilizations.

Edward P. Lanning, *Peru Before the Incas* (Englewood Cliffs, NJ: Prentice-Hall, 1967). The best survey of pre-Inca civilizations.

*Indicates paperback edition available.

CHAPTER 3

Religious Rivalries and India's Golden Age

KEY TERMS

Brahman
Ganges River
caste system
dharma
karma
Buddha
stupas
nirvana
Alexander the Great
Chandragupta Maurya
Ashoka
Gupta Empire
Hinduism

DISCUSSION QUESTIONS

How did classical Indian society reflect the teachings of Hinduism?

Compare Hinduism with its offshoot, Buddhism.

INTRODUCTION

The development of a new civilization in India after the long period of disruption following Harappa's fall around 1500 B.C.E. completed—along with those in China and the Mediterranean—the basic roster of classical civilizations that arose after 1000 B.C.E. The new foundations for this civilization were laid between 1500 and 500 B.C.E. by the nomadic Aryan invaders who were moving into India during the centuries when Harappa collapsed. By the end of this period, fairly large states, ruled by kings who claimed divine descent, controlled much of the fertile farmland that made up the Ganges River plains. Cities had developed, originally around the palaces of these monarchs and later at the sites of important religious shrines and regional market centers. A rich and increasingly influential merchant class joined the Aryan priests and warriors at the top of the Indian social hierarchy.

Ritual divisions and restrictions on intermarriage between these three groups grew more rigid as the increasingly complex caste hierarchy became a pervasive force in Indian life. Above all, the Vedic priests, or brahmans, emerged as the dominant force in Indian society and culture. Their literacy and the magical aura that surrounded the vital ceremonies they performed rendered them the makers and chief advisors of kings, the dispensers of the blessings (or curses) of the gods, and the most revered and privileged of India's elite social groups.

Even as the brahmans' power peaked, however, forces were building in Indian society that threatened to alter fundamentally the course of civilized development in South Asia. Weary of the empty rituals associated with sacrifices to the gods and the power-seeking and materialism of the priestly class, numerous holy men and religious seers had arisen by the 6th century B.C.E. From these holy men a number of major religious thinkers emerged who tried to discover and propagate more meaningful forms of religious belief and worship.

The most successful of these thinkers, the Buddha, founded one of the great world religions—a religion that for centuries provided a powerful challenge to the brahmans and many of the ancient Vedic beliefs and practices. The rivalry that developed between the brahmans and the followers of the Buddha helped define and reshape India's cultural core. The brahmans defended and reinvigorated the ancient Vedic rites and beliefs, and, drawing heavily on these beliefs, they promoted the growth of the religion we know as *Hinduism.* By the first centuries C.E., it was clear that a revived Hinduism had survived the Buddhist challenge. Though Buddhism would remain an important force in many parts of India for another millennium, it would eventually all but die out in the land of its birth.

The Buddha's teachings also contributed to the establishment of India's first genuine empire. Beginning in the late 4th century B.C.E., the rulers of a local dynasty in eastern India, the Maurya, began to build what would become the largest empire in premodern India. The most successful of the Mauryan monarchs, Ashoka (268–232 B.C.E.), converted to Buddhism and then tried to govern according to Buddhist precepts and to spread the religion to neighboring parts of Asia. The Mauryan Empire proved to be short-lived, however. When it collapsed, it was followed by another round of nomadic invasions through the Himalayan passes in the northwest, and the subcontinent was again fragmented politically. Many of the dynasties that followed the Mauryas dedicated themselves to the promotion of either Buddhism or the brahman counteroffensive. But in the early 4th century C.E., there arose in north India a powerful new dynasty, the Gupta, that was firmly committed to the reassertion of the brahmans' dominance.

The Gupta rulers' patronage of Hinduism reaffirmed the position of the brahmans as high priests and political advisors and led to an age of splendid Hindu achievement in architecture, painting, and sculpture as well as philosophy, literature, and the sciences. The Gupta Empire was considerably smaller than that estab-

1600–1000 Period of Aryan invasions

1200–700 Sacred Vedas composed

c. 1500 Fall of Harappan civilization

700–c. 550 Era of unrivaled Brahman dominance

c. 542–483 Life of the Buddha

322–185 Time of the Mauryan Empire

322–298 Chandragupta Maurya rules

327–325 Alexander the Great's invasion

1600 B.C.E. **1200 B.C.E.** **700 B.C.E.** **500 B.C.E.**

Perhaps the most frequently depicted Indian religious image is the god Shiva, here portrayed in a South Indian bronze. The position of the god's hands or the objects held in them each represent a different aspect of his power, which is simultaneously creative and destructive.

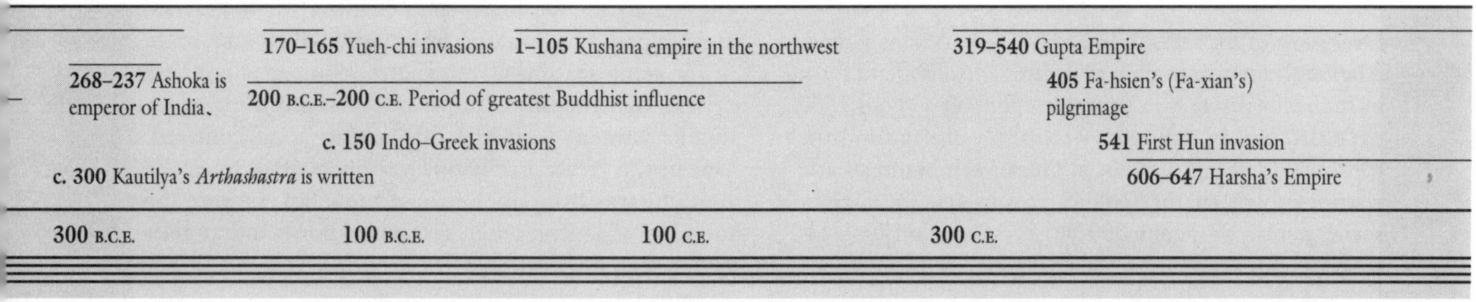

268–237 Ashoka is emperor of India.
c. 300 Kautilya's *Arthashastra* is written
170–165 Yueh-chi invasions
200 B.C.E.–200 C.E. Period of greatest Buddhist influence
c. 150 Indo-Greek invasions
1–105 Kushana empire in the northwest
319–540 Gupta Empire
405 Fa-hsien's (Fa-xian's) pilgrimage
541 First Hun invasion
606–647 Harsha's Empire
300 B.C.E.
100 B.C.E.
100 C.E.
300 C.E.

lished by the Mauryas, and the dynasty did not rule a good deal longer. But the ideas and institutions that were solidified during the Gupta era gave Indian civilization the strength and resilience to withstand the shock of yet another round of foreign invasions, beginning with the ravages of the Huns in the first half of the 6th century C.E.

This overview of the critical millennium of Indian history between c. 500 B.C.E. and 500 C.E. suggests several underlying patterns. One of the most critical of these patterns is the predominance in Indian history of political disunity and the short-lived character of even the most powerful Indian empires and dynasties. In contrast to China, where unity was the norm and disunity was viewed as unnatural and harmful, India has been divided into rival kingdoms throughout most of its history. This has meant that regional cultural diversity and local identities have been more pronounced in India than in China. In fact, the very name *India* and the idea of the continent as a single political unit did not exist until foreign rulers, the British, conceived them in the 19th century C.E.

Also in contrast to China, where scholar-bureaucrats and strong states were the mainstays of civilization, the brahmans, and social institutions such as the caste system, have been the key to the remarkable persistence of civilization in India. Rather than vanquish the brahmans and destroy the caste system, foreign invaders have frequently been converted by them and have established themselves as warrior-kings near the top of the caste hierarchy. Thus, despite periodic foreign invasions and persistent political divisions, common religious ideas and distinctive forms of social organization have provided the basis for an underlying unity for most of the diverse ethnic groups of South Asia, from Vedic times to the present. Religion and social organization held Indian civilization together durably but more loosely than political culture united China.

The Age of Brahman Dominance

Over most of the areas in India where the Aryans settled, religious leaders or brahmans became the dominant force in Indian civilization in the millennium after about 1500 B.C.E. In this era, the *caste system* also came to form the backbone of the Indian social order, with brahman and warrior groups sharing political power and the highest social status. By about 500 B.C.E., several major challenges to this social order had emerged. The most enduring and serious of these proved to be the new religion that coalesced around the teachings of the Buddha.

The forces that made for the renewal of civilization in South Asia after the fall of Harappa were initially centered not on the great plains of the Ganges and Indus river systems but in the foothills of the *Himalaya Mountains.* Tribes of Aryan warrior-herders settled in the lush valleys of the cool hills. The hills provided abundant pasturage for their herds of horses and cattle, and the wooded valleys were easier to clear for farming than the jungle-covered plains along the Ganges and its tributaries. In the hill regions, single Aryan tribes or confederations of tribal groups developed small states—in many ways similar to those in Homeric Greece—that were based on a combination of sedentary agriculture and livestock breeding. The territories of most of these states extended no farther than the hills surrounding a single large valley or several adjoining valley systems. Most of the states were republics ruled collectively by a council made up of the free warrior elite. Individual leaders were usually called kings, even though their offices and powers more closely resembled those of tribal chieftains. They were elected or removed from office by a vote of the warriors' councils.

The hill republics provided an environment well suited to the preservation of traditional Aryan values and lifestyles. Wars between the numerous hill states were frequent, as were feuds and cattle raids. Thus, the warrior elites were kept busy at pastimes that brought them both wealth and honor. The republics nurtured the spirit of independence that had been strong among the invading Aryan tribes and hostility toward those who attempted to concentrate political authority in the hands of a single ruler.

The warrior elites were also careful to keep the power of the brahmans in check, and the hill cultures fostered a healthy skepticism with regard to the priests and the gods they worshiped. One early hymn reported, for example, that "One and another say, There is no Indra [the god of thunder and war]. Who hath beheld him? Whom then shall we honor?" In another hymn the brahmans, chanting their prayers, are compared to croaking frogs gathered about a pond in the rainy season. Given these trends, it is not surprising that the hill regions were major centers of religious ferment from the 6th century B.C.E. onward. One of the greatest religious reformers of all time, the Buddha, was from one of these republics, as were the founders of several other, less well-known Indian religions, such as Jainism.

The Kingdoms of the Ganges Plains

As Aryan settlement spread in the last millennium B.C.E. from the Indus region and Himalayan foothills to vast plains of the Ganges River system, republics and religious skeptics gave way to kings and powerful brahman priests. Though these regions eventually became the heartlands of great empires, in the middle centuries of the last millennium B.C.E. they were divided into a patchwork of rival kingdoms. The lowland rulers were usually drawn from the warrior elite, but they held power in their own right rather than deriving it from selection by warrior councils. Excepting their influential brahman advisors, there were no formal checks on the power and authority of the kings. Many kings claimed descent from divine ancestors, and their thrones were normally inherited by their sons. All considered themselves to be the supreme war leaders, chief judges, and protectors of the peoples in their domains.

As these roles suggest, the powers and privileges these kings enjoyed were justified by the duties they performed. The great Indian epic the *Ramayana* and other sources from this period stress the duties and obligations of righteous monarchs. They were expected to protect the realm from outside invaders and internal social conflicts. They were instructed to revere the brahmans and follow their advice, to patronize public works, and to rule in ways that promoted the welfare of their people. Ideally, Vedic kings were supposed to be hardworking, honest, and accessible to their most lowly subjects. There are even passages in the ancient texts that justify the violent overthrow of evil rulers.

It is highly unlikely that monarchs who lived up to all these high ideals would have long survived the court intrigues and the assaults of rival rulers that were commonplace in the Vedic era. In fact, the sources from this period suggest a darker side to kingship that may have been closer to the realities of the age. Kings lived in constant fear for their thrones and lives. They were threatened by internal rivals, including their own sons, and also by neighboring monarchs who periodically tested their strength in battle. A ruler's survival depended on the extensive use of spies and informers, a strong and loyal palace guard, and his courage and skills as a military commander.

Sources of Brahman Power

Though most of the rulers of the kingdoms on the Ganges plains were members of the warrior elite, brahmans residing at the court centers often exercised more real power. Their positions as the educators of the princes who would someday rule and as the chief advisors to the rulers themselves naturally made them influential figures in the ruling circles. Like the scholar-gentry in China, their literacy in a society where few could read or write made the brahmans obvious candidates for administrative positions, from heads of bureaucratic departments to judges and tax collectors. In addition, only the brahmans knew how to perform the sacred rituals that were essential to the coronation of a new king. They alone knew the rites that conferred divine status on a monarch—and without divine status a ruler's legitimacy was in doubt. Once the ruler was installed, brahman astrologers foretold his future and regulated his daily schedule, instructing him when to make war or mate with his wives.

As the brahmans' pivotal role in court ceremonies and prophecy indicates, their positions of power and prestige were linked above all to their capacity to mediate between the gods and humans. The key function of the priests of the early Aryan invaders was to offer sacrifices to the gods and spirits who intervened continuously in human affairs. By the 7th and 6th centuries B.C.E., the sacrifices themselves had in a very real sense become more powerful than the gods to whom they were offered. By this time it was widely believed that if the sacrifice was done correctly, the god to whom it was directed had no choice but to grant the wish of the petitioner for whom the brahmans had performed the ceremony. Thus, a king could ensure victory, a peasant village sufficient rainfall, or a barren woman fertility if the proper ceremony was conducted flawlessly. Only the brahmans were capable of performing the ceremony and allowed to read the sacred Vedic texts where the prayers and instructions for various types of sacrifices were set forth. Only they had memorized the steps of the sacrificial rituals and mastered the techniques of preparing the sacrificial offerings correctly. Their monopoly over the sacred rites ensured that brahmans would be honored and feared, even by the strongest of warrior-kings.

Only a small percentage of the brahmans in a given kingdom served as advisors at the court or as state administrators. Many were the personal priests or physicians of wealthy high-caste families; most were village priests, schoolteachers, and wandering ascetics. Some were alchemists and sorcerers, and even downright charlatans, living off the gullibility of the masses, who believed in their ability to tell fortunes and turn magic spells to good and evil purposes. But all brahmans, from the palaces of kings to the most remote villages, were privileged beings, exempt from taxes and protected from bodily injury by the harsh punishments meted out to

Like many of the larger Indian towns, the one portrayed in this artist's recreation (based on classical Indian stone sculptures from the last centuries B.C.E.*) depicts an Indian city that has walls, a moat, and building constructed mainly of intricately carved wood.*

those who dared to assault them. As the following passage from one of the ancient Vedas makes clear, not even kings were considered exempt from the horrible fate that befell those who did injury to a brahman.

Whenever a king, fancying himself mighty,
seeks to devour a Brahman, [his] kingdom is broken up.
[Ruin] overflows that kingdom as water swamps
a leaky boat;
Calamity smites that country in which a priest is
wronged.
Even trees . . . repel, and refuse their shade to, the man
who claims a right to the property of a Brahman.

In addition to the power exercised by the brahmans, and the services they provided, religion shaped the daily lives of the peoples of South Asia through the ethical prescriptions found in the sacred Vedic texts. These texts were orally compiled and systematically transmitted by the brahman priests between 1200 and 900 B.C.E. In the last centuries B.C.E., the *Vedas* were written in the Sanskrit language, which thereafter became the standard and scholarly language of India, akin to Greek and Latin in the West. From the chants and ritual formulas of the early Vedas, the texts were increasingly devoted to religious and philosophical speculation and moral prescriptions for the faithful. This highly religious culture provided the context for further changes as Indian civilization moved to even greater complexity.

An Era of Widespread Social Change

The rise of kings and increasing brahman dominance were only two of the many social changes that occurred as full civilization took shape for the second time in Indian history. Around the court centers of the lowland kings, towns grew up as servant, artisan, and merchant groups catered to the needs of the rulers, their courtiers, and often large numbers of brahman advisors and administrators. Along the Ganges and other rivers, towns developed that were mainly trading centers or were devoted to the specialized manufacture of key products such as pottery, tools, and cotton textiles. With the increase in commerce and specialized production, merchants and artisans became established as distinctive social groups. The great wealth amassed by the larger trading houses allowed the merchants to win a prominent place in the Indian social hierarchy, which became both more complex and more rigid in this era.

Another social stratum that assumed major importance in this period was the peasantry. As farming supplanted herding as the basis for the economies of the lowland kingdoms, peasants came to make up a large percentage of India's population. Mud-walled farming villages spread across the plains of northern India, though throughout the classical era they continued to be dwarfed in most places by massive primeval rain forests. Irrigation networks and new agricultural tools steadily increased productivity and hence the capacity of the peasants to support ever larger numbers of nonfarming specialists. Most peasants grew staples such as rice, millet, and wheat, but some villages specialized in cotton, plants for dyes such as indigo, and luxury crops such as sugar cane. Though presumably eager to market their surplus or specialized crops, the peasants only grudgingly paid the tribute demanded by the tax collectors of the lowland monarchs. If a ruler was weak and his court in disarray, it is likely that the peasants paid nothing at all.

The Caste System

The tripartite class division in India between warriors, priests, and commoners that made up the tribal social order of the early Aryan invaders had altered radically over the centuries. New social groups, such as merchants and peasants, were added to these broad social categories *(varnas),* and each was subdivided into occupational subgroups, or castes. Broad categories and occupational subgroups were arranged in a hierarchical pyramid based on the degree to which the tasks they performed were considered polluting. Those who dealt with human waste or slaughtered animals, for example, were regarded as extremely defiling, while scholars and wandering holy men who eschewed physical labor and refused to eat animal flesh were revered for their purity.

At the top of the pyramid were the brahman, warrior, and merchant castes, whose members made up only a small minority of the total population. The bulk of the population belonged to peasant and artisan castes, which made up most of the central and lower layers of the caste pyramid. Beneath the peasants and artisans were the untouchables, who performed the most despised tasks in Indian society, including removing human waste from towns and villages, sweeping the streets, and tanning leather hides. The Indians' reverence for cows, which may have been present in Harappan society, and their aversion to dead animals rendered the latter occupation particularly polluting. Even the untouchables were divided into caste subgroups, with sweepers looking down upon manure handlers, and they in turn despising leatherworkers.

Over the centuries, the boundaries between caste groups hardened. In addition to occupation, a caste's position in the Indian social hierarchy was distinguished by its diet and by the caste groups with which its members could dine or exchange different kinds of food. A caste's status also determined the social groups with which it was allowed to intermarry and whether or not it was permitted to read the Vedas. Only members of castes belonging to the three highest varnas (brahmans, warriors, and merchants) were allowed to read the texts. *Rama,* perhaps the greatest of Indian cultural heroes, was celebrated in the *Ramayana* for cutting off the head of a peasant holy man who presumed to recite hymns from the Vedas while hanging upside down from a tree.

A person was born into a caste group and could not change his or her caste status. Over considerable periods of time, a caste group could collectively rise or fall in status, but individuals were tied to the fortunes of their caste as a whole. An individual's refusal to accept the duties and status associated with the caste into which he or she was born could lead to beatings and other forms of physical abuse. If the rebellious individual continued to violate caste laws, he or she would be ostracized or quite literally outcast. This penalty normally meant certain death because no one, including a member of their own family, was allowed to pay them for labor or offer them food, drink, or other services.

In addition to physical punishment and local sanctions, the caste system was upheld by Indian rulers and the belief that it was supernaturally ordained. One of the chief duties of a righteous monarch was to preserve the caste hierarchy and see to it that persons at each level carried out the tasks and behaved in the manner appropriate to those at that rank. Ideally, the caste system was to provide for a harmonious exchange of products and services at all levels of Indian society. Peasants, for example, provided food for the brahmans, who saw to their religious and ritual needs, and for the warriors, who defended them from bandits and foreign invaders. In reality, high-caste groups, particularly brahmans and warriors, enjoyed a disproportionate share of wealth and power. But except in times of severe natural calamity or social crisis, even the lowliest of untouchables was guaranteed a livelihood, however meager.

The caste position and career determined by a person's birth was called one's *dharma.* The concept of transmigration of the soul helped to explain why some were given the enviable dharma of a brahman whereas others were consigned to the lowly status of an untouchable tanner. In the Vedic era, it was widely accepted that a person's soul existed through many human lives and was transferred from one body to another after death. In each of its lives, the soul accumulated varying amounts of merit and demerit, depending on the actions of the person in whose body it dwelled. The sum of these merits and demerits at any given point in time made up one's *karma.* An individual's karma in turn determined the sort of person that soul would be attached to in its next reincarnation. Thus, a person who was born as a brahman possessed a soul that had built up a large surplus of merit; a person born as a sweeper was paying the penalty for the sins of his or her past lives.

One of the greatest sins was to violate one's dharma—to refuse the duties and status attached to the caste into which one was born. The only way to ensure a better situation in the next rebirth was to accept one's situation in the present and fully perform the tasks one was allotted. Thus, the concepts of the transmigration of the soul and reincarnation provided not only an explanation for the inequities of the caste system but also a religious rationale for an individual's acceptance of his or her place in the caste hierarchy.

The Family and the Changing Status of Women

Some of our best insights into family life and gender relationships in this era are provided by the two great Indian epics, the *Mahabharata* and the *Ramayana.* Though these tales of war and princely honor, love and social duty were not written down until the last centuries B.C.E., they were related in oral form long before. They suggest that by the middle centuries of the last millennium B.C.E., the extended family was increasingly regarded as the ideal. Those who could support the large household that extended family arrangements required, which normally meant only the highest caste groups, gathered all the male members of a given family and their wives and children under the same roof. At times up to four generations, from great-grandfathers and-grandmothers to great-grandsons and-granddaughters, lived together in the same dwelling or family compound.

Though these arrangements restricted individual privacy and often led to family quarrels, they also provided a high degree of security and human companionship. Lower-caste groups from the peasants and artisans rarely possessed the wealth required to support extended households. As a consequence, the great majority of Indian families were *nuclear families,* or made up of parents and their children, with perhaps a widowed grandparent sharing their dwelling.

Somewhat contradictory visions of the positions and roles of women emerge from the epics, which suggest that attitudes toward women may have been in flux. On one hand, women are seen as weak, passionate, frivolous, and fond of gossip and slander. Female demons in the *Ramayana* take on the roles of jealous temptresses and vengeful jilted lovers. Within the family, women remain clearly subordinated to men. Though youths are charged to obey and honor their mothers, parental veneration is focused on the father to whom complete obedience and loyalty are expected. Wives are instructed to be attentive to their husbands' needs and be ready to obey their every command. Rama's wife Sita is chosen for her physical beauty and absolute devotion to her husband. When he is forced into exile in the forest, she follows without question or complaint. When she is carried off to Sri Lanka by the demon Ravanna, Rama races to defend her honor and his own. Having rescued her after a mighty battle with Ravanna and his evil minions, Rama then refuses to take her back because he suspects that she may have been raped while in captivity. Only when she proves her virtue by walking unscathed through a fire will he accept her again as his wife. Throughout both epics, the fate of women is controlled by men, be they gods, demons, or mortal humans.

On the other hand, some passages in the epics (and other sources from this period) indicate that in certain ways women had greater freedom and opportunities for self-expression than was the case by the last centuries B.C.E. Women in the epics are often depicted as strong-willed and cunning. Sita and Draupadi, two of the wives of the five Pandava brothers who are the heroes of the *Mahabharata,* display remarkable courage and strength of character at various points in their respective ordeals. Contemporary sources mention women who were renowned scholars of the sacred Vedic texts, which later they would not even be permitted to read. Women in this era also made their mark as teachers, poets, musicians, and artists, though the last two activities were not highly esteemed. Like their brothers, girls from high-caste families were allowed to undergo the special ceremonies that celebrated their twice-born or exalted status—an honor boys continued to enjoy but that gradually died out for young women. Women were

An Indian village with its sacred tree. The thatched roofs of the cottages can be seen in the background as women bring their offerings of rice to the Buddha, who is not pictured in accord with early artistic practice.

even famed for their skills in the martial arts, as the amazon (female warrior) palace guards of several monarchs demonstrated.

The End of an Era

Roughly 1000 years after the first Aryan tribes entered India, a new civilization had come into being that was very different from the Harappan complex it replaced. Sedentary agriculture was well established and was productive enough to support a variety of specialized elites, true cities, extensive trade, and nonagrarian artisan manufacturers. In the caste system, the Indians had developed perhaps the most complex scheme of social stratification and labor division known to human history. They had also made notable accomplishments in philosophy and religious speculation, invention, and artistic creativity, though most of the art works were done in wood and thus have perished over time.

These considerable achievements, however, pale in comparison with what was about to occur in the final centuries B.C.E. The absolute and increasingly self-serving dominance of the brahmans, the endless succession of petty wars between the kings they advised, and the religious bankruptcy displayed by the excesses of the sacrificial cults all prompted major challenges. These challenges and the brahman responses to them would both remake and enrich Indian civilization in the millennium between 500 B.C.E. and 500 C.E.

Religious Ferment and the Rise of Buddhism

For nearly a millennium, the Buddhist challenge to the brahmanical order was a central theme in South Asian history. Once institutionalized in monastic orders and great *stupas*, or temple mounds housing relics of the Buddha, the new religion provided a clear alternative to the sacrifice-oriented faith of the brahmans and the caste system that had been the dominant feature of Indian society for centuries. The Buddhist challenge was strengthened further by the patronage of the later rulers of the powerful Mauryan empire. Taking advantage of the political chaos left by the Greek invasions of northwest India beginning in the 4th century B.C.E., the Mauryas became the first dynasty to rule large portions of the subcontinent. The decline of the Mauryas, however, and changes within Buddhism itself, opened the way for a brahman counteroffensive that came to full fruition in the Gupta era in the first centuries C.E.

The 6th and 5th centuries B.C.E. were a time of great social turmoil and philosophical speculation throughout Eurasia. In China, Confucius and Laozi proposed very different views of the proper organization of human society and purposes of life. In Persia, Zoroaster founded a new religion, while the prophets Ezekiel and Isaiah strove to improve the Hebrews' understanding of the intentions of their single, almighty God. In Greece, the writings of Thales and Pythagoras laid the basis for unprecedented advances in philosophy, the sciences, and mathematics. India too was caught up in this transcontinental trend of social experimentation and intellectual probing.

Indian reformers questioned the brahmans' dominance and the efficacy of the sacrifices on which it ultimately rested. They sought to find alternatives to the caste system as the basis for India's social order. They posed questions about the nature of the universe and the end of life that the Vedic thinkers had debated for centuries, and often came up with very different answers. Some experimented with new techniques of meditation and self-mortification; others promoted new religions that would free the masses from what were viewed as the oppressive teachings of the brahmans. One holy man and thinker, the *Buddha,* did all of these things and in the process made the most influential religious and philosophical breakthroughs of an age of remarkable intellectual ferment. Though Zoroaster transformed Persian thinking and Confucius proclaimed an ethical system that was adopted in China and neighboring lands, the Buddha founded a religion that became a key ingredient in the life of civilized peoples throughout most of Asia.

The Making of a Religious Teacher

Accounts of the Buddha's life are so cluttered with myths and miracles that it is difficult to know what kind of man he actually was and what sort of message he originally preached. We are fairly certain, however, that he lived from the middle of the 6th century to the second decade of the 5th century B.C.E. He was born into one of the warrior clans of the hill states south of the Himalayas, where, as we have seen, the rule of kings and the hold of the brahmans was weak. Buddhist traditions relate that he was the son of the local ruler who was haunted by a prophecy made by a religious seer, or holy person with prophetic powers, at the time of the Buddha's birth. The seer predicted that the child would someday become a wandering ascetic like himself, thus refusing his father's throne.

To prevent this, the king confined his son to the palace grounds and provided him with every imaginable human pleasure and comfort. But as he approached manhood the prince grew curious about the world beyond the palace gardens and walls. With the aid of a trusted servant, the Buddha ventured forth into the nearby countryside, where he encountered for the first time illness, old age, death, and a wandering ascetic (a holy person who has renounced the pleasures of the material world). Unsettled by these encounters with human suffering, the prince became moody and withdrawn. Finally, as the holy man had predicted, he renounced all claims to succeed his father as king and set off with a group of wandering ascetics to meditate and ponder the many questions posed by his discoveries beyond the palace walls.

In the wilderness, the Buddha experimented with the many ways Indian *gurus,* or religious teachers, had devised to reach a higher understanding of the nature of humanity and the supernatural world. He did yogic exercises, fasted almost to death, chanted sacred prayers for days on end, and conversed with every seer he encountered. Discouraged by his failure to find the answer to the questions that had driven him to take up the life of a wandering ascetic, and exhausted by the self-punishment he had inflicted, the Buddha collapsed, legend has it, under a huge Bo tree. Saved from death by the care of a young girl who took pity on him, the Buddha turned to meditation in his search for understanding. Ultimately, by disciplining his mind and body, he achieved enlightenment, which rested on his discovery of what Buddhists came to call the Four Noble Truths.

The central issue for the Buddha was the problem of suffering, which he believed all living things experience because all living things and the objects to which they are attached are impermanent. The moment we are born we begin to die, he reasoned. Individuals whom one loves or befriends may turn indifferent or hostile or simply move away; love and friendship are inevitably ended by death. The goals to which humans devote their lives, such as fame and wealth, are empty and, once attained, can easily be lost. These attachments to the illusory and impermanent things of the world are the source of suffering. One can escape suffering only by ceasing to desire the things of the world and realizing that even one's sense of self is part of the illusion. This realization, or enlightenment, can be achieved by following the eight-step process of right action, thinking, and meditation. Once enlightenment has been attained, the individual is released from suffering because she or he is free from desire and attachment. He or she has attained *nirvana*—not heaven in the Christian sense, but simply an eternal state of tranquility.

Having attained enlightenment, the Buddha, because of his great compassion for all living creatures, set out to spread his message to all humanity (and, Buddhist legends relate, to the creatures of the forest as well). He became the most successful of the numerous seers and gurus who traveled through the hill and lowland kingdoms in this era, challenging the teachings of the brahmans and offering alternative modes of worship and paths to salvation. The Buddha soon gained a considerable following, which ranged from exalted monarchs to humble sweepers and included both men and women. As he feared, his followers turned his teachings into an organized religion. In the process, what had begun as a starkly pessimistic and antiworldly vision of existence, without gods or a god or the promise of heaven, became one of the great salvationist faiths of all human history.

The Emergence of Buddhism as a Religion

After his death (again as he feared), the Buddha was worshiped as a deity. His most faithful disciples became monks who devoted their lives to spreading his message and achieving nirvana. They held conferences where they attempted to compile authoritative collections of his teachings and the traditions concerning his life. Not surprisingly, disagreements over points of doctrine and meaning arose at these sessions. These disputes led to the formation of rival schools of monks, who vied with each other, the brahmans, and other sects to build a popular following.

Over time, the rival schools created elaborate philosophical systems. But in their efforts to attract a broader following, the monks stressed more accessible aspects of what had become a new religion. They offered miraculous tales of the Buddha's life, which included traditions that his mother had been a virgin and that he had been visited by revered scholars from afar soon after his birth. In the popular mind, nirvana became equated with heaven. Graphic visions of heavenly pleasures and the tortures of hell became central features of popular Buddhism. The Buddha was worshiped as a savior who returned periodically to help the faithful find the way to heaven. Though within the monastic communities Buddhist monks continued their emphasis on meditation and the achievement of nirvana, lay people were encouraged to perform good deeds that would earn enough merit for their souls to go to one of the Buddhist heavens after death.

The Buddhist Challenge

Though other philosopher-ascetics criticized the religious beliefs and caste system that the brahmans had done so much to establish, none was as successful as the Buddha and the many monastic orders committed to his teachings at winning converts among the Indian people. The monks and monastic organizations provided a very viable alternative to the brahman priesthood as centers of scholarship, education, and religious ritual, and often directly opposed the beliefs that the brahmans championed. Though the Buddha retained the ideas of karma and reincarnation, he rejected the Vedas as divinely inspired teachings that ought to be accepted as the ultimate authority on all issues. He ridiculed the powers the brahmans claimed for their sacrifices and the gods for whom they were intended. He favored introspection and self-mastery over ritual. In so doing, he struck at the very heart of the brahmans' social and religious dominance.

The Buddha rejected the lifestyles of both the brahmans who had become addicted to worldly power and the brahman ascetics who practiced extreme forms of bodily mortification. He tried to do away with the caste system, an aim that gave his teachings great potential appeal among the untouchables and other groups. The Buddha also accepted women as his followers and taught that they were capable of attaining nirvana. These opportunities were institutionalized in Buddhist monastic organizations, which normally included provisions for communities of nuns. The evidence we have suggests that the monastic life became a fulfilling career outlet for women in many parts of India. This outlet proved doubly meaningful in an era when educational and other occupational opportunities for women were declining, and upper-caste women in particular were increasingly confined to the home. Thus, in virtually all spheres of life from religious worship to social organization, Buddhism offered potentially revolutionary challenges to the long-established brahmanical order.

The Greek Interlude

The intellectual and social ferment that swept northern India in the 6th century B.C.E. was intensified by political

DOCUMENT

Buddha, The Sermon at Benares

On seeing their old teacher approach, the five bhikkhus agreed among themselves not to salute him, nor to address him as master, but by his name only. "For," so they said, "he has broken his vow and has abandoned holiness. He is no bhikkhu but Gotama, and Gotama has become a man who lives in abundance and indulges in the pleasures of worldliness."

But when the Blessed One approached in a dignified manner, they involuntarily rose from their seats and greeted him in spite of their resolution. Still they called him by his name and addressed him as "friend Gotama."

When they had received the Blessed One, he said: "Do not call the Tathāgata by his name nor address him as 'friend,' for he is the Buddha, the Holy One. The Buddha looks with a kind heart equally on all living beings, and they therefore call him 'Father.' To disrespect a father is wrong; to despise him is wicked.

"The Tathāgata," the Buddha continued, "does not seek salvation in austerities, but neither does he for that reason indulge in worldly pleasures, nor live in abundance. The Tathāgata has found the middle path

"There are two extremes, O bhikkhus, which the man who has given up the world ought not to follow—the habitual practice, on the one hand, of self-indulgence which is unworthy, vain and fit only for the worldly-minded—and the habitual practice, on the other hand, of self-mortification, which is painful, useless and unprofitable.

"Neither abstinence from fish or flesh, nor going naked, nor shaving the head, nor wearing matted hair, nor dressing in a rough garment, nor covering oneself with dirt, nor sacrificing to Agni, will cleanse a man who is not free from delusions.

"Reading the Vedas, making offerings to priests, or sacrifices to the gods, self-mortification by heat or cold, and many such penances performed for the sake of immortality, these do not cleanse the man who is not free from delusions.

"Anger, drunkenness, obstinacy, bigotry, deception, envy, self-praise, disparaging others, superciliousness and evil intentions constitute uncleanliness; not verily the eating of flesh.

"A middle path, O bhikkhus, avoiding the two extremes, has been discovered by the Tathāgata—a path which opens the eyes, and bestows understanding, which leads to peace of mind, to the higher wisdom, to full enlightenment, to Nirvāna!

"What is that middle path, O bhikkhus, avoiding these two extremes, discovered by the Tathāgata—that path which opens the eyes, and bestows understanding, which leads to peace of mind, to the higher wisdom, to full enlightenment, to Nirvāna?

"Let me teach you, O bhikkhus, the middle path, which keeps aloof from both extremes. By suffering, the emaciated devotee produces confusion and sickly thoughts in the mind. Mortification is not conducive even to worldly knowledge; how much less to a triumph over the senses!

"He who fills his lamp with water will not dispel the darkness, and he who tries to light a fire with rotten wood will fail. And how can anyone be free from self by leading a wretched life, if he does not succeed in quenching the fires of lust, if he still hankers after either worldly or heavenly pleasures. But he in whom self has become extinct is free from lust; he will desire neither worldly nor heavenly pleasures, and the satisfaction of his natural wants will not defile him. However, let him be moderate, let him eat and drink according to the needs of the body.

"Sensuality is enervating: the self-indulgent man is a slave to his passions, and pleasure-seeking is degrading and vulgar.

"But to satisfy the necessities of life is not evil. To keep the body in good health is a duty, for otherwise we shall not be able to trim the lamp of wisdom, and keep our mind strong and clear. Water surrounds the lotus-flower, but does not wet its petals.

"This is the middle path, O bhikkhus, that keeps aloof from both extremes."

This beautifully detailed sandstone statue of the enlightened Buddha meditating in a standing position was carved in the 5th century C.E. *Note the nimbus or halo—which was commonly employed in later Buddhist iconography—as well as the calm and composure radiated by the Buddha's facial expression.*

upheavals touched off by the invasion of northwestern India by Alexander the Great in 327 B.C.E. Alexander had several reasons for invading India. To begin with, he believed that except for India, Arabia, North Africa, and some remote and barbaric parts of Europe, he had run out of places to conquer. He knew of the Indians because some of them had fought with the Persians against his armies; he knew little or nothing of the Chinese. A new campaign would keep his soldiers in fighting trim and his generals from quarreling among themselves. It is also likely that Alexander found the prospect of further adventures in India a good deal more exciting than the humdrum tasks involved in administering the huge empire his armies had won in less than a decade.

Whatever his motives, in 327 B.C.E. Alexander's armies crossed the Hindu Kush into India, thus beginning what would be his last major campaign of conquest. It was a rousing success. His greatly outnumbered armies won a series of battles against the peoples living in the upper Indus valley. As had been the case in his Persian campaigns, Alexander's well-trained troops proved more than a match for the war chariots, archers, and massed cavalry of his Indian adversaries. Once the surprise wore off, his veteran soldiers also proved able to cope with the numbers of war elephants that had spooked their horses.

Victory stirred Alexander's passion for further conquests. But his soldiers, weary of endless battles and fearful of the stiffening resistance of numerous Indian princes in an exotic and very distant land, refused to go farther to the east. After considerable debate, Alexander agreed to lead his forces out of India. Those in his armies who survived an epic march through the desert wastes to the north and west of the Indus River returned to Persia in 324 B.C.E. Alexander's death a year later left his Indian conquests to be fought over by the commanders who divided up his empire.

Though several Greek rulers controlled territory in India's northwest for decades after Alexander's invasion, the impact of his campaign was largely indirect. It stimulated some trade and considerable cultural exchange between India and the Mediterranean region. Of particular importance was the flow of Greek astronomical and mathematical ideas to India as well as the impact of Indian thinking on religious movements in the Mediterranean. Greek Stoicism and the mystery religions that swept the eastern Mediterranean in the centuries around the birth of Christ owe much to Indian philosophical influences. In the arts, the combination of Indian and Greek styles led to an Indo-Greek school of sculpture that was both distinctive and influential in shaping approaches to the depiction of the Buddha. Indian motifs were blended with Greek physical features and artistic techniques.

The Rise of the Mauryas

Appropriately, the most lasting effects of Alexander's invasion were military and political. The defeats suffered by the kingdoms in the northwest created a political vacuum that was soon filled by the ablest of the regional lords, *Chandragupta Maurya* (322–298 B.C.E.). After some initial setbacks, Chandragupta embarked on a sustained campaign to build a great empire. After conquering much of the northwest and driving the Greek successors of Alexander out of India, his armies began the conquest of the kingdoms of the Ganges plain that would later form the heartland of the Maurya Empire.

As Chandragupta's empire grew, the folksy atmosphere of earlier localized court centers gave way to a new imperial style. He reigned from an elaborately carved and decorated palace set in large and well-tended gardens. Adopting the Persian example, Chandragupta proclaimed himself an absolute emperor and on state occasions sat on a high throne above hundreds of his splendidly attired courtiers. He was guarded by a special corps of amazons, and elaborate precautions were taken to safeguard his life. The food Chandragupta ate was first tasted by servants to ensure that *he* did not die of poisoning. Parrots were bred for the trees of the palace gardens to make sure that poisonous snakes did not find their way into the ruler's chambers. There were hollow pillars in which to hide palace spies, secret passages to enable the king to move about the palace undetected, and an obligatory bath and frisking for all who entered. Chandragupta built a standing army that Greek writers estimated (overly generously) was 500,000 strong, and he tried with some success to replace regional lords with his own administrators.

Chandragupta's son and successor, Bindusara, extended the Maurya Empire to the east along the Ganges plains and far to the south of the subcontinent. Little is known about Bindusara, but he was apparently a highly cultured man. He once requested wine, figs, and a philosopher as presents from one of the Greek rulers in western Asia. He received the wine and figs, but not the philosopher because, as the ruler informed him, the Greeks did not trade in philosophers. Bindusara's son, *Ashoka*, completed the conquests begun by his father and grandfather, and in his long reign from 268–232 B.C.E., northern India enjoyed a time of unprecedented political unity, prosperity, and cultural splendor.

Ashoka's Conversion and the Flowering of Buddhism in the Mauryan Age

In the early years of his rule, Ashoka showed little of the wisdom and tolerance that were to set off his reign as one of the great periods in Indian history. He won his throne only after a bloody struggle in which he eliminated several brothers. He was apparently bad-tempered and impetuous, as evidenced by his order that a woman from his harem be put to death for telling him that he was ugly. He also delighted in conquest—at least until he witnessed the horrible sufferings that were caused by his conquest of Orissa in eastern India. That experience, and regret for his earlier dissolute life, led to his conversion to Buddhism.

From the time of his conversion onward, Ashoka became a ruler who strove to serve his people and promote their welfare. He ceased to enlarge his domains by conquest; used his revenues to build roads, hospitals, and rest houses; and sought to reduce the slaughter of animals in his kingdom by encouraging vegetarianism. His attempts to curb the slaughter of cows were particularly important, since those attempts, in conjunction with a long-standing reverence for cattle, contributed to the sacred status that this animal attained in Indian civilization. Because Ashoka's edicts were also aimed at restricting animal sacrifices, they aroused the anxiety of the brahmans, who saw them as a threat to the rituals that were vital to their dominance in Indian society.

The influence of Buddhism on Ashoka's personal life spilled over into his state policy. Drawing on the Buddhist concept of a righteous world ruler spreading peace and good government, Ashoka attempted to build an imperial bureaucracy that would enforce his laws and sanctions against war and animal slaughter. Though his efforts to establish meaningful control by a centralized administration met with some success, they also aroused considerable opposition. The brahmans, resentful of their displacement as political advisors and administrators by Ashoka's bureaucrats, tried to stir up local resistance to imperial edicts. Warrior families that had once ruled the small states also sought to retain their control over local politics. They waited for signs of dynastic weakness in the hope of reviving their lost kingdoms.

Several social groups, however, gained greatly from Ashoka's attempts to recast Indian society in a Buddhist mold. The period of Maurya rule coincided with a great expansion from the Roman Empire in the west to China in the east. Indian merchants and artisans participated eagerly in this process. India established itself as one of the great preindustrial manufacturing centers of the classical world, specializing in cotton cloth and clothing. In fact, Indian cloth makers were so skilled that for many centuries Roman writers would lament the flow of gold to the east to pay for Indian textiles, for which the Romans had little else to exchange. Seeing in Buddhism an advantageous alternative to the caste system, merchants and artisans supported Ashoka's efforts. They generously patronized the different orders of Buddhist monks that increased greatly in wealth and membership. Women also had good reasons to support the Buddhist alternative. Their position within the family was strengthened under Buddhist law. In addition, the monastic life gave them opportunities for achievement and self-expression as nuns, scholars, and artists.

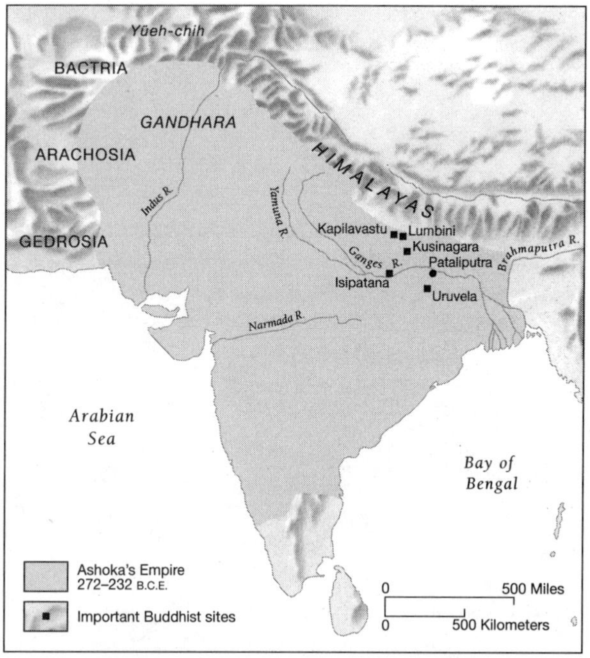

India at the Time of Ashoka

One of the chief signs of the Buddhist surge under Ashoka and his successors was the spread of great monastery complexes throughout the subcontinent. Most of the monasteries were made of wood and thus were lost in fires or destroyed by later invaders. But the Buddhist architectural legacy was preserved in the great stone shrines, or *stupas,* that were built to house pieces of bone or hair and personal possessions, which were said to be relics of the Buddha. Most of the freestanding stupas were covered mounds of dirt surrounded by intricately carved stone gateways and fences.

Another major effect of Ashoka's dedication to Buddhism resulted from his efforts to spread the faith beyond the Indian subcontinent. He sent missions, including one led by one of his sons, to Sri Lanka to the south and to the Himalayan kingdoms and the steppes of central Asia to the north. The establishment of Buddhism in each region was critical, because converted rulers and monks in these areas were instrumental in spreading the religion to much of the rest of Asia. From Sri Lanka Buddhism was carried to Burma, Java, and many other parts of Southeast Asia. From Nepal and central Asia it was disseminated into Tibet, China, and the rest of East Asia.

Ashoka's Death and the Decline of the Mauryas

Ashoka's bold experiments in religious and social change and the empire that he and his forebears had established did not long survive his death. Weaker rulers followed him to the throne. The empire was first divided between rival claimants within the Maurya household and then pulled apart by internal strife and local lords who attempted to reestablish the many kingdoms that had been absorbed into the Maurya imperium. By 185 B.C.E., the Mauryan Empire had disappeared. Political fragmentation returned to the subcontinent, and new warrior invaders compounded the rapidly growing divisions. Though some of these conquerors built substantial empires and were devoted to the continued spread of Buddhism, none of them could match Ashoka in power and resolution. Within the fragmented political order that emerged after the decline of the Mauryas, the brahmans initiated a religious revival that gradually, and usually without overt persecution, pushed Buddhism to the fringes of Indian social and intellectual life.

Brahmanical Recovery and the Splendors of the Gupta Age

Across the Indian subcontinent in the centuries between the fall of the Mauryas and the rise of the Guptas in the late 3rd century C.E., Buddhism and Hin-

The great Buddhist stupa at Sanchi in central India. Stupas were built to house relics of the Buddha, and they became major sites of pilgrimage for the Buddhist faithful.

duism, as the brahmanical beliefs and modes of worship would come to be known, vied largely without violence for the patronage of Indian rulers and the support of the Indian masses. By the time of the founding of the Gupta Empire in the 4th century C.E., it was clear that the brahmans would be able to meet the Buddhist challenge. Gupta patronage fortified the brahman revival, which in turn produced one of India's most glorious ages of philosophical and artistic creativity and social sophistication.

In the centuries after the end of the Mauryan Empire, new waves of invaders entered the Indian subcontinent. Indo-Greek rulers, whose kingdoms were based in central Asia, attempted to establish provinces in the northwest. Their kingdoms were attacked by Scythian nomads, who then raided and plundered and later settled in north India. The Scythians were overrun by a new wave of nomads, the Yueh-chih, from the eastern steppes. The Yueh-chih conquests gave rise to the Kushana dynasty, which was based in the northwest and was the most powerful in India between the end of the 1st and the early 3rd centuries C.E. Under the Kushanas, Buddhism experienced its last great era of imperial patronage. But the Kushanas' domains did not extend to the Ganges plains or central and south India, so in those areas kingdoms arose where the brahmans were able to reestablish their old political and religious dominance.

As the numbers of the converts to Buddhism multiplied in the last centuries B.C.E., the brahmans grew more and more sensitive to the challenge posed by the new faith. But they drew comfort from the fact that they still controlled the kings of the lowland states, where most of the population and Indian civilization was concentrated. The kings in turn were committed to upholding their positions and the caste hierarchy that was the key to the world they dominated. When, in the 4th and 3rd centuries B.C.E. these kings had been displaced by the powerful Mauryan Empire, and when the most talented ruler of that empire converted to Buddhism, the brahmans could no longer ignore their peril. The rise of the Mauryan Empire then was very much a precipitant of a largely peaceful, but nonetheless increasingly intense, struggle between the brahmans and the Buddhist monastic orders for dominance in Indian civilization.

Brahman Revival and Buddhist Decline

Even in the centuries immediately after the fall of the Mauryan dynasty, when the influence of Buddhism in Indian society was at its height, patterns had developed that rendered it quite vulnerable to a brahman counteroffensive. Over time, Buddhist monks became more and more concentrated in huge monasteries. Increasingly isolated from village and urban life, the monks grew obsessed with fine points of philosophy that often had little or no relevance to ordinary believers. Because Buddhism in India had not developed a sequence of family and life cycle rituals or folk festivals, the monks had little occasion to interact with the mass of the people. They focused their services more and more on wealthy patrons, whose donations supported the monasteries. This support made the daily rounds to collect alms unnecessary for the monks in many areas, and led to luxurious lifestyles and lax discipline at some of the more prominent Buddhist centers.

While the Buddhist monks became more remote from the Indian populace, the brahmans strove to effect changes in belief and worship that would make Hinduism more appealing to ordinary people. They played down the need for grand and expensive sacrifices and stressed the importance of personal worship and small, everyday offerings of food and prayers to the gods. Increasing emphasis was placed on intense devotion to gods such as Shiva and Vishnu and their female consorts Kali and Lakshmi. Special gods were allotted to particular occupational groups, such as Ganesh, the elephant-headed, pot-bellied deity who was especially revered by merchants.

Temples, both large and small, sprang up to house the multitude of statues that provided the focus for popular worship of the gods. Devotional cults were open to persons at all caste levels, including in some cases the untouchables. Women were also allowed to participate, at times, as cult poets and singers. In addition, the brahmans multiplied or enriched special festivals and rites-of-passage ceremonies, such as child-naming celebrations, weddings, and funerals, which enlarged the role they played in the everyday life of the Indian people. Over centuries, revived Hinduism simply absorbed the salvationist Buddhism that alone had a mass appeal. The brahmans treated the Buddha as another god of the Hindu pantheon and allowed their followers to worship him as one of the worldly forms of the preserver god Vishnu.

At the elite level, brahman philosophers and gurus placed increasing emphasis on the sophisticated and sublime philosophical ideas associated with the later books of the Vedas, the *Upanishads*. Not heavens or hells but the release of the soul from the endless cycle of rebirths was stressed in these teachings. Moderate asceticism and meditation were the means by which this release was achieved. In contrast to the Buddha, who preached that the soul itself was an illusion, the orthodox Hindu schools taught that the soul was real and its ultimate purpose was to fuse with the godhead from which it had come. The world was *maya*, or illusion, only because it was wrongly perceived by most humans. Those who had achieved realization and release understood that the world was in fact an extension of a single reality that encompassed everything.

In addition to monastic weaknesses and brahman reforms, Buddhism in India was weakened by underlying economic changes that altered the social circumstances that had favored the new religion. Most critical was the decline of the Rome-China trading axis with the fall of the Han empire in the 3rd century C.E. Not only did this undermine the position of the merchant groups that had been major patrons of Buddhism, it made large-scale traders more and more dependent on local kings and warrior households, which remained the chief allies of the brahmans.

The damage done to Buddhism by the losses of the mercantile classes was compounded by the collapse of the Mauryan and later the Kushana empires, which had been the monastic orders' supreme source of patronage. Their eventual replacement by the Guptas, who were enthusiastic supporters of the brahmans and Hinduism, all but sealed the fate of Buddhism in India. Its demise would be gradual and only occasionally hastened by violent persecution. But centuries of rule by the Guptas in north India and Hindu kingdoms in the south left only pockets of Buddhist strength, which would decay over time.

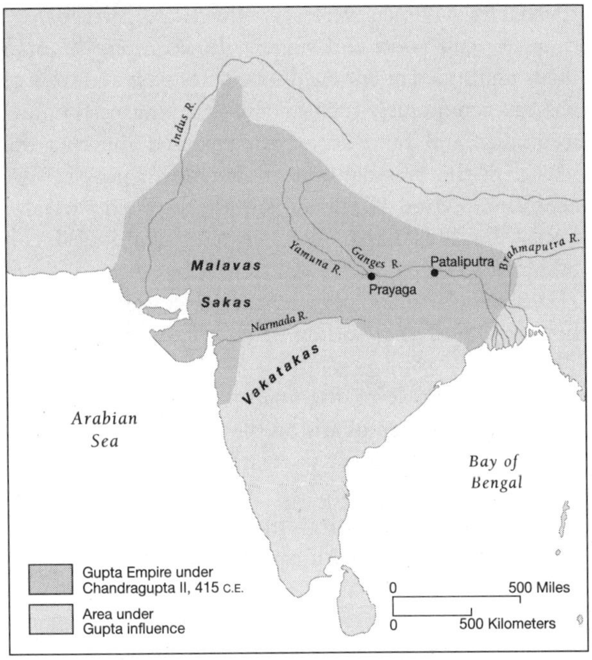

The Gupta Empire

The Gupta Empire

In the last decades of the 3rd century C.E., a family of wealthy landholders in the eastern Ganges plains first infiltrated the court of the local ruler and then seized his throne. Through a succession of clever alliances and timely military victories, the Gupta family built an empire that by the end of the 4th century C.E. extended across most of northern India. The *Guptas'* domains were not nearly as extensive as those of the Mauryas, and they had far less control over the regional lords and villages that fell under their sway than had briefly been the case with the Mauryas, particularly under Ashoka. The Gupta rulers never attempted to build a genuine bureaucracy or to regulate affairs at the local level effectively. Their empire was in fact a massive tributary edifice, in which former kings were left to rule in the name of the Guptas, and regional warrior elites were virtually autonomous governors of all but the empire's heartlands in the Ganges basin.

The Guptas were content to be acknowledged as supreme overlords and to draw as much tribute as possible from the many vassals who were forced to accede to their rule. Weak control from the center meant that local lords periodically revolted or squabbled among themselves. Though internal warfare continued, it was at a low level compared to the centuries after the fall of the Mauryas. Until the 5th century, foreign invaders were kept beyond the Himalayas and internal conflicts were short and localized. Gupta dominance brought over two and a half centuries of relative peace and unprecedented prosperity to much of north India.

A Hindu Renaissance

From the outset, the Guptas had been staunch defenders of Hinduism and patrons of the brahmans. With the family's rise to power, the brahmans' roles as sanctifiers of and advisors to kings were fully restored. Buddhist monks were increasingly confined to their monasteries, which, lacking the patronage of the imperial court, had to depend on wealthy local merchants or landowners for support. The brahmans' roles as gurus, or teachers, for the princes of the imperial court and the sons of local notables also became entrenched. Brahmans regained the aura of mystery and supernatural power that they had enjoyed in the Vedic age. In *The Signet Ring of Rakshasa,* one of the great dramas that was produced in the Gupta epoch, King Chandragupta prostrates himself at the feet of his teacher and advisor, Chanyaka. The ruler lavishes presents on brahmans linked to the court and relies on their stratagems to thwart the schemes of his adversaries. With their power base and sources of patronage restored, brahman priests, poets, scholars, and patrons of the arts became the driving force behind an era of splendid achievement in literature, music, art, architecture, and the natural sciences.

The most dramatic expressions of the Hindu resurgence were the great temples that rose above the rapidly growing urban centers, both within the Gupta domains and in the independent kingdoms in the far south. In many cases the temples themselves provided the impetus for urban growth. Merchants, artisans, servants, and laborers migrated to the towns where the temples were located to serve the growing numbers of pilgrims who journeyed to the sacred sites to worship and win favors from the Hindu deities. The intricately carved stone gateways and sanctuary towers of these edifices proclaimed the majesty of the Hindu gods and goddesses to the townspeople and peasants of the nearby villages. In eastern India and elsewhere, the temple towers literally teemed with sculptures of deities and friezes of their legendary exploits; with animals, which were often the vehicles or manifestations of major gods or goddesses; and with humans in all manner of activities, including explicit depictions of sexual intercourse.

The jumble of sculpture and the structure of the temples as a whole were very much reflections of the Hindu worldview. Compared with medieval European cathedrals and Muslim mosques, which soar to the heavens, Hindu temples were heavy and earthbound. These qualities were in part explained by limitations in construction techniques, but they resulted equally from the Hindu view that the divine is everywhere, not simply in the heavens. The towers, cluttered with statuary, mirrored the Hindu view of space as a realm alive with life. The worldly and even profane preoccupations of gods and goddesses (as well as ordinary mortals) depicted in temple sculptures suggest the Hindu conviction that divinity encompasses all life. It also reflects the symbolic parallels drawn in Indian religions between the union of male and female and the individual's search for oneness with the divine.

As these examples suggest, Hindu art stressed symbolism rather than accurate representation, which was so highly valued by the ancient Greeks. The sculpture and the god or goddess it depicted stood for something else—including creation (Brahma), destruction (*Shiva*), fertility (Lakshmi), and death (Kali as Durga). In fact, the temple complexes as a whole were massive *mandalas,* or cosmic diagrams, measured precisely and laid out according to established conventions.

Achievements in Literature and the Sciences

Though written languages had developed in India during the centuries before the rise of the Gupta dynasty, the Gupta reign initiated one of the great ages of Indian literary achievement. In the Gupta period and the following centuries, many of the great classics of *Sanskrit,* the sacred and classical Indian language, and Tamil, one of the major languages of the South, were written. The poet Kalidasa, who is acknowledged as the greatest of Sanskrit authors, lived in a period when Gupta power was at its height. In the "Cloud Messenger" and numerous other poems, he provided vivid pictures of life in the Gupta age. In the following passage, for example, the clouds bringing the monsoon rains pass over a town where the poet exclaims:

Your body will grow fat with the smoke of incense from open windows where women dress their hair.
You will be greeted by palace peacocks, dancing to welcome you, their friend.
If your heart is weary from travel you may pass the night above mansions fragrant with flowers
Whose pavements are marked with red dye from the feet of lovely women.

In addition to poetry and drama, Hindu scholars in the classical era wrote treatises on the nature of time, space, and causality, which contain arguments that have much in common with the findings of modern science on these issues. In fact, the era of the Hindu revival was a time of great Indian achievement in both mathematics and the sciences. In addition to advances in geometry and algebra that were made quite independently of the work in these fields by the Greeks, Indian thinkers calculated the circumference of the globe and the value of π with remarkable accuracy. They also used the concept of zero and devised decimals, and, most critically, formulated the "Arabic" number system that we use today. In the Gupta age and afterward, the Indians also made major breakthroughs in medicine. They developed hospitals, surgical techniques, and sophisticated treatments for a variety of illnesses.

Intensifying Caste and Gender Inequities

As the brahmans recovered their earlier social dominance, the caste hierarchy they had long promoted was established as the backbone of the Indian social system. Caste divisions grew even more complex and came to vary significantly between different areas in the subcontinent. Styles of dress increasingly distinguished members of each varna grouping, and the restrictions on untouchables and other low-caste groups grew harsher and more pervasive. In some areas, for example, untouchables traveling on roadways between towns had to clap sticks together or continually shout that they were on the road in order to warn high-caste groups that they were in danger of being polluted. If a brahman or merchant was seen approaching, the untouchable was required to leave the road and pass by through the fields at a considerable distance. The untouchables were not allowed to use any wells but their own or to worship in the temples frequented by other caste groups. Even their living quarters were segregated from the rest of the towns and rural villages.

Like the untouchables, women at all caste levels suffered a further reduction of their status and restriction of career outlets. They were no longer allowed to read the sacred Vedas, though a few remained prominent in the devotional cults. Hindu law declared that women were legally minors, subject to the supervision and protection

An approaching pilgrim's view of the temple towers in the city of Madurai in south India. Like medieval cathedrals and Islamic mosques, these great structures attest to the intense faith and outpouring of devotion that were associated with the Hindu resurgence of the early centuries C.E.

of their fathers, husbands, and, if widowed, their sons. Except for their personal clothing and jewelry, women were not allowed to inherit property. The fact that family fortunes could pass only from father to son and that large dowries were required to arrange marriages with suitable spouses meant that girls were increasingly seen as an economic liability. As popular sayings and poems from this period attest, sons were prized and pampered, while daughters were overlooked and neglected. In some regions where dowry amounts were highly inflated, female infanticide was practiced to save families from financial ruin.

Women were tied to the home, their lives decided by males. Marriages were primarily a means of establishing alliances between families. They were arranged with the groom having little say and the bride none. Child marriages were not uncommon among the upper castes. Young girls left the familiar surroundings of their own homes to live with their husband's families. In their new households, they were at the mercy of their mothers-in-law, who could be caring and reassuring but, if the literature from this and later periods is any gauge, were very often bossy and critical. A young girl's place in the new household depended almost wholly on her ability to bear sons, who would be devoted to her and would care for her in old age. A woman whose husband died before she bore him a son was doomed to a lonely life in the remote corners of the family compound. Even widows who bore sons were not to be envied. They were not allowed to remarry or go out alone lest they defile the memory of their deceased husbands.

Other than marriage, few avenues were open to women. A single woman was regarded as an economic liability and a blot on her family's honor. As the Buddhist monasteries shrank in numbers and size, the possibility of becoming a nun diminished sharply. Only by becoming a courtesan, or a woman accomplished in all the arts including sexual intercourse, could a woman establish some degree of independence. Courtesans, who are sometimes celebrated in the literature of this period, could become well educated, acquire wealth, and find outlets for their talents. But though they were far above the despised common prostitutes in status, they could not hope to have social respectability or raise families of their own. Unlike married women, whose husbands were duty bound to provide them with the requirements of life, courtesans were dependent on the tastes and whims of males, who dominated all aspects of interaction between the sexes in the Gupta age.

The Pleasures of Elite Life

Though women were restricted in career options and largely confined to their households, life for those of the upper castes was not without its rewards—at least, once a woman had established her place in her husband's family

Stylized sculptures depicting young women from the Hindu temple at Khajuraho in eastern India. These figures represent a standardized form of feminine beauty in South Asian culture: large breasts, small waist, and ornate jewelry.

by having sons. Well-to-do families lived in large compounds set in gardens filled with flowering plants and colorful birds. They were waited on by servants and entertained at periodic festivals and in their own compounds by swings, games such as chess and parchesi (both of which the Indians invented), and wandering musicians. Males and females dressed in silks and fine cottons and at mealtimes enjoyed one of the world's great cuisines. When they ventured away from the family compound, the very wealthy were carried in litters borne by servants and given the place of honor to which their caste rank entitled them.

Males from the upper castes were particularly privileged. They were expected to experience the four stages of the ideal Hindu life that were firmly established in this era for men only. In their youth they were to work hard as students, but many diversions and pleasures were available to the fashionable sons of well-to-do families. Many of these pastimes are described in the famous (or infamous) *Kamasutra* by Vatsayana, who lived in the Gupta era. Though often dismissed as little more than a glorified sex manual, Vatsayana's work in fact contains detailed instructions on virtually all aspects of the life of the young man-about-town. There are recommendations for grooming and hygiene, discussions of good etiquette in various situations, advice on the best way to select a wife, and, of course, instructions in making love to either a witty and knowledgeable courtesan or one's future wife. There was, of course, a double standard: young men were expected to come to marriage knowledgeable in the ways of love; girls who were not virgins were disgraced and unmarriageable.

The student was expected in the second stage of life to become a householder and, ideally, a faithful husband. Preserving or adding to the family fortune was a major task in this phase of life, and bearing sons to perform one's funeral rites and continue the family line was essential. At some point in middle age, the householder was supposed to bid farewell to his family and go off to the forest to join the hermits in meditation. In his final years, the upper-caste man was expected to enter the fourth stage of life by becoming a wandering holy man, completely dependent on the charity of others. Few individuals actually advanced beyond the householder stage. But the fact that the sequence had become the social ideal indicates that Indian religion and society could readily accommodate scholarship and worldly pursuits, bodily denial, and meditation as valid paths to self-fulfillment.

Lifestyles of the Ordinary People

For most Indians who labored as peasants, artisans, or sweepers at the lower levels of the caste system, the delights of upper-caste youths or the ability to set off as a wandering holy man were unattainable. Most Indians experienced lives of hard work, if not sheer drudgery. Most knew no deference from others but rather spent their lives bowing to and serving their caste superiors. At the lower-caste levels, women were somewhat freer in their ability to move about the town and countryside and buy and sell in the local marketplace. But they had no servants to perform their many household chores and were required to do backbreaking farming tasks, such as weeding fields or transplanting rice.

There were, of course, small pleasures. Even low-caste groups could attend temple festivals, watch dances and dramatics performed in the open air, and risk their meager wages in dice games or betting on roosters specially bred to fight with each other. In an age when India was one of the most fertile and productive regions on the earth, it is probable that all but the untouchables lived as well as ordinary people did anywhere in the world.

The Indian economy continued to grow in the Gupta age, despite the decline of long-distance trade with China and Rome. Leadership in international commerce increasingly shifted to the trading cities on the east and west coasts and the southern seaports of the subcontinent. Strong trading links were maintained with kingdoms in Sri Lanka and throughout Southeast Asia, which were strongly influenced by Indian cultural exports. In fact, India became the pivot of the great Indian Ocean trading network that stretched from the Red Sea and Persian Gulf in the west to the South China Sea in the east—a position it would maintain until the age of European overseas expansion after the 16th century C.E. It is no small wonder that India was known by the time of the Guptas as a land of great wealth as well as the home of many religions. A Chinese Buddhist, Fa-hsien, on a pilgrimage to India, exclaimed:

> **The people are many and happy. They do not have to register their households with the police. There is no death penalty. Religious sects have houses of charity where rooms, couches, beds, food, and drink are supplied to travelers.**

Gupta Decline and a Return to Political Fragmentation

For nearly 250 years, the Guptas managed to hold together the collection of vassal kingdoms that they passed off as an empire. Signs of future danger appeared in the northwest with the first of the Hun probes across the Himalayas in the early decades of the 5th century C.E. Preoccupied by the growing threat on their northern frontier, the later Gupta rulers failed to crush resistance from their vassals and challenges from states to the south of the Gupta domains. By the middle of the century, Gupta efforts to hold back repeated assaults by greater and greater numbers of Hun invaders were faltering. With the death of *Skanda Gupta,* the last of the truly able Gupta monarchs, a flood of nomadic invaders broke into the empire. Their pillaging and widely dispersed assaults finished off what remained of Gupta military might, and the empire dissolved into a patchwork of local kingdoms and warring states. From the mid-7th century until the establishment of the Delhi Sultanate in the early 13th century, northern India was divided and vulnerable to outside invasions.

CONCLUSION

The Legacy of the Classical Age in India

The civilization the Aryan invaders began to build in the centuries after settling in India in the middle of the second millennium B.C.E. proved a good deal more adaptable and long-lasting than the Harappan complex it replaced. Though its growth was marked by a couple of notable attempts to build a centralized political system to shield and nurture it, unlike China its genius and strength did not rest in political organization or military innovation. By the last centuries B.C.E., the central bulwarks of civilization in India were the caste system and the Hindu religion that provided its ideological underpinnings. What has come to be viewed as a system of social oppression served then as an intricate and ingenious mode of dividing labor and allotting social roles. The Hindu social order that rested on the caste hierarchy not only proved able to withstand the very formidable challenge of Buddhism but managed to absorb wave after wave of foreign invaders.

Though the contributions of the Buddhists and other nonbrahmanical religions were not inconsiderable, the brahman-dominated, caste-ordered civilization of India produced some of humanity's most sublime art and philosophy; important breakthroughs in mathematics, the sciences, and technology; prosperous urban centers; and a population that in numbers has been second only to that of China through much of human history. Neither the rigidity of the caste system nor the pronounced religious emphasis of Indian culture prevented the range of diversity common in the achievements of the other classical civilizations. In India's case, these achievements included an often sensual art and literature, a sizeable corpus of tough-minded political theory, and a sophisticated trading system—all of which defy persisting characterizations of India as otherworldly and antimaterial.

FURTHER READING

Perhaps the most readable introductions to life and society in India's classical age can be found in A. L. Basham's *The Wonder That Was India* (1954) and Jeannine Auboyer's *Daily Life in Ancient India* (1961). The works of Romilla Thapar, especially her *Ashoka and the Decline of the Mauryas* (1961), are the best on the political history of the era. But even her more general *A*

History of India (1966) is very detailed and quite technical—certainly a challenge for the beginner. Fine narrative histories of all aspects of Indian civilization in this period can be found in the appropriate chapters of *The History and Culture of the Indian People* (1964), ed. R. C. Majumdar, A. K. Majumdar, and D. K. Ghose. One of the best works on the position of women and social life more generally is Pandharinath Prabhu's *Hindu Social Organization* (1940). A wide range of other aspects of ancient Indian culture is covered in the fine essays in A. L. Basham's *A Cultural History of India* (1975).

Superb introductions to various branches of Indian religious and philosophical thinking, with well-selected portions of the appropriate texts, can be found in S. Radhakrishnan and Charles Moore, eds., *A Source Book in Indian Philosophy* (1957). Of the many books on Buddhism, Trevor Ling's *The Buddha* (1973) has the dual advantage of incorporating recent scholarship and being very readable. S. Radhakrishnan's *Hindu View of Life* (1927) provides a useful insider's view of Hindu religious beliefs and social organization. Heinrich Zimmer's *Philosophies of India* (1956), though somewhat dated, remains a good place to begin an exploration of the riches and diversity of Indian mythology and religious thinking. Benjamin Rowland's *The Art and Architecture of India* (1953) is the most objective and comprehensive work available in English on Indian art. For a taste of Indian literature in the classical age, there are English translations of the Ramayana and the Mahabharata and P. Lal's fine translations of *Great Sanskrit Plays* (1957).

CHAPTER 4

Classical Chinese Civilization

KEY TERMS

Chou Dynasty	*Legalism*
Warring States Period	*Ch'in / Qin Dynasty*
li	*Ch'in Shih Huang-ti (First Emperor)*
Confucius	*Liu Pang*
Analects	*Han Dynasty*
Taoism	*scholar-gentry*
Lao-tzu	*Wu Ti*
Mencius	*Pax Sinica*

DISCUSSION QUESTIONS

Compare and contrast Confucianism, Legalism, and Taoism. Compare the dynasties (Ch'in and Han) that adopted the first two of these schools of thought.

How did China participate in international trade under the Han?

The Chou Dynasty: The Feudal Age

Around 1040 B.C.E., the leader of the Chou (Zhou) tribe overthrew the Shang ruler, who, it was claimed, had failed to rule fairly and benevolently. The Chou leader announced that Heaven *(T'ien)* had given him a mandate to replace the Shang. This was more than a rationalization of the seizure of power. It introduced a new aspect of Chinese thought: The cosmos is ruled by an impersonal and all-powerful Heaven, which sits in judgment over the human ruler, who is the intermediary between Heaven's commands and human fate.

The Chou was a western frontier tribe that had maintained its martial spirit and fighting ability. The other Chinese tribes switched their loyalty to the Chou leader, who went on to establish a dynasty that lasted for almost 800 years (1040– 256 B.C.E.), the longest in Chinese history.

Comprising most of North China and the Yangtze valley, the large Chou domain made the establishment of an effective central authority impossible. Consequently, the Chou kings set up a feudal system of government by delegating local authority to relatives and noble magnates. These 50 or more vassal lords, whose power was hereditary, recognized the overlordship of the Chou kings and supplied them with military aid.

The early Chou kings were vigorous leaders who were able to retain the allegiance of their vassals (when necessary, by their superior military power) and fend off attacks from barbarians on the frontiers. In time, however, weak kings succeeded to the throne, and the power and independence of their vassals increased. By the eighth century B.C., the vassals no longer went to the Chou capital for investiture by the Son of Heaven, as the Chou king called himself.

The remnants of Chou royal power disappeared completely in 771 B.C.E., when an alliance of dissident vassals and barbarians destroyed the capital and killed the king. Part of the royal family managed to escape eastward to Lo-yang, however, where the dynasty survived for another five centuries (until c. 250 B.C.E.) doing little more than performing state religious rituals as the Son of Heaven. Seven of the stronger feudal princes gradually conquered their weaker neighbors. In the process they assumed the title *wang* ("king"), formerly used only by the Chou ruler, and began to extinguish the feudal rights of their own vassals and establish centralized administrations. Warfare among these emerging centralized states was incessant, particularly during the two centuries known as the Period of Warring States (c. 400–221 B.C.E.). By 221 B.C.E., the ruler of the Ch'in, the most advanced of the seven Warring States, had conquered all his rivals and established a unified empire with himself as absolute ruler.

Chou Economy and Society

Despite its political instability, the Chou period is unrivaled by any later period in Chinese history for its material and cultural progress. These developments led the Chinese to distinguish between their own high civilization and the nomadic ways of the "barbarians" beyond their frontiers. A sense of the superiority of their own civilization became a lasting characteristic of the Chinese.

During the sixth century B.C.E., iron was introduced and mass producing cast iron objects from molds came into general use by the end of the Chou period. (The first successful European attempts at casting iron were not made until the end of the Middle Ages.)

The ox-drawn iron-tipped plow, together with the use of manure and the growth of large-scale irrigation and water-control projects, led to great population growth based on increased agricultural yields. Canals were constructed to facilitate moving commodities over long distances. Commerce and wealth grew rapidly, and a merchant and artisan class emerged. Brightly colored shells, bolts of silk, and ingots of precious metals were the media of exchange; by the end of the Chou period, small round copper coins with square holes were being minted. Chopsticks and finely lacquered objects, today universally considered as symbols of Chinese and East Asian culture, were also in use by the end of the period.

Class divisions and consciousness became highly developed under Chou feudalism and have remained until modern times. The king and the aristocracy were sharply separated from the mass of the people on the basis of land ownership and family descent.

The core units of aristocratic society were the elementary family, the extended family, and the clan held together by patriarchal authority and ancestor worship. Marriages were formally arranged unions between families. Among the peasants, the father also exercised autocratic power over the family. Marriage, however, usually took place after a girl became pregnant following the Spring Festival at which boys and girls, beginning at age 15, sang and danced naked.

The customs of the nobles can be compared in a general way to those of Europe's feudal nobility. Underlying the society was a complex code of chivalry, called *li,* practiced in both war and peace. It symbolized the

DOCUMENT

Legalism: The Theories of Han Fei Tzu (d. 233 B.C.E.)

When the sage rules the state, he does not count on people doing good of themselves, but employs such measures as will keep them from doing any evil. If he counts on people doing good of themselves, there will not be enough such people to be numbered by the tens in the whole country. But if he employs such measures as will keep them from doing evil, then the entire state can be brought up to a uniform standard. Inasmuch as the administrator has to consider the many but disregard the few, he does not busy himself with morals but with laws.

... Therefore, the intelligent ruler upholds solid facts and discards useless frills. He does not speak about deeds of humanity and righteousness, and he does not listen to the words of learned men.

Those who are ignorant about government insistently say: "Win the hearts of the people." If order could be procured by winning the hearts of the people, then even the wise ministers Yi Yin and Kuan Chung would be of no use. For all that the ruler would need to do would be just to listen to the people. Actually, the intelligence of the people is not to be relied upon any more than the mind of a baby. If the baby does not have his head shaved, his sores will recur; if he does not have his boil cut open, his illness will go from bad to worse. However, in order to shave his head or open the boil someone has to hold the baby while the affectionate mother is performing the work, and yet he keeps crying and yelling incessantly. The baby does not understand that suffering a small pain is the way to obtain a great benefit.

... The sage considers the conditions of the times ... and governs the people accordingly. Thus though penalties are light, it is not due to charity; though punishment is heavy, it is not due to cruelty. Whatever is done is done in accordance with the circumstances of the age. Therefore circumstances go according to their time, and the course of action is planned in accordance with the circumstances.

... Now take a young fellow who is a bad character. His parents may get angry at him, but he never makes any change. The villagers may reprove him, but he is not moved. His teachers and elders may admonish him, but he never reforms. The love of his parents, the efforts of the villagers, and the wisdom of his teachers and elders—all the three excellent disciplines are applied to him, and yet not even a hair on his shins is altered. It is only after the district magistrate sends out his soldiers and in the name of the law searches for wicked individuals that the young man becomes afraid and changes his ways and alters his deeds. So while the love of parents is not sufficient to discipline the children, the severe penalties of the district magistrate are. This is because men become naturally spoiled by love, but are submissive to authority. ...

ideal of the noble warrior, and men devoted years to its mastery.

The art of horseback riding, developed among the nomads of central Asia, greatly influenced late Chou China. In response to the threat of mounted nomads, rulers of the Warring States period began constructing defensive walls. Inside China itself, chariots were largely replaced by swifter and more mobile cavalry troops wearing tunics and trousers adopted from the nomads.

The peasant masses, still attached serflike to their villages, worked as tenants of noble landholders, paying one-tenth of their crop as rent. Despite the increased agricultural production resulting from large-scale irrigation and the ox-drawn iron-tipped plow, the peasants had difficulty eking out an existence. Many were forced into debt slavery. A major problem in the Chinese economy, evident by late Chou times, has been that the majority of farmers have worked fields so small that they could not produce a crop surplus to tide them over periods of scarcity.

The Rise of Philosophical Schools

By the fifth century B.C.E., the increasing warfare among the feudal lords and Warring States had destroyed the stability that had characterized Chinese society under the Shang and early Chou dynasties. Educated Chinese had become aware of the great disparity between the traditions inherited from their ancestors and the conditions in which they themselves lived. The result was the birth of a social consciousness that focused on the study of humanity and the problems of society. Some scholars have noted the parallel between the flourishing intellectual life of China in the fifth century B.C.E. and Greek philosophy and Indian religious thought at the same time. It has been suggested that these three great centers of world civilization stimulated and influenced each other. However, little or no historical evidence exists to support such an assertion. The birth of social consciousness in China, isolated from the other centers of civilization, can best be understood in terms of internal developments rather than external influences.

Confucianism: Rational Humanism

The first, most famous, and certainly most influential Chinese philosopher and teacher was K'ung-fu-tzu ("Master K'ung, the Sage," 551–479 B.C.E.), known in the West as Confucius after Jesuit missionaries to China in the seventeenth century latinized his name.

Later Confucianists attributed to the master the role of composing or editing the Five Confucian Classics (two books of history and one book each on poetry, divination, and ceremonies), which were in large part a product of the early Chou period. But the only work that can be accurately attributed to Confucius is the *Analects* ("Selected Sayings"), a collection of his responses to his disciples' questions.

Confucius, who belonged to the lower aristocracy, was more or less a contemporary of the Buddha in India, Zoroaster in Persia, and the early philosophers of Greece. Like the Buddha and Zoroaster, Confucius lived in a troubled time—an age of political and social turmoil—and his prime concern, like theirs, was the improvement of society. To achieve this goal, Confucius did not look to the gods and spirits for assistance; he accepted the existence of Heaven *(T'ien)* and spirits, but he insisted it was more important "to know the essential duties of man living in a society of men." "We don't know yet how to serve men," he said, "how can we know about serving the spirits?" And, "We don't yet know about life, how can we know about death?" He advised a ruler to "respect the ghosts and spirits but keep them at a distance" and "devote yourself to the proper demands of the people."

Confucius believed that the improvement of society was the responsibility of the ruler and that the quality of government depended on the ruler's moral character: "The way *(Tao)* of learning to be great consists in shining with the illustrious power of moral personality, in making a new people, in abiding in the highest goodness." Confucius's definition of the Way as "moral personality" and the "highest goodness" was in decided contrast to the old premoral Way in which gods and spirits, propitiated by offerings and ritual, regulated human life for good or ill. Above all, Confucius's new Way meant a concern for the rights of others, the adherence to a Golden Rule:

> **Tzu-king [a disciple] asked saying, "Is there any single saying that one can act upon all day and every day?" The Master said, "Perhaps the saying about consideration: 'Never do to others what you would not like them to do to you.'"**

Although Confucius called himself "a transmitter and not a creator," his redefinition of *Tao* was a radical innovation. He was, in effect, putting new wine into old bottles. He did the same thing with two other key terms, *li* and *chün-tzu. Li,* meaning "honorable behavior," was the chivalric code of the constantly fighting *chün-tzu,* the hereditary feudal "noblemen" of the Chou period. As refined and reinterpreted by Confucius, *li* came to embody such ethical virtues as righteousness and love for one's fellow humans. The *chün-tzu,* under the influence of the new definition of *li,* became "noble men," or "gentlemen," whose social origins were not important. As Confucius said, "The noble man understands what is right; the inferior man understands what is profitable." Confucius's teachings have had a greater and longer-lasting influence on China, and much of East Asia, than those of any other philosopher.

Taoism: Intuitive Mysticism

A second philosophical reaction to the troubled life of the late Chou period was the teaching of Lao-tzu ("Old Master"), a semilegendary figure who was believed to have been a contemporary of Confucius. As with Confucius, the key term in Lao-tzu's teaching is *Tao,* from which his philosophy derives its name. But while Confucius defined *Tao* as a rational standard of ethics in human affairs, Lao-tzu gave it a metaphysical meaning—the course of nature, the natural and inevitable order of the universe.

The goal of Taoism, like Confucianism, is a happy life. Lao-tzu believed that this goal could be achieved by living a life in conformity with nature, retiring from the chaos and evils of contemporary Warring States society and shunning human institutions and opinions as unnatural and artificial "outside things." Thus at the heart

DOCUMENT

Confucius
Analects
(c. 500 B.C.E.)

Mêng I Tzu asked about the treatment of parents. The Master said, Never disobey! When Fan Ch'ih was driving his carriage for him, the Master said, Meng asked me about the treatment of parents and I said, Never disobey! Fan Ch'ih said, In what sense did you mean it? The Master said, While they are alive, serve them according to ritual. When they die, bury them according to ritual and sacrifice to them according to ritual.

Mêng Wu Po asked about the treatment of parents. The Master said, Behave in such a way that your father and mother have no anxiety about you, except concerning your health.

Tzu-yu asked about the treatment of parents. The Master said, 'Filial sons' nowadays are people who see to it that their parents get enough to eat. But even dogs and horses are cared for to that extent. If there is no feeling of respect, wherein lies the difference?

Tzu-hsia asked about the treatment of parents. The Master said, It is the demeanour that is difficult. Filial piety does not consist merely in young people undertaking the hard work, when anything has to be done, or serving their elders first with wine and food. It is something much more than that.

Tzu-kung asked about the true gentleman. The Master said, He does not preach what he practises till he has practised what he preaches.

The Master said, A gentleman can see a question from all sides without bias. The small man is biased and can see a question only from one side.

The Master said, 'He who learns but does not think, is lost.' He who thinks but does not learn is in great danger.

The Master said, He who sets to work upon a different strand destroys the whole fabric.

The Master said, Yu, shall I teach you what knowledge is? When you know a thing, to recognize that you know it, and when you do not know a thing, to recognize that you do not know it. That is knowledge.

The Master said, Hear much, but maintain silence as regards doubtful points and be cautious in speaking of the rest; then you will seldom get into trouble. See much, but ignore what it is dangerous to have seen, and be cautious in acting upon the rest; then you will seldom want to undo your acts. He who seldom gets into trouble about what he has said and seldom does anything that he afterwards wishes he had not done, will be sure incidentally to get his reward.

Duke Ai asked, What can I do in order to get the support of the common people? Master K'ung replied, If you 'raise up the straight and set them on top of the crooked,' the commoners will support you. But if you raise the crooked and set them on top of the straight, the commoners will not support you.

Chi K'ang-tzu asked whether there were any form of encouragement by which he could induce the common people to be respectful and loyal. The Master said, Approach them with dignity, and they will respect you. Show piety towards your parents and kindness towards your children, and they will be loyal to you. Promote those who are worthy, train those who are incompetent; that is the best form of encouragement.

Someone, when talking to Master K'ung, said, How is it that you are not in the public service? The Master said, The Book says: 'Be filial, only be filial and friendly towards your brothers, and you will be contributing to government.' There are other sorts of service quite different from what you mean by 'service.'

of Taoist thought is the concept of *wu-wei,* or "nonaction"—a manner of living which, like nature itself, is nonassertive and spontaneous. Lao-tzu pointed out that in nature all things work silently; they fulfill their function and, after they reach their bloom, they return to their origins. Unlike Confucius's ideal gentleman, who is constantly involved in society in order to better it, Lao-tzu's sage is a private person, an egocentric individualist, resigned to accepting life's burdens.

Taoism is a revolt not only against society but also against the intellect's limitations. Intuition, not reason, is the source of true knowledge; and books, Taoists

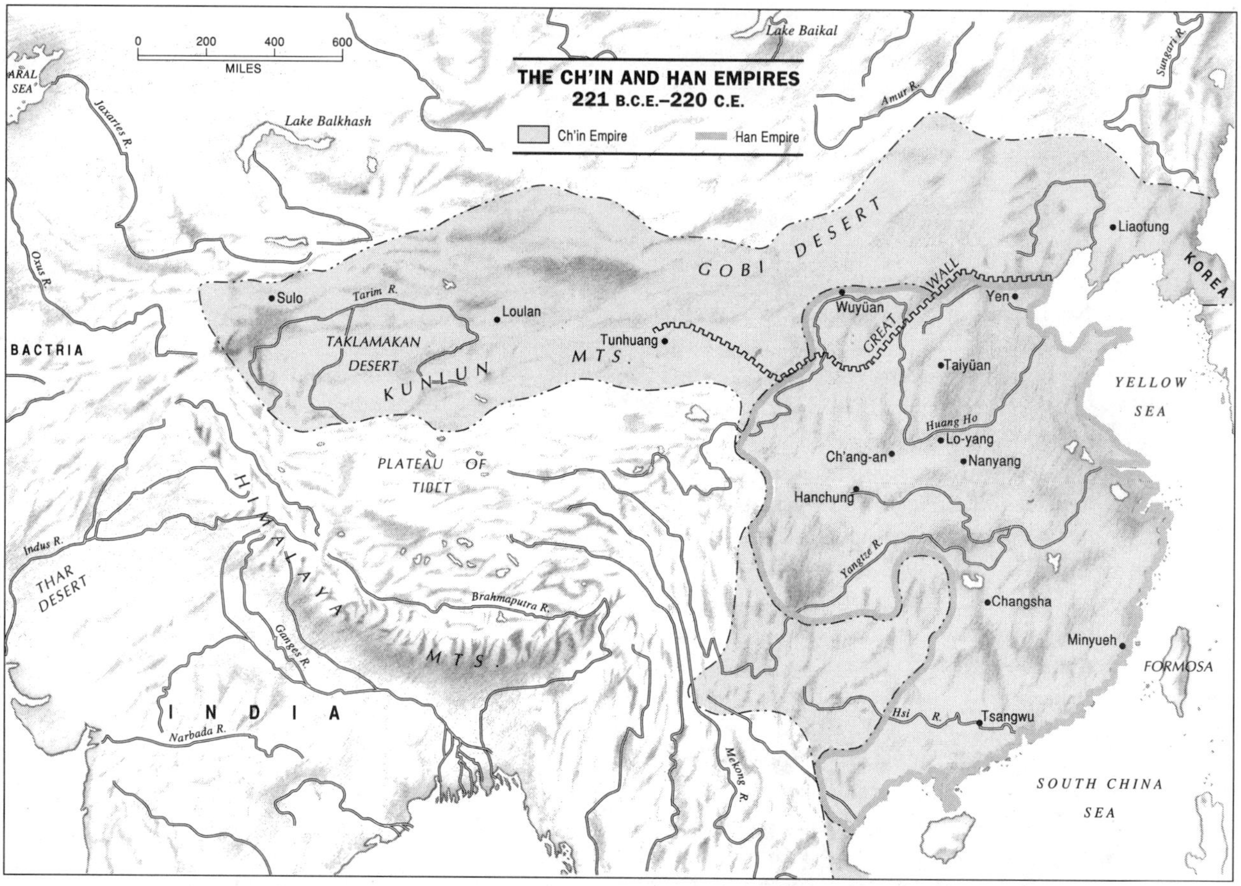

said, are "the dregs and refuse of the ancients." One of the most famous Taoist philosophers, Chuang-tzu (fourth century B.C.E.), who made fun of Confucians as tiresome busybodies, even questioned the reality of the world of the senses. He said that he once dreamed that he was a butterfly, "flying about enjoying itself." When he awakened he was confused: "I do not know whether I was Chuang-tzu dreaming that I was a butterfly, or whether now I am a butterfly dreaming that I am Chuang-tzu."

Similar anecdotes and allegories abound in Taoist literature, as in all mystical teachings that deal with subjects that are difficult to put into words. (As the Taoists put it, "The one who knows does not speak, and the one who speaks does not know.") But Taoist mysticism is more philosophical than religious. Unlike Upanishadic philosophy or Christian mysticism, it does not aim to extinguish the personality through the union with the Absolute or God. Rather, its aim is to teach how one can obtain happiness in this world by living a simple life in harmony with nature.

Confucianism and Taoism became the two major molds that shaped Chinese thought and civilization. Although these rival schools frequently sniped at one another, they never became mutually exclusive outlooks on life. Taoist intuition complemented Confucian rationalism; during the centuries to come, Chinese were often Confucianists in their social relations and Taoists in their private life.

Mencius's Contribution to Confucianism

The man whose work was largely responsible for the emergence of Confucianism as the most widely accepted philosophy in China was Mencius, or Meng-tzu (372–289 B.C.E.). Born a century after the death of Confucius, Mencius added important new dimensions to Confucian thought in two areas—human nature and government.

Although Confucius had only implied that human nature is good, Mencius emphatically insisted that all people are innately good and tend to seek the good just as water tends to run downhill. But unless people strive to preserve and develop their innate goodness, which is the source of righteous conduct, it can be corrupted by the bad practices and ideas existing in the environment. Mencius taught that the opposite of righteous conduct is selfishness, and he attacked the extreme individualism of the Taoists as a form of selfishness. He held that "all men are brothers," and he would have agreed with a later Confucian writer who summed up in one sentence the teaching of a famous Taoist: "He would not pluck so much as a hair out of his head for the benefit of his fellows."

The second area in which Mencius elaborated on Confucius's teaching was political theory. Mencius distinguished between good kings, who ruled benevolently, and the rulers of his day (the Period of Warring States), who governed by naked force and spread violence and disorder. Because good rulers are guided by ethical standards, he said, they will behave benevolently toward the people and provide for their well-being. Unlike Confucius, who did not question the right of hereditary kings to rule, Mencius said that the people have a right to rebel against bad rulers and even kill them if necessary, because they have lost the Mandate of Heaven.

As we have seen, this concept had been used by the Chou to justify their revolt against the Shang. On that occasion, the concept had a religious meaning, being connected with the worship of Heaven, who supported the ruler as the Son of Heaven. Mencius, however, secularized and humanized the Mandate of Heaven by equating it with the people: "Heaven hears as the people hear; Heaven sees as the people see." By redefining the concept in this way, Mencius made the welfare of the people the ultimate standard for judging government. Indeed, he even told rulers to their faces that the people were more important than the rulers were.

Modern commentators, both Chinese and Western, have viewed Mencius's definition of the Mandate of Heaven as an early form of democratic thought. Mencius did believe that all people were morally equal and that the ruler needed the consent of the people, but he was clearly the advocate of benevolent monarchy rather than popular democracy.

Legalism

Another body of thought emerged in the fourth and third centuries B.C.E. and came to be called the School of Law, or Legalism. It had no single founder, as did Confucianism and Taoism, nor was it ever a school in the sense of a teacher leading disciples. What it did have in common with Confucianism and Taoism was the desire to establish stability in an age of turmoil.

The Legalists emphasized the importance of harsh and inflexible law as the only means of achieving an orderly and prosperous society. They believed that human nature was basically bad and that people acted virtuously only when forced to do so. Therefore they argued for an elaborate system of laws defining fixed penalties for each offense, with no exceptions for rank, class, or circumstances. Judges were not to use their own conscience in estimating the gravity of the crime and arbitrarily deciding on the punishment. Their task was solely to define the crime correctly; the punishment was provided automatically by the code of law. This procedure is still a characteristic of Chinese law.

Since the enforcement of law required a strong state, the immediate goal of the Legalists was to enhance the power of the ruler at the expense of other elements, particularly the nobility. Their ultimate goal was the creation of a centralized state strong enough to unify all China and end the chaos of the Warring States period. The unification of China in 221 B.C.E. by the Ch'in was largely the result of putting Legalist ideas of government into practice.

China: The First Empire

The unification of China and the creation of a centralized empire was the proud achievement of two dynasties, the Ch'in (Qin) and the Han. The Ch'in dynasty collapsed soon after the death of its founder, but the Han lasted for more than four centuries. Together the two dynasties transformed China, but the changes were the culmination of earlier developments during the Warring States period.

Rise of Legalist Ch'in

Throughout the two centuries of the Warring States period (c. 400–221 B.C.E.) there was the hope that a king would emerge who would unite China and inaugurate a great new age of peace and stability. While the Confucians believed that such a king would accomplish the task by means of his outstanding moral virtue, the Legalists substituted overwhelming might as the essential element of effective government. The political philosophy of the Legalists, who liked to sum up and justify their doctrine in two words—"It works"—triumphed, and no state became more adept at practicing that pragmatic philosophy than the Ch'in.

A soldier of the terra cotta army buried at the tomb of the First Emperor. The weapon he held is missing.

The Ch'in's rise to preeminence began in 352 B.C.E., when its ruler selected Lord Shang, a man imbued with Legalist principles, to be chief minister. Recognizing that the growth of Ch'in's power depended on a more efficient and centralized bureaucratic structure than could exist under feudalism, Lord Shang undermined the old hereditary nobility by creating a new aristocracy based on military merit. He also introduced a universal draft beginning at approximately age 15. As a result, chariot and cavalry warfare, in which the nobility had played the leading role, was replaced in importance by masses of peasant infantry equipped with iron weapons.

Economically, Lord Shang further weakened the old landowning nobility by abolishing the peasants' attachment to the land and granting them ownership of the plots they tilled. Thereafter the liberated peasants paid taxes directly to the state, thereby increasing its wealth and power. These reforms made Ch'in the most powerful of the Warring States.

Ch'in Unites China

Nearly a hundred years after Lord Shang, another Legalist prime minister helped the king of Ch'in prepare and carry out the conquest of the other Warring States, bring an end to the powerless Chou dynasty in 256 B.C.E., and unite China in 221 B.C.E. The king then declared himself the "First August Supreme Ruler" (Shih Huang-ti) of China, or "First Emperor," as his new title is usually translated. He also enlarged China—a name derived from the word Ch'in—by conquests in the south as far as the South China Sea.

The First Emperor moved the leading members of the old nobility to near the capital, where they could be closely watched. To further forestall rebellion, he ordered the entire civilian population to surrender its weapons to the state. A single harsh legal code, which replaced all local laws, was so detailed in its provisions that it was said to have been like "a fishing net through which even the smallest fish cannot slip out." The population was organized in groups of ten families, and each person was held responsible for the actions of all the members of the group. This ensured that all crimes would be reported; it also increased loyalty to the state at the expense of family loyalty. The entire realm, which extended into South China and Vietnam, was divided into 48 provinces, administrative units drawn to obliterate traditional feudal units and to facilitate direct rule by the emperor's centrally controlled civil and military appointees. To destroy the source of the aristocracy's power and to permit the emperor's agents to tax every farmer's harvest, private ownership of land by peasants, promoted a century earlier in the state of Ch'in by Lord Shang, was decreed for all of China. Thus the Ch'in Empire reflected the emerging social forces at work in China—the peasants freed from serfdom, the merchants eager to increase their wealth within a larger political area, and the new military and administrative upper class.

Among the many public works—all constructed by forced labor—of the First Emperor's short 11-year reign were 4000 miles of highways and thousands of miles of canals and waterways, one of which connected the Yangtze to the Hsi River and Canton (Guangzhou). The written language was standardized, as were weights and measures—and even the length of axles so that cart wheels would fit the grooves cut in the highways. Although the First Emperor, like some Warring States rulers before him, built walls to impede the incursion of nomadic tribes from central Asia, it is no longer believed that he built the 1400-mile Great Wall of China. In its present form the Great Wall was mainly the work of the sixteenth-century Ming dynasty.

The First Emperor tried to enforce intellectual conformity and make the Ch'in Legalist system appear to be the only natural political order. He suppressed all other schools of thought—especially the Confucians who idealized Chou feudalism by stressing the obedience of sons to their fathers, of nobles to the lord, and of lords to the king. To break the hold of the past, the emperor put into effect a Legalist proposal requiring all privately owned books reflecting past traditions to be burned and "all those who raise their voice against the present government in the name of antiquity [to] be beheaded together with their families."

Near the Ch'in capital at Ch'ang-an (Xi'an), the First Emperor employed over half a million laborers to construct a huge mound tomb for himself and, nearby, three large pits filled with the life-sized terra cotta figures of his imperial guard. The mausoleum has not been excavated, but the partial excavation of the pits revealed some 7500 soldiers aligned in military formation. Strangely, each head is a personal portrait—no two faces are alike.

When the First Emperor died in 210 B.C.E. while on one of his frequent tours of inspection, he was succeeded by an inept son who was unable to control the rivalry among his father's chief aides. Ch'in policies had alienated not only the intellectuals and the old nobility but also the peasants, who were subjected to ruinous taxation and forced labor. Rebel armies rose in every province of the empire, some led by peasants, others by aristocrats. Anarchy followed, and by 206 B.C.E. the Ch'in dynasty, which the First Emperor had claimed would endure for "ten thousand generations," had completely disappeared. But the Chinese Empire itself, which Ch'in created, would last for more than 2000 years (until 1912, when China became a republic), the longest-lived political institution in world history.

At issue in the fighting that continued for another four years was not only the question of succession to the throne but also the form of government. The peasant and aristocratic leaders, first allied against Ch'in, became engaged in a furious and ruthless civil war. The aristocrats sought to restore the oligarchic feudalism of pre-Ch'in times. Their opponents, whose main leader was Liu Pang, a peasant who had become a Ch'in general, desired a centralized state. In this contest between the old order and the new, the new was the victor.

The Han Dynasty: The Empire Consolidated

In 206 B.C.E. the peasant Liu Pang defeated his aristocratic rival and established the Han dynasty. Named after the Han River, a tributary of the Yangtze, the new dynasty had its capital at Ch'ang-an. It lasted for more than 400 years and is traditionally divided into two parts: the Earlier Han, from 206 B.C.E to C.E. 8, and the Later Han, from C.E. 25 to C.E. 220, with its capital at Loyang. In time and importance, the Han corresponded to the late Roman Republic and early Roman Empire; ethnic Chinese still call themselves "Men of Han."

The empire and power sought by Liu Pang and his successors were those of the Ch'in, but they succeeded where the Ch'in had failed because they were tactful and gradual in their approach. Liu Pang reestablished for a time some of the vassal kingdoms and feudal states in regions distant from the capital. Peasant discontent was mollified by lessened demands for taxes and forced labor. But the master stroke of the Han emperors was to enlist the support of the Confucian intellectuals. They provided the empire with an ideology that would last until 1912. The Ch'in's extreme Legalistic ideology of harsh punishment and terror had alienated most Chinese.

The Han emperors recognized that an educated bureaucracy was necessary for governing so vast an empire. The ban on the Confucian classics and other Chou literature was lifted, and the way was open for a revival of the intellectual life that had been suppressed under the Ch'in.

In accord with Legalist principles, now tempered by Confucian insistence on the ethical basis of government, the Han emperors established administrative organs staffed by a salaried bureaucracy to rule their empire. Talented men were chosen for government service through an examination system based on the Confucian classics. Confucius's emphasis on loyalty as the most important duty—son to father within the family, minister to king within the state—pleased the Han and all later emperors.

The examinations were theoretically open to all Chinese except merchants. (The Han inherited both the Confucian bias against trade as an unvirtuous striving for profit and the Legalist suspicion of merchants who put their own interests ahead of those of the state and society.) The bureaucrats were drawn from the landlord class because wealth was necessary to obtain the education needed to pass the examinations. Consequently, the earlier division of Chinese society between aristocrats and peasants was transformed into a division between peasants and landowner-bureaucrats. The latter are also called scholar-gentry, a term first used in the eighteenth century by the British. They saw a parallel with the gentry who dominated the countryside and administration of their own country.

Wu Ti and the *Pax Sinica*

After 60 years of consolidation, the Han Empire reached its greatest extent and development during the long reign of Wu Ti ("Martial Emperor"), who ruled from 141 to 87 B.C.E. To accomplish his goal of territorial expansion, he raised the peasants' taxes but not those of the great landowners, who remained virtually exempt from taxation. In addition, he increased the amount of labor and military service the peasants were forced to contribute to the state.

The Martial Emperor justified his expansionist policies in terms of self-defense against Mongolian nomads, the Hsiung-nu, known to the West later as the Huns. Their attacks had caused the First Emperor to construct a wall to obstruct their raiding cavalry. To outflank the nomads in the west, Wu Ti extended the wall and annexed a large corridor extending through the Tarim River basin of central Asia to the Pamir Mountains close to Bactria. This corridor has ever since remained a part of China.

Wu Ti failed in an attempt to form an alliance with the Scythians in Bactria, but his envoy's report of the interest shown in Chinese silks by the peoples of the area was the beginning of a commercial exchange between China and the West. This trade brought great profits to Chinese and Kushan merchant families.

Wu Ti also outflanked the Hsiung-nu in the east by the conquest of southern Manchuria and northern Korea. In addition, he completed the conquest of South China, begun by the Ch'in, and he added northern Vietnam to the Chinese Empire. All the conquered lands experienced considerable Chinese emigration. Thus at a time when the armies of the Roman Republic were laying the foundation of the *Pax Romana* in the West, the Martial Emperor was establishing a *Pax Sinica* ("Chinese Peace") in the East.

Han Decline

Wu Ti's conquests led to a fiscal crisis. As costs increased, taxes increased, and the peasants' burdens led to revolt. The end result was that the central government had to rely more and more on local military commanders and great landowners for control of the population, giving them great power and prestige at its own expense. This cycle of decline after an initial period of increasing prosperity and power has been the pattern of all Chinese dynasties. During the Han this "dynastic cycle," as Western historians of China call it, led to a succession of mediocre rulers after Wu Ti's death and a temporary usurpation of the throne (C.E. 9–25), which divided the Earlier from the Later Han.

The usurper, Wang Mang, the Confucian chief minister of the court, united Confucian humanitarianism with Legalist practice. Like his contemporary in the West, the Roman emperor Augustus, his goal was the rejuvenation of society by employing the power of the state. By Wang Mang's day the number of large tax-free estates had greatly increased while the number of tax-paying peasant holdings had declined. This was a by-product of the private landownership that, under the Ch'in, had replaced the old communal use of the land. Rich officials and merchants were able to acquire the lands of impoverished peasant-owners, who became tenants paying exorbitant rents.

More and more peasants fell behind in their rents and were forced to sell themselves or their children into debt slavery. To remedy this situation and increase the government's tax income, Wang Mang abolished debt slavery and decreed that the land was the property of the nation and should be portioned out to peasant families, who would pay taxes on their allotments.

Wang Mang sought to solve the long-standing problem of inflation—which had greatly increased since Wu Ti first began debasing the coinage when he found himself in financial difficulties—by setting maximum prices on basic commodities. He also sought to stabilize prices by a program called "leveling"—the government bought surplus commodities when prices fell and sold them when scarcity caused prices to rise. (In 1938, a chance reading of Wang Mang's "leveling" proposal inspired the "ever-normal granary" program of President Roosevelt's New Deal.)

Wang Mang's remarkable reform program failed, however; officials bungled the difficult administrative task, and the powerful landowners rebelled against the ruler who proposed to confiscate their land. Although Wang Mang rescinded his reforms, he was killed by the rebels in C.E. 23. The conflict of landlordship and tenancy, along with the concentration of power of great families, became a major problem in Chinese history.

The Later Han dynasty never reached the heights of its predecessor. Warlords who were members of the rich landowner class seized more and more power, and widespread peasant rebellions (one band was led by "Mother Lu," a woman skilled in witchcraft) sapped the state's resources. Surviving in name only during its last 30 years, the Han dynasty ended in C.E. 220, when the throne was usurped by the son of a famous warlord. Three-and-a-half centuries of disunity and turbulence followed—the longest in China's long history and often called China's "Middle Ages"—as it did in Europe after the fall of the Roman Empire. But China eventually succeeded where Europe failed: in C.E. 589 the Sui dynasty united China again. With minor exceptions, it has remained united to this day.

Han Scholarship, Art, and Technology

Politically and culturally, the relation of the Han to the Chou paralleled that of ancient Rome to Greece. Politically, the disunity of Greece and the Chou was followed by the imperial unity and administrative genius of the Romans and the Han. Culturally, just as the Romans owed a great debt to the Greeks, so did the Han to the Chou. Furthermore, Greek and Chou intellectual creativity was not matched by the Romans and the Han.

Scholarship flourished under the Han, but it was mainly concerned with collecting and interpreting the classics of Chinese thought produced in the Chou period. As the basis of education for prospective bureaucrats, Wu Ti established an imperial university in 124 B.C.E.; a century later it had about 3000 students. The Han scholars venerated Confucius as the ideal wise man, and Confucianism became the official philosophy of the state. Great respect for learning, together with the system of civil service examinations based on the Five Confucian Classics, became fundamental characteristics of Chinese civilization.

Han scholars started another scholarly tradition with their historical writings. Their antiquarian interest in researching the past produced a comprehensive history of China, the *Historical Records (Shih chi)*. This voluminous work of 130 chapters has been highly praised, in part for its inclusion of a vast amount of information, beginning with the Hsia dynasty through the Han emperors up to Wu Ti (who had the author castrated when he spoke out in defense of a cashiered general), but even more for its freedom from superstition and careful weighing of evidence. In the Later Han a scholar wrote the *History of the (Earlier) Han*, and thereafter it was customary for each dynasty to write the official history of its immediate predecessor. The Chinese believed that the successes and failures of the past provided guidance for one's own time and for the future.

A masterpiece of nearly 2000 years is a unique, lively horse of bronze, galloping and neighing with its head and tail high. To show its speed the unknown craftsman, with a bold imagination, placed its right hind hoof on a flying swallow, and the other three hooves in the air. The craftsmanship is extremely fine and conforms to the principles of mechanics.

As stated in the *Historical Records*, "Events of the past, if not forgotten, are teachings about the future."

Archaeological investigation was used as an aid to the writing of history. One scholar anticipated modern archaeologists by more than a thousand years in classifying human history by "ages": "stone" (Old Stone Age), "jade" (New Stone Age), "bronze," and "the present age" when "weapons are made of iron."

Another monument to Han scholarship was the world's first dictionary, *Shuo Wen (Words Explained)*, produced during Wu Ti's reign. It listed the meaning and pronunciation of more than 9000 Chinese characters.

In contrast to Han scholarship, Han art was clearly creative. The largely decorative art of the past, which served a religious purpose, was replaced by a realistic pictorial art (foreshadowed earlier by the individually sculpted soldiers buried near the First Emperor's tomb) portraying ordinary life. The result was the first great Chinese flowering of sculpture, both in relief and in the round. Some of the finer examples of this realistic secular art are the sculptured models of the tall and spirited horses that Wu Ti imported from Bactria. The Han greatly admired these proud "celestial" and "blood-sweating" horses from the West, and their artists brilliantly captured their high spirit.

During the Han period, China surpassed the level of technological development in the rest of the world. Notable inventions included a primitive seismograph capable of indicating earthquakes several hundred miles away; the use of water power to grind grain and to operate a piston bellows for iron smelting; the horse collar, which greatly increased the pulling power of horses; paper made from cloth rags, which replaced cumbersome bamboo strips and expensive silk cloth as writing material; and the humble but extremely useful wheelbarrow. By the end of the first century B.C.E., the Han Chinese had recognized sunspots and accurately determined the length of the calendar year.

Popular Taoism and Buddhism

By the time the First Emperor united China and ended the Warring States period in 221 B.C.E., a decadent or popular form of Taoism had emerged. Popular Taoism was a religion of spirits and magic that provided the spiritual comfort not found in either philosophical Taoism or Confucianism. Its goals were long life and personal immortality. These goals were to be achieved not so much as a reward for ethical conduct but through magical charms and spells and by imbibing an "elixir of immortality." The search for such an elixir, which was thought to contain the vital forces of nature, led to an emphasis on diet and ultimately to the culinary art for which the Chinese are famous.

Popular Taoism also became a vehicle for the expression of peasant discontent. In C.E. 184 the Yellow Turbans (one of many such uprisings throughout China's history) led a widespread peasant revolt inspired by Taoist followers of a now-deified Lao-tzu. Over 300,000 rebels destroyed much of China and greatly contributed to the anarchy that fatally weakened the Later Han dynasty.

The breakdown of the political and social order during the Later Han also produced an upsurge in philosophical Taoism. Educated Chinese began to turn inward in their thinking, discouraged with Confucianism and its concern for society.

Mahayana Buddhism, which appeared in China at this time, provided another answer to the need for religious assurance. It was brought to China by missionaries and traders through central Asia. About C.E. 184 a Buddhist missionary established a center for the translation of Buddhist writings into Chinese at the Later Han capital. However, relatively few Chinese were attracted to the religion during this period. Buddhism's great attraction of converts and influence on Chinese culture came after the fall of the Han dynasty, when renewed political turmoil made its emphasis on otherworldly salvation appealing to the great majority of Chinese.

The Meeting of East and West in Ancient Times

In the centuries immediately preceding and following the birth of Christ, the great civilizations of the world—Roman, Indian, and Chinese—were connected by commercial and diplomatic exchanges. These contacts began to decline in the third century C.E. and were eventually cut off. But each civilization remembered that beyond the mountains and the deserts to the east or to the west lay other great civilizations.

Beyond the Roman Frontiers

During the first and second centuries C.E., the prosperous years of the *Pax Romana,* the peoples of the Roman Empire maintained trade contacts extending far beyond the imperial boundaries. Chinese silk, which the Romans believed was produced from the leaves of trees, was sold in the market quarter of Rome, and Indian cotton was converted into cloth at Alexandria. Contacts between West and East had progressively increased after 334 B.C.E., when Alexander the Great invaded Asia, until a chain of intercommunicating states stretched across Eurasia from the Atlantic to the Pacific.

After Alexander's death, the Seleucid and Ptolemaic kingdoms of the Hellenistic Age maintained trade contacts with India over two routes, one by land and the other by sea. The most frequented route was the caravan road that began in Syria or Asia Minor, crossed Mesopotamia, then skirted the Iranian plateau to either Bactra (modern Balkh) or Kandahar before crossing the Hindu Kush to reach Taxila in India. The sea route began either at the Red Sea ports of Egypt or at the head of the Persian Gulf and moved along the coast to India.

Sea Traffic to India

By the late first century B.C.E., after Egypt and Syria had succumbed to Rome, Roman capital and appetite for the luxury goods of India—ivory, pearls, spices, dyes, and cotton—greatly stimulated trade with the East. By this time, however, the existing trade routes had serious disadvantages. The Parthians, whose kingdom extended from the Euphrates to the borders of Bactria, were levying heavy tolls on the caravan trade, and the Sabaean Arabs of southwest Arabia had cut off the Red Sea route at Aden and were in control of much of the overseas trade with India. From Aden, the Sabaeans sent Indian goods north by caravan to Petra, which grew rich as a distribution point to Egypt via Gaza and to the north via Damascus.

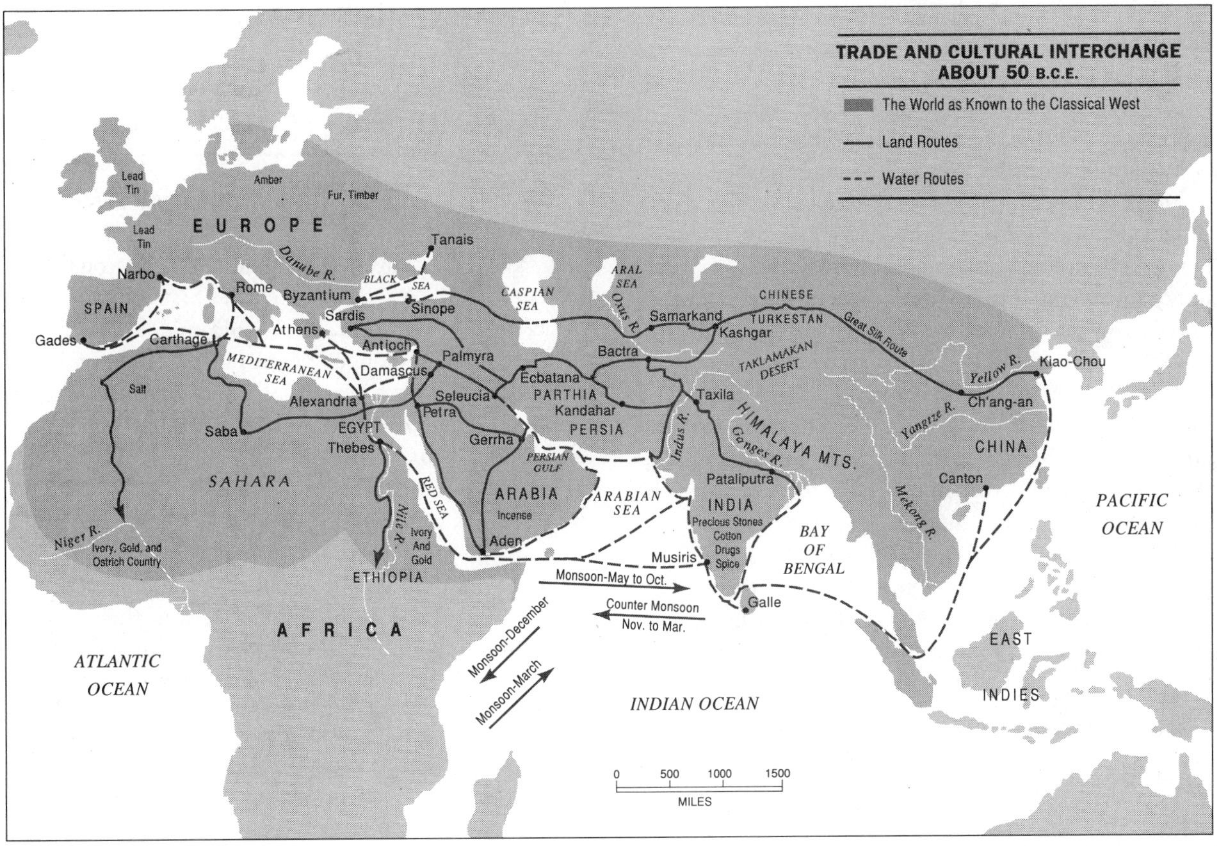

Augustus broke the hold of the Parthian and Arab middlemen on the Eastern trade by establishing direct commercial connections by sea with India. By 1 B.C.E. he had reopened the Red Sea by forcing the Sabaeans out of Aden and converting it into a Roman naval base. Ships were soon sailing from Aden directly to India across the Arabian Sea, blown by the monsoon winds recently discovered by a Greek mariner named Hippalus. From May to October the monsoon blows from the southwest across the Arabian Sea, while the countermonsoon blows from the northeast between November and March. Thus direct round-trip voyages, eliminating middlemen and the tedious journey along the coasts, could be made in eight months. Strabo, a Greek geographer during the time of Augustus, stated that 120 ships sailed to India every year from Egyptian ports on the Red Sea. Augustus claimed that "to me were sent embassies of kings from India," probably to specify the towns within the Roman Empire and in India where foreign merchants might freely conduct their business and practice their own customs and religions.

During the first century C.E., Roman-financed ships reached the rich markets of southern India and Ceylon (Sri Lanka). Christianity may have reached India at this time. Indian Christians today claim that their small group of about 2 million was founded by St. Thomas, one of Jesus' original 12 disciples, who may have sailed to India about C.E. 50. In C.E. 166, according to the Chinese *History of the Later Han Dynasty,* some merchants from Ta Ch'in ("Great Ch'in," the Chinese name for Rome), claiming to represent "King Antun" (the emperor Marcus Aurelius Antoninus), arrived in South China by sea across the Bay of Bengal and around the Malay Peninsula.

The Silk Trade with China

The Chinese made the first move to pierce the land barrier separating them from the West. In 138 B.C.E. the Han emperor Wu Ti dispatched an envoy to Bactra to seek allies against the Hsiung-nu (Mongolian nomads). Although the envoy failed to secure an alliance, the information he brought back amounted to the Chinese discovery of the West.

Intrigued above all by his envoy's report indicating great interest in Chinese silks and his description of the magnificent Western horses, Wu Ti resolved to open trade relations with the West. His armies pushed across the Pamir Mountains to a location close to Alexandria Eschate (Khojend), founded by Alexander the Great as the northern limit of his empire. Shortly after 100 B.C.E. silk began arriving in the West, conveyed by the Parthians. Wealthy private merchants carried on this trade, organized into caravans of shaggy packhorses and two-humped Bactrian camels that required large outlays of capital. When the Chinese soon moved back across the Pamirs, the Kushans of India became middlemen, selling the silk to the Parthians and later to Western merchants coming by sea to India.

It was not until about C.E. 120 that the Parthians allowed some Western merchants to cross their land. The information they brought back about the Chinese was used by Ptolemy in constructing his map of the world.

The Economic Consequences for the West

To satisfy the Roman world's insatiable appetite for luxury goods, Western trade with the East grew immensely in the first two centuries C.E. But because such Roman exports as wool, linen, glass, and metalware to the East did not match in value Rome's imports of silk, spices, perfumes, gems, and other luxuries, the West suffered seriously from an adverse balance of trade. Gold and silver had to be continually exported to Asia. Late in the first century A.D., Pliny estimated that India, China, and Arabia drained away annually at least 100 million *sesterces* (the daily wage of an unskilled Roman laborer was four *sesterces*), declaring, "That is the sum which our luxuries and our women cost us." The discovery of large hoards of Roman coins in India supports Pliny's statement. This serious drain was one of the factors in the general economic decline of the Roman world in the third century C.E.

Severance of East-West Contacts

Beginning in the third century C.E., contacts between the East and the West gradually declined. With the overthrow of the Han dynasty in C.E. 220, China's power and prestige dwindled in central Asia. By coincidence, the Kushan Empire in northeast India fell at the same time, and India entered a period of change and transition. But probably the most significant factor in the disruption of East-West relations was the political and economic decline of the Roman world in the third century C.E.

CONCLUSION

An Era of Accomplishment and Affluence

The four centuries of Han rule from roughly 200 B.C.E. to 200 C.E., represented the first wave in a cyclic succession of dynasties that would rule China until the 20th century. Prolonged periods of political division and civil strife followed the fall of some dynasties, most notably the Han. Yet there was considerable social and institutional continuity from one dynasty to the next. Though Chinese civilization expanded and changed significantly in areas as fundamental as the social composition of the ruling elite, marriage arrangements, and religion, key elements came together in the Han period that persisted into the 20th century. Among them were the assumption that political unity was natural and desirable, the principle of rule by an emperor served by a professional bureaucracy, and the dominance in political, social, and cultural life of the educated scholar-gentry elite. Most Chinese also had a deep veneration for tradition and their ancestors, and they laid great stress on the importance of maintaining social harmony, self-restraint, and decorum in dealings within the family and in the wider society.

Classical China did not produce an entirely unified culture or complete social harmony. Major philosophical and religious schools disagreed widely about the nature of "man" and the goals of life. Many ordinary people knew little of the ideas of the great Chinese philosophers such as Confucius and Lao-tzu. They continued to believe in a variety of gods and spirits, which were often associated with the home and kitchen, and developed rituals and offerings to placate these supernatural beings. The gap between elite and masses in Chinese culture was considerable, in part because Chinese writing was so difficult to master that only a small elite had time and money enough to learn to read and write.

Despite these divisions and differences, the short-lived Ch'in dynasty and four centuries of Han rule had established the basic components of a civilization that would last for thousands of years. As the achievements of the classical age demonstrate, it was to be one of the most creative and influential civilizations of all human history. The strength of its agrarian base has allowed China to carry about one-fourth of the total human population from the last centuries B.C.E. to the present day.

The productivity of its peasants has allowed the Chinese to support some of the world's largest cities and one of history's largest and most creative elites. Over the centuries, Chinese textiles, porcelain, and inventions have been traded over much of the globe and have spurred technological revolutions in societies as diverse as those found in Japan and Europe. The civilization of China that came together in the classical age of the Ch'in and Han was destined to dominate the history of much of Asia and contribute significantly to the advance of civilized life throughout the globe.

FURTHER READING

Good introductions to life in China in the classical age can be found in Wolfram Eberhard's *A History of China (1977),* Dun J. Li's *The Ageless Chinese (1965),* and E. Reischauer's and J. K. Fairbank's *East Asia: The Great Tradition (1960). China's Civilization (1976)* by Arthur Cotterell and David Morgan contains useful illustrations and incorporates more recent interpretations of developments in early China. Two works deal extensively with the life and reign of Shi Huangdi: Arthur Cotterell's *The First Emperor of China (1981)* and Li Yu-Ning's *The First Emperor of China (1975).*

A relatively brief and clear introduction to Chinese thought is provided by Frederic Mote's *Intellectual Foundations of China (1971).* A much more detailed study that places Chinese thought in a comparative context can be found in Benjamin Schwartz's *The World of Thought in Ancient China (1983).* Michael Loewe's *Everyday Life in Early Imperial China (1968)* is excellent on Han society, as is the more detailed and scholarly work *Han Social Structure (1972)* by T'ung-Tsu Ch'u, which includes extensive quotations from Chinese texts and valuable insights into the position of women, merchants, artisans, and eunuchs. A detailed survey of the archeological work done on Han sites and what they tell us about Han society is provided by Wang Shongshu's *Han Civilization (1982).* Micháele Pirazzoli-t'Serstevens's lavishly illustrated study, *The Han Civilization of China (1982),* contains the most comprehensive, up-to-date, and readable overview of Han civilization available. Edmund Capon's and William MacQuitty's *Princes of Jade (1973)* is less informative and reliable, but it also contains superb plates and illustrations. The most authoritative and detailed account of science and technology in the Han and later dynastic periods can be found in Joseph Needham's multivolume study, *Science and Civilization in China (1954–).* Burton Watson's *Courtier and Commoner in Ancient China (1974),* which is a translation of portions of Ban Ku's *History of the Former Han,* can be perused for examples and anecdotes that allow the student to gain a vivid sense of the day-to-day workings of Han society.

CHAPTER 5

Greece and the Hellenistic World

KEY TERMS

Crete	*citizen*
Minoan	*Pericles*
Mycenaean	*Peloponnesian War*
Dark Age	*Socrates*
Iliad	*Plato*
Odyssey	*Aristotle*
Archaic Period	*Macedon*
ethnos	*Alexander the Great*
polis	*Hellenism*
Aeropolis	*Cynics*
tyrant	*Epicureans*
Sparta	*Stoics*
Athens	*Euclid*
Persian Wars	*Archimedes*
Delian League	

DISCUSSION QUESTIONS

Compare and contrast the city-states of Athens and Sparta.

Why is Greek philosophy so important to western thought?

How did Greek culture blend with the traditions of the ancient near East in the Hellenistic period?

Greece in the Bronze Age to 700 B.C.E.

Unlike the rich floodplains of Mesopotamia and Egypt, Greece is a stark world of mountains and sea. The rugged terrain of Greece, only ten percent of which is flat, and the scores of islands that dot the Aegean and Ionian seas favor the development of small, self-contained agricultural societies. The Greek climate is uncertain, constantly threatening Greek farmers with failure. Rainfall varies enormously from year to year, and arid summers alternate with cool, wet winters. Greek farmers struggled to produce the Mediterranean triad of grains, olives, and wine, which first began to dominate agriculture around 3000 B.C.E. Wheat, barley, and beans were the staples of Greek life. Constant fluctuations in climate and weather from region to region helped break down the geographical isolation by forcing isolated communities to build contacts with a wider world in order to survive and to establish colonies and communities across the Mediterranean from what is now France to modern Turkey. Throughout its history, Greece was less a geographical than a cultural designation.

Minoan Society: Crete, Island of Peace

Knowledge of Minoan civilization burst upon the modern world suddenly in 1899. In that year the English archaeologist Sir Arthur Evans made the first of a series of extraordinary archaeological discoveries at Knossos, the legendary palace of Minos. Crete's location between the civilizations of the Fertile Crescent and the less urbanized worlds of the north and west made the island a natural point of exchange and amalgamation of cultures. Still, during the golden age of Crete, roughly between 2000 and 1550 B.C.E., the island developed its unique traditions of monumental architecture, social stratification, peace, and the participation of women in public life.

Great palace complexes were constructed at Knossos, Phaistos, Hagia Triada, and elsewhere on the island. They appear as a maze of storerooms, workrooms, and living quarters clustered around a central square. Larger public rooms may have existed at an upper level, but all traces of them have disappeared. Palace bureaucrats, using a unique form of syllabic writing known as Linear A, controlled agricultural production and distribution as

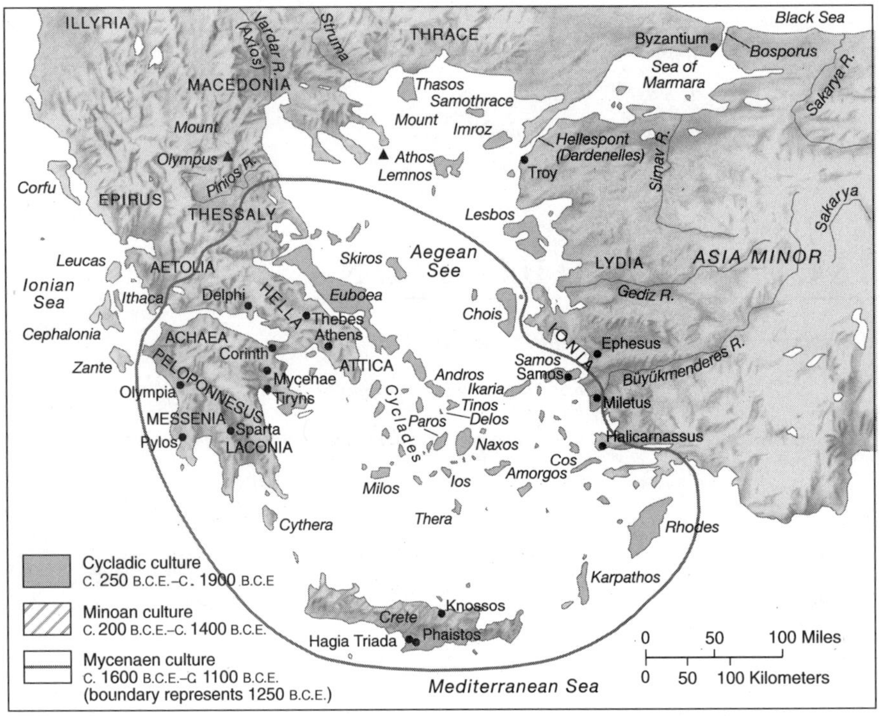

Early Greece

Societies and Cultures in World History
Chapter 2: Early Greece, 2500–500 B.C.E.

well as the work of skilled artisans in their surrounding areas. Towns with well-organized street plans, drainage systems, and clear hierarchies of elite and lesser homes dotted the landscape.

Like other ancient civilizations, Minoan Crete was a strongly stratified system in which the vast peasantry paid a heavy tribute in olive oil and other produce. Tribute or taxes flowed to local and regional palaces and ultimately to Knossos, which stood at the pinnacle of a four-tier network uniting the island. To some extent, the palace elites redistributed this wealth back down the system through their patterns of consumption.

Though the system may have been exploitative, it was not militaristic. None of the palaces or towns of Crete was fortified. Nor was the cult of the ruler particularly emphasized. Monumental architecture and sculpture designed to exalt the ruler and to overwhelm the commoner is entirely absent from Crete. A key to this unique social tone may be Cretan religion and, with it, the unusually high status of women. Although male gods received veneration, Cretans particularly worshiped female deities. Bulls and bull horns as well as the double-headed ax, or *labris*, played an important if today mysterious role in the worship of the gods. Chief among the female deities was the mother goddess, who was the source of good and evil. However, one must be careful not to paint too idyllic an image of Cretan religion. Children's bones found in excavations of the palace of Knossos show traces of butchering and the removal of slices of flesh.

Faience statuette of a priestess, or perhaps a deity, from the Palace of Minos, holding two squirming snakes. The stiff, flounced skirt and bare breasts are typical of female figures found in Cretan frescoes and on gold signet rings.

Although evidence such as the frequent appearance of women participating in or watching public ceremonies and the widespread worship of female deities cannot lead to the conclusion that Minoan society was a form of matriarchy, it does suggest that Minoan civilization differed considerably from the floodplain civilizations of the Near East and the societies developing on the mainland. At least until the fourteenth century B.C.E., Cretan society was truly unique. Both men and women seem to have shared important roles in religious and public life and together built a structured society without the need for vast armies or warrior kings.

Around 1450 B.C.E., a wave of destruction engulfed all of the Cretan cities except Knossos, which finally met destruction around 1375 B.C.E. The causes of this catastrophe continue to inspire historical debate. Some argue that a natural disaster such as an earthquake or the eruption of a powerful volcano on Thera was responsible for the destruction. More likely, given the martial traditions of the continent and their total absence on Crete, the destruction was the work of mainland Greeks taking control of Knossos and other Minoan centers. An Egyptian tomb painting from the fifteenth century B.C.E. graphically illustrates the transition. An ambassador in Cretan dress was overpainted by one wearing a kilt characteristic of that worn by mainland Greeks. Around this same time, true warrior graves equipped with weapons and armor begin to appear on Crete and at Knossos for the first time. Following this violent conquest, only Knossos and Phaistos were rebuilt, presumably by Greek lords who had eliminated the other political centers on the island. A final destruction hit Knossos around 1200 B.C.E.

Mycenaean Civilization: Mainland of War

Around 1600 B.C.E., a new and powerful warrior civilization arose on the Peloponnesus at Mycenae. The only remains of the first phase of this civilization are thirty graves found at the bottom of deep shafts arranged in two circles. The swords, axes, and armor that fill the graves emphasize the warrior lives of their occupants. This entire civilization, which encompassed not only the mainland but also parts of the coast of Asia Minor, is called Mycenaean, although there is no evidence that the city of Mycenae actually ruled all of Greece.

The Mycenaeans quickly adopted artisanal and architectural techniques from neighboring cultures, especially from the Hittites and from Crete. However, the Mycenaeans incorporated these techniques into a distinctive tradition of their own. Unlike the open Cretan palaces and towns, Mycenaean palaces were strongly walled fortresses. From these palaces Mycenaean kings, aided by a small military elite, organized and controlled the collection of taxes and tribute from subordinate towns and rural districts. Their palace administrators adopted the Linear A script of Crete, transforming it to write their own language, a Greek dialect, in a writing known as Linear B, which appears to have been used almost exclusively for record-keeping in palaces.

Mycenaean domination did not last for long. Around 1200 B.C.E., many of the mainland and island fortresses and cities were sacked and totally destroyed. In some areas, such as Pylos, the population fell to roughly ten percent of what it had been previously. Centralized government, literacy, urban life, civilization itself disappeared from Greece for over four hundred years. Why and how this happened is one of the great mysteries of world history.

In later centuries the Greeks believed that following the Trojan War, new peoples, especially the Dorians, had migrated into Greece, destroying Mycenae and most of the other Achaean cities. More recently, some historians have argued that catastrophic climatic changes, volcanic eruptions, or some other natural disaster wrecked the cities and brought famine and tremendous social unrest in its wake. Neither theory is accurate. Mycenaean Greece was destroyed neither by barbarian invaders nor by natural disasters. It self-destructed. Its disintegration was part of the widespread crisis affecting the eastern Mediterranean in the twelfth century B.C.E. The pyramid of Mycenaean lordship, built by small military elites commanding maritime commercial networks, was always threatened with collapse. Overpopulation, the fragility of the agrarian base, the risks of overspecialization in cash crops such as grain in Messenia and in sheep raising in Crete, and rivalry among states—all made Mycenaean culture vulnerable. The disintegration of the Hittite empire and the near-collapse of the Egyptian disrupted Mediterranean commerce, exacerbating hostilities among Greek states. As internal warfare raged, the delicate structures of elite lordship disappeared in the mutual sackings and destructions of the palace fortresses. The Dark Age poet Hesiod (ca. 800 B.C.E.), although writing about his own time, probably got it about right:

> ***Father will have no common bond with son***
> ***Neither will guest with host, nor friend with friend***
> ***The brother-love of past days will be gone . . .***
> ***Men will destroy the towns of other men.***

The Dark Age: 1200–700 B.C.E.

With the collapse of the administrative and political system on which Mycenaean civilization was built, the tiny elite that had ruled it vanished as well. Some of these rulers probably migrated to the islands, especially Cyprus, and the eastern Mediterranean. Others took to piracy. What later Greeks remembered as the Trojan War may have been a cloudy recollection of the last raids of freebooters along the edge of the collapsing Hittite empire. From roughly 1200 until 700 B.C.E., the Aegean world entered what is generally termed the Dark Age, a confused and little-known period during which Greece returned to a more primitive level of culture and society.

Everywhere in this world, between roughly 1100 and 1000 B.C.E., architecture, urban traditions, even writing disappeared along with the elites whose exclusive benefit these achievements had served. The Greece of this Dark Age was much poorer, more rural, and more simply organized. It was also a society of ironworkers. Iron began to replace bronze as the most common metal for ornaments, tools, and weapons. At first this was a simple necessity. The collapse of long-distance trade deprived Greeks of access to tin and copper, the essential ingredients of bronze. Gradually, however, the quality of iron tools and weapons began to improve as smiths learned to work hot iron into a primitive steel.

What little is known of this period must be gleaned from archaeology and from two great epic poems written down around 750 B.C.E., near the end of the Dark Age. The archaeological record is bleak. Pictorial representation of humans and animals almost disappears. Luxury goods and most imports are gone from tombs. Pottery made at the beginning of the Dark Age shows little innovation, crudely imitating forms of Mycenaean production.

Gradually, beginning in the eleventh century B.C.E., things began to change a bit. New geometric forms of decoration begin to appear on pottery. New types of iron pins, weapons, and decorations appeared, which owe little or nothing to the Mycenaean tradition. Cultural changes accompanied these material changes. Around the middle of the eleventh century B.C.E., Greeks in some locations stopped burying their dead and began to practice cremation. Whatever the meaning of these changes, they signaled something new on the shores of the Aegean.

The two epic poems, the *Iliad* and the *Odyssey*, hint at this something new. The *Iliad* is the older poem, dating probably to the second half of the eighth century B.C.E. The *Odyssey* dates from perhaps fifty years later. Traditionally ascribed to Homer, these epics were actually the work of oral bards, or performers who composed as they chanted. The world in which the action of the Homeric epics takes place was already passing away when the poems were composed, but the world described is not really that of the late Bronze Age. Although the poems explicitly harken back to the Mycenaean age, much of the description of life, society, and culture actually reflects Dark Age conditions.

Homer's heroes were petty kings, chieftains, and nobles, whose position rested on their wealth, measured in land and flocks, on personal prowess, on networks of kin and allies, and on military followings. The Homeric hero Odysseus is typical of these Dark Age chieftains. In the *Iliad* and the *Odyssey* he is king of Ithaca, a small island on the west coast of Greece. To the Homeric poets he was "goodly Odysseus" as well as "the man of wiles" and "the waster of cities." He retained command of his men only as long as he could lead them to victory in the raids against their neighbors, which formed the most honorable source of wealth. Odysseus describes with pride his departure for home after the fall of Troy:

> ***"The wind that bore me from Ilios brought me . . . to Ismarus, whereupon I sacked their city and slew the people. And from the city we took their wives and much goods, and divided them among us, that none through me might go lacking his proper share."***

Present, the king was judge, gift giver, lawgiver, and commander. Absent, no legal or governmental institutions preserved his authority. Instead the nobility, lesser warriors who were constantly at odds with the king, sought to take his place. In the *Odyssey* only their mutual rivalry saves Odysseus' wife, Penelope, from being forced to marry one of these haughty aristocrats eager to replace the king.

These nobles, warriors wealthy enough to possess horses and weapons, lived to prove their strength and honor in combat against their equals, the one true test of social value. The existence of chieftains such as Odysseus was a threat to their honor, and by the eighth century B.C.E., the aristocracy had eliminated kings in most places. Ranking beneath these proud warriors was the populace. Some of this group were slaves, but most were shepherds or farmers too mired down in the laborious work of subsistence agriculture to participate in the

This red-figured Greek vase from the fifth century B.C.E. depicts the hero Odysseus resisting the Sirens. He is tied to the mast of his ship to prevent him from being lured to destruction by the song of the bird-bodied temptresses.

heroic lifestyle of their social betters. Still, even the populace were not entirely excluded from public life. Odysseus' son Telemachus summoned the assembly of the people, the *demos*, to listen to his complaints against the noble suitors of his mother. This does not mean that the assembly was particularly effective. They listened to both sides and did nothing. Still, a time was coming when changes in society would give a new and hitherto unimagined power to the silent farmers and herdsmen of the Dark Age.

From the Bronze Age civilizations, Greek speakers had inherited distant memories of an original, highly organized urban civilization grafted onto the rural, aristocratic warrior society of the Dark Age. Most importantly, this common, dimly recollected past gave all Greek-speaking inhabitants of the Mediterranean world common myths, values, and identity.

Archaic Greece, 700–500 B.C.E.

Between roughly 700 and 500 B.C.E., extraordinary changes took place in the Greek world. The descendants of the farmers and herdsmen of Homer's Dark Age brought about a revolution in political organization, artistic traditions, intellectual values, and social structures. In a burst of creativity forged in conflict and competition, Greeks of the Archaic Age (ca. 700-500 B.C.E.) laid the foundations for the Western notions of politics, abstract thought, and the individual.

The first sign of radical change in Greece was a major increase in population in the eighth century B.C.E. In Attica, for example, between 780 and 720 B.C.E., the population increased perhaps sevenfold. The reasons for this extraordinary increase are obscure, but it may have resulted from a shift from herding to agriculture. In any case the consequences were enormous. First, population increase meant more villages and towns, greater communication among them, and thus the more rapid circulation of ideas and skills. Second, the rising population placed impossible demands on the agricultural system of much of Greece. Third, it led to greater division of labor and, with an increasingly diverse population, to fundamental changes in political systems. The old structure of loosely organized tribes and chieftains became inadequate to deal with the more complex nature of the new society.

The multiplicity of political and social forms developing in the Archaic Age set the framework in which developed the first flowering of Greek culture. Economic and political transformations laid the basis for intellectual advance by creating a broad class with the prosperity to enjoy sufficient leisure for thought and creative activity. Finally, maritime relations brought people and ideas from around the Greek world together, cross-fertilizing artists and intellectuals in a way never before seen in Western Eurasia.

GREECE IN THE BRONZE AGE

c. 2500 B.C.E.	Beginning of Minoan civilization in Crete
c. 2000–1500 B.C.E.	Golden Age of Crete
c. 1600 B.C.E.	Beginning of Mycenaean civilization in Greece
c. 1450 B.C.E.	Cretan cities, except Knossos, destroyed
c. 1375 B.C.E.	Knossos destroyed
c. 1200–700 B.C.E.	Greek Dark Age
c. 1200 B.C.E.	Mycenaean sites in Greece destroyed; Knossos destroyed again
c. 1100–1000 B.C.E.	Writing disappears from Greece

Ethnos and Polis

In general, two forms of political organization developed in response to the population explosion of the eighth century B.C.E. On the mainland and in much of the western Peloponnesus, people continued to live in large territorial units called *ethne* (sing. *ethnos*). In each ethnos people lived in villages and small towns scattered across a wide region. Common customs and a common religion focusing on a central religious sanctuary united them. The ethnos was governed by an elite, or *oligarchy*, meaning "rule by the few," made up of major landowners who met from time to time in one or another town within the region. This form of government, which had its roots in the Dark Age, continued to exist throughout the classical period.

A much more innovative form of political organization, which developed on the shores of the Aegean and on the islands, was the *polis* (pl. *poleis*), or city-state. Initially, *polis* meant simply "citadel." Villages clustered around these fortifications, which were both protective structures and cult centers for specific deities. These high, fortified sites—*acropolis* means "high citadel"—were sacred to specific gods: in Athens and Sparta, to Athena; in Argos and Samos, to Hera; at Corinth and Thermon, to Apollo. In addition to protection, the polis

The scene painted on this Corinthian vase shows hoplites in close formation marching into battle.

offered a marketplace, or *agora*, where farmers and artisans could trade and conduct business. The rapid population growth of the eighth century B.C.E. led to the fusion of these villages and the formation of real towns. Each town was independent, each was ruled by a monarch or an oligarchy, and each controlled the surrounding region, the inhabitants of which were on an equal footing with the townspeople. At times of political or military crisis, the rulers might summon an assembly of the free males of the community to the agora to participate in or to witness the decision-making process. In the following centuries, these city-states became the center for that most dramatic Greek experiment in government—democracy.

Within the polis, political power was not the monopoly of the aristocracy. The gradual expansion of the politically active population resulted largely from the demands of warfare. In the Dark Age, warfare had been dominated by heavily armed, mounted aristocrats who engaged their equals in single combat. In the Archaic Age, such individual combat between aristocratic warriors gave way to battles decided by the use of well-disciplined ranks of infantrymen called *phalange* (sing. *phalanx*). While few Greeks could afford costly weapons, armor, and horses, between 25 and 40 percent of the landowners could provide the shields, lances, and bronze armor needed by the infantrymen, or *hoplites*.

The democratization of war led gradually to the democratization of political life. Those who brought victory in the phalanx were unwilling to accept total domination by the aristocracy in the agora. The rapid growth of the urban population, the increasing impoverishment of the rural peasantry, and the rise of a new class of wealthy merchant commoners were all challenges that traditional forms of government failed to meet. Everywhere traditional aristocratic rule was being undermined, and cities searched for ways to resolve this social conflict. No one solution emerged, and one of the outstanding achievements of Archaic Greece was the almost limitless variety of political forms elaborated in its city-states.

Colonists and Tyrants

Colonization and tyranny were two intertwined results of the political and social turmoil of the seventh century B.C.E. Population growth, changes in economy, and opposition to aristocratic power led Greeks to seek change externally through emigration and internally through political restructuring.

Late in the eleventh century B.C.E., Greeks began to migrate to new homes on the islands and along the coast of Asia Minor, in search of commercial advantages or a better life. By the eighth century B.C.E., Greeks had pushed east as far as Al Mina in northern Syria and Tarsus in eastern Asia Minor.

Beginning around 750 B.C.E., a new form of colonization began in the western Mediterranean. The impetus for this expansion was not primarily trade, but rather the need to reduce population pressure at home. The first noteworthy colony, Cumae near Naples, was founded by emigrants from Euboea. Soon other cities sent colonists to southern Italy and Sicily. Around 700 B.C.E., similar colonies appeared in the northeast in Thrace, on the shores of the Black Sea, and as far as the mouth of the Don River.

Colonists were not always volunteers. At Thera, for example, young men were chosen by lot to colonize Cyrene. The penalty for refusing to participate was death and confiscation of property. Usually colonists included only single males, the most volatile portion of the community. Colonies were thus a safety valve to release the pressures of population growth and political friction. Although colonies remained attached culturally to their mother cities, they were politically independent. The men who settled them were warriors as well as farmers or traders and carved out their new cities at the expense of the local population.

Colonization relieved some of the population pressure on Greek communities, but it did not solve the problem of political conflict. As opposition to en-

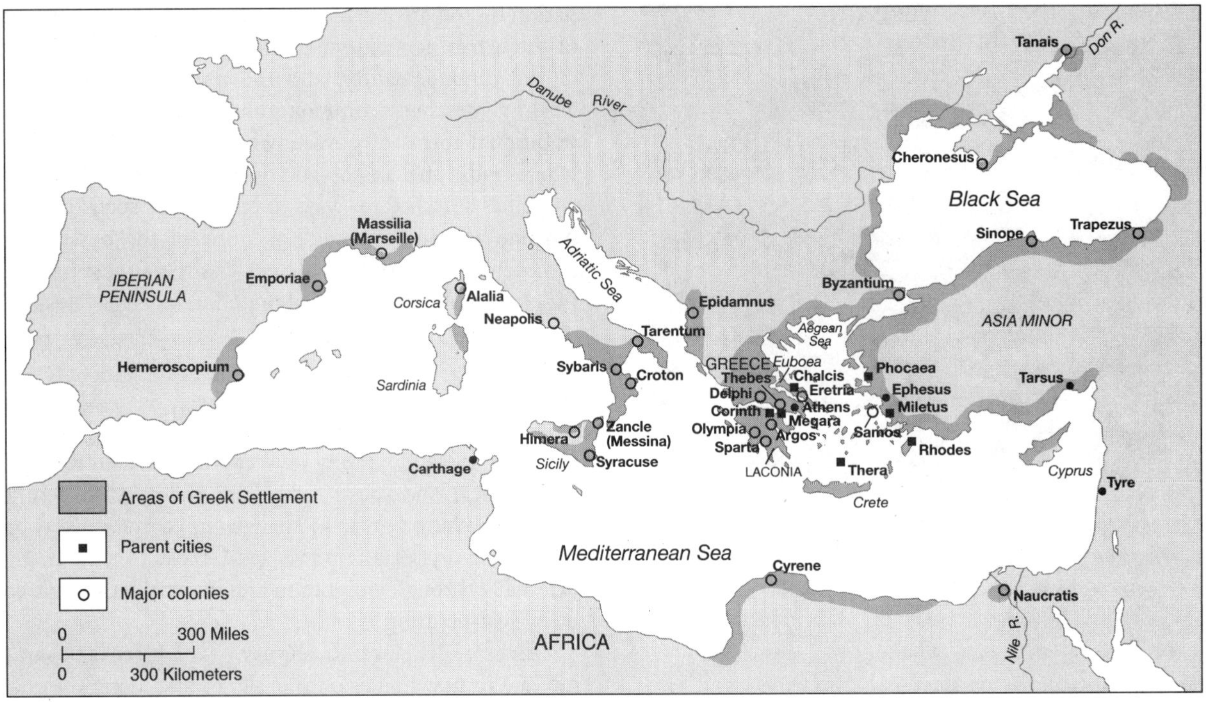

Greek Cities and Colonies of the Archaic Age

trenched aristocracies grew, first in Argos, then at Corinth, Sicyon, Elis, Mytilene, and elsewhere, individuals supported by those opposed to aristocratic rule seized power. These rulers were known as *tyrants*, a term that originally meant the same as *king*. In the course of the later sixth century B.C.E., *tyrant* came to designate those who had achieved supreme power without benefit of official position. Often, this rise to power came through popularity with hoplite armies. However, the term *tyrant* did not carry the negative connotation associated with it today. Early tyrants were generally welcomed by their fellow citizens and played a crucial role in the destruction of aristocratic government and the creation of civic traditions.

The great weakness of tyrannies was that they depended for their success on the individual qualities of the ruler. Tyrants tended to pass their powers on to their sons and, as tyrannies became hereditary, cities came to resent incompetent or excessively harsh heirs' arbitrary control of government. As popular tyranny gave way to harsh and arbitrary rule, opposition brought on civil war and the deposition or abdication of the tyrant. Gradually tyranny acquired the meaning it bears today, and new forms of government emerged. Still, in spite of the bitter memory Greek tyranny left in people's minds, in many cities tyrants had for a time solved the crisis of political order and had cleared the way for broader participation in public life than had ever before been known.

Gender and Power

Military, political, and cultural life in the city-states became more democratic, but this democratization did not extend to women. Greek attitudes toward gender roles and sexuality were rigid. Except in a few cities, and in certain religious cults, women played no public role in the life of the community. They remained firmly under male control throughout their lives, passing from the authority of their fathers to that of their husbands. For the most part friendship existed only between members of the same sex, and these friendships were often intensely sexual. Thus bisexuality was the norm in Greek society, although neither Greek homosexuality nor heterosexuality were the same as they are in modern society. Rather, both coexisted within a sexuality of domination by those considered superior in age, rank, or sex over others. Mature men took young boys as their lovers, helped educate them, and inspired them by word and deed to grow into ideal warriors and citizens. We know less about such practices among women, but teachers

Societies and Cultures in World History
Chapter 2: Early Greece, 2500–500 B.C.E.

such as Sappho of Lesbos (ca. 610–ca. 580 B.C.E.) formed similar bonds with their pupils, even while preparing them for marriage.

Those women who were in public life were mostly slaves, frequently prostitutes. These ranged from impoverished streetwalkers to educated, sophisticated courtesans who entertained men at *symposia* (sing. *symposion*), or male banquets, which were the centers of cultural and social life. Greek society did not condemn or even question infanticide, prostitution, and sexual exploitation of women and slave boys. These practices formed part of the complex and varied social systems of the developing city-states.

Gods and Mortals

Greeks and their gods enjoyed an ambivalent, peculiar, almost irreverent relationship. On the one hand, Greeks made regular offerings to the gods, pleaded with them for help, and gave them thanks for assistance. On the other, the gods were thoroughly human, sharing in an exaggerated manner not only human strengths and virtues but also weaknesses and vices.

Greeks offered sacrifices to the gods on altars, which were raised everywhere—in homes, in fields, in sacred groves. No group had the sort of monopoly on the cult of the gods enjoyed by Mesopotamian and Egyptian priests. Unlike the temples of other societies, Greek temples were houses of the gods, especially the gods seen to have a particular relationship with individual cities, not centers of ritual. The so-called Doric temple, which housed a statue of the god, consisted of an oblong or rectangular room covered by a pitched roof and circled by columns. These temples reflected the wealth and patriotism of the city. They stood as monuments to the human community rather than to the divine.

Though gods were petitioned, placated, and pampered, they were not privileged or protected. Unlike the awe-inspiring gods of the Mesopotamians and Egyptians, the traditional Greek gods, inherited from the Dark Age, were represented in ways that showed them as all too human, vicious, and frequently ridiculous. Zeus was infamous for his frequent rapes of boys and girls. His lust was matched only by the fury of his jealous wife, Hera. The Greek gods were immortal, superhuman in strength, and able to interfere in human affairs. But in all things, they reflected the values and weaknesses of the Greek mortals, who could bargain with them, placate them, and even trick them.

Religious cults were not under the exclusive control of any priesthood or political group. Thus, there were no official versions of stories of gods and goddesses. This is evident both from Greek poetry, which often presents contradictory stories of the gods, and from pottery, which bears pictorial versions of myths that differ greatly from written ones. No one group or sacred site enjoyed a monopoly on access to the gods. Like literacy and government, the gods belonged to all.

Myth and Reason

The glue holding together the individual and frequently hostile Greek poleis and ethne scattered throughout the Mediterranean was their common stock of myths and a common fascination with the Homeric legends. Stories of gods and heroes, told and retold, were fashioned into *mythoi* (myths, literally, "formulated speech"), which explained and described the world both as it was and as it should be. Myths were told about every city, shrine, river, mountain, and island. Myths explained the origins of cities, festivals, the world itself. What is the place of humans in the cosmos? They stand between beasts and gods because Prometheus tricked Zeus and gave men fire with which they cook their food and offer the bones and fat of sacrificial animals to the gods. Why is there evil and misfortune? Because, Greek men explained, in revenge for Prometheus' trickery, Zeus offered man Pandora (the name means "all gifts"), the first woman, whose beauty hid her evil nature. By accepting this gift, humans brought evil and misfortune on themselves. Such stories were more than simply fanciful explanations of how things came to be. Myths sanctioned and supported the authority of social, political, and religious traditions. They presented how things had come to be in a manner that prescribed how they were to remain. In the process of revising and retelling, myths became a powerful and dynamic tool for reasoning about the world.

By the sixth century B.C.E., a number of Ionian Greeks began to investigate the origins and nature of the universe, not in terms of myth or religion, but by observation and rational thought. Living on the coast of Asia Minor, these Ionians were in contact with the ancient civilizations of Mesopotamia and learned much from the Babylonian traditions of astronomy, mathematics, and science. However, their primary interest went beyond observing and recording to speculating. They were the first philosophers, intellectuals who sought natural explanations for the world around them.

Thales of Miletus (ca. 625–ca. 547 B.C.E.) regarded water as the fundamental substance of the universe. For Anaximander (610–ca. 527 B.C.E.) the primary substance was matter—eternal and indestructible. It was Anaximenes of Miletus (d. ca. 545 B.C.E.) who regarded air as the primary substance of the universe. Heraclitus of Ephesus (ca. 540-ca. 480) saw the universe not as one unchanging substance but rather as change itself. For him, the universe is constantly in flux, changing like a flickering fire. Thus all is constantly in a state of becoming, not in a static state of being. And yet this constant change is not random. The cosmic tension between stability and flux is regulated by laws that human reason can determine. The universe is rational.

The significance of such speculative thought was not in the conclusions reached, but rather in the method employed. The Ionian philosophers no longer spoke in myth but rather in plain language. They reached their conclusions through observation and rational thought in which religion and the gods played no direct role. As significant as their original speculations was the manner in which these philosophers were received. Although as late as the fourth century B.C.E., intellectuals still occasionally fell prey to persecution, by the sixth century B.C.E., much of Greek society was ready to tolerate such nonreligious, rational teaching, which in other times and places would have been thought scandalous or atheistic.

ARCHAIC GREECE

c. 780-720	Population increase in Greece
776 B.C.E.	First Olympic Games held
c. 750-700 B.C.E.	Greeks develop writing system based on Phoenician model; Greeks begin colonizing western Mediterranean
c. 700-500 B.C.E.	Archaic Age of Greece
c. 700 B.C.E.	First stone temples appear in Greece
c. 650 B.C.E.	Cypselus breaks rule of Bacchiads in Corinth; rules city as tyrant
594 B.C.E.	Solon elected chief archon of Athens; institutes social and political reforms
586 B.C.E.	Death of Periander ends tyrants' rule in Corinth
499 B.C.E.	Ionian cities revolt

Archaic bronze statuette of a Spartan girl exercising. (About 500 B.C.E.)

Development of the Polis

The political, social, and cultural transformations that occurred in the Archaic Age took different forms across the Greek world. No community or city-state was typical of Greece. The best way to understand the diversity of Archaic Greece is to examine two very different cities that, by the end of the sixth century B.C.E., had become leading centers of Greek civilization. Sparta and Athens present something of the spectrum of political, cultural, and social models of the Hellenic world. Sparta developed into a state in which citizenship was radically egalitarian but restricted to a small military elite. In Athens, the Archaic Age saw the foundations of an equally radical democracy.

Martial Sparta

At the beginning of the eighth century B.C.E., the Peloponnesus around Sparta and Laconia faced circumstances similar to those of Corinth and other Greek communities. Population growth, increasing disparity between rich and poor, and an expanding economy created powerful tensions. However, while Corinthian society developed into a complex mix of aristocrats, merchants, artisans, and peasants, ruled by an oligarchy, the Spartan solution presented a rigid, two-tiered social structure. By the end of the Archaic Age, a small, homogeneous class of warriors called equals ruled a vast population of state serfs, or *helots*. The two classes lived in mutual fear and mistrust. Spartans controlled the helots through terror and ritual murder. The helots in turn were "an enemy constantly waiting for the disasters of the Spartans." And yet, throughout antiquity the Spartans were the Greeks most praised for their courage, simplicity of life, and service to the state.

War was the center of Spartan life, and war lay at the origin of the Spartans' extraordinary social and political organization. In the eighth century B.C.E., the Spartans conquered the fertile region of Messenia and compelled the vanquished Messenians to turn over one-half of their harvests. The spoils were not divided equally, but went to increase the wealth of the aristocracy, thus creating resentment among the less privileged. Early in the seventh century B.C.E., the Spartans attempted a similar campaign to take the plain of Thyreatis from the city of Argos. This time they were defeated, and resentment of the ordinary warriors toward their aristocratic leaders flared into open conflict. The Messenians seized this opportunity to revolt, and for a time Sparta was forced to fight for its very existence at home and abroad. In many cities, such crises gave rise to tyrants. In Sparta, the crisis led to radical political and social reforms that transformed the polis into a unique military system.

The Spartans attributed these reforms to the legendary lawgiver Lycurgus (seventh century B.C.E.). Whether or not Lycurgus ever existed and was responsible for all of the reforms, they saved the city. But in the process Sparta abandoned the mainstream of Greek development. Traditionally, Greeks had placed personal honor above communal concerns. During the crisis of the second Messenian war, Spartans of all social ranks were urged to look not to individual interest but to good order and obedience to the laws, which alone could unite Spartans and bring victory.

United, the Spartans crushed the Messenians. In return for obedience, poor citizens received equality before the law and benefited from a land distribution that relieved their poverty. Conquered land, especially that in Messenia, was divided and distributed to Spartan warriors. However, the Spartan warriors were not expected to work the land themselves. Instead, the state reduced the defeated Messenians to the status of helots and assigned them to individual Spartans. While this system did not erase all economic inequalities among the Spartans (aristocrats continued to hold more land than others), it did decrease some of the disparity. It also provided a minimum source of wealth for all Spartan citizens and allowed them to devote themselves to full-time military service.

This land reform was coupled with a political reform that incorporated elements of monarchy, oligarchy, and democracy. The state was governed by two hereditary kings and a council of elders, the *gerousia*. In peacetime, the authority of the two royal families was limited to familial and religious affairs. In war, they commanded the army and held the power of life and death.

The key to the success of Sparta's political reform was an even more radical social reform that placed everyone under the direct supervision and service of the state from birth until death. Although admiring aristocratic visitors often exaggerated their accounts of Spartan life, the main outlines are clear enough. Good order and obedience to the laws was the sole guiding principle, and service to the state came before family, social class, and every other duty or occupation.

Spartan equals were made, not born. True, only a man born of free Spartan parents could hope to become an equal, but birth alone was no guarantee of admission to this select body, or even of the right to live. Public officials examined infants and decided whether they were sufficiently strong to be allowed to live or should be exposed on a hillside to die. From birth until age seven, a boy lived with his mother, but then he entered the state education system, living in barracks with his contemporaries and enduring thirteen years of rigorous military training.

At age twelve, training with swords and spears became more intense, as did the rigors of the lifestyle. Boys were given only a single cloak to wear and slept on thin rush mats. They were encouraged to supplement their meager diet by stealing food, although if caught they were severely whipped, not for the theft but for the failure. All of this they were expected to endure in silence.

Much of the actual education of the youths was entrusted to older accomplished warriors who selected boys as their homosexual lovers. Not only did the lover serve as tutor and role model, but in time the two became a fighting team, each inspiring the other to show the utmost valor. At age twenty, a Spartan youth was sent out into the countryside with nothing but a cloak and a knife and forbidden to return until he had killed a helot.

If a youth survived the rigors of his training until age thirty, he could at last be incorporated into the rank of equals, provided he could pass the last obstacle. He had to be able to furnish a sufficient amount of food from his own lands for the communal dining group to which he would be assigned. This food might come from inherited property or, if he had proved himself an outstanding warrior, from the state. Those who passed this final qualification became full members of the assembly, but they continued to live with the other warriors. Men could marry at age twenty, but family life in the usual sense was nonexistent. A man could not live with his wife until age thirty because he was bound to the barracks.

Although their training was not as rigorous as that of males, Spartan women were given an education and allowed a sphere of activity unknown elsewhere in Greece. Girls, like boys, were trained in athletic competition and, again like them, competed naked in wrestling, footraces, and spear throwing. This training was based not on a belief in the equality of the sexes but simply on the desire to improve the physical stamina and childbearing abilities of Spartan women. Women were able to own land and to participate widely in business and agricultural affairs, the reason being that since men were entirely involved in military pursuits, women were expected to look after economic and household affairs.

Few inhabitants of Sparta ever became equals. In addition to the great numbers of helots, there were many inhabitants of the region who were free citizens of their local communities but were not allowed into the state educational system. Others were washed out, unable to endure the harsh life, and still others lacked the property qualifications to supply their share of the communal meals. Thus for all the trappings of egalitarianism, equality in Sparta was the privilege of a tiny minority.

The total dedication to military life was reinforced by a deliberate rejection of other activities. From the time of the second Messenian war, Sparta withdrew from the mainstream of Greek civilization. Equals could not engage in crafts, trade, or any other forms of economic activity. Because Sparta banned silver and gold coinage, it could not participate in the growing commercial network of the Greek world. Although a group of free citizens of subject towns could engage in such activities, the role of Sparta in the economic, architectural, and cultural life of Greece was negligible after the seventh century B.C.E. Militarily, Sparta cast a long shadow across the Peloponnesus and beyond, but the number of equals was always too small to allow Sparta both to create a vast empire and to maintain control over the helots at home. Instead, Sparta created a network of alliances and nonaggression pacts with oligarchic neighbors. In time this network came to be known as the Peloponnesian League.

Democratic Athens

Athens did not enjoy the advantages of a strategic site, nor was it surrounded by rich plains like Sparta. However, the "goodly citadel of Athens" was one of the few Mycenaean cities to have escaped destruction at the start of the Dark Age. Gradually Athens united the whole surrounding region of Attica into a single polis, by far the largest in the Greek world. Well into the seventh century B.C.E., Athens followed the general pattern of the polis. Like other Dark Age communities, Athens was ruled by aristocratic clans. Only the members of these clans could participate in the *areopagus*, or council. Until the seventh century B.C.E., Athens escaped the social pressures brought on by population growth and economic prosperity that led to civil strife, colonialism, and tyranny elsewhere. This was due largely to its relative abundance of arable land and its commercial prosperity based on the export of grain.

By the late seventh century B.C.E., however, Athens began to suffer from the same class conflict that had shaken other cities. Sometime around 630 B.C.E., an aristocrat named Cylon attempted to seize power as tyrant. His attempt failed, but when he was murdered, a decade of strife ensued as aristocratic clans, wealthy merchants, and farmers fought for control of the city. Violence between groups and families threatened to tear the community apart. Finally in 594 B.C.E., Solon (ca. 630 B.C.E.–ca. 560 B.C.E.), an aristocratic merchant, was elected chief archon and charged with restructuring the city's government. Solon based his reform on the ideal of eunomia, as had the Spartans, but he followed a very different path to secure good order.

In Sparta, Lycurgus had begun with a radical redistribution of land. In Athens, Solon began with the less extreme measure of eliminating debt bondage. Athenians who had been forced into slavery or into sharecropping because of their debts were restored to freedom. A law forbade mortgaging free men and women as security for debts. Athenians might be poor, but they would be free. This free peasantry formed the basis of Athenian society throughout its history.

Solon also reorganized the rest of the social hierarchy and broke the aristocracy's exclusive control of the areopagus by dividing the society into four classes based on wealth rather than birth and opening the archonship to the top two classes. He further weakened the areopagus by establishing a council of four hundred members drawn from all four classes, to which citizens could appeal decisions of the magistrates.

Although Solon's reforms established the framework for a resolution of Athens' social tensions, they did not entirely succeed. Solon himself did not consider his new constitution perfect, only practical. Resistance from the still-powerful aristocracy prompted some Athenians to urge Solon to assume the powers of a tyrant in order to force through his reforms. He refused, but after his death, Peisistratus (d. 527 B.C.E.), an aristocrat strongly supported by the peasants against his own class, hired a mercenary force to seize control of the city. After two abortive attempts, Peisistratus ruled as tyrant from 545 B.C.E. until his death.

Peisistratus might have governed the city, for a while at least, as an absolute tyrant. Instead, he and later his son Hippias (d. 490 B.C.E.), who succeeded him until 510 B.C.E., continued to rule through Solon's constitution but simply ensured that the archons elected each year were their agents.

Peisistratus and Hippias drew their support from the demos, or people at large, rather than from an aristocratic faction. They claimed divine justification for their rule and made a great show of devotion to the Athenian gods. Peisistratus promoted annual festivals, and in so doing began the great tradition of Athenian literature. At the festival of Athena, professional reciters of epic poetry recited large portions of the *Iliad* and the *Odyssey*. During a festival in honor of the god Dionysus, actors performed the first tragedies and comedies. The tyrants also directed a series of popular, nationalistic public works programs that beautified the city, increased national pride, and provided work for the poor. They rebuilt the temple of Athena on the acropolis. These internal measures were accompanied by support for commerce and export, particularly of grain. Soon, Athens was challenging Corinth as the leading commercial power and trading in grain as far away as the Black Sea.

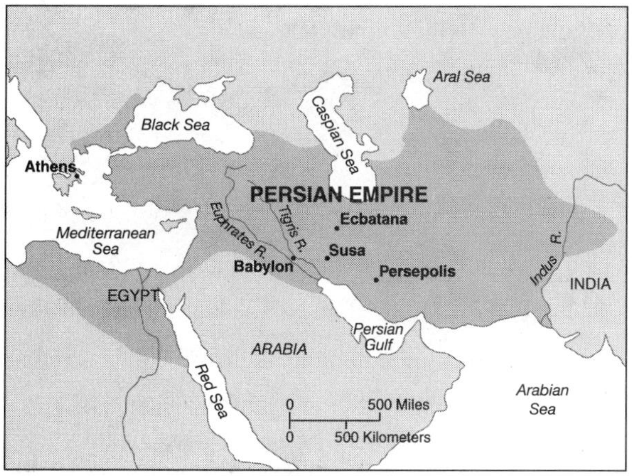

The Persian Empire, 500 B.C.E.

Peisistratus was firm. His son Hippias was harsh. Still, even Hippias enjoyed the support of the majority of the citizens of both popular and aristocratic factions. Only after the assassination of his younger brother did Hippias become sufficiently oppressive to drive his opponents into exile. Some of these exiles obtained the assistance of Sparta and returned to overthrow Hippias in 510 B.C.E. Hippias' defeat ended the tyrants' rule in Athens and won for Sparta an undeserved reputation as the opponent of all tyranny.

Neither Sparta nor Athens was a typical archaic Greek city—there was no such thing. However each faced similar problems: deep conflict between old aristocratic families and wider society, growing population pressure, and threats from within and from without. Their solutions, a period of tyranny followed radical democracy in Athens or, in the case of Sparta, the creation of a small but egalitarian military elite, suggest the spectrum of alternatives from which cities across the Greek world sought to meet these challenges.

The Coming of Persia and the End of the Archaic Age

By the end of the sixth century B.C.E., the products of Greek experimentation were evident throughout the Mediterranean. Greek city-states had resolved the crises of class conflict. Greek merchants and artisans had found ways to flourish despite poor soil and uncertain climate. Greek philosophers, poets, and artists had begun to celebrate the human form and the human spirit. Still, these achievements were the product of small, independent, and relatively weak communities on the fringe of the civilized world.

In the second half of the sixth century B.C.E., this changed. The Persian Empire, under its dynamic king Cyrus II, began a process of conquest and expansion west into Asia Minor. The Persian Empire, which eventually reached from what is today western Turkey to India, was an extraordinary amalgam of ancient imperial traditions of Mesopotamia, the dynamic Zoroastrian religion of the supreme deity Ahura Mazda, and an eagerness to tolerate wide varieties of religious and cultural traditions. Cyrus granted the provinces of his empire great autonomy and preserved local forms of government wherever possible, being careful only to impose governors, or satraps, loyal to him and his Achaemenid dynasty.

War and Politics in the Fifth Century B.C.E.

The vast Persian army, moving west in 490 B.C.E., threatened the fruits of three centuries of Greek political, social, and cultural experimentation. The shared ideal of freedom within community and the common bond of language and culture seemed no basis on which to build an effective resistance to the great Persian Empire. Moreover, Darius I of Persia was not marching against the Greeks as such but against the allies of the rebellious Ionian cities. Few Greek states other than Athens had supported the Ionians against their Persian conquerors. Many Greeks saw the Persians as potential allies or even rulers preferable to their more powerful Greek neighbors and rivals within their own states. Separated by political traditions, intercity rivalries, and cultural differences, the Greeks felt no sense of national or ethnic unity. Particular interest, rather than patriotism or love of freedom, determined which cities opposed the Persian march. In the end, only Eretria, a badly divided Athens, and the small town of Plataea were prepared to refuse the Persian king's demand for gifts of earth and water, the traditional symbols of submission.

The Persian Wars

Initially, the Persian campaign followed the pattern established in Ionia. In the autumn of 490 B.C.E., Darius quickly destroyed the city of Eretria and carried off its population in captivity. The victorious Persian forces, numbering perhaps twenty thousand infantrymen and mounted archers, then landed at the Bay of Marathon. The total Athenian and Plataean force was no more than half that of its enemies, but the Greeks were better armed and commanded the hills facing the Marathon plain on which the Persian troops had massed. The Athenians also benefited from the leadership of Miltiades (ca. 544–489 B.C.E.), an experienced soldier who had served Darius and who knew the Persian's strengths and weaknesses. For over a week the two armies faced each other in a battle of nerves. Growing dissension in the Athenian ranks finally led the Greek generals to make a desperate and unexpected move. Abandoning the high ground, the Athenian hoplites rushed in disciplined phalanxes over almost a mile of open fields and then attacked the amazed Persian forces at a run. Although the Persians broke through the center of the Greek lines, the Athenians routed the Persian flanks and then turned in, enveloping the invaders in a deadly trap. In a few hours it was all over. Six thousand Persians lay dead, while fewer than two hundred Athenians were buried in the heroes' grave that still marks the Marathon plain. The Persians retreated to their ships and sailed for the Bay of Phalerum near Athens, hoping to attack the city itself before its victorious troops could return. However, the Athenians, though exhausted from the battle, rushed the twenty-three miles home in under eight hours, beating the Persian fleet. When the Persians learned that they had lost the race, they turned their ships for Asia.

The almost miraculous victory at Marathon had three enormous consequences for Athens and for Greece in general. First, it established the superiority of the hoplite phalanx as the finest infantry formation in the Mediterranean world. Second, Greeks expanded this belief in military superiority to a faith in the general superiority of Greeks over the "barbarians" (those who spoke other languages). Finally, by proving the value of the citizen army, the victory of the Athenians solidified and enhanced the democratic reforms of Cleisthenes.

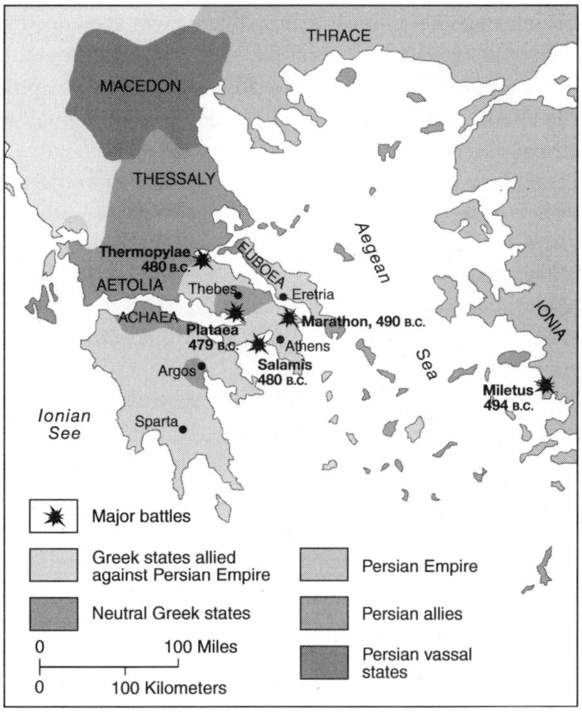

Persian Wars

Societies and Cultures in World History
Chapter 3: Classical and Hellenistic Greece, 500–100 B.C.E.

For six years Persia was occupied by problems elsewhere in their vast empire and paid little attention to Greece. After the unexpected death of Darius I in 486 B.C.E., his son Xerxes (486–465 B.C.E.) began to amass foodstuffs, weapons, and armies for a land assault on his Greek enemies. In response to these preparations, Greek cities attempted to close ranks against the invaders. However, many Greek communities still saw their neighbors as greater threats than the Persians. Some states, including Thebes, Argos, and Thessaly, more or less willingly allied with the Persians against Athens or Sparta. North of the Peloponnesus only Athens, Plataea, and a few other small states were willing to fight the Persians. Sparta was prepared to defend itself and its league, but was not interested in campaigns far from home. Finally, in 481 B.C.E., when the Persian invasion was imminent, representatives of what a contemporary called "the Greeks who had the best thoughts for Greece" met in Sparta to plan resistance. The allies agreed that the Spartans would take command of the combined land and sea forces, which totaled roughly 35,000 helots, 5,000 hoplites, and 378 ships.

Although larger than those mustered by Athens against Darius, the Greek forces were puny compared with Xerxes' estimated two hundred thousand infantry and one thousand light and highly maneuverable Ionian and Phoenician ships. The Spartan commanders sought a strategic point at which the numerical superiority of the Persian forces would be neutralized. The choice fell on the narrow pass of Thermopylae and the adjacent Euboean strait. While a select force of hoplites held the pass, the Greek fleet, following a strategy devised by Themistocles, harried the larger Persian one. Neither action produced a Greek victory, but none could have been expected.

At Thermopylae, the Greeks held firm for days against wave after wave of assaulting troops. Finally, Greek allies of the Persians showed them a narrow mountain track by which they were able to attack the Greek position from the rear. Seeing that all was lost, the Spartan king Leonidas (490-480 B.C.E.) sent most of his allies home. Then he and his three hundred Spartan equals faced certain death with a casual disdain characterized by the comment made by one Spartan equal. Told that when the Persians shot their arrows, they were so numerous that they hid the sun, the Spartan replied, "Good. If the Persians hide the sun, we shall have our battle in the shade." The epitaph raised later by the Spartan state to Leonidas and his men read simply, "Go tell the Spartans, you who read: we took their orders, and are dead."

While the Persian troops were blocked at Thermopylae, their fleet was being battered by fierce storms in the Euboean straits and harassed by the heavier Greek ships. Here the Greeks learned that in close quarters, they could stand up to Xerxes' navy. This lesson proved vital a short time later. While the Persian army burned Athens and occupied Attica, Themistocles lured the fleet into the narrow strait between Salamis and the mainland. There the slower Greek vessels bottled up the larger and vastly more numerous enemy ships and cut them to pieces.

After Salamis, Xerxes lost his appetite for fighting Greeks. Without his fleet, he could not supply a vast army far from home in hostile territory. Leaving a force to do what damage it could, he led the bulk of his forces back to Persia. At Athenian urging, the Greek allies under Leonidas' kinsman Pausanias (d. ca. 470 B.C.E.) met the Persians at Plataea in 479 B.C.E. Once more hoplite discipline and Greek determination meant more than numerical superiority. That night the Spartan king dined in the splendor of the captured tent of the defeated Persian commander. Athenian sea power and Spartan infantry had proven invincible. Soon the Athenians were taking the offensive, liberating the Ionian cities of Asia Minor and, in the process, laying the foundations of an Athenian empire every bit as threatening to their neighbors as that of Xerxes.

The Athenian Empire

Sparta, not Athens, should have emerged as the leader of the Greek world after 479 B.C.E. However, the constant threat of a helot revolt and the desire of the members of Sparta's Peloponnesian League to go their separate ways left Sparta too preoccupied with internal problems to fill the power vacuum left by the Persian defeat.

Athens, on the other hand, was only too ready to take the lead in freeing the Greek world from the Persian menace. With Sparta out of the picture, the Athenian fleet was the best hope of liberating the Aegean from Persians and pirates. In 478 B.C.E. Athens accepted control of what historians have come to call the Delian League, after the island of Delos where the league met. Athens and some of the states with navies provided ships; others contributed annual payments to the league. Initially, the league pursued the war against the Persians, driving them back along the Aegean and the Black Seas. At the same time, Athens hurriedly rebuilt its defensive fortifications, a move correctly interpreted by Sparta and other states as directed more against them than against the Persians.

Athens' domination of the Delian League assured its prosperity. Attica, with its fragile agriculture, depended on Black Sea wheat, and the league kept these regions under Athenian control. Since Athens received not only cash "contributions" from league members but also one-half of the spoils taken in battle, the state's public coffers were filled. The new riches made possible the reconstruction of the city that was burned by the Persians into the most magnificent city of Greece.

The Athenian empire was an economic, judicial, religious, and political union held together by military might. Athens controlled the flow of grain through the Hellespont to the Aegean, ensuring its own supply and heavily taxing cargoes to other cities. Athens controlled the law courts of member cities and used them to repress anti-Athenian groups. Athenian citizens—rich and poor alike—acquired territory throughout the empire. The rich took over vast estates confiscated from local opponents of Athenian dominance, while the poor replaced hostile populations in the colonies. Control over this empire depended on the Athenian fleet to enforce cooperation. Athenian garrisons were established in each city and "democratic" puppet governments ruled according to the wishes of the garrison commanders. Revolt, resignation from the league, or refusal to pay the annual tribute resulted in brutal suppression. Persian tyranny had hardly been worse than Athenian imperialism, and Sparta and its allies looked with growing fear upon this dangerous new imperial power.

Private and Public Life in Athens

During the second half of the fifth century B.C.E., Athens, enriched by tribute from its over 150 subject states, was a vital, crowded capital drawing merchants, artisans, and laborers from throughout the Greek world. At its height, the total population of Athens and surrounding Attica numbered perhaps 350,000. However, probably fewer than 60,000 were citizens, that is, adult males qualified to own land and participate in Athenian politics. Over one-quarter of the total population were slaves. Great landowners, unable to force ordinary free men to work their estates, had turned to slave labor. Slaves were also vital in mining and other forms of craft and industrial work.

Greek slaves were not distinguished by race, ethnicity, or physical appearance. Anyone could become a slave. Prisoners of war, foreigners who failed to pay taxes, victims of pirate raids, could all end up on the auction blocks of the ancient world. Slaves were as much the

A small clay plaque discovered in Corinth shows workmen laboring in a pit quarrying clay for the pottery industry, which brought prosperity to the city. Refreshments are being lowered to the workers in the jar at the center.

Sixth-century B.C.E. *Attic black figure vase showing women spinning and weaving wool.*

property of their owners as their land, houses, cattle, and sheep. Many masters treated their slaves well, but beatings, tattooing, starvation, and shackling were all too common as a means of enforcing obedience.

Roughly half of Athens' free population were foreigners called metics. These were primarily Greek citizens of the tributary states of the empire, but they might also be peoples from Africa or from Asia Minor, such as Lydians. The number of metics increased after the middle of the fifth century B.C.E. both because of the flood of foreigners into the empire's capital and because Athenian citizenship was restricted to persons with two parents who were of citizen families. Metics could not own land in Attica nor could they participate directly in politics. They were required to have a citizen protector and to pay a small annual tax. Otherwise, they were free to engage in every form of activity. The highest concentration of metics was found in the port of Piraeus, where they participated in commerce, manufacturing, banking, and skilled crafts.

More than half of those born into citizen families were entirely excluded from public life. These were the women, who controlled and directed the vital sphere of the Athenian home, but who were considered citizens only for purposes of marriage, transfer of property, and procreation. From birth to death, every female citizen lived under the protection of a male guardian, either a close relative such as father or brother, or a husband or son. Women spent almost their entire lives in the inner recesses of the home. Fathers arranged marriages, the purposes of which are abundantly clear from the ritualized exchange of words sealing the betrothal:

> ***I give this woman for the procreation of legitimate children.***
> ***I accept.***
> ***And (I give a certain amount as) dowry.***
> ***I am content.***

A wife had no control over her dowry, which passed to her son. In the event of divorce or the death of her husband, the woman and her dowry returned to her father. An honorable Athenian woman stayed at home and managed her husband's household. Only the poorest citizens sent their wives and daughters to work in the marketplace or the fields. Even the most casual contact with other men without permission was strictly forbidden, although men were expected to engage in various sorts of extramarital affairs. In the words of one Athenian male, "Hetairai we have for our pleasure, mistresses for the refreshment of our bodies, but wives to bear us legitimate children and to look after the house faithfully." The household, as Athenians never tired of repeating, was the foundation of all society. Thus the role of women was indeed important, even though the public sphere was entirely closed to them.

The male citizens of fifth-century B.C.E. Athens were free to an extent previously unknown in the world. But Athenian freedom was freedom in community, not freedom from community. The essence of their freedom lay in their participation in public life, especially self-government, which was their passion. This participation was always within a complex network of familial, social, and religious connections and obligations, each of which placed different and even contradictory demands on its members. The impossibility of satisfying all of these demands, of responding to the special interests of each, forced citizens to make hard choices, to set priorities, and to balance conflicting obligations. The sum of these overlapping groupings was Athenian society, in which friends and opponents alike were united.

Unity did not imply equality. Even in fifth-century B.C.E. Athens, not all Athenians were socially or economically equal. Most were farmers who looked to military service as a means of increasing their meager income. Others engaged in trade or industry, although metics, with their commercial contacts in their cities of origin, dominated much of these activities in Athens. However, the aristocracy was still strong, and most of the popular leaders of the century came from the ranks of old wealth and influence. Still, sovereignty lay not with these aristocrats but with the demos, the people, who formed the assembly and large juries, always composed of several hundred citizens, who decided legal cases less on law than on the political merits of the case and the quality of the orators who pleaded for each side. Such large bodies were too unwieldy to deal with the daily tasks of government. Thus, control of these tasks fell to the council, composed of five hundred members selected by lot by the tribes; the magistrates, who were also chosen by lot; and ten military commanders or generals, the only major officeholders elected rather than chosen at random.

Paradoxically, the resolute determination of Athenian democrats to prevent individuals from acquiring too much power helped create a series of extraconstitutional power brokers. Since most offices were filled by lot and turned over frequently, real political leadership came not from officeholders but from generals and from popular leaders. These so-called demagogues, while at times holding high office, exercised their power through their speaking skills, informal networks, and knowledge of how to get things done. Demagogues tended to be wealthy aristocrats who could afford to put in the time demanded by these largely voluntary services.

For the next thirty years, one individual dominated Athenian public life, the general Pericles (ca. 495–429 B.C.E.). Although not an original thinker, he was a great orator and a successful military commander, who proved to be the man most able to win the confidence of Athens and to lead it during the decades of its greatest glory. Athens' system of radical democracy reached its zenith under the leadership of Pericles, even while its imperial program drew it into a long and fatal war against Sparta, the only state powerful enough to resist it.

Pericles and Athens

Pericles was descended from the greatest aristocratic families of Athens. Nevertheless, as one ancient author put it, he "took his side, not with the rich and the few, but with the many and the poor."

Pericles led Athens, but he never ruled it. As a general he could only carry out the orders of the assembly and the council, and as a citizen he could only attempt to persuade his fellows. Still he was largely responsible for the extension of Athenian democracy to all free citizens. Under his influence Athens abolished the last property requirements for officeholding. He convinced the state to pay those who served on juries, thus making it possible for even the poorest citizens to participate in this important part of Athenian government. But he was also responsible for restricting citizenship to those whose mothers and fathers had been Athenians—a law that would have denied citizenship to many of the most illustrious Athenians of the sixth century B.C.E., including his own ancestors. The law also prevented citizens of Athens' subject states from developing a real stake in the fate of the empire.

Pericles' policies ultimately drew Athens into deadly conflict with Sparta. The source of the conflict was not a clash between democracy and oligarchy but rather the threat to Sparta and its allies posed by the growth of the Athenian empire. With the disappearance of the Persian threat, Pericles saw Sparta and its allies as the only threat to Athens' domination of the Greek world. For their part, neutral cities and those allied with Sparta looked on Athens' mix of radical democracy at home and brutal imperialism abroad with growing fear.

Neither Athens with its prosperous trading empire nor Sparta with its internal problems wanted war, but so precarious was the balance of power between the two that the whole Greek world was a tinderbox ready to burst into flame. The spark came when Athens aided a breakaway colony of Corinth, a Spartan ally. This assistance infuriated Corinth, and in 432 B.C.E., the Corinthians convinced the Spartans that Athenian imperial ambitions were insatiable. In the words of the great historian of the war, Thucydides (d. ca. 401 B.C.E.), "What made war inevitable was the growth of Athenian power and the fear which this caused in Sparta." The next year, Sparta invaded Attica. The Peloponnesian War, which would destroy both great powers, had begun.

The Peloponnesian War

The Peloponnesian War was actually a series of wars and rebellions. Athens and Sparta waged two devastating ten-year wars, from 431 B.C.E. to 421 B.C.E. and then again from 414 B.C.E. to 404 B.C.E. At the same time, cities in each alliance took advantage of the wars to revolt against the great powers, eliciting terrible vengeance from both Athens and Sparta. Within many of the

Greek city-states, oligarchs and democrats waged bloody civil wars for control of their governments. Moreover, between 415 B.C.E. and 413 B.C.E., Athens attempted to expand its empire in Sicily, an attempt that ended in disaster. Before it was over, the Peloponnesian War had become an international war, with Persia, always interested in promoting disunity among the Greeks, entering the fray on the side of Sparta. In the end, there were no real victors, only victims.

Initially, Sparta and Athens both hoped for quick victory. Sparta's strength was its army, and its strategy was to invade Attica, devastate the countryside, and force the Athenians into an open battle. Pericles urged Athens to a strategy of conserving its hoplite forces while exploiting its naval strength. Athens was a naval power and, with its empire and control of Black Sea grain, could hold out for years behind its fortifications, the great walls linking Athens to its port of Piraeus. At the same time, the Athenian fleet could launch raids along the coast of the Peloponnesus, thus bringing the war home to the Spartans. Pericles hoped in this way to outlast the Spartans. In describing the war, Thucydides uses the same word for "survive" and "win."

The first phase of the war, called the Archidamian War after the Spartan king Archidamus (431–427 B.C.E.), was indecisive. Sparta pillaged Attica but could not breach the great wall nor starve Athens. In 430 B.C.E., the Spartans received unexpected help in the form of plague, which ravaged Athens for five years. By the time it ended in 426 B.C.E., as much as one-third of the Athenian population had died, including Pericles. Still Athens held out, establishing bases encircling the Peloponnesus and urging Spartan helots and allies to revolt. Exhausted by a decade of death and destruction, the two sides contracted peace in 421 B.C.E. Although Athens was victorious in that its empire was intact, the peace changed nothing and tensions festered for five years.

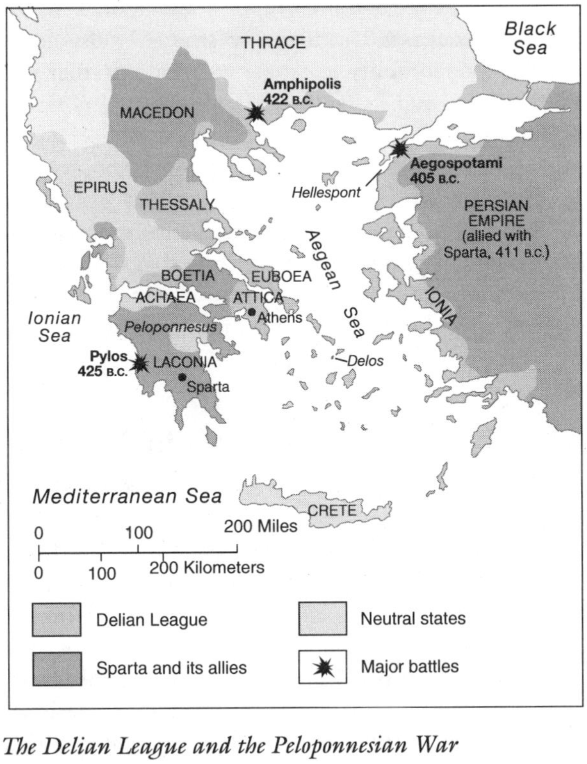

The Delian League and the Peloponnesian War

After the peace of 421 B.C.E., Pericles' kinsman Alcibiades (ca. 450–404 B.C.E.) dominated the demos. Well-spoken, handsome, and brave, but also vain, dissolute, and ambitious, Alcibiades led the city into disaster. Although a demagogue who courted popular support, he despised the people and schemed to overturn the democracy. In 415 B.C.E., he urged Athens to expand its empire west by attacking Syracuse, the most prosperous Greek city of Sicily, which had largely escaped the devastation of the Archidamian War. The expedition went poorly and Alcibiades, accused at home of having profaned one of the most important Athenian religious cults, was ordered home. Instead, he fled to Sparta, where he began to assist the Spartans against Athens. The Sicilian expedition ended in disaster. Athens lost over two hundred ships and fifty thousand men. At the same time, Sparta resumed the war, this time with naval support provided by Persia.

Suddenly Athens was fighting for its life. Alcibiades soon abandoned Sparta for Persia and convinced the Athenians that if they would abandon their democracy for an oligarchy, Persia would withdraw its support of Sparta. In 411 B.C.E., the desperate Athenian assembly established a brutal oligarchy controlled by a small faction of antidemocratic conspirators. Alcibiades' promise proved hollow and the war continued. Athens reestablished its democracy, but the brief oligarchy left the city bitterly divided. The Persian king renewed his support for Sparta, sending his son Cyrus (ca. 424–401 B.C.E.) to coordinate the war against Athens. Under the Spartan general Lysander (d. 395 B.C.E.), Sparta and its allies finally closed in on Athens. Lysander captured the Athenian fleet in the Hellespont, destroyed it, and severed Athens' vital grain supply. Within months Athens was entirely cut off from the outside world and starving. In 404 B.C.E., Sparta accepted Athens' unconditional surrender. Athens' fortifications came down, its empire vanished, and its fleet, except for a mere twelve ships, dissolved.

The Peloponnesian War showed not only the limitations of Athenian democracy but the potential brutality of oligarchy as well. More ominously, it demonstrated the catastrophic effects of disunity and rivalry among the Greek cities of the Mediterranean.

Athenian Culture in the Hellenic Age

Most of what we today call Greek is actually Athenian: throughout the Hellenic age (the fifth and early fourth centuries B.C.E., as distinct from the Hellenistic period of roughly the later fourth through second centuries), the turbulent issues of democracy and oligarchy, war and peace, hard choices and conflicting obligations found expression in Athenian culture even as the glory of the Athenian empire was manifested in art and architecture. The great dramatists Aeschylus, Sophocles, and Euripides were Athenian, as were the sculptor Phidias, the Parthenon architects Ictinus and Callicrates, the philosophers Socrates and Plato. To Athens came writers, thinkers, and artists from throughout the Greek world.

The Examined Life

A primary characteristic of Athenian culture was its critical and rational nature. In heated discussions in the assembly and the agora, the courtroom and the private symposium, Athenians and foreigners drawn to the city no longer looked for guidance to the myths and religion of the past. Secure in their identity and protected by the openness of their radical democracy, they began to examine past and present and to question the foundations of traditional values. From this climate of inquiry emerged the traditions of moral philosophy and its cousin, history.

Throughout the Hellenic age interest in natural philosophy, the explanation of the universe in rational terms, remained high. But philosophers also began to turn their attention to the human world, in particular to the powers and limitations of the individual's mind and the individual's relationship with society. The philosopher Heraclitus examined the rational faculties themselves rather than what one could know with them. In part, this meant a search for personal, inner understanding that would lead to proper action within society, in other words, to the search for ethics based in reason. Moreover, such an inquiry led to a study of how to formulate arguments and persuade others through logic. This study of rhetoric, the art of persuasion, was particularly important in fifth-century Athens because it was the key to political influence. Teachers, called *sophists* ("wise people"), traveled throughout Greece offering to provide an advanced education for a fee. Sophist teachers such as Gorgias (ca. 485–ca. 380 B.C.E.) and Protagoras (ca. 490–421 B.C.E.) trained young men in the arts of rhetoric and in logic. By exercising their students' minds with logical puzzles and paradoxical statements, the sophists taught a generation of wealthy Greeks the powers and complexities of human reason.

Socrates (ca. 470–399 B.C.E.) was considered a sophist by many of his contemporaries, but he himself reacted against what he saw as the amoral and superficial nature of sophistic education. As a young man he was interested in natural philosophy, but he abandoned this tradition in favor of the search for moral self-enlightenment urged by Heraclitus. "Know thyself" was Socrates' plea. An unexamined life, he argued, was not worth living. Socrates refused any pay for his teaching, arguing that he had nothing to teach. He knew nothing, he said, and was superior to the sophists only because he recognized his ignorance while they professed wisdom.

Socrates' method threatened and infuriated many of his contemporaries who prized their reputations for wisdom or skill. He engaged them in discussion and then, through a series of disarmingly simple questions, forced them to defend their beliefs. The inevitable result was that in their own words the outstanding sophists, politicians, and poets of the day demonstrated the inadequacy of their beliefs. Condemned to death in 399 B.C.E. on the trumped-up charges of corrupting the morals of the Athenian youth and introducing strange gods, he rejected the opportunity to escape into exile. Rather than reject Athens and its laws, he drank the fatal potion of hemlock given him by the executioner. Since Socrates refused to commit any of his teaching to writing, we have no direct knowledge of the content of his instruction. We know of him only from the conflicting reports of his former students and opponents. Two things about him are certain, however. Socrates never doubted the moral legitimacy of the Athenian state and he demanded that every aspect of life be investigated.

From City-States to Macedonian Empire, 404–323 B.C.E.

The Peloponnesian War touched every aspect of Greek life. The war brought changes to the social and political structures of Greece by creating an enduring bitterness between elites and populace and a distrust of both democracy and traditional oligarchy. The mutual exhaustion of Athens and Sparta left a vacuum of power in the Aegean. Finally, the war raised fundamental questions

Man and Youth, a fifth–century B.C.E. *drinking cup in terra–cotta from Attica in Greece. The cup is signed by Douris. Over two hundred extant vases are ascribed to him.*

about the nature of politics and society throughout the Greek world.

Politics After the Peloponnesian War

Over the decades-long struggle, the conduct of war and the nature of politics had changed, bringing new problems for victor and vanquished alike. Lightly armed professional mercenaries willing to fight for anyone able to pay gradually replaced hoplite citizen soldiers as the backbone of the fighting forces. The rise of mercenary armies undermined democracies such as Athens as well as Sparta with its class of equals.

Victory left Sparta no more capable of assuming leadership in 404 B.C.E. than it had been in 478 B.C.E. Years of war had reduced the population of equals to less than three thousand. The Spartans proved extremely unpopular imperialists. As a reward for Persian assistance, Sparta returned the Ionian cities to Persian control. Elsewhere it established hated oligarchies to rule in a way favorable to Sparta's interests. In Athens, a brutal tyranny of thirty men took control in 404 B.C.E. With Spartan support, they executed fifteen hundred democratic leaders and forced five thousand more into exile. The Thirty Tyrants evoked enormous hatred and opposition. Within a year the exiles recaptured the city, restored democracy, and killed or expelled the tyrants.

Similar opposition to Spartan rule emerged throughout the Greek world, shattering the fragile peace created by Athens' defeat. For over seventy years the Greek world boiled in constant warfare. Mutual distrust, fear of any city that seemed about to establish a position of clear superiority, and the machinations of the Persian

Empire to keep Greeks fighting each other produced a constantly shifting series of alliances.

Persia turned against its former ally in 401 B.C.E. when Sparta supported an unsuccessful attempt by Cyrus to unseat his brother Artaxerxes II. Soon the unlikely and unstable alliance of Athens, Corinth, Argos, Thebes, and Euboea, financed by Persia, entered a series of vicious wars against Sparta. The first round ended in Spartan victory, due to the shifting role of Persia, whose primary interest was as ever the disunity of the Greeks. By 377 B.C.E., however, Athens had reorganized its league and with Thebes as ally was able to break Spartan sea power. The decline of Sparta left a power vacuum soon filled by Thebes. Athens, concerned by this new threat, shifted alliances, making peace with its old enemy. However, Spartan military fortunes had so declined that when Sparta attacked Thebes in 371 B.C.E., its armies were destroyed and Spartan power broken. The next year Thebes invaded the Peloponnesus and freed Messenia, the foundation of Sparta's economic prosperity. Sparta never recovered. Deprived of its economic base, its body of equals reduced to a mere eight hundred, and its fleet gone, Sparta never regained its historic importance. Theban hegemony was short-lived. Before long the same process of greed, envy, and distrust that had devastated the other Greek powers destroyed Thebes. Athens' reconstituted league disintegrated as members opposed Athenian attempts once more to convert a free association of states into an empire. By the 330s, all of the Greek states had proven themselves incapable of creating stable political units larger than their immediate polis.

Philosophy and the Polis

The failure of Greek political forms, oligarchy and democracy alike, profoundly affected Athenian philosophers. Plato (ca. 428–347 B.C.E.), an aristocratic student of Socrates, grew up during the Peloponnesian War and had witnessed the collapse of the empire, the brutality of the Thirty Tyrants, the execution of Socrates, and the revival of the democracy and its imperialistic ambitions. From these experiences he developed a hatred for Athenian democracy and a profound distrust of ordinary people's ability to tell right from wrong. Disgusted with public life, Plato left Attica for a time and traveled in Sicily and Italy, where he encountered different forms of government and different philosophical schools. Around 387 B.C.E., he returned to Athens and opened the Academy, a school to provide Athenian youth with what he considered to be knowledge of what was true and good for the individual and the state.

For transmitting his teachings Plato chose a most unlikely literary form, the dialogue. He developed his ideas through discussions between his teacher, Socrates, and a variety of students and opponents. While Plato shared with his mentor the conviction that human actions must be grounded in self-knowledge, Plato's philosophy extended much further. His arguments about the inadequacy of all existing forms of government and the need to create a new form of government through the proper education of elite philosopher rulers were part of a complex understanding of the universe and the individual's place in it.

Plato argued that true knowledge is impossible as long as it focuses on the constantly changing, imperfect world of everyday experience. Real knowledge consists of only that which is eternal, perfect, and beyond the experience of the senses, the realm of what Plato calls the Forms. When we judge that individuals or actions are true or good or beautiful, we do so not because these particular persons or events are truly virtuous, but because we recognize that they participate in some way in the Idea or Form of truth or goodness or beauty.

The evils of the world, and in particular the vices and failures of government and society, result from ignorance of the truth. Most people live as though chained in a cave in which all they can see are the shadows cast by a fire on the walls. In their ignorance, they mistake these flickering, imperfect images for reality. Their proper ruler must be a philosopher, one who is not deceived by the shadows. The philosopher's task is to break their chains and turn them toward the source of the light so that they can see the world as it really is.

Plato's idealist view of knowledge (so called because of his notion of Ideas or Forms) dominated much of ancient philosophy. His greatest student, Aristotle (384–322 B.C.E.), however, rejected this view in favor of a philosophy rooted in the natural world. Aristotle came from a medical family of northern Greece and, although a student in Plato's Academy for almost twenty years, he never abandoned observation for speculation. Systematic investigation and explanation characterize Aristotle's vast work, and his interests ranged from biology to statecraft to the most abstract philosophy. In each field, he employed essentially the same method. He observed as many individual examples of the topic as possible and from these specific observations extracted general theories. His theories, whether on the nature of matter, the species of animals, the working of the human mind, ethics, or the proper form of the state, are distinguished by clarity of logical thinking, precision in the use of terminology, and respect for the world of experience.

The ruins of the Athenian Acropolis are dominated by the Parthenon. This temple of Athena was largely intact until 1687, when the Turks, attempting to conquer Athens, used it as a powder magazine. The powder exploded and devastated the building.

Aristotle brought this empirical approach to the question of life in society. He defined humans as "political animals," that is, animals particularly characterized by life in the polis. Unlike Plato, he did not regard any particular form of government as ideal. Rather, he concluded that the type of government ultimately mattered less than the balance between narrow oligarchy and radical democracy. And yet, during the very years that Aristotle was teaching, the vacuum created by the failure of the Greek city-states was being filled by the dynamic growth of the Macedonian monarchy, which finally ended a century of Greek warfare and with it, the independence of the Greek city-states.

The First Utopia

If the Greeks were fixated on good government, it might be because they had seen so many examples of bad. The bewildering variety of political forms that replaced the tyrants of the sixth century had proved no better than the evil they had sought to correct. By the end of the fourth century B.C.E., Lysander's brutal rule disillusioned many about the advantages of the Spartan mixture of monarchy, oligarchy, and democracy. The oligarchy of Corinth and the federalism of Thebes proved no better. And the radical democracy of Athens had brought disaster not only to the city but to all of Greece.

Aristotle and Plato tackled the problem, each according to his own philosophical inclinations. Aristotle, ever the empiricist, collected over 150 city constitutions, which he hoped to analyze in order to discover the best form of government. His teacher Plato would have thought such an exercise a waste of time. To Plato, all existing constitutions were bad. No place had the perfect form of government. He thus set about in his *Republic* to describe the constitution of "no place" (in Greek, *utopia*, a term coined over eighteen hundred years later), the ideal government.

In his description, Plato tackles the ultimate problem of politics: how should the state be ordered? His answer is a disturbing and fascinating image of a just society, created by a philosopher-king and ruled by a hand-picked body of Guardians.

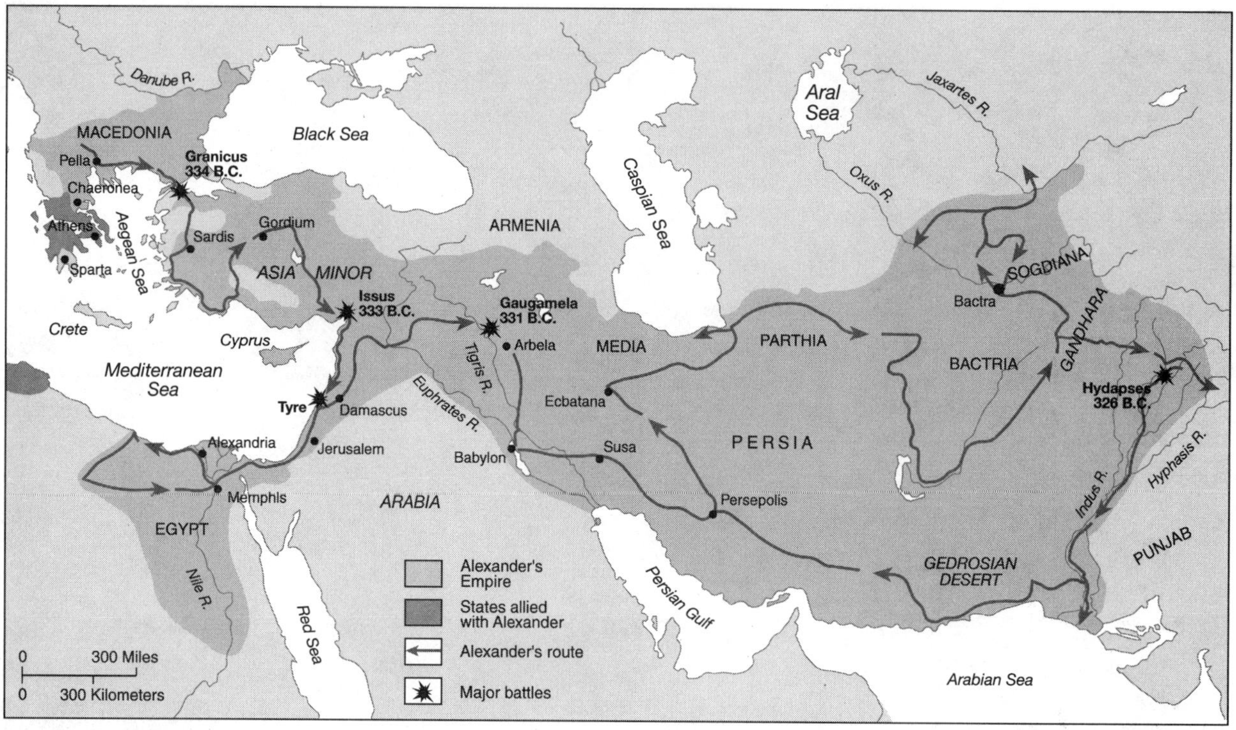

Empire of Alexander the Great

Plato's ideal state resembles the Greek polis in size. A relatively small, territorially limited state is all that he can imagine. It is committed to equality of the sexes and populated by four groups of people: slaves, craftsmen, auxiliaries, and Guardians. The first group is implied but never discussed. Plato, like any other Greek, could not have imagined a society existing without slave labor. The bulk of the citizens are farmers, craft workers, and tradesmen, each specializing in that form of economic activity for which he or she is most suited. They are the only property owners in the republic, form the basis of its prosperity, and lead lives much like those of the ordinary citizens of a Greek polis, except that they have no role in defense or government.

The third group, in part self-perpetuating, in part recruited from the most promising children of the first, are the auxiliaries, who devote themselves exclusively to protecting the state from internal and external dangers. Auxiliaries are made, not born, and the program of education outlined by Plato is the critical ingredient in his ideal state. Boys and girls destined to be auxiliaries must be trained to know what is true and good and must be protected from lies and deception. Thus Plato bans poets and dramatists from his educational program. After all, Homer, Hesiod, Aeschylus, and Sophocles clothe fictions about the immorality of the gods and men in language of great beauty. Instead, the auxiliaries will be taught music and lyric poetry to instill in them a love of the harmony and order of the world. They also undertake physical training appropriate for soldiers, which not only prepares them for battle but, like music, develops the proper harmony of body and soul.

The auxiliaries must be free of private interests or ambitions, which would distract them from the needs of the state. Thus, they must live without private property or private family. Their needs are to be provided for by the craft worker class, making it unnecessary and impossible for the auxiliaries to amass anything of their own. Because family concerns might distract them from their duty, they must live in a garrison-like arrangement. Rulers would select appropriate male and female auxiliaries to mate and produce the best offspring. The children of such unions would be brought up together, regarding themselves and the adult auxiliaries as one large family identical with the state.

The best of these children, distinguished by their intellectual and moral ability, are to be selected as rulers, or Guardians. They undergo further education in the exact sciences and logic to train them to recognize the fundamental principles on which all truth depends. Finally, at the age of thirty-five, after years of study, a Guardian undertakes the hard task of governing, which Plato sees as a process of sharing with those less fortunate the enlightenment that education has given them.

Plato did not consider his republic an exercise in imagination. He firmly believed that it was practical and possible. The best person to establish it was a philosopher-king, a ruler in whom "political power and philosophy meet together."

Plato's contemporaries as well as subsequent generations have been at once fascinated and horrified by this ideal state. For many, the idea of total equality of the sexes was too absurd to consider. For others, the abolition of the family or the banning of poetry went beyond the realm of reason. Aristotle thought that the effects of such a system would be the opposite of what Plato intended, creating dissension and rebellion rather than reducing them. Modern readers praise or condemn Plato's republic because it smacks of communism, thought control, and totalitarianism. The modern social philosopher Karl Popper, for example, has termed Plato's political demands "purely totalitarian and antihumanitarian," and considers Plato the most determined enemy of freedom ever known. Goaded by Plato's challenge, political theorists ever since have taken up the task of devising their own image of the perfect society, seeking their own answer to Plato's challenge, "Where shall we find justice?"

The Rise of Macedon

The polis had never been the only form of the Greek state. Alongside the city-states of Athens, Corinth, Syracuse, and Sparta were more decentralized ethne ruled by traditional hereditary chieftains and monarchs. Macedonia, in the northeast of the mainland, was one such ethnos. Its kings, chosen by the army from within a royal family, ruled in cooperation with nobles and clan leaders. The Macedonian people spoke a Greek dialect, and Macedonian kings and elite identified with Greek culture and tradition. Macedonia had long served as a buffer between the barbarians to the north and the Greek mainland, and its tough farmers and pastoralists were geared to constant warfare. As Athens, Sparta, and Thebes fought each other to mutual exhaustion, Macedonia under King Philip II (359-336 B.C.E.) moved into the resulting power vacuum. Philip showed a particular genius for rapidly organizing and leading armies and for conducting complex, multiple campaigns each year. He secured his borders against northern barbarians and captured the northern coast of the Aegean, including the gold and silver mines of Mount Pangaeus, which gave him a ready source of money for his campaigns. Then he turned his attention to the south.

Philip forced himself into the center of Greek affairs in 346 B.C.E. when he intervened to end the war between Thebes and Phocis. From then on he was relentless in his efforts to swallow up one Greek state after another. The Greek states had united against the Persians but resisted cooperating against Philip, and one by one they fell. In 338 B.C.E., Philip achieved a final victory at Chaeronea and established a new league, the League of Corinth. However, unlike all those that had preceded it, this league was no confederation of sovereign states. It was an empire ruled by a king and supported by wealthy citizens whose cooperation Philip rewarded well. This new model of government, a monarchy drawing its support from a wealthy elite, became a fixture of the Mediterranean world for the next two thousand years.

Philip's success was based on his powerful military machine, which combined both Macedonian military tradition and the new mercenary forces that had emerged over the past century in Greece. The heart of his army was the infantry, which was trained in the use of pikes some fourteen feet long, four feet longer than those of the Greek hoplites. Macedonian phalanxes moved forward in disciplined ranks, pushing back their foes, whose shorter lances could not reach the Macedonians. When the enemy were contained, the Macedonian cavalry charged from the flank and cut them to pieces. The cavalry, known as the Royal Companions, were the elite of Macedon and the greatest beneficiaries of Philip's conquests.

No sooner had Philip subdued Greece than he announced a campaign against Persia. He intended to lead a combined Greek force in a war of revenge and conquest to punish the great empire for its invasion of Greece 150 years earlier and its subsequent involvement in the Greek world. Before he could begin, however, he met the fate of his predecessors. At the age of forty-six he was cut down by an assassin's knife, leaving his twenty-year-old son, Alexander (336–323 B.C.E.), to lead the expedition. Within thirteen years Alexander conquered not only the Persians but western Asia as far as India.

The Empire of Alexander the Great

Alexander was less affected by his teacher, the philosopher Aristotle, than he was by the poet Homer. Envisioning himself a new Achilles, Alexander sought to imitate and surpass that legendary warrior and hero of the

DOCUMENT

Aristotle

Politics

(4th century B.C.E)

Aristotle (384–322 B.C.E.) was the third of the great Greek philosophers and was arguably the most influential of all. The Politics was an attempt to establish principles of government along scientific lines. Aristotle was the first philosopher to explore the basic forms of government and to discuss their inherent strengths and weaknesses.

We now proceed to a point out of what natural disposition the citizens ought to be: but this surely any one would easily perceive who casts his eye over those states of Greece which bear a high repute, and indeed over all the habitable world, as it is divided among the nations. Those who live in cold countries, as the north of Europe, are full of courage, but wanting in understanding and in art; therefore they remain free for a long time; but, not being versed in the political science, they cannot reduce their neighbours under their power. But the Asiatics, whose understandings are quick, and who are conversant in the arts, are deficient in courage; and therefore they continue to be always conquered, and the slaves of others. But the Greeks, placed as it were between these two parts, partake of the nature of both, so as to be at the same time both courageous and intellectual; for which reason Greece continues free, and governed in the best manner possible, and capable of commanding the whole world, could it be combined into one system of policy. The races of the Greeks have the very same difference among themselves: for part of them possess but one of these qualities, whereas in the other they are both happily blended together. Hence it is evident, that those persons ought to be both intelligent and courageous who will be readily obedient to a legislator, whose object is virtue.

We are now to consider what those things are without which a city cannot possibly exist; for what we call parts of the city must of necessity be inherent in it. And this we shall more plainly understand, if we know the number of things necessary to a city. First, the inhabitants must have food: secondly, arts, for many instruments are necessary in life: thirdly, arms, for it is necessary that the community should have an armed force within themselves, both to support their government against the disaffected of themselves, and also to defend it from those who seek to attack it from without: fourthly, a certain revenue, as well for the internal necessities of the state, as for the business of war: fifthly, and indeed chief of all, the care of the service of gods: sixthly in order, but most necessary of all, a court to determine both civil and criminal causes. These things are matters which are absolutely required, so to speak, in every state: for a city is a number of people, not accidentally met together, but with a purpose of insuring to themselves sufficient independency and self-protection; and if any thing necessary for these purposes is wanting, it is impossible that in such a situation these ends can be obtained. It is necessary therefore that a city should be composed with reference to these various trades; for this purpose a proper number of husbandmen are necessary to procure food; as also artificers and soldiers, and rich men, and priests, and judges, to determine what is necessary and beneficial.

Since we are inquiring what is the best government possible, and as it is admitted to be that in which the citizens are happy, and that, as we have already said, it is impossible to obtain happiness without virtue; it follows, that in the best governed states, where the citizens are really men of intrinsic and not relative goodness, none of them should be permitted to exercise any low mechanical employment or traffic, as being ignoble and destructive to virtue: neither should they who are destined for office be husbandmen; for leisure is necessary in order to improve in virtue, and to perform the duty which they owe to the state.

It is necessary that the citizens should be rich, and these are the men proper for citizens; for no low mechanic ought to be admitted to the rights of a citizen, nor any other sort of people, whose employment is not productive of virtue.

Societies and Cultures in World History
Chapter 3: Classical and Hellenistic Greece, 500–100 B.C.E.

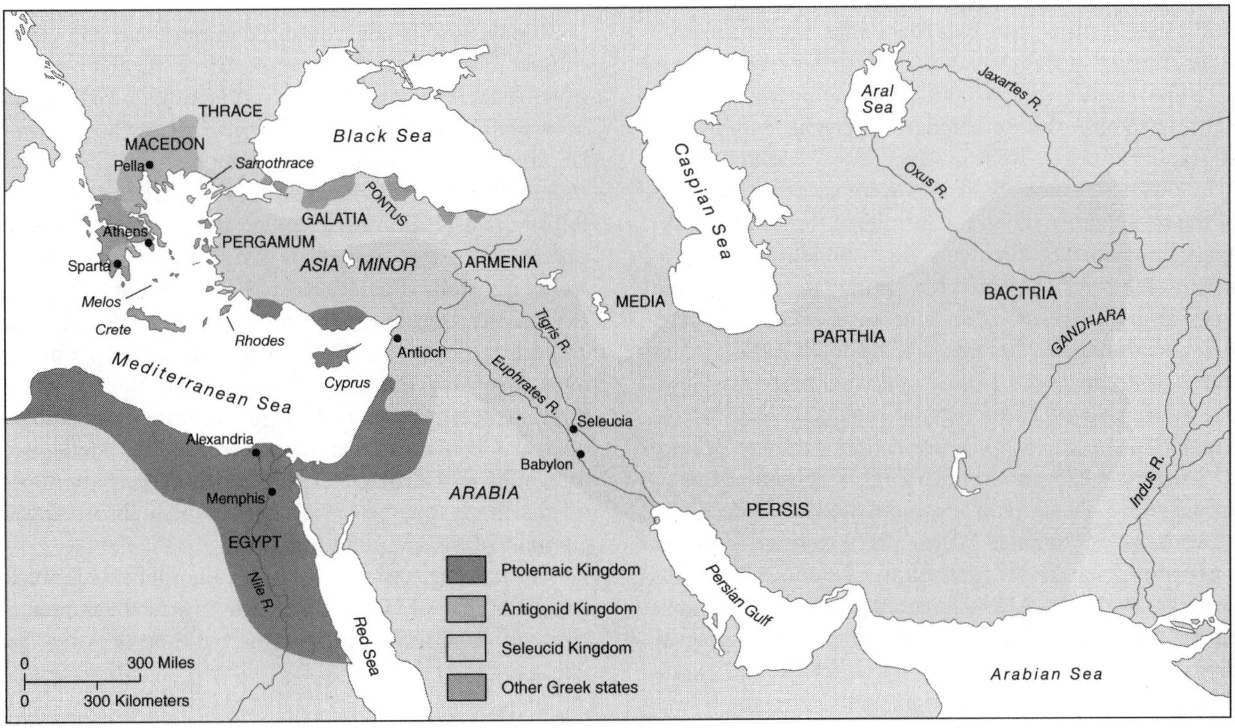

The Hellenistic Kingdoms

Iliad. Alexander's military genius, dedication to his troops, reckless disregard for his own safety, and ability to move both men and supplies across vast distances at great speed inspired the war machine developed by Philip and led it on an odyssey of conquest that stretched from Asia Minor to India. In 334 B.C.E., the first year of his campaign, Alexander captured the Greek cities of Asia Minor. Then he continued east. At Gordium, according to legend, he confronted an ancient puzzle, a complex knot tied to the chariot of the ancient king of that city. Whoever could loosen the knot, the legend said, would become master of Asia. Alexander solved that puzzle, as he did all of his others, with his sword. Two months later he defeated the Persian king Darius III at Issus and then headed south toward the Mediterranean coast and Egypt. After his victories there, he turned again to the north and entered Mesopotamia. At Gaugamela in 331 B.C.E., he defeated Darius a second, decisive time. Shortly after, Darius was murdered by the remnants of his followers. Alexander captured the Persian capital of Persepolis with its vast treasure and became the undisputed ruler of the vast empire.

The conquest of Persia was not enough. Alexander pushed on, intending to conquer the whole world. His armies marched east, subduing the rebellious Asian provinces of Bactria and Sogdiana. He negotiated the Khyber Pass from what is now Afghanistan into the Punjab, crossed the Indus River, and defeated the local Indian king. Everywhere he went he reorganized or founded cities on trade routes, entrusting them to loyal Macedonians and other Greeks, settling there veterans of his campaigns, and then pushed on toward the unknown. On the Hyphasis River in what is now Pakistan, his Macedonian warriors finally halted. Worn out by years of bloody conquest and exhausting travel, they refused to go further, and Alexander led his troops back to Persepolis in 324 B.C.E. No mortal had ever before accomplished such a feat. Even in his own lifetime, Alexander was venerated as a god.

Alexander is remembered as a greater conqueror than ruler, but his plans for his reign, had he lived to complete them, might have won him equal fame. Unlike his Macedonian followers, who were interested mainly in booty and power, he recognized that only by merging local and Greek peoples and traditions could he forge a lasting empire. Thus, even while founding cities on the Greek model throughout his empire, he carefully respected the local social and cultural traditions of the conquered peoples. Whether his program of cultural and social amalgamation could have succeeded is a moot point.

In 323 B.C.E., less than two years after his return from India, he died at Babylon at the age of thirty-two.

The empire did not outlive the emperor. Vicious fighting soon broke out among his generals and his kin. Alexander's wife Roxana and son Alexander IV (323–317 B.C.E.) were killed, as were all other members of the royal family. The various units of the empire broke apart into separate kingdoms and autonomous cities in which each ruler attempted to continue the political and cultural tradition of Alexander in a smaller sphere. Alexander's empire became a shifting kaleidoscope of states, kingdoms, and cities, dominated by priest-kings, native princelings, and territorial rulers, all vying to enhance their positions while preserving a relative balance of power. By 275 B.C.E., three large kingdoms—Egypt, an expanded Persia, and a combination of Greece and Macedonia—dominated Alexander's former domain. The most stable was Egypt, acquired upon Alexander's death by Ptolemy I (323–285 B.C.E.), one of Alexander's closest followers, and ruled by Ptolemy and his descendants until 31 , when Cleopatra VII (51–30 B.C.E.) was defeated by the Roman Octavian. In the east, the Macedonian general Seleucus (246–226 B.C.E.) captured Babylon in 312 B.C.E., and he and his descendants ruled a vast kingdom reaching from what is today western Turkey to Afghanistan. Gradually whittled away from all sides, the Seleucid kingdom gradually shrank to a small region of northern Syria before it fell to Rome in 64 B.C.E. The third kingdom, in Macedon and Greece, was secured by Antigonus II Gonatas (276–239 B.C.E.), the grandson of another of Alexander's commanders, after fifty years of conflict. His Antigonid successors ruled the kingdom until it fell to the Romans in 168 B.C.E.

Alexander's conquests transformed the political map of southern Europe, western Asia, and Egyptian Africa. They swept away or absorbed old traditions of government, brought Greek traditions of urban organization, and replaced indigenous ruling elites with Hellenized dynasties. Within this vast region, rulers encouraged commercial and cultural contact, enriching their treasuries and creating a new form of Greek culture. Still, Alexander's successors never developed the interest or ability to integrate this Greek culture and the more ancient indigenous cultures of their subjects. Ultimately, this failure proved fatal for the Hellenistic kingdoms.

The Hellenistic World

Although vastly different in geography, language, and custom, the Hellenistic kingdoms shared two common traditions, west Asian centralized government and Greek culture. First, great portions of the Hellenistic world, from Asia Minor to Bactria and south to Egypt, had been united at various times by the Assyrian and Persian empires. During these periods they had absorbed much of Mesopotamian civilization and in particular the administrative traditions begun by the Assyrian Tiglath-pileser. Thus the Hellenistic kings ruled kingdoms already accustomed to centralized government and could rely on the already existing machinery of tax collection and administration to control the countryside. For the most part, however, these kings had little interest in the native populations of their kingdoms beyond the amount of wealth that they could extract from them. Hellenistic monarchs remained Greek and lavished their attentions on the newly created Greek cities, which absorbed vast amounts of the kingdom's wealth.

The second unifying factor in the Hellenistic world was the spread of Greek culture and the establishment of cities on the Greek model. In the tradition of Alexander

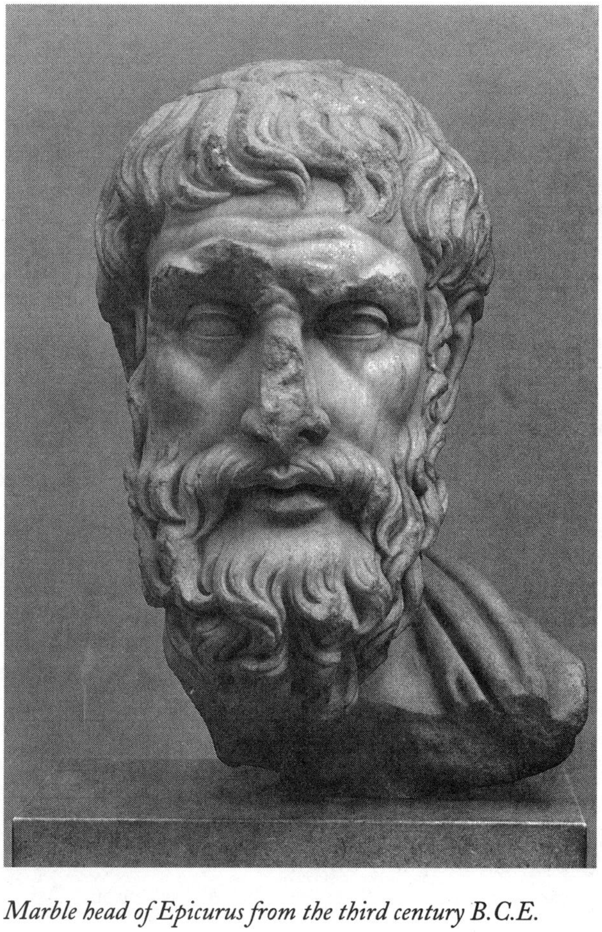

Marble head of Epicurus from the third century B.C.E.

himself, the Ptolemys, Seleucids, and Antigonids cultivated Greek urban culture and recruited Greeks for the most important positions of responsibility. Alexander had founded over thirty-five cities during his conquests. The Seleucids established almost twice as many throughout their vast domain, even replacing the ancient city of Babylon with their capital, Seleucia, on the Tigris. In Egypt the Ptolemys replaced the ancient capital of Memphis with the new city of Alexandria. These cities became the centers of political control, economic consumption, and cultural diffusion throughout the Hellenistic world.

These two common traditions aided the creation, across the Hellenistic world, of a vastly expanded commercial network, resulting in greatly increased wealth for its elites. Caravans crossed the Seleucid Empire from Seleucia-on-the-Orentes to the Black Sea, Alexandria in Egypt became the port for trade up the Nile into Africa, and Rhodes served as a commercial center for trade throughout the Mediterranean. From India and China came silks and spices. Syrian and Egyptian workshops produced luxury goods such as jewelry and glass. The Aegean world exported wine and oil, while the Black Sea territories, Egypt, and Sicily shipped wheat throughout the Mediterranean. Greek-speaking merchants dominated this trade, their language becoming the common means of communication in far-flung ports and caravan towns. Likewise, everywhere Hellenistic governments involved themselves directly in these commercial enterprises, especially in Egypt, where the Ptolemies used Greek colonists to rationalize and organize agriculture and trade for the benefit of the dynasty.

Urban Life and Culture

The Hellenistic kingdoms lived in a perpetual state of warfare with one another. Kings needed Greek soldiers, merchants, and administrators and competed with their rivals in offering Greeks all the comforts of home. Hellenistic cities were Greek in physical organization, constitution, and language. Each had an agora, or marketplace, that would not have been out of place in Attica. They boasted temples to the Greek gods and goddesses, theaters, baths, and most importantly, a *gymnasion*, or combination sports center and school. In the gymnasion young men competed in Greek sports and absorbed Greek poetry and philosophy just as did their cousins in the Peloponnesus. Sophocles' tragedies played to enthusiastic audiences in an enormous Greek theater in what is today Ai Khanoum on the Oxus River in Afghanistan, and the rites of Dionysus were celebrated in third-century B.C.E. Egypt with processions of satyrs, maenads, free wine for all, and a golden phallus 180 feet long. These Greeks were drawn from throughout the Greek-speaking world, and in time a universal Greek dialect, *koine*, became the common language of culture and business.

CLASSICAL GREECE

525–456 B.C.E.	Aeschylus
c. 500–c. 430 B.C.E.	Phidias
496–406 B.C.E.	Sophocles
490 B.C.E.	Battle of Marathon
485–406 B.C.E.	Euripides
c. 484–c. 420 B.C.E.	Herodotus
480 B.C.E.	Battles of Thermopylae and Salamis
478 B.C.E.	Athens assumes control of Delian League
c. 470–399 B.C.E.	Socrates
c. 460–430 B.C.E.	Pericles dominates Athens
c. 450–c. 388 B.C.E.	Aristophanes
431–421; 414–404 B.C.E.	Peloponnesian War
c. 428–347 B.C.E.	Plato
384–322 B.C.E.	Aristotle
384–322 B.C.E.	Demosthenes
338 B.C.E.	Philip of Macedon defeats Athens
336–323 B.C.E.	Reign of Alexander the Great

For all their Greek culture, Hellenistic cities differed fundamentally from Greek cities and colonies of the past. Not only were they far larger than any earlier Greek cities, but their government and culture were different from those of other cities or colonies. Colonies had been largely independent poleis, but the Hellenistic cities were never politically sovereign. The regional kings maintained firm control over the cities, even while working to attract Greeks from the mainland and the islands to them. This policy weakened the political significance of Greek life and culture. Theoretically, these cities were democracies, although kings firmly controlled city government, and participation in the city councils and magistracies was the province of the wealthy.

In the new cities of the east, Greeks from all over were welcomed as soldiers and administrators regardless of their city of origin. By the second century B.C.E., Greeks no longer identified themselves by their city of origin but as "Hellenes," that is, Greeks. The great social and geographical mobility possible in the new cities extended to women as well as men. No longer important simply as transmitters of citizenship, women began to assume a greater role in the family, in the economy, and in public life. Marriage contracts, particularly in Ptolemaic Egypt, emphasized the theoretical equality of husband and wife. In one such contract, the husband and wife were enjoined to take no concubines or male or female lovers. The penalty for the husband was loss of the wife's dowry; for the wife, the punishment was divorce.

Since women could control their own property, many engaged in business and some became wealthy. Wealth translated into civic influence and power. Phyle, a woman of the first century B.C.E. from Priene in Asia Minor, spent vast sums on a reservoir and aqueducts to bring water to her city. She was rewarded with high political office, as was a female archon in Histria on the Black Sea in the second century.

The most powerful women in Hellenistic society were queens, especially in Egypt, where the Ptolemys adopted the Egyptian tradition of royal marriages between brothers and sisters. Arsinoë II (ca. 316–270 B.C.E.) ruled as an equal with her brother-husband Ptolemy II (285–246 B.C.E.). She inaugurated a tradition of powerful female monarchs that ended only with Cleopatra VII, the last independent ruler of Egypt, who successfully manipulated the Roman generals Julius Caesar (100–44 B.C.E.) and Mark Antony (81–30 B.C.E.) to maintain Egyptian autonomy.

Just as monarchs competed with one another in creating Greek cities, they vied in making their cities centers of Greek culture. Socially ambitious and newly wealthy citizens supported poets, philosophers, and artists and endowed gymnasia and libraries. The largest library was in Alexandria in Egypt. In time the library housed half a million book-rolls, including all of the great classics of Greek literature. Generations of poet-scholars edited and commented on the classics, in the process inventing literary criticism and preserving much of what is known about classical authors.

Hellenistic writers were not simply book collectors or critics. They developed new forms of literature, including the romance, which often recounted imaginary adventures of Alexander the Great, and the pastoral poem, which the Sicilian Theocritus (ca. 310–250 B.C.E.) developed out of popular shepherd songs.

Political rivalry also encouraged architectural and artistic rivalry, as kings competed for the most magnificent Hellenistic cities. Temples, porticoes, and public buildings grew in size and ornamentation. Hellenistic architects not only developed more elaborate and monumental buildings, they also combined these buildings in harmonious urban ensembles. In cities such as Rhodes and Pergamum, planners incorporated their constructions into the terrain, using natural hills and slopes to create elegant terraced vistas.

Hellenistic Philosophy

Philosophy, too, flourished in the Hellenistic world, but in directions different from those initiated by Plato and Aristotle, who were both deeply committed to political involvement in the free polis. Instead, Cynics, Epicureans, and Stoics turned inward, advocating types of morality less directly tied to the state and society. These philosophies appealed to the rootless Greeks of the Hellenistic east no longer tied by bonds of religion or patriotism to any community. Each philosophy was as much a way of life as a way of thought and offered different answers to the question of how the individual, cut loose from the security of traditional social and political networks, should deal with the whims of fate.

The Cynic tradition, established by Antisthenes (ca. 445–ca. 365 B.C.E.), a pupil of Socrates, and Diogenes of Sinope (d. ca. 320 B.C.E.), taught that excessive attachment to the things of this world was the source of evil and unhappiness. An individual achieves freedom by renouncing material things, society, and pleasures. The more one has, the more one is vulnerable to the whims of fortune. The Cynics' goal was to reduce their possessions, connections, and pleasures to the absolute minimum. "I would rather go mad than enjoy myself," Antisthenes said.

Like the Cynics, the Epicureans sought freedom, but from pain rather than from the conventions of ordinary life. Epicurus (341–270 B.C.E.) and his disciples have often been attacked for their emphasis on pleasure. "You need only possess perception and be made of flesh, and you will see that pleasure is good," Epicurus wrote. But this search for pleasure was not a call to sensual indulgence. Pleasure must be pursued rationally. Today's pleasure can mean tomorrow's suffering. The real goal is to reduce desires to that which is simple and attainable. Thus Epicureans urged retirement from politics, retreat from public competition, and concentration instead on friendship and private enjoyment. For Epicurus, reason properly applied illuminates how best to pursue pleasure. The traditional image of the Epicurean as an indulgent sensualist is a gross caricature. As Epicurus advised one follower, an Epicurean "revels in the pleasure of the body—on a diet of bread and water."

The Stoics also followed nature, but rather than leading them to retire from public life, it led them to greater participation in it. Stoic virtue consists in applying reason to one's life in such a way that one knowingly lives in conformity to nature. Worldly pleasures, like worldly pain, have no particular value. Both are to be accepted and endured. Just as the universe is a system in which stars and planets move according to fixed laws, so too is human society ordered and unified. As the founder of Stoicism, Zeno (ca. 335–ca. 263 B.C.E.) expressed it, "All men should regard themselves as members of one city and people, having one life and order." Every person has a role in the divinely ordered universe, and all roles are of equal value. True happiness consists in freely accepting one's role, whatever it may be, while unhappiness and evil result from attempting to reject one's place in the divine plan.

Cynicism, Epicureanism, and Stoicism all emphasized the importance of reason and the proper understanding of nature. Hellenistic understanding of nature was one area in which Greek thinkers were influenced by the ancient Near Eastern traditions brought to them through the conquests of Alexander.

Mathematics and Science

Particularly for mathematics, astronomy, and engineering, the Hellenistic period was a golden age. Ptolemaic Egypt became the center of mathematical studies. It was the home of Euclid (fl. ca. 300 B.C.E.), whose *Elements* was the fundamental textbook of geometry until the twentieth century, and of his student Apollonius of Perga (ca. 262–ca. 190 B.C.E.), whose work on conic sections is one of the greatest monuments of geometry. Both Euclid and Apollonius were as influential for their method as for their conclusions. Their treatises follow rigorous logical proofs of mathematical theorems, which established the form of mathematical reasoning to the present day. Archimedes of Syracuse (ca. 287–212 B.C.E.) corresponded with the Egyptian mathematicians and made significant contributions to geometry, such as the calculation of the approximate value of π—as well as to mechanics with the invention of Archimedes' screw for raising water—and to arithmetic and engineering. Archimedes was famous for his practical applications of engineering, particularly to warfare, and legends quickly grew up about his marvelous machines, with which he helped Syracuse defend itself against Rome.

Many mathematicians, such as Archimedes and Apollonius, were also mathematical astronomers, and the application of their mathematical skills to the exact data collected by earlier Babylonian and Egyptian empirical astronomers greatly increased the understanding of the heavens and earth. Archimedes devised a means of measuring the diameter of the sun, and Eratosthenes of Cyrene (ca. 276–194 B.C.E.) calculated the circumference of the earth to within two hundred miles. Aristarchus of Samos (fl. ca. 270 B.C.E.) theorized that the sun and fixed stars were motionless and that the earth moves around the sun. His theory, unsupported by mathematical evidence and not taking into account the elliptical nature of planetary orbits or the planets' nonuniform speeds, was rejected by contemporaries.

Like astronomy, Hellenistic medicine combined theory and observation. In Alexandria, Herophilus of Chalcedon (ca. 335–ca. 280 B.C.E.) and Erasistratus of Ceos (fl. ca. 250 B.C.E.) conducted important studies in human anatomy. The Ptolemaic kings provided them with condemned prisoners whom they dissected alive and thus were able to observe the functioning of the organs of the body. The terrible agonies inflicted on their experimental subjects were considered to be justified by the argument that there was no cruelty in causing pain to guilty men to seek remedies for the innocent.

Hellenistic science and mathematics were, like other aspects of Hellenistic culture, blends of Greek reason and Near Eastern experience with a strong practical orientation. The same combination of indigenous and Greek traditions was largely lacking in other aspects of Hellenistic life, leaving Hellenistic culture an elite and fragile veneer.

The Limits of Hellenism

For all of the vitality of the Hellenistic civilization, these cities remained parasites on the local societies. No real efforts were made to integrate them into a new civilization. Some ambitious members of the indigenous elites tried to adopt the customs of the Greeks, while others plotted insurrection. The clearest example of these conflicting tensions was that of the Jewish community. Early in the second century B.C.E., a powerful Jewish faction in Jerusalem, which included the High Priest of Yahweh, supported Hellenization. With the assistance of the Seleucid king, this faction set up a gymnasion in Jerusalem where Jewish youths and even priests began to study Greek and participate in Greek culture. Some even underwent painful surgery to reverse the effects of circumcision so that they could pass for Greeks in naked athletic contests. This rejection of tradition infuriated a large portion of the Jewish population. When the Seleucids finally attempted to introduce pagan cults into the temple in 167 B.C.E., open rebellion broke out and, under the leadership of the family of the Maccabees, continued intermittently until the Jews gained independence in 141 B.C.E. Such violent opposition was repeated elsewhere from time to time, especially in Egypt and Persia, where, as in Judea, old traditions of religion and monarchy provided rallying points against the transplanted Greeks. In time the Hellenistic kingdoms' inability to bridge the gap between Greek and indigenous populations proved fatal. In the East, the non-Greek kingdom of Parthia replaced the Seleucids in much of the old Persian Empire. In the West, continuing hostility between kingdoms and within kingdoms prepared the way for their progressive absorption by the new power to the west: Rome.

In the fifth century B.C.E., the rugged slopes, fertile plains, and islands of the Greek world developed characteristic forms of social, political, and cultural organization that have reappeared in varying forms that have become an integral part of world civilization. In Athens, which emerged from the ruins of the Persian invasion as the most powerful and dynamic state in the Hellenic world, the give-and-take of a direct democracy challenged men to raise fundamental questions about the relationship between individual and society, freedom and absolutism, gods and mortals. At the same time, this society of free males excluded the majority of its inhabitants—women, foreigners, and slaves—from participation in government and fought a long and ultimately futile war to hold together an exploitative empire.

The interminable wars among Greek states ultimately left the Greek world open to conquest by a powerful, semi-Greek monarchy that went on to spread Athenian culture throughout the Mediterranean world and western Asia. Freed from the particularism of individual city-states, Hellenistic culture became a universal tradition emphasizing the individual rather than the community of family, tribe, or religious association. And yet, this universal Hellenistic cultural tradition remained a thin veneer, hardly assimilated into the masses of the ancient world. Its proponents, except for Alexander the Great, never sought a real synthesis of Greek and barbarian tradition. Such a synthesis would begin only with the coming of Rome.

CHAPTER 6

The Roman World

KEY TERMS

Carthage	*Julius Caesar*
Etruscans	*Gaul*
Rome	*Octavian / Augustus*
Senate	*Pax Romana*
patrician	*veteran colonies*
plebian / pleb	*Virgil*
republic	*Judaism*
oligarchy	*Jesus*
Struggle of the Orders	*Paul of Tarsus*
citizenship	*Christianity*
Punic Wars	*Stoicism*
paterfamilias	*barbarians*
optimates	*Constantine*
populares	*Origen*
the Gracchi brothers	*Augustine of Hippo*
Marius	*monk*

DISCUSSION QUESTIONS

How did Rome, which began as a small city in the backward western Mediterranean, conquer its large empire?

How was the Roman republic weakened by the empire?

What caused the division and fall of the Roman Empire?

The Western Mediterranean to 509 B.C.E.

Early Romans were a mix of indigenous and migrant pastoralists and warriors whose villages stood between Greek and Phoenician merchant adventurers to the south and Etruscan cities to the north. Rome's formula for success lay in learning from all of these neighbors, then dominating and conquering them, and finally adapting and incorporating elements of their traditions into those of Rome itself.

Civilization came late to the western Mediterranean, carried in the ships of Greeks and Phoenicians. While the great floodplain civilizations of Mesopotamia and Egypt and the Greek communities of the eastern Mediterranean were developing sophisticated systems of urban life and political organization, western Europe and North Africa knew only the scattered villages of simple farmers and pastoralists. However, Europe was rich in metals, and an indigenous Bronze Age culture developed slowly between 1500 and 1000 B.C.E., spreading widely north of the Alps and south into Italy and Spain.

Mercantile Carthage

Around 800 B.C.E., Phoenicians arrived in the west, first as traders and then as colonists. Setting out in warships from the regions of Tyre, Sidon, and Byblos, they ventured beyond the Strait of Gibraltar in search of supplies of silver and tin. They established a trading post at Cadiz (*Gadir*, "walled place" in Phoenician) at which they could trade with the local inhabitants for silver from the Sierra Morena and for tin, which the Spanish (Iberians) obtained from distant Britain and Ireland. The Phoenicians established a series of bases along the route to and from Spain on the coast and on the islands of Corsica, Sicily, Ibiza, and Motya in the Mediterranean and at Utica and Carthage on the coast of North Africa. Carthage was initially no more than a small anchorage for ships. Gradually, its population grew as overcrowding forced emigration from Tyre. When, in the sixth century B.C.E., Tyre was conquered by Nebuchadnezzar and incorporated into the Babylonian Empire, Carthage became an independent city and soon established itself as the center of an expanding Phoenician presence in the western Mediterranean.

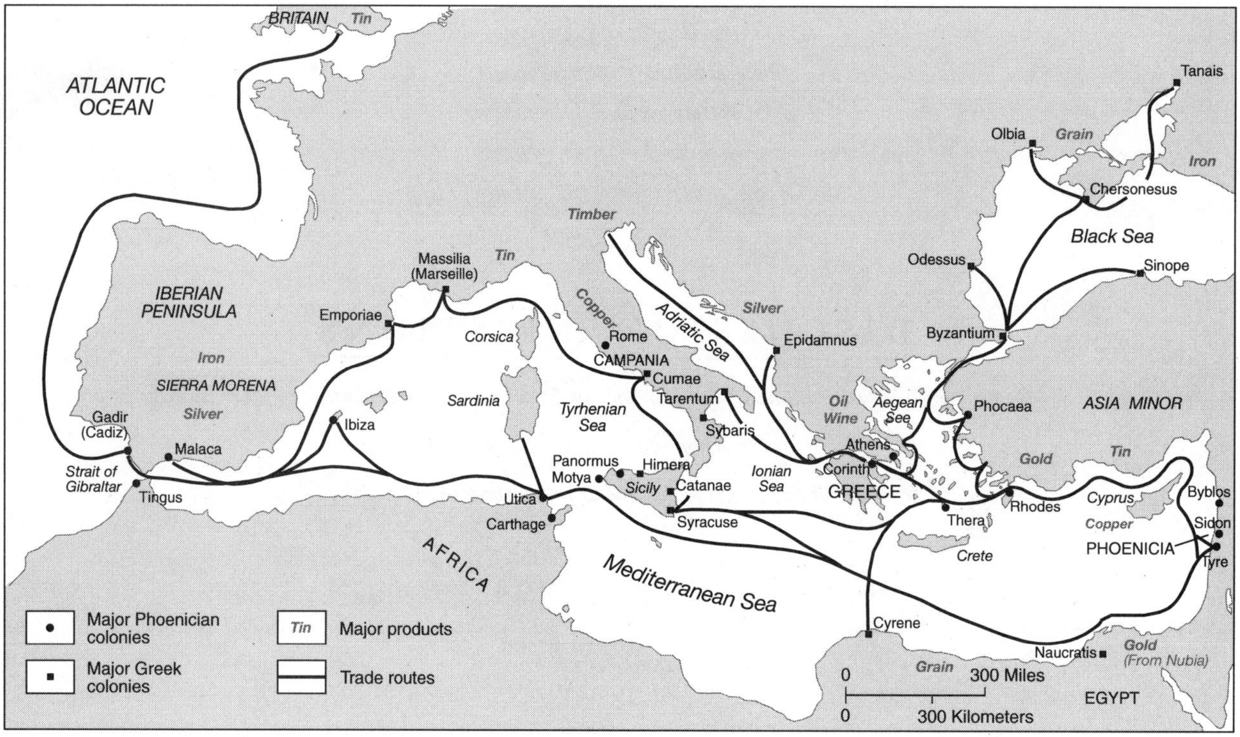

Western Mediterranean

The city was perfectly situated to profit both from the land and the sea. Its excellent double harbor, which had attracted the Phoenicians initially, made it an ideal port. The city was equally protected on land, situated on a narrow isthmus and surrounded by massive walls. As long as Carthage controlled the sea, its commercial center was secure from any enemies. The wealth of Punic (from *Puni* or *Poeni*, the Roman name for the Carthaginians) commerce was supplemented by the agricultural riches of the surrounding region, which produced grain and fruits for export in abundance, while inland the subject native population engaged in cattle raising and sheepherding for their masters.

By the middle of the sixth century B.C.E., Carthage was the center of a real empire. But in contrast with the Athenian empire of the following century, that of Carthage was much more successful at integrating other cities and peoples into its military and thus sharing the burden of warfare. As a society of merchants, Carthaginians mistrusted military leaders and carefully subordinated them to civil authority. Their choice was often based more on their trustworthiness than on military ability. These generals commanded mercenary armies consisting of Libyan light infantry, Numidian cavalry, Spanish hill people, Balearic sling throwers, Gallic infantry, Italians, and often Greeks. Only the fleet was composed primarily of Carthaginians. This multiethnic empire proved far more stable than any of those created by the Greeks, succeeding in victory and withstanding defeat to endure for over three centuries.

Stable and prosperous, Carthage was the master of the western Mediterranean. But its dominion was not undisputed. From the sixth century B.C.E., the Punic empire felt the pressure of ambitious Greek cities eager to compete in the western Mediterranean.

The Western Greeks

The Greek arrival in the west was the result of a much more complex process than the trading policy of the Phoenicians. Toward the end of the Dark Age, commerce, overpopulation, and civic tension sent Greek colonists out in all directions. In the eighth century B.C.E., Crete, Rhodes, Corinth, Argos, Chalcis, Eretria, and Naxos all established colonies in Sicily and southern Italy.

Both commercial rivalry and open warfare characterized the relationship between Greeks and Phoenicians in the western Mediterranean. Early in their struggle with the Greeks, the Carthaginians found allies in the third major civilization of the West. These were the Etruscans, who in the seventh century B.C.E. dominated the western part of central Italy known as Etruria.

Etruscan Civilization

Etruscan civilization was the first great civilization to emerge in Italy. It coalesced slowly in Etruria over the course of the seventh century B.C.E. from diverse regional and political groups sharing a similar cultural and linguistic tradition. In the mid-sixth century B.C.E., in the face of Greek pressure from the south, twelve of these groups united in a religious and military confederation. Over the next one hundred years, the confederation expanded north into the Po Valley and south to Campania. Cities, including Rome, each initially ruled by a king, were the centers of Etruscan civilization, and everywhere the Etruscans spread they either improved upon existing towns or founded new ones. Still, the Etruscan confederation never developed into a centralized empire. Etruscan kings assumed power in conquered towns, but between the sixth and fifth centuries B.C.E., Etruscan kingship gave way to oligarchic governments, much as Greek monarchies did a bit earlier.

While the Etruscans were consolidating their hegemony in western Italy, they were also establishing their maritime power. From the seventh to the fifth centuries B.C.E., Etruscans controlled the Italian coast of the Tyrrhenian Sea as well as Sardinia, from which their ships could reach the coast of what is today France and Spain. Attempts to extend farther south into Greek southern Italy and toward the Greek colonies on the modern French coast brought the Etruscans and the Greeks into inevitable conflict. Etruscan cities fought sporadic sea battles against Greek cities in the waters of Sicily as well as off the coasts of Corsica and Etruria. Through the fifth century B.C.E., Etruscan cities lost control of the sea to the Greeks. Around the same time, Celts from north of the Alps invaded and conquered the Po Valley. And to the south, Etruscans saw their inland territories progressively slipping into the hands of their former subjects, the Romans, who had expelled their last king in 509 B.C.E.

These Romans had learned and profited from their domination by the Etruscans as well as from their dealings with Greek and Carthaginian civilizations. From these early civilizations on the western shores of the Mediterranean Sea, Rome had begun to acquire the commercial, political, and military expertise to begin its long development from a small city to a great empire.

From City to Empire, 509 B.C.E.-146 B.C.E.

What manner of people were these who came from obscure origins to rule an empire? Their own answer would have been simple: They were farmers and soldiers, simple people accustomed to simple, straightforward actions. Throughout their long history, Romans liked to refer to the clear-cut models provided by their semilegendary predecessors: Cincinnatus, the farmer, called away to the supreme office of dictator in time of danger, then returning to his plow; Horatius Cocles, the valiant warrior who held back an Etruscan army on the Tiber bridge until it could be demolished and then, despite his wounds, swam across the river to safety; Lucretia, the wife who chose death after dishonor. These were myths, but they were important myths to Romans, who preferred concrete models to abstract principles. They were indeed part of the Roman success formula: devotion to family and to the state, determination and steadfastness, a willingness to incorporate other peoples and their cultures into those of Rome, and a genius for organization and administration at home and abroad.

Latin Rome

Prior to the seventh century B.C.E., civilization in Italy meant Etruria to the north and Greater Greece to the south. In between lay Latium, a marshy region punctured by hills on which a sparse population could find protection from disease and enemies. This population was an amalgam of aboriginal Ligurians and the more recently arrived Latins and Sabines who lived a pastoral life in small scattered villages, one of which became Rome.

Early Roman society was composed of households; clans, or *gentes*; and village councils, or *curiae* (sing. *curia*). The male head of each household, the *paterfamilias*, had power of life and death over its members and was responsible for the proper worship of the spirits of the family's ancestors, on whom continued prosperity depended. Within some villages, these families were grouped into gentes, which claimed descent from a semimythical ancestor.

Male members of village families formed councils, which were essentially religious organizations but also provided a forum for public discussion. These curiae tended to be dominated by gentes, but all males could participate, including *plebeians*, those who belonged to the *plebs*, that is, families not organized into gentes. Later, the leaders of the gentes called themselves *patricians* ("descendants of fathers") and claimed superiority to the plebs.

Villages grouped together for military and voting purposes into ethnic *tribus*, or tribes, each composed of a number of curiae. Assemblies of all members of the curiae expressed approval of major decisions, especially declaration of war and the selection of new kings, and thus played a real if limited political role. More powerful although less formal was the role of the *senate* (assembly of elders), which was composed of heads of families. Kings served as religious leaders, the primary means of communication between gods and men. Through the early Latin period royal power remained fundamentally religious and limited by the senate, curiae, gentes, and families.

Etruscan Rome

The Etruscans introduced in Latium and especially in Rome their political, religious, and economic traditions. Etruscan kings and magistrates ruled Latin towns, increasing the power of traditional Latin kingship. The kings were not only religious leaders, directing the cults of their humanlike gods, but also led the army, served as judges, and held supreme political power. As Latium became an integral part of the Etruscan world, the Tiber became an important commercial route. For the first time, Rome began to enter the wider orbit of Mediterranean civilization. The town's population swelled with the arrival of merchants and craft workers.

As Rome's importance grew, so did its size. Etruscan engineers drained the marshes into a great canal flowing to the Tiber, thus opening to settlement the lowlands between the hills. This improvement enabled them to create and pave the Forum, the center of civic, religious, and commercial life. The Etruscans were also builders, constructing a series of vast fortifications encircling the town. Under Etruscan influence, the fortified Capitoline hill, which served much like a Greek acropolis, became the cult center with the erection of the temple to Jupiter, the supreme god; Juno, his consort; and Minerva, an Etruscan goddess of craftwork similar to Athena. In its architecture, religion, commerce, and culture, Latin Rome was deeply indebted to its Etruscan conquerors.

As important as the physical and cultural changes brought by the Etruscans was their reorganization of the society. As in Greece, this restructuring was tied to changes in the military. The Etruscans had learned from the Greeks the importance of hoplite tactics, and King Servius Tullius (578 B.C.E.–534 B.C.E.) introduced this system of warfare into Rome. This change led to the abolition of the earlier curia-based military and political system in favor of one based only on property holding. The king divided Roman society into two groups. Those landowners wealthy enough to provide armed military service were organized into five *classes* (from which the word *class* is derived), ranked according to the quality of their arms and hence their wealth. Each class was further divided into military units called centuries. Members of these centuries constituted the centuriate assembly, which replaced the older curial assemblies for such vital decisions as the election of magistrates and the declaration of war. The rest of the society was *infra classem* (literally "under class"). Owning no property, they were excluded from military and political activity.

With this military and political reorganization came a reconstruction of the tribal system. Servius Tullius abolished the old tribal organization in favor of geographically organized tribes into which newcomers could easily be incorporated. Henceforth, while the family remained powerful, involvement in public life was based on property and geography. Latins, Sabines, Ligurians, and Etruscans could all be active citizens of the growing city.

By the middle of the second century B.C.E., *the Roman republic had evolved to the point where private citizens could cast private ballots. This Roman coin of 137* B.C.E. *features a Roman voter dropping a stone tablet into a voting urn.*

As the old tribal units and curiae declined, divisions between the patricians and the plebeians grew more distinct. During the monarchy the patricians became an upper stratum of wealthy nobles. They forbade marriage outside their own circle, forming a closed, self-perpetuating group that monopolized the senate, religious rites, and magisterial offices. Although partially protected by the kings, the plebeians, whether rich or poor, were pressed into a second-class status and denied access to political power.

In less than two centuries, the Etruscans transformed Rome into a prosperous, unified urban center that played an important role in the economic and political life of central Italy. They laid the foundations of a free citizenry, incorporating Greek models of military and social organization. The transformations brought about by the Etruscan kings became an enduring part of Rome. The Etruscans themselves did not. Around 509 B.C.E. the Roman patricians expelled the last king, Tarquin the Proud, and established a republic—a term derived from the Latin *res publica*, public property, as opposed to *res privata*, private property of the king.

Rome and Italy

Later Roman historians, always the moralizers, made the expulsion of King Tarquin the dramatic result of his son's lust. According to legend, Sextus, the son of Tarquin, raped Lucretia, a virtuous Roman matron. She told her husband of the crime and then took her own life. Outraged, the Roman patricians were said to have driven the king and his family from the city. Actually, monarchy was giving way to oligarchic republics across Etruria in the sixth century B.C.E. Rome was hardly exceptional. However, the establishment of the Roman republic coincided roughly with the beginning of the Etruscan decline, allowing Rome to assert itself and to develop its Latin and Etruscan traditions in unique ways. The patrician oligarchy had engineered the end of the monarchy and patricians dominated the new republic at the expense of the plebs who, in losing the king, lost their only defender. Governmental institutions of the early republic developed within this context of patrician supremacy.

Characteristic of republican institutions was that at every level, power was shared by two or more equals elected for fixed terms. This practice of shared power was intended to ensure that magistrates would consult with each other before making decisions and that no individual could achieve supreme power at any level. Replacing the king were the two *consuls*, each elected by the assembly for a one-year term.

During the early republic, wealthy patricians, aided by their clients, monopolized the senate and the magistracies. Patricians also controlled the system of priesthoods, which they held for life. With political and religious power came economic power. The poorer plebs were increasingly indebted to wealthy patricians, losing their property, and with it the basis for military service and political participation.

The plebs began to organize in response to patrician control. On several occasions in the first half of the fifth century B.C.E., the whole plebeian order withdrew a short distance from the city, refusing to return or to serve in the military until conflicts with the patricians were resolved. In time the plebs created their own assembly, the Council of the Plebs, which enacted laws binding on all plebeians. This council founded its own temples and elected magistrates called *tribunes*, who protected the plebs from arbitrary patrician power. Anyone harming the tribunes, whether patrician or plebeian, could be killed by the plebs without trial. With their own assembly, magistracies, and religious cults, the plebeians were well on the way to creating a separate republic.

This conflict between the plebeians and the patricians, known as the Struggle of Orders, threatened to tear the Roman society apart at the same moment that pressure from hostile neighbors placed Rome on the defensive. Roman preeminence in Latium had ended with the expulsion of the last king and enemies both north and south began periodic attacks against Rome.

This military pressure, and the inability of the patricians to meet it alone, ultimately forced them to a compromise with the plebeians. Around 450 B.C.E. the plebs won a victory with the codification of basic Roman law, the Law of the Twelve Tables, which announced publicly the basic rights of all free citizens. Around the same time, the state began to absorb the plebeian political and religious organizations intact. Gradually, priesthoods, magistracies, and thus the senate were opened to plebeians. The consulship was the last prize finally won by the plebs in 367 B.C.E. In 287 B.C.E., as the result of a final secession of the plebs, the decisions of the plebeian assembly became binding on all citizens, patrician and plebeian alike.

Bitter differences at home did not prevent patricians and plebs from presenting a united front against their enemies abroad. External conquest deflected internal hostility and profited both orders. By the beginning of the fourth century B.C.E., the united patrician-plebeian state had turned back its enemies and was expanding its rule both north and south. Roman legions, commanded by patricians but formed of the whole spectrum of property-owning Romans, reestablished Roman preeminence in Latium and then began a series of wars that brought most of Italy under Roman control. By 265 B.C.E., Rome had absorbed the Etruscan cities of the north and the Hellenistic cities of the south.

The Roman conquest benefited patrician and plebeian alike. While the patricians acquired wealth and power, the plebeians received a prize of equal value: land. Since landowning was a prerequisite for military service, this distribution created still more peasant soldiers for further expeditions. Still, while the constant supply of new land did much to diffuse the tensions between orders, it did not actually resolve them. Into the late third century B.C.E., debt and landlessness remained major problems creating tensions in Roman society. Probably not more than one-half of the citizen population owned land by 200 B.C.E.

The Roman manner of treating conquered populations was radically different from anything seen before, and contributed to Rome's success. In war, no one could match the Roman legions for ruthless, thorough destruction. Yet no conquerors had ever shown themselves so generous in victory. After crushing the Latin revolt of 338 B.C.E., the Romans incorporated virtually all of the Latins into the Roman citizenry. Later colonies founded outside Latium were given the same status as Latin cities. Other

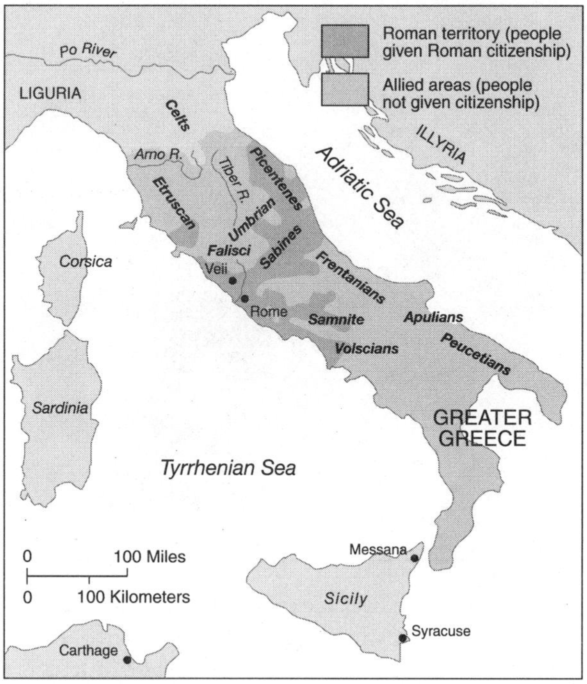

Rome in 264 B.C.E.

more-distant conquered peoples were considered allies and required to provide troops but no tribute to Rome. In time, they too might become citizens.

This statue of a Roman patrician—the class that filled the Senate—comes from the time of the empire. The family patriarch, clad in his toga, holds the busts of his two sons.

The implications of these measures were revolutionary. By extending citizenship to conquered neighbors and by offering the future possibility to allies, Rome tied their fate to its own. Rather than potentially subversive subjects, conquered populations became strong supporters. Thus, in contrast to the Hellenistic cities of the east where Greeks jealously guarded their status from the indigenous population, Rome's colonies acted as magnets, drawing local populations into the Roman cultural and political orbit. Greeks were scandalized by the Roman tradition of giving citizenship even to freed slaves. By the end of the fourth century B.C.E., some of the sons of these freedmen were finding a place in the senate. Finally, in all of its wars of conquest, Rome claimed a moral mandate. Romans went to great lengths to demonstrate that theirs were just wars, basing their claims on alleged acts of aggression by their enemies, on the appeal to Rome by its allies, and, increasingly, by presenting themselves as the preservers and defenders of Greek traditions of freedom. Both these political and propagandistic measures proved successful. Between 265 B.C.E. and 91 B.C.E., few serious revolts shook the peace and security of Italy south of the Po.

Benevolent treatment of the conquered spurred further conquest. Since subject cities and peoples did not pay tribute, the only way for Rome to benefit from its conquests or to exercise its authority was to demand and use troops. By 264 B.C.E., all of Italy was united under Roman hegemony. Roman expansion finally brought Rome into conflict with the great Mediterranean power of the west, Carthage.

Rome and the Mediterranean

Since its earliest days, Rome had allied itself with Carthage against the Greek cities of Italy. The zones of interest of the two cities had been quite separate. Carthage was a sea empire, while Rome was a land-based power without a navy. The Greeks, aspiring to power on land and sea, posed a common threat to both Rome and Carthage. However, once Rome had conquered the Greek cities to the south, it became enmeshed in the affairs of neighboring Sicily, a region with well-established Carthaginian interests. There, in 265 B.C.E., a group of Italian mercenary pirates in Messana, threatened by Syracuse, requested Roman assistance. The senate refused but the plebeian assembly, eager for booty, exercised its newly won right to legislate for the republic and accepted. Shortly afterward the Romans invaded Sicily, and Syracuse turned to its old enemy, Carthage, for assistance. The First Punic War had begun.

The First Punic War, which lasted from 265 to 241 B.C.E., was a costly, brutal, and drawn-out affair, which Rome won by dint of persistence and methodical calculation rather than strategic brilliance. Carthage paid a huge indemnity and abandoned Sicily. Syracuse and Messana became allies of Rome. In a break with tradition, Rome obligated the rest of Sicily to pay a true tribute in the form of a tithe (one-tenth) of their crops. Shortly after that, Rome helped itself to Sardinia as well, from which it again demanded tribute, not simply troops. Rome had established an empire.

During the next two decades Roman legions defeated the Ligurians on the northwest coast, the Celtic Gauls south of the Alps, and the Illyrians along the Adriatic coast. At the same time, Carthage fought a bitter battle against its own mercenary armies, which it had been unable to pay off after its defeat. Carthage then began the systematic creation of an empire in Spain. Trade between Carthage and Rome reached the highest level in history, but trade did not create friendship. On both sides, powerful leaders saw the treaty of 241 B.C.E. as just a pause in a fight to the death. Fearful and greedy Romans insisted that Carthage had to be destroyed for the security of Rome.

Fear of Carthagenian successes in Spain provoked Rome to war in 218 B.C.E. As soon as this Second Punic War had begun Carthegian general Hannibal began an epic in march north out of Spain, along the Mediterranean coast, and across the Alps. In spite of great hardships, he was able to transport over 23,000 troops and approximately eighteen war elephants into the plains of northern Italy. Hannibal's brilliant generalship brought victory after victory to the Carthaginian forces. Soon many of Rome's Gallic, Italian, Etruscan, and Greek allies turned against Rome, hoping to benefit from a Carthaginian victory.

Three things saved the Roman state. First, while some important allies and colonies defected, the majority held firm. Rome's traditions of sharing the fruits of victory with its allies, extending the rights of Roman citizenship, and protecting central and southern Italy against its enemies proved stronger than the appeals of Hannibal. The second reason for Rome's survival was the tremendous social solidarity all classes and factions of its population showed during these desperate years. In spite of the internal tensions between patricians and plebeians, their ultimate dedication to Rome never faltered. The final reason for Rome's ultimate success was Publius Cornelius Scipio (236 B.C.E.-184 B.C.E.), also known as Scipio the Elder, a commander able to force Hannibal from Italy. Scipio, who earned the title Africanus for his victory, accomplished this not by attacking Hannibal directly, but by taking the war home to the enemy, first in Spain and then in Africa, where at Zama in 202 B.C.E. he defeated Hannibal and destroyed the Carthaginian army. Saddled with a huge indemnity and forced to abandon all of its territories and colonies to Rome, Carthage had become in effect a Roman subject.

But still this humiliating defeat was not enough for Rome. While some Roman senators favored allowing Carthage to survive as a means of keeping the Roman plebs under senatorial control, others demanded destruction. Ultimately trumped-up reasons were found to renew the war in 149 B.C.E. In contrast to the desperate, hard-fought campaigns of the Second Punic War, the Third was an unevenly matched slaughter. In 146 B.C.E., Scipio Aemilianus (184 B.C.E.–129 B.C.E.), or Scipio the Younger, the adopted grandson of Scipio the Elder, overwhelmed Carthage and sold its few survivors into slavery. As a symbolic act of final destruction, he then had the site razed, plowed, and cursed. Carthage's fertile hinterland became the property of wealthy Roman senators.

In the same year that Carthage was destroyed, Roman armies destroyed Corinth, a second great center of Mediterranean commerce. This victory marked the culmination of Roman imperialist expansion east into the Greek and Hellenistic world, which had begun with the conquest of Illyria. This expansion was not simply the result of Roman imperialist ambitions. The Hellenistic states, in their constant warring and bickering, had drawn Rome into their conflicts against their neighbors. Greek states asked the Roman senate to arbitrate their disputes. Appealing to Rome's claims as "liberator," cities pressed the senate to preserve their freedom in the face of aggressive expansion by their more powerful neighbors. In a series of intermittent, uncoordinated, and sporadic engagements, Rome did intervene, although its real focus was on its life-and-death struggle with Carthage. Roman intentions may not have been conquest, but Roman intervention upset the balance of power in the Hellenistic world. The price of Roman arbitration, intervention, and protection was loss of independence. Gradually the Roman shadow fell over the eastern Mediterranean.

By 146 B.C.E., the Roman republic controlled the whole rim of the Mediterranean from Rhodes in the east across Greece, Dalmatia, Italy, southern Gaul, Spain, and North Africa. Even Syria and Egypt, although nominally independent, bowed before Roman will. Roman perseverance and determination, its citizen army, republican government, and genius for adaptation and organization, had brought Rome from obscurity to the greatest power the West had ever known. The republic had endured great adversity. It would not survive prosperity.

Republican Civilization

Territorial conquest, the influx of unprecedented riches, and exposure to sophisticated Hellenistic civilization ultimately overwhelmed earlier Roman civilization. This civilization had been created by stubborn farmers and soldiers who valued above all else duty, simplicity, and piety and whose political and cultural institutions had been flexible and accommodating. This unique blend was the source of strength that led Rome to greatness, but its limitations prevented the republic from resolving its internal social tensions and the external problems caused by the burden of empire.

Farmers and Soldiers

Rome rose to world power on the strength of its military, composed neither of aristocrats nor professional soldiers but of farmers. The ideal Roman farmer was not the great estate owner of the Greek world, but the smallholder, the dirt farmer of central Italy. The most important crop of Roman farms was citizens. Nor was the ideal Roman soldier the gallant cavalryman but rather the solid foot soldier. Sometime in the early republic the Greek phalanx was transformed into the Roman legion, a flexible unit composed of thirty companies of 120 men each.

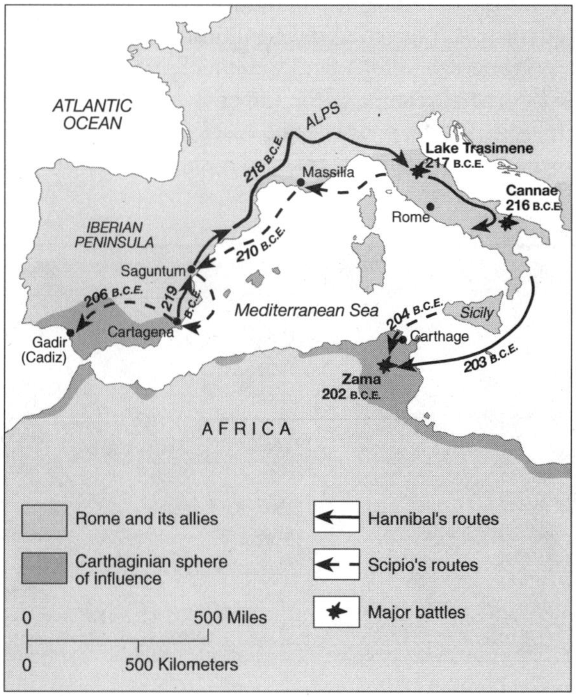

The Punic Wars

THE ROMAN REPUBLIC

509 B.C.E.	Expulsion of the last Etruscan king; beginning of Roman republic
295 B.C.E.	Rome extends rule north to Po Valley
265–241 B.C.E.	First Punic War
264 B.C.E.	All of Italy under Roman control
218–202 B.C.E.	Second Punic War
149–146 B.C.E.	Third Punic War; Carthage is destroyed
136–132 B.C.E.	First Sicilian slave war
133–121 B.C.E.	Gracchi reform programs
91–82 B.C.E.	Social War and civil war (Marius vs. Sulla)
79–27 B.C.E.	Era of civil wars
63 B.C.E.	Cicero elected consul; Pompey conquers eastern Mediterranean
60 B.C.E.	First Triumvirate (Pompey, Crassus, Caesar)
49–48 B.C.E.	Civil war (Caesar defeats Pompey)
44 B.C.E.	Caesar murdered
43–32 B.C.E.	Second Triumvirate (Antony, Lepidus, Octavian)
31 B.C.E.	Octavian defeats Antony and Cleopatra at Actium

These solid, methodical troops, the backbone of the republican armies that conquered the Mediterranean, were among the victims of that conquest. The pressures of constant international warfare were destroying the farmer-soldiers whom the traditionalists loved to praise. When the Roman sphere of interest had been confined to central Italy, farmers could do their planting in spring, serve in the army during the summer months, and return home to care for their farms in time for harvest. When Rome's wars became international expeditions lasting for years, many soldiers, unable to work their lands while doing military service, had to mortgage their farms in order to support their families. When they returned they often found that during their prolonged absences they had lost their farms to wealthy aristocratic moneylenders. Without land, they and their sons were excluded from further military service and sank into the growing mass of desperately poor, disenfranchised citizens.

The Roman Family

The family was the basic unit of society and of the state. In Roman tradition, the *paterfamilias* was the master of the family, which in theory included his wife, children, and slaves, over whom he exercised the power of life and death. This authority lasted as long as he lived. Only at his death did his sons, even if long grown and married, achieve legal and financial independence.

Roman women were not kept in seclusion as in Greece, but they rarely exercised independent power in this male-dominated world. Before marriage, a Roman girl was subject to the authority of her father. When she married, her father traditionally transferred legal guardianship to her husband, thus severing her bonds to her paternal family. A husband could divorce his wife at will, returning her and her dowry to her father. However, within the family, wives did exercise real though informal authority. Part of this authority came from their role in the moral education of their children and the direction of the household. Part also came from their control over their dowries. Widows might exercise even greater authority in the raising of their children.

Paternal authority over children was absolute. Not all children born into a marriage became members of the family. The Law of the Twelve Tables allowed defective children to be killed for the good of the family. Newborn infants were laid on the ground before the father, who decided whether the child should be raised. By picking up a son, he accepted the child into the family. Ordering that a daughter be nursed similarly signified acceptance. If there were too many mouths to feed or the child was simply unwanted, the father could command that the infant be killed or abandoned. Nor were all sons born into Roman families. Romans made use of adoption for many purposes. Families without heirs could adopt children. Powerful political and military figures might adopt promising young men as their political heirs. These adopted sons held the same legal rights as the natural offspring of the father and thus were integral members of his family.

Slaves, too, were members of the family. On the one hand, slaves were property without personal rights. On the other, they might live and work alongside the free members of the family, worship the family gods, and enjoy the protection and endure the authority of the paterfamilias. In fact, the authority of the paterfamilias was roughly the same over slave and free members of the family. If he desired, he could sell the free members of the family into slavery.

In the wake of imperial conquests, the Roman family and its environment began to change in ways disturbing to many of the oligarchy. Some women, perhaps in imitation of their more liberated Hellenistic sisters, began to take a more active role in public life. One example is Cornelia, a daughter of Scipio Africanus. After her husband's death in 154 B.C.E., she refused to remarry, devoting herself instead to raising her children, administering their inheritance, and directing their political careers.

Not every Roman family could afford its own *domus* and in the aftermath of the imperial expansion, housing problems for the poor became acute. In Rome and other towns of Italy, shopkeepers lived in small houses attached

The progress of a Roman son. At left the baby nurses while the proud father looks on. The toddler in his father's arms soon gives way to the young boy playing with a donkey and cart. The maturing youth is seen at right reciting his lessons.

A street in Herculaneum. This Roman town was buried in the eruption of Mt. Vesuvius in 79 C.E., along with the nearby city of Pompeii. A blanket of volcanic ash and pumice preserved the archeological treasures until the sites were rediscovered in modern times.

to their shops or in rooms behind their workplaces. Peasants forced off their land and crowded into cities found shelter in multistory apartment buildings, an increasingly common sight in the cities of the empire. In these cramped structures, families crowded into small, low rooms about ten feet square. In Roman towns throughout Italy, simple dwellings, luxurious mansions, shops, and apartment buildings existed side by side. The rich and the poor rubbed shoulders every day, producing a friction that threatened to burst into flame.

Roman Religion

Romans worshiped many gods, and the list expanded with their empire's boundaries. Every aspect of daily life and work was the responsibility of individual powers, or *numina.* Every man had his *genius*, or personal *numen*, just as every woman had her *juno.* Each family had its household powers, the *lares familiares*, whose proper worship was the responsibility of the paterfamilias. *Vesta* was the spirit of the hearth fire. The *lares* were the deities of farmland, the *domus*, and the guardians of roads and travelers. The *penates* guarded the family larder or storage cupboard. These family spirits exercised a binding power, a *religio*, upon the Romans, and the pious Roman householder recognized these claims and undertook the *officia*, or duties, to which the spirits were entitled. These basic attitudes of religion, piety, and office lay at the heart of Roman reverence for order and authority. They extended to other traditional Roman and Latin gods such as Jupiter, the supreme god; Juno, his wife; Mars, the god of war; and the two-faced Janus, spirit of gates and new beginnings.

Outside the household, worship of the gods and the reading of the future in the entrails of sacrificed animals, the flight of birds, or changes in weather were the responsibilities of colleges of priests. Unlike those in Mesopotamia and Egypt, Roman priests did not form a special caste but rather were important members of the elite who held priesthoods in addition to other public offices. Religion was less a matter of personal relationship with the gods than a public, civic activity binding society together. State-supported cults with their colleges of priests, Etruscan- and Greek-style temples, and elaborate ceremonies were integral parts of the Roman state and society. The world of the gods reflected that of mortals. As the Roman mortal world expanded, so did the divine. Romans were quick to identify foreign gods with their own. Thus Zeus became Jupiter, Hera became Juno, and Aphrodite became Venus.

Republican Letters

As Rome absorbed foreign gods, it also absorbed foreign letters. From the Etruscans the Romans adopted and adapted the alphabet, the one in which most Western languages are written to this day. Early Latin inscriptions are largely funeral monuments and some public notices such as the Law of the Twelve Tables. The Roman high priest responsible for maintaining the calendar of annual feasts also prepared and updated annals, short accounts of important religious and secular events of each year. However, prior to the third century B.C.E., apart from extravagant funerary eulogies carefully preserved within families, Romans had no apparent interest in writing or literature as such. The birth of Latin letters began with Rome's exposure to Greek civilization.

Early in the third century B.C.E., Greek authors had begun to pay attention to expanding Rome. The first serious Greek historian to focus on this new western power was Timaeus (ca. 356 B.C.E.–ca. 260 B.C.E.), who spent most of his productive life in Athens. There he wrote a history of Rome, interviewing Roman and Greek witnesses to Roman victories against Greeks in southern Italy. Polybius (ca. 200 B.C.E.–ca. 118 B.C.E.), the greatest of the Greek historians to record Rome's rise to power, gathered his information firsthand. As one of a thousand eminent Greeks deported to Rome for political investigation, he became a close friend of Scipio Aemilianus and accompanied him on his Spanish and African campaigns. Polybius' history is both the culmination of the traditions of Greek historiography and its transformation, since it centers on the rise of a non–Greek power to rule "almost the whole inhabited world."

At the same time that Greeks began to take Rome seriously, Romans themselves became interested in Greece and in particular in the international Hellenistic culture of the eastern Mediterranean. The earliest Latin literary works were clearly adaptations if not translations of Hellenistic genres and texts. Already in 240 B.C.E., plays in the Greek tradition were said to have been performed in Rome. The earliest of these that survive are the plays of Plautus (ca. 254 B.C.E.–184 B.C.E.) and Terence (186 B.C.E.–159 B.C.E.), lightly adapted translations of Hellenistic comedies.

Determined soldier-farmers, disciplined by familial obligations and their piety toward the gods and the Roman state, spread Roman rule throughout the Mediterranean world. Confident of their military and governmental skills and lacking pretensions to great skill in arts, literature, and the like, they were eager to absorb the achievements of others, even while adapting them to their own needs.

The Price of Empire, 146 B.C.E.-121 B.C.E.

Rome's rise to world power within less than a century profoundly affected every aspect of republican life and ultimately spelled the end of the republican system. Roman society could not withstand the tensions caused by the enrichment of the few, the impoverishment of the many, and the demands of the excluded populations of the empire to share in its benefits. Traditional Roman culture could not survive the attraction of Hellenistic civilization with its wealth, luxuries, and individualistic values. Fi-

Relief of Roman comic actors at work. The action of many Roman comedies took place on a street. The back wall of the stage represented house fronts with doorways for entrances and exits.

nally, Roman government could not restrain the ambitions of its oligarchs or protect the interests of its ordinary citizens. The creation of a Mediterranean empire brought in its wake a century of revolutionary change before new, stable social, cultural, and political forms emerged in the Roman world.

Winners and Losers

Rome had emerged victorious in the Punic and Macedonian wars against Carthage and Macedon, but the real winners were the members of the oligarchy—the *optimates*, or the "best," as they called themselves—whose wealth and power had grown beyond all imagining. These optimates included roughly three hundred senators and magistrates, most of whom had inherited wealth, political connections, and long-established clientages. Since military command and government of the empire were entrusted to magistrates who were answerable only to the senate of which they were members, the empire was essentially their private domain.

But new circumstances created new opportunities for many others. Italian merchants, slave traders, entrepreneurs, and bankers, many of lowly origin, poured into the cities of the east in the wake of the Roman legions. These newly enriched Romans constituted a second elite and formed themselves into a separate order, that of the *equites*, or equestrians, distinguished by their wealth and honorific military service on horseback, but connected with the old military elite. Gradually, some of these "new men," their money "laundered" through investments in land, managed to achieve lower magistracies and even move into the senatorial order. Still, the upper reaches of office were closed to all but a tiny minority. By the end of the Punic wars, only some twenty-five families could hope to produce consuls.

The losers in the wars included the vanquished who were sold into slavery by the tens of thousands, the provincials who bore the Roman yoke, the Italian allies who had done so much for the Romans, and even the citizen farmers, small shopkeepers, and free craft workers of the republic. All four groups suffered from the effects of empire, and over the next century all resorted to violence against the optimates.

The slaves revolted first, beginning in 135 B.C.E. Thousands of them, captured in battle or taken after victory, flooded the Italian and Sicilian estates of the wealthy. Estimates vary, but in the first century B.C.E., the slave population of Italy was probably around two million, fully one-third of the total population. This vastly expanded slave world overwhelmed the traditional role of slaves within the Roman *familia*. Rural slaves on absentee estates enjoyed none of the protections afforded traditional Roman servants. Some Romans sold off their slaves who reached old age; others simply worked them to death. Many slaves, born free citizens of Hellenistic states, found such treatment unbearable. Revolts profoundly disturbed the Roman state, all the more because not just slaves revolted. In many cases poor free peasants and disgruntled provincials rose up against Rome.

Optimates and Populares

The despair that led ordinary Roman citizens to armed rebellion grew from the social and economic consequences of conquests. While aristocrats amassed vast landed estates worked by cheap slaves, ordinary Romans often lacked even a family farm capable of supporting themselves and their families. Many found their way to Rome, where they swelled the ranks of the unemployed, huddled into shoddily constructed tenements, and lived off the public subsidies.

While many senators bemoaned the demise of the Roman farmer-soldier, few were willing to compromise their own privileged position to help. In the face of the oligarchy's unwillingness to deal with the problem, the tribune Tiberius Gracchus (ca. 163 B.C.E.–133 B.C.E.) in 133 attempted to introduce a land-reform program that would return citizens to agriculture. Gracchus was the first of the *populares*, political leaders appealing to the masses. His motives were probably a mixture of compassion for the poor, concern over the dwindling number of citizens who qualified for military service, and personal

Roman slaves sifting grain. Roman victories in the Punic and Macedonian wars brought in a huge influx of slaves from the conquered lands. Slaves were pressed into service on the estates and plantations of wealthy landowners.

ambition. Gracchus attempted to get around senatorial opposition to reform by using the plebeian assembly to acquire unprecedented powers. To his opponents, these measures smacked of an attempt to make himself sole ruler, a democratic tyrant on the Greek model. A group of senators and their clients, led by one of Gracchus' own cousins, broke into the assembly meeting at which the election was to take place and murdered the tribune and three hundred of his supporters.

The optimates in the senate could eliminate Tiberius Gracchus, but they could not so easily eliminate the movement he had led. In 123 B.C.E., his younger brother, Gaius Gracchus (153 B.C.E.–121 B.C.E.), became tribune and during his two one-year terms initiated an even broader and more radical reform program. Tiberius had been concerned only about poor citizens. Gaius attempted to broaden the citizenry and shift the balance of power away from the senate. Alarmed by the revolts of the Latin allies, he sought to extend citizenship to all Latins and improve the status of Italian allies by extending to them the right to vote in the assembly. In order to check the power of senatorial magistrates in the provinces, he transferred to the equestrians the right to investigate provincial corruption. This move brought the wealthy equestrian order into politics as a counterbalance to the senate.

Gaius also improved the supply and distribution of grain in Rome and other Italian cities to benefit the urban poor. He reestablished his brother's land-distribution project, extended participation to Latins and Italians, and encouraged colonization as a means to provide citizens with land. Finally, in order to protect himself and his party from the anticipated reaction of the senate and to avenge his brother's death, he pushed through a law stipulating that only the people could condemn a citizen to death.

Gaius' program was extraordinary for several reasons. In the first place, it was exactly that, a program, the first comprehensive attempt to deal with the problems facing Roman society. Secondly, it proposed a basic shift of power, for the first time drawing the equestrian order into the political arena opposite the senate and making the assembly rather than the senate the initiator of legislation. In the short run, however, Gaius' program was a failure. In 121 B.C.E., he failed to be reelected for a third term and thus lost the immunity of the tribunate. Recalling the fate of his brother, he armed his supporters. Once more the senate acted, ordering the consul to take whatever measures he deemed necessary. Gaius and some three thousand of his supporters died.

The deep inequalities within the Roman citizenry and the increasingly brutal treatment of slaves and allies flared into violence in the second and first centuries The only serious attempts to restructure the state to settle these conflicts ended with the deaths of Tiberius and Gaius Gracchus.

The End of the Republic, 121 B.C.E.–27 B.C.E.

The murders of the Gracchi also marked a new beginning in Roman politics and provided a model for future attempts at reform. Henceforth reformers would look not to the senate or the aristocracy for their support but to the people, and competition for power would be settled by violence. In the following century, personal ambition replaced dedication to the state, and power as an end in itself replaced power in the service of Rome.

With the Gracchi dead and the core of their reforms dismantled, the senate appeared victorious against all challengers. At home, the masses of ordinary Roman citizens and their political leadership were in disarray. The conquered lands of North Africa and the Near East filled the public coffers as well as the private accounts of Roman senators and publicans.

In reality, Rome had solved neither the problem of internal conflict between rich and poor nor that of how to govern its enormous empire. The apparent calm ended when revolts in Africa and Italy exposed the fragility of the senate's control and ushered in an ever increasing spiral of violence and civil war.

The Crisis of Government

In 112 B.C.E., the senate declared war against Jugurtha (ca. 160–104 B.C.E.), the king of a North African client state who, in his war against a rival, had killed some Roman merchants. The war dragged on for five years amid accusations of corruption, incompetence, and treason. Finally in 107 B.C.E., the people elected as consul Gaius Marius (157–86 B.C.E.), a "new man" who had risen through the tribunate, and entrusted him with the conduct of the war. In order to raise an army, Marius ignored property qualifications and enlisted many impoverished Romans and armed them at public expense. Generals had recruited landless citizens before, but never in such an overt and massive manner. Senators looked on Marius' measure with great suspicion, but the poor citizen recruits, who had despaired of benefiting from the land re-

DOCUMENT

Plutarch
The Life of Cato the Elder
(c. 115 C.E.)

Plutarch (46–124 C.E.) was a Greek philosopher and biographer and is one of the best-known sources for information about ancient personalities. Although educated in Athens, Plutarch traveled extensively in the Roman Empire and may even have achieved high office within it. Plutarch wrote extensively on ethical and philosophical issues, but his most popular work was his Lives, which he began in middle age.

Marcus Cato, we are told, was born at Tusculum, though (till he betook himself to civil and military affairs) he lived and was bred up in the country of the Sabines, where his father's estate lay. His ancestors seeming almost entirely unknown, he himself praises his father Marcus, as a worthy man and a brave soldier, and Cato, his great grandfather too, as one who had often obtained military prizes, and who, having lost five horses under him, received, on the account of his valor, the worth of them out of the public exchequer.

He gained, in early life, a good habit of body by working with his own hands, and living temperately, and serving in war; and seemed to have an equal proportion both of health and strength. And he exerted and practiced his eloquence through all the neighborhood and little villages; thinking it as requisite as a second body, and an all but necessary organ to one who looks forward to something above a mere humble and inactive life. He would never refuse to be counsel for those who needed him, and was, indeed, early reckoned a good lawyer, and, ere long, a capable orator.

Hence his solidity and depth of character showed itself gradually, more and more to those with whom he was concerned, and claimed, as it were, employment in great affairs, and places of public command. Nor did he merely abstain from taking fees for his counsel and pleading but did not even seem to put any high price on the honor which proceeded from such kind of combats, seeming much more desirous to signalize himself in the camp and in real fights; and while yet but a youth, had his breast covered with scars he had received from the enemy; being (as he himself says) but seventeen years old, when he made his first campaign; in the time when Hannibal, in the height of his success, was burning and pillaging all Italy. In engagements he would strike boldly, without flinching, stand firm to his ground, fix a bold countenance upon his enemies, and with a harsh threatening voice accost them, justly thinking himself and telling others, that such a rugged kind of behavior sometimes terrifies the enemy more than the sword itself. In his marches, he bore his own arms on foot, whilst one servant only followed, to carry the provisions for his table, with whom he is said never to have been angry or hasty, whilst he made ready his dinner or supper, but would, for the most part, when he was free from military duty, assist and help him himself to dress it. When he was with the army, he used to drink only water; unless, perhaps, when extremely thirsty, he might mingle it with a little vinegar; or if he found his strength fail him, take a little wine.

Cato grew more and more powerful by his eloquence, so that he was commonly called the Roman Demosthenes, but his manner of life was yet more famous and talked of. For oratorical skill was, as an accomplishment, commonly studied and sought after by all young men; but he was very rare who would cultivate the old habits of bodily labor, or prefer a light supper, and a breakfast which never saw the fire; or be in love with poor clothes and a homely lodging, or could set his ambition rather on doing without luxuries than on possessing them. For now the state, unable to keep its purity by reason of its greatness, and having so many affairs, and people from all parts under its government, was fain to admit many mixed customs, and new examples of living. With reason, therefore, everybody admired Cato, when they saw others sink under labors, and grow effeminate by pleasures; and yet beheld him unconquered by either, and that not only when he was young and desirous of honor, but also when old and greyheaded, after a consulship and triumph; like some famous victor in the games, persevering in his exercise and maintaining his character to the very last.

He gave most general annoyance, by retrenching people's luxury; for though (most of the youth being thereby already corrupted) it seemed almost impossible to take it away with an open hand and directly, yet going, as it were, obliquely around, he caused all dress, carriages, women's ornaments, household furniture, whose price exceeded one thousand five hundred drachmas, to be rated at ten times as much as they were worth; intending by thus making the assessments greater, to increase the taxes paid upon them. And thus, on the one side, not only those were disgusted at Cato, who bore the taxes for the sake of their luxury, but those, too, who on the other side laid by their luxury for fear of the taxes. For people in general reckon, that an order not to display their riches, is equivalent to the taking away their riches; because riches are seen much more in superfluous, than in necessary, things.

forms proposed by the Gracchi, looked forward to receiving a grant of land at the end of their military service.

Marius quickly defeated Jugurtha in 106 B.C.E. In the next year Celtic and Germanic barbarians crossed the Alps into Italy and, although technically disqualified from further terms, Marius was elected consul five times between 104 and 100 B.C.E.to meet the threat. During this period he continued to recruit soldiers from among the poor and on his own authority extended citizenship to allies. To his impoverished soldiers, Marius promised land but, after his victory in 101 B.C.E., the senate refused to provide veterans with farms. As a result, Marius' armies naturally shifted their allegiance away from the Roman state and to their popular commander. Soon this pattern of loyalty became the norm. Politicians forged close bonds with the soldiers of their armies. Individual commanders, not the state or the senate, ensured that their recruits received their pay, shared in the spoils of victory, and obtained land upon their retirement. In turn, the soldiers became fanatically devoted to their commanders. Republican armies had become personal armies, potent tools in the hands of ambitious politicians.

During the last generation of the republic, idealists continued their hopeless struggle to prop up the dying republican system while more forward-thinking generals fought among themselves for absolute power.

The Civil Wars

The real threat to the existence of the republic was posed by the ambitions of powerful military commanders—Pompey (Gnaeus Pompeius Magnus, 106–48 B.C.E.), Crassus (Marcus Licinius Crassus, ca. 115–53 B.C.E.), and Julius Caesar (Gaius Julius Caesar, 100–44 B.C.E.).

Pompey and Crassus, rose rapidly and unconstitutionally through a series of special commands by judicious use of fraud, violence, and corruption. Pompey first won public acclaim by commanding a victorious army in Africa and Spain. Upon his return to Rome in 70 B.C.E., he united with Crassus, who had won popularity for suppressing a slave rebellion. Together they worked to dismantle the constitution to the benefit of the populares. In return, Pompey received an extraordinary command over all of the coasts of the Mediterranean, in theory to suppress piracy but actually to give him control over all of the provinces of the empire. His army conquered Armenia, Syria, and Palestine, acquired an impressive retinue of client kings and increased the income from the provinces by some 70 percent.

While Pompey was extending the frontiers of the empire to the Euphrates, Crassus, whose wealth was legendary—"no one should be called rich," he once observed, "who is not able to maintain an army on his income"—was consolidating his power in Rome. He allied himself with Julius Caesar, a young, well-connected orator from one of Rome's most ancient patrician families, who nevertheless promoted the cause of the populares.

When Pompey returned triumphant from Asia in 62 B.C.E., he expected to find Italy in need of a military savior. Instead, all was in order. Pompey disbanded his army and returned to private life, asking only that the senate approve his organization of the territories he had conquered and grant land to his veterans. The senate refused. In response Pompey formed an uneasy alliance with Crassus and Caesar. This alliance was known as the first triumvirate (from the Latin for "three men"). Caesar was elected consul in 59 B.C.E. and the following year received command of the province of Cisalpine Gaul in northern Italy.

Pompey and Crassus may have thought that this command would remove the ambitious young man from the political spotlight. Instead, Caesar, who has been called with only some exaggeration "the sole creative genius ever produced by Rome," used his province as a staging ground for the conquest of a vast area of western Europe to the mouth of the Rhine. His brilliant military skills beyond the Alps and his dedication to his troops made him immensely popular with his legions. His ability for self-promotion ensured that this popularity was matched at home, where the populares eagerly received news of his Gallic wars. In 53 B.C.E. Crassus died leading an army in Syria, leaving Pompey and the popular young Caesar to dispute supreme power. As word of Caesar's military successes increased his popularity in Rome, it also increased Pompey's suspicion of his younger associate. Finally, in 49 B.C.E., Pompey's supporters in the senate relieved Caesar of his command and ordered him to return to Italy.

Return he did, but not as commanded. Rather than leave his army on the far side of the Rubicon River, which marked the boundary between his province of Cisalpine Gaul and Italy, as ordered, he marched on Rome at the head of his legions. This meant civil war, a vicious bloodletting that convulsed the whole Mediterranean world. In 48 B.C.E., Caesar defeated Pompey in northern Greece, and Pompey was assassinated shortly after. Still the wars went on between Pompey's supporters and Caesar until 45 B.C.E., when with all his enemies defeated, Caesar returned to Rome. There he showed his opponents clemency as he sought to heal the wounds of war and to undertake an unprecedented series of reforms. He enlarged the senate to nine hundred and widened its representation, appointing soldiers, freedmen, provincials, and above all wealthy men from the Italian towns. He increased the number of magistracies to broaden participation in government, founded colonies at Carthage and Corinth, and settled veterans in colonies elsewhere in Italy, Greece, Asia, Africa, Spain, and Gaul. Still, he made no pretense of returning Rome to republican government. In early 44 B.C.E., although serving that year as consul together with his general Mark Antony (Marcus Antonius, ca. 81 B.C.E.–30 B.C.E.), Caesar had himself declared perpetual dictator. This move was finally too much for some sixty diehard republican senators. On March 15, a group led by two enemies whom Caesar had pardoned, Cassius Longinus and Marcus Junius Brutus, assassinated him as he entered the senate chamber.

The republic was dead long before Caesar died, and the assassination simply returned Rome to civil war, a civil war that destroyed Cicero himself. Antony, Marcus Lepidus (Marcus Aemilius Lepidus, d. 12 B.C.E.), another of Caesar's generals, and Caesar's grandnephew and adopted son Octavian (Gaius Octavius, 63 B.C.E. –14 B.C.E.), who took the name of his great uncle, soon formed a second triumvirate to destroy Caesar's enemies. After a bloody purge of senatorial and equestrian opponents, including Cicero, Antony and Octavian set out after Cassius and Brutus, who had fled into Macedonia. At Philippi in 42 B.C.E. Octavian and Antony defeated the armies of the two assassins (or, as they called themselves, liberators), who chose suicide rather than capture.

After the defeat of the last republicans at Philippi, the members of the Second Triumvirate began to look suspiciously at one another. Antony took command of the east, protecting the provinces of Asia Minor and the Levant from the Parthians to the east and bleeding them dry in the process. Lepidus received Africa, and Octavian was left to deal with the problems of Italy and the west.

Initially Octavian had cut a weak and unimposing figure. Still, he had the magic of Caesar's name with which to inspire the army, he had a visceral instinct for politics and publicity, and he combined these with an absolute determination to succeed at all costs. Aided by more competent and experienced commanders, notably Marcus Agrippa (Marcus Vipsanius Agrippa, ca. 63–12 B.C.E.), and Gaius Maecenas (ca. 70 B.C.E.–8 B.C.E.), he began to consolidate his power at the expense of his two colleagues. Lepidus attempted to gain a greater share in the empire but found that his troops would not fight

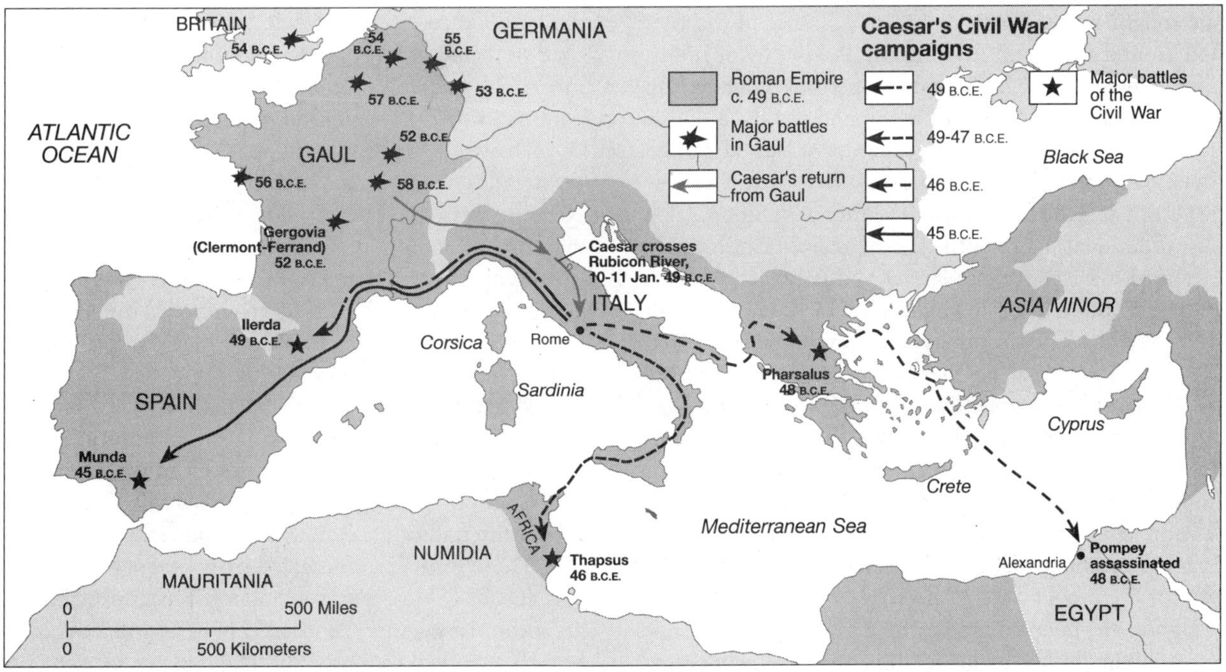

The Roman Empire and Career of Julius Caesar

against Octavian. He was forced out of his position and allowed to retire in obscurity, retaining only the honorific title of *pontifex maximus*.

Antony, to meet his ever growing demand for cash, became dependent on the Ptolemaic ruler of Egypt, the clever and competent Cleopatra. For her part, Cleopatra manipulated Antony in order to maintain the integrity and independence of her kingdom. Octavian seized the opportunity to portray Antony as a traitor to Rome, a weakling controlled by an alien woman who planned to move the capital of the empire to Alexandria. Antony's supporters replied with propaganda of their own, pointing to Octavian's humble parentage and his lack of military ability. The final break came in 32 B.C.E. Antony, for all his military might, could not attack Italy as long as the despised Cleopatra was with him. Nor could he abandon her without losing her essential financial support. Instead, he tried to lure Octavian to a showdown in Greece. His plan misfired. Agrippa forced him into a naval battle off Actium in 31 B.C.E. in which Antony was soundly defeated. He and Cleopatra committed suicide and Octavian ruled supreme in the Roman Empire.

The Good Life

Mere survival was a difficult and elusive goal through the last decades of the republic. Still, some members of the elite sought more. They tried to make sense of the turmoil around them and formulate a philosophy of life to provide themselves with a model of personal conduct. By now Rome's elite were in full command of Greek literature and philosophy, and they naturally turned to the Greek tradition to find their answers. However, they created from it a distinctive Latin cultural tradition. The most prominent figure in the late republic is Cicero, who combined his active life as lawyer and politician with an abiding devotion to Stoic philosophy. In stoicism's belief in divine providence, morality, and duty to one's allotted role in the universe, he found a rational basis for his deeply committed public life. In a series of written dialogues, Cicero presented Stoic values in a form that created a Latin philosophical language freed from slavish imitation of Greek. He also wrote a number of works of political philosophy, particularly *The Republic* and *The Laws*, in conscious but creative imitation of Plato's concern for the proper order of society. For Cicero, humans and gods are bound together in a world governed not simply by might but by justice. The universe, while perhaps not fully intelligible, is nonetheless rational, and reason must be the basis for society and its laws.

These same concerns for virtue are evident in the writings of the great historians of the late republic, Sallust (Gaius Sallustius Crispus, 86–ca. 34 B.C.E.) and Livy (Titus Livius, 59 B.C.E.–17 C.E.). Sallust was a supporter of Julius Caesar, who had written his own stylistically powerful histories of the Gallic and Civil wars. For him as well as for his younger contemporary Livy, the chaos of civil war was the direct result of moral corruption and decline that followed the successes of the empire. For Sallust, the moral failing was largely that of the senate and its members, who trampled the plebs in their quest for power and personal glory. Livy, who was much more conservative, condemned plebeian demagogues as well as power-hungry senators. Only those aristocratic conservatives who had stood for the ancient Roman traditions merited praise. In the second century B.C.E. the Greek historian Polybius had been fascinated with the rise of the Roman republic to world supremacy. A century later the Roman historians were even more fascinated with its decline.

The Augustan Age

It took Octavian two years following his victory at Actium in 31 B.C.E. to eliminate remaining pockets of resistance and to reconcile his rule with Roman constitutional traditions without surrendering any power. That power rested on three factors: his immense wealth, which he used to secure support; his vast following among the surviving elites as well as among the populares; and his total command of the army. Octavian's power also rested on the exhaustion of the Roman people, who were eager, after decades of civil strife, to return to peace and stability. Remembering the fate of Julius Caesar, however, Octavian had no intention of rekindling opposition by establishing an overt monarchy. Instead, in 27 B.C.E., he returned the republic from his own charge to the senate and the people of Rome. In turn the senate decreed him the title of *Augustus*, meaning "exalted."

What this meant was that Augustus, as he was now called, continued to rule as strongly as before, but not through an autocratic office or title—he preferred to be called simply the "first citizen," or *princeps*. Thus he preserved the traditional Roman magistracies.

These formalities deceived no one. Augustus' power was absolute. However, by choosing not to exercise it in an absolutist manner, he forged a new constitutional system that worked well for himself and his successors. This system included a renewed senate, an equestrian order removed from politics, a professional army, and a cultural renewal with the emperor's cult at its center. So successful was this system that for two centuries the empire enjoyed stability and peace, the *Pax Romana.*

The Empire Renewed

Key to Augustus' program of renewal was the senate, which he made, if not a partner, then a useful subordinate in his reform. He gradually reduced the number of senators, which had grown to over a thousand, back down to six hundred. In the process he eliminated the unfit and incompetent as well as the impoverished and those who failed to show the appropriate reverence toward the emperor. At the same time he made senate membership hereditary, although he continued to appoint individuals of personal integrity, ability, and wealth to the body. Most conspicuous among the "new men" to enter the senate under Augustus were the wealthy leaders of Italian cities and colonies. These small-town notables formed the core of Augustus' supporters and worked closely with him to renew the Roman elite.

Augustus also shared with the senate the governance of the empire, although again not on an equal footing. The senate named governors to the peaceful provinces, while Augustus named commanders to those frontier "imperial" provinces where the bulk of the legions were stationed. Senators themselves served as provincial governors and military commanders. The senate also functioned as a court of law in important cases. Nonetheless, the senate remained a creature of the emperor, seldom asserting itself even when asked to do so by Augustus or his successors. Senators competed with each other to see who could be first to do the emperor's bidding.

Augustus also addressed the land crisis that had provoked much of the unrest in the late republic. After Actium, he had to satisfy the need for land among the loyal soldiers of his sixty legions. Drawing on his immense wealth, acquired largely from the estates of his proscripted enemies, he pensioned off thirty-two legions, sending them to colonies he purchased for them throughout the empire. The remaining twenty-eight legions became a permanent professional army stationed in imperial provinces. In time the normal period of enlistment became fixed at twenty years, after which time Augustus provided the legionnaires with land and enough cash to settle in among the notables of their colonies.

These measures created a permanent solution to the problem of the citizen-soldier of the late republic. Veteran colonies—all built as model Roman towns with their central forum, baths, temples, arenas, and theaters as well as their outlying villas and farms—helped Romanize the far provinces of the empire. These colonies, unlike the independent colonies of Greece in an earlier age, remained an integral part of the Roman state. Thus Romanization and political integration went hand in hand, uniting through peaceful means an empire first acquired by arms. Likewise, ambitious provincials, through service as auxiliaries and later as citizens, acquired a stake in the destiny of Rome.

Divine Augustus

A cornerstone of Augustus' renewal was religious reform. He assumed the office of *pontifex maximus* and used it to direct a reinvigoration of Roman religion. In 17 B.C.E. he celebrated three days of sacrifices, processions, sacred games, and theater performances, known as the secular games. He restored numerous temples and revived ancient Roman cults. He established a series of public religious festivals, reformed priesthoods, and encouraged citizens to participate in the traditional cults of Rome. Augustus' goals in all these religious reforms were twofold. He was determined to restore the traditions of Roman piety, morality, sacred order, and faith in the relationship between the gods and Roman destiny. An equally important goal was Augustus' promotion of his own cult. His adoptive father, Julius Caesar, had been deified after his death, and Augustus benefited from this association with a divine ancestor. His own *genius*, or guiding spirit, received special devotion in temples throughout the western portion of the empire dedicated to "Rome and Augustus." In the eastern regions he was worshiped as a living god. In this manner the emperor became identical with the state and the state religion closely akin to emperor worship. After his death Augustus and virtually all of the emperors after him were worshiped as official deities in Rome.

Closely related to his fostering of traditional cults was Augustus' attempt to restore traditional Roman family virtues. Like the reformers of the late republic, he believed that the declining power of the paterfamilias was at the root of Rome's ills. To reverse the trend and to restore the declining population of free Italians, Augustus encouraged marriage, procreation, and the firm control of husbands over wives. He imposed penalties for those who chose not to marry and bestowed rewards on those who produced large families.

Augustus actively patronized those writers who shared his conservative religious and ethical values and who might be expected to glorify the *princeps*, and he used his power to censor and silence writers he considered immoral. Chief among the favored was poet Virgil (70 B.C.E.–19 B.C.E.).

Virgil began his poetic career with pastoral poems celebrating the joys of rural life and the bitterness of the loss of lands in the civil wars. Later, under the patronage of Augustus, Virgil turned directly to glorifying the *princeps* and the new age. The ultimate expression of this effort was the *Aeneid*, an epic consciously intended to serve for the Roman world the role of the Homeric poems in the Greek.

As Virgil reworked the legend of Aeneas—a Trojan hero who escaped the destruction of the city, wandered throughout the Mediterranean, and ultimately came to Latium—he presented a panoramic history of Rome and its destiny. In the midst of his wanderings, Aeneas (like Odysseus before him) enters the underworld to speak with his dead father. Here he sees a vision of Rome's future greatness. He sees the great heroes of Rome, including Augustus, "son of a god," and he is told of the particular mission of Rome:

> ***Let others fashion in bronze more lifelike, breathing images***
> ***Let others (as I believe they will) draw living faces from marble***
> ***Others shall plead cases better and others will better***
> ***Track the course of the heavens and announce the rising stars.***
> ***Remember, Romans, your task is to rule the peoples***
> ***This will be your art: to teach the habit of peace***
> ***To spare the defeated and to subdue the haughty.***

An idealized marble portrait statue of the emperor Augustus addressing his army. Augustus ruled without benefit of any aristocratic office or title. He preferred to be called simply the "first citizen," or princeps.

Augustus' Successors

Through the poetry of Virgil, Augustus' fame was immortal. His flesh was not. The problem of succession occupied him throughout much of his long reign and was never satisfactorily solved. Unfortunately, Augustus outlived all of his first choices. His final choice, his stepson Tiberius (14–37 C.E.) proved to be a gloomy and unpopular successor but nevertheless a competent ruler under whom the machinery of the empire functioned smoothly. The continued smooth functioning of the empire even under the subsequent members of Augustus' family—the mad Gaius, also known as Caligula (37–41 C.E.), the bookish but competent Claudius (41–54 C.E.), and initially under Nero (54–68 C.E.)—is a tribute to the soundness of Augustus' constitutional changes.

The first emperors had rounded off the frontiers of the empire, transforming the client states of Cappadocia, Thrace, Commagene, and Judaea in the east and Mauritania in North Africa into provinces. Claudius (41–54 C.E.) presided over the conquest of Britain in 43 C.E. These emperors introduced efficient means of governing and protecting the empire, and tied together its inhabitants, roughly fifty million in the time of Augustus, in networks of mutual dependence and common interest.

Augustus established peaceful relations with the Parthians, the successors of the Seleucids, who ruled a vast empire from the Euphrates to the Indus River. The Parthian Empire was open to ancient Mesopotamian, Greek, and Indian religious, political, and cultural traditions. Peace with Parthia permitted unhampered trade between the Roman world and China and India.

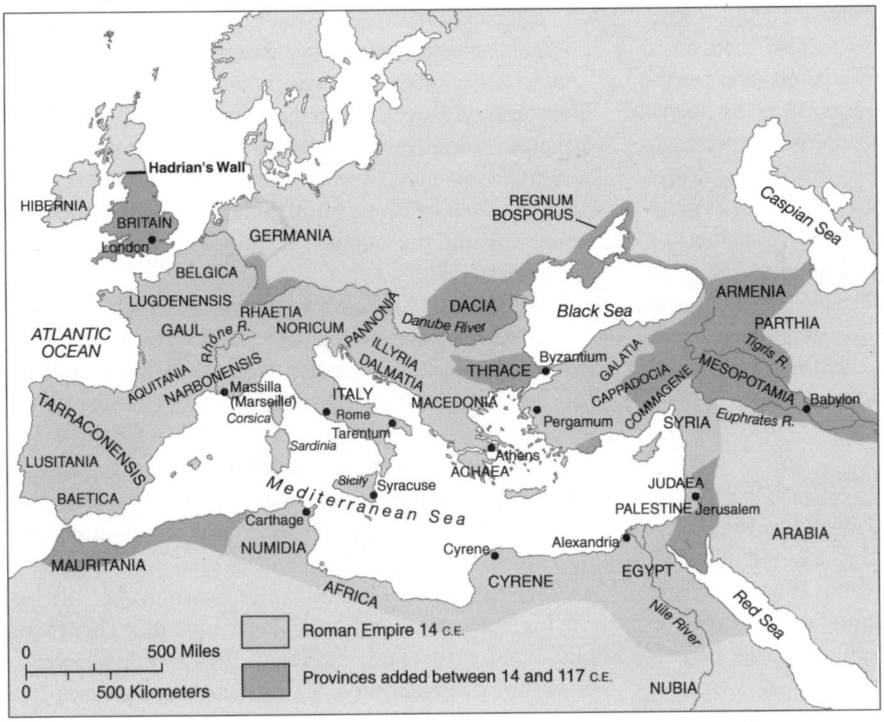

Roman Empire 14 and 117 C.E.

In the western portions of the Roman Empire, after a disastrous attempt to expand the empire to the Elbe River ended in the loss of three legions in 9 C.E., the frontier was fixed at the Rhine. In the east, the northern border stopped at the Danube. The deserts of Africa, Nubia, and southern Arabia formed what in the first century many saw as the "natural" southern boundaries of the empire.

Augustus' concentration of all power in his own hands, combined with his reforms of the senate, equestrian order, and military, proved a formula that for over two centuries provided the empire, through good emperors and bad, with peace and stability.

The Pax Romana, 27 B.C.E.–180 C.E.

From 27 B.C.E. to 180 C.E., no major enemies appeared to challenge the Roman Empire. The imperial bureaucracy collected taxes, enforced law, and kept the peace. Trade flourished and the standard of living rose. Within the vast empire, a system of military camps, towns, and rural estates constituted a remarkably homogeneous and prosperous civilization. Not only merchants but teachers circulated freely within the empire, spreading Greek philosophical ideas of universal harmony and Christian ideas of the kingdom of God.

Administering the Empire

The imperial government of this vast empire was as oppressive as it was primitive. Taxes, rents, forced labor service, military levies and requisitions, and outright extortion weighed heavily on its subjects. To a considerable extent, the inhabitants of the empire continued to be governed by the indigenous elites whose cooperation Rome won by giving them broad autonomy. In return for their participation in Roman rule, these elites received Roman citizenship, a prize that carried prestige, legal protection, and the promise of further advancement in the Roman world.

Finally, much of the governing of the empire was done by the vast households of the Roman elite, particularly that of the princeps. Freedmen and slaves from the emperor's household often governed vast regions, oversaw imperial estates, and managed imperial factories and mines. The descendants of the old Roman nobility might look down their noses at imperial freedmen, but they obeyed their orders.

The empire worked because it rewarded those who worked with it and left alone those who paid their taxes and kept quiet. Local elites, auxiliary soldiers, and freedmen could aspire to rise to the highest ranks of the power elite. As provincials were drawn into the Roman system, they were also drawn into the world of Roman culture. Proper education in Latin and Greek, the ability to hold one's own in philosophical discussion, the absorption of Roman styles of dress, recreation, and religious cults, all were essential for ambitious provincials. Thus, in the course of the first century C.E., the disparate portions of the empire competed, not to free themselves from the Roman yoke but to become Roman themselves.

The Rise of Christianity

The same openness that permitted the spread of Latin letters and Roman baths to distant Gaul and the shores of the Black Sea provided paths of dissemination for other, distinctly un-Roman, religious traditions. For many in the empire, the traditional rituals offered to the household gods and the state cults of Jupiter, Mars, and the other official deities were insufficient objects of religious devotion.

Since the second century B.C.E. the Roman world had been caught up in the emotional cult of Dionysus, an ecstatic, personal, and liberating religion entirely unlike the official Roman cults. Again in the first century C.E., so-called mystery cults, that is, religions promising immediate, personal contact with a deity that would bring immortality, spread throughout the empire. Some were officially introduced into Rome as part of its open polytheism. Generally, Rome tolerated these alien cults as long as they could be assimilated or at least reconciled in some way into the cult of the Roman gods and the genius of the emperor.

With one religious group this assimilation was impossible. The Jews of Palestine had long refused any accommodation with the polytheistic cults of the Hellenistic kingdoms or with Rome. Roman conquerors and emperors, aware of the problems of their Hellenistic predecessors, went to considerable lengths to avoid antagonizing this small group of people. When Pompey seized Jerusalem in 63 B.C.E., he was careful not to interfere in Jewish religion and even left Judaea (the Roman name for the old Kingdom of Judah) under the control of the Jewish high priest. Later, Judaea was made into a client kingdom under the puppet Herod. Jews were allowed to maintain their monotheistic cult and were excused from making sacrifices to the Roman gods.

Still, the Jewish community remained deeply divided about its relationship with the wider world and with Rome. At one end of the spectrum were the Sadducees, a party composed largely of members of priestly families

Spoils From the Temple in Jerusalem, *a marble relief from the Arch of Titus. The arch was begun by Titus's father, the emperor Vespasian, to commemorate Titus's victory over the Jews in 78 C.E.*

who enjoyed considerable influence with their foreign rulers. They were staunch defenders of the ancient Jewish law, or Torah, but not to the exclusion of other later religious and legal traditions. They were willing to work with Rome and even adopt some elements of Hellenism, as long as the services in the temple could continue.

At the other end of the spectrum were the Hasidim (meaning "the pious," "the loyal ones"), those who rejected all compromise with Hellenistic culture and collaboration with foreign powers. Many expected the arrival of a messiah, a liberator who would destroy the Romans and reestablish the kingdom of David. One party within the Hasidim were the Pharisees, who practiced strict dietary rules and rituals to maintain the separation of Jews and Gentiles (literally, "the peoples," that is, all non-Jews). The Pharisees accepted the writings of the Hebrew prophets along with the Torah and abided by a still larger body of orally transmitted law, the "tradition of the elders."

For all their insistence on purity and separation from other peoples, the Pharisees did not advocate violent revolt against Rome. They preferred to await divine intervention. Another group of Hasidim, the Zealots, were less willing to wait. After 6 B.C.E., when Judaea, Samaria, and Idumaea were annexed and combined into the province of Judaea administered by imperial procurators, the Zealots began to organize sporadic armed resistance to Roman rule. As ever, armed resistance was met with violent suppression. Through the first century C.E., clashes between Roman troops and Zealot revolutionaries grew more frequent and more widespread.

The already complex landscape of the Jewish religious world became further complicated by the brief career of Joshua ben Joseph (ca. 6 C.E.–30 C.E.), known to history as Jesus of Nazareth and to his followers as Jesus the Messiah or the Christ. Jesus came from Galilee, an area known as a Zealot stronghold. However, while Jesus preached the imminent coming of the kingdom of God, he did so in an entirely nonpolitical manner. He was, like many popular religious leaders, a miracle worker. When people flocked around him to see his wonders, he preached a message of peace and love of God and neighbor. His teachings were entirely within the Jewish tradition—with one major exception. While many contemporary religious leaders announced the imminent coming of the messiah, Jesus informed his closest followers, the apostles and disciples, that he himself was the messiah.

For roughly three years Jesus preached in Judaea and Galilee, drawing large, excited crowds. Many of his followers pressed him to lead a revolt against Roman authority and reestablish the kingdom of David, even though he insisted that the kingdom he would establish was not of this world. Other Jews saw his claims as blasphemy and his assertion that he was the king of Jews, even if a heavenly one, as a threat to the status quo. Jesus became more and more a figure of controversy, a catalyst for violence. Ultimately the Roman procurator (imperial representative), Pontius Pilate, decided that he posed a threat to law and order. Pilate, like other Roman magistrates, had no interest in the internal religious affairs of the Jews. However, he was troubled by anyone who caused political disturbances, no matter how unintentionally. Pilate ordered Jesus scourged and put to death by crucifixion, a common Roman form of execution for slaves, pirates, thieves, and noncitizen troublemakers.

The cruel death of this gentle man ended the popular agitation he had stirred up, but it did not deter his closest followers. They soon announced that three days after his death he had risen and had appeared to them numerous times over the next weeks. They took this resurrection as proof of his claims to be the messiah and confirmation of his promise of eternal life to those who believed in him. Soon a small group of his followers, led by Peter (d. ca. 64 C.E.), formed another Jewish sect, preaching and praying daily in the temple. New members were initiated into this sect, soon known as Christianity, through baptism, a purification rite in which the initiate was submerged briefly in flowing water. They also shared a ritual meal in which bread and wine were distributed to members. Otherwise, they remained entirely within the Jewish religious and cultural tradition, and Hellenized Jews and pagans who wished to join the sect had to observe strict Jewish law and custom.

Christianity spread beyond its origin as a Jewish sect because of the work of one man, Paul of Tarsus (ca. 5–ca. 67 C.E.). Although Paul was an observant Jew, he was part of the wider cosmopolitan world of the empire and from birth enjoyed the privileges of Roman citizenship. He saw Christianity as a separate tradition, completing and perfecting Judaism but intended for the whole world.

Paul set out to spread his message, crisscrossing Asia Minor, Greece, and even traveling to Rome. Wherever he went, Paul won converts and established churches, called *ecclesiae*, or assemblies. Everywhere Paul and the other disciples went they worked wonders, cast out demons, cured illnesses, and preached. Paul's teachings, while firmly rooted in the Jewish historical tradition, were radically new. God had created the human race, he taught, in the image of God and destined it for eternal life. However, by deliberate sin of the first humans, Adam and Eve, humans had lost eternal life and introduced evil and death into the world. Even then God did

DOCUMENT

The Sermon on the Mount (c. 28–35 C.E.)

The Sermon on the Mount was delivered by Jesus sometime after the beginning of his ministry in C.E. 27 and was recorded by the Apostle Matthew. It is a classic example of Jesus' method of teaching, but more importantly its message lies at the heart of the religion that he founded. Unlike most teachers and prophets of his day, Jesus did not teach in a synagogue; rather he brought his message directly to the people by traveling to various centers of population where he would preach in the open air. Thus the setting of the Sermon on the Mount, while unusual in the context of his contemporaries, was typical of Jesus' style.

And he went about all Galilee, teaching in their synagogues and preaching the gospel of the kingdom and healing every disease and every infirmity among the people. So his fame spread throughout all Syria, and they brought him all the sick, those afflicted with various diseases and pains, demoniacs, epileptics, and paralytics, and he healed them. And great crowds followed him from Galilee and the Decapolis and Jerusalem and Judea and from beyond the Jordan.

Seeing the crowds, he went up on the mountain, and when he sat down his disciples came to him. And he opened his mouth and taught them, saying:

"Blessed are the poor in spirit, for theirs is the kingdom of heaven.

"Blessed are those who mourn, for they shall be comforted.

"Blessed are the meek, for they shall inherit the earth.

"Blessed are those who hunger and thirst for righteousness, for they shall be satisfied.

"Blessed are the merciful, for they shall obtain mercy.

"Blessed are the pure in heart, for they shall see God.

"Blessed are the peacemakers, for they shall be called sons of God.

"Blessed are those who are persecuted for righteousness' sake, for theirs is the kingdom of heaven.

"Blessed are you when men revile you and persecute you and utter all kinds of evil against you falsely on my account. Rejoice and be glad, for your reward is great in heaven, for so men persecuted the prophets who were before you.

"You are the salt of the earth; but if salt has lost its taste, how shall its saltness be restored? It is no longer good for anything except to be thrown out and trodden under foot by men.

"You are the light of the world. A city set on a hill cannot be hid. Nor do men light a lamp and put it under a bushel, but on a stand, and it gives light to all in the house. Let your light so shine before men, that they may see your good works and give glory to your Father who is in heaven.

"Think not that I have come to abolish the law and the prophets; I have come not to abolish them but to fulfill them. For truly, I say to you, till heaven and earth pass away, not an iota, not a dot, will pass from the law until all is accomplished. Whoever then relaxes one of the least of these commandments and teaches men so, shall be called least in the kingdom of heaven; but he who does them and teaches them shall be called great in the kingdom of heaven. For I tell you, unless your righteousness exceeds that of the scribes and Pharisees, you will never enter the kingdom of heaven.

"You have heard that it was said to the men of old, 'You shall not kill; and whoever kills shall be liable to judgment.' But I say to you that every one who is angry with his brother shall be liable to judgment; whoever insults his brother shall be liable to the council, and whoever says, 'You fool!' shall be liable to the hell of fire. So if you are offering your gift at the altar, and there remember that your brother has something against you, leave your gift there before the altar and go; first be reconciled to your brother, and them come and offer your gift. Make friends quickly with your accuser, while you are going with him to court, lest your accuser hand you over to the judge, and the judge to the guard, and you be put in prison; truly, I say to you, you will never get out till you have paid the last penny."

not abandon his people but began, through the Jews, to prepare for their eventual redemption. That salvation was accomplished by Jesus, the son of God, through his faith, a free and unmerited gift of God to his elect. Through faith, the Christian ritual of baptism, and participation in the church, men and women can share in the salvation offered by God.

How many conversions resulted from Paul's theological message and how many resulted from the miracles he and the other disciples worked will never be known, but another factor certainly played a part in the success of conversions. That was the courage Christians showed in the face of persecution.

Even the tolerance and elasticity of Rome for new religions could be stretched only to a point. Their stubborn refusal to acknowledge the existence of the other gods and to participate in the cult of the genius of the emperor was intolerable. Christianity was an aggressive and successful cult, attracting followers throughout the empire. This was not religion, it was subversion. Beginning during Nero's reign, Roman officials sporadically rounded up Christians, destroyed their sacred scriptures, and executed those who refused to sacrifice to the imperial genius. But instead of decreasing the cult's appeal, persecution only aided it. For those who believed that death was birth into a new and better life, martyrdom was a reward, not a penalty.

This new religious movement, strengthened by a message of salvation, a reputation for wonders, a decentralized network of churches, and an enthusiasm for martyrdom, soon reached every corner of the empire. Progressively, an ever greater percentage of the empire's population looked to it for answers to life's problems.

The Cultural Legacy of Imperial Rome

During the two centuries of the Pax Romana, both members of old Roman families and provincials cultivated Latin and Greek letters as the mark of their status. Writers sought to mold character as well as to entertain and inform.

In the later second century, Romans in general preferred the study and writing of philosophy, particularly stoicism, over history. The most influential Stoic philosopher of the century was Epictetus (ca. 55–135 C.E.), a former slave who taught that man could be free by the control of his will and the cultivation of inner peace. Like the early Stoics, Epictetus taught the universal brotherhood of humankind and the identity of nature and divine providence. He urged his pupils to recognize that dependence on external things was the cause of unhappiness and therefore they should free themselves from reliance on material possessions and public esteem.

The slave's philosophy found its most eager pupil in an emperor. Marcus Aurelius (161–180 C.E.) reigned during a period when stresses on the Empire were beginning to show in an alarming manner. Once more the Parthians attacked the eastern frontier, while in Britain and Germany barbarians struck across the borders. In 166 a confederation of barbarians known as the Marcomanni crossed the Danube and raided as far south as northern Italy. A plague, brought west by troops returning from the Parthian front, ravaged the whole empire. Aurelius spent virtually the whole of his reign on the Danubian frontier, repelling the barbarians and shoring up the empire's defenses.

Throughout his reign Aurelius found consolation in the Stoic philosophy of Epictetus. In his soldier's tent at night he composed his *Meditations*, a volume of philosophical musings. Like the slave, the emperor sought freedom from the burden of his office in his will and in the proper understanding of his role in the divine order. He called himself to introspection, to a constant awareness, under the glories and honors heaped upon him by his entourage, of his true human nature: "A poor soul burdened with a corpse."

During these two hundred years, Roman culture had put down deep roots from Britain to Mesopotamia, uniting provincial and Roman elites in a common Greco-Roman tradition of literature, philosophy, and governance. At the same time, non-Roman cultural traditions, especially Christianity, spread across this same vast area, beginning a new, internal transformation of the empire. The violence and unrest that once more convulsed the empire affected them both.

Crisis, Restoration, Division, 192–376 C.E.

From the reign of Septimius Severus (193–211) to the time of Diocletian (284–305), both internal and external challenges shook the Roman Empire. The empire survived these third-century crises but its social, political, and economic structures were radically transformed. Stabilization of the empire under Diocletian meant the creation of a new, autocratic constitution. Reform under his successor Constantine (306–337) meant the abandonment of its old gods for that of the Christians.

The reasons for the third-century crisis were both internal and external. The sheer size of the empire was a fundamental problem. Haphazard expansion in many regions overextended the frontiers. The manpower and resources needed to maintain this vast territory strained the economic system of the empire.

The economic system itself was part of the reason for this strain on resources. For all of its commercial networks, the economy of the empire remained tied to agriculture. To the aristocrats of the ancient world, agriculture was the only honorable source of wealth. The goal of the successful merchant was to liquidate his commercial assets, buy estates, and rise into the leisured landholding elite. As a result, liquid capital either for investment or taxation was always scarce.

The failure of the empire to develop a stable political base complicated its economic problems. In times of emergency, imperial control relied on the personal presence and command of the emperor. As the empire grew, it became impossible for this presence to be felt everywhere. Moreover, the empire never developed a regular system of imperial succession. Control of the army, which was the ultimate source of imperial power, was possible only as long as the emperor was able to lead his armies to victory.

An Empire on the Defensive

Through much of the late second and third centuries, emperors failed dismally to lead their armies to victory. The barely Romanized provincials in the military bore the brunt of these attacks. When the emperors selected by the distant Roman senate failed to win victory, frontline armies unhesitatingly raised their own commanders to the imperial office. These commanders set about restructuring the empire in favor of the army. They opened important administrative posts to soldiers, expanded the army's size, raised military pay, initiated expensive building programs in frontier settlements, and in general introduced authoritarian military discipline throughout society. To finance these costly measures, the new military government confiscated senatorial wealth, introduced new forms of taxation, and increasingly debased the coinage.

Soon, however, the military control of the empire turned into a nightmare even for the provinces and their armies. Exercising their newly discovered power, armies raised and then destroyed a succession of pretenders, offering support to whichever imperial candidate promised them the greatest riches. The army's incessant demands for higher pay led emperors to lower the amount of silver in the coins with which the soldiers were paid. But the less the coins were worth, the more of them were necessary to purchase goods. Such drastic inflation wrecked the economic stability of the empire and spurred the army on to greater and more impossible demands for raises.

The crisis of the third century did not result only from economic and political instability within the empire. Rome's internal crises coincided with increased attacks from outside

This relief shows landowners collecting rents from peasants. The peasantry, displaced by slaves, congregated in the capital and formed a poverty-stricken urban underclass.

the empire. In Africa, Berber tribes harassed the frontiers. The Sassanid dynasty in the new Persian Empire, which replaced the Parthians in 224 C.E., threatened Rome's eastern frontier. When the Emperor Valerian (253–260 C.E.) attempted to prevent the Persian king of kings Shapur I from seizing Roman Mesopotamia and Armenia, he was captured and held prisoner for the rest of his life.

While Rome most feared this empire to the east, its greatest danger lay rather in the west. Along both the Rhine and the Danube, new barbarian peoples raided deep into the empire and harassed Roman commerce on sea and land. The central administration of the empire simply could not deal effectively with these barbarian attacks. Left on their own, regional provincial commanders at times even headed separatist movements. Provincial aristocrats who despaired of receiving any help from distant Rome often supported these pretenders.

Barbarians at the Gate

The external attacks of the barbarians compounded the internal violence that threatened to destroy the Roman Empire. Along the Rhine, various Germanic tribes known collectively as the Franks and the Alemanni began raiding expeditions into the empire. Along the lower Danube and in southern Russia, a barbarian confederation known as the Goths raided the Balkans and harassed Roman shipping on the Black Sea. These attacks reflected changes within the Germanic world as profound as those within the empire. Between the second and fifth centuries the Germanic world was transformed from a mosaic of small, decentralized, agricultural tribes into a number of powerful military tribal confederations capable of challenging Rome itself.

The Germanic peoples typically inhabited small villages organized into patriarchal households, integrated into clans, which in turn composed tribes. For the most part, clans governed themselves, and except in war tribal leaders had little authority over their followers. In the second century many tribes had kings, but they were religious rather than political leaders.

Germanic communities lived by farming, but cattle raising and especially warfare carried the highest social prestige. Women took care of agricultural chores and household duties. Like the number of cattle, the number of wives showed a man's social position.

Warfare defined social groupings and warriors dominated public life. Conflict took the form of feuds, and each act of aggression was repaid in kind. If an individual within a clan had a grievance with an individual within another clan, all his kinsmen were obliged to assist him. Thus a single incident could result in a continuous escalation of acts of revenge.

This intratribal and intertribal violence produced a rough equilibrium of power and wealth as long as small Germanic tribes lived in isolation. The presence of the Roman Empire, felt both directly and indirectly in the barbarian world, upset this equilibrium. Unintentionally,

An ivory plaque portraying Stilicho, a Vandal by birth, who rose to be Master of Soldiers and Consul of Rome. He is shown here in the patrician robes of a consul and carrying the weapons of a soldier, suggesting his dual role.

Rome itself helped transform the Germanic tribes into the major threat to the imperial system since the attraction of Roman luxury goods and the Romans' efforts to establish friendly Germanic buffer zones along the borders drew even distant tribes into the Roman imperial system.

In return for payments of gold and foodstuffs, chieftains of these "federated" tribes opposed tribes hostile to Rome and supplied warriors for the Roman army. Others even led their people into Roman service. By the late third century the Roman army included Franks, Goths, and Saxons serving as far away from their homes as Egypt. Greater wealth and Roman military backing led to increasingly powerful warrior leaders among the Germanic barbarians, who created new tribes and tribal confederations.

The Empire Restored

By the last decades of the third century, the empire seemed in danger of crumbling under combined internal and external pressure. That it did not was largely due to the efforts of the soldier-emperor Aurelian (270–275), who was able to repulse the barbarians, restore the unity of the empire, and then set about stabilizing the internal imperial structure.

Diocletian, a Dalmatian soldier who had risen through the ranks to become emperor, completed the process of stabilization and reorganization of the imperial system begun by Aurelian. The result was a regime that in some ways increased imperial power and in other ways simply did away with the pretenses that had previously masked the emperor's true position.

No longer was the emperor *princeps*, or "first citizen." Now he was *dominus*, or "lord," the term of respect used by slaves in addressing their masters. He also assumed the title of *Iovius*, or Jupiter, thus claiming divine status, and demanded adoration as a living god. Diocle-tian recognized that the empire was too large and complex for one man to rule. To solve the problem, he divided the empire into eastern and western parts, each part to be ruled by both an augustus and a junior emperor, or caesar. Diocletian was augustus in the east, supported by his caesar, Galerius. In the west the rulers were the augustus Maximian and his caesar, Constantius.

In theory this tetrarchy, or rule by four, provided for regular succession. The caesars, who were married to daughters of the augusti, were to succeed them. Although from time to time subsequent emperors would rule alone, Diocletian's innovation proved successful and enduring. The empire was divided administratively into eastern and western parts until the death of Julius Nepos, the last legitimate emperor in the west, in 480.

In addition to this constitutional reform, Diocletian enacted or consolidated a series of measures to improve the functioning of the imperial administration. He reorganized and expanded the army, approximately doubled the number of provinces, separated their military and civil administration, and greatly increased the number of bureaucrats to administer them. He attempted to stem runaway inflation by increasing the amount of silver in coins and fixing maximum prices and wages throughout the empire. He restructured the imperial tax system, basing it on payments in goods and produce in order to distribute the burden more equitably on all citizens and to avoid problems of currency debasement.

The pillar of Diocletian's success was his victorious military machine. He was effective because, like the barbarian chieftains who had turned their tribes into armies, he militarized society and led this military society to victory. Like Diocletian himself, his soldiers were drawn from provincial, marginal regions. They showed tremendous devotion to their god-emperor.

All of these measures were designed to marshal the entire population in the monumental task of preserving Roman culture. Central to this task was the proper reverential attitude toward the divine emperors who directed it. One group seemed stubbornly opposed to this heroic effort: the Christians. Their opposition led to the beginning of the Great Persecution, which formally began in 303 and lasted sporadically until 313. It resulted in the death of hundreds of Christians who refused to sacrifice to the pagan gods.

Constantine the Emperor of God

In 305, in the midst of the Great Persecution, Diocletian and his co-augustus Maximian took the extraordinary step of abdicating in favor of their caesars, Galerius and Constantius. This abdication was intended to provide for an orderly succession. Instead, the sons of Constantius and Maximian, Constantine and Maxentius (306–312), drawing on the prejudice of the increasingly barbarian armies toward hereditary succession, set about wrecking the tetrarchy. In so doing they plunged the empire once more into civil war as they fought over the western half of the empire.

Victory in the west came to Constantine in 312, when he defeated and killed Maxentius in a battle at the Milvian Bridge outside Rome. Constantine attributed his victory to a vision telling him to paint a ⳨ on the shields of his soldiers. For pagans this symbol indicated the solar

Colossal head of Constantine with eyes upraised to show that the emperor thought of himself as close to God.

emblem of the cult of the Unconquered Sun. For Christians it was the Chi-Rho, ☧, formed from the first two letters of the Greek word for Christ. The next year in Milan Constantine and his co-emperor Licinius (308–324) rescinded the persecution of Christians and granted Christian clergy the same privileges enjoyed by pagan priests. Constantine himself was not baptized until near death, a common practice in antiquity. However, during his reign Christianity grew from a persecuted minority to the most favored cult in the empire.

Almost as important as Constantine's conversion to Christianity was his decision to establish his capital in Byzantium, a city founded by Greek colonists on the narrow neck of water connecting the Black Sea to the Mediterranean. He transformed and enriched this small town, calling it the New Rome. Later it was known as Constantinople, the city of Constantine. For the next eleven centuries Constantinople served as the heart of the Roman and then the Byzantine world. From his new city, Constantine began to transform the empire into a Christian state and Christianity into a Roman state religion.

The effects of Constantine's conversion on the empire and on Christianity were far-reaching. Constantine himself continued to maintain cordial relations with representatives of all cults and to use ambiguous language that would offend no one when talking about "the deity." His successors were less broad-minded. They quickly reversed the positions of Christianity and paganism.

While paganism was being disestablished, Christianity was rapidly becoming the established religion. Constantine made enormous financial contributions to Christian communities to repay them for their losses during persecutions. He erected rich churches on the model of Roman basilicas, or administrative buildings, and converted temples into Christian places of worship. He gave bishops the authority to act as magistrates within the Christian community. Constantine attempted to make himself the de facto head of the Church. Constantine and his successors sought to use the cult of the one God to strengthen their control over the empire.

Over the course of the fourth century, the number of Christians rose from five to thirty million. Imperial support was essential to the spread of Christianity in the fourth century but other factors encouraged conversion as well. Christian miracles, particularly that of exorcism, or casting out of demons, made Christian preachers seem more competent than others to deal with these supernatural creatures whose existence no one doubted. Finally, persecution of polytheists by Constantine's successors and local Christian authorities played a large part as well.

During the third and fourth centuries, the empire endured crises from within and without. It survived by transforming itself from a decentralized civilian system to an autocratic military one; from a Roman, Latin empire to an increasingly Greek, eastward-looking one; by enlisting its external enemies in its armies; and by making a persecuted sect its official religion. All of these measures were undertaken by powerful and ruthless emperors who sought, by whatever means, to bolster their position.

The Empire Transformed, 376–500 C.E.

The emperor and the empire needed bolstering in 376 when the Huns, a nomadic horse people from central Asia, swept into the Black Sea region and threw the entire barbarian world into chaos once more. In the following century, the empire was profoundly changed. In the east, emperors ruled a shrinking and increasingly Hellenized empire, while in the west, barbarian kings replaced imperial governors as rulers of former Roman provinces.

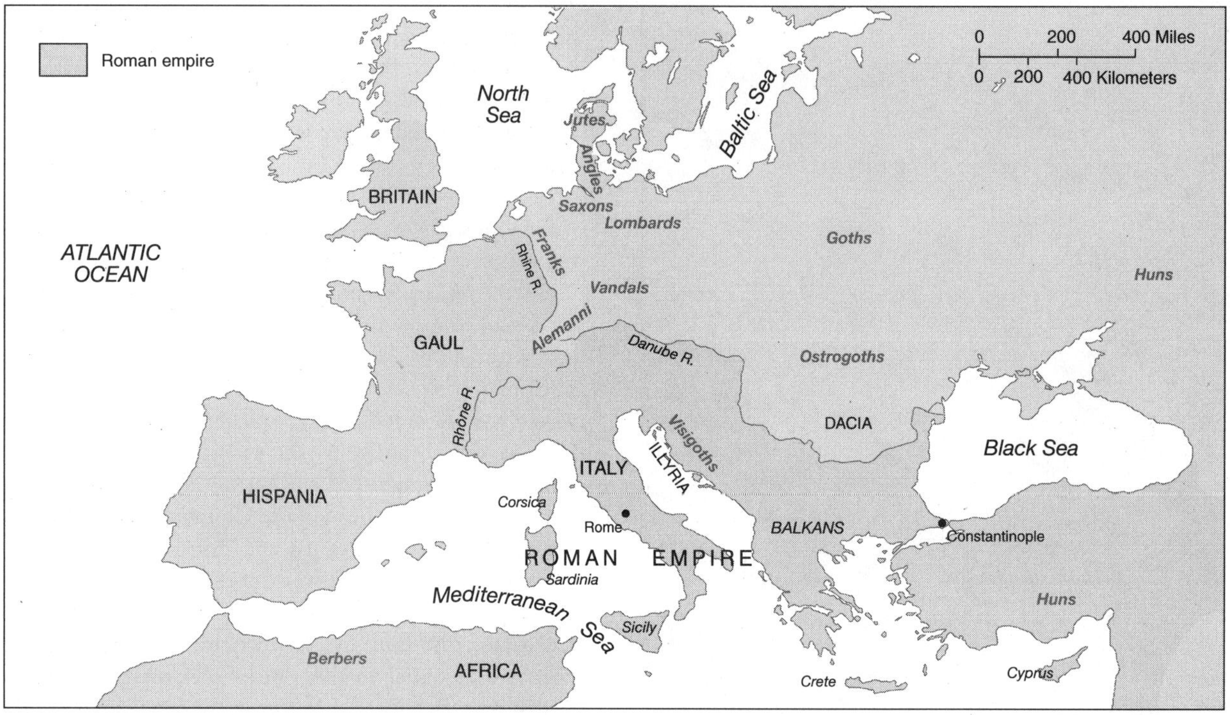

Barbarian Tribes

At the same time that the political traditions of the empire were being transformed, new and powerful forms of religious expression transformed its cultural traditions.

The Huns quickly destroyed the Gothic confederation and absorbed many of the peoples who had constituted the Goths. Others, such as the Visigoths, sought protection in the empire. But the Roman authorities treated them as brutally as had the Huns, forcing some to sell their children into slavery in return for morsels of dog flesh. In despair the Visigoths rose up against the Romans, and against all odds, annihilated an imperial army at Adrianople in 378, killing the emperor Valens himself. His successor, Theodosius (379–395), was forced to allow the Visigoths to settle along the Danube and to be governed by their own leaders.

Theodosius' treaty with the Visigoths set an ominous precedent. Never before had a barbarian people been allowed to settle as a political unit within the empire. Within a few years, the Visigoths were again on the move, traveling across the Balkans into Italy under the command of their chieftain Alaric (ca. 370–410). In 410 they captured Rome and sacked it for three days, an event that sent shock waves throughout the entire empire. Ultimately the Visigoths settled in Spain and southern Gaul with the approval of the emperor.

The Barbarization of the West

Rome did not fall. It was transformed. Romans participated in and even encouraged this transformation. Roman accommodation with the Visigoths set the pattern for subsequent settlement of barbarians in the western half of the empire. By this time, barbarians made up the bulk of the imperial army, and were frequently themselves its commanders. Indeed, these so-called imperial Germans had often proven even more loyal to Rome than the Roman provincial populations they were to protect. In the late fourth and fifth centuries, emperors accepted whole barbarian peoples as integral parts of the Roman army and settled them within the empire.

The establishment of barbarian kingdoms within the Roman world meant the end of the western empire as a political entity. However, the emperors continued to pretend that all these barbarian peoples were Roman troops commanded by loyal Roman officers who happened to be of barbarian origin. Occasionally emperors granted them portions of abandoned lands or existing estates. Local Roman elites considered these leaders rude and uncultured barbarians who nevertheless could be made to serve these elites' own interests more easily than better educated imperial bureaucrats.

Barbarian military leaders needed local ties by which to govern the large indigenous populations over whom they ruled. They found cooperation with these aristocrats both necessary and advantageous. Thus while individual landowners might have suffered in the transition from Roman to barbarian rule, for the most part this transition took place with less disturbance of the local social or political scene than was once thought.

The Hellenization of the East

The eastern half of the empire, in contrast to the west, managed to survive and even to prosper in the fifth and sixth centuries. In the east, beginning in 400, the trends toward militarization and barbarization of the administration were reversed, the strength of the imperial government was reaffirmed, and the vitality and integrity of the empire were restored.

Several reasons account for the contrast between east and west. First, the east had always been more urbanized and civilized than the west. It had an old tradition of civil control that antedated the Roman Empire itself. When the decay of Roman traditions allowed regionalism and tribalism to arise in the west, the same decay brought in the east a return to Hellenistic traditions. Second, the east had never developed the tradition of public poverty and private wealth characteristic of the west. In the east tax revenues continued to support an administrative apparatus, which remained in the hands of civilians rather than barbarian military commanders. Moreover, the local aristocracies in the eastern provinces never achieved the wealth and independence of their western counterparts. Finally, Christian bishops, frequently divided over doctrinal issues, never managed to monopolize either sacred power, which was shared by itinerant holy men and monks, or secular power, which was wielded by imperial agents. Thus under the firm direction of its emperors, especially Theodosius and later Zeno, the eastern empire not only survived but prepared for a new expansionist phase under the emperor Justinian.

Everywhere, the patina of Latin culture began to wear thin as provincials began to rise to positions of prominence and power. In the east, this meant the reemergence of regional cultures and especially of Hellenistic traditions. It also meant that Christian and pagan thinkers would use these traditions to interpret the crises of their world.

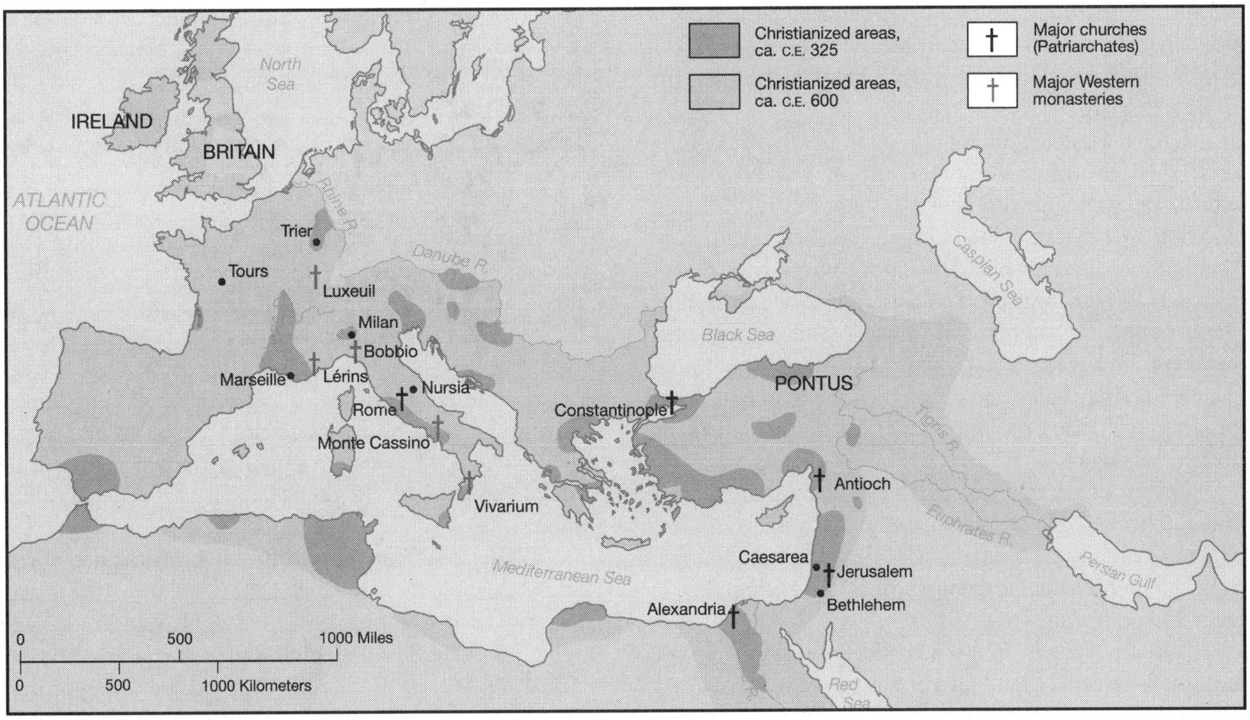

The Spread of Christianity

The Transformation of Elite Culture

The transformation of the classical world from a pagan empire, secure in its mastery over the civilized world, to a fragmented Christian one was as profoundly felt in the cultural sphere as it was in the political and social spheres. Crisis forces choice, and in the third through fifth centuries the choices faced by intellectuals were as profound as those faced by emperors. Where should one look for peace—within or without? Ought Christians to reject the intellectual tradition of the Greco-Roman world or recast it in Christian form? Finally, was the Roman political system in which Christianity had become so deeply embedded essential to its survival?

Two very different thinkers—Origen and Augustine—set the stage for future European cultural developments.

Origen (185–254) began to intellectualize the meaning of the Christian Scriptures and transformed pagan philosophy into a Christian intellectual tradition. As a result of his work Christian intellectuals could no longer be dismissed as "wool seekers, cobblers, laundry workers, and the most illiterate and rustic yokels." In the following century Augustine of Hippo (354–430) faced a new, internal challenge. Victory over paganism was quickly followed by serious disagreements over the proper relationship between the Christian community and the Christian empire. In the early period of Christianity the question was whether to be a Christian meant to be a Jew. Now Augustine had to decide whether to be a Christian meant to be a Roman.

Origen was born into a Christian family in Alexandria, then the most cultivated city of the Hellenistic world, and grew up with an acute sense of the challenge of being a Christian. When Origen was seventeen his father was executed for his faith and his property was confiscated. Origen himself would perish in a subsequent persecution. To support his mother and six younger brothers, he began to teach rhetoric, that is, traditional pagan learning. Later he headed the Christian education program of Alexandria. Important Christians and pagans sought his advice.

Origen invented a new sort of Christian, the Christian intellectual. He moved Christian teaching from a literal to a symbolic understanding of Scripture, and he gave it a sound philosophical foundation by synthesizing it with Neoplatonism.

Initially, Origen interpreted Scripture literally, but eventually rejected literal interpretation when he realized the importance of symbolism. For Origen the Scriptures were a symbol of God's eternal teaching—incomprehensible to those who sought a literal meaning but apparent to those who looked for the hidden spiritual message. This allegorical tradition would dominate Christian biblical studies for over a thousand years. He also insisted that, since God endowed man with reason, he must have intended that humans reach true wisdom through reason. Origen's insistence that there was no contradiction between faith and reason established a continuing intellectual basis for Christianity.

Origen was the father of Christian philosophy. Augustine was the father of Christian political science. Born into a well-off North African family in the town of Tagaste, he was quickly drawn into the good life and upward mobility open to bright young provincials in the fourth century. His skills in rhetoric took him to the provincial capital of Carthage and then on to Rome and finally Milan, the western imperial residence, where he gained fame as one of the foremost rhetoricians of the empire.

While in Milan, Augustine came into contact with kinds of people he had never encountered in Africa, particularly with Neoplatonists and Christians. The encounter with a spiritual philosophy and a Christianity compatible with it profoundly changed the young professor. After a period of agonized searching, Augustine converted to the new religion. Abandoning his Italian life, he

THE ROMAN EMPIRE AND THE TRANSFORMATION OF THE CLASSICAL WORLD

27 -68 C.E.	Julio-Claudian period
27 –14 C.E.	Augustus
c. 30 C.E.	Death of Jesus
54–68 C.E.	Nero
69	Year of the Four Emperors
69–96	Flavian period
96–193	Antonine period
161–180	Marcus Aurelius
193–211	Septimius Severus
224–636	Sassanid dynasty
284–305	Diocletian
303–313	Great Persecution
306–337	Constantine
313	Edict of Milan
364–378	Valens
378	Battle of Andrianople
410	Sack of Rome by Visigoths
430	Death of Augustine
480	Death of Julius Nepos

returned to the North African town of Hippo where he soon became bishop.

Augustine elaborated a new Christian understanding of human society and the individual's relationship to God, which dominated Western thought for the next fifteen centuries. He argued that the true members of God's elect necessarily coexisted in the world with sinners. No earthly community, not even the empire or the Church, was the true "city of God." Earthly society participated in the true "city of God" through Christian rituals and did so quite apart from the individual worthiness of the recipients or even of the ministers of these rites. Salvation came through the Church, but the saved were not identified solely with any particular group of Christians. In this way, Augustine argued for a distinction between the visible Christian empire and the Christian community, a vital distinction at a moment when barbarians were threatening the empire's very existence.

Gold plaque from a sixth-century Syrian reliquary. The subject is Simeon Stylites on his pillar. The snake represents the vanquished devil. Clients could consult the holy man by climbing up the ladder on the left.

The Transformation of Popular Culture

The responses of Origen and Augustine to the choices of late antiquity were fundamental for the subsequent intellectual development of Western civilization. On a more popular level a different sort of Christian had an equally profound influence on the future. This was the hermit, monk, or recluse, who taught less by words than life, a life often so unusual that even the most ignorant and worldly citizen of the late empire could recognize in it the power of God. Beneath the apparent eccentricity, however, lay a fundamental principle: the radical rejection of society's values in favor of absolute dedication to God's.

Shortly after Origen had died fighting for the integrity of the Christian intellectual tradition, another Egyptian was undertaking a different path to enduring fame. Anthony (ca. 250–355), a well-to-do peasant, heard the same Biblical text that later converted Augustine, "Go, sell all you have and give to the poor and follow me." Anthony was uneducated; it was said that he had been too shy as a boy to attend school. This straightforward peasant did exactly what the text commanded. He disposed of all his goods and left his village for the Egyptian desert. There, for the next seventy years, he sought to follow Christ in a life of constant self-mortification and prayer.

This dropout from civilization deeply touched his fellow Christians, many of whom were disturbed by the abrupt transformation of their religion from persecuted minority to privileged majority. By the time of his death this monk—the word comes from the Greek *monos*, alone—found himself the head of a large, loosely knit community of like-minded persons who looked to him as spiritual father, or abbot. These men and women sought spiritual perfection through physical self-mortification and through the subordination of their own wills to that of the abbot. Monks drank no wine, ate no meat, used no oil. They spent their days in prayer, either communal or individual. During the fourth century this monastic tradition spread east to Bethlehem, Jerusalem, and Constantinople and west to Rome and Gaul. In the following centuries it reached beyond the borders of the empire when Egyptian-style monasticism was introduced into Ireland. Over the next centuries thousands rejected the worldliness of civilization and the easy life of the average Christian to lead a monastic life in the wildernesses of the empire.

Although Anthony had begun as a hermit, he and most Egyptian monks eventually settled into communal lives. Elsewhere, particularly in the desert of Syria, the model of the monk remained the individual hermit. Here

Christian hermits were wild men and women who came down from the mountainsides and galvanized the attention of their contemporaries by their lifestyles. The most famous of the hermits, Simeon Stylites (ca. 390–459), spent thirty-six years perched at the top of a pillar fifty feet high.

Their lack of ties to human society made such people of God the perfect arbitrators in the constant disputes that threatened to disrupt village life. They were "individuals of power," whose proven ability to cast out demons and work miracles made them ideal community patrons at a time when traditional power brokers of the village were being lured away to imperial service or provincial cities.

Unlike the eastern monks, the Syrian hermits of the fourth and fifth centuries had few parallels in the west and these exceptions did not establish themselves either as independent sources of religious power or as political power brokers. In the west, in spite of the creation of the barbarian kingdoms, cultural and political leadership remained firmly in the hands of the aristocracy. Aristocratic bishops, rather than hermits, monopolized the role of mediators of divine power just as their lay brothers, in cooperation with barbarian rulers, monopolized the role of mediators of secular power.

During the first and second centuries, a deeply Hellenized Roman civilization tied together the vast empire by incorporating the wealthy and powerful of the Western world into its fluid power structure while brutally crushing those who would not or could not conform. The binding force of the Roman Empire was great and survived the political crises of the third century, which were as serious as those that had brought down the republic three hundred years before.

Thereafter, the fundamental differences between east and west led to a divergent transformation of the two halves of the Roman Empire at the close of late antiquity. The east remained more firmly attached not only to Roman traditions of government but also to the much more ancient traditions of social complexity, urban life, and religious culture that stretched back to the dawn of civilization.

The west experienced a transformation even more profound than that of the east. The triple heritage of late Roman political and military forms, barbarian society, and Christian culture coalesced into a new civilization that was perhaps less the direct heir of antiquity than that of the east, but the more dynamic for its distinctiveness. In culture, politics, and patterns of urban and rural life, the west and the east had gone separate ways, and their paths diverged ever more in the centuries ahead.

FURTHER READING

Primary Sources

Major selections of the works of Tacitus, Plutarch, Suetonius, and Marcus Aurelius are available in English translation from Penguin Books. The second volume, *Naphtali Lewis and Meyer Reinhold, *Roman Civilization, Selected Readings, Vol. II: The Empire* (1951), contains a wide selection of documents with useful introductions.

The Augustan Age

G. W. Bowersock, *Augustus and the Greek World* (New York: Oxford University Press, 1965). A cultural history of the Augustan Age.

D. A. West and A. J. Woodman, *Poetry and Politics in the Age of Augustus* (New York: Cambridge University Press, 1984). The cultural program of Augustus.

J. B. Campbell, *The Emperor and the Roman Army* (New York: Oxford University Press, 1984). Essential for understanding the military's role in the Roman Empire.

Richard Duncan-Jones, *The Economy of the Roman Empire*, 2d ed. (New York: Cambridge University Press, 1982). A series of technical studies on Roman wealth and its economic context and social applications.

The Pax Romana, 27 b.c.e.–180 c.e.

Fergus Millar, *The Roman Empire and Its Neighbors*, 2d ed. (New York: Holmes & Meier, 1981). A collection of essays surveying the diversity of the empire.

Peter Garnsey and Richard Saller, *The Roman Empire: Economy, Society, and Culture* (Berkeley: University of California Press, 1987). A topical study of imperial administration, economy, religion, and society, arguing the coercive and exploitative nature of Roman civilization on the agricultural societies of the Mediterranean world.

Fergus Millar, *The Emperor in the Roman World* (Ithaca, NY: Cornell University Press, 1977). A study of emperors, stressing their essential passivity, responding to initiatives from below.

Philippe Ariäs and Georges Duby, eds., *History of Private Life., Vol. 1., From Pagan Rome to Byzantium* (Cambridge, MA: Harvard University Press, 1986). Essays on the interior, private life of Romans and Greeks by leading French and British historians.

*Judith P. Hallett, *Fathers and Daughters in Roman Society & the Elite Family* (Princeton, NJ: Princeton University Press, 1984). A study of indirect power exercised by elite women in the Roman world as daughters, mothers, and sisters.

* Ramsay MacMullen, *Paganism in the Roman Empire* (New Haven, CT: Yale University Press, 1981). A description of the varieties and levels of pagan religion in the Roman world.

Jane E. Gardner, *Women in Roman Law and Society* (Bloomington, IN: Indiana University Press, 1986). A study of the extent of freedom and power over property enjoyed by Roman women.

Edward Champlin, *Fronto and Antonine Rome* (Cambridge, MA: Harvard University Press, 1980). A cultural history of Antonine court life through the letters of the second century's greatest rhetorician.

*Joseph Jay Deiss, *Herculaneum: Italy's Buried Treasure* (New York: Harper and Row, 1985). A vividly written and well-illustrated introduction to Herculaneum for a general audience.

Crisis, Restoration, Division, 192–376 c.e.

* A. H. M. Jones, *The Later Roman Empire, 284–602: A Social, Economic and Administrative Survey*, 2 vols. (Baltimore: The Johns Hopkins University Press, 1986). The standard, detailed survey of late antiquity by an administrative historian.

* Peter Brown, *The World of Late Antiquity, A.D. 150–750* (New York: Harcourt Brace Jovanovich, 1971). A brilliant essay on the cultural transformation of the ancient world.

E. A. Thompson, *The Early Germans* (Oxford: Oxford University Press, 1965). An important social and economic view of Germanic society.

The Empire Transformed 376–500 c.e.

* Ramsay MacMullen, *Paganism in the Roman Empire* (New Haven, CT: Yale University Press, 1981). A sensible introduction to the varieties of Roman religion in the imperial period.

T. D. Barnes, *The New Empire of Diocletian and Constantine* (Cambridge, MA: Harvard University Press, 1982). A current examination of the transformations brought about under these two great emperors.

* Philip Willis Dixon, *Barbarian Europe* (Oxford: Elsevier Phaidon, 1976), an introduction to Germanic societies.

* Herwig Wolfram, *History of the Goths* (Berkeley, CA: University of California Press, 1988). An ethnologically sensitive history of the formation of the Gothic peoples.

* Ramsay MacMullen, *Christianizing the Roman Empire* (100-400) (New Haven, CT: Yale University Press, 1984). A view of Christianity's spread from the perspective of Roman history.

* Judith Herrin, *The Formation of Christendom* (Princeton, NJ: Princeton University Press, 1987). A history of early Christianity from the perspective of a noted Byzantinist.

* Karl E. Morrison, ed., *The Church in the Roman Empire* (Chicago: University of Chicago Press, 1986). Major documents of early Christianity.

Peter Brown, *Society and the Holy in Late Antiquity* (Berkeley, CA: University of California Press, 1982). Imaginative essays on religion and society, emphasizing the role of saints.

* David Knowles, *Christian Monasticism* (New York: McGraw-Hill, 1969). A very readable introduction by a great historian of monastic history.

CHAPTER 7

The Islamic Empire

KEY TERMS

Arabia	*Sharia*
Bedouins	*Umayyads*
Mecca	*caliph*
Kaaba	*Ridda Wars*
Muhammad	*jihad*
Hijrah	*Sunni*
Medina	*Shi'a*
ummah	*Peoples of the Book*
Quran	*Abbasids*
monotheism	*mawali*
Five Pillars of Islam	*Crusades*

DISCUSSION QUESTIONS

How did Islam succeed in uniting Arab tribes and, eventually, non-Arab peoples into a single empire?

Why was selection of a successor to Muhammad such a difficult problem in the Islamic Empire?

Arabia was the birthplace of the Islamic religion; and the Arabic language was the "tongue of the angels," since God chose to reveal himself through that vehicle to Muhammad, the founder of the faith. Arabia became the center of the Islamic world, and the source of renewal and inspiration for the faithful believers throughout an emerging Islamic Empire.

The Arabian peninsula with its deserts, high temperatures, and exposed frontiers was, however, an unlikely place for one of history's most dynamic movements to begin. The geographical conditions encouraged nomadic tribes and strong individualism, not settled civilizations with overbearing governments. From outside Arabia commerce, religious influences, and military domination followed along the trade routes and affected the Bedouins in a variety of ways. In the midst of this crossroads between Asia, Europe, and Africa emerged Muhammad, to whom Allah chose to speak.

From this one man came a religion that shaped every aspect of individual and community life: from diet to politics, from family to law, and from prayer to conquest. From this hostile environment, within one century, the power of Islam would be felt from the Indian Ocean to the Pacific and change age-old religious, intellectual, and political patterns.

Arabia Before the Prophet

The Arabian peninsula is one-third the size of the continental United States. Most of the land is arid and desert; rainfall is scarce, vegetation scant, and very little of the land is suitable for agriculture. Arabia before the birth of Muhammad was a culturally isolated and economically underdeveloped region. However, in the relatively more fertile southwestern corner of the peninsula, several small Arabic kingdoms once flourished in the area now known as Yemen. The most notable of these early kingdoms, Saba' (the biblical Sheba), existed as early as the eighth century B.C.E. until the third century C.E., when the kingdom was overtaken by the Himyarites from the south. Aided by the domestication of the camel (c. 400 B.C.E.), several small Arabic kingdoms became prosperous due to growing trade in frankincense and spices, and established contacts with kingdoms both within and outside of the Arabian peninsula. In the north of the region, several Arabic kingdoms were able to establish contacts with the Byzantine and the Persian (Sassanian) Empires as early as the fifth century C.E. Among the most notable of these small kingdoms were Nabataea in northwest Arabia, which dominated Arabian trade routes until the Romans annexed the kingdom in the second century C.E., and that of the Lakhmids in the northeast, whose prominence was greatest c. C.E. 250 to 600, when the kingdom was destroyed by the Sassanids. But in the interior, the vast desert dotted only with occasional oases, the nomadic life was the only successful existence.

The Bedouins

The nomads, or Bedouins, lived according to ancient tribal patterns; at the head of the tribe was the elder, or sheik, elected and advised by the heads of the related families comprising the tribe. Driven from place to place in their search for pastures to sustain their flocks, the Bedouins led a precarious existence. Aside from maintaining their herds, some relied on plunder from raids on settlements, on passing caravans, and on one another.

The Bedouins enjoyed a degree of personal freedom unknown in more agrarian and settled societies. Sheiks could not always limit the freedom of their tribesmen, who often rode off and hired themselves out as herdsmen or warriors if the authority of the tribe became too restrictive. The Bedouins developed a code of ethics represented in the word muru'ah, or "manly virtue." Far from being abrasive and rough, muru'ah was proven through grace and restraint, loyalty to obligation and duty, a devotion to do that which must be done, and a respect for women.

Bedouin women also enjoyed a great degree of independence. They were allowed to engage in business and commerce; they could choose their own lovers and conduct their lives without great restriction by the control of their husbands. The freedom and independence of Bedouins sprang from the realities of life in the desert, as did the values and ethics of the Arabs. One rule of conduct was unqualified hospitality to strangers. A nomad never knew when the care of a stranger might be essential to provide the necessary water and shade to save his or her own life.

The Bedouins of the seventh century lacked a unifying religious system. Most looked at life as a brief time within which to take full advantage of daily pleasure. Ideas of an afterlife were not well defined or described. The Bedouins worshipped a large number of gods and spirits, many of whom were believed to inhabit trees, wells, and stones. Each tribe had its own gods, generally symbolized by sacred stones, which served as altars where communal sacrifices were offered.

Although the Bedouins of the interior led a primitive and largely isolated existence, some parts of Arabia were highly influenced by the neighboring and more highly sophisticated cultures of Byzantium, Persia, and Ethiopia. By the latter half of the sixth century, Christian and Jewish residents were found throughout the Arabian peninsula; their religious systems and philosophical positions surely had a growing influence on the Bedouin population.

Early Mecca

On the western side of the Arabian peninsula is a region known as the Hejaz, or "barrier." The Hejaz rises from the western coastal plain from Yemen in the south to the Sinai peninsula in the north. One of the oases in the Hejaz is Mecca, set among the barren hills 50 miles inland from the sea. This site had several advantages: Mecca possessed a well (the Zemzem) of great depth, and two ancient caravan routes met there. An east-to-west route ran from Africa through the peninsula to Iran and central Asia, and a northwest-southeast route brought the spices of India to the Mediterranean world.

Another significant advantage for Mecca was its importance as a religious sanctuary. An ancient temple, an almost square structure built of granite blocks, stood near the well of Mecca. Known as the Kaaba ("cube"), this square temple contained the sacred Black Stone, which was said to have been brought to Abraham and his son Ishmael by the angel Gabriel. According to tradition, the stone, probably a meteorite, was originally white but had become blackened by the sins of all those who touched it.

For centuries the Kaaba had been a holy place of annual pilgrimage for the Arabic tribes and a focal point of Arabic cultural and linguistic unity. The Kaaba itself was draped with the pelts of sacrificial animals and supposedly held the images and shrines of 360 gods and goddesses.

By the sixth century, Mecca was controlled by the Quraysh tribe, whose rulers organized themselves into an aristocracy of merchants and wealthy businessmen. The Quraysh held lucrative trading agreements with Byzantine and Persian contacts, as well as with the southern Arabian tribes and the Kingdom of Axum across the Red Sea in what is now Ethiopia. In addition, a number of annual merchant fairs, such as one usually held at nearby Ukaz, were taken over by the Quraysh to extend the economic influence of Mecca. The Quraysh were also concerned with protecting the religious shrine of the Kaaba, in addition to ensuring that the annual pilgrimage of

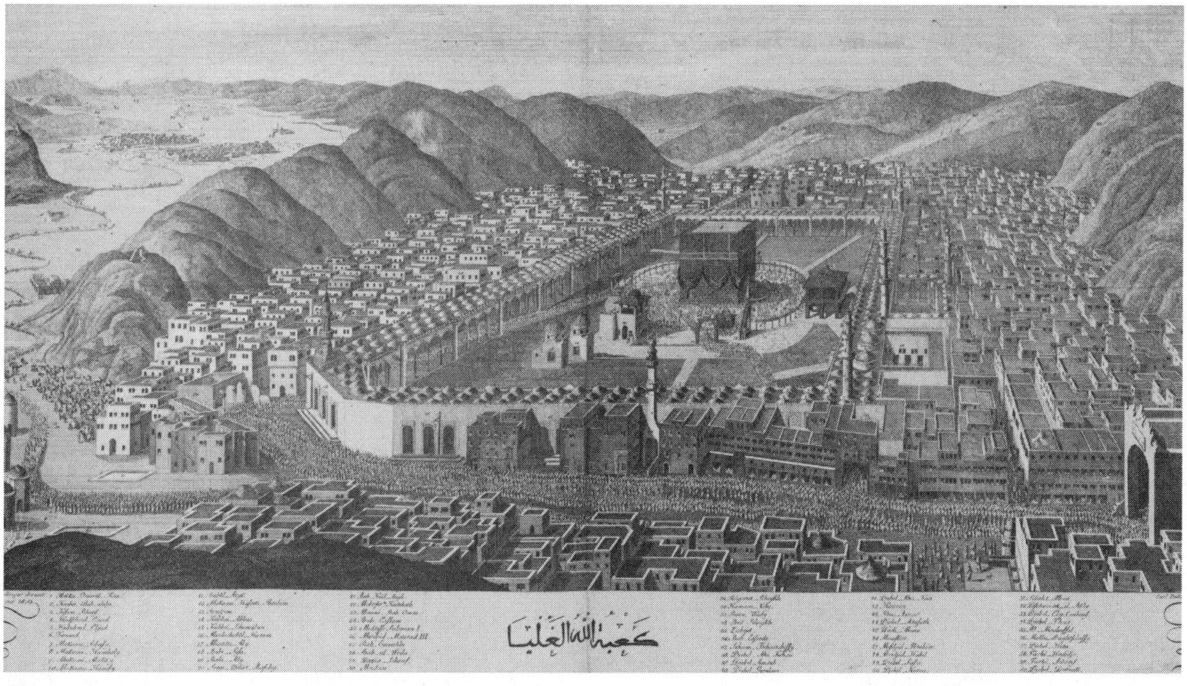

At the center of this drawing of the city of Mecca is the Kaaba, a square temple of uncut stones housing the sacred Black Stone. Each year thousands of Muslims make a pilgrimage to worship at the Kaaba, the most sacred shrine of Islam.

tribes to the holy place would continue as a source of large revenue for the merchants of the city.

Muhammad, Prophet of Islam

Into this environment at Mecca was born a man who would change completely the religious, political, and social organization of his people. Muhammad (c. 570–632) came from a family belonging to the Quraysh. His early years were difficult because of the deaths of both his parents and his grandfather who cared for him after his parents' loss. He was raised by his uncle, Abu Talib, a prominent merchant of Mecca. His early years were spent helping his uncle in the caravan trade. Even as a young man, Muhammad came to be admired by his fellow Meccans as a sincere and honest person, and earned the nickname al-Amin, "the trustworthy." When he was about 25 years old, he accepted employment by a wealthy widow, Khadija, whose caravans traded with Syria. He later married Khadija and began to take his place as a leading influential citizen of Mecca. Muhammad's marriage to Khadija was a long and happy one, and produced two sons, who both died as infants, and two daughters, of whom the younger, Fatima, is best known because of her eventual role in Islam's future.

A description of Muhammad, and probably a very accurate one, has been preserved in the Sira, the traditional biography of the Prophet. He is described as a handsome, large man with broad shoulders, black, shining eyes flecked with brown, and a fair complexion. His personality was reserved and gentle, but he was a man of impressive energy. He walked quickly, and always seemed to make it difficult for his friends to keep up with him. Although he was a popular companion, an energetic businessman, and a responsible husband and father, Muhammad was a very introspective man. Often he would escape from Meccan society, which he considered too materialistic and irreligious, and spend long hours alone in a cave on nearby Mount Hira. During these hours of meditation Muhammad searched for answers to the metaphysical questions that many thoughtful Arabs were beginning to contemplate. Muhammad's meditations many times produced nearly total mental and physical exhaustion. But during one such solitary meditation, Muhammad heard a call that was to alter history.

Muhammad's initial communication from heaven came in the form of a command:

> ***Recite! In the name of your Lord, who created all things, who***
> ***created man from a clot (of blood).***
> ***Recite! And your Lord is Most Bounteous***
> ***Who teaches by the Pen,***
> ***teaches man that which he would not have otherwise known. (Quran 96:1–5)***

The Arabic word for "recitation" or "reading" is qur'an, and the collected revelations given to Muhammad are known to us as the Quran. The revelations that continued to come over the next 20 years or so were sometimes terse and short, at other times elaborate and poetic. The early revelations did not immediately convince Muhammad that he was a messenger of God. In fact, his first reaction was fear and self-doubt. During his depressions brought on by fears over the source and nature of his revelations, he sought the comfort and advice of Khadija.

As the revelations continued, Muhammad finally became convinced that the message he was receiving was the truth and that he had been called to be a messenger of divine revelation. He came to think of himself and his mission as one similar to prophets and messengers who had preceded him in announcing the existence of the one God, Allah. Allah, "the God," was the same God worshipped by the Christians and Jews, but Allah had now chosen Muhammad to be his last and greatest prophet to perfect the religion revealed earlier to Abraham, Moses, the Hebrew prophets, and Jesus. The religion Muhammad preached is called Islam, which means "surrender" or "submission" to the will of God. The followers of Islam are called Muslims. The term Muslim refers to one who submits to God's law.

Muhammad's Message and Early Followers

At first Muhammad had little success in attracting followers in Mecca. The early message Muhammad brought to the Arabs was strong and direct: that Allah was one and majestic, all-powerful and demanding of the faith of his followers. Furthermore, Allah demanded that his followers be compassionate, ethical, and just in all their dealings:

> ***In the name of Allah, the most Beneficent, the Most Merciful***
> ***by the night as it enshrouds***
> ***by the day as it illuminates***
> ***by Him Who created the male and female***
> ***indeed your affairs lead to various ends.***

For who gives (of himself) and acts righteously, and conforms to goodness,
We will give him ease.
But as for him who is niggardly cleaning himself, self-sufficient and rejects goodness,
We will indeed ease his path to adversity.
Nor shall his wealth save him as he perishes
for Guidance is from Us
and to Us belongs the Last and First. (Quran 96:1–14)

Muhammad was able to win the early support of some of his relatives and close friends. His first converts were his wife, his cousin Ali, and Abu Bakr, a leading merchant of the Quraysh tribe who was highly respected for his integrity. Abu Bakr remained the constant companion of the Prophet during his persecution and exile and later became the first caliph (leader) of Islam. But opposition to Muhammad's message was very strong, especially from Mecca's leading citizens. Many thought Muhammad was an ambitious poet attempting to pass on his own literary creations as the word of God. Others believed him to be possessed by demons. Muhammad's strong monotheism worried those residents of Mecca who obtained their income from the pilgrims to the Kaaba. Most of Muhammad's early converts were among the poorest of the city's residents, and as a result Mecca's leading citizens feared the possibility of social revolution.

Since Muhammad was himself a member of the Quraysh tribe, its leaders first tried to convince Abu Talib to persuade his nephew to stop preaching. Next they tried to bribe Muhammad himself with the promise of a lucrative appointment as a tribal official. When such offers were rejected, actual persecution of Muhammad's converts began, and the Quraysh attempted a commercial and social boycott of the Prophet's family. During these times of trial Abu Talib and Khadija both died, and Muhammad's faith and resolution were greatly tested. But inspired by the spirit and example of earlier prophets such as Abraham and Moses, who were also tested and persecuted, Muhammad persevered in his faith and continued his preaching.

The Hijrah

To the north of Mecca is the city of Medina, which was then called Yathrib. The residents of Medina were somewhat familiar with monotheistic beliefs, perhaps because of the Jewish community in residence there. They also had no dependence on the revenues from a pagan site of pilgrimage, as the Meccans had. While visiting Mecca, some pilgrims from Medina judged Muhammad to be a powerful and influential leader and invited him to come to Medina to settle differences among that city's tribal chiefs. As opposition to his message increased in Mecca, Muhammad sent some of his followers to take up residence in Medina in order to escape persecution. But Muhammad and Abu Bakr were the last to flee Mecca when it became known that the Quraysh intended to kill the Prophet. They were followed, but escaped, the story goes, by hiding in a narrow cave whose entrance was quickly covered by a spider's web. The web convinced the Quraysh that the cave had been abandoned for a great length of time.

The Hijrah, or "migration" from Mecca to Medina (often transliterated as Hegira), took place in September in the year 622. The event was such a turning point in the history of Islam that the year is counted as Year 1 of the Islamic calendar. In Medina, the Prophet met with entirely different circumstances than in his birthplace. Muhammad's leadership turned Medina (Madinat al Nali, or the "City of the Prophet") into the leading center of power in the Arabian peninsula.

The Community at Medina

Muhammad was received in Medina as a leader and a spiritual visionary. He and his followers set about the establishment of a genuine community, or Ummah, free of pressure and persecution. This community at Medina included a number of Jewish and Christian families, whom Muhammad tried to convert. His efforts were successful with some Jewish residents, but the Jews who did not choose to accept Muhammad's faith were allowed to continue their way of life, since they were also thought to be "people of the Book" to whom Allah had made himself known through earlier prophets.

The welfare of the community at Medina was of grave concern to Muhammad. Many of those who followed the Prophet to Medina were without work, and necessary food was sometimes obtained by plundering the caravans passing Medina on the way to Mecca. Also, Muhammad and his followers became steadily more aggressive in their attempts to win converts to Islam. The word jihad, meaning "struggle," was applied to the early efforts of the Ummah to win converts and strengthen its own recruiting.

Military encounters with the pagan opponents of Islam began in 624, with the Battle of Bedr. Muhammad defeated the stronger Quraysh army of Mecca, and the victory reinforced the resolve of the new religion's fol-

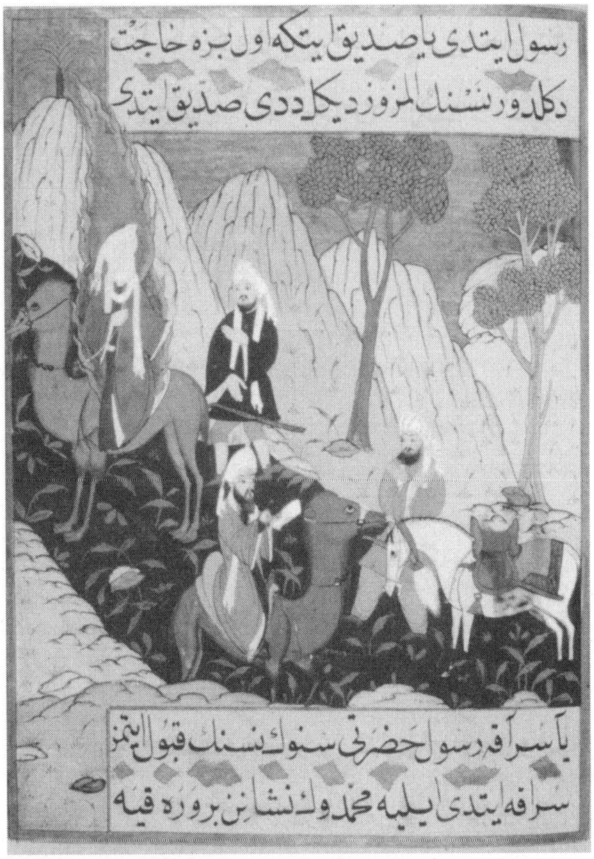

This Turkish illustration depicts one of the incidents said to have occurred during the Hijrah. A man from Mecca, chasing the Prophet and his companion, Abu Bakr, on their way to Medina, has been thrown from his horse. The Meccan, having repented of his pursuit, is pardoned by Muhammad; the written pardon is delivered by Abu Bakr.

lowers. Succeeding battles established the Muslims as the dominant force in Arabia, and finally a truce with Mecca was arranged, under which the Muslims could visit the holy shrines in the city.

Return to Mecca

In 629 Muhammad returned with his followers to take control of the city of Mecca and to cleanse the Kaaba of pagan idols. The temple itself, together with the Black Stone, was preserved as the supreme religious center of Islam, the "Mecca" to which all devout Muslims are to attempt to make a pilgrimage during their lifetimes. Muhammad urged unbelievers and his old enemies to accept Islam and become part of the Ummah. By 632 almost all of the Arabian peninsula had accepted Islam, and Muhammad had even sent ambassadors to the neighboring Byzantine and Persian Empires to announce the new religion and encourage converts. Clearly Muhammad did not look upon Islam as only a religion of the Arabs and eagerly sought converts other than the residents of the Arabian peninsula.

The Death of Muhammad

Muhammad died on June 8, 632, in Medina. He succumbed to a fever, probably induced by the great strains brought on by constant campaigns for new converts and the unrelenting demands for his attention. Muslims at first refused to accept his death, but were reassured by Abu Bakr, who recited this verse from the Quran:

> ***Muhammad is only a messenger: many are the messengers who have died before him; if he dies, or is slain, will you turn back on your heels? (3:144)***

On the day of Muhammad's death, the question of leadership of the faithful was solved by the democratic election of Abu Bakr, who became the Prophet's first successor or caliph (from the Arabic khalifa). Abu Bakr was not looked upon as a prophet; Muhammad was seen as the last and the greatest of Allah's messengers. The caliph was regarded as the head of the Islamic Ummah.

The significance of Muhammad to the birth and growth of Islam is impossible to overestimate. The Prophet and his message inspired his followers to create and work for the betterment of a society united by the Islamic faith. Tribal loyalties were replaced by faith in the One God, who chose to speak to his people in their own language through a messenger who was also one of their own.

Soon after Muhammad's death, his followers and companions, many of whom were scholars and teachers, began to collect and codify his teachings and actions. The result of their efforts was the hadith, or reports of the activities and sayings of Muhammad. The hadith has become an important source of values and ethical paths of behavior for the Islamic world. The Sunnah, the custom or practice of the Prophet, is grounded in the hadith and serves as a pattern for a model way of life to be imitated by the faithful. Sunni Islam is therefore based on imitation of the Prophet's behavior as a proper goal for a meaningful life. Approximately 85 percent of the modern world's Muslims are Sunni.

The Islamic Faith and Law

Islam places great emphasis on the necessity of obedience to God's law in addition to faith. The Quran is the fundamental and ultimate source of knowledge about Allah and the proper actions of his followers. This holy book contains the theology of Islam, in addition to the patterns of ethical and appropriate conduct to which a Muslim must subscribe. Included in the Quran are some basic concepts which are held in common by the Islamic community as fundamental to the faith.

The Quran

Muslims believe that the Quran contains the actual word of God as it was revealed to Muhammad through divine inspiration. These revelations to the Prophet took place over a period of more than 20 years. Before Muhammad's death, many of these messages had been written down in order to be preserved. Muhammad himself began the work of preservation, and Abu Bakr, the first caliph, continued the process by compiling revelations which up to that time had been memorized by the followers and passed on by word of mouth. A complete written text of the Quran was produced shortly after Muhammad's death, with particular care taken to eliminate discrepancies and record only one standard version. This authorized and final edition was then transmitted to various parts of the new Islamic Empire and used to assist in the conversion of unbelievers. The text of the Quran has existed virtually unchanged for 14 centuries.

The Quran was intended to be recited aloud; much of the power of the Quran comes from the experience of reciting, listening, and feeling the message. It was in this manner that Muhammad converted his followers. The Quran is never to be translated from the Arabic for the purpose of worship. Because the followers of Islam had to learn the Quran in Arabic, the spread of Islam created a great amount of linguistic unity. Arabic replaced many local languages as the language of daily use, and the great majority of the Muslim world from Morocco to Iraq is still Arabic-speaking. In addition, the Quran remains the basic document for the study of Islamic theology, law, social institutions, and ethics. The study of the Quran remains at the heart of all Muslim scholarship, from linguistics and grammatical inquiry to scientific and technical investigation.

The Tenets of Islamic Faith

Monotheism is the central principle of Islam. Tahwid means the unity or oneness of God; there is no other God but Allah, and this belief is proclaimed five times daily as the believers are called to prayer with these words:

> ***God is most great. I testify that there is no God but Allah. I testify that Muhammad is the Messenger of Allah. Come to prayer, come to revelation, God is most great! There is no God but Allah.***

Allah is the one and only God, unchallenged by other false divinities and unlike all others in the strength of his creative power. All life, in fact all creation, is the responsibility of Allah alone. His nature is described in many ways and through many metaphors, one of the most beautiful as "light."

> ***Allah is the light of the heaven and the earth. . . . His light is as a niche wherein is a lamp. The lamp is in a glass. The glass is as it were a shining star. [The lamp is] kindled from a blessed tree, an olive neither of the East or the West, whose oil would almost glow forth [of itself] though no fire touched it. Light upon light, Allah guided unto His light whom He will. And Allah speaketh to mankind in allegories, for Allah is Knower of all things.***
>
> ***[This lamp is found] in houses which Allah hath allowed to be exalted and that His name shall be remembered therein. Therein do offer praise to Him at noon and evening. (Quran, 24:35)***

Islam also recognizes the significance and the contributions of prophets who preceded Muhammad. From the beginnings of human history, Allah has communicated with his people either by the way of these prophets, or by written scriptures:

This Quran leaf from the eighth or ninth century illustrates the austere formality and elegance of the Kufic form of Arabic calligraphy. Vowel marks appear as dots of various colors, while the tenth verse marker (in the third line) is a triangle of six dots. It is not unusual for as few as three lines of calligraphy to appear on a single page.

> ***Lo! We inspire thee as We inspired Noah and the Prophets after him, as We inspired Abraham and Ishmael and Isaac and Jacob and the tribes, and Jesus and Job and Jonah and Aaron and Solomon and as We imparted unto David the Psalms. (Quran, 4:164)***

Twenty-eight such prophets are mentioned in the Quran as the predecessors of Muhammad, who is believed to have been the last and greatest of all of Allah's messengers. Muhammad is given no divine status by Muslims, even though he was the one chosen to proclaim Allah's message of salvation in its perfected form and final revelation; in fact, Muhammad took great care to see that he was not worshipped as a god.

The creation of the universe and all living creatures within it is the work of Allah; harmony and balance in all of creation was ensured by God. In addition to humans and other creatures on the earth, angels exist to protect humans and to pray for forgiveness for the faithful. Jinn are spirits who may be good or bad, and forces known as "the unseen" exist on a level unknown to humans.

Men and women are given a special status in the pattern of the universe, since Allah has endowed them with the ability to know and react to him better than any other living creatures. They can choose to obey, or to reject Allah's will and deny him. Allah's message includes the belief in a Day of Resurrection when people will be held responsible for their actions and rewarded or punished accordingly for eternity.

Geographic imagery played an important role in the Prophet's description of heaven and hell: Both are depicted in a manner that brings forth an immediate reaction from people living in the desert. Those who have submitted to Allah's law—the charitable, humble, and forgiving—and those who have preserved his faith, shall dwell in a Garden of Paradise, resting in cool shade, eating delectable foods, attended by "fair ones with wide, lovely eyes like unto hidden pearls," and hearing no vain speech or recrimination but only "Peace! Peace!" This veritable oasis is far different from the agonies of the desert hell that awaits the unbelievers, the covetous, and the erring. Cast into a pit with its "scorching wind and shadow of black smoke," they will drink boiling water and suffer forever.

The Five Pillars

Islam is united in the observance of the Five Pillars, or five essential duties that all Muslims are required to perform to the best of their ability. These obligations are accepted by Muslims everywhere and thus serve to further unite the Islamic world. The first obligation is a basic profession of faith, by which a believer becomes a Muslim. The simple proclamation (shahada) is repeated in daily prayers. Belief in the One God and imitation of the exemplary life led by his Prophet are combined in the profession of faith.

Prayer (salat) is said five times a day, when Muslims are called to worship by the muezzin ("caller to prayer") who leads the recitation of the faithful from atop the minaret of the mosque (masjid, or "place of prostration"). During prayer, Muslims face Mecca, and in so doing give recognition to the birthplace of Islam and the unity of the Islamic community. Prayer can be given alone, at work, at home, or in the mosque.

A Muslim is required to give alms (zakat) to the poor, orphans, and widows, and to assist the spread of Islam. The payment of alms is not considered to be a charitable activity, but rather a social and religious obligation to provide for the welfare of the Ummah. Muslims are generally expected to contribute a percentage (usually 2.5 percent) of their total wealth and assets annually in alms.

Muslims are requested to fast (siyam) during the holy month of Ramadan, the ninth month of the Islamic lunar calendar. From sunrise to sunset, adult Muslims in good health are to avoid food, drink, and sexual activity. Finally, every Muslim is called to make a pilgrimage (hajj) to Mecca at least once in his or her lifetime, in the twelfth month of the Islamic year. The focus of the pilgrimage is the Kaaba in the Grand Mosque of Mecca. The hajj once again emphasizes the unity of the Islamic world community and the adherence to Islamic law no matter where a Muslim may reside.

Islamic Law

It is not possible to separate Islam from its law, because law in the Muslim community is religious by its nature. Islam is a way of life as well as a religion, and at its heart is the Sharia, or "path," the law provided by Allah as a guide for a proper life. The Sharia gives the believers a perfect pattern of human conduct and regulates every aspect of a person's activities. Islamic law is considered to be established by God, and therefore unquestionably correct; God's decrees must be obeyed even if humans are incapable of understanding, since the Sharia is greater than human reason.

Islamic law, then, permeates all aspects of human conduct and all levels of activity—from private and personal concerns to those involving the welfare of the whole state. Family law is set forth in the Quran and is based on much earlier Arabic tribal patterns of develop-

DOCUMENT

The Quran

The Quran, dictated to Muhammad by Allah, is one of the most significant of all religious works. It is also one of the world's most beautiful works of literature. The following is a selection from Surah XXIII, entitled "The Believers."

In the name of Allah, the Beneficent, the Merciful.
Successful indeed are the believers
Who are humble in their prayers,
And who shun vain conversation,
And who are payers of the poor-due;
And who guard their modesty—
Save from their wives or the (slaves) that their right hands possess, for then they are not blameworthy,
But whoso craveth beyond that, such are transgressors—
And who are shepherds of their pledge and their covenant, and who pay heed to their prayers.
These are the heirs
Who will inherit Paradise. There they will abide.
Verily We created man from a product of wet earth;
Then placed him as a drop (of seed) in a safe lodging;
Then fashioned We the drop a clot, then fashioned We the clot a little lump, then fashioned We the little lump bones, then clothed the bones with flesh, and then produced it as another creation. So blessed be Allah, the Best of Creators!
Then lo! after that ye surely die.
Then lo! on the Day of Resurrection ye are raised (again).
And We have created above you seven paths, and We are never unmindful of creation.
And We send down from the sky water in measure, and We give it lodging in the earth, and lo! We are able to withdraw it.
Then We produce for you therewith gardens of date-palms and grapes, wherein is much fruit for you and whereof ye eat;
And a tree that springeth forth from Mount Sinai that groweth oil and relish for the eaters.
And lo! in the cattle there is verily a lesson for you. We give you to drink of that which is in their bellies, and many uses have ye in them, and of them do ye eat;
And on them and on the ship we are carried.
Then We sent Moses and his brother Aaron with Our tokens and a clear warrant
Unto Pharaoh and his chiefs, but they scorned (them) and they were despotic folk.
And they said: Shall we put faith in two mortals like ourselves, and whose folk are servile unto us?
So they denied them, and became of those who were destroyed.
And We verily gave Moses the Scripture, that haply they might go aright.
And We made the son of Mary and his mother a portent, and We gave them refuge on a height, a place of flocks and water-springs.
O ye messengers! Eat of the good things, and do right. Lo! I am Aware of what ye do.
And lo! this your religion is one religion and I am your Lord, so keep your duty unto Me.
Say: In Whose hand is the dominion over all things and He protecteth, while against Him there is no protection, if ye have knowledge?
They will say: Unto Allah (all that belongeth). Say: How then are ye bewitched?
Nay, but We have brought them the Truth, and lo! they are liars.
Allah hath not chosen any son, nor is there any God along with Him; else would each God have assuredly championed that which he created, and some of them would assuredly have overcome others. Glorified be Allah above all that they allege.
Knower of the invisible and the visible! and exalted be He over all that they ascribe as partners (unto Him)!

From *The Meaning of the Glorious Koran, An Explanatory Translation* by Muhammed Marmaduke Pickthall. Published by Unwin Hyman, of HarperCollins Publishers Limited. Reprinted by permission.

ment. Islamic law emphasizes the patriarchal nature of the family and society. Marriage is expected of every Muslim man and woman unless physical infirmity or financial inability prohibits it. Muslim men can marry non-Muslim women, preferably Christians or Jews, since they too are "people of the Book," but Muslim women are forbidden to marry non-Muslim men. The Quran had the effect of improving the status and opportunities of women in Islam, as opposed to the older and traditional Arabic patterns of conduct. Women can contract their own marriages, keep and maintain their own dowries, and manage and inherit property.

The Quran allows Muslim men to marry up to four wives, but polygamy is not required. Co-wives must be treated with equal support and affection. Many modern-day Muslims interpret the Quran as encouraging monogamy; the practice of polygamy may have arisen in order to provide protection and security in early Islamic society, when women outnumbered men because of the toll of constant warfare.

For Islamic society as a whole, the law is considered to be universal and equally applied. Islamic law is considered to be God's law for all humankind, not only for the followers of Islam. In addition to its theology, Islam offers to its believers a system of government, a legal foundation, and a pattern of social organization. The Islamic Ummah was and is an excellent example of a theocratic state, one in which all power resides in God, in whose behalf political, religious, and other forms of authority are exercised. In fact, there is not even the combination of church and state in Islam, because there is no "church" or religious organization. The role of the state is to serve as the guardian of religious law. Also a characteristic of Islam is the principle of religious equality. There is no priesthood—no intermediaries between people and God. There are leaders of worship in the mosques as well as the ulema, a class of learned experts in the interpretation of the Quran, but they are all members of the secular community.

The Arab Empire of the Umayyads

Muhammad's victory over the Quraysh and the resulting allegiance of many of the Bedouin tribes of Arabia created a wholly new center of power in the Middle Eastern cradle of civilization. A backward, nonagrarian area outside the core zones of Egypt, Mesopotamia, and Persia suddenly emerged as the source of religious and political forces that would eventually affect the history of much of the known world. But when the prophet Muhammad died quite suddenly in 632, it appeared that his religion might altogether disappear. Despite internal disputes, the Muslim community held together and soon expanded beyond Arabia. Muhammad's old adversaries, the Quraysh tribe of the Ummaya clan, emerged after several years' struggle as the dominant force within the Islamic community. Under Umayyid rule, the Arabs rapidly built a vast empire, which had established the foundations for an enduring Islamic civilization by the time of its fall in the middle of the 8th century C.E.

Many of the Bedouin tribes that had converted to Islam renounced the new faith in the months after Muhammad's death, and his remaining followers quarreled over who should succeed him. Though these quarrels were never fully resolved, the community managed to find new leaders who directed a series of campaigns to force those who had abandoned Islam to return to the fold. Having united most of Arabia under the Islamic banner by 633, Muslim military commanders began to mount serious expeditions beyond the peninsula, where only probing attacks had occurred during the lifetime of the prophet and in the period of tribal warfare after his death. The courage, military prowess, and religious zeal of the warriors of Islam, and the weaknesses of the empires that bordered on Arabia, resulted in stunning conquests in Mesopotamia, North Africa, and Persia, which dominated the next two decades of Islamic history. The empire built from these conquests was Arab rather than Islamic. Most of it was ruled by a small Arab warrior elite, led by the Umayyads and other prominent clans, who had little desire to convert the subject populations, either Arab or otherwise, to the new religion.

Consolidation and Division in the Islamic Community

The leadership crisis brought on by Muhammad's death in 632 was compounded by the fact that he had not appointed a successor or even established a procedure by which a new leader might be chosen. Opinion within the Muslim community was deeply divided as to who should succeed him. In this moment of extreme danger, a strong leader who could hold the Islamic community together was urgently needed. On the afternoon Muhammad died, one of the clans that remained committed to the new faith called a meeting to select a new leader who would be designated as the caliph, the political and religious successor to Muhammad. Several choices were possible, and a deadlock between the clans appeared likely—a deadlock that would almost certainly have been fatal to a community threatened by enemies on all sides. One of the main candidates, Ali, the cousin and son-in-law of Muhammad, was passed over because he was considered too young to assume a position of such great responsibility. This decision was later to prove a major source of division in the Islamic community. But in 632, it appeared that a difficult reconciliation had been won by the choice of one of Muhammad's earliest followers and closest friends, Abu Bakr (caliph from 632 to 634).

In addition to his personal courage, warmth, and wisdom, Abu Bakr was well versed in the genealogical histories of the Bedouin tribes, which meant that he was well placed to determine which tribes could be turned against each other and which ones could be enticed into alliances. Initially at least, his mandate was very limited. He received no financial support from the Muslim community. Thus, he had to continue his previous occupation as a merchant on a part-time basis, and he only loosely controlled the better military commanders of the faithful.

These commanders turned out to be very able indeed. After turning back attacks on Mecca, the Islamic faithful routed one after another of the Bedouin tribes. The defeat of rival prophets and some of the larger clans in what were known as the Ridda Wars soon brought about the return of the Arabian tribes to the Islamic fold. Emboldened by the proven skills of his generals and the swelling ranks of the Muslim faithful, Abu Bakr oversaw raids to the north of Arabia into the sedentary zones in present-day Iraq and Syria and eastward into Egypt.

The unified Bedouin forces had originally intended merely to raid for booty and then retreat back into the desert. But their initial probes revealed the deep-seated rot and vulnerability of the Byzantine and Persian empires, which dominated or ruled directly the territories into which the Muslim warriors rode. The invaders were also prodded onward by the growing support of the Arab Bedouin peoples who had been migrating into the Fertile Crescent for centuries. These peoples had long served as the vassals and frontier guardians of the Byzantine and Persian empires. Now they joined their Arab brethren in a combined assault on the two empires.

Motives for Arab Conquests

The Arab warriors were driven by many forces. The unity provided by the Islamic faith gave them a new sense of common cause and strength. United, they could stand up to the non-Arab rulers who had so long played them against each other and despised them as unwashed and backward barbarians from the desert wastelands. It is also probable that the early leaders of the community saw the wars of conquest as a good way to release the pent-up energies of the martial Bedouin tribes they now sought to lead. Above all, the Bedouin warriors were drawn to the campaigns of expansion by the promise of a share in the booty to be won in the rich farmlands raided and the tribute that could be exacted from the towns and cities that came under Arab rule. As an early Arab writer observed, the Bedouins forsook their life as desert nomads not out of a promise of religious rewards, but because of a "yearning after bread and dates."

The chance to glorify their new religion may have been a motive for the Arab conquests, but they were not driven by a desire to win converts to it. In fact, other than fellow Bedouin tribes of Arab descent, the invaders had good reason to avoid mass conversions. Not only would Arab warriors have to share the booty of their military expeditions with ever larger numbers if converts were made, but Muslims were exempted from some of the more lucrative taxes levied on Christian and other non-Muslim groups. Thus, the vision of Islamic jihads, or holy wars, launched to forcibly spread the faith, which has long been associated with Islam in the Christian West, distorts the forces behind the early Arab expansion.

Weaknesses of the Adversary Empires

Of the two great empires that had once contested for dominance in the Fertile Crescent transit zone, the Sassanian Empire of Persia proved the more vulnerable. Power in the extensive Sassanian domains was formally concentrated in the hands of an autocratic emperor. By the time of the Arab explosion, the emperor was manipulated by a landed, aristocratic class that harshly exploited the cultivators who made up most of the population of the empire. Zoroastrianism, the official religion of the emperor, lacked popular roots. By contrast, the religion of a visionary reformer named Mazdak, which had won considerable support among the peasantry, had been brutally suppressed by the Sassanian rulers in the period before the rise of Islam.

At first, the Sassanian commanders had little more than contempt for the Arab invaders and set out against them with poorly prepared forces. By the time the seriousness of the Islamic threat was made all too clear by decisive Arab victories in the Fertile Crescent region and the defection of the Arab tribes on the frontier, Muslim warriors had broken into the Sassanian heartland. Further Muslim victories brought about the rapid collapse of the vast empire. The Sassanian rulers and their forces retreated eastward in the face of the Muslim advance. The capital was taken, armies were destroyed, and generals were slain. When, in 651, the last of the Sassanian rulers was assassinated, Muslim victory and the destruction of the empire were ensured.

Despite an equally impressive string of Muslim victories in the provinces of their empire, the Byzantines proved a more resilient adversary. Their ability to resist the Muslim onslaught, however, was impeded both by the defection of their own frontier Arabs and the support the Muslim invaders received from the Christians of Syria and Egypt. Members of the Christian sects dominant in these areas, such as the Copts and Nestorians, had long resented the rule of the Orthodox Byzantines, who taxed them heavily and openly persecuted them as heretics. When it became clear that the Muslims would not only tolerate the Christians but tax them less heavily than the Byzantines did, these Christian groups rallied to the Arabs.

Weakened from within and exhausted by the long wars fought with Persia in the decades before the Arab explosion, the Byzantines reeled from the Arab assaults. Syria, western Iraq, and Palestine were quickly taken by the Arab invaders, and by 640 a series of probes had been made into Egypt, one of the richest provinces of the empire. In the early 640s, the ancient center of learning and commerce, Alexandria, was taken, most of Egypt was occupied, and Arab armies extended their conquests into Libya to the west. Perhaps even more astounding from the point of view of the Byzantines, by the mid-640s the desert Bedouins were putting together war fleets that increasingly challenged the long-standing Byzantine mastery of the Mediterranean. The rise of Muslim naval supremacy in the eastern end of the sea sealed the loss of Byzantium's rich provinces in Syria and Egypt and opened the way to further Muslim conquests in North Africa, the Mediterranean islands, and even southern Italy. For a time the Byzantines managed to rally their forces and stave off further inroads into their Balkan and Asia Minor heartlands. But the early triumphs of the Arab invaders had greatly reduced the strength and magnificence of the Byzantine Empire. Though it would survive for centuries, it would henceforth be a kingdom under siege.

The Problem of Succession and the Sunni-Shi'ite Split

The stunning successes of Muslim armies and the sudden rise of an Arab empire covered over, for a time, continuing divisions within the community. The old division between the tribes of Mecca and Medina was compounded by differences between the tribes of north and south Arabia as well as between those who came to identify Syria as their homeland and those who settled in Iraq. Though these divisions were often generations old and the result of personal animosities, resentments had also begun to build over how the booty from the conquests ought to be divided among the tribal blocks that made up the Islamic community. In 656, just over two decades after the death of the prophet, the growing tensions broke into open violence.

The spark that began the conflict was the murder of the third caliph, Uthman, by mutinous warriors returning from Egypt. His death was the signal for the supporters of Ali to proclaim him as caliph. Uthman's unpopularity among many of the tribes, particularly those from Medina and the prophet's earliest followers, arose in part from the fact that he was the first caliph to be chosen from Muhammad's early enemies, the Umayyad clan. Already angered by the murder of their kinsman, the Umayyads rejected Ali's claims and swore revenge when he failed to punish Uthman's assassins. Warfare erupted between the two factions.

Ali was a famed warrior and experienced commander, and his deeply committed supporters soon gained the upper hand. After his victory at the Battle of the Camel in late 656, most of the Arab garrisons shifted to his side in opposition to the Umayyads, whose supporters were concentrated in the province of Syria and the holy city of Mecca. Just as Ali was on the verge of routing the Umayyad forces at the Battle of Siffin in 657, he was won over by a plea for mediation of the dispute. His decision to accept arbitration was fatal to his cause. Some of his most fervent adherents repudiated his leadership and had to be violently suppressed. While representatives of both parties tried unsuccessfully to work out a compromise, the Umayyads regrouped their forces and added Egypt to the provinces backing their claims. In 660, Mu'awiya, the new leader of the Umayyads, was proclaimed caliph in Jerusalem, thereby directly challenging Ali's position. A year later, Ali was assassinated, and his son, Hasan, was pressured by the Umayyads into renouncing his claims to the caliphate.

In the decades after the prophet's death, the question of succession generated deep divisions within the Muslim community. The split between the Sunnis, who backed the Umayyads, and the Shi'ites, or dissenters who supported Ali, remains to this day the most fundamental in the Islamic world. Hostility between these two branches of the Islamic faithful was further heightened in the years after Ali's death by the continuing struggle between the Umayyads and Ali's second son, Husayn. After being abandoned by the clans in southern Iraq, who had promised to rise in a revolt supporting his claims against the Umayyads, Husayn and a small party were overwhelmed and killed at Karbala in 680. From that point on, the Shi'ites mounted determined and sustained resistance to the Umayyad caliphate.

Over the centuries, factional disputes about who had the right to succeed Muhammad, with the shi'ites recognizing none of the early caliphs except Ali, have been compounded by differences in belief, ritual, and law that have steadily widened the gap between Sunnis and Shi'is. These divisions have been further complicated by the formation of splinter sects within the Shi'ite community in particular, beginning with those who defected from Ali when he agreed to arbitration of his and the Umayyads' claims.

The Umayyad Imperium

After a pause to settle internal disputes over succession, the remarkable sequence of Arab conquest was renewed in the last half of the 7th century. Muslim armies broke into central Asia, thus inaugurating a rivalry with Buddhism in the region that continues to the present day. By the early 8th century, the southern prong of this advance had reached into northwest India. Far to the west, Arab armies swept across North Africa and crossed the Straits of Gibraltar to conquer Spain and threaten France. Though the Muslim advance into western Europe was in effect checked by the hard-fought victory of Charles Martel and the Franks at Poitiers in 732, the Arabs did not fully retreat beyond the Pyrenees into Spain until decades later. Muslim warriors and sailors dominated much of the Mediterranean—a position that would be solidified by the conquest of key islands, such as Crete, Sicily, and Sardinia, in the early decades of the 9th century. By the early 700s, the Umayyads ruled an empire that extended from Spain in the west to the steppes of central Asia in the east. Not since the Romans had there been an empire to match it; never had an empire of its size been built so rapidly.

Though Mecca remained the holy city of Islam, under the Umayyads the political center of community shifted to Damascus in Syria, where the Umayyads chose to reside after the murder of Uthman. From Damascus a succession of Umayyad caliphs strove to build a bureaucracy that would bind together the vast domains they claimed to rule. The empire was very much an Arab conquest state. Except in the Arabian peninsula and in parts of the Fertile Crescent, a small Arab and Muslim aristocracy ruled over peoples who were neither Arab nor Muslim. Only Muslim Arabs were first-class citizens of this great empire. They made up the core of the army and imperial administration, and only they received a share of the booty derived from the ongoing conquests. They could be taxed only for charity. The Umayyads sought to keep the Muslim warrior elite concentrated in garrison towns and separated from the local population. It was hoped that isolation would keep them from assimilating to the subjugated cultures, because intermarriage meant conversion and the loss of taxable subjects.

Umayyad Decline and Fall

The ever-increasing size of the royal harem was just one manifestation of the Umayyad caliphs' growing addiction to luxury and soft living. Their legitimacy had been disputed by various Muslim factions from the outset of their seizure of the caliphate. But the Umayyads further alienated the Muslim faithful as they became more aloof in the early decades of the 8th century and retreated from the dirty business of war into their pleasure gardens and marble palaces. Their abandonment of the frugal, simple lifestyle followed by Muhammad and the earliest caliphs—including Abu Bakr, who made a trip to the market the day after he was selected to succeed the prophet—enraged the dissenting sects and sparked revolts throughout the empire. The uprising that would prove fatal to the short-lived dynasty began among the frontier warriors who had fought and settled in distant Iran.

By the middle decades of the 8th century, more than 50,000 warriors had settled near the oasis town of Merv in the eastern Iranian borderlands of the empire. Many of them had married local women, and over time they had come to identify with the region and to resent the dictates of governors sent from distant Damascus. The warrior settlers were also angered by the fact that they were rarely given the share of the booty, which was now officially tallied in the account books of the royal treasury, that they had earned by fighting the wars of expansion and defending the frontiers. They were contemptuous of the Umayyads and the Damascus elite, whom they viewed as corrupt and decadent. In the early 740s, an attempt by Umayyad palace officials to introduce new troops into the Merv area touched off a revolt that soon spread over much of the eastern portions of the empire.

Marching under the black banners of the Abbasid party, which traced its descent from Muhammad's uncle, al-Abbas, the frontier warriors were openly challenging

Umayyad armies by 747. Deftly forging alliances with Shi'ite rebels and other dissident groups that challenged the Umayyads throughout the empire, their leader, Abu al-Abbas, the great-great-grandson of the prophet's uncle, led his forces from victory to victory. Persia and then Iraq fell to the rebels. In 750, they met an army led by the Umayyad caliph himself in a massive Battle on the River Zab near the Tigris. The Abbasid victory resulted in the conquest of Syria and the capture of the Umayyad capital.

Desiring to eliminate the Umayyad family altogether to prevent recurring challenges to his rule, Abu al-Abbas invited numerous members of the clan to what was styled as a reconciliation banquet. As the Umayyads were enjoying the feast, guards covered them with carpets and they were slaughtered by Abbas's troops. An effort was then made to hunt down and kill all the remaining members of the family throughout the empire. Most were slain, but the grandson of a former caliph fled to distant Spain, and founded there the Caliphate of Cordoba, which was to live on for centuries after the rest of the empire had disappeared.

In this 15th-century Persian miniature, the Tigris River is shown flooding portions of the Abbasid capital at Baghdad.

From Arab to Islamic Empire: The Early Abbasid Era

The sudden shift from Umayyad to Abbasid leadership within the Islamic Empire reflected a series of even more fundamental transformations within the evolving Islamic civilization. The revolts against the Umayyads were fundamentally a product of growing regional identities and divisions within the Islamic world. As Islamic civilization spread even farther under the Abbasids, these regional interests and religious divisions made it increasingly difficult to hold together the vast areas the Arabs had conquered. They also gave rise to new cleavages within the Islamic community that have sapped its strength from within, from Abbasid times to the present day. The victory of the Abbasids led to bureaucratic expansion, absolutism, and luxury on a scale beyond the wildest dreams of the Umayyads. The Abbasids also championed a policy of active conversion and the admission of converts as full members of the Islamic community. As a result, Islam was transformed from the religion of a small, Arab warrior elite into a cosmopolitan and genuinely universal faith with tens of millions of adherents from Spain to the Philippine islands.

The rough treatment the Umayyad clan had received at the hands of the victorious Abbasids ought to have forewarned their Shi'ite and mawali allies of what was to come. But the Shi'ite and other dissenting groups continued the support that allowed the Abbasids to level all other centers of political rivalry until it was too late. Gradually, the Abbasids rejected many of their old allies, becoming in the process more and more righteous in their defense of Sunni Islam and increasingly less tolerant of what they termed the heretical views of the various sects of Shi'ism. With the Umayyads all but eliminated and their allies brutally suppressed, the way was clear for the Abbasids to build a centralized, absolutist imperial order.

The fact that they chose to build their new capital, Baghdad, in Iraq near the ancient Persian capital of Ctesiphon was a clear sign of things to come. Soon the Abbasid caliphs were perched atop jewel-encrusted thrones, reminiscent of those of the ancient Persian emperors,

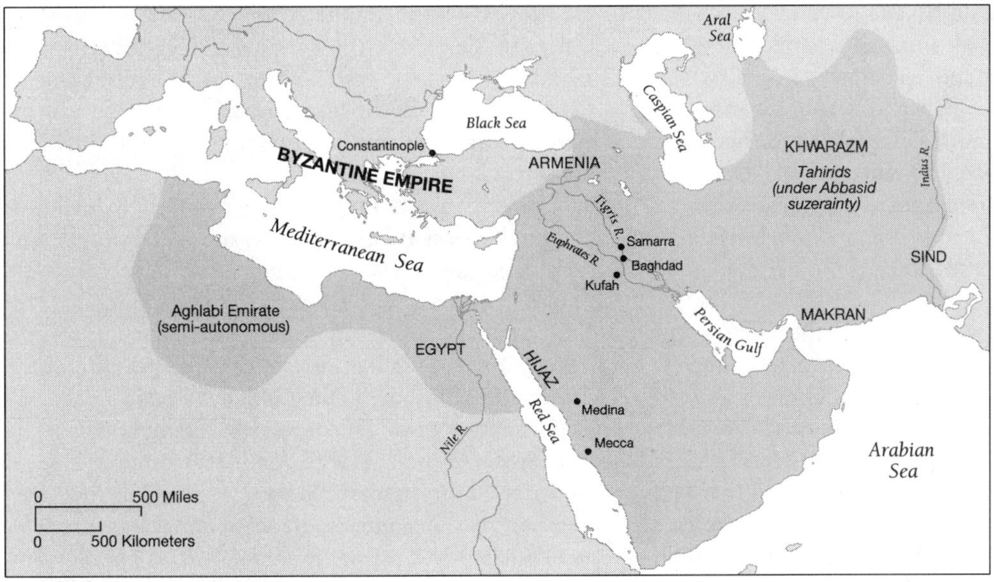

The Abbasid Empire at Its Peak, c. 900 C.E.

gazing down on the great gatherings of courtiers and petitioners who bowed before them in their gilt and marbled audience halls. The caliphs' palaces and harems expanded to keep pace with their claims to absolute power over the Islamic faithful as well as the non-Muslim subjects of their vast empire.

The ever-expanding corps of bureaucrats, servants, and slaves who strove to translate Abbasid political claims into reality lived and worked within the circular walls of the new capital at Baghdad. The bureaucratization of the Islamic Empire was reflected above all in the growing power of the wazir, or chief administrator and head of the caliph's inner councils, and of the sinister figure of the royal executioner, who stood close to the throne in the public audiences of the Abbasid rulers. The wazirs oversaw the building of an administrative infrastructure that allowed the Abbasids to project their demands for tribute to the most distant provinces of the empire. Sheer size, poor communications, and collusion between Abbasid officials and local notables meant that the farther the town or village was from the capital, the less effectively royal commands were carried out. But for well over a century, the Abbasid regime was fairly effective at collecting revenue from its subject peoples and preserving law and order over much of the empire.

The presence of the executioner perhaps most strikingly symbolized the absolutist pretensions of the Abbasid rulers. With a wave of his hand, a caliph could condemn the highest of Muslim nobles to death. Thus, even in matters of life and death, the Abbasids claimed a status above the rest of the Muslim faithful and even above Islamic law that would have been rejected as heretical by the early community of believers. Though they stopped short of declaring themselves divine, the Abbasid rulers styled themselves the "shadow of God on earth," beings clearly superior to ordinary mortals—Muslim or otherwise. The openness and accessibility of the earlier caliphs, including the Umayyads, had become more and more unimaginable. The old days, when members of the Muslim community could request an audience with the caliph merely by ringing a bell announcing their presence in the palace, were clearly gone. Now, just to get into the vast and crowded throne room, one had to bribe and petition numerous officials, and more often than not the best result would be to win a few minutes with the wazir or one of his assistants. If an official or notable were lucky enough to buy and beg an audience with the caliph, he had to observe an elaborate sequence of bowing and prostration in approaching the throne.

The "Good Life" in the Abbasid Age

The luxurious lifestyle of the Abbasid rulers and their courtiers reflected the new wealth of the political and commercial elites of the Islamic Empire and also intensified sectarian and social divisions within the Islamic community. As the compilation of folk tales, *The Thousand and One Nights* from many parts of the empire testifies, life for much of the elite in Baghdad and other major urban centers was luxurious and was oriented to the delights of the flesh. Caliphs and wealthy merchants lived in palatial residences of stone and marble, complete with gurgling fountains and elaborate gardens, which served as retreats from the glare and heat of the southern Mediterranean climate. In the Abbasid palaces, luxurious living and ostentation soared to fantastic heights. In the Hall of the Tree, for example, there was a huge artificial tree, made entirely of gold and silver and filled with gold mechanical birds that chirped to keep the caliph in good cheer.

Sexual enjoyment, which within the confines of marriage had been condoned rather than restricted by the Quran, often degenerated into eroticism for its own sake. The harem, replete with fierce eunuchs, insatiable sultans, and veiled damsels, provided outside observers with a stereotypic image of the Abbasid world that had little to do with the life of the average citizen of the empire—and often even little to do with that of the caliph and high officials. Yet, as is illustrated by the following passage from *The Thousand and One Nights* describing the interior of the mansion of a Baghdad notable, the material delights of the Abbasid era were enjoyed beyond the confines of the palace:

> ***They reached a spacious ground-floor hall, built with admirable skill and beautified with all manner of colors and carvings, with upper balconies and groined arches and galleries and cupboards and recesses whose curtains hung before them. In the midst stood a great basin full of water surrounding a fine fountain, and at the upper end on the raised dais was a couch of juniper wood set with gems and pearls, with a canopy-like mosquito curtain of red satin-silk looped up with pearls as big as filberts and bigger.***

Since the tales were just that—tall stories—there is some exaggeration of the wealth, as well as the romantic exploits and human excesses, of the world depicted. But for the free-living members of the elite classes, the luxuries, frivolities, and vices of the Abbasid age were very real indeed.

Islamic Conversion and Mawali Acceptance

The Abbasid era saw the full integration of new converts, both Arab and non-Arab, into the Islamic community. In the last decades of the Umayyad period, there was a growing acceptance of the mawali as equals and some effort to win new converts to the faith, particularly among Arab peoples outside the Arabian peninsula. In the Abbasid era, mass conversions to Islam were encouraged for all peoples of the empire, from the Berbers of North Africa in the west to the Persians and Turkic peoples of Central Asia in the east. Converts were admitted on an equal footing with the first generations of believers, and over time the distinction between mawali and the earlier converts all but disappeared.

Most converts were won over peacefully, owing to the great appeal of Islamic beliefs and to the considerable advantages they enjoyed over non-Muslim peoples in the empire. Not only were converts exempt from paying the head tax, but greater opportunities were open to them to get advanced schooling and launch careers as administrators, traders, or judges. No group demonstrated the new opportunities open to converts as dramatically as the Persians, who soon came to dominate the upper levels of imperial administration. In fact, as the Abbasid rulers became more dissolute and consequently less interested in affairs of state, several powerful Persian families close to the throne became the real locus of power within the imperial system.

Imperial Breakdown and Agrarian Disorder

In the last decades of the 9th century, the dynasty brought the slave armies under control for a time, but at a great cost. Incessant civil violence drained the treasury and alienated the subjects of the Abbasids. A further strain was placed on the empire's dwindling revenues by some caliphs' attempts to escape the perils and turmoil of Baghdad by establishing new capitals in the vicinity of the original capital. The construction of palaces, mosques, and public works for each of these new imperial centers added to the already exorbitant costs of maintaining the court and imperial administration. The burden of footing the bill, of course, fell heavily on the already hard-pressed peasantry of the central provinces of the empire, where some semblance of imperial control still remained.

The need to support growing numbers of mercenary troops also increased the revenue demands on the peasantry. Lacking the bureaucratic means to pay a regular salary to the commanders of the mercenary forces and stipends for their troops, the Abbasid regime farmed out the revenues from various parts of the empire to these military chiefs and their retainers. Some of the commanders were concerned for the welfare of the village populations under their control and tried to make improvements in irrigation and cropping patterns that would enhance the revenues they received over the long term. Unfortunately, the majority of the mercenary leaders tried to exact as much as possible from the hapless peasants.

Spiraling taxation and outright pillaging led to the destruction or abandonment of many villages in the richest provinces of the empire. The great irrigation works that had for centuries been essential to agricultural production in the fertile Tigris-Euphrates basin fell into disrepair and in some areas collapsed entirely. Some peasants perished through flood, famine, or violent assault; others fled to wilderness areas beyond the reach of the Abbasid tax farmers or to neighboring kingdoms. Some formed bandit gangs that grew in size and audacity or joined the crowds of vagabonds that trudged the highways and camped in the towns of the imperial heartland. At times, bandits and vagabonds were involved in the food riots in the towns or the local peasant rebellions that broke out periodically during the later Abbasid period. In many cases, dissident religious groups, such as the various Shi'ite sects, instigated these uprisings, thereby making them movements that not only challenged the legitimacy of the Abbasid regime but were dedicated to its utter destruction.

A forest of graceful arches fills the interior of the mosque at Cordoba in Spain. Such an architectural feat testifies to the depth and expansive power of Islamic civilization.

Nomadic Incursions and the Eclipse of Caliphal Power

Preoccupied by struggles in the capital and central provinces, the caliphs and their advisors were powerless to prevent further losses of territory in the outer reaches of the empire in addition to areas as close to the capital as Egypt and Syria. More alarmingly, by the mid-10th century, kingdoms that had formed in areas once part of the empire had begun to aspire to supplant the Abbasids as paramount lords of the Islamic world. In 945, the armies of one of these regional splinter dynasties, the *Buyids* of Persia, invaded the heartlands of the Abbasid Empire and captured Baghdad. From this point onward, the caliphs were little more than puppets controlled by families such as the Buyids, whose heads took the title of sultan and became the real rulers of what was left of the Abbasid Empire.

The Buyids controlled the caliph and the court, but they could not prevent the further disintegration of the empire. In just over a century, the Buyids' control over the caliphate was broken, and they were supplanted in 1055 by another group of nomadic invaders from central Asia via Persia, the *Seljuk Turks*. For the next two centuries, Turkic military leaders ruled the remaining portions of the Abbasid Empire in the name of caliphs, who were usually of Arab or Persian extraction. The Seljuks were staunch Sunnis, and they moved quickly to purge the Shi'ite officials who had risen to power under the Buyids and to rid the caliph's domains of the Shi'ite influences the Buyids had tried to promote.

For a time, the Seljuk military machine was also able to restore political initiative to the much-reduced caliphate. Seljuk victories ended the threat of conquest by a rival Shi'ite dynasty centered in Egypt, and it humbled the Byzantines, who had hoped to take advantage of Muslim divisions to regain some of their long-lost lands. The Byzantines' crushing defeat was particularly important because it opened the way to the settlement of Asia Minor, or Anatolia, by nomadic peoples of Turkic origins. The region later formed the nucleus for the powerful Ottoman Empire, and it comprises today the greater part of Turkey, the national home of the Turkic peoples.

The Impact of the Christian Crusades

Soon after seizing power, the Seljuks were confronted by another and very different challenge to Islamic civilization. It came from Christian Crusaders, knights from western Europe who were determined to capture the portions of the Islamic world that made up the Holy Land of biblical times. Muslim divisions and the element of surprise made the first of the Crusaders' assaults between 1096 and 1099 by far the most successful. Much of the Holy Land was captured and divided into Christian kingdoms. In June 1099, the main objective of the Crusade, Jerusalem, was taken while its Muslim and Jewish inhabitants were massacred by the rampaging Christian knights.

For nearly two centuries, the Europeans, who eventually mounted eight Crusades that varied widely in strength and success, were able to maintain their precarious beachhead in the eastern Mediterranean. But they posed little threat to the more powerful Muslim princes, whose disregard for the Christians was demonstrated by the fact that they continued to quarrel among themselves despite the intruders' aggressions. When united under a strong leader, as they were under Saladin in the last decades of the 12th century, the Muslims rapidly reconquered most of the crusader outposts. Saladin's death in 1193 and the subsequent breakup of his kingdom gave the remaining Christian citadels some respite, but the last of the crusader kingdoms was lost with the fall of Acre in 1291.

Undoubtedly, the impact of the Crusades was much greater on the Christians who launched them than on the Muslim peoples who had to fend them off. Because there had long been so much contact between western Europe and the Islamic world through trade and the Muslim kingdoms in Spain and southern Italy, it is difficult to be sure which influences to attribute specifically to the Crusades. But the Crusaders' firsthand experiences in the eastern Mediterranean certainly intensified the European borrowing from the Muslim world that had been going on for centuries. Muslim weapons, such as the famous damascene swords (named after the city of Damascus), were highly prized and sometimes copied by the Europeans, who were always eager to improve on their methods of making war. Muslim techniques of building fortifications were adopted by many Christian rulers, as can be seen in the castles built in Normandy and coastal England by William the Conqueror and his successors in the 11th and 12th centuries. Richard the Lionhearted's legendary preference for Muslim over Christian physicians was but one manifestation of the Europeans' avid and centuries-old interest in the superior scientific learning of Muslim peoples.

From Muslims and Jews in Spain, Sicily, Egypt, and the Middle East, the Europeans recovered much of the Greek learning that had been lost to northern Europe during the waves of nomadic invasions after the fall of Rome. They also mastered Arabic numerals and the decimal system, and they benefited from the great advances Arab and Persian thinkers had made in mathematics and many of the sciences. The European demand for Middle Eastern rugs and textiles is amply demonstrated by the Oriental rugs and tapestries that adorned the homes of the upper classes in Renaissance and early modern paintings as well as by such names for cloth as *fustian, taffeta, muslin,* and *damask,* which are derived from Persian terms or the names of Muslim cities where the cloth was produced and sold.

Muslim influences, from Persian and Arabic words and games such as chess (passed on from India) to chivalric ideals, troubadour ballads, and foods like dates, coffee, and yogurt, permeated both the elite and popular cultures of much of western Europe in this period. Some of these imports—namely, the songs of the troubadours—can be traced quite directly to the contacts the Crusaders made in the Holy Land. But most were part of a process of exchange that extended over centuries. In fact, the Italian merchant communities that remained after the political and military power of the Crusaders had been extinguished in the Middle East probably contributed a good deal more to this exchange than all the forays of Christian knighthood.

Of perhaps even greater significance, the "exchange" was largely a one-way process. Though they imported items such as fine glassware, weapons, and horses from Christian Italy and Byzantium, and beeswax, slaves, and timber from Russia and the Balkans, Muslim peoples in this era displayed little interest in the learning and products of the West. The Crusades reflected this imbalance. They had only a marginal effect on political and military developments in the Middle East, and, if anything, their cultural impact on Islamic civilization was even less.

Islamic Society and Culture

The driving force in Islamic civilization was the teachings of Muhammad, but wherever Islam spread, it assimilated native cultures. The result was the creation of a distinctive civilization, with major centers of culture in Damascus, Baghdad, Cairo, Córdoba, and, later, Delhi and Constantinople. The economy and the culture of the Islamic world had a substantial impact on the peoples of Europe and Asia.

Economic Life

As a merchant, Muhammad gave Islam a keen appreciation of commerce and, indeed, of all forms of productive activity, provided they were carried out in an honest, charitable spirit. Sayings attributed to him in the Hadith describe merchants as "the couriers of the horizons and God's trusted servants on earth," who, if honest, "will stand with the martyrs on the Day of Judgment." Tilling and sheepherding were occupations also created and blessed by God, but "the best of gain is from honorable trade and from a man's work with his own hands."[1] Muhammad condemned moneychangers, prostitutes, hoarders, greedy merchants, and lenders who charged usury (interest). Similar ethical maxims are found in contemporary Christian teaching and underscore the common attempt to curtail acquisitiveness and dishonesty on the one hand while instilling thrift and humaneness on the other. However, contemporary Christianity did not place a comparable positive emphasis on commerce per se.

Muslim trade routes eventually extended from the Pyrenees to the Indus. Muslim traders also traveled far beyond the boundaries of Islamic states, ranging as far as India, Southeast Asia, and China. Others crossed the Sahara into western and central Africa or sailed down Africa's east coast as far as Kilwa (in modern Tanzania). They traded as well with the peoples of Byzantium, western Europe, and Russia, though much of this commerce was in the hands of Jewish and Christian merchants. Ships carried most of the trade with Europe and Asia, but the primary route with China, the "Great Silk Way," ran overland through northern Persia and Turkestan. The fact that non-Muslim merchants could live and work in Islamic states enhanced commercial growth. Around 1285, for instance, the sultan of Egypt formally welcomed merchants "who come to his realm, as to the garden of Eden, by whatever gate they may choose to enter, from Iraq, from Persia, from Asia Minor, from the Hijaz [in Arabia], from India, and from China."[2] The absence of internal tariff barriers in the Muslim world between the eighth and twelfth centuries also fostered commercial expansion. So too did the development of bills of exchange (checks) and joint-stock companies, which enabled many people to invest in business activities, thus sharing both profits and risks.

Manufacturing in the Islamic world was extensive and varied. Linen, cotton, wool, and silk were among the products, as were glass, ceramics, metals, soaps, dyes, and perfume. Some areas were renowned for their manufactures: Córdoba for its leather, Egypt for glass and linens, Toledo and Damascus for steel, Kufah for silk kerchiefs, Baghdad and Samarkand for porcelain, and Bukhara (in central Asia) for carpets. The Muslims learned how to make paper from the Chinese in the eighth century and later founded their own mills. The widespread availability of paper stimulated scholarship and encouraged publishing.

Islamic Society

"The noblest among you in the eyes of God is the most pious," said Muhammad, "for God is omniscient and well informed." This principle could serve as a new basis for social valuation, in contrast to the traditional Arab recognition of an aristocracy based on birth and family ties. A similar position is expressed in the New Testament, but as Islam and Christianity evolved, each accommodated notions of a social hierarchy. Muhammad himself reportedly gave preeminence to the Arabs: "The best of mankind are the Arabs." "Love the Arabs," he insisted, "for three reasons: because I am an Arab, because the Koran is in Arabic, and because the inhabitants of Paradise speak Arabic."[3]

During the Umayyad period, Muslims recognized four social classes, the first of which comprised Arab Muslims, the de facto aristocracy. The government in Damascus recorded their names in a special registry and gave each Arab Muslim a regular payment from the imperial treasury. Initially, the government reserved the new garrison towns, such as Cairo and Kufah, for them alone. Arab families discouraged their female members from marrying non-Arabs.

Non-Arab Muslims made up the second class. Because they typically affiliated themselves with an Arab clan or family, they were known as *mawali,* or clients. By the early eighth century not only were they more numerous than the Arabs, but they resented their inferior status, especially since some of them were more educated than their Arab counterparts. Some mawali reacted by embracing Shi'ite views, while others claimed to have become Arabs through clientage. In time the Arabs of the conquered lands tended to intermarry with the mawali, giving rise to a broader definition of an Arab as one who spoke Arabic and embraced Islam.

The third class in Islamic society consisted of free non-Muslims, primarily Jews, Christians, and Zoroastrians. Such persons, known as *dhimmis,* or covenanted people, received personal security and substantial local autonomy in return for accepting Muslim rule and paying additional taxes. Dhimmis were free to worship according to their own rites, engage in business activities, own property, and for the most part govern themselves through their own laws and in their own courts. They could not hold public office, bear arms, testify in court against Muslims, dress in Muslim fashion, or use saddles on their horses. One such pact, dating from about the seventh century, specifically prohibited missionary activity: "We shall not manifest our religion publicly nor convert anyone to it. We shall not prevent any of our kin from entering Islam if they wish it." The same pact also made the dhimmis' inferior status very apparent: "We shall show respect toward the Muslims, and we shall rise from our seats when they wish to sit."[4] For the most part the dhimmis received more tolerance and respect than medieval European Christians accorded Jews. Periodically, repression occurred, however, as when the dhimmis' commercial success threatened the Muslims, when the latter suspected the dhimmis of collaborating with the crusaders or the Mongols, or when the dhimmis ignored the terms of their covenant.

Slaves were the lowest class in Islamic society. Although Muhammad had reservations about slavery, he accepted its legality. A saying in the Hadith may reveal his true feelings: "The worst of men are those who buy and sell men."[5] Muslims could not be enslaved, but conversion did not automatically bring manumission. Nor could masters and slaves marry, though the former could take slaves as concubines. The children of such a union were free, and their mother enjoyed a special status, could not be sold, and received her freedom when her master died. Children of slave parents, however, were born slaves.

The Islamic economy was not heavily dependent on slaves, as was the Roman Empire or the southern United States before the American civil war, but large numbers of slaves were traded and used primarily in the military or as servants. Some caliphs were the sons of slave mothers. The wealthiest Muslims possessed thousands of slaves. The Arabs enslaved prisoners, but they also purchased many slaves in markets. There were slaves of nearly all races and from a wide variety of places, including Spain, Greece, sub-Saharan Africa, India, and central Asia. So plentiful and varied was the supply that handbooks were available to guide consumers in the art of purchase. The advice included observations on the strengths and weaknesses of the various peoples: Greek women, for instance, "are good as treasurers because they are meticulous and not very generous," whereas Slavic women "live long because of their excellent digestion, but . . . are barren because they are never clean from menstrual blood."[6] Despite the popularity of slavery, Islamic teaching recommended manumission and urged that slaves be allowed to purchase their freedom.

Muslim Women

Women in traditional Arabic society, although important in the home, were subordinate to men. They could neither inherit nor claim a share of spoils won on the battlefield, and their husbands enjoyed an absolute right of divorce. In some instances baby girls were regarded with such disdain that they were buried alive at birth or killed at the age of 5 or 6. The Quran alludes to this practice—disapprovingly—in several places, as in an account of the Last Judgment, "when the buried infant shall be asked for what sin she was slain."[7]

Muhammad sought to improve the treatment of women, according them spiritual if not social equality. They were to be obedient to men, who were responsible for the management of affairs.

> ***Men are the managers of the affairs of women for that God has preferred . . . one of them over another, and for that they have expended of their property. Righteous women are therefore obedient. . . . And those you fear may be rebellious admonish; banish them to their couches, and beat them.***[8]

The proper relationship between husbands and wives, according to Muhammad, entailed love. Muslims conceived of marriage in contractual terms, with each party having rights and responsibilities. According to the Koran, a man could have up to four wives, but no woman was entitled to more than one husband. In practice, the expense of supporting more than one wife generally confined polygamy to the wealthy. Behind the practice of polygamy was the conviction that procreation was a fundamental purpose of marriage. "Your women," said Muhammad, "are a tillage [cultivated land] for you; so come unto your tillage as you wish."[9] Muhammad's comment hints at Islam's recognition of the importance of sexual pleasure for both men and women, an attitude strikingly different from the medieval Christian view of sex in essentially negative terms.

The Quran exhorted women to dress circumspectly, taking special care to cover their breasts and to draw their veils around them when they left the home. Such admonitions led free-born Muslim women in the towns to veil their faces in public and to seclude themselves within their own part of the home, known as the harem. The harem system did not originate with Islam but had roots in ancient Mesopotamia and was similar to the Byzantine practice of providing private apartments for women in their own homes. The harem became a characteristic part of Islamic society by the late eighth century. The seclusion of women in harems or behind veils, the practice of polygamy, and a willingness to beat disobedient wives underscore the fact that Islam, though making important advances over traditional Arab society, was far from establishing the social equality of the sexes. This is also apparent with respect to the inheritance of property; in pre-Islamic Arabic society, women could not inherit at all. The Quran lifted this absolute prohibition but still limited women's rights in specified circumstances.

In practice, the role of women in medieval Islam varied substantially. Some played an active part in politics, including the scheming that became a regular part of determining succession to the caliphate. The wife of the Ummayad caliph al-Walid I (705–715) engaged in political activities to promote justice and encouraged her husband to enlarge mosques. One of the greatest of the Abbasid caliphs, Harun al-Rashid (786–809), apparently owed his position to his fabulously wealthy mother, Khayzuran, a former slave, who may have had a rival son assassinated. Harun's wife, Zubaydah, contributed money to build an aqueduct in Mecca and took an interest in urban development, much as aristocratic Turkish women patronized hospitals and schools. Women were de facto rulers of Egypt in the 1020s, late 1040s, and 1250s.

Muslim women participated in a wide range of cultural and intellectual pursuits. During the Umayyad caliphate they provided salons in which scholars, poets, and other educated people could gather; prominent among such women was Muhammad's great-granddaughter, Sukaina. As in pre-Islamic society, women wrote poetry, and female professionals sang elegies at funerals. Throughout the Umayyad period, women studied law and theology, while in the caliphate of Córdoba women as well as men taught in schools. Female scholars were prominent in the towns of Muslim Spain, and some lectured at the universities of Córdoba and Valencia. Women were also active in the Sufi movement. The Abbasids employed women to spy against the Byzantines in the guise of merchants, physicians, and travelers, which suggests that they undertook such activities in their own society.

The status of Muslim women began to decline in the late Umayyad period owing to the large increase in the number of slave women that occurred during the territorial expansion of Islam. Increasingly, men saw women as objects, the possession of which reflected wealth. During the Abbasid caliphate, government decrees increasingly regulated the public appearances and clothing of women. Women were banned from public ceremonies. In twelfth-century Seville "decent women" could not dress like prostitutes or hold their own parties, even with their husbands' permission. Some of these regulations were intended to stress female modesty. In Seville women could not run hostels because of the possibility of sexual improprieties, and they could not enter Christian churches because the priests had reputations as fornicators and sodomites. In markets they could deal only with merchants of good reputation, and they could not sit by the riverbank in the summer in the presence of men. For the most part such regulations, though patronizing, suggest concern for the protection of women in Islamic society.

The Muslim Synthesis in Medicine, Science, and Philosophy

The Muslims assimilated and advanced the medical and scientific knowledge of classical antiquity. Because Muhammad had reportedly praised the study of medicine, the subject received considerable attention from medieval Muslim scholars, especially after the works of Galen, Hippocrates, and other classical writers were available in Arabic translations. The great age of medical advance occurred in the Abbasid period, when Muslims founded schools of medicine and hospitals; Baghdad alone had 860 physicians in the year 931.

The contributions of two men are especially noteworthy in this field: the Persian physician al-Razi (Rhazes; died c. 925), head of the Baghdad hospital, who wrote approximately 120 medical books, including a pioneering study of smallpox and measles; and the Persian scholar Ibn Sina (Avicenna; d. 1037), whose *Canon of Medicine* synthesized classical and Islamic medical knowledge, appeared in Latin translation in the twelfth century, and served as the leading medical text in Europe as late as the seventeenth century. Among the topics Ibn Sina explored were the contagious nature of tuberculosis, psychological disorders, and skin diseases. One of the keys to his success was his willingness to learn from practice: "I . . . attended the sick, and the doors of medical treatments based on experience opened before me to an extent that cannot be described."[10]

The importance of experimentation was evident in other sciences as well. Although alchemy—the attempt to transform common metals into gold and other valuable substances—failed to achieve its goal, its practitioners acquired valuable chemical knowledge and developed the world's first laboratories. Al-Razi classified all matter

DOCUMENT

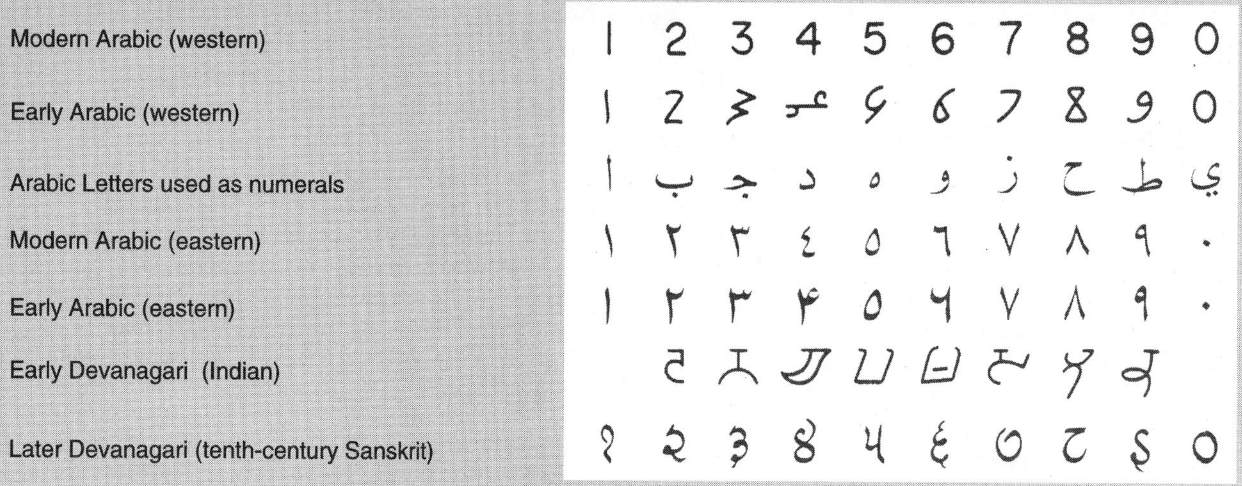
Modern Arabic (western)
1 2 3 4 5 6 7 8 9 0
Early Arabic (western)
Arabic Letters used as numerals
ا ب ج د ه و ز ح ط ي
Modern Arabic (eastern)
١ ٢ ٣ ٤ ٥ ٦ ٧ ٨ ٩ ٠
Early Arabic (eastern)
Early Devanagari (Indian)
Later Devanagari (tenth-century Sanskrit)

Arabic Numerals

The system of numeration employed throughout the greater part of the world today was probably developed in India, but because it was the Arabs who transmitted this system to the West the numerals it uses have come to be called Arabic.

After extending Islam throughout the Middle East, the Arabs began to assimilate the cultures of the peoples they had subdued. One of the great centers of learning was Baghdad, where Arab, Greek, Persian, Jewish, and other scholars pooled their cultural heritages and where in 771 an Indian scholar appeared, bringing with him a treatise on astronomy using the Indian numerical system.

Until that time the Egyptian, Greek, and other cultures used their own numerals in a manner similar to that of the Romans. Thus the number 323 was expressed like this:

Egyptian	999	∩∩	III
Greek	HHH	ΔΔ	III
Roman	CCC	XX	III

The Egyptians actually wrote them from right to left, but they are set down above from left to right to call attention to the similarities of the systems.

The Indian contribution was to substitute a single sign (in this case meaning "3" and meaning "2") indicating the number of signs in each cluster of similar signs. In this manner the Indians would render Roman CCC XX 111 as:

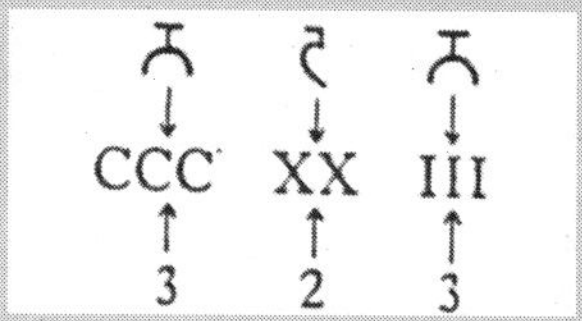

This new way of writing numbers was economical but not flawless. The Roman numeral CCC II, for instance, presented a problem. If a 3 and a 2 respectively were substituted for the Roman clusters CCC and II, the written result was 32. Clearly, the number intended was not thirty-two but three hundred and two. The Arab scholars perceived that a sign representing "nothing" or "nought" was required because the place of a sign gave as much information as its unitary value did. The place had to be shown even if the sign which showed it indicated a unitary value of "nothing." It is uncertain whether the Arabs or the Indians filled this need by inventing the zero, but in any case the problem was solved: now the new system could show neatly the difference between XXX II (32) and CCC II (302).

If the origin of this new method was Indian, it is not at all certain that the original shapes of the Arabic numerals also were Indian. In fact, it seems quite possible that the Arab scholars used their own numerals but manipulated them in the Indian way. The Indian way had the advantage of using much smaller clusters of symbols and greatly simplifying written computations. The modern forms of the individual numbers in both eastern Arabic and western Arabic, or European, appear to have evolved from letters of the Arabic alphabet.

The Semites and Greeks traditionally assigned numerical values to their letters and used them as numerals. This alphabetical system is still used by the Arabs, much as Roman numerals are used in the West for outlines and in enumerating kings, emperors, and popes.

The new mathematical principle on which the Arabic numerals were based greatly simplified arithmetic. Their adoption in Europe began in the tenth century after an Arabic mathematical treatise was translated by a scholar in Spain and spread throughout the West.

From "ARAMCO and Its World: Arabia and the Middle East," edited by Ismail I. Nawwab, Peter C. Speers, and Paul F. Hoye, Islam and Islamic History Section, published in 1980 by Arabian American Oil Company, Washington D.C.

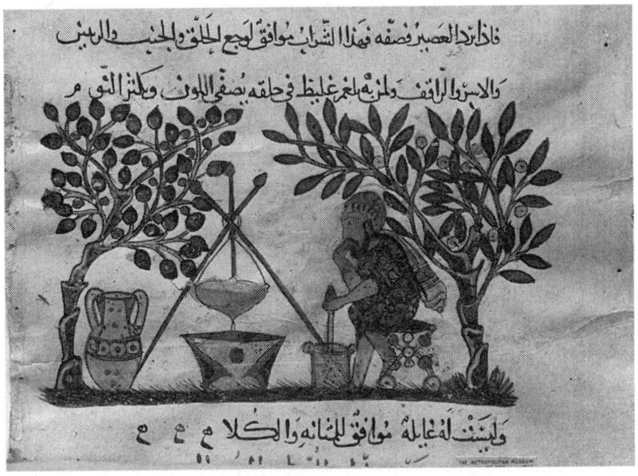

This Arabic miniature, which was painted around 1222–23, contains a recipe for cough medicine and shows an apothecary preparing it.

as animal, vegetable, or mineral and distinguished between volatile and nonvolatile substances. In the field of optics, Ibn al-Haytham (Alhazen; d. 1039) of Cairo rejected the classical theory that the eye emits visual rays, arguing instead that it sees by receiving rays of light. He devised experiments to study refraction, eclipses, and the atmosphere.

The Muslim ability to synthesize is perhaps best illustrated in the field of mathematics, where Islamic scholars adopted "Arabic" numerals from India, including zero and the placement of numbers in series to denote units, tens, hundreds, and so forth, and geometry and simple trigonometry from the Greeks. One of the leading scholars in this field was Muhammad ibn-Musa al-Khwarizmi, whose ninth-century treatises on arithmetic and algebra (*al-jabr*, "integration") later influenced Europeans. Later mathematical work involved quadratic and cubic equations and led to the development of analytical geometry and spherical trigonometry.

Beginning primarily in the twelfth century, Muslim advances in mathematics and science spread to Europe through Sicily and Spain, where the Jews played a crucial role as cultural intermediaries. In the sixteenth century those achievements provided much of the foundation for the scientific revolution.

Islamic philosophy was heavily indebted to the works of Plato, Aristotle, and the Neoplatonists. No question was more basic to Muslim philosophers than the proper relationship of reason to revelation. The most prominent of the early Arab philosophers, Yaqub al-Kindi (d. c. 870), attempted to reconcile Plato and Aristotle while insisting on the importance of knowing God and the universe as the key to immortality, a doctrine essentially derived from the Neoplatonists. When some philosophers insisted that reason was equal in importance to revelation as a means to acquire religious knowledge, al-Ghazali (d. 1111) sought to restore the primacy of belief, thereby preventing Islamic doctrine from becoming the monopoly of an educated clique of theologians. God, he insisted, could reveal divine mercy to the common people as well, for belief is

> ***a light which God bestows on the hearts of His creatures as the gift and bounty from Him, sometimes through an unexplainable conviction from within, sometimes because of a dream in sleep, sometimes by seeing the state of bliss of a pious man. . . sometimes through one's own state of bliss.***[11]

Al-Ghazali's attack on rationalist theologians prompted a defense of Aristotelian and Neoplatonic philosophy by the celebrated Ibn Rushd (Averroës, 1126–1198) of Córdoba, a judge and court physician. Like Ibn Sina, he was convinced that the truths of reason and revelation were compatible. The same truth, he argued, could be expressed either philosophically or symbolically; when, therefore, the Quran seemed to advocate an irrational belief, he resolved the apparent contradiction by interpreting the sacred texts allegorically. Through his extensive commentaries on Aristotle, which appeared in Latin translation in the thirteenth century, Ibn Rushd had a major impact on the development of scholastic thought in medieval universities. His views were equally influential in shaping late medieval Jewish philosophy, as reflected especially in the teaching of Gersonides (1288– c. 1344), a French rationalist noted for his commentaries on Aristotle. The Western religious and philosophical heritage is greatly indebted to Islam, not least for introducing European thinkers to much of Aristotle's work.

Islamic Literature

Medieval Muslims were fond of verse. Indeed, the Quran itself was written in quasi-verse form. A ninth-century Arabic scholar aptly summarized the importance of verse:

> ***Poetry is the mine of knowledge of the Arabs, the book of their wisdom, the muster roll of their history, the repository of their great days, the rampart protecting their heritage, the trench defending their glories, the truthful witness on the day of dispute, the final proof at the time of argument.***[12]

Verse was the medium used by Firdawsi (c. 935–c. 1020) to compose what became the Iranian national epic, the *Shah-Nameh* ("Book of Kings"), which recounted Persian history from legendary times to 641. Nearly 60,000 verses long, it was instrumental in establishing the definitive form of the Persian language, much as the King James Bible and the works of Shakespeare did for English.

Another Iranian poet, Shams ud-din Hafiz (c. 1325– c. 1389), composed some 500 short lyric poems using simple language and proverbial expressions. Most have three levels of meaning: a reflection of contemporary life in the Persian town of Shiraz, with much to say about wine and love; an expression of tribute to Hafiz' courtly patrons; and a statement of his Sufi beliefs through images readily understood by Iranian readers. Hafiz' works reveal sympathy for the common people, dislike of hypocrisy, and preoccupation with love:

> ***When your beauty radiated on creation's morn,***
> ***The world was set ablaze by love freshly born.***[13]

Hafiz influenced another major Sufi poet, Jami (1414–1492), whose mystical lyrics explored ethics and existence. His contemporary, the Indian poet Kabir (d. 1518), was also a mystic. Raised as a Muslim and influenced by Hindu teachings, Kabir taught the equality of all persons and their ability to achieve unity with God through personal devotion.

Apart from the Quran, the best-known Islamic literary work was *The Thousand and One Nights,* a collection of stories from the Middle East and Asia that were originally transmitted orally, much like the ancient Homeric epics. In their extant form, most are set against the background of Baghdad during the caliphate of Harun al-Rashid or Cairo under the Fatimids. A fragment of the work existed by the ninth century, although it was another 600 years or so before a final version emerged.

Final mention must be made of history as a literary form. The greatest medieval Muslim historian was the Tunisian Ibn Khaldun (1332–1406), a pioneer of sociological methodology in explaining the past. To write history, he insisted, required a knowledge of geography, climate, economics, religion, and culture. He called attention to the necessity of evaluating documents preparatory to writing history, since all records are likely to contain inaccuracies. These errors, he explained, are the result of partisanship, overconfidence, a chronicler's failure to grasp the meaning of what he has recorded, excessive faith in one's sources, the inability to place an event in proper context, a desire to gain favor from patrons, a reliance on myth, and exaggeration. A sense of group consciousness was basic to Ibn Khaldun's philosophy of history; a strong communal identity enabled a people to triumph, but their civilization decayed as that spirit weakened. This theory, he believed, explained the decline of the Abbasid caliphate and the triumph of two less cultured nomadic peoples, the Seljuk Turks and the Mongols.

The Legacy of the Abbasid Age

Though problems of political control and succession continued to plague the kingdoms and empires that divided the Muslim world, the central position of Islamic civilization in global history was solidified during the centuries of Abbasid rule. Its role as the go-between for the other, more ancient civilizations of the Eastern Hemisphere grew as Arab trading networks expanded and reached into new areas. More than ever, it became the civilizer of nomadic peoples, from the Turks and Mongols of central Asia to the Berbers of North Africa and the camel herders of the Sudan. Equally critically, Islam's original contributions to the growth and refinement of civilized life greatly increased. From its great cities and universities and the accomplishments they generated in the fine arts, sciences, and literature to its vibrant religious and philosophical life, Islam pioneered patterns of organization and thinking that would affect the development of human societies in major ways for centuries to come.

In the midst of all this achievement, however, there were tendencies that would put the Muslim peoples at a growing disadvantage, particularly in relation to their long-standing European rivals. Muslim divisions would leave openings for political expansion that the Europeans would eagerly exploit, beginning with the island Southeast Asian extremities of the Islamic world and then working their way across Muslim North India. The Muslims' inclination to leave commerce and entrepreneurship increasingly in the hands of non-Muslim groups, such as Jews and Christians, would hamper effective responses to their growing economic dependence on the West and other civilizations, particularly China, and their increasing backwardness relative to them. Above all, the growing orthodoxy and intolerance of the ulama, as well as the Muslim conceit that the vast Islamic world contained all requirements for civilized life, caused Muslim peoples to grow less receptive to outside influences and innovations. These tendencies became increasingly pronounced at precisely the time when their Christian rivals were entering a period of unprecedented curiosity, experimentation, and exploration of the world beyond their own civilized regions. The combination of these trends would put the Islamic world at a growing disadvantage vis-à-vis the West and would eventually engender a profound crisis in Islamic civilization that continues in the present day.

NOTES

1. B. Lewis, trans. and ed., *Islam from the Prophet Muhammad to the Capture of Constantinople* (New York: Walker, 1974), vol. 2, pp. 125–129.
2. Ibid., p. 166.
3. Ibid., pp. 195–196.
4. Ibid., p. 218.
5. Ibid., p. 128.
6. Ibid., pp. 246–247, 250.
7. *Koran Interpreted,* vol. 2, p. 326.
8. Ibid., vol. 1, pp. 105–106.
9. Ibid., p. 59.
10. Lewis, *Islam,* vol. 2, p. 179.
11. Ibid., p. 21.
12. Ibid., p. 173.
13. *The Divan,* 87:1–2.

CHAPTER 8

African Civilizations and the Spread of Islam

KEY TERMS

stateless society
Sahara
Nubia
Ethiopia
Sudanic kingdoms
Mali
Sundiata
Songhay
slavery
Swahili
Yoruba
Benin
Kongo
Mwene Mutapa
Great Zimbabwe

DISCUSSION QUESTIONS

How was Islam transmitted to Africa?

How did Islam adapt itself to African customs?

To what extent did traditional African societies remain untouched by Islam?

INTRODUCTION

The spread of Islam, from its heartland in the Middle East and North Africa to India and Southeast Asia, revealed the power of the religion and its commercial and sometimes military attributes. Civilizations were altered without being fully drawn into a single Islamic statement. A similar pattern developed in sub-Saharan Africa as Islam provided new influences and contacts without amalgamating African culture as a whole to the Middle Eastern core. New religious, economic, and political patterns developed in relation to the Islamic surge, but great diversity remained.

Africa below the Sahara was never totally isolated from the centers of civilization in Egypt, west Asia, or the Mediterranean, but for long periods the contacts were difficult and intermittent. During the ascendancy of Rome, sub-Saharan Africa, like northern Europe, was on the periphery of the major centers of civilization. After the fall of Rome, the civilizations of Byzantium and the Islamic world provided a link between the civilizations of the Middle East and the Mediterranean as well as the areas, such as northern Europe and Africa, on their frontiers. In Africa, between roughly 800 and 1500 C.E., the frequency and intensity of contact with the outside world increased as part of the growing international network. Social, religious, and technological changes took place that influenced many of the different peoples throughout the vast and varied continent. Chief among these changes was the arrival of the followers of the Prophet Muhammad.

The spread of Islam across much of the northern third of Africa produced profound effects on both those who converted and those who resisted the new faith. Islamization also served to link Muslim Africa even more closely to the outside world through trade, religion, and politics. Trade and long-distance commerce, in fact, was carried out in many parts of the continent and linked regions beyond the orbit of Muslim penetration. Until about 1450, however, Islam provided the major external contact between sub-Saharan Africa and the world.

State building took place in many areas of the continent under a variety of conditions. West Africa, for example, experienced both the cultural influence of Islam and its own internal dynamic of state building and civilizational developments that produced, in some places, great artistic accomplishments. The formation of some powerful states, such as Mali and Songhay, depended more on military power and dynastic alliances than on ethnic or cultural unity. In this aspect and in the process of state formation itself, Africa paralleled the roughly contemporaneous developments of western Europe. The development of city-states, with strong merchant communities in West Africa and on the Indian Ocean coast of East Africa, bore certain similarities to the urban developments of Italy and Germany in this period. However, disparities between the technologies and ideologies of Europeans and Africans by the end of this period also created marked differences in the way in which their societies developed. The arrival of western Europeans—the Portuguese—in the 15th century set in motion a series of exchanges that would draw Africans increasingly into the world economy and create a new set of relationships that would characterize African development for centuries to come.

Several emphases thus highlight the history of Africa in the postclassical centuries. Northern Africa and the East African coast became increasingly incorporated into the Arab Muslim world, but even other parts of the continent reflected the power of Islamic thought and institutions. New centers of civilization and political power arose in several parts of sub-Saharan Africa, illustrating the geographical diffusion of civilization. African civilizations, however, built somewhat less clearly on prior precedent than was the case in other postclassical societies. Some earlier themes, such as the Bantu migration and the formation of large states in the western Sudan, persisted. Overall, sub-Saharan Africa remained a varied and distinctive setting; parts of it were drawn into new contacts with the growing world network, but much of it retained a certain isolation.

100–200 Camels introduced for trade in the Sahara

300 Origins of the kingdom of Ghana

600–700 Islam spreads across North Africa

1000 Ghana at height of its power

1100 Almoravid movement in the Sahara

100 C.E. — **600** C.E. — **1000** C.E.

African Societies: Diversity and Similarities

African societies developed diverse forms from large centralized states to stateless societies organized around kinship or age sets rather than central authority. Within this diversity were many commonly shared aspects of language and beliefs. Universalistic faiths did penetrate the continent and serve as the basis for important cultural developments in Nubia and Ethiopia.

The continent of Africa is so vast and its societies are so diverse that it is almost impossible to generalize about them. Differences in geography, language, religion, politics, and other aspects of life contributed to the diversity and to Africa's lack of political unity over long periods of time. Unlike many parts of Asia, Europe, and North Africa, neither universal states nor universal religions characterized the history of sub-Saharan Africa. Yet universal religions, first Christianity and later Islam, did find adherents in Africa and sometimes contributed to the formation of large states and empires.

Stateless Societies

While some African societies had rulers who exercised control through a hierarchy of officials in what can be called states, other African societies were "stateless": organized around kinship or other forms of obligation and lacking the concentration of political power and authority we normally associate with the state. The African past reveals that the movement from stateless to state societies was not necessarily an evolutionary development. Stateless peoples who lived in villages organized around either lineages or age sets—that is, groups of people of the same age who are considered to have similar responsibilities to society—did not need rulers or bureaucracies and existed side by side with states. Sometimes the *stateless societies* were larger and more extensive than the neighboring states. Stateless societies had forms of government, but the authority and power normally exercised by a ruler and his court in a kingdom could be held instead by a council of families or by the community, with no need to tax the population to support the ruler, the bureaucrats, the army, or the nobles as was usually the case in state-building societies. Stateless societies had little concentration of authority, and that authority affected only a small part of the peoples' lives. In these societies, government was rarely a full-time occupation.

Other alternatives to formal government were also possible. Among peoples of the West African forest, secret societies of men and women exercised considerable control over customs and beliefs and were able to limit the authority of rulers. Especially among peoples who had sharp rivalries between lineages or family groupings, secret societies developed that cut across the lineage divisions. The secret societies incorporated their members after an initiation that might have been based on knowledge, skills, physical tests, an initiation fee, or all of these. Members took on an allegiance to the society that transcended their lineage ties. The secret societies settled village disputes; enforcement or punishment was carried out by masked junior members acting on behalf of the secret society so that no feuding between families resulted. The secret societies acted to maintain stability within the community, and they served as an alternative to the authority of state institutions.

Throughout Africa many stateless societies thrived, perhaps aided by the fact that internal social pressures or disputes could often be resolved by the splitting off of dissidents and the establishment of a new village in the relatively sparsely populated continent. Fragmentation and a "frontier" open to new settlement were constant features in much of African history. Still, stateless societies found it difficult to meet external pressures, mobilize for warfare, organize large building projects, or create stable conditions for continuous long-distance trade with other peoples. All these needs or goals contributed in various ways to the formation of states in sub-Saharan Africa.

1200 Rise of the empire of Mali

1260 Death of Sundiata; earliest stone buildings at Zimbabwe; Lalaibela rules in Ethiopia; Yoruba culture flourishes at Ile-Ife

1300 Mali at its height; Kanem Empire as a rival

1324 Pilgrimage of Mansa Musa

1400 Flourishing of cities of Timbuktu and Jenne; Ethiopian Christian kingdom; Swahili cities flourish on East Africa coast

1417, 1431 Last Chinese trade voyages to East Africa

1500 Songhai Empire flourishes; Benin at height of its power

1200 C.E. — **1400** C.E.

DOCUMENT

Ibn Battuta
Travels in Africa
(1364)

Muhammad Ibn Abdullah Ibn Battuta (1304–1377) spent most of his long life traveling in Asia and Africa. He was born in Tangier and made the first of his four pilgrimages to Mecca at the age of 25. After performing his religious obligations Ibn Battuta kept traveling for 24 years. He visited all of the Muslim states of the Middle East as well as Sri Lanka, India, and China. Ibn Battuta remains one of the central sources of knowledge about African and Muslim civilization in this early period.

These people have remarkable and strange ways. As for their men, they feel no jealousy. None of them traces his descent through his father, but from his maternal uncle, and a man's heirs are the sons of his sister only, to the exclusion of his own sons. This is something that I have seen nowhere in the world except among the Indian infidels in the land of Mulāybar, whereas these are Muslims who observe the prayer and study fiqih and memorize the Quran. As for their women, they have no modesty in the presence of men and do not veil themselves in spite of their assiduity in prayer. If anybody wishes to marry one of them he may do so, but they do not travel with the husband, and if one of them wished to do so her family would prevent her.

The women there have friends and companions among the foreign men, just as the men have companions from among the foreign women. One of them may enter his house and find his wife with her man friend without making any objection.

One day I went into the presence of Abū Muhammad Yandakān al-Masūfi in whose company we had come and found him sitting on a carpet. In the courtyard of his house there was a canopied couch with a woman on it conversing with a man seated. I said to him: "Who is this Woman?" He said: "She is my wife." I said: "What connection has the man with her?" He replied: "He is her friend." I said to him: "Do you acquiesce in this when you have lived in our country and become acquainted with the precepts of the Shar'?" He replied: "The association of women with men is agreeable to us and a part of good conduct, to which no suspicion attaches. They are not like the women of your country." I was astonished at his laxity. I left him, and did not return thereafter. He invited me several times but I did not accept.

WHAT I APPROVED OF AND WHAT I DISAPPROVED OF AMONG THE ACTS OF THE SŪDĀN

One of their good features is their lack of oppression. They are farthest removed of people from it and their sultan does not permit anyone to practise it. An-

Common Elements in African Societies

Even amid the diversity of African cultures, certain similarities in language, thought, and religion provided some underlying unities. The spread of the Bantu-speaking peoples provided a linguistic base across much of Africa, so that even though specific languages differed, structure and vocabulary allowed for some mutual understanding between neighboring Bantu speakers.

The same might be said of the animistic religion that characterized much of Africa. The belief in the power of natural forces personified as spirits or gods and the role of ritual and worship—often in the form of dancing, drumming, divination, and sacrifice—in influencing their actions was central to the religion of many African peoples, although local practice varied widely. African religions had well-developed concepts of good and evil. Africans, like Europeans, believed that some evil, disasters, and illnesses were produced by witchcraft. Specialists were needed to combat the power of evil and eliminate the witches. This led in many societies to the existence of a class of diviners or priests who guided religious practice and helped protect the community. Above all, African religion provided a cosmology—a view of how the universe worked—and a guide to ethics and behavior.

other is the security embracing the whole country, so that neither traveller there nor dweller has anything to fear from thief or usurper. Another is that they do not interfere with the wealth of any white man who dies among them. They simply leave it in the hands of a trustworthy white man until the one to whom it is due takes it. Another is their assiduity in prayer and their persistence in performing it in congregation and beating their children to make them perform it. If it is a Friday and a man does not go early to the mosque he will not find anywhere to pray because of the press of the people. It is their habit that every man sends his servant with his prayer-mat to spread it for him in a place which he thereby has a right to until he goes to the mosque. Their prayer-carpets are made from the fronds of the tree resembling the palm which has no fruit. Another of their good features is their dressing in fine white clothes on Friday. If any one of them possesses nothing but a ragged shirt he washes it and cleanses it and attends the Friday prayer in it. Another is their eagerness to memorize the great Quran. They place fetters on their children if there appears on their part a failure to memorize it and they are not undone until they memorize it.

I went into the house of the qadi on the day of the festival and his children were fettered so I said to him: "Aren't you going to let them go?" He replied: "I shan't do so until they've got the Quran by heart!" One day I passed by a youth of theirs, of good appearance and dressed in fine clothes, with a heavy fetter on his leg. I said to those who were with me: "What has this boy done? Has he killed somebody?" The lad understood what I had said and laughed, and they said to me: "He's only been fettered so that he'll learn the Quran!"

One of their disapproved acts is that their female servants and slave girls and little girls appear before men naked, with their privy parts uncovered. During Ramadan I saw many of them in this state, for it is the custom of the farariyya to break their fast in the house of the sultan, and each one brings his food carried by twenty or more of his slave girls, they all being naked. Another is that their women go into the sultan's presence naked and uncovered, and that his daughters go naked. On the night of 25 Ramadan I saw about 200 slave girls bringing out food from his palace naked, having with them two of his daughters with rounded breasts having no covering upon them. Another is their sprinkling dust and ashes on their heads out of good manners. Another is what I mentioned in connection with the comic anecdote about the poets' recitation. Another is that many of them eat carrion, and dogs, and donkeys.

Many African peoples shared an underlying belief in a creator deity whose power and action were expressed through spirits or lesser gods and through the founding ancestors of the group. The ancestors were often viewed as the first settlers and thus the "owners" of the land or the local resources, and through them the fertility of the land, the game, the people, and the herds could be ensured. Among some groups, working the land took on religious significance, so the land itself had a meaning beyond its economic usefulness.

Religion, economics, and history were thus closely intertwined. Then too, the family, lineage, or clan around which many African societies were organized had an important role in dealing with the gods. Deceased ancestors were often a direct link between their living relatives and the spirit world. Veneration of the ancestors and gods was part of the same system of belief. Such a system was strongly linked to specific places and people. It showed remarkable resiliency even in the face of contact with the more generalized principles of religions such as Islam and Christianity.

The economies of Africa are harder to describe in common terms than some basic aspects of politics and culture. North Africa, fully involved in the Mediterranean and Arab economic world, stands clearly apart. Sub-Saharan Africa varied greatly from one region to the next. In many areas, settled agriculture and skilled ironwork had been established before the postclassical period or advanced rapidly during the period itself. Specialization encouraged active local and regional trade, the basis for many lively markets and the many large cities that grew both in the structured states and in the decentralized areas. The bustle and gaiety of market life were important ingredients of African society, and women as well as men participated actively. Trade was handled by professional merchants, in many cases in hereditary kinship groupings. Participation in international trade increased in many regions in this period, mainly toward the Islamic world and often through the intermediary of Arab traders.

While African states benefited from their ability to tax the trade, they stood at some disadvantage in trading unprocessed goods, such as gold, ivory, salt, or slaves, for more elaborate products made elsewhere. International trade stimulated political and cultural change and furthered the growth of African merchant groups, but it did not induce rapid technical or manufacturing shifts within Africa, except for some important innovations in the excavation of mines.

Finally, we should note that one of the least known aspects of African societies prior to the 20th century is the size and dynamic of their populations. This is true not only of Africa but of much of the world. Archeological evidence, travelers' reports, and educated guesses are used to estimate the population of early African societies, but in truth, our knowledge of how Africa fits into the general trends of the world population is very slight. By 1500, Africa may have had 30 to 60 million inhabitants.

The Arrival of Islam in North Africa

Africa north of the Sahara had long been part of the world of classical antiquity, where Phoenicians, Greeks, Romans, and Vandals traded, settled, built, battled, and destroyed. The Greek city of Cyrene (c. 600 B.C.E.) in modern Libya and the great Phoenician outpost at Carthage (founded c. 814 B.C.E.) in Tunisia attest to the part North Africa played in the classical world. After the age of the Pharaohs, Egypt (conquered by Alexander in 331 B.C.E.) had become an important part of the Greek world and then later a key province in the Roman Empire, valued especially for its grain. Toward the end of the Roman Empire, Christianity had taken a firm hold in Mediterranean Africa, but in the warring between the Vandals and the Byzantines in North Africa in the 5th and 6th centuries C.E., considerable disruption had taken place. During that period, the Berber peoples of the Sahara had raided the coastal cities. As we have seen with Egypt, North Africa was also linked across the Sahara to the rest of Africa in many ways. With the rise of Islam, those ties became even closer.

Between 640 and 700 C.E., the followers of Muhammad swept across North Africa from Suez to the Pillars of Hercules on Morocco's Atlantic shore. By 670 C.E., Muslims ruled Tunisia, or *Ifriqiya*—what the Romans had called Africa. (The Arabs originally used this word as the name for eastern North Africa and *Maghrib* for lands to the West.) By 711, Arab and Berber armies had crossed into Spain. Only their defeat in France by Charles Martel at Poitiers in 732 brought the Muslim advance in the West to a halt. The message of Islam found fertile ground among the populations of North Africa. Conversion took place rapidly within a certain political unity provided by the Abbasid dynasty. This unity eventually broke down, and North Africa divided into several separate states and competing groups.

In opposition to the states dominated by the Arabic rulers, the peoples of the desert, the Berbers, formed states of their own at places such as Fez in Morocco and at Sijilimasa, the old city of the trans-Saharan caravan trade. By the 11th century, under pressure from new Muslim invaders from the East, a great puritanical reformist movement, whose followers were called the *Almoravids,* grew among the desert Berbers of the western Sahara. Launched on the course of a jihad—a holy war waged to purify, spread, or protect the faith—the Almoravids moved southward against the African kingdoms of the savanna and westward into Spain. In 1130 another reformist group, the *Almohadis,* followed the same pattern. These North African and Spanish developments were an essential background to the penetration of Islam into sub-Saharan Africa.

Islam offered many attractions within Africa. Its fundamental teaching that all Muslims are equal within the community of believers made the acceptance of conquerors and new rulers easier. The Islamic tradition of uniting the powers of the state and religion in the person of the ruler or caliph appealed to some African kings as a way of reinforcing their authority. The concept that all members of the umma, or community of believers, were equal put the newly converted Berbers and later Africans on an equal footing with the Arabs, at least in law. Despite these egalitarian and somewhat utopian ideas within Islam, practices differed considerably at local levels. Social stratification remained important in Islamicized societies and ethnic distinctions also divided the believers. Despite certain teachings on the relative equality between men and women, the law recognized that the monetary penalty for killing a man was twice that for killing a woman. The disparity between law and practice—between equality before God and inequality within the world—sometimes led to reform movements of a utopian type. Groups like the Almohades are characteristic within Islamic history, often developing in peripheral areas and dedicated to a purification of society by returning to the original teachings of the Prophet.

The Christian Kingdoms: Nubia and Ethiopia

Islam, of course, was not the first universalistic religion to take root in Africa, and the wave of Arab conquests across northern Africa had left behind it islands of Christianity at various places. Christianity had made converts in Egypt and Ethiopia even before the conversion of the Roman Empire in the 4th century C.E. Aside from the Christian kingdom of Axum, Christian communities thrived in Egypt and Nubia. The Christians of Egypt, the *Copts,* developed a rich tradition in contact with Byzantium, translating the gospels and other religious literature from Greek to Coptic, their own tongue, which was based on the language of ancient Egypt. On doctrinal and political issues they eventually split from the Byzantine connection. When Egypt was conquered by Arab armies and then converted to Islam, the Copts were able to maintain their faith; they were recognized by Muslim rulers as followers of a revealed religion and thus entitled to a certain tolerance. The Coptic influence had already spread up the Nile into Nubia, the ancient land of Kush. Muslim attempts to penetrate Nubia were met with such stiff resistance in the 9th century that the Christian descendants of ancient Kush were left in relative peace as independent Christian kingdoms until the 13th century.

The *Ethiopian kingdom* that grew from Axum was perhaps the most important of the African Christian outposts. Cut off from Christian Byzantium by the Muslim conquest of Egypt and the Red Sea coast, surrounded by pagan neighbors, and probably influenced by pagan and Jewish immigrants from Yemen, the Christian kingdom turned inward. Its people occupied the Ethiopian highlands, living in fortified towns and supporting themselves with agriculture on terraced hillsides. Eventually, through a process of warfare, conversion, and compromise with non-Christian neighbors, a new dynasty appeared, which under King Lalaibela (d. 1221) sponsored a remarkable building project in which 11

The 13th-century churches of Lalaibela, some cut from a single rock, represent the power of early Christianity in Ethiopia.

great churches were sculpted from the rock in the town that bore his name.

In the 13th and 14th centuries, an Ethiopian Christian state emerged under a dynasty that traced its origins back to the marriage of Solomon and Sheba. Using the Geez language of Axum as a religious language and Amharic as the common speech, this state maintained its brand of Christianity in relative isolation while facing constant pressure from its increasingly Muslim neighbors.

The struggle between the Christian state in the Ethiopian highlands and the Muslim peoples in Somalia and on the Red Sea coast shaped much of the consequent history of the region and continues to do so today. When one of these Muslim states, with help from the Ottoman Turks, threatened the very existence of the Ethiopian kingdom, a Portuguese expedition arrived in 1542 at Massawa on the Red Sea and turned the tide in favor of its Christian allies. Portuguese attempts thereafter to bring Ethiopian Christianity into the Roman Catholic church failed, and Ethiopia remained isolated, Christian, and fiercely independent.

Kingdoms of the Grasslands

In the sahel grasslands, several powerful states emerged that combined Islamic religion and culture with local practices. The kingdoms of *Mali*and *Songhay* and the *Hausa states* represented an African adaptation of Islam and its fusion with African traditions.

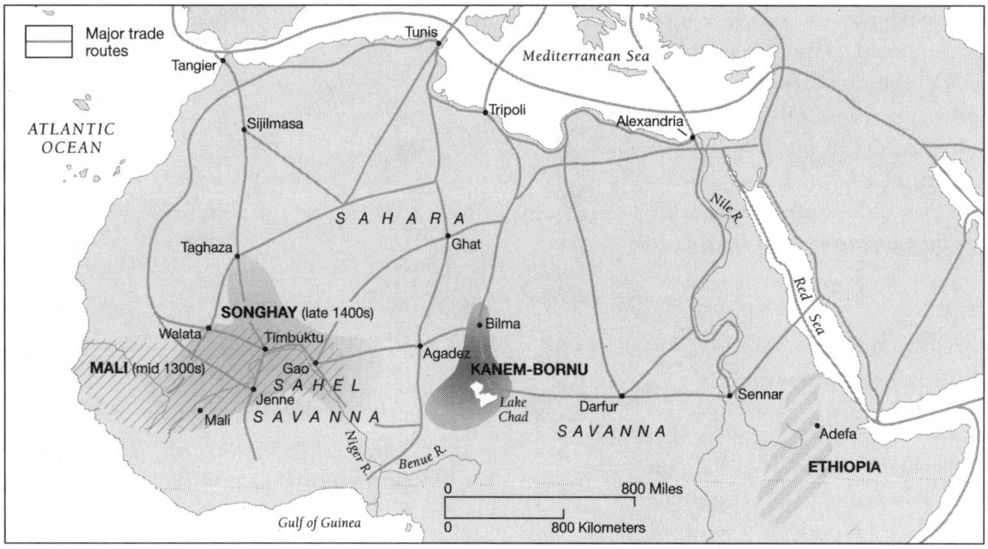

The Savanna Kingdoms, About 1400 C.E.

As the Islamic wave spread across North Africa, it sent ripples across the Sahara, not in the form of invading armies but at first in the merchants and travelers who trod the dusty and ancient caravan routes toward the savanna. Africa had three important "coasts" of contact: the Atlantic, the Indian Ocean, and the savanna on the southern edge of the Sahara.

On the edge of the desert, where several resource zones came together, African states such as Ghana had already formed by the 8th century by exchanging gold from the forests of West Africa for salt or dates from the Sahara or for goods from Mediterranean North Africa. Camels, which had been introduced from Asia to the Sahara between the 1st and 5th centuries C.E., had greatly improved the possibilities of trade, but these animals, which thrived in arid and semiarid environments, could not penetrate into the humid forest zones because of disease. Thus, the *Sahel,* the extensive grassland belt at the southern edge of the Sahara, became a point of exchange between the forests to the south and North Africa—an active "coast" where ideas, trade, and people from the Sahara and beyond arrived in increasing numbers. Along that coast, several African states developed between the trading cities, taking advantage of their position as intermediaries in the trade. But location on the relatively open plains of the dry Sahel also meant that these states were subject to attack and periodic droughts.

Founded probably in the 3rd century C.E., Ghana rose to power by taxing the salt and gold exchanged within its borders. By the 10th century, its rulers had converted to Islam, and Ghana was at the height of its power. At a time when William the Conqueror could muster perhaps 5000 troops for his invasion of England, Muslim accounts reported that the king of Ghana could field an army many times that size. Eventually, however, Almoravid armies invaded Ghana from North Africa in 1076, and although the kingdom survived, its power was in decline so that by the beginning of the 13th century, new states had risen in the savanna to take its place of leadership.

Sudanic States

There were several Sudanic kingdoms, and even during the height of Ghana's power, neighboring and competing states persisted, such as Takrur on the Senegal River to the west and Gao (Kawkaw) on the Niger River to the east. Before we deal with the most important kingdoms that followed Ghana, it will be useful to review some of the elements these states had in common.

The *Sudanic states* were often led by the patriarch or council of elders of a particular family or group of lineages that established control over its neighbors. Usually these states had a territorial core area in which the people were of the same linguistic or ethnic background, but their power extended over subordinate communities. These were conquest states, which drew on the taxes, tribute, and military support of the subordinate areas, lineages, and villages. The effective control of subordinate societies and the legal or informal control of their sovereignty are the usual definition of empires. Ghana, Mali, and Songhay and some of their neighbors were imperial states.

The rulers of these states were considered to be sacred individuals and were surrounded with rituals that separated them from their subjects. With the conversion of the rulers of Ghana and Takrur after the 10th century, Islam was used to reinforce indigenous ideas of kingship, so that Islam became something of a royal cult. Much of the population never converted, and the Islamicized ruling families also drew on their traditional powers to fortify their rule.

Several savanna states rose among the various peoples in the Sudan. We can trace the development and the culture of two of the most important, Mali and Songhay, as an example of the fusion of Islamic and indigenous African cultures, within the context of trade and military expansion, that these states represented.

The Empire of Mali and Sundiata, the "Lion Prince"

The empire of Mali, centered between the Senegal and Niger rivers, was the creation of the Malinke peoples, who in the 13th century broke away from the control of Ghana, which was by then in steady decline. In Mali the old forms of kingship were reinforced by Islam. As in many of the Sudanic states, the rulers supported Islam by building mosques, attending public prayers, and supporting preachers. In return, sermons to the faithful emphasized obedience and support of the king. Mali became a model of these Islamicized Sudanic kingdoms. The economic basis of society in the Mali Empire was successful agriculture. This was combined with an active tradition of trade in many products, although like Ghana, Mali also depended on its access to gold-producing areas to the south. Malinke merchants, or *juula,* formed small partnerships and groups to carry out trade throughout the area. They spread beyond the borders of the empire and throughout much of West Africa.

The beginning of Malinke expansion is attributed to *Sundiata* (sometimes written Sunjata), a brilliant leader whose exploits serve as the foundation of a great oral tradition. The griots, professional oral historians who also served as keepers of traditions and advisors to kings, began their epic histories of Mali with Sundiata, the "Lion Prince."

> ***Listen then sons of Mali, children of the black people, listen to my word, for I am going to tell you of Sundiata, the father of the Bright Country, of the savanna land, the ancestor of those who draw the bow, the master of a hundred vanquished kings. . . . He was great among kings, he was peerless among men; he was beloved of God because he was the last of the great conquerors.***

After a difficult childhood, Sundiata emerged from a period of interfamily and regional fighting to create a unified state. Oral histories ascribed to him the creation of the basic rules and relationships of Malinke society and the outline of the government of the empire of Mali. He became the mansa, or emperor. Sundiata, it was said, "divided up the world," which meant that he was considered the originator of social arrangements. Sixteen clans of freemen were entitled to bear arms and carry the bow and quiver of arrows as the symbol of their status, five clans were devoted to religious duties, and four clans were specialists and tradesmen, such as blacksmiths and griots. Division and grouping by clans had apparently existed and represented traditional patterns among the peoples of the savanna in ancient Ghana as well, but Sundiata as the hero of origins was credited with the creation of this social arrangement. While he created the political institutions of rule that allowed for considerable regional and ethnic differences in the federated provinces, he also stationed garrisons to maintain loyalty and security. Travel was secure and crime was severely punished, as *Ibn Battuta,* the Arab traveler, reported: "Of all peoples," he said, "the Blacks are those who most hate injustice, and their emperor pardons none who is guilty of it." The security of travelers and their goods was an essential element in a state where commerce played so important a role.

Sundiata died about 1260, but his successors expanded the borders of Mali until it controlled most of the Niger valley almost to the Atlantic coast. A sumptuous court was established and hosted a large number of traders. Mali grew wealthy from the trade. Perhaps the most famous of Sundiata's successors was Mansa Kankan Musa (c. 1312–1337), who made a pilgrimage to Mecca in 1324 and brought the attention of the Muslim world to Mali.

City Folk and Villagers

The cities of the western Sudan began to resemble those of North Africa, but with a distinctive local architectural style. The towns were commercial and often included craft specialists and a resident foreign merchant community. The military expansion of states such as

The spread of Islam and the importance of trade in Africa is represented by the great mosque at Jenne on the Niger River in the modern Republic of Mali.

Ghana, Mali, and later Songhay contributed to their commercial success because the power of the state protected traders.

A cosmopolitan court life developed as merchants and scholars were attracted by the power and protection of Mali. Mandinka juula traders ranged across the Sudan and exploited their position as middlemen. "Port" cities flourished, such as Jenne and *Timbuktu,* which lay just off the flood plain on the great bend in the Niger River. Timbuktu was reported to have a population of 50,000, and by the 14th century, its great Sankore mosque contained a library and an associated university where scholars, jurists, and Muslim theologians studied. The book was the symbol of civilization in the Islamic world, and it was said that the book trade in Timbuktu was the most lucrative business of all.

For the vast majority of people in the empire of Mali and the other Sudanic states, life was not centered on the royal court, the great mosque, or long-distance trade but rather on the agricultural cycle and the village. Making a living from the land was the preoccupation of most people, and about 80 percent of the villagers lived by farming. This was a difficult life. The soils of the savanna were sandy and shallow. Plows were rarely used. The villagers were people of the hoe, who looked to the skies in the spring for the first rains to start their planting. Rice in the river valleys, millet, sorghums, some wheat, fruits, and vegetables provided the basis of daily life in the village and supplied the caravan trade. Even a large farm would rarely exceed ten acres and most were much smaller. Clearing land was often done communally, accompanied by feasts and competition, but the farms belonged to families and were worked by them. A man with two wives and several unmarried sons could work more land than a man with one wife and a smaller family. Polygamy, or the practice of having multiple wives, was therefore, common in the region, and it remains so today.

Given the difficulties of the soil, the periodic droughts, insect pests, storage problems, and the limitations of technology, the farmers of the Sudanic states—by the methods of careful cultivation, crop rotation, and, in places like Timbuktu, the use of irrigation—were able to provide for their people the basic foods that supported them and the imperial states on which they were based. The hoe and the bow became symbols of the common people of the savanna states.

The Songhay Kingdom

As the power of Mali began to wane, a successor state from within the old empire was already beginning to emerge. The people of Songhay dominated the middle reaches of the Niger valley. Traditionally, the society of Songhay was made up of "masters of the soil," that is, farmers, herdsmen, and "masters of the waters," or fisher-folk. Songhay had begun to form in the 7th century as an independent kingdom, perhaps under a Berber dynasty. By 1010, a capital was established at Gao on the Niger River, and the rulers had become Muslims, although the majority of the population remained pagan. Dominated by Mali for a while, by the 1370s Songhay had established its independence again and began to thrive as new sources of gold from the West African forests began to pass through its territory. Gao became a large city with a resident foreign merchant community and several mosques. Under a dynamic leader, Sunni Ali (1464–1492), the empire of Songhay was forged.

Sunni Ali was a great tactical commander and a ruthless leader. His cavalry expanded the borders and seized the traditional trading cities of Timbuktu and Jenne. The whole middle Niger valley fell under his control, and he developed a system of provincial administration to mobilize recruits for the army and rule the far-flung conquests. Although apparently a Muslim, he met any challenge to his authority even when it came from the Muslim scholars of Timbuktu, whom he persecuted. Sunni Ali was followed by a line of Muslim rulers who took the military title of askia. These rulers, especially

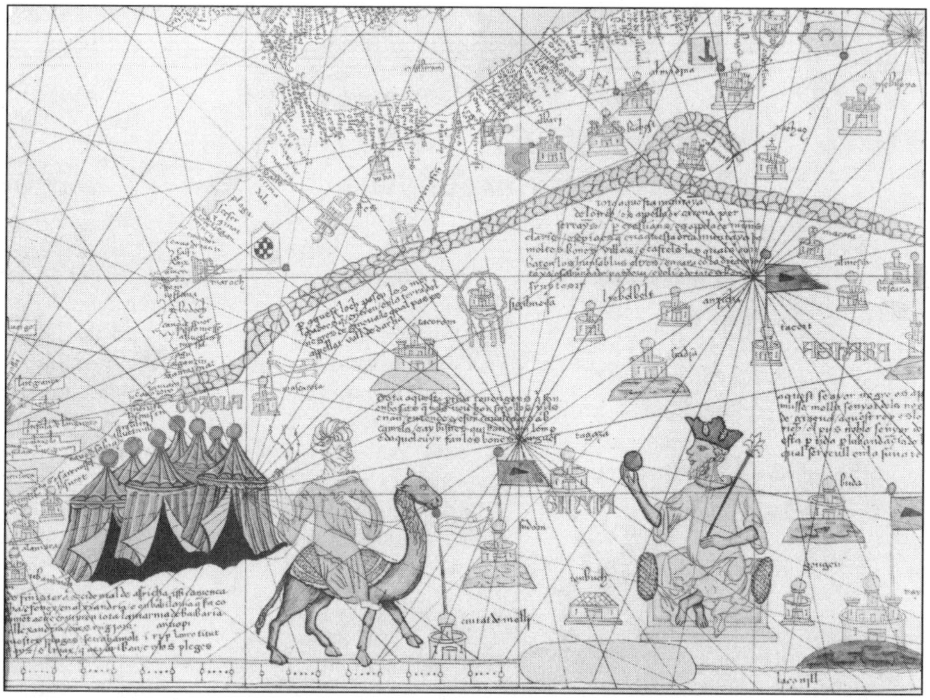

Mansa Musa of Mali from a facsimile of a 14th century Catalan atlas by Abraham Cresques.

Askia *Muhammad the Great,* extended the boundaries of the empire so that by the mid-16th century Songhay dominated the central Sudan.

Life in the Songhay Empire followed many of the patterns established in the previous savanna states. The fusion of Islamic and pagan populations and traditions continued. Muslim clerics and jurists were sometimes upset by the pagan beliefs and practices that continued among the population, and even more by the local interpretation of Islamic law. They wanted to impose a strict interpretation of the law of Islam and were shocked that men and women mixed freely in the markets and streets, that women went unveiled, and that at Jenne young girls went naked.

Songhay remained the dominant power in the region until the end of the 16th century. In 1591, a Muslim army from Morocco, equipped with muskets, crossed the Sahara and defeated the vastly larger forces of Songhay. This sign of weakness stimulated internal revolts against the ruling family, and eventually the parts of the old empire broke away.

The demise of the Songhay imperial structure did not mean the end of the political and cultural tradition of the western Sudan. Other states that combined Muslim and pagan traditions rose among the Hausa peoples of northern Nigeria, based on cities such as Kano. The earliest Muslim ruler of Kano took control in the late 14th century and turned the city into a center of Muslim learning. In Kano, Katsina, and other Hausa cities of the region, an urbanized royal court in a fortified capital ruled over the essentially animistic villages, where the majority of the population lived. With powerful cavalry forces these states were able to extend their rule and protect their active trade in salt, grains, and cloth. While these later Islamicized African states tended to be small in size and local in their goals, they reproduced many of the social, political, and religious forms of the great empires of the grasslands.

Beyond the Sudan, Muslim penetration came in various forms. Merchants became established in most of the major trading cities, and religious communities developed in each of these, often associated with particular families. Networks of trade and contact were established widely over the region as juula merchants and groups of pastoralists established their outposts in the area of Guinea. Muslim traders, herdsmen, warriors, and religious leaders became important minorities within these segmented African societies, composed of elite families, occupational groups, free men, and slaves. Intermarriage often took place, but Muslim influence varied widely from region to region. Nevertheless, families of juula traders and lineages that became known as specialists in Muslim law spread widely through the region, so that by the 18th century there were Muslim minorities scattered widely throughout West Africa, even in those areas where no Islamicized state had emerged.

DOCUMENT

The Great Oral Tradition and the Epic of Sundiata

Oral traditions are of various kinds. Some are simply the shared stories of a family or people, but in many West African societies, the mastery of oral traditions is a skill practiced by griots. Although today's griots are professional musicians and bards, historically they held important places at the courts of West African kingdoms. The epic of Sundiata, the great ruler of Mali, has been passed down orally for centuries. In the following excerpts from a version collected among the Mandingo (Malinke) people of Guinea by the African scholar D. T. Niane, the role of the griot and the advantages of oral traditions are outlined.

> We are now coming to the great moments in the life of Sundiata. The exile will end and another sun will rise. It is the sun of Sundiata. Griots know the history of kings and kingdoms and that is why they are the best counselors of kings. Every king wants to have a singer to perpetuate his memory, for it is the griot who rescues the memories of kings from oblivion, as men have short memories. Kings have prescribed destinies just like men, and seers who probe the future know it. They have knowledge of the future, whereas we griots are depositories of the knowledge of the past. But whoever knows the history of a country can read its future.
>
> Other peoples use writing to record the past, but this invention has killed the faculty of memory among them. They do not feel the past any more, for writing lacks the warmth of the human voice. With them everybody thinks he knows, whereas learning should be a secret. The prophets did not write and their words have been all the more vivid as a result. What paltry learning is that which is concealed in dumb books!

The following excerpt describes the preparation for a major battle fought by Sundiata against the forces of Soumaoro, king of the Sossos, who had taken control of Mali and who is referred to in the epic as an evil sorcerer. Note the interweaving of proverbs, the presence of aspects of Muslim and animist religion, the celebration of Sundiata's prowess, the recurring references to iron, and the high value placed on the cavalry, the key to military power in the savanna. Note how the story of Alexander the Great inspires this "African Alexander."

Political and Social Life in the Sudanic States

We can generalize from these brief descriptions of Mali and Songhay about the nature of the Sudanic states. The village communities, clans, and various ethnic groups continued to organize many aspects of life in the savanna. The development of unified states provided an overarching structure that allowed the various groups and communities to coexist. The large states usually represented the political aims and power of a particular group and often of a dominant family. Many states pointed to the immigrant origins of the ruling families, and in reality the movement and fusion of populations was a constant feature in the Sudan. Islam provided a universalistic faith that served the interests of many groups. Common religion and law provided solidarity and trust to the merchants who resided in the cities and whose caravans brought goods to and from the savanna. The ruling families used Islamic titles, such as emir or caliph, to reinforce their authority, and they surrounded themselves with literate Muslim advisors and scribes, who aided in the administration of government. The Muslim concept of a ruler who united civil and religious authority reinforced traditional ideas of kingship. It is also important to note that in Africa, as elsewhere in the world, the formation of states heightened social differences and made these societies more hierarchical.

In all the Sudanic states, Islam was fused with the existing traditions and beliefs. Rulership and authority

Every man to his own land! If it is foretold that your destiny should be fulfilled in such and such a land, men can do nothing against it. Mansa Tounkara could not keep Sundiata back because the destiny of Songolon's son was bound up with that of Mali. Neither the jealousy of a cruel stepmother, nor her wickedness could alter for a moment the course of great destiny.

The snake, man's enemy, is not long-lived, yet the serpent that lives hidden will surely die old. Djata (Sundiata) was strong enough now to face his enemies. At the age of eighteen he had the stateliness of the lion and the strength of the buffalo. His voice carried authority, his eyes were live coals, his arm was iron, he was the husband of power.

Moussa Tounkara, king of Mema, gave Sundiata half of his army. The most valiant came forward of their own free will to follow Sundiata in the great adventure. The cavalry of Mema, which he had fashioned himself, formed his iron squadron. Sundiata, dressed in the Muslim fashion of Mema, left the town at the head of his small but redoubtable army. The whole population sent their best wishes with him. He was surrounded by five messengers from Mali, and Manding Bory [Sundiata's brother] rode proudly at his side. The horsemen of Mema formed behind Djata a bristling iron squadron. The troop took the direction of Wagadou, for Djata did not have enough troops to confront Soumaoro directly, and so the king of Mema advised him to go to Wagadou and take half the men of the king, Soumaba Cissé. A swift messenger had been sent there and so the king of Wagadou came out in person to meet Sundiata and his troops. He gave Sundiata half of his cavalry and blessed the weapons. Then Manding Bory said to his brother, "Djata, do you think yourself able to face Soumaoro now?"

"No matter how small a forest may be, you can always find there sufficient fibers to tie up a man. Numbers mean nothing; it is worth that counts. With my cavalry I shall clear myself a path to Mali."

Djata gave out his orders. They would head south, skirting Soumaoro's kingdom. The first objective to be reached was Tabon, the iron-gated town in the midst of the mountains, for Sundiata had promised Fran Kamara that he would pass Tabon before returning to Mali. He hoped to find that his childhood companion had become king. It was a forced march and during the halts the divines, Singbin Mara Cissé and Mandjan Bérété, related to Sundiata the history of Alexander the Great and several other heroes, but of all of them Sundiata preferred Alexander, the king of gold and silver, who crossed the world from west to east. He wanted to outdo his prototype both in the extent of his territory and in the wealth of his treasury.

were still based on the ability to intercede with local spirits, and while Sundiata or Sunni Ali might be nominally Muslim, they did not ignore the traditional basis of their rule. Because of this, Islam in these early stages in the Sudan tended to accommodate pagan practice and belief. Large proportions of the populations of Mali and Songhay never converted to Islam, and those who did convert often maintained many of the old beliefs as well.

We can see this fusion of traditions clearly in the position of women. Several Sudanic societies were matrilineal, and some recognized the role of women within the lines of kinship, contrary to the normal patrilineal customs inscribed in the *Sharia,* or Islamic law. As we have just noted in the case of Songhay, North African visitors to the Sudan were shocked by the easy familiarity between men and women and the freedom enjoyed by women.

Finally, we must also take note that slavery and the slave trade between black Africa and the rest of the Islamic world had a major impact on women and children in these societies. Various forms of slavery and dependent labor had existed in Africa prior to the arrival of Islam. While we know little about slavery in central Africa in this period, slavery had been a relatively marginal aspect of the Sudanic states. Africans had been enslaved by others before, and Nubian (African) slaves had been known in the classical world, but with the Muslim conquests of North Africa and commercial penetration to the south, slavery became a more widely diffused phenomenon, and a slave trade in Africans developed on a new scale.

In theory, slavery was viewed by Muslims as a stage in the process of conversion—a way of preparing pagans to become Muslims—but in reality, conversion did not guarantee freedom. Slaves in the Islamic world were used in a variety of occupations, such as domestic servants and laborers, but they were also used as soldiers and administrators who, having no local ties and affiliations, were considered to be dependent and thus trustworthy by their masters. Slaves were also used as eunuchs and concubines; thus the emphasis on women and children. The trade caravans from the Sahel across the Sahara often transported slaves as well as gold, and as we shall see, other slave-trade routes developed from the African interior to the east African coast. The tendency for the children of slave mothers to eventually be freed and integrated into Muslim society, while positive in one sense, also meant a constant demand for more slaves. Estimates of the volume of this trade vary widely. One scholar places the total in the trans-Saharan trade at 4.8 million, with another 2.4 million sent to the Muslim ports on the Indian Ocean coast. Actual figures may have been considerably lower, but the trade extended over 700 years and affected a large area. In a way, it was one more fashion in which the Islamic civilization touched and modified sub-Saharan Africa.

The Swahili Coast of East Africa

A string of Islamicized African ports tied to the trade of the Indian Ocean dotted the East African coast. Although these cities were Islamicized, African customs and the Bantu Swahili language remained so strong that they represented a cultural fusion, mostly limited to the coast.

While the kingdoms of West Africa came under the influence of Islam from across the Sahara, another center of Islamic civilization was developing on the seaboard and offshore islands of Africa's Indian Ocean coast. Along that coast, extending southward from the horn of Africa to modern-day Mozambique, a string of Islamicized trading cities developed that reflected their cosmopolitan contacts with trading partners from Arabia, Persia, India, and China. Islam provided the residents of these towns a universal set of ethics and beliefs that made their maritime contacts easier, but in East Africa, as in the savanna kingdoms of West Africa, Islamization was slow to penetrate among the general population. When it did, the result was often a compromise between indigenous ways and the new faith.

The Coastal Trading Ports

A 1st-century Greek account of the Indian Ocean, *The Periplus of the Erythraean Sea,* mentioned some ports in East Africa but was somewhat vague about the nature of the local inhabitants—that is, whether they were Africans or immigrants from the Arabian peninsula. From that century to the 10th century, the wave of Bantu migration had clearly reached the East African interior. Bantu-speaking pastoralists in the north and agriculturalists in the south mixed with older populations in the region. Other peoples were also moving to the African coast. Contact across the Indian Ocean dated back to at least the 2nd century B.C.E. From Indonesia or Malaya, seaborne immigrants settled on the large island of Madagascar and from there introduced foods such as bananas and coconuts to the African coast. These were widely adopted and spread rapidly along the coast and into central Africa. Small coastal villages of fishermen and farmers, making rough pottery and working iron, dotted this coast. By the 8th and 9th centuries, visitors and refugees from Oman and the Persian Gulf had established themselves at some of these villages, attracted by the possibilities of trade with the land of *Zanj,* the Arabic term for the East African coast. The villages were transformed from relatively homogeneous and egalitarian societies with shared language, ancestors, and traditions into more cosmopolitan and diverse communities.

By the 13th century, a string of urbanized *East African trading ports* had developed along the coast. These towns shared the common Bantu-based and Arabic-influenced Swahili language and other cultural traits, although they were governed by separate Muslim ruling families. Towns such as Mogadishu, Mombasa, Malindi, Kilwa, Pate, and Zanzibar eventually contained mosques, tombs, and palaces of cut stone and coral. Ivory, gold, iron, slaves, and exotic animals were exported from these ports in exchange for silks from Persia and porcelain from China for the ruling Muslim families. The Arab traveler Ibn Batuta was impressed with the beauty and refinement of these towns. He described Kilwa as "one of the most beautiful and well-constructed towns in the world" and was also impressed by the pomp and luxury of its ruler. Kilwa, in fact, was particularly wealthy because it controlled the southern port of Sofala,

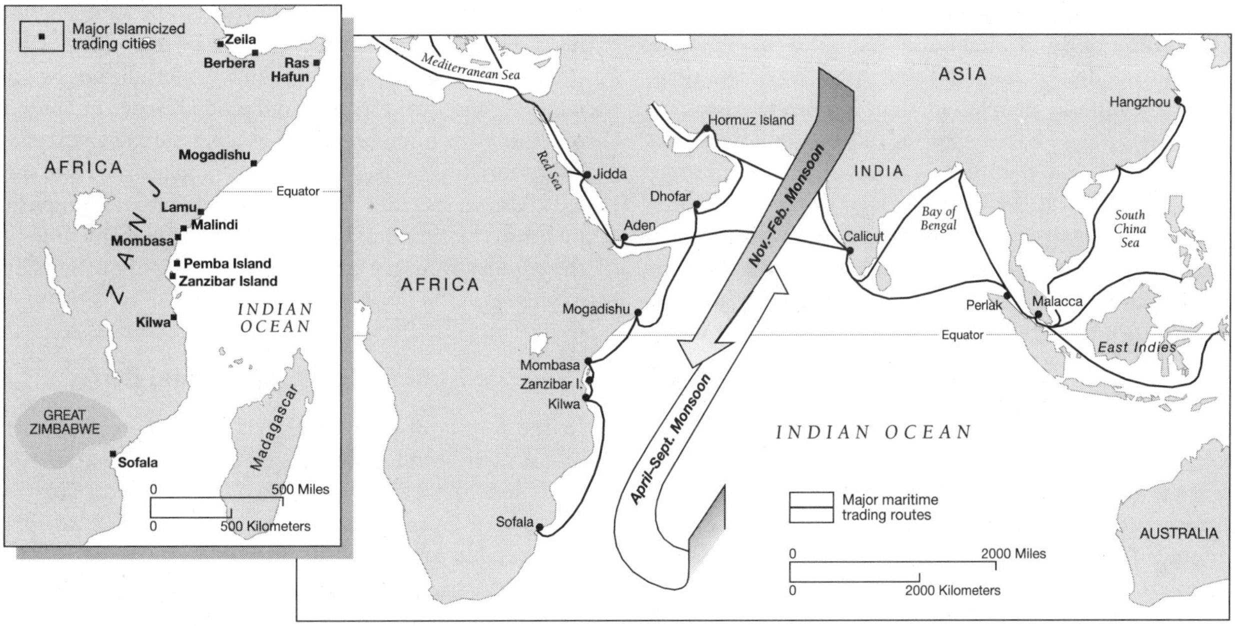

The Swahili Coast; African Monsoon Routes and Major Trade Routes

which had access to the gold produced in the interior (near "Great Zimbabwe"), and because of its location as the farthest point south at which ships from India could hope to sail and return in a single monsoon season.

From the 13th to the 15th centuries, Kilwa flourished in the context of international trade, but it was not alone. At their height, perhaps as many as 30 of these port towns dotted the coast. These were tied to each other by an active coastal commerce and, in a few places, to the interior by a caravan trade, although it was usually Africans who brought the goods to the coast. Textiles from India and porcelain from China were brought by Arab traders. Some Chinese ports sent goods directly to Africa in the 13th century, and as late as 1417 and 1431, state-sponsored expeditions sailing directly from China stopped at the East African coast to load ivory, gold, and rare woods. Such contact was discontinued after 1431 by the Chinese, and goods from China came to the coast thereafter in the ships of Arab or Indian traders.

The Mixture of Cultures on the Swahili Coast

The Islamic overlay in these towns benefited this long-distance commerce. The 13th century was a period of considerable Islamic expansion, and as that faith spread eastward to India and Indonesia, it provided a religious bond of trust and law that facilitated trade throughout ports of the Indian Ocean. The ruling families in the East African trading ports built mosques and palaces; the mosque at Mogadishu was begun in 1238. Many of these ruling families claimed to be descendants of immigrants from Shiraz in Persia—a claim intended to legitimize their position and orthodoxy. In fact, some evidence indicates that the original Muslim families had emigrated to the Somali coast and from there to other towns farther south.

The institutions and forms of the Muslim world operated in these cities. While Islam tended to be the faith of the rulers and the merchants, the majority of the population on the East African coast, and perhaps even in the towns themselves, retained their previous beliefs and culture.

African culture remained strong throughout the area. The Swahili language was essentially a Bantu language containing a large number of Arabic words, though many of these words were not incorporated until the 16th century. The language was written in an Arabic script some time prior to the 13th century; the ruling families could also converse in Arabic. Islam itself penetrated very little into the interior among the hunters, pastoralists, and farmers. Even the areas of the coast near the trading towns remained relatively unaffected. In the towns, the stone and coral buildings of the Muslim elite were surrounded by mud and thatch houses of the non-Muslim common people, so that Islamization was to some extent class based. Still, a culture developed that fused Islamic and traditional elements. Family lineage, for example, was traced both through the maternal line, which controlled property (the traditional African practice), and through the paternal line, as was the Muslim custom. Swahili culture was a dynamic hybrid, and the Swahili people spread their language and culture along the coast of East Africa.

By the time the Portuguese arrived on this coast around 1500, the Swahili culture was widely diffused. Kilwa was no longer the predominant city, and the focus of trade had shifted to Malindi and Mombasa on the Kenya coast; but the commerce across the Indian Ocean continued. Eventually, the Portuguese raided Kilwa and Mombasa in an attempt to shift the focus of trade into their own hands. Their outpost on Mozambique island and their control of Sofala put much of the gold trade in their hands. Although the Portuguese built a major outpost at Fort Jesus in Mombasa in 1592, they were never able to control the trade on the northern Swahili coast. The East African patterns, as established by 1500, persisted even more straightforwardly than those of the Sudanic kingdoms.

Peoples of the Forest and Plains

Across Central Africa, kingdoms developed that were supported by complex agrarian societies capable of great artistic achievements. At Benin, in the Kongo, in the Yoruba city-states, and at Great Zimbabwe, royal authority—often considered divinely inspired—led to the creation of powerful states.

As important as the Islamic impact was on the societies of the savanna and the East African coast, other African peoples in the continent's interior and in the forests of West Africa were following their own trajectories of development. By 1000 C.E., most of these societies were based on a varied agriculture sometimes combined with herding, and most societies used iron tools and weapons. Many were still organized in small village communities. In various places, however, states had formed. Some of them began to resolve the problems of integrating large territories under a single government and ruling subject peoples. While Egypt, Kush, and Ethiopia had developed writing, and other areas borrowed the Arabic script, many sub-Saharan African societies were preliterate and transmitted their knowledge, skills, and traditions by oral methods and direct instruction. The presence or absence of writing has often been used as a measure of civilization by western observers, but as in pre-Columbian Peru, various African societies produced considerable accomplishments in the arts, building, and statecraft—sometimes in the context of highly urbanized settings without a system of writing.

Artists and Kings: Yoruba and Benin

In the forests of central Nigeria, objects in terra-cotta of a realistic and highly stylized form have been discovered near the village of *Nok.* These objects, most of which date from about 500 B.C.E. to 200 C.E., display considerable artistic skill. The inhabitants of ancient Nok and its region practiced agriculture and used iron tools. They remain something of a mystery, but it appears that their artistic traditions spread widely through the forest areas and influenced other peoples. Nevertheless, there is a long hiatus in the historical and archeological record between the Nok sculptures and the renewed flourishing of artistic traditions in the region after about 1000 C.E.

Among the Yoruba-speaking peoples of Nigeria, at the city of Ile-Ife, remarkable terra-cotta and bronze portrait heads of past rulers were produced in the period after 1200 C.E. The lifelike representations of these portraits and the skill of their execution place them among the greatest achievements of African art. The craftsmen of Ile-Ife also worked in wood and ivory. Much of the art seems to be associated with kings and the authority of kingship. Ile-Ife, like other *Yoruba* states, seems to have been an agricultural society supported by a peasantry and dominated by a ruling family and an aristocracy. Ile-Ife was considered by many peoples in the region to be the original cultural center, and many of them traced their own beginnings to it.

Yoruba origins are, in fact, obscure. Ile-Ife was seen as the holiest city of the Yoruba, their place of birth. Another legend maintained by the royal historians was that Oduduwa, a son of the king of Mecca, migrated from the east and settled in Yoruba. Modern historians have suggested that the real origins were perhaps Meroe and Nubia, or at least in the savanna south of the Sahara. In any case, the Yoruba spoke a non-Bantu language of the West African Kwa family and recognized a certain affinity between themselves and neighboring peoples, such as the Hausa, who spoke Afro-Asian languages.

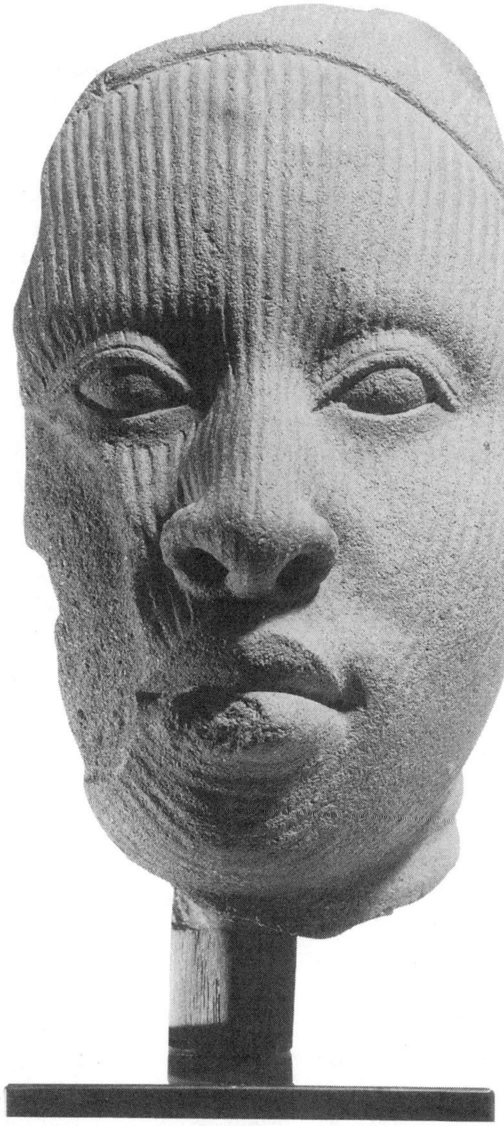

In the 13th and 14th centuries, Ife artists worked in terra-cotta, as well as bronze, and produced personalized portraits.

The Yoruba were organized in small city-states, each controlling a radius of perhaps 50 miles. The Yoruba were, in fact, highly urbanized, although many of the town inhabitants farmed in the surrounding countryside. These city-states developed under the strong authority of regional kings, who were considered divine. The person of the king was surrounded with a royal court of great size that included secondary wives, musicians, magicians, and bodyguards of soldier-slaves. His rule was not absolute, however, and it was limited by other forces in society. We can use the example of the Yoruba state of Oyo, which had emerged by the 14th century. Its king, the alafin, controlled subject peoples through "princes" in the provinces, drawn from local lineages, who were allowed to exercise traditional rule as long as they continued to pay tribute to Oyo. In the capital a council of state, made up of nobles from the seven city districts, advised the ruler and limited his power, and the Ogboni, or secret society of religious and political leaders, reviewed decisions of the king and the council. The union of civil and supernatural powers in the person of the ruler was the basis of power. The highly urbanized nature of Yoruba society and the flourishing of artisan traditions within these towns bear some similarity to the city-states of medieval Italy or Germany.

Patterns similar to the Yoruba city-states could be found among Edo peoples to the east of Yoruba. A large city-state called *Benin* was formed sometime in the 14th century under Ewuare the Great (1440–1473). Benin's control extended from the Niger River to the coast near modern Lagos. Benin City was described by early European visitors in the 16th century as a city of great population and broad avenues. The Oba, or ruler, lived in a large royal compound surrounded by a great entourage, and his authority was buttressed by ritual and ceremony.

That authority was also the theme of the magnificent artistic output in ivory and cast bronze that became characteristic of Benin. Tradition had it that Iguegha, an artisan in bronze casting, was sent from Ile-Ife to introduce the techniques of making bronze sculptures. Benin then developed its own distinctive style, less naturalistic than that of Ile-Ife but no less impressive. Celebration of the powers and majesty of the royal lineage as well as objects for the rituals surrounding kingship were the subjects of much of this art. When the first Europeans, the Portuguese, visited Benin in the 1480s, they were impressed by the power of the ruler and the extent of his territory. Similarly, the artists of Benin were impressed with the Portuguese, and Benin bronzes and ivories began to include representations of Portuguese soldiers and other themes that reflected the contact with outsiders.

Central African Kingdoms

South of the rain forest that stretched across Africa almost to Lake Victoria lay a broad expanse of savanna and plain, cut by several large rivers such as the Kwango and the Zambezi. From their original home in Nigeria, the Bantu peoples had spread into the southern reaches of the rain forest along the Congo River, then southward onto the southern savannas, and eventually to the east coast. By the 5th century C.E., Bantu farmers and fishermen had reached beyond the Zambezi, and by the 13th century they were approaching the southern end of the continent. Mostly beyond the influence of Islam, many of these central African peoples had begun their own process of state formation by about 1000 C.E., replacing the pattern of kinship-based societies with forms of political authority based on kingship.

Whether the idea of kingship developed in one place and was diffused elsewhere or had multiple origins is unknown, but the older system based on seniority within the kinship group was replaced with rule based on the control of territory and the parallel development of rituals that reinforced the power of the ruler. Several important kingdoms developed. In Katanga, the Luba peoples modified the older system of village headmen to a form of divine kinship in which the ruler and his relatives were thought to have a special power that ensured fertility of people and crops; thus, only the royal lineage was fit to rule. A sort of bureaucracy grew to administer the state, but it was hereditary, so that brothers or male children succeeded to the position. In a way, this system was a half step toward more modern concepts of bureaucracy, but it provided a way of integrating large numbers of people in a large political unit.

The Kingdoms of Kongo and Mwene Mutapa

Beginning about the 13th century, another kingdom was forming on the lower Congo River. By the late 15th century this kingdom of the *Kongo* was flourishing. On a firm agricultural base, its people also developed the skills of weaving, pottery, blacksmithing, and carving. Individual artisans, skilled in the working of wood, copper, and iron, were highly esteemed. There was a sharp division of labor between men and women. Men took responsibility for clearing the forest and scrub, producing palm oil and palm wine, building houses, hunting, and long-distance trade. Women took charge of cultivation in all its aspects, the care of domestic animals, and household duties. On the seacoast, women made salt from sea water, and they also collected the seashells that served as currency in the Kongo kingdom. The population was distributed in small family-based villages and in towns. The area around the capital, Mbanza Kongo, had a population of 60,000 to 100,000 by the early 16th century.

The kingship of the Kongo was hereditary but local chieftainships were not, and this gave the central authority considerable power to control subordinates. In a way, the Kongo kingdom was a confederation of smaller states brought under the control of the manikongo, or king, and by the 15th century it was divided into eight major provinces. The word *mani* means "blacksmith," and it demonstrated the importance of iron and the art of working it in its association with political and ritual power.

Farther to the east, another large Bantu confederation developed among the farming and cattle-herding Shona-speaking peoples in the region between the Zambezi and Limpopo rivers. Beginning in the 9th century C.E., migrants from the west began to build royal courts in stone, to which later immigrants added more polished constructions. There were many of these zimbabwe, or stone house, sites (about 200 have been found) that housed local rulers and subchiefs, but the largest site, called *Great Zimbabwe,* was truly impressive. It was the center of the kingdom and had a religious importance as well, associated with the "bird of God," an eagle that served as a link between the world and the spirits. The symbol of the "bird of God" is found at the ruins of Great Zimbabwe and throughout the area of its control. Great Zimbabwe (not to be confused with the modern nation of Zimbabwe) included several structures, some with strong stone walls 15 feet thick and 30 feet high, a large conical tower, and extensive cut-stone architecture made without the use of mortar to join the bricks together. Observers in the 19th century suspected that Phoenicians or Arabs had built these structures, but archeologists have since established that a Bantu kingdom had begun construction in stone by the 11th century C.E. and had done its most sophisticated building in the 14th and 15th centuries.

By the 15th century, a centralized state centered on Great Zimbabwe had begun to form. It controlled a large portion of the interior of southeast Africa all the way to the Indian Ocean. Under a king who took the title of Mwene Mutapa (which the Portuguese later pronounced as Mono-motapa), this kingdom experienced a short period of considerable expansion in the late 15th and 16th centuries. Its dominance over the sources of gold in the interior eventually gave it great advantages in commerce, which it developed with the Arab port of Sofala on the coast. Evidence of this trade is found in the glass beads and porcelain unearthed by archeologists at Great Zimbabwe. By the 16th century, internal divisions and rebellion had split the kingdom apart, but control of the gold fields still provided a source of power and trade. Representatives of the Mwene Mutapa called at the East Coast ports to buy Indian textiles, and their

Great Zimbabwe was one of several stone settlement complexes in southeastern Africa. Added to at different times, it served as the royal court of the Monomotapa empire.

regal bearing and fine iron weapons impressed the first Europeans who saw them. As late as the 19th century, a much reduced kingdom of Muenemutapa survived in the interior and provided some leadership against European encroachment.

CONCLUSION

Internal Development and External Contacts

This chapter has concentrated on the Sudanic states and the Swahili coast, where the impact of Islam was the most profound and where, because of the existence of written sources, it is somewhat easier to reconstruct the region's history. Sub-Saharan Africa had never been totally isolated from the Mediterranean world or other outside contacts, but the spread of Islam obviously brought large areas of Africa to the global community more intensely, even though Africa remained something of an Islamic frontier. Still, the fusion of Islamic and indigenous African cultures created a synthesis that restructured the life of many Africans.

While the arrival of Islam in Africa in the period from 800 to 1500 was clearly a major event, it would be wrong to see Africa's history in this period exclusively in terms of the Islamic impact. Great Zimbabwe and the Kongo kingdom, to cite only two examples, represented the development of Bantu concepts of kingship and state building relatively independently of trends taking place elsewhere on the continent. Similar processes and accomplishments could also be noted in Benin and among the Yoruba of West Africa. Meanwhile in Ethiopia, East Africa, and the eastern Sudan, the impact of the pre-Islamic Mediterranean world had been long felt.

By the late 15th century when the first Europeans, the Portuguese, began to arrive on the west and east coasts of Africa, they encountered in many places well-developed, powerful kingdoms that were able to deal with the Portuguese as equals from a position of strength. This was even more the case in those parts of Africa that had come under the influence of Islam and through it had established various links with other areas of Muslim civilization. In this period, Africa had increasingly become part of the general cultural trends of the wider world, even though many of these contacts had been brought by outsiders rather than Africans. Moreover, the intensification of the export trade in ivory, slaves, and especially gold from Africa drew Africans, even those far from the centers of trade, into a widening network of relations. With the arrival of Europeans in sub-Saharan Africa in the late 15th century, the pace and intensity of the cultural and commercial contacts became even greater, and many African societies were presented with new and profound challenges.

FURTHER READING

Several of the books recommended on Africa in Chapter 10 are also useful for further reading in relation to this chapter. The period covered in this chapter is summarized in Roland Oliver's and Anthony Atmore's *The African Middle Ages, 1400–1800* (1981). Basil Davidson has produced many excellent popular books that provide a sympathetic view of African development. A good example, prepared to accompany a television series, is *The Story of Africa* (1984). A readable book that gives an overview of African history and emphasizes broad common themes and everyday life is Robert W. July's *Precolonial Africa* (1975). Essential reading on Central Africa is Jan Vansina, *Paths in the Rainforests* (1990).

A very good survey of the early history of Africa with interesting comments on the Nok culture is Susan Keech McIntosh's and Roderick J. McIntosh's "From Stone to Metal: New Perspectives on the Later Prehistory of West Africa," *Journal of World History* vol. 2, no. 1 (1988), 89–133. Basil Davidson has also written, with F. K. Buah, *A History of West Africa* (1966), which presents a good introduction for that region. More detailed, however, is J. F. Ade Ajayi's and Michael Crowder's *History of West Africa*, 2 vols. (1971), which contains excellent review chapters by specialists. For the East African coast, an excellent survey and introduction is provided by Derek Nurse and Thomas Spear in *The Swahili: Reconstructing the History and Language of an African Society* (1985).

Two good books on the Kongo kingdom are Anne Hilton's *The Kingdom of the Kongo* (1985), which shows how African systems of thought accommodated the arrival of Europeans and their culture, and Georges Balandier's *Daily Life in the Kingdom of the Kongo* (1969), which makes good use of travelers' reports and other documents to give a rounded picture of Kongo society. David Birmingham's and Phyllis Martin's *History of Central Africa*, 2 vols. (1983) provides an excellent regional history.

Two multivolume general histories of Africa, which provide synthetic articles by leading scholars on many of the topics discussed in this chapter, are *The Cambridge History of Africa*, 8 vols. (1975–1986) and the UNESCO *General History of Africa*, 7 vols. to date (1981–).

Some important source materials on African history for this period are D. T. Niane's *Sundiata, an Epic of Old Mali* (1986); G. R. Crone, ed., *The Voyages of Cadamosto*, 2d series, vol. 80 (1937), which deals with Mali, Cape Verde, Senegal, and Benin; and H. A. R. Gibb's *The Travels of Ibn Batuta*, 2 vols. (1962), which in vol. 2 includes his visit to the Swahili coast.

CHAPTER 9

Islam in South and Southeast Asia

KEY TERMS

Harsha
Arabic numerals
Mahmud of Ghazni
Delhi Sultanate
Sufi mystics
bhaktic cults

DISCUSSION QUESTIONS

How was Islam "a religious system that was in many ways the opposite... of Hinduism"?

By what means did Islam spread to South and Southeast Asia? Who was most likely to convert to Islam?

In what ways did Islam influence Hindu culture? How was Islam affected by Hindu tradition?

The Coming of Islam to South Asia

Focal Point: From the 7th century onward, successive waves of Muslim invaders, traders, and migrants carried the Islamic faith and elements of Islamic civilization to much of the vast Indian subcontinent. By the 12th and 13th centuries, Muslim dynasties ruled much of north and central India. Muslim conquests and growing numbers of conversions elicited a variety of Hindu responses, and efforts on the part of some of the adherents of both religions to reconcile their very significant differences. Though these efforts resulted only in an uneasy standoff between the two communities, Islamic influences had clearly become a major force in South Asian historical development. They added further layers of richness and complexity to Indian civilization as well as some of its most enduring channels to the peoples and cultures of neighboring lands.

All through the millennia when a succession of civilizations from Harappa to the Brahmanic Empire of the Guptas developed in the subcontinent, foreigners had entered India in waves of nomadic invaders or as small bands of displaced peoples seeking refuge. Invariably, those who chose to remain were assimilated into the civilizations they encountered in the lowland areas. They converted to the Hindu or Buddhist religion, found a place in the caste hierarchy, and adopted the dress, foods, and lifestyles of the farming and city-dwelling peoples of the subcontinent. This capacity to absorb peoples moving into the area owed much to the strength and flexibility of India's civilizations and also to the fact that India's peoples usually enjoyed a higher level of material culture than peoples entering the subcontinent. As a result, the persistent failure of Indian rulers to unite in the face of aggression on the part of outsiders meant periodic disruptions and localized destruction, but not fundamental challenges to the existing order. All of this changed with the arrival of the Muslims in the last years of the 7th century C.E.

With the coming of the Muslims, the peoples of India encountered for the first time a large-scale influx of bearers of a civilization as sophisticated, if not as ancient, as their own. They were also confronted by a religious system that was in many ways the very opposite of their own. Hinduism, the predominant Indian religion at that time, was open, tolerant, and inclusive of widely varying forms of religious devotion—from idol worship to meditation in search of union with the supernatural source of all creation. Islam was doctrinaire, proselytizing, and committed to the exclusive worship of a single, transcendent God.

In contrast to the egalitarianism of Islam, which proclaimed all believers equal in the sight of God, Hindu beliefs did much to validate the caste hierarchy, which rested on the acceptance of inborn differences between individuals and groups and the widely varying levels of material wealth, status, and religious purity these differences produced. Thus, where the faith of the invading Muslims was religiously more rigid than that of the absorptive and adaptive Hindus, the caste-based social system of the great majority of the indigenous peoples was much more compartmentalized and closed than those of the Muslim invaders, with their emphasis on mobility and the community of believers.

Because growing numbers of Muslim warriors, traders, Sufi mystics, and ordinary farmers and herders were able to enter the subcontinent and settle in it, extensive interaction between invaders and the indigenous peoples was inevitable. In the early centuries of the Muslim influx, conflict—often involving violent clashes between the two—predominated. But there was also a good deal of trade and even religious interchange between them. As time passed, peaceful (if wary) interaction became the norm. Muslim rulers employed large numbers of Hindus to govern the largely non-Muslim populations they ruled; mosques and temples dominated different quarters within Indian cities; and Hindu and Muslim mystics strove to find areas of agreement between their two faiths. Tensions remained, and periodically they erupted into communal rioting or sustained warfare between Hindu and Muslim lords.

North India on the Eve of the Muslim Invasions

In the years after the collapse of the Gupta Empire at the end of the 5th century, the heads of numerous regional dynasties aspired to restore imperial unity in North India. But until *Harsha* in the early 7th century, all imperial ambitions were frustrated by timely alliances of rival lords that checked the rise of a single and unifying power center. Harsha was the second son of one of these rival kings, who through a series of wars had carved out a modest domain in the Panjab region to the southeast of the Indus River system. Upon his father's death in 604, Harsha's elder brother ascended the throne. He was soon killed—some accounts say he was treacherously murdered by the agents of a rival confederation of kings centered in Bengal. Although still a youth, Harsha agreed to accept the imperiled throne and was soon at war with the kingdoms of Bengal. The young king proved skillful at forging alliances with other rulers who were the enemies of those in the Bengali confederation; he also was a talented military commander. Soon after ascending the throne, he won a series of battles that both avenged the murder of his brother and led to a great increase in the territories under his control. Within a matter of years, he had pieced together the largest empire India had seen since the fall of the Gupta dynasty over a century earlier.

At the height of his power, Harsha ruled much of the central and eastern Gangetic plain, but his "empire" was a good deal smaller than that of the Guptas. He beat the Bengali lords in battle but was unable to control their lands on a sustained basis, and his attempts to expand into southern and northwest India were unsuccessful. Thus, though he was one of the most powerful rulers India was to know from the time of the Guptas until the establishment of the Delhi sultanate in the 13th century, Harsha's conquests fell far short of uniting even the northern regions of the Indian subcontinent.

The wars that dominated the early years of Harsha's reign gave way to a long period of peace and prosperity for his empire. Content with his early conquests, and too greatly feared by rival rulers to be attacked, Harsha turned his considerable energies to promoting the welfare of his subjects. Like Ashoka, he built roads and numerous rest houses for weary travelers, established hospitals, and endowed temples and Buddhist monasteries. A Chinese pilgrim named Xuan Zang, who visited the Buddhist shrines of India during Harsha's reign, wrote that as the king toured the provinces he would hold audiences for the common people in a special pavilion that was set up alongside the main roads. Judging from Xuan Zang's account, the prosperity of the Gupta age had been largely restored during Harsha's reign. This was particularly true in large towns such as the capital, *Kanauj*, which had formidable walls, palatial homes, and beautiful gardens with artificial tanks or pools. Some of the artistic creativity of the Gupta age was also revived during Harsha's long reign. The ruler was an author of some talent and wrote at least three Sanskrit plays, and he befriended and generously patronized philosophers, poets, artists, and historians.

Though he was probably a Hindu devotee of the god Shiva in his early years, Harsha was tolerant of all faiths and became increasingly attracted to Buddhism. His generous patronage of Buddhist monasteries and the Buddhist monastics attracted pilgrims like Xuan Zang. If Xuan Zang's account can be trusted, Harsha came close to converting to Buddhism in the last years of his life. He sponsored great religious assemblies, which were dominated by Buddhist monks and religious rituals, and he prohibited eating meat and putting an end to human life. His lavish patronage of the Buddhists led on one occasion to a Brahmin-inspired assassination attempt, which appears only to have strengthened his preference for Buddhist ceremonies and beliefs.

Political Divisions and the First Muslim Invasions

Harsha died without a successor in 646, and his kingdom was quickly pulled apart by ambitious ministers who were attempting to found new dynasties of their own. Though Hindu culture flourished in both north and south India in the centuries after Harsha's death—as evidenced by the great temples that were constructed and the works of sculpture, literature, and music that were produced—no paramount kingdom emerged. Political divisions in the north and west-central regions of the subcontinent proved the most significant, because they left openings for a succession of invasions by different Muslim peoples.

The first and least enduring Muslim intrusion, which came in 711, resulted indirectly from the peaceful trading contacts that had initially brought Muslims into contact with Indian civilization. Since ancient times, Arab seafarers and traders had been major carriers in the vast trading network that stretched from Italy in the Mediterranean to the South China Sea. After converting to Islam, these traders continued to frequent the ports of India, particularly those on the western coast. An attack by pirates sailing from Debul (in Sind in western India) on ships owned by some of these Arab traders prompted *Hajjaj*, the viceroy of the eastern provinces of the Umayyad Empire, to launch a punitive expedition against the king of Sind. An able Arab general, *Muhammad ibn Qasim*, who was only 17 years old when the campaign began, led over 10,000 horse- and camel-mounted warriors into Sind to avenge the assault on Arab shipping.

After victories in several fiercely fought battles and successful sieges of the great stone fortresses that stood guard over various parts of the arid and thinly peopled Sind interior, Muhammad ibn Qasim declared the region, as well as the Indus valley to the northeast, provinces of the Umayyad Empire. Soon after the territories had been annexed, a new caliph, who was a bitter enemy of Hajjaj, came to power in Damascus. He purged Hajjaj, and he recalled and executed his son-in-law, Muhammad ibn Qasim. Though the personnel of the ruling Arab elite shifted as a result, the basic policies established by Muhammad ibn Qasim were followed by his Umayyad and Abbasid successors for several centuries.

In these early centuries, the coming of Islam brought little change for most of the inhabitants of the Indian subcontinent. In fact, in many areas, local leaders and the mass of the populace had surrendered towns and districts willingly to the conquerors, who offered the promise of lighter taxation and greater religious tolerance. The Arab overlords decided to treat both Hindus and Buddhists as protected "people of the book," despite the fact that their faiths had no connection to the Bible, the book in question. This meant that although they were obliged to pay special taxes, non-Muslims enjoyed the freedom to worship as they pleased and to maintain their temples and monasteries.

As in other areas conquered by the Arabs, most of the indigenous officials and functionaries retained their positions, which did much to reconcile them to Muslim rule. The status and privileges of the Brahmin castes were also respected. Virtually all the Arabs, who made up only a tiny minority of the population, lived in the cities or special garrison towns. Because little effort was expended in converting the peoples of the conquered areas, they remained overwhelmingly Hindu or Buddhist and, initially at least, displayed scant interest in the beliefs or culture of their new overlords.

Indian Influences on Islamic Civilization

Though the impact of Islam on the Indian subcontinent in this period was limited, the Arab foothold in Sind provided contacts by which Indian learning could be transmitted to the Muslim heartlands in the Middle East. As a result, Islamic civilization was enriched by the skills and discoveries of yet another great civilization. Of particular importance was Indian scientific learning, which rivaled that of the Greeks as the most advanced of the ancient world. Hindu mathematicians and astronomers traveled to Baghdad after the Abbasids came to power in the mid-8th century. Their works on algebra and geometry were translated into Arabic, and their instruments for celestial observation were copied and improved upon by Arab astronomers.

Most critically, Arab thinkers in all fields began to use the numerals that Hindu scholars had devised centuries earlier. Because these numbers were passed on to the Europeans through contacts with the Arabs in the early Middle Ages, we call them Arabic numerals today, but they originated in India. Due to the linkages between civilized centers established by the spread of Islam, this system of numerical notation has proved central to two scientific revolutions: the first in the Middle East, which was discussed previously, and a second, in Europe and subsequently in much of the rest of the world from the 16th century onward, which was a more sustained and fundamental transformation.

In addition to science and mathematics, Indian treatises on subjects ranging from medicine to music were translated and studied by Arab scholars. Indian physicians were brought to Baghdad to run the well-endowed hospitals that the Christian Crusaders found a source of wonderment and a cause for envy. On several occasions, Indian doctors were able to cure Arab rulers and high officials whom Greek physicians had pronounced beyond help. Indian works on statecraft, alchemy, and palmistry were also translated into Arabic, and it is believed that some of the tales in the Arabian Nights were based on ancient Indian stories. Indian musical instruments and melodies made their way into the repertoires of Arab performers, and the Indian game of chess became a favorite of both princes and ordinary townspeople.

Arabs who emigrated to Sind and other Muslim-ruled areas often adopted Indian dress and hairstyles, ate Indian foods, and rode on elephants as the Hindu rajas (kings) did. In this era, additional Arab colonies were established in coastal areas, such as Malabar to the south and Bengal in the east. These trading enclaves would later provide the staging areas from which Islam was transmitted to island and mainland Southeast Asia.

From Booty to Empire: The Second Wave of Muslim Invasions

After the initial conquests by Muhammad ibn Qasim's armies, little territory was added to the Muslim foothold on the subcontinent. In fact, disputes between the Arabs occupying Sind and quarrels with first the Umayyad and later the Abbasid caliphs gradually weakened the Muslim hold on the area and led to the reconquest of parts of the lower Indus valley by Hindu rulers. The slow Muslim retreat was dramatically reversed by a new series of military invasions, this time launched by a Turkish slave dynasty that in 962 had seized power in Afghanistan to the north of the Indus valley. The third ruler of this dynasty, *Mahmud of Ghazni,* led a series of expeditions that initiated nearly two centuries of Muslim raiding and conquest in northern India. Drawn by the legendary wealth of the subcontinent and a zeal to spread the Muslim faith, Mahmud repeatedly raided northwest India in the first decades of the 11th century. He defeated one confederation of Hindu princes after another, and he drove deeper and deeper into the subcontinent in the quest of ever richer temples to sack and loot.

Built in 1626 at Agra, this exquisite tomb of white marble encrusted with semiprecious stones provides a superb example of the blending of Islamic and Hindu architectural forms and artistic motifs.

The raids mounted by Mahmud of Ghazni and his successors gave way in the last decades of the 12th century to sustained campaigns aimed at seizing political control in north India. The key figure in this transition was a tenacious military commander of Persian extraction, *Muhammad of Ghur.* The breakup of the *Ghazni Empire* as a result of the ceaseless quarrels of Mahmud's successors made it possible for the small mountain kingdom of Ghur, near Herat in western Afghanistan, to emerge as a formidable regional power center. After barely surviving several severe defeats at the hands of Hindu rulers, Muhammad put together a string of military victories that brought the Indus valley and much of north-central India under his control. In the following years, Muhammad's conquests were extended along the Gangetic plain as far as Bengal, and into west and central India, by several of his most gifted subordinate commanders. After Muhammad was assassinated in 1206, *Qutb-ud-din Aibak,* one of his slave lieutenants, formed a separate kingdom in the Indian portions of the Ghuri Empire.

Significantly, the capital of the new kingdom was at Delhi along the Jumna River on the Gangetic plain. Delhi's location in the very center of northern India graphically proclaimed that a Muslim dynasty rooted in the subcontinent itself, not an extension of a central Asian empire, had been founded. For the next 300 years, a succession of dynasties would rule much of north and central India. Alternately of Persian, Afghan, Turkic, and mixed descent, the rulers of these imperial houses, who proclaimed themselves the sultans of Delhi, fought each other, Mongol and Turkic invaders, and the indigenous Hindu princes for control of the Indus and Gangetic heartlands of Indian civilization.

All the dynasties that laid claim to the sultanate based their power on large military machines, which were anchored on massive contingents of cavalry and increasingly on corps of war elephants patterned after those that indigenous rulers had used for centuries. The support of their armies and sumptuous court establishments became the main objectives of the extensive bureaucracies that each of the rulers at Delhi attempted to maintain. Though some rulers patronized public works projects, the arts, and charitable relief, most concentrated on maximizing the revenues they could collect from the peasants and townspeople in their domains. Throughout the Delhi sultanate era, however, factional struggles among the ruling Muslims, and their dependence on Hindu lords and village notables in administration at the local level, greatly limited the actual control exercised by any of the dynasties that emerged.

Patterns of Conversion and Accommodation

Though the Muslims literally fought their way into India, their interaction with the indigenous peoples soon came to be dominated by accommodation and peaceful exchanges. Over the centuries when much of the north was ruled by dynasties centered at Delhi, sizable Muslim communities developed in different areas of the subcontinent, particularly in Bengal to the east and in the northwestern provinces in the Indus valley that were the points of entry for most of the Muslim peoples who migrated into India. Few of these converts were won by forcible conversion. The main carriers of the new faith were traders, who played a growing role in both coastal and inland trade, and especially Sufi mystics, who shared much with Indian gurus and wandering ascetics, in both style and message. Belief in their magical and healing powers did much to enhance the Sufis' stature and increase their following. Their mosques and schools often became centers of regional political power. Sufis organized their devotees in militias to fend off bandits or the depredations of rival princes, oversaw the clearing of forests for farming and settlement, and welcomed low and outcaste Hindu groups into the Muslim brotherhood. After their deaths, the tombs of Sufi mystics became objects of veneration for Indian Muslims as well as Hindu and Buddhist pilgrims.

Most of the indigenous converts, who came to form a majority of the Muslims living in India, were drawn from specific regions and social groups. Surprisingly small numbers of converts were found in the Indo-Gangetic centers of Muslim political power—a fact that suggests the very limited importance of forced conversions. Most Indians who converted to Islam were from Buddhist or low-caste groups. In areas such as western India and Bengal, where Buddhism had survived as a popular religion until the era of the Muslim invasions, esoteric rituals and corrupt practices had debased Buddhist teachings and undermined the morale of the monastic orders. This decline was accelerated by Muslim raids on Buddhist temples and monasteries, which provided vulnerable and lucrative targets for the early invaders. Without monastic supervision, local congregations sank further into orgies and experiments with magic, and in some areas into practices, such as human sacrifice, that also disregarded the Buddha's social concerns and religious message. Disorganized and misdirected, Buddhism proved no match for the confident and vigorous new religion the Muslim invaders carried into the subcontinent, particularly when those who were spreading the new faith possessed the charisma and organizing skills of the Sufi mystics.

Though Buddhist converts probably made up the larger portion of the Indians who converted to Islam, untouchables and low-caste Hindus, as well as animistic tribal peoples, were also attracted to the more egalitarian social arrangements promoted by the new faith. As was the case with the Buddhists, group conversions were essential, since those who remained in the Hindu caste system would have little to do with those who converted. Some conversions were also prompted by the desire of Hindus or Buddhists to escape the hated head tax the Muslim rulers levied on unbelievers, and by intermarriage between the indigenous peoples and Muslim migrants. The migrants themselves also increased the size of the Muslim population in the subcontinent. This was particularly true in periods of crisis in central Asia, as in the 13th and 14th centuries when Turkic, Persian, and Afghan peoples retreated to the comparative safety of India in the face of the Mongol and Timurid conquests.

Although Islam won large numbers of converts in certain areas and communities, it initially made little impression on the Hindu community as a whole. Despite military reverses and the imposition of Muslim political rule over large areas of the subcontinent, high-caste Hindus in particular persisted in regarding the invaders as the bearers of an upstart religion and as polluting outcasts. Al-Biruni, one of the chief chroniclers of the Muslim conquests, complained openly about the prevailing Indian disdain for the newcomers:

> ***The Hindus believe that there is no country but theirs, no nation like theirs, no kings like theirs, no religion like theirs, no science like theirs. They are haughty, foolishly vain, self-conceited and stolid.***

Many Hindus were quite willing to take positions as administrators in the bureaucracies of Muslim overlords or as soldiers in their armies and to trade with Muslim merchants. But they remained socially aloof from their conquerors. Separate living quarters in both cities and rural villages were established everywhere Muslim communities developed. Genuine friendships between mem-

DOCUMENT

Mahmūd of Ghanzi and the Conquest of India

Mahmūd of Ghazni (r. 998–1030) is one of the most controversial figures in Indian historiography. His raids mark the beginning of the Turkish conquest of India. For Hindus, he was a fearsome fanatic, a destroyer of temples, and an enemy of Hindu culture; for Muslims, he was a model combination of a king and a holy warrior.

[From Bîrūnî, trans, by E. C. Sachau, Alberuni's India, pp. 19–22]

[The Hindus] totally differ from us in religion, as we believe in nothing in which they believe, and vice versa. On the whole, there is very little disputing about theological topics among themselves; at the utmost, they fight with words, but they will never stake their soul or body or their property on religious controversy. On the contrary, all their fanaticism is directed against those who do not belong to them—against all foreigners. They call them *mleccha*, i.e., impure, and forbid having any connection with them, be it by intermarriage or any other kind of relationship, or by sitting, eating, and drinking with them, because thereby, they think, they would be polluted. They consider as impure anything which touches the fire and the water of a foreigner; and no household can exist without these two elements. Besides, they never desire that a thing which once has been polluted be purified and thus recovered. . . . They are not allowed to receive anybody who does not belong to them, even if he wished it, or was inclined to their religion. This, too, renders any connection with them quite impossible and constitutes the widest gulf between us and them. . . .

But then came Islam; the Persian empire perished, and the repugnance of the Hindus against foreigners increased more and more when the Muslims began to make their inroads into their country, for Muhammad Ibn Qasim entered Sindh [in 711]. He entered India proper, and penetrated even as far as Kanauj, marched through the country of Gandhara, and on his way back, through the confines of Kashmir, sometimes fighting sword in hand, sometimes gaining his ends by treaties, leaving to the people their ancient belief, except in the case of those who wanted to become Muslims. All these events planted a deeply rooted hatred in their hearts.

Now in the following times no Muslim conqueror passed beyond the frontier of Kabul and the river Sindh until the days of the Turks when they seized the power of Ghazni under the Sāmānî dynasty, and the supreme power fell to the lot of Sabuktagîn. This prince chose the holy war as his calling and therefore called himself *Al-ghāzî* (i.e., warring on the road of Allāh). In the interest of his successors he constructed, in order to weaken the Indian frontier, those roads on which he afterwards his son Mahmud marched into India during a period of thirty years and more. God be merciful to both father and son! Mahmud utterly ruined the prosperity of the country and performed there wonderful exploits, by which the Hindus became like atoms of dust scattered in all directions and like a tale of old in the mouth of the people. Their scattered remains cherish, of course, the most inveterate aversion towards all Muslims. This is the reason, too, why Hindu sciences have retired far away from those parts of the country conquered by us and have fled to places which our hand cannot yet reach, to Kashmîr, Benares, and other places. And there the antagonisms between them and all foreigners receives more and more nourishment both from political and religious sources.

bers of high-caste groups and Muslims were rare, and sexual liaisons between them were severely restricted.

During the early centuries of the Muslim influx, the Hindus were convinced that like so many of the peoples who had entered the subcontinent in the preceding millennia, the Muslims would soon be absorbed by the superior religions and more sophisticated cultures of India. Many signs pointed to that outcome. Hindus staffed the bureaucracies and made up a good portion of the armies of Muslim rulers. In addition, Muslim princes adopted regal styles and practices that were Hindu-inspired and contrary to the Quran. Some Hindus proclaimed themselves to be of divine descent, while others minted coins decorated with Hindu images such as Nandi, the bull associated with a major Hindu god, Shiva.

More broadly, Muslim communities became socially divided along caste lines. Recently arrived Muslims were generally on top of the hierarchies that developed, and even they were divided depending on whether they were Arab, Turk, or Persian. High-caste Hindu converts came next, followed by "clean" artisan and merchant groups. Lower-caste and untouchable converts remained at the bottom of the social hierarchy, which may well explain why conversions in these groups were not as numerous as one would expect from the original egalitarian thrust of Islam. Muslims also adopted Indian foods and styles of dress and took to chewing pan, or betel leaves. The Muslim influx had unfortunate consequences for women in both Muslim and Hindu communities. The invaders increasingly adopted the lower age of women at the time of their marriage, and the prohibitions against the remarriage of widows found especially at the high-caste levels of Indian society. Some upper "caste" Muslim groups even performed the ritual of *sati*, the immolation of widows with the bodies of their deceased husbands.

Islamic Challenge and Hindu Revival

Despite a significant degree of acculturation to Hindu lifestyles and social organization, Muslim migrants to the subcontinent held to their own quite distinctive religious beliefs and rituals. The Hindus found Islam impossible to absorb and soon realized that they were confronted by an actively proselytizing religion with great appeal to substantial segments of the Indian population. Partly in response to this challenge, the Hindus placed ever greater emphasis on the devotional cults of gods and goddesses that earlier had proved so effective in neutralizing the challenge of Buddhism. Membership in these devotional, or *bhaktic*, cult groups was open to all, including women and untouchables. In fact, some of the most celebrated writers of religious poetry and songs of worship were women, such as Mira Bai. Saints from low-caste origins were revered by warriors and brahmans as well as by farmers, merchants, and outcasts. Because many songs and poems were composed in regional languages, such as Bengali, Marathi, and Tamil, they were more accessible to the common people and became prominent expressions of popular culture in many areas.

Bhaktic mystics and gurus stressed the importance of a strong emotional bond between the devotee and the god or goddess who was the object of veneration. Chants, dances, and in some settings drugs were used to reach the state of spiritual intoxication that was the key to individual salvation. Once one had achieved the state of ecstasy that came through intense emotional attachment to a god or goddess, all past sins were removed and caste distinctions were rendered meaningless. The most widely worshiped deities were the gods *Shiva* and *Vishnu* (particularly in the guise of Krishna the goatherder) and the goddess Kali in any of several manifestations. By increasing popular involvement in Hindu worship and by enriching and extending the modes of prayer and ritual, the bhaktic movement may have done much to stem the flow of converts to Islam, particularly at the level of low-caste groups. Once again, the Hindu tradition demonstrated its remarkable adaptability and tolerance for widely varying modes of divine worship.

Stand-Off: The Muslim Presence in India at the End of the Sultanate Period

The attempts of mystics like Kabir to minimize the differences between Hindu and Islamic beliefs and worship won only small numbers of the followers of either faith. They were also strongly repudiated by the guardians of orthodoxy in each religious community. Sensing the long-term threat to Hinduism posed by Muslim political dominance and conversion efforts, the Brahmins denounced the Muslims as infidel destroyers of Hindu temples and polluted meat-eaters. Later Hindu mystics, such as the 15th-century holy man Chaitanya, composed songs that focused on love for Hindu deities and set out to convince Indian Muslims to renounce Islam in favor of Hinduism.

For their part, Muslim ulama, or religious experts, grew increasingly aware of the dangers that Hinduism posed for Islam. Attempts to fuse the two faiths were rejected on the grounds that though Hindus might ar-

This Indian miniature painting of milkmaidens serving the Hindu god, Krishna, reflects the highly personalized, devotional worship that was characteristic of the bhaktic movement.

gue that specific rituals and beliefs were not essential, they were fundamental for Islam. If one played down the teachings of the Quran, prayer, and the pilgrimage, one was no longer a true Muslim. Thus, the ulama and even some Sufi mystics stressed the teachings of Islam that separated it from Hinduism. They worked to promote unity within the Indian Muslim community and to strengthen its contacts with Muslims in neighboring lands and the Middle Eastern centers of the faith.

After centuries of invasion and migration, a sizable Muslim community had been established in the Indian subcontinent. Converts had been won, political control had been established throughout much of the area, and strong links had been forged with Muslims in other lands such as Persia and Afghanistan. But non-Muslims, particularly Hindus, remained the overwhelming majority of the population of the vast and diverse lands south of the Himalayas. Unlike the Zoroastrians in Persia or the animistic peoples of the Maghrib and the Sudan, most of the Indians showed little inclination to convert to the religion of the Muslim conquerors.

On the contrary, despite their subjugation, they remained convinced that they possessed a superior religion and civilization and that the Muslims would eventually be absorbed into the expansive Hindu fold. The Muslim adoption of Hindu social forms and Indian customs certainly pointed in this direction. The teachings of Hindu and Muslim mystics threatened to blur the religious boundaries between the two faiths—a process that favored the ascendancy of the more amorphous faith of the Hindu majority. Thus, though Muslim conquests and migration had carried Islam into the heart of one of the most ancient and populous centers of civilization, India remained, after centuries of political dominance and missionary activity, one of the least converted and integrated of all the areas to which the message of Muhammad had spread.

The Spread of Islam to Southeast Asia

Focal Point: The spread of Islam to various parts of coastal India set the stage for its further expansion to island Southeast Asia. Arab traders and sailors regularly visited the ports of Southeast Asia long before they converted to Islam. From the 13th century, these traders, and the Sufi mystics they sometimes carried aboard their ships, spread Islam to Java and much of the rest of island Southeast Asia. As was the case in India, conversion was generally peaceful, and the new believers combined Islamic teachings and rituals with elements of the animist, Hindu and Buddhist religions that had spread through the area in preceding centuries.

From a world history perspective, island Southeast Asia had long been mainly a middle ground, where the Chinese segment of the great Euroasian trading complex met the Indian Ocean trading zone to the west. At ports on the coast of the Malayan peninsula, east Sumatra, and somewhat later north Java, goods from China were transferred from East Asian vessels to Arab or Indian ships, and products from as far west as Rome were loaded into the emptied Chinese ships to be carried to East Asia. By the 7th and 8th centuries C.E., sailors and ships from areas within Southeast Asia—particularly Sumatra and Malaya—had become active in the seaborne trade of the region. Southeast Asian products, especially luxury items—such as aromatic woods from the rain forests of Borneo and Sumatra and spices such as cloves, nutmeg, and mace from the far end of the Indonesian archipelago—had also become important exports to both China in the east and India and the Mediterranean regions in the west. These trading links were to prove even more critical to the expansion of Islam in Southeast Asia than they had earlier been to the spread of Buddhism and Hinduism.

As the coastal trade of India came to be controlled (from the 8th century onward) increasingly by Muslims from such regions as Gujarat and various parts of south India, elements of Islamic culture began to filter into island Southeast Asia. But only in the 13th century after the collapse of the far-flung trading empire of *Shrivijaya,* which was centered on the Strait of Malacca between Malaya and the north tip of Sumatra (see map on p. 284), was the way open for widespread proselytization by Islam. Indian traders, Muslim or otherwise, were welcome to trade in the chain of ports controlled by Shrivijaya. But since the rulers and officials of Shrivijaya were devout Buddhists, there was little incentive for the traders and sailors of Southeast Asian ports to convert to Islam, the religion of growing numbers of the merchants and sailors from India. With the fall of Shrivijaya, the way was open for the establishment of Muslim trading centers and efforts to preach the faith to the coastal peoples.

Trading Contacts and Conversion

As was the case in most of the areas to which Islam spread, peaceful contacts and voluntary conversion were far more important than conquest and force in spreading the faith in Southeast Asia. Throughout the islands of the region, trading contacts paved the way for conversion. Muslim merchants and sailors introduced local peoples to the ideas and rituals of the new faith and impressed on them how much of the known world had already been converted. Muslim ships also carried Sufis to various parts of Southeast Asia, where they were destined to play as vital a role in conversion as they had in India. The first areas to be won to Islam in the last decades of the 13th century were several small port centers on the northern coast of Sumatra. From these parts, the religion spread in the following centuries across the Strait of Malacca to Malaya.

On the mainland the key to widespread conversion was the powerful trading city of *Malacca,* whose smaller trading empire had replaced the fallen Shrivijaya. From Malacca, Islam spread along the coasts of Malaya to east Sumatra and to the trading center of *Demak* on the north coast of Java. From Demak, the most powerful of the trading states on north Java, the Muslim faith was disseminated to other Javanese ports and, after a long struggle with a Hindu-Buddhist kingdom in the interior, to the rest of the island. From Demak, Islam was also carried to the Celebes and the spice islands in the eastern archipelago, and from the latter to Mindanao in the southern Philippines.

This progress of Islamic conversion shows that port cities in coastal areas were particularly receptive to the new faith. Here the trading links were critical. Once one of the key cities in a trading cluster converted, it was in the best interest of others to follow suit in order to enhance personal ties and provide a common basis in Muslim law to regulate business deals. Conversion to Islam also linked these centers, culturally as well as economically, to the merchants and ports of India, the Middle East, and the Mediterranean.

Islam made slow progress in areas such as central Java, where Hindu-Buddhist dynasties contested its spread. But the fact that the earlier conversion to these Indian religions had been confined mainly to the ruling elites in Java and other island areas left openings for mass conversions to Islam that the Sufis eventually exploited. The island of Bali, where Hinduism had taken deep root at the popular level, remained largely impervious to the spread of Islam. The same was true of most of mainland Southeast Asia, where centuries before the coming of Islam, Theravada Buddhism had spread from India and Ceylon and won the fervent adherence of both the ruling elites and the peasant masses.

Sufi Mystics and the Nature of Southeast Asian Islam

Because Islam came to Southeast Asia primarily from India and was spread in many areas by Sufis, it was often infused with mystical strains and displayed a high tolerance for coexistence with earlier animist, Hindu, and Buddhist beliefs and rituals. Just as they had in the Middle East and India, the Sufis who spread Islam in Southeast Asia varied widely in personality and approach. Most were believed by those who followed them to have magical powers, and virtually all Sufis established mosque and school centers from which they traveled in neighboring regions to preach the faith.

In winning converts, the Sufis were willing to allow the inhabitants of island Southeast Asia to retain pre-Islamic beliefs and practices that orthodox scholars would clearly have found contrary to Islamic doctrine. Pre-Islamic customary law remained important in regulating social interaction, whereas Islamic law was confined to specific sorts of agreements and exchanges. Women retained a much stronger position, both within the family and in society, than they had in the Middle East and India. Trading in local and regional markets, for example, continued to be dominated by small-scale female buyers and sellers. In such areas as western Sumatra, lineage and inheritance continued to be traced through the female line after the coming of Islam, despite its tendency to promote male dominance and descent through the male line. Perhaps most tellingly, pre-Muslim religious beliefs and rituals were incorporated into Muslim ceremonies. Indigenous cultural staples, such as the brilliant Javanese puppet shadow plays that were based on the Indian epics of the Brahmanic age, were refined, and they became even more central to popular and elite belief and practice than they had been in the pre-Muslim era.

ANALYSIS

Conversion and Accommodation in the Spread of World Religions

Although not all great civilizations have produced world religions, the two have tended to be closely associated throughout human history. World religions are those that have the capacity to spread across many cultures and societies, to forge links between civilized centers, and to diffuse civilized lifestyles to nomadic pastoral or shifting-cultivating peoples. Religions with these characteristics had appeared before the rise of Islam. As we have seen, India alone produced two of these faiths in ancient times: Hinduism, which spread to parts of Southeast and central Asia, and Buddhism, which spread even more widely in the Asian world. At the other end of the Eastern Hemisphere, Christianity spread throughout the Mediterranean region before claiming northern and western Europe as its core area. Judaism spread not because it won converts in non-Jewish cultures but because the Jewish people were driven from their homeland by Roman persecution and scattered throughout the Middle East, North Africa, and Europe.

Because religious conversion affects all aspects of life, from the way one looks at the universe to more mundane decisions about whom one may marry or how one ought to treat others, a world religion must be broad and flexible enough to permit the retention of much of the existing culture of peoples who are potential converts. At the same time, it must possess core beliefs and practices that are well enough defined to allow its followers to maintain a clear sense of common identity despite their great differences in culture and society. These beliefs and practices must also be sufficiently profound and sophisticated to convince potential converts that their own cultures can be enriched and their lives improved by adopting the new religion.

Until the 16th century, when Christianity claimed the two continents of the Western Hemisphere, no world religion could match Islam in the extent to which it spread across the globe and in the diversity of peoples and cultures that identified themselves as Muslims. Given its uncompromising monotheism, very definite doctrines, and elaborately prescribed rituals and principles of social organization, Islam's success at winning converts from very different cultural backgrounds is at first glance quite surprising. This is particularly true if it is compared with the much more amorphous beliefs and more variable ceremonial patterns of earlier world religions such as Buddhism and Hinduism. Closer examination, however, reveals that the apparent rigidity of Islamic beliefs and social practices, as written in the Quran and interpreted in the abstract by the ulama, proved much more flexible and adaptable in the actual situations in which the religion was introduced into new, non-Islamic cultures. Like all world religions, Islam had the capacity to adjust to widely varying cultural norms and modes of expression even as it was converting the peoples who exhibited these differences to a common set of religious beliefs, ritual forms, and social practices.

The fact that Islam won converts overwhelmingly through peaceful contacts between long-distance traders and the preaching and organizational skills of Sufis exemplifies this capacity for accommodation in the conversion process. Those adopting the new religion did not do so because they were pressured or forced to convert but because they saw Islam as a way to enhance their understanding of the supernatural, enrich their ceremonial expression, improve the quality of their social interaction, and establish ongoing links to a transcultural community beyond their local world.

Because Islam was adopted rather than imposed, those who converted had a good deal to say about how much of their own cultures they would change and which aspects of Islam they would emphasize or accept. Certain beliefs and practices were obligatory for all true believers—the worship of a single God, adherence to the prophet Muhammad and the divine revelations he received as recorded in the Quran, observance of the five pillars of the faith, etc.—but even these were liable to reinterpretation and reworking. In virtually all cultures to which it spread, for example, Islamic monotheism supplanted but did not eradicate the animistic veneration of nature spirits or personal and place deities. Allah was acknowledged as the most powerful and all-purpose of supernatural forces, but people continued to make offerings to spirits that could heal, bring fertility, protect their home, or punish their enemies. In such areas as Africa and western China, where the veneration of ancestral spirits was a key aspect of religious life, the spirits were retained not as powers in themselves but as emissaries to Allah. In cultures like those found in India and Southeast Asia, Islamic doctrines were recast in a heavily mystical, even magical, mode.

The capacity of Islam for accommodation was exhibited in the social as well as the religious sphere. In Islamic Southeast Asia and, as we shall see in the next chapter, sub-Saharan Africa, the position of women remained a good deal stronger in critical areas, such as occupational outlets and family law, than it had become in the Middle East and India. In both regions, the malecentric features of Islam that had grown more pronounced through centuries of accommodation in ancient Middle Eastern and Persian cultures were played down as Islam adapted to societies where women had traditionally enjoyed considerable influence, both within the extended family and in occupations such as farming, marketing, and craft production. Even an institution like the caste system of India, which in principle is so opposed to the strong egalitarian strain in Islam, developed among Muslim groups that migrated into the subcontinent and survived in indigenous South Asian communities that converted to Islam.

Beyond basic forms of social organization and interaction, Islam accommodated diverse aspects of the societies into which it spread. The African solar calendar, for example, which was essential for the coordination of the planting cycle, was retained alongside the Muslim lunar calendar. In India, Hindu-Buddhist symbols of kingship were appropriated by Muslim rulers and acknowledged by both their Hindu and Muslim subjects. In island Southeast Asia, exquisitely forged knives, called *krises*, which were believed to have magical powers, were among the most treasured possessions of local rulers both before and after they converted to Islam.

There was always the danger that accommodation could go too far—that in winning converts, Islamic precepts and rituals would be so watered down and remolded that they no longer resembled and, in fact, actually contradicted the teachings of the Quran. Sects that came to worship Muhammad or his nephew Ali as godlike, for example, had clearly moved beyond the Muslim pale. This danger was a key source of the periodic movements for purification and revival that have been a notable feature of virtually all Islamic societies, particularly those on the frontier fringes of the Islamic world. But even these movements, which were built around the insistence that the Muslim faith had been corrupted by alien ideas and practices and that there had to be a return to Islamic fundamentals, were invariably cast in the modes of cultural expression of the peoples who rallied to them. What was considered fundamental varied according to culture, and perhaps more important, the ways in which basic beliefs were interpreted and rituals enacted differed significantly from one Islamic culture to the next.

Questions: Can you think of ways in which world religions, such as Christianity, Hinduism, and Buddhism, changed to accommodate the cultures and societies to which they spread? Do these religions strike you as more or less flexible than Islam? Why? Do you think it is possible for a set of religious beliefs and practices to become a world religion without changing as it moves from one culture to the next? If not, why? If so, can you think of a religion that has?

CONCLUSION

The Legacy of the Abbasid Age

Though problems of political control and succession continued to plague the kingdoms and empires that divided the Muslim world, the central position of Islamic civilization in global history was solidified during the centuries of Abbasid rule. Its role as the go-between for the other, more ancient civilizations of the Eastern Hemisphere grew as Arab trading networks expanded and reached into new areas. More than ever, it became the civilizer of nomadic peoples, from the Turks and Mongols of central Asia to the Berbers of North Africa and the camel herders of the Sudan. Equally critically, Islam's original contributions to the growth and refinement of civilized life greatly increased. From its great cities and universities and the accomplishments they generated in the fine arts, sciences, and literature to its vibrant religious and philosophical life, Islam pioneered patterns of organization and thinking that would affect the development of human societies in major ways for centuries to come.

In the midst of all this achievement, however, there were tendencies that would put the Muslim peoples at a growing disadvantage, particularly in relation to their long-standing European rivals. Muslim divisions would leave openings for political expansion that the Europeans would eagerly exploit, beginning with the island Southeast Asian extremities of the Islamic world and then working their way across Muslim North India. The Muslims' inclination to leave commerce and entrepreneurship increasingly in the hands of non-Muslim groups, such as Jews and Christians, would hamper effective responses to their growing economic dependence on the West and other civilizations, particularly China, and their increasing backwardness relative to them. Above all, the growing orthodoxy and intolerance of the ulama, as well as the Muslim conceit that the vast Islamic world contained all requirements for civilized life, caused Muslim peoples to grow less receptive to outside influences and innovations. These tendencies became increasingly pronounced at precisely the time when their Christian rivals were entering a period of unprecedented curiosity, experimentation, and exploration of the world beyond their own civilized regions. The combination of these trends would put the Islamic world at a growing disadvantage vis-à-vis the West and would eventually engender a profound crisis in Islamic civilization that continues in the present day.

FURTHER READING

M. A. Shaban's *Islamic History: An Interpretation,* 2 vols. (1971) contains the most readable and thematic survey of early Islam, concentrating on the Abbasid period. Though Philip Hitti's monumental *History of the Arabs* (1967) and J. J. Saunders's *A History of Medieval Islam* (1965) are now somewhat dated, they contain much valuable information and some fine insights into Arab history. Also useful are the works of G. E. von Gruenenbaum, especially *Classical Islam* (1970), which covers the Abbasid era. On changes in Islamic religion and the makeup of the Muslim community, Marshall Hodgson's *Venture of Islam* (1974, vol. 2) is indispensable, but again it should not be tackled by the beginner. *The Cambridge History of Islam,* 2 vols. (1970), Ira Lapidus's *A History of Islamic Societies* (1988), and Albert Hourani's *A History of the Islamic Peoples* (1991) provide excellent reference works for the political events of the Abbasid era and Muslim achievements in various fields. D. M. Dunlop's *Arab Civilization to A.D. 1500* (1971) also contains detailed essays on the latter aspects of Islamic culture as well as an article on the accomplishments of Muslim women in this era.

On social history, B. F. Musallam's *Sex and Society in Islam* (1983) has material on the Abbasid period, and Ira Lapidus's study, *Muslim Cities in the Later Middle Ages* (1967), remains the standard work on urban life in the premodern era. Two essential works on the spread of Islam to India are S. M. Ikram's *Muslim Civilization in India* (1964) and Aziz Ahmad's *Studies in Islamic Culture in the Indian Environment* (1964). For the role of the Sufis in Islamic conversion, Richard Eaton's *Sufis of Bijapur* (1978) and *The Rise of Islam and the Bengal Frontier* (1993) are particularly revealing. The best introduction to the pattern of Islamic conversion in Southeast Asia is H. J. de Graaf's essay in *The Cambridge History of Islam* (1976, vol. 2). Clifford Geertz's *Islam Observed* (1968) provides a sweeping and provocative interpretation of the process of conversion in general and of the varying forms Islam takes in the Javanese and Moroccan milieux in particular.

CHAPTER 10

A Golden Age in East Asia

KEY TERMS

T'ang Dynasty	*Korea*
Empress Wu	*Nara Period*
Yangtze River	*Shinto*
Ch'ang An	*Heian Period*
Sung Dynasty	*Fujiwara*
Jurchen	*Lady Murasaki*
Mongols	*Kamakura Period*
Yuen Dynasty	*shogun*
Kubilai Khan	*Ashikaga*

DISCUSSION QUESTIONS

How did the T'ang and Sung Dynasties succeed in uniting China?

Why was the Sung Dynasty eventually overthrown?

In what ways has Japan been influenced by Chinese culture?

What aspects of Japanese tradition were not transformed by Chinese influences?

The period from the sixth to the fourteenth centuries saw the reunification of China following a long period of division. After 600 years of renewed imperial splendor under the T'ang dynasty and its successor, the Sung (Song), China was overrun by the Mongols and ruled as part of their short-lived empire from 1279 to 1368, when a new Chinese dynasty, the Ming, restored Chinese power. During the same period, Korean civilization matured, produced a series of effective dynasties, and added innovations to the Chinese culture it had adopted from the earlier Han dynasty in China. In the eighth century Japan evolved a literate civilization on the model of T'ang China and in subsequent centuries produced a highly sophisticated court culture. Japan slowly dissolved into chronic fighting between rival clans until unity was reimposed by the founders of the Tokugawa shogunate by 1600.

Emperor T'ang T'ai-tsung (626–649) was a brilliant field commander whose campaigns reestablished Chinese control over Sinkiang and northern Vietnam, conquered Tibet, and even extended imperial rule into central Asia. An astute administrator, T'ai-tsung also restored and extended the imperial bureaucratic system of the Han.

Reunification in China

For nearly four centuries after the fall of the Han dynasty in 220 China was divided into many separate kingdoms, with much of the north under barbarian control. Buddhism flourished, perhaps as a response to the troubled times, and was promoted also by the Sinicized rulers of the north. The chief such kingdom, known as the Northern Wei, controlled most of North China from 386 to 534. It built a number of splendid Buddhist cave temples with statues of the Buddha and his devotees whose style, though Chinese, reveals Indian influence, as do the many pagodas, a temple form adapted from the Indian stupa.

The Chinese cultural and political tradition proper was carried on by a succession of rival dynasties vying for supremacy in the south, which was enriched by a flood of wealthy and educated refugees from the north. Nanking (Nanjing) was the chief southern capital and major urban center, but none of the southern dynasties or kingdoms was able either to unify the region or to provide strong government. Literature, philosophy, and the arts continued vigorously despite the absence of political unity, and Buddhism also became popular in the south. This was the period of both Indian Buddhist missions to China and Chinese pilgrim visits to India; it was also a time of new technological achievements, including gunpowder, advances in medicine, refinements in the use of a magnetized needle for indicating direction (the forerunner of the compass), and the use of coal as a fuel.

Most politically conscious Chinese wanted to see the Han model of greatness restored, but first the country had to be reunified and the imperial machine rebuilt. This was primarily the work of the short-lived Sui dynasty, which in 589 welded contending Chinese states together by conquest. Interestingly, the Sui base was the same Wei valley from which the Ch'in had erupted, and like the Ch'in, the Sui built roads and canals to connect their empire, radiating out from their capital at Ch'ang An.

The second Sui emperor, Yang Ti (604–618), heady with new power, is often compared to Ch'in Shih Huang Ti. He too rebuilt the Great Wall, at a cost of an additional million lives, and reconquered northern Vietnam as well as much of Sinkiang and Mongolia, although his campaign in Korea was defeated by fierce resistance. Yang Ti built a magnificent new capital at Loyang, following the model of the Chou and the Han, but at heavy expense. Perhaps his most notable project was the building of the Grand Canal, from Hangchou (Hangzhou) in the south to Kaifeng in the north, to bring rice from the productive Yangtze delta for troops and officials in semiarid northern China. But his megalomaniacal behavior caused great suffering to his exhausted troops, forced laborers, taxpayers, and tyrannized officials. Rebellion spread, as in the last years of the Ch'in, and Yang Ti was assassinated by a courtier in 618 after only 14 years on the throne. A frontier general swept away the pretensions of the Sui heir and proclaimed a new dynasty, the T'ang. Although the new dynasty was to last nearly 300 years, it owed its success in large part to the foundations laid by the Sui, as the Han had rested on those of the Ch'in.

The T'ang Dynasty

Under T'ang rule China achieved a new high point in prosperity, cultural sophistication and greatness, and imperial power. The cosmopolitan T'ang capital at Ch'ang An (Qangan), where the Han had ruled, was the world's largest city, with about 2 million inhabitants. The imper-

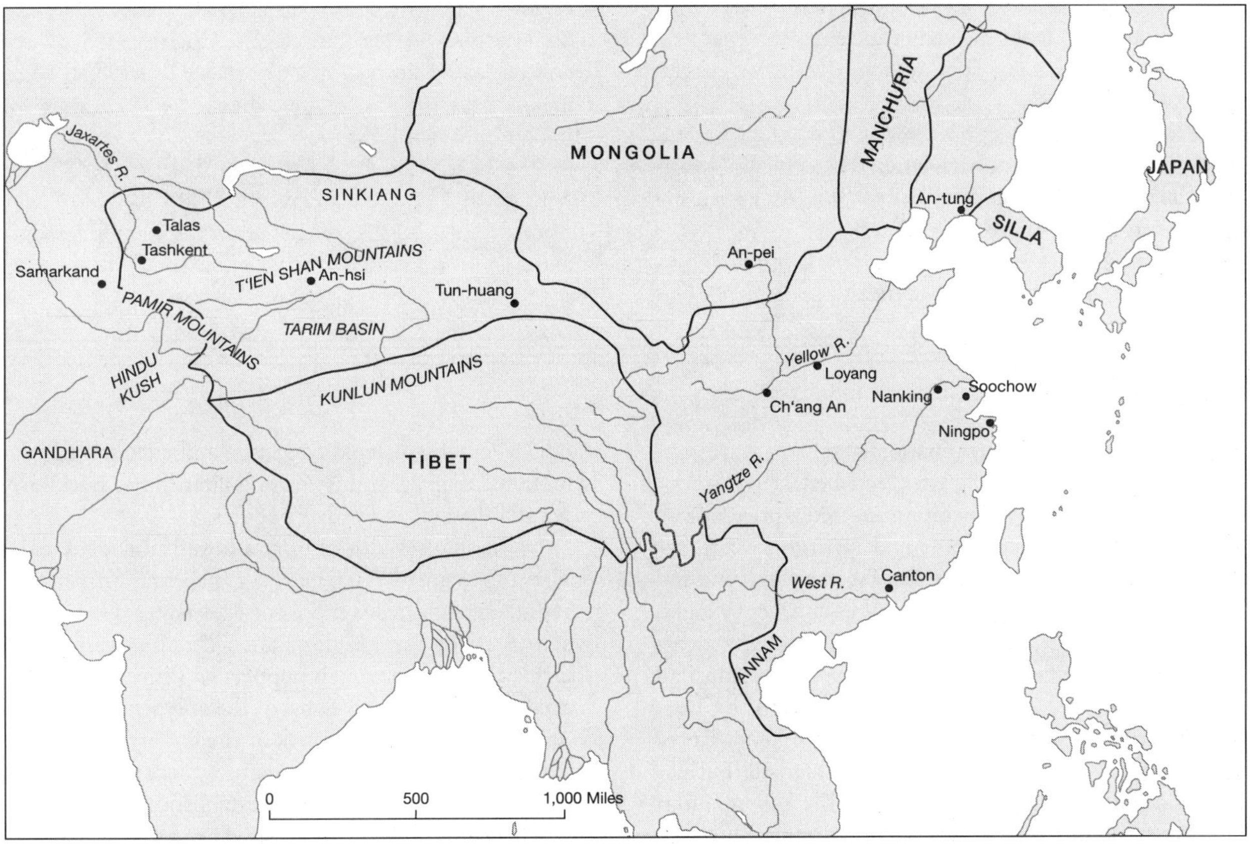

China Under the T'ang

DOCUMENT

The Examination System During the T'ang Dynasty
(8th century)

The importance of the examination system in identifying the future governors of China inevitably led to snobbery and hypocrisy. Stories of abuses became a part of folk culture and served both as warnings and instruction for succeeding generations. The following are a selection of such tales.

Hsiao Ying-shih passed the imperial examination in 735. Proud of his talent, he was unequaled in conceit and arrogance. He often took a pot of wine and went out to visit rural scenic areas. Once during such an outing, he stayed at an inn, drinking and chanting poetry by himself. Suddenly a storm arose, and an old man dressed in a purple robe came in with a page boy to take shelter. Because of their informality, Hsiao Ying-shih treated them rather insolently. In a short while, the storm was over, the rain stopped, carriages and retinues came, and the old man was escorted away. Flustered, Hsiao Ying-shih inquired about the old man's identity, and the people around him said, "That was the Minister of the Board of Civil Office."

Now, Hsiao Ying-shih had gone to see the Minister many times, yet had not been received. When he heard that the old man was none other than the Minister himself, he was flabbergasted.

The next day Hsiao brought a long letter with him and went to the Minister's residence to apologize. The Minister had him brought into the hallway and scolded him severely. "I regret that I am not related to you in any way, otherwise I would like to give you some good 'family discipline,'" said the Minister. "You are reputed to be a literary talent, yet your arrogance and poor manners are such that it is perhaps better for you to remain a mere *chin-shih* (presented scholar)."

Hsiao Ying-shih never got anywhere in officialdom, dying as a Chief Clerk in Yang prefecture.

Lu Chao was from I-ch'un of Yuan-chou. He and Huang P'o, also from the same prefecture, were equally famous. When they were young, Huang P'o was wealthy, but Lu Chao was very poor. When they were ready for the imperial examination, the two of them decided to set out on the trip together. The Prefect gave a farewell dinner at the Pavilion of Departure, but Huang P'o alone was invited. When the party was at its peak, with lots of wine and music, Lu Chao passed by the Pavilion, riding an old, weak horse. He traveled some ten *li* out of the city limits, then stoped to wait for Huang P'o to join him.

The next year, Lu Chao came back to his hometown, having been awarded the title of *chuang-yüan* [number one]. All the officials from the Regional Commander on down came out to welcome him, and the Prefect of Yuan-chou was greatly embarrassed.

ial civil service and the examination system were reestablished, and learning and the arts flourished.

The rebuilding of the empire exacted a price, for all its glory. Most of the Han-ruled territories were reclaimed by conquest after they had fallen away at the end of the Sui, including northern Vietnam, but Tibet, Sinkiang, Mongolia, and southern Manchuria were wisely left as tributary regions, after their inhabitants had been defeated in a brilliant series of campaigns by Emperor T'ang T'ai-tsung (Tang Taizong, 626–649). Korea again fought the Chinese armies to a standstill but accepted tributary status, and much of the mountainous southwest, home of the Thai and other groups, remained outside imperial rule. T'ai-tsung is remembered as a model ruler who fostered education and encouraged conscientious officials. In his cosmopolitan time, Buddhism was still tolerated and widely popular.

In the late seventh century a beautiful concubine of T'ai-tsung's named Wu Chao (Wuzhao) was made a consort and empress by his successor Kao-tsung (Gao-zong), whom she soon came to dominate. After his death in 683 she ruled alone or through puppets and then proclaimed herself emperor of a new dynasty, the only female emperor in Chinese history. She struck at the old aristocracy, her chief opposition, and ordered many of them executed. She drew support from the Buddhist establishment, which she strongly favored and which declared her a reincarnation of the Bodhisattva Maitreya, the Buddhist messiah. Wu

Once when the Prefect invited him to watch the Dragon Boat Race, Lu Chao composed a poem during the banquet which read:

"It is a dragon," I told you.
But you had refused to believe.
Now it returns with the trophy,
Much in the way I predicted.

Lu Hui's mother's brother was Cheng Yü. As his parents died when he was small, Lu Hui was brought up in his mother's family, and Cheng Yu often encouraged him to take the imperial examination and become a *chin-shih.* Lu Hui was recommended for the examinations for the "widely brilliant" in the early part of 870, but in 880, bandits encroached on the capital, forcing him to flee to the south. At that same time Cheng Yü's son Hsü was stationed in Nanhai as a Regional Commander. Lu Hui and Cheng Hsü had gone to school together, but when Hsü was already a county official, Hui was still a commoner. The two of them, however, equally enjoyed the favor of Cheng Yü.

During the ten years in which Cheng Hsü rose to become a Governor-General, Lu Hui remained a destitute scholar. Once again he managed to escape an uprising and came back to Cheng Hsü, carrying but one sack of personal belongings. Cheng Hsü still treated him kindly. At this time, the Emperor was on the expedition to Shu, and the whole country was in turmoil. Cheng Hsü encouraged Lu Hui to seize the opportunity to advance himself. "How long can a man live?" he said to Lu Hui. "If there is a shortcut to riches and fame, why insist on going through the examination?"

But Lu Hui was adamant. Cheng Hsü asked his friends and assistants to try to persuade Lu Hui to give up the exams; he even left the seat on his right-hand side vacant for Lu Hui to occupy. Lu Hui therefore said to him, "Our great nation has established the examination system for the outstanding the talented. I do not have the ability and dare not dream of such honors. However, when he was alive, my uncle again and again encouraged me to take the examinations. Now his study is empty and quiet, but I cannot bring myself to break our agreement. If I have to die as a mere student, it is my fate. But I will not change my mind for the sake of wealth. I would sooner die."

When Cheng Hsü saw Lu Hui's determination, he respected him even more than before. Another ten years passed before Lu Hui finally passed the examination under the Lord of Hung-nung, and he died as one of the highest officials in the whole empire.

Chao had become a Buddhist nun after T'ai-tsung's death in 650, but she soon grew restless without greater scope for her talents. Empress Wu, as she is called, was denounced by Chinese historians, although their criticism has clear sexist overtones. She was a strong and effective, if ruthless, ruler, obviously opposed to the Confucian establishment and promoting its rival, the alien faith of Buddhism. Her being a woman in addition was just too much for her opponents to deal with, and she was deposed in a palace coup.

The gradual Sinification of the originally non-Han south below the Yangtze valley continued under the imperial momentum. By the late T'ang most of the empire's revenue came from the more productive south, including the Yangtze valley, and most Chinese lived in that area. The north, where the empire had been born, suffered as always from recurrent drought, erosion, and the silting of its vital irrigation works. But now the south, progressively cleared of its earlier forests, more than made up the difference. Agricultural techniques were slowly adapted to the wetter and hillier conditions and the far longer growing season of the south. The increasing use of human manure ("night soil") improved the less fertile soils outside the alluvial river valleys, supporting a continued increase of population, which thus provided still more night soil. Many northerners had fled south after the fall of the Han dynasty; now they and their descendants were joined by new streams seeking greater economic opportunity than in the overcrowded and often marginal north. Imperial tradition and the defense of the troublesome northwest frontiers kept the capital in the north, but the south was the empire's principal economic base.

Renewing their contacts with more distant lands westward, the Chinese found no other civilization that could rival the Celestial Empire. The Son of Heaven, as the emperor was called, was seen as the lord of "all under heaven," meaning the four corners of the known world, within which China was clearly the zenith of power and sophistication. Did not all other people the Chinese encountered acknowledge this, by tribute, praise, and imitation of Chinese culture, the sincerest form of flattery?

In fact, even beyond the world the Chinese knew, they had no equal. Rome was long gone, and the Abbasid caliphate was no match for the T'ang or its great successor, the Sung. A coalition of Arabs and western Turks did repulse a T'ang expeditionary force at the battle of the Talas River near Samarkand in 751, but the battle is perhaps more significant in that some captured Chinese transmitted the recently developed T'ang arts of printing and papermaking to the West. The mass production of paper dated from the late first century C.E., although it had been invented a century earlier. Printing, which began about 700, was first done from carved wooden blocks a page at a time, but by 1030 the Chinese, and only slightly later the Koreans, had developed movable-type printing, with individual characters made of wood, ceramics, or metal. Only in the fifteenth century would this technique reach Europe.

Paper and printing were typical creations of the Chinese, with their love of written records and of learning, literature, and painting. They were only two of China's basic gifts to the West, along with cast iron, the crossbow, gunpowder, the compass, the use of coal as fuel, the water wheel, paper currency, the wheelbarrow, wallpaper, and porcelain, to mention only a few. Porcelain had matured by T'ang times, and from it were made objects of exquisite beauty whose refinement was never matched elsewhere. Porcelain, silk, and later tea became China's chief exports.

The secret of making silk had been supposedly smuggled out of China by two monks at the time of the eastern Roman emperor Justinian (527–565) in the form of cocoons concealed in hollow walking sticks. But later Western silk production in Italy and France never equaled the Chinese in quality, just as European porcelain, developed in the eighteenth century, never reproduced the perfection of form and finish of the Chinese models.

Tea was introduced from Southeast Asia as a medicine and an aid to meditation and began to be drunk widely in fifth-century China. It became the basic Chinese drink during the T'ang, grown in quantities in the misty hills of the south. By the eighteenth century it was a major item of export to the West. Seeds and cuttings of the tea plant were smuggled out of China by the English East India Company in 1843 to start plantation production in India and Ceylon, and tea became the world's most popular drink.

Ch'ang An in an Age of Imperial Splendor

The splendor of the T'ang and its empire was symbolized in its capital at Ch'ang An, where the Han and the Ch'in had also ruled. It was the eastern terminus of trade routes linking China with central Asia and lands beyond and also presided over the largest empire the world had yet seen, exceeding even the Han and Roman empires. People from all over Asia—Turks, Indians, Persians, Syrians, Vietnamese, Koreans, Japanese, Jews, Arabs, and even Nestorian (eastern) Christians—thronged its streets and added to its cosmopolitan quality. It was probably also the largest wholly planned city ever built, covering some 30 square miles and including within its massive walls about a million people. The imperial census also recorded nearly another million living in the urban area outside the walls.

Like all Chinese administrative centers, Ch'ang An was laid out on a checkerboard pattern, with broad avenues running east-west and north-south to great gates at the cardinal compass points. These were closed at night, and the main avenues leading to them divided the city into major quarters. These were further subdivided by other principal streets into groups of 110 blocks, each constituting an administrative unit, with its own internal pattern of alleyways. The emperor's palace faced south down a 500-foot-wide central thoroughfare to the south gate, the one used by most visitors and all official envoys and messengers. This arrangement was designed to awe and impress all who came to Ch'ang An with the power and greatness of the empire. Kaifeng and Peking were later designed similarly, and for the same purpose.

Within the city, people lived in rectangular wards, each surrounded by walls with gates closed at night. The West Market and the East Market, supervised by the government, occupied larger blocks to serve their respective halves of the city. There and elsewhere in the city, in open spaces and appointed theaters, foreign and Chinese players, acrobats, and magicians performed dramas, operas, skits, and other amusements. Women of fashion paraded their fancy clothing and coiffures. For men and women alike, one of the most popular pastimes was polo, which had been adopted from Persia; T'ang paintings showing polo matches make it clear that women played too. As later in India, the wealthy prided themselves on their stable of good polo ponies and their elegant turnout for matches.

Artists and sculptors also found horses popular subjects; despite their apparent mass production, T'ang paintings and clay figurines of horses are still full of life and movement. Another favorite subject for art was the endless variety of foreigners in this cosmopolitan center, depicted faithfully in both painting and figurines, so that one can easily recognize, by dress and physical features, which people are being represented.

T'ang culture was worldly, elegant, and urbane, but Buddhism was still in vogue and in official favor. Buddhist temples and pagodas also gave Chinese architects an outlet for their talents, and the first half of the T'ang was a golden age of temple architecture and sculpture, the latter showing clear artistic as well as religious influences from the Indian home of Buddhism. A cosmopolitan center for all of Asia, Ch'ang An was also, like China, the cultural model for the rest of East Asia. Official emissaries and less formal visitors and merchants or adventurers came repeatedly from Korea, Japan, and lesser states to the south and west to bask in the glories of Ch'ang An and to take back with them as much as they could for building their own versions of T'ang civilization.

Persian Zoroastrians, Muslims, Jews, Indian Buddhists and Hindus, and Nestorian Christians and Byzantines from the eastern Mediterranean, representing nearly all the great world religions, were among the city's permanent residents, all welcomed in this center of world culture and all leaving some evidence of their presence. Ch'ang An flourished for two and one half centuries, from the early seventh to the mid-ninth, when the capital, like the empire, fell into chaos. But from 618 to around 860 it shone with a cosmopolitan brilliance perhaps never equaled until modern times.

Cultural Achievement and Political Decay

The T'ang is still seen as the greatest period of Chinese poetry, especially in the work of Li Po (Li Bo, 701–762) and Tu Fu (Du Fu, 712–770). Some 1,800 samples of Li Po's 20,000 poems survive, including these lines:

Beside my bed the bright moonbeams glimmer
Almost like frost on the floor.
Rising up, I gaze at the mountains bathed in moonlight:
Lying back, I think of my old home.
A girl picking lotuses beside the stream—
At the sound of my oars she turns;

The poet Li Po (701–762) is perhaps the most appealing T'ang figure. His poetry is still learned and quoted by successive generations of Chinese.

She vanishes giggling among the flowers,
And, all pretense, declines to come out.
Amid the flowers with a jug of wine
The world is like a great empty dream.
Why should one toil away one's life?
That is why I spend my days drinking. . . .
Lustily singing, I wait for the bright moon.
I drink alone with no one to share
Raising up my cup, I welcome the moon. . . .
We frolic in revels suited to the spring.

The legend, almost certainly untrue but appealing, is that Li Po drunkenly leaned out of a boat to embrace the reflection of the moon and drowned, happy in his illusion.

Tu Fu was a more sober poet than Li Po, but equally admired. Here are some samples of his lines:

Frontier war drums disrupt everyone's travels.
At the border in autumn a solitary goose honks.

Tonight the hoar frost will be white. . . .
I am lucky to have brothers, but all are scattered. . . .
The letters I write never reach them.
How terrible that the fighting cannot stop.
Distant Annam sends the court a red parrot,*
Gaudy as a peach blossom and as talkative as we are.
But learning and eloquence are given the same treatment:
The cage of imprisonment. Is one ever free?
The capital is captured, but hills and streams remain.
With spring in the city the grass and trees grow fast.
Bewailing the times, the flowers droop as if in tears.
Saddened as I am with parting, the birds make my heart flutter.
Army beacons have flamed for three months.
A letter from home now would be worth a king's ransom.
In my anxiety I have scratched my white hairs even shorter.
What a jumble! Even hairpins cannot help me.

Relatively little T'ang painting or literature has survived, apart from a few tomb walls and a few texts, but we have many accounts of the great painters of the time and of fiction writers of whose work we have only a few samples. What have survived in great abundance are the magnificent glazed pottery figures used to furnish tombs and adorn houses and palaces, probably the best-known aspect of T'ang art. Learning and the arts enjoyed a further blossoming under Emperor Hsuan-tsung (Xuanzong, 712–756) and at his elegant court. But in his old age Hsuan-tsung became infatuated with a son's concubine, the beautiful Yang Kuei-fei, who with her relatives and protégés gained control of the empire but ran it badly. Rebellion resulted, and the capital was sacked in 755. Hsuan-tsung fled south with Lady Yang, but his resentful guards strangled her as the cause of all the empire's troubles, and Hsuan-tsung abdicated in sorrow. The rebellion was finally put down, and order was restored.

Although there were to be no more outstanding T'ang emperors and the power of court factions and great families grew, the economy thrived and culture flourished. A Confucian revival occurred in the ninth century, and partly as a result, the state moved to confiscate the wealth and destroy the political power of Buddhist temples, monasteries, and monks in the 840s. Most temple and monastic properties and tax-free estates, which had grown to immense size, were taken over by the state, and most monasteries were destroyed. The move was similar to that undertaken by King Henry VIII of England seven centuries later, and with similar motives—the need to regain undivided power and control over lost revenues. Chinese Buddhism never recovered from this blow and remained thereafter a small minority religion in a Confucian and Taoist society. Buddhism was also resented by many Chinese because of its foreign origins, especially orthodox Confucianists and dedicated Taoists, as Christianity was to be later. Its association with Empress Wu did not help.

Like its Han predecessor, the T'ang dynasty lost effectiveness over time and was weakened by corruption. A series of rebellions broke out after 875, prompted first by a great drought in the north but spreading quickly among disaffected subjects all over the country. Rival generals or their puppets succeeded one another on the throne after 884, and in 907 the dynasty dissolved. After a period of confusion, a young general proclaimed a new dynasty in 960, the Sung, which was to last more than three centuries.

The Sung Dynasty

In many ways, the Sung is the most exciting period in Chinese history. Later Chinese historians have criticized it because it failed to stem the tide of barbarian invasion and was ultimately overwhelmed by the hated Mongols. But it lasted from 960 to 1279, roughly the 300-year average for most dynasties, and presided over a period of unprecedented growth, innovation, and cultural flowering. For a long time the Sung policy of defending the empire's essential territories and appeasing neighboring barbarian groups with money and flattery worked well. It made sense to give up the exhausting Han and T'ang effort to hold Sinkiang, Tibet, Mongolia, Manchuria, Vietnam, and even the more marginal arid fringes of northern China. These areas were all unprofitable from the Chinese point of view; they never repaid, in any form but pride, the immense costs of controlling them. Most of them were arid or mountainous wastelands thinly settled by restless nomads who took every chance to rebel and who were very effective militarily.

Vietnam and Korea had been chronic drains on China's wealth and military strength; both were determined to fight relentlessly against Chinese control but willing to accept a more or less nominal tributary status, which satisfied Chinese pride and avoided bloody struggles. The Sung wisely concentrated on the productive center of Han Chinese settlements south of the Great Wall and even accepted barbarian control of what is now the Peking area and a similar arrangement with another barbarian group in the arid northwestern province of

*Annam is central Vietnam, beyond the empire's direct rule, but, as implied here, tributary.

Kansu (Gansu). Little of value was lost by these agreements, and the remarkable flowering of Sung China had much to do with its abandonment of greater imperial ambitions. What remained under Chinese control was still roughly the size of non-Russian Europe and, with a population of some 100 million, was by far the largest, most productive, and most highly developed state in the world.

The Sung capital was built at Kaifeng, near the great bend of the Yellow River. In addition to its administrative functions, it became a huge commercial entrepôt and a center of manufacturing, served in all respects by the Grand Canal, which continued to bring rice and other goods from the prosperous south. There was a notable boom in iron and steel production and metal industries, using coal as fuel. China in the eleventh century probably produced more iron, steel, and metal goods than the whole of Europe until the mid-eighteenth century and similarly preceded Europe by seven centuries in smelting and heating with coal. Kaifeng was better located to administer and to draw supplies from the Yangtze valley and the south than Ch'ang An, whose role in frontier pacification was in any case no longer so necessary. The Sung army was large, mobile, equipped with iron and steel weapons, and well able for some time to defend the state's new borders. Kaifeng probably exceeded a million inhabitants, with merchants and artisans proportionately more important than in the past, although there were also swarms of officials, soldiers, providers, servants, and hangers-on of various sorts.

The early Sung emperors prudently eliminated the power of the court eunuchs and the great landed families and reestablished the scholar-officialdom as the core of administration. Civil servants recruited through examination had no power base of their own but did have a long tradition of public service and could even check the abuses of the powerful. To ensure their loyalty to the empire, their local postings were changed every three years, and they never served in their native places, lest they become too identified with the interests of any one area. In each county and at each higher level the emperor appointed both a civil administrator—a magistrate or governor—and a military official, each with his own staff, who with other officials such as tax collectors and the imperial censors or inspectors had overlapping jurisdictions and could check on each other. It was an efficient system that ensured good administration most of the time. The spread of mass printing promoted literacy and education and opened wider opportunities for commoners to enter the elite group of the scholar-gentry from whom officials were recruited or to prosper in trade.

The eleventh century was in many ways a golden age of good government, prosperity, and creativity. Paper promissory notes and letters of credit, followed by mass government issue of paper currency, served the growth of commerce. Government officials distributed printed pamphlets and promoted improved techniques in agriculture: irrigation, fertilization, ingenious new metal tools and mechanical equipment, and improved crop strains. Population grew even beyond the T'ang levels. Painting had a glorious development, often supported by rich urban merchants as well as by the Sung court. Literature also flourished, aided by the spread of cheap printing. Fiction proliferated, some now in the vernacular. The most famous Sung literary figure is the poet-painter-official Su Shih (Su Tung-p'o, Su Dongpo, 1037–1101), perhaps the best known in China's long tradition of poetic nature lovers. It was a confident, creative time.

Su Shih was, like so many of the scholar-gentry, a painter as well as a poet. In several of his poems he tries to merge the two media, inviting the reader to step into the scene and be immersed in a mind-emptying union with the great world of nature. He also used dust as a symbol for both official life (dead files and lifelessness, as in our own culture) and the capital on the dusty plains of the north, where he served for many years as an official.

Foggy water curls and winds around the brook road;
Layered blue hills make a ring where the brook runs east.
On a white moonlit shore a long-legged heron roosts.
And this is a place where no dust comes.
An old man of the stream looks, says to himself:
"What is your little reason for wanting so much to be a bureaucrat?
You have plenty of wine and land;
Go on home, enjoy your share of leisure!"
A boat, light as a leaf, two oars squeaking frighten wild geese.
Water reflects the clear sky, the limpid waves are calm.
Fish wriggle in the weedy mirror, herons dot misty foreshores.
Across the sandy brook swift, the frost brook cold, the moon brook bright.
Layer upon layer like a painting, bend after bend like a screen.
Remember old Yen Ling long ago—"Lord," "Minister"—a dream, Now gone, vain fames.
Only the far hills are long, the cloudy hills tumbled, the dawn hills green.
Drunk, abob in a light boat, wafted into the thick of flowers,
Fooled by the sensory world, I hadn't meant to stop here.
Far misty water, thousand miles' slanted evening sunlight,
Numberless hills, riot of green like rain—
I don't remember how I came.

Life along the river near Kaifeng at spring festival time. These two scenes come from a long scroll that begins with the rural areas and moves through suburbs into the capital, giving a vivid picture of the bustling life in and around Kaifeng, at the time the largest city in the world. The painting, by Chang Tse-tuan, was done in the early twelfth century.

Defeat in the North

But trouble was brewing on the northern frontiers. A barbarian group, the Jurchen, spilled over from their homeland in southern Manchuria in the early twelfth century. In alliance with the Sung, in 1122 they defeated another barbarian group that had ruled the northeastern border area, returning it to Chinese control. The warlike Jurchen were not overly impressed by the army of their Sung allies, and the Sung foolishly treated them as inferiors. The Jurchen advanced southward, besieged Kaifeng, which was heavily defended, and sacked the city in 1127 after the Chinese failed to pay them an extravagant indemnity. The war continued for a decade, with Jurchen armies briefly penetrating south of the Yangtze. But the Sung armies regrouped and drove them back into northern China, finally concluding a treaty that left the Jurchen in control of the area north of the Yangtze valley with the Sung as a tribute-paying vassal. Now called Southern Sung, the dynasty built a new capital at Hangchou (Hangzhou) at the southern edge of the Yangtze delta. The Sung had lost the north, but now they could concentrate on China's heartland, the Yangtze valley and the south. Another century of brilliance and innovation ensued, with no loss of momentum.

The Southern Sung Period

Cut off from normal overland trade routes through the northwest, the Sung turned in earnest to developing sea passages to Southeast Asia and India. Permanent colonies of Chinese merchants grew in many Southeast Asian trade centers, and ports on China's southeast coast, from Hangchou south, flourished. These included large numbers of resident foreigners, mostly Arabs, who lived in special quarters under their own headmen. Foreign accounts agree that these were the world's largest port cities at the time. Taxes on maritime trade provided a fifth of the imperial revenue, an unheard-of proportion that betokened new commercial prosperity. There was a striking advance in the size and design of oceangoing ships, some of which could carry over 600 people plus cargo, far larger than any elsewhere until modern times. The compass, an earlier Chinese invention, was a vital navigational aid, and these ships also pioneered in the use of multiple masts (important for manageability as well as speed), separate watertight compartments (not known elsewhere until much later), and the stern-post rudder, which replaced the awkward and unseaworthy steering oar. In all these respects, Sung ships presaged modern ships by many centuries. Ironically, they helped make it possible much later for Europeans to undertake the sea voyage to Asia using the compass, rudder, and masts—plus gunpowder—originally developed by China and to record their conquests and profits on Chinese-invented paper.

Domestically too commerce and urbanization flourished. The Yangtze delta and the southeast coast had long been China's commercial centers, thanks to their high productivity and the easy movement of goods by

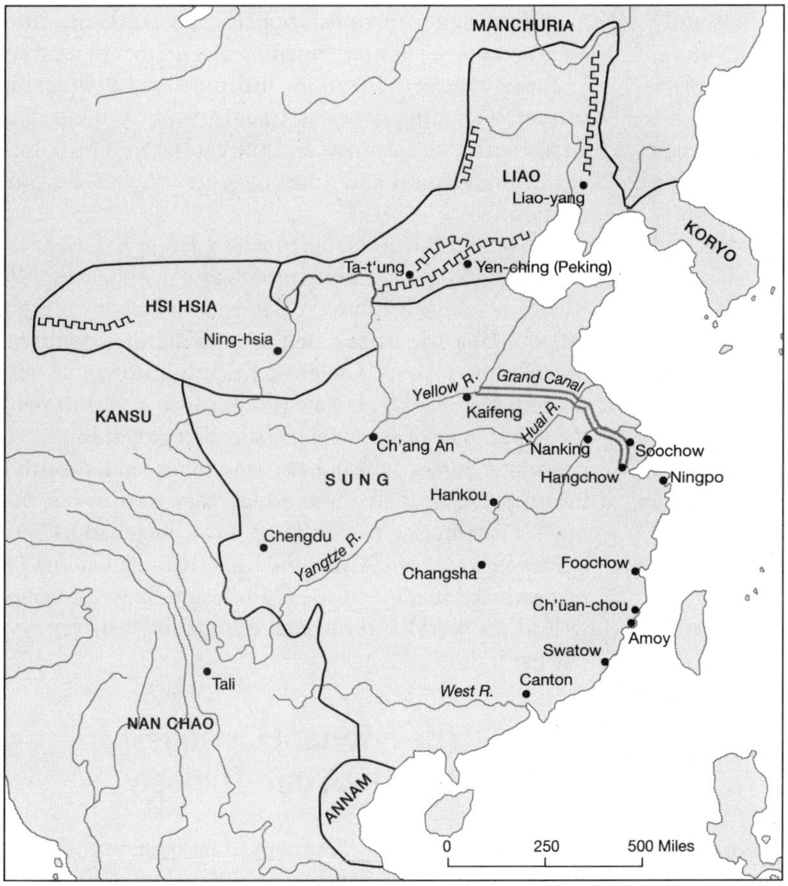

CHINA AND KOREA IN 1050

river, sea, and canal. An immense network of canals and navigable creeks covered the Yangtze and Canton deltas, serving a system of large and small cities inhabited increasingly by merchants managing a huge and highly varied trade. The capital at Hangchou, with its additional administrative role, grew to giant size and may have reached a million and a half in population, making it one of the world's largest cities before the age of railways. Water transport made this possible for Hangchou and other big cities, including Pataliputra, Rome, Ch'ang An, Istanbul, Edo (Tokyo), and eighteenth-century London. The proliferation of Chinese cities included for the first time several as big as or bigger than the capital and many only slightly smaller. Suchou (Soochow, Suzhou) and Fuchou (Foochow, Fuzhou) each had well over a million people, and according to Marco Polo, there were six other large cities in the 300 miles between those two. Chinese medicine became still more sophisticated, incorporating even the practice of vaccinating against smallpox, learned from Guptan India but unknown in the West until 1798.

We know a good deal about Hangchou, both from voluminous Chinese sources and from the accounts of several foreigners who visited it, including Marco Polo, who saw it only under Mongol rule after its great period had long passed. Nevertheless, he marveled at its size and wealth and called it the greatest city in the world, by comparison with which even Venice, his hometown and probably then the pinnacle of European urbanism, was, he says, a poor village. The great Arab traveler Ibn Battuta, 50 years later in the fourteenth century, says that even then Hangchou was three days' journey in length and subdivided into six towns, each larger than anything in the West. His approximate contemporary, the traveling Italian friar John of Marignolli, called Hangchou "the first, the biggest, the richest, the most populous, and altogether the most marvelous city that exists on the face of the earth."

These were all men who knew the world; even allowing for the usual hyperbole of travelers' tales, they were right about Hangchou. Its rich merchant and scholar-official community and its increasingly literate population of shopkeepers, artisans, and the upwardly mobile supported an exuberance of painting, literature, drama, music, and opera, while for the unlettered there were public storytellers in the ancient Chinese oral tradition. Southern Sung (and the Yuan or Mongol dynasty that followed it) is the great period of Chinese landscape painting, with its celebration of the beauties of the misty mountains, streams and lakes, bamboo thickets, and green hills of the south.

Innovation and Technological Development

The Southern Sung period was also a time of technological innovation. The philosopher Chu Hsi (Zhuxi, 1130–1200), the founder of what is called Neo-Confucianism, was in many ways a Leonardo-like figure, interested in and competent at a wide range of practical subjects as well as philosophy. This was in the tradition of the Confucian scholar-gentleman, but Chu Hsi and some of his contemporaries carried what Confucius called "the investigation of things" still further into scientific inquiry. Chu Hsi's journals record, for example, his observation that uplifted rock strata far above current sea level contained marine fossils. Like Leonardo, but three centuries earlier, he made the correct deduction and wrote the first statement of the geomorphological theory of uplift. But Chu Hsi was primarily concerned with personal development. He argued that through the Confucian discipline of self-cultivation, every man could be his own philosopher and sage, a doctrine similar to Plato's.

Rapid developments in agriculture, manufacturing, and transport led to a great variety of new tools and machines for cultivation and threshing; for lifting water (pumps); for carding, spinning, and weaving textile fibers; and for making windlasses, inclined planes, canal locks, and refinements in traction for water and land carriers. Water clocks were widespread, as were water-powered mills, to grind grain and to perform some manufacturing functions. Superficially at least, thirteenth-century China resembled eighteenth-century Europe: commercialization, urbanization, a widening market (including overseas trade), rising demand, and hence both the incentive and the capital to pursue mechanical invention and other measures to increase production.

Would these developments have led to a true industrial revolution, with all its profound consequences? We will never know, because the Mongol onslaught cut them off, and later dynasties failed to replicate the conditions of late Sung society. The great English historian of early modern Europe, R. H. Tawney, warns us against "giving the appearance of inevitableness by dragging into prominence the forces which have triumphed and thrusting into the background those which they have swallowed up."[1] It is tempting to think that if the Sung had had just a little longer—or if Chinggis Khan had died young (as he nearly did many times)—China might have continued to lead the world and modern Europe might never have risen as it did.

The Mongol Conquest and the Yuan Dynasty

The Mongols overran Southern Sung because they were formidable fighters, but they were aided by some serious Sung errors. The Mongol leader, Chinggis (Genghis) Khan (1155–1227), first attacked the Jurchen territories in the north and then the other non-Chinese groups in the northwest. In 1232 the Sung made an alliance with the Mongols to crush the remnants of the Jurchen and within two years reoccupied Kaifeng and Loyang. A year later they were desperately defending northern China against an insatiable Mongol army, other wings of which had already conquered Korea, central Asia, the Near East, and eastern Europe.

EAST ASIA, 600–1500

	China	Korea	Japan
c. C.E. 600–900	Sui dynasty (589–618) T'ang dynasty (618–907)	Paekche kingdom (c. 220–660) Koguryo kingdom (c. 220–669) Silla kingdom (c. 220–935)	Nara period (c. 710–794) Heian era (794–1185)
c. 900–1200	Sung dynasty (960–1279) Jurchen invasion (1120s) Chu Hsi (1130–1200)	Koryo kingdom (935–1218)	
c. 1200–1500	Chinggis Khan (1155–1227) Yuan dynasty (1279–1368)	Mongol rule (1218–1364) Yi dynasty (1392–1910)	Kamakura period (1185–1333) Ashikaga shogunate (1333–1573)

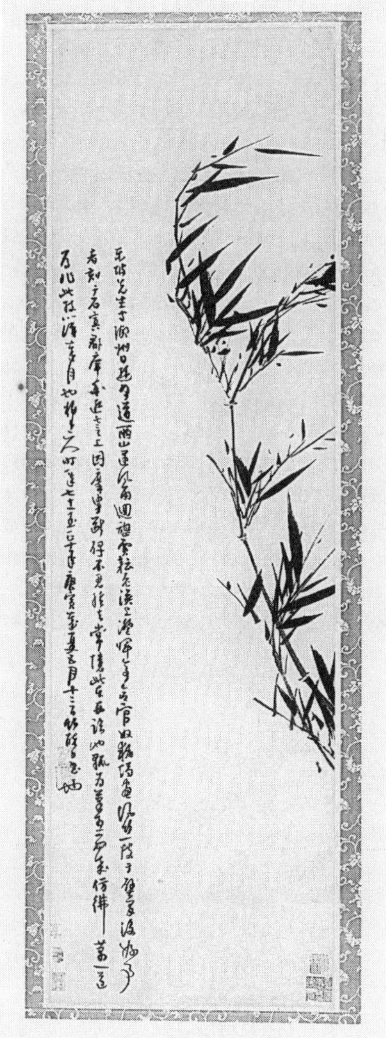

Bamboo, by Wu Chan (Yuan dynasty). Chinese artists loved to paint the graceful fronds of bamboo, each leaf created with a single stroke of the brush, in black ink. The techniques of bamboo painting were akin to those of calligraphy, and hence such paintings often include gracefully written text.

For 40 years the fighting raged in the north, where the heavily fortified Chinese cities were both defended and attacked with the help of explosive weapons. Gunpowder had been used much earlier in China for fireworks and for warfare too as an explosive and a "fire powder." Fire arrows using naphtha as fuel and part propellant had been known in early Han times, and by the tenth century fire lances, spear-tipped bamboo tubes filled with a gunpowder propellant, were in use. In the struggle between the Chinese and the Mongols, cast-metal barrels using gunpowder to propel a tight-fitting projectile appeared, marking the first certain occurrence of cannon in warfare. This devastating new technology, especially helpful in sieges, quickly spread to Europe and was in use there by the early fourteenth century.

The Sung were fatally weakened by divided counsels and inconsistent strategies, worsened by factionalism. By 1273 the Mongols had triumphed. They soon poured into the south, where Hangchou surrendered in 1276. Resistance continued in the Canton area until 1279, when the Sung fleet was defeated in a great sea battle. During much of the long struggle it was touch and go, but the Mongols made few mistakes and the Sung many, although they put up a far longer and more effective resistance to the Mongols than any of their many other continental opponents except the Delhi sultanate of Alaud-din Khalji and his mameluke troops. (The Mongols' seaborne expeditions to Japan and Java left them at a serious disadvantage; their fleet was twice scattered by major storms at critical points, and their invasion attempts were abandoned.)

The Mongols could indeed never have conquered China without the help of Chinese technicians, including siege engineers, gun founders, artillery experts, and naval specialists. Chinggis died in 1227, but he had already planned the conquest of Sung China, which was completed by his grandson Kubilai (1260–1294), who fixed his capital at Peking as early as 1264 and adopted the dynastic title of Yuan. Korea, northern Vietnam, and the previously non-Chinese southwest were also conquered; southern Vietnam, Siam, Burma, and Tibet were forced to accept tributary status as vassals. The Mongol conquest of China's southwest included the defeat of the Thai kingdom of Nan Chao based at Tali (Dali) and forced a major wave of Thais out of their homeland southward into Siam, where they joined earlier migrants.

Korea

Korean culture, though adopting much from China, added its own innovations and retained a strong sense of separate identity, together with a fierce determination to preserve its political independence. The Korean peninsula, set off from the mainland of Asia, is separated by mountains along its northwestern frontier adjacent to Manchuria and by the gorge of the Yalu River, which marks the boundary. The Korean people probably came originally from eastern Siberia and northern Manchuria, as their spoken language, which is unrelated to Chinese, suggests. They brought with them or evolved their own culture, which was already well formed before they were exposed to heavy Chinese influence at the time of the Han occupation in the late second century B.C.

Rice, wheat, metals, written characters, paper, printing, lacquer, porcelain, and other innovations spread to Korea after they appeared in China. As in Vietnam, literate Chinese-style culture in Korea was an elite phenomenon that rested on an already developed indigenous cultural base that remained distinctive. A Chinese-style state arose in the north around P'yongyang in the century before Han Wu-ti's conquest. On the withdrawal of the Chinese military colonies after the fall of the Han in C.E. 220, Korea regained its freedom and was thenceforward self-governing (except for the brief Mongol interlude) until the Japanese takeover in 1910, although Chinese cultural influence continued and was openly welcomed.

Three Kingdoms: Paekche, Silla, and Koguryo

Three Korean kingdoms arose after 220: Paekche in the southwest, Silla in the southeast, and Koguryo in the north, the largest and closest to China. Confucianism and Chinese forms of government, law, literature, and art spread widely throughout the peninsula, followed by Buddhism as it grew in China. But Korea's long tradition of a hereditary aristocracy in a hierarchically ordered society of privilege prevented the adoption of China's more open official system of meritocracy based on examinations. Like the Japanese, the Koreans departed from the Chinese pattern in providing an important place for a military aristocracy.

In 669, with help from the T'ang, Silla succeeded in conquering Koguryo, after having earlier demolished Paekche. With its now united strength, Silla repelled T'ang efforts at reconquest, a remarkable feat given the power and proximity of T'ang China. As a formal Chinese vassal, Silla presided over a golden age of creativity. T'ang culture was a natural model, but in many respects Korean adaptations were at least the equal of their Chinese models. Korean ceramics, fully as accomplished as anything produced in China, had a magnificent development, particularly in pottery and fine porcelain. This included the beautiful celadon ware, with its subtle milky green jade-colored glaze, whose secret formula was admired and envied by the Chinese, though it was extinguished by the Mongol conquest of the thirteenth century and never recovered. Silla Korea also went beyond Chinese written characters and began a system of phonetic transcription, derived from the sound of characters but designed to reproduce spoken Korean. By the fifteenth century this had been further refined into the *han'gul* syllabary.

Silla control weakened by the tenth century. The kingdom was taken over by a usurper in 935, who named his new united state Koryo, an abbreviation of Koguryo and the origin of the name Korea. The Koryo capital at Kaesong, just north of Seoul, was built on the planned imperial model of the T'ang city of Ch'ang An and incorporated most of the Chinese system of government. Interest in Buddhism and its texts, as well as a refinement of Sung techniques, stimulated a virtual explosion of woodblock printing in the eleventh century, and magnificent celadon pieces were again produced. Koryo rule dissolved into civil war on the eve of the Mongol invasion, and Chinggis Khan easily overran the peninsula in 1218. The Mongols exacted heavy tribute and imposed iron rule, even forcing Koreans to aid them in their later expeditions against Japan. But in the 1350s the Mongol empire collapsed, and in 1392 a new dynasty arose, the Yi, which was to preside over a united Korea until 1910.

This masterpiece of Korean art in bronze, depicting Maitreya, the "Buddha of the future," dates from the Silla period, sixth or seventh century C.E.

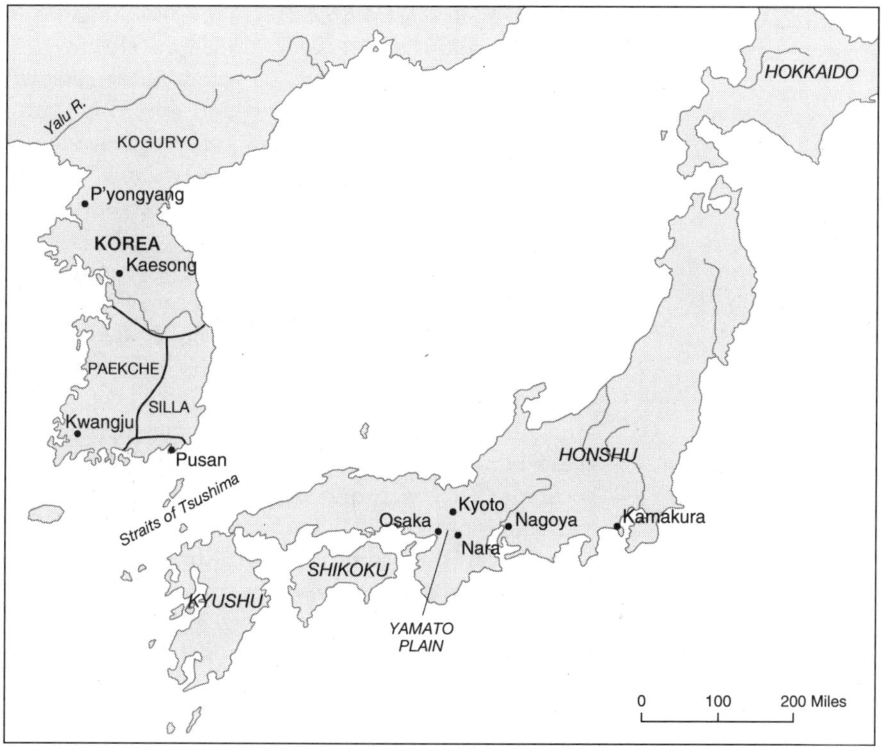

Korea and Japan, c. 500–1000

The Yi Dynasty

Under the Yi dynasty Korea continued the adaptation of Chinese civilization to a greater extent than any of its predecessors, including the incorporation of the imperial examination system, the Confucian bureaucracy, and the division of the country into eight centrally administered provinces on the Chinese model. Although Confucian ideology spread, in practice officeholding was still dominated by hereditary aristocrats. From their capital at Seoul, Yi rulers continued to accept the formal status of a Chinese tributary state, a relationship that both parties spoke of amicably as that between "younger brother and elder brother." Buddhism declined almost completely, while Confucianism and Chinese-style painting and calligraphy flourished. A group called the *yangban,* originally landowners, acquired most of the functions and status of the Chinese gentry as an educated elite but remained a hereditary class, providing both civil and military officials, unlike the Chinese model.

Korean economic development was retarded by the country's mountainous landscape, which, like that of Japan and Greece, is divided into separate small basins, and by its long harsh winter, especially severe in the north. Only about one-seventh of the total land area could be cultivated, and trade and concentrated urban growth were also disadvantaged. But although most Koreans remained materially poorer than most Chinese, elite culture, technology, and the arts prospered in distinctively Korean styles, including the still superb ceramics. Korean dress, house types, diet, lifestyles, marriage and inheritance customs, and the volatile, earthy, robust, spontaneous Korean temperament remained their own as well. Food was flavored by the peppery pickled cabbage called *kimchi,* as it still is. Korea's indigenous cultural fabric was basic and showed through the Chinese overlay. There was thus no risk that Korea would be absorbed into Chinese culture, and Koreans remained proud of their independence and of their own sophisticated cultural tradition.

The first century or so of Yi rule was a brilliant period in Korean and East Asian history. The fifteenth century saw a new explosion of printing, now vigorously supported by a Confucian state that put a high value on texts and learning. The Koreans further perfected the art of movable metal type, which was used among other things to reproduce the libraries burned by the Mongols and the wooden plates from which those books had been made. Eight other ambitious printing projects were carried out between 1403 and 1484. This was the first ex-

YI DYNASTY KOREA

tensive use of movable type anywhere in the world. The technique originated in eleventh-century Sung China and was further developed in Korea a century or so later. In contrast, movable-type printing began in Europe only in the mid-fifteenth century.

The same century in Korea also saw important new developments in mathematics and in the manufacture of astronomical instruments. More closely related to printing was the perfection of the *han'gul* alphabet and syllabary, not only to write Korean but to give the Korean pronunciation of Chinese characters as well. Traditional characters continued to be used for official documents and elite literature, but the development and popularity of *han'gul* was an affirmation of Korea's proud and confident distinctiveness.

The vigor of the Yi order was slowly weakened by bureaucratic factionalism, which the throne never really overcame. Factionalism already had a long and disruptive history in Korea, from the time of the three early kingdoms, and it progressively eroded the effectiveness and authority of the Yi state. No strong rulers emerged after the early sixteenth century, and toward its end a divided and enfeebled Korea had to face the invasion of the Japanese warlord Hideyoshi between 1592 and 1598. His army overran and ravaged the country until, with aid from China, the invaders were driven back almost to the coast and stalemated there. The gifted Korean admiral Yi Sun-sin then repeatedly defeated Japanese naval detachments and disrupted their supply lines with his ingenious "turtle ships." These vessels, covered with overlapping plates of iron and copper and armed fore and aft with beak-shaped metal prows that could ram and sink any ship, were the first armored warships. They were powered by rowers protected by the outer "turtle shell." The invasion was abandoned when Hideyoshi died in 1598, but Korea never fully recovered from its devastation.

The Yi dynasty continued, plagued by perennial factional fighting, although it still supported learning, the arts, and major new printing projects. Considerable economic growth resulted from improved agriculture and a rising commercial sector, and population probably doubled between 1600 and 1800. Merchants began to buy their way to *yangban* (gentry) status, as did prosperous farmers. Korea thus followed the path of Sung, Ming, and Manchu China and of Tokugawa Japan. But its political and administrative health was poor, ultimately inviting Japanese intervention after 1894.

Japan

Composed of four main islands off the southern tip of Korea, Japan had been both protected by its insularity from turmoil on the Asian mainland and to a degree also isolated from its development. The Straits of Tsushima between Korea and Japan are approximately 120 miles wide, and although Japan has been periodically involved with the mainland, the connection has never been as close as that between China and other areas of East Asia or between Britain and Europe. Japan has had the advantage of a clearly separate identity and as a result of its insularity has been able to make its own choices at most periods about what it wanted to adopt from abroad. Like Korea, Japan is mainly mountainous, and settlement has remained heavily concentrated on the narrow coastal plain between Tokyo and Osaka, an area roughly equivalent to the coastal corridor between Boston and Washington, D.C. All in all, Japan is about the size of

California, but the northernmost island of Hokkaido was settled by the Japanese on a major scale only in this century. Mountains also retarded Japanese economic development and political unification. As in Korea, only a little over a seventh of the country is cultivated even now, although the climate, conditioned by the surrounding sea, is far milder and better watered. Coastal sea routes have also helped link settled areas and carry trade.

Early Culture and Development

The spoken language of the Japanese, unrelated to Chinese but in the same linguistic group as Korean, suggests that they too came originally from the Asian mainland north of China via the sea passage from Korea, although other migrants and cultural influences may have come into Japan from the tropical Pacific. The migrants slowly defeated, displaced, or absorbed the islands' original inhabitants, including a physically very different group called the Ainu, who now live as a tiny and dwindling minority on reservations on the northernmost island of Hokkaido. Early Japanese history is cloudy, in part because written records do not begin until the eighth century C.E., after Japan had adopted the Chinese art of writing from Korea. We have no firm dates before that time and can only guess when the people we now call Japanese arrived or when they emerged as a separate culture, but it was probably sometime between the third century B.C.E. and the first century C.E., partly through interbreeding with earlier inhabitants. Earlier preliterate and premetallic cultures had developed in Japan, producing pottery perhaps as early as in any part of Asia. Bronze tools and weapons from China entered via Korea about the first century B.C.E., and implements made of iron, a technology also imported from Korea, were being produced by around 200 C.E.

It seems clear that Korea played an important role in Japan until the fifth century C.E. By the time of the first Japanese records in the eighth century, a third of the nobility claimed Korean or Chinese descent, and clearly such lineage was perceived as a mark of superiority. Close interaction with Korea continued, with large numbers of Korean artisans, metallurgists, and technologists living in Japan, as well as Korean nobles and perhaps even rulers. There were also invasions and raids in both directions, until by about 400 such violent interactions faded and the Japanese continued to move northward from the southernmost island of Kyushu, closest to Korea, onto the main island of Honshu. There they established a central core on the Yamato Plain in the Nara–Kyoto–Osaka area, where it was to remain for approximately the next 1,000 years. The imperial capital, however, was not moved northeast to Tokyo until 1868, and the frontier with the Ainu lay just north of Kyoto for centuries.

The Nara Period

Chinese cultural infusions continued from Korea, including, sometime before 500, Chinese written characters and an increasing knowledge of Chinese culture and of Buddhism. By the end of the sixth century and increasingly in the seventh, missions were dispatched to China to observe and to bring back to Japan as much of Chinese civilization as possible. In the mid-seventh century a sweeping series of measures called the *Taika* ("Great Reform") began the process of transforming Japan and the Japanese imperial administration into a version of China's. By 710 the first permanent capital was inaugurated at Nara, a smaller-scaled copy of Ch'ang An, which presided over a modified Chinese-style government.

The ensuing century (until 794) is known as the Nara period, during which the transplantation of Chinese civilization continued, helped by successive Japanese missions to China. Currency and coins on the Chinese model were introduced. The Chinese scholars' habit of recording everything they observed was transmitted too, and important accounts of T'ang China come from Japanese sources of this period, as well as the first official histories of Japan. Buddhism spread, but Confucianism

Traditional Japanese stone garden at the Ryoanji Temple, Kyoto. Originally from T'ang China, this orderly and peaceful form of landscaping became characteristically Japanese and is still widely practiced.

also entered from China and became important for the upper classes. As Taoism was retained in China, the original animistic and naturalistic Japanese religion of Shinto remained, in part no doubt as an assertion of Japanese distinctiveness but also because of its close connection with the imperial family. Beautiful wood-crafted Shinto shrines remain in "natural" areas even in contemporary Japan.

Artistic styles, gardens, court and official clothing, and sophisticated tastes all strove to replicate the Chinese model, and although they slowly diverged from that standard, Japanese high culture still retains the unmistakable marks of its seventh- and eighth-century Chinese origins. Even the straw mats *(tatami)* that still today cover the floor in traditional Japanese rooms, the prominence of raw fish and pickled vegetables in the diet, and the tea ceremony all came from T'ang China. Korean and Chinese artists, artisans, and technicians remained important in the Nara period as teachers and implementers of cultural reform. But Japan was a very different place, and the cultural transplant was never complete, nor did it ever penetrate very deeply into the mass of the people, most of whom remained peasants until the late nineteenth century. Unlike Chinese society, but as in Korea, descent and inherited status continued to be important, and society as a whole remained more tightly organized and more hierarchically controlled. Feudal-style lords and hereditary nobles remained the chief wielders of power. Japan tried the Chinese examination system, but, as in Korea, hereditary aristocrats undercut it by reserving most official positions for themselves. The Japanese emperor, considered divine and hence the bearer of a sacred mandate, was above politics or even administration.

The Heian Era

In 794 a vigorous young emperor, Kammu, moved the capital to Kyoto (then called Heian), in part to break away from the growing influence of Buddhist institutions in Nara. With the support of the powerful Fujiwara family, he and his successors began to modify or discard some aspects of the Chinese model so enthusiastically adopted earlier. Art and architecture increased their characteristically Japanese concern for textures and the use of natural materials. T'ang China was in turmoil, and Japanese missions stopped going there, while new interest arose in indigenous cultural patterns. Chinese written characters were increasingly supplemented and later somewhat displaced by a phonetic system known as *kana*. Most of its symbols combined a consonant and a vowel and made it possible to transcribe spoken Japanese accurately, as Chinese characters could not do. Chinese characters remained important among the educated elite and for official use, but the *kana* system was understandably preferred for most purposes, including popular literature.

The effort to follow Chinese patterns of government was largely given up, and power came increasingly into the hands of the Fujiwara clan and its appointees or hereditary officeholders. Because the new capital was called Heian, the centuries from 794 to 1185 are called the Heian era. The period is famous for its aristocratic and court culture, where noble gentlemen and ladies devoted their lives to aesthetic refinement. The best-known Heian work is Lady Murasaki's *Tale of Genji,* considered the world's first psychological novel.

Lady Murasaki and Heian Court Literature

Lady Murasaki's birth date is not known precisely, though it was probably around 978 C.E., nor are we sure of the date of her death, though it was probably around 1015. We do not even know her real name, since in Heian Japan it was considered improper to record the personal names of aristocratic women outside of the imperial family. It is known that she came from a junior branch of the great Fujiwara clan and that her father was a provincial governor. The name Murasaki may derive from that of a major figure in her novel, *The Tale of Genji,* or from its meaning of "purple," a pun on the *Fuji* of Fujiwara, which means "wisteria." She was far from alone as a woman author; mid-Heian period literature is dominated by women, who, particularly at court, were apparently less conventional than men. The absence of harems and extensive concubinage in Japan left women freer to express their talents in other ways.

Lady Murasaki's journal is our only source of information about her life. It records that she was a precocious child and became literate early:

> **My father was anxious to make a good Chinese scholar of [my brother], and often came to hear him read his lessons. . . . So quick was I at picking up the language that I was soon able to prompt my brother. . . . After this I was careful to conceal the fact that I could write a single Chinese character.**[2]

But she acquired a wide knowledge of both Chinese and Japanese works and also became a talented calligrapher, painter, and musician, attainments considered suitable for an aristocratic girl. At about age 21 she was married to a much older man, a distant Fujiwara cousin, and bore a daughter. The next year her husband died, and in her grief she considered becoming a Buddhist nun but turned instead to reflection on the problem of human happiness, especially for women. Around that time, approximately the year 1001, she began work on her masterpiece, *The Tale of Genji,* which was probably nearly finished when, some six years later, she became a lady-in-waiting at the imperial court.

Her journal describes the refined and colorful life at court, as well as its less glamorous rivalries and intrigues. Both are the subject of her great novel, which combines a romantic as well as a psychological approach with realistic detail and subtle insight into human behavior. *Genji* is still praised as the masterpiece of Japanese literature. Her people are real, despite the highly mannered world in which they lived, and through her journal we also have a picture of her as an extraordinarily alive, imaginative, and compelling person. A collection of her poems has also survived, which further mark her as an accomplished stylist.

The Tale of Genji deals with the life of a prince and his seemingly endless affairs with various court ladies. It includes careful attention to manners, dress, and court politics—perhaps not the most rewarding of subjects, but in the hands of Lady Murasaki they become not mere details but a means of revealing character. Although the hero is idealized, this is far more than a conventional romantic tale, and the portrayal of Genji as he grows older is a subtle one. Toward the end of her journal, Lady Murasaki gives us a candid glimpse of herself: People think, she wrote, that "I am very vain, reserved, unsociable . . . wrapped up in the study of ancient stories, living in a poetical world all my own. . . . But when they get to know me, they find that I am kind and gentle."[3] Perhaps she was all these things. Bold as she was in her writings, when describing herself Lady Murasaki still felt compelled to present her character in terms of the traditional "feminine" virtues.

Political Disorder and the Rise of Feudalism

Heian court culture was delightful, no doubt, but may suggest a lack of adequate Fujiwara concern with the real world of politics. Elite life at the capital was deeply involved with elegance, refinement, and aesthetic sensitivity but gave little thought to increasingly pressing economic problems, the poverty of most Japanese, or growing political disorder. In the end Fujiwara power was undermined and finally destroyed by new families who used their private armies to become de facto rulers over lands they had originally guarded for noble families. Some of these armies, and the new group of warriors *(samurai),* with their pronounced military ethic, had developed out of frontier wars as Japanese settlement spread slowly northeastward beyond the Yamato area after the ninth century. Armed followers of Buddhist temples increasingly took part in political struggles. Armies began to interfere in factional conflicts at court or were called in by different factions, including clans within the Fujiwara family. By the twelfth century, armies had become the real powers.

The Kamakura Period

In 1185 one of the warrior lineages, the Minamoto clan, set up a rival capital in its then frontier base at Kamakura (now a southern suburb of Tokyo). The refined culture and court-based politics of Heian were now supplemented by a less cultivated but far more politically effective system based on a combination of new bureaucratic methods, military power, and the security offered by the samurai. The samurai leaders were hereditary aristocrats who became both literate and educated and were more administrators than fighting men. Through them and other educated aristocrats Heian culture spread and in time influenced even the warrior clans. However, the rise of noble families and the samurai armies under their control led to the emergence of Japanese feudalism, a phenomenon parallel to that of medieval Europe but different from the imperial civil bureaucracy and meritocracy of China.

The emperor became increasingly a figurehead during this period, and real power rested with whoever could grasp and hold it—first the Fujiwara and then the Minamoto and other military clans. The Kamakura-based administration presided over a feudal hierarchy of warriors and nobles who were bound in fealty assured by oaths, financial and service obligations, and promises of military support. In return, the Kamakura ruler, or *shogun,* the emperor's chief military commander and agent, granted his vassal-lords hereditary rights to their lands. As in medieval Europe, this was a symptom of limited central state power, an arrangement of mutual convenience, but it was also inherently unstable as ambitious or upstart vassals sought to improve their positions or rebel against the shogun's authority. Political power was seldom unified under any single control for long. Each vassal maintained both his own group of samurai and his army, but the loyalty of these forces could not always be ensured, whether to local lords or to the shogun. The patterns that emerged in the Kamakura shogunate (1185–1333) were to dominate Japan until the nineteenth century.

In 1268 the Mongol emperor Kubilai Khan demanded the submission of the Japanese, and when they refused, the Mongols forced the recently conquered Koreans to build and man a fleet for the invasion of Japan, which arrived in 1274. Soon after the first landings a great storm wrecked many of the invaders' ships and forced their withdrawal. The Japanese executed subsequent Mongol envoys, and in 1281 a far larger expedition manned by both subject Koreans and Chinese arrived, only to be swept away by an even greater storm. This storm was typical of the late summer typhoons along the coasts of East Asia, though the Japanese can perhaps be forgiven for attributing their double deliverance to a "divine wind," or *kamikaze*. However, the costs of meeting the terrible Mongol threat and of the preparation that went on against an expected third expedition drained Kamakura resources and diverted large numbers of people from productive occupations. With the weakening of Kamakura power, political divisions and open revolts multiplied. In 1333 an unusually active emperor, Go-Daigo, whom the dominant faction at Kamakura had tried to depose, gathered support and attracted dissidents from the crumbling Kamakura structure. One of his commanders overran Kamakura and ended its power. But another of his supporters turned against him, put a different member of the imperial line on the throne, and had himself declared shogun.

The Ashikaga Shogunate

The Ashikaga shoguns, who established themselves in Kyoto from 1339, were never able to build effective central control. A rival faction supporting another member of the imperial family remained in power in southwestern Honshu and could not be dislodged, while Kyushu continued under the control of one or more other groups. Civil war became endemic, and as one consequence feudal lords beyond the reach of central control supported highly profitable piracy along the coasts of China. This caused chronic trouble between the Ashikaga and the Ming dynasty. The government tried to suppress piracy, but its power to do so was inadequate. For a time the Chinese felt obliged to abandon large stretches of their own coast and pull settlements back to more easily protected sites up rivers and estuaries. From the mid-fifteenth century, political chaos in Japan was endemic, despite the country's small size and the even smaller dimensions of its settled areas. By 1467 effective Ashikaga rule was ended and much of Kyoto had been destroyed, although the emasculated shogunate continued in name. Rival Buddhist sects and their monasteries also fought bloody wars against each other with armed monks as troops. Peasant revolts and bitter conflicts among petty feudal lords continued to ravage the countryside.

Yet despite the growing political disorder, especially after 1450, the last century of the Ashikaga shogunate saw a remarkable flowering of culture. In part this was the result of a conscious fusion of aristocratic Heian traditions with those of the newer samurai culture. Millions also found solace in popular Buddhist sects, including Shin, Nichiren, and Zen, originally Chinese but adapted to Japanese tastes and styles. These popular and egalitarian or, in the case of Zen, contemplative and mystical approaches concentrated on salvation, self-cultivation, and the apprehension of eternal truths rather than on the turmoil of political life. The discipline of Zen appealed to the warrior class but also stressed unity with nature, a traditional Japanese interest. Less detached but clearly related to a turning away from worldly strife was the further blossoming of temple and palace architecture, consciously and ingeniously integrated with peaceful natural settings, of landscape gardening, and of nature painting, much of it in the Southern Sung mode. The literature of the period, meanwhile, commented on the shifting fortunes of politics and the foibles of people grasping for power or gloried in the simple beauty of nature and the joys of untroubled rural life. The shogunate patronized Zen as it supported art and literature, continuing the Heian tradition.

Even more specifically Japanese was the Ashikaga evolution of the tea ceremony as a graceful, soothing, contemplative, and aesthetic ritual. Although its origins too were in T'ang China, it became and remains a distinctively Japanese assertion of cultural identity and personal serenity. Delicate teahouses set in naturally landscaped gardens in unobtrusive elegance provided havens of tranquillity and aesthetic enjoyment for samurai and other members of the elite, who took additional pleasure from the exquisite beauty of the teacups. It was a striking and thoroughly Japanese counterpart to the bloody and often ruthless life of the times.

Finally, the Ashikaga era saw the evolution of traditional dances into a stylized and distinctively Japanese form, the *Noh* drama. This subtle, Zen-inspired blending of dance, gesture, speech, and costume evolved into a unique theatrical style capable of communicating rich meaning and emotion. Every step and every movement are precisely measured to achieve a state of controlled tension, a slow-moving, concentrated experience of understatement and disciplined expression.

The production of artisans too—including, appropriately, the making of fine swords—developed still further. The arrival of the Portuguese early in the sixteenth century stimulated trade, already growing for some time, as the Europeans' more powerful vessels supplanted those of local pirates.

The Ashikaga shogunate dissolved completely into still more chaotic civil war in the 1570s, and Japan was torn by rival clans and their armies until the end of the century. In 1568 a minor but able and determined feudal lord, Oda Nobunaga (1534–1582), won control of Kyoto. He broke the military power of the major Buddhist monasteries and their fortified strongholds in the capital region, including the great fortress of the Shin sect at Osaka. As a counterweight against Buddhism, Nobunaga encouraged Portuguese and other Jesuit missionaries, but his tactics against opponents were ruthless, including the burning alive of captives and the slaughter of noncombatants.

When Nobunaga was murdered by one of his own commanders in 1582, his chief general, Toyotomi Hideyoshi (1536–1598), seized power and by the early 1590s controlled most of Honshu, Kyushu, and Shikoku, thus unifying most of Japan for the first time. A peasant by birth, Hideyoshi tried to disarm all non-samurai to ensure that commoners were kept down and unable to challenge his authority. He nationalized and centralized the taxation system and further separated warriors from cultivators. As a self-made man, he feared the possible rivalry of others like him. His famous "sword hunt" among all commoners, in which houses were searched and all swords confiscated, reestablished rigid class lines and was accompanied by new laws prohibiting farmers or common soldiers from becoming merchants or even laborers. Hideyoshi rose to power in a period of change and instability; he saw this instability as a threat and tried to stop it. Hideyoshi seems ultimately to have succumbed to megalomania, as evidenced by his grandiose plan for the conquest of China, for which he carried out an invasion of Korea as a first step in 1592. The story of that misadventure has already been told.

Hideyoshi at first welcomed the Christian missionaries and the profitable trade with the Portuguese, but suddenly he turned against all foreigners. He seems to have feared that Christianity was becoming a disruptive factor in Japanese society and a political menace as the foreigners, already rivals among themselves, became involved in internal conflicts and as Japanese converts developed loyalties to a foreign pope. Hideyoshi placed a ban on missionaries in 1587, but this was not strictly enforced until 1597, when he crucified nine Catholic priests and 17 Japanese converts as an example.

In the chaos following Hideyoshi's death in 1598, Tokugawa Ieyasu (1542–1616), originally a vassal and ally of Nobunaga and then of Hideyoshi, emerged victorious in 1600 to found the far more effective and lasting order of the Tokugawa shogunate, which was to rule Japan under a centralized feudal administration until 1868.

Summary

This chapter has summarized the renaissance of Chinese civilization after the time of troubles following the fall of the Han dynasty in 220 and the golden ages of the T'ang and the Sung until those impressive developments were cutoff by the Mongol conquest late in the thirteenth century. Despite Mongol brutality, Chinese civilization continued under alien domination, and the hated invaders were eventually thrown off. Korean culture had arisen before the Han conquest and retained its distinctiveness. It borrowed heavily from Chinese civilization at the elite level while creating innovations in ceramics and printing by movable type and shaping institutions adopted from China to Korean tradition. Korea was first unified by the Silla dynasty from 669 to 995 and continued under the Koryo dynasty until it was destroyed by the Mongol invasion in 1218. Yi dynasty Korea from 1392 to 1910 saw a new burst of cultural and technological growth, although its political vigor was slowly eroded by factionalism.

Japanese civilization, having been largely created on the Chinese model and with Korean help, in time asserted its own separate cultural identity and produced a graceful elite culture that coexisted with rural poverty and chronic political division and conflict. Japanese feudalism and the role of the samurai evolved after the Heian period (794–1185) under the Kamakura and Ashikaga shogunates (1185–1568), but such methods were unable to unify the country or to end endemic civil war until the emergence of the Tokugawa clan in 1600. Despite political turmoil, Japan also produced great art, literature, and architecture and a refined culture for the upper classes. Chinese influence on the major East Asian societies was thus limited. Koreans and Japanese made what they took from China their own and went on to modify or develop it further in distinctive ways while retaining and building on their own indigenous culture.

NOTES

1. R. H. Tawney, *The Agrarian Problem in the Sixteenth Century* (London: Longman, Green, 1912), p. 177.
2. All quotations from Lady Murasaki's journal are taken from Arthur Waley's introduction to his translation of *The Tale of Genji* (New York: Doubleday, 1955), pp. ix, xxi.
3. Ibid., p. xxi.

FURTHER READING

China

Allen, T. T. *Mongol Imperialism.* Berkeley: University of California Press, 1987.

Carter, T. F., and Goodrich, L. C. *The Invention of Printing in China and Its Spread Westward.* New York: Ronald Press, 1955.

Chaffee, J. W. *The Thorny Gates of Learning: A Social History of Examinations in Sung China.* Cambridge: Cambridge University Press, 1995.

Dawson, R. S. *Imperial China.* London: Oxford University Press, 1972.

De Crespigny, R. *Under the Brilliant Emperor: Imperial Authority in T'ang China.* Canberra: Australian National University Press, 1985.

Dien, A. E., ed. *State and Society in Medieval China.* Stanford, Calif.: Stanford University Press, 1990.

Franke, H. *China Under Mongol Rule.* Aldershot, England: Varioram Press, 1994.

Gernet, J. *Daily Life in China on the Eve of the Mongol Invasion,* trans. H. M. Wright. London: Macmillan, 1962.

Hymes, R. *Statesmen and Gentlemen: Elites of the Southern Sung.* New York: Cambridge University Press, 1986.

Lo, W. W. *An Introduction to the Civil Service of Sung China.* Honolulu: University Press of Hawaii, 1987.

McKnight, B. *Law and Order in Sung China.* New York: Cambridge University Press, 1993.

McMullen, D. L. *State and Scholars in T'ang China.* Cambridge: Cambridge University Press, 1987.

Olschki, L. *Marco Polo's Asia.* Berkeley: University of California Press, 1960.

Rossabi, M. *Kubilai Khan: His Life and Times.* Berkeley: University of California Press, 1988.

Spuler, B. *History of the Mongols.* Berkeley: University of California Press, 1972.

Waley, A. *The Poetry and Career of Li Po.* London: Allen & Unwin, 1960.

Weinstein, S. *Buddhism Under the T'ang.* New York: Cambridge University Press, 1988.

Korea

Deuchler, M. *The Confucian Transformation of Korea.* Cambridge, Mass.: Harvard University Press, 1993.

Henthorn, G. *History of Korea.* Glencoe, Ill.: Free Press, 1971.

Lee, K.-B. *A New History of Korea,* trans. E. Wagner. Cambridge, Mass.: Harvard University Press, 1985.

Japan

Berry, M. E. *Hideyoshi.* Cambridge, Mass.: Harvard University Press, 1986.

Dunn, C. J. *Everyday Life in Traditional Japan.* London: Batsford, 1969.

Duus, P. *Feudalism in Japan.* New York: Knopf, 1969.

Elison, E., and Smith, B., eds. *Warlords, Artists, and Commoners: Japan in the Sixteenth Century.* Honolulu: University Press of Hawaii, 1981.

Hall, J. W., ed. *Japan Before Tokugawa.* Princeton, N.J.: Princeton University Press, 1986.

Hane, M. *Japan.* New York: Scribner, 1972.

———. *Premodern Japan,* 2nd ed. Boulder, Colo.: Westview Press, 1990.

Keene, D. *No: The Classical Theatre of Japan.* Stanford, Calif.: Stanford University Press, 1966.

Mass, J. P. *Warrior Government in Early Medieval Japan.* New Haven, Conn.: Yale University Press, 1974.

Morris, I. *The World of the Shining Prince.* Oxford: Oxford University Press, 1964.

Reischauer, E. O. *Japan: The Story of a Nation.* London: Duckworth, 1970.

Tiedemann, A. E., ed. *An Introduction to Japanese Civilization.* New York: Columbia University Press, 1974.

Totman, C. Japan Before Perry: A Short History. Berkeley: University of California Press, 1981.

Sources of the West
35: The Examination System During the T'ang Dynasty

CHAPTER 11

The Last Great Nomadic Challenge: The Mongol Empire

KEY TERMS

Chinggis Khan	*Golden Horde*
nomads	*Moscow*
Karakorum	*Kubilai Khan*
Batu	*Yuan Dynasty*
Russia	*Marco Polo*
Tartars	*Black Death*

DISCUSSION QUESTIONS

Why were Mongol nomads a serious threat to sedentary civilizations?

Why did the Mongol Yuan Dynasty threaten the power of traditional Chinese elites?

What impact did the Mongols have on both eastern and western cultures?

From the first explosion of Mongol military might from the steppes of central Asia in the early decades of the 13th century to the death of Timur in 1405, the nomads of central Asia made a last, stunning return to center stage in world history. Mongol invasions ended or interrupted many of the great empires of the postclassical period and also extended the world network that had increasingly defined the period. Under Chinggis Khan—who united his own Mongol tribesmen and numerous nomadic neighbors into the mightiest war machine the world had seen to that time—central Asia, northern China, and eastern Persia were brought under Mongol rule. Under Chinggis Khan's sons and grandsons, the rest of China, Tibet, Persia, Iraq, much of Asia Minor, and all of southern Russia were added to the vast Mongol imperium. Though the empire was divided between Chinggis Khan's sons after his death in 1227, the four *khanates* or kingdoms—which emerged in the struggles for succession—dominated most of Asia for the next one and a half centuries. The Mongol conquests and the empires they produced represented the most formidable nomadic challenge to the growing global dominance of the sedentary peoples of the civilized cores since the great nomadic migrations in the first centuries C.E. Except for Timur's devastating but short-lived grab for power at the end of the 14th century, nomadic peoples would never again mount a challenge as massive and sweeping as that of the Mongols.

In most histories, the Mongol conquests have been depicted as a savage assault by backward and barbaric peoples on many of the most ancient and developed centers of human civilization. Much is made of the ferocity of Mongol warriors in battle; their destruction of great cities, such as Baghdad, in reprisal for resistance to Mongol armies; and their mass slaughters of defeated enemies. Depending on the civilization from whose city walls a historian recorded the coming of the Mongol "hordes," they were depicted as the scourge of Islam, devils bent on the destruction of Christianity, persecutors of the Buddhists, or defilers of the Confucian traditions of China. Though they were indeed fierce fighters and capable of terrible acts of retribution against those who dared to defy them, the Mongols' conquests brought much more than death and devastation.

At the peak of their power, the domains of the Mongol khans, or rulers, made up a vast realm in which once hostile peoples lived together in peace and virtually all religions were tolerated. From the Khanate of Persia in the west to the empire of the fabled Kubilai Khan in the east, the law code first promulgated by Chinggis Khan gave order to human interaction. The result was an important new stage in international contact. From eastern Europe to southern China, merchants and travelers could move across the well-policed Mongol domains without fear for their lives or property. The great swath of Mongol territory that covered or connected most of Europe, Asia, and the Middle East served as a bridge between the civilizations of the Eastern Hemisphere. The caravans and em-

1130–c. 1250 Almohads rule North Africa and Spain

1215 First Mongol attacks on North China; Beijing captured

1236–1240 Mongol conquest of Russia

1234 Mongols take all of North China; end of Qin dynasty

1037–1194 Seljuk Turks dominant in the Middle East

1235–1279 Mongol conquest of South China; end of southern Song dynasty

1115–1234 Jurchens (Qin dynasty) rules North China

1227 Death of Chinggis Khan; Ogedei named successor

907–1118 Khitan conquest of North China

1219–1223 First Mongol invasions of Russia and the Islamic world

1126 Song dynasty flees to South China

1206 Temujin takes the name of Chinggis Khan; Mongol state is founded

900 C.E. **1100** C.E. **1200** C.E.

World Civilizations: The Global Experience, Second Edition
Chapter 20: The Last Great Nomadic Challenges: From Chinggis Kahn to Timur

bassies that crossed the Mongol lands transmitted new foods, inventions, and ideas from one civilized pool to the others and from civilized pools to the nomadic peoples who served as intermediaries. Like the Islamic expansion that preceded it, the Mongol explosion did much to lay the foundations for more human interaction on a global scale, extending and intensifying the world network that had been building since the classical age.

This chapter will explore the sources of the Mongol drive for a world empire and the course of Mongol expansion. Particular attention will be given to the nomadic basis of the Mongol war machine and the long-standing patterns of nomadic–sedentary interaction that shaped the character, direction, and impact of Mongol expansion. After a discussion of the career and campaigns of Chinggis Khan, separate sections of this chapter will deal with the Mongol conquest and rule in Russia and eastern Europe, the Middle East, and China. The chapter will conclude with an assessment of the meaning of the Mongol interlude for the development of civilization and the growth of cross-cultural interaction on a global scale. In both their destructive and constructive roles, the Mongols generated major changes within the framework of global history.

The Mongol Empire of Chinggis Khan

The Mongols had long been one of the nomadic peoples that intervened periodically in Chinese history. But tribal divisions and rivalries with neighboring ethnic groups—particularly Turkic peoples—had long blunted the expansive potential of Mongol warrior culture. In the early 13th century, these and other obstacles to Mongol expansion were overcome, primarily because of the leadership of an astute political strategist and brilliant military commander who took the title *Chinggis Khan.* Within decades, the Mongols and allied nomadic groups built an empire that stretched from the Middle Eastern heartlands of the Islamic world to the China Sea.

In most ways, the Mongols epitomized nomadic society and culture. Their survival depended on the well-being of the herds of goats and sheep they drove from one pasture area to another according to the cycle of the seasons. Their staple foods were the meat and milk products provided by their herds, supplemented in most cases by grain and vegetables gained through trade with sedentary farming peoples. They also traded hides and dairy products for jewelry, weapons, and cloth manufactured in urban centers. They dressed in sheepskins, made boots from tanned sheep hides, and lived in round felt tents that were processed from wool sheared from their animals. The tough little ponies they rode to round up their herds, hunt wild animals, and make war were equally essential to their way of life. Both male and female Mongol children could ride as soon as they were able to walk. Mongol warriors could literally ride for days on end, sleeping and eating in the saddle.

Like the Arabs and other nomadic peoples we have encountered, the basic unit of Mongol society was the

1240–1241 Mongol invasion of western Europe

1253 Mongol victory over Seljuk Turks; rise of Ottoman Turks in Middle East

1258 Mongol destruction of Baghdad

1260–1294 Reign of Kubilai Khan in China

1260 Mamluk (slave) rulers of Egypt defeat Mongols at Ain Jalut; end of drive west

1271–1368 Reign of the Yuan (Mongol) dynasty in China

1271–1295 Journey of Marco Polo to central Asia, China, and Southeast Asia

1274, 1280 Failed Mongol invasions of Japan

1290s First true guns used in China

1336–1405 Life of Timur

mid-14th century Spread of the Black Death in Eurasia

1368 Yuan dynasty overthrown; Ming period in China begins

c. 1370 Gunpowder weapons effectively deployed in China and Europe

1380 Russian victory at Kulikova; power of the (Mongol descended) Golden Horde is broken

1250 C.E. — **1300** C.E. — **1350** C.E.

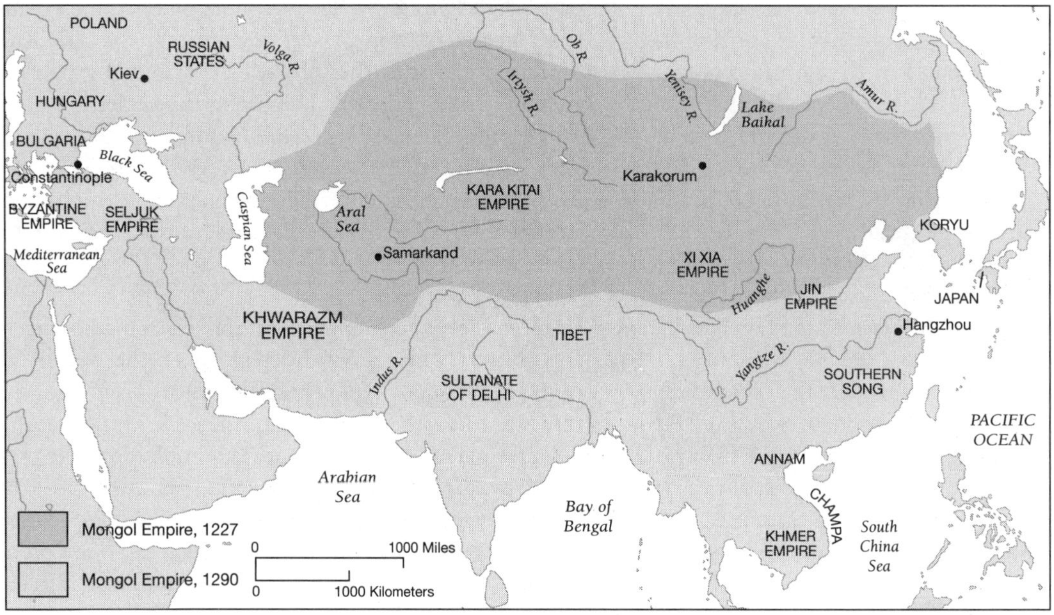

The First Mongol Empire of Chinggis Khan

tribe, which was divided into kin-related clans whose members camped and herded together on a regular basis. When threatened by external enemies or in preparation for raids on other nomads or invasions of sedentary areas, clans and tribes could be combined in great confederations. Depending on the skills of their leaders, these confederations could be held together for months or even years. But when the threat had passed or the raiding was done, clans and tribes invariably drifted back to their own pasturelands and campsites. At all organizational levels, leaders were elected by the free males of the group. Though women exercised considerable influence within the family and had the right to be heard in tribal councils, males dominated positions of leadership.

Courage in battle, usually evidenced from youth by bravery in the hunt, and the capacity to forge alliances and attract dependents were vital leadership skills. A strong leader could quickly build up a large following of chiefs from other clans and tribal groups. Some of these subordinates might be defeated rivals who had been enslaved by the victorious chief, though often the lifestyles of master and slave differed little. Should the leader grow old and feeble or suffer severe reverses, his once loyal subordinates would quickly abandon him. He expected this to happen, and the subordinates felt no remorse. Their survival and that of their dependents hinged on attaching themselves to a strong tribal leader.

The Making of a Great Warrior: The Early Career of Chinggis Khan

Indo-European and then Turkic-speaking nomads had dominated the steppes and posed the principal threat to Asian and European sedentary civilizations in the early millennia of recorded history. But peoples speaking Mongolian languages had enjoyed moments of power and had actually carved out regional kingdoms in north China in the 4th and 10th centuries C.E. In fact, in the early 12th century, Chinggis Khan's great-grandfather, Kabul Khan, led a Mongol alliance that had won glory by defeating an army sent against them by the Qin kingdom of north China. Soon after this victory, Kabul Khan became ill and died, and his successors could neither defeat their nomadic enemies nor hold the Mongol alliance together. Divided and beaten, the Mongols fell on hard times.

Chinggis Khan, who as a youth was named Temujin, was born in the 1170s into one of the splinter clans that fought for survival in the decades after the death of Kabul Khan. Temujin's father was an able leader, who managed to build up a decent following and negotiate a promise of marriage between his eldest son and the daughter of a stronger Mongol chief. According to Mongol accounts, just when the family fortunes seemed to be on the upswing, Temujin's father was poisoned by the agents of a rival nomadic group. Suddenly, Temujin,

Though it was a cumbersome process, even large Mongol tents could be moved when mounted on huge wagons, which were pulled by large teams of oxen.

who was still a teenager, was thrust into a position of leadership. But most of the chiefs who had attached themselves to his father refused to follow a mere boy, whose prospects of survival appeared to be slim.

In the months that followed, his much-reduced encampment was threatened and finally attacked by a rival tribe. Temujin was taken prisoner in 1182, locked into a wooden collar, and led in humiliation to the camp of his enemies. After a daring midnight escape, Temujin rejoined his mother and brothers and found refuge for his tiny band of followers deep in the mountains. Facing extermination, Temujin did what any sensible nomad leader would have done: he and his people joined the camp of a more powerful Mongol chieftain, who had once been aided by Temujin's father. With the support of this powerful leader, Temujin avenged the insults of the clan that had enslaved him and another that had taken advantage of his weakness to raid his camp for horses and women. These successes and Temujin's growing reputation as a warrior and military commander soon won him allies and clan chiefs eager to attach themselves to a leader with a promising future. Within a decade, the youthful Temujin had defeated his Mongol rivals and routed the forces sent to crush him by other nomadic peoples. In 1206, at a *kuriltai*, or meeting of all of the Mongol chieftains, Temujin—renamed Chinggis Khan—was elected the *khagan*, or supreme ruler, of the Mongol tribes. United under a strong leader, the Mongols prepared to launch a massive assault on an unsuspecting world.

Building the Mongol War Machine

The men of the Mongol tribes that had elevated Chinggis Khan to leadership were in many ways natural warriors. Trained from youth not only to ride but also to hunt and fight, they were physically tough, mobile, and accustomed to killing and death. They wielded a variety of weapons, including lances, hatchets, and iron maces. None of their weapons was as devastating as their powerful short bows. A Mongol warrior could fire a quiver of arrows with stunning accuracy without breaking the stride of his horse. He could hit enemy soldiers as distant as 400 yards (compared with a range of 250 yards for the English longbow) while charging straight ahead, ducking under the belly of his pony, or leaning over the horse's rump while retreating from superior forces. The fact that the Mongol armies were entirely cavalry meant that they possessed speed and a mobility that were demoralizing to enemy forces. Leading two or three horses to use as remounts, Mongol warriors could spend more than one week in the saddle and, when pressed, cover 80 or 90 miles per day. They could strike before their enemies had prepared their defenses, hit unanticipated targets, retreat back to the steppes after suffering temporary reverses, and then suddenly reappear in force.

To a people whose very lifestyle bred mobility, physical courage, and a love of combat, Chinggis Khan and his many able subordinate commanders brought organization, discipline, and unity of command. The old quarrels and vendettas between clans and tribes were overridden by loyalty to the khagan, and energies once devoted to infighting were now directed toward conquest and looting in the civilized centers that fringed the steppes on all sides. The Mongol forces were divided into armies made up of basic fighting units called *tumens*, each consisting of 10,000 cavalrymen. Each tumen was further divided into units of 1000, 100, and 10 warriors. Commanders at each level were responsible for the training, arming, and discipline of the cavalrymen under their charge. The tumens were also divided into heavy cavalry, which carried lances and wore some metal armor, and light cavalry, which relied primarily on the bow and arrow and leather helmets and body covering. Even more lightly armed and protected were the scouting parties that rode ahead of Mongol armies and, using flags and special signal fires, kept the main force apprised of the enemy's movements.

Chinggis Khan also created a separate messenger force, whose bodies were tightly bandaged to allow them to remain in the saddle for days, switching from horse to horse to carry urgent messages between the khagan and his commanders. Military discipline had long been secured by personal ties between commanders and ordinary soldiers. Mongol values, which made courage in battle a prerequisite for male self-esteem, were also buttressed by a formal code that dictated the immediate execution of a warrior who deserted his unit. Chinggis Khan's swift executions left little doubt about the fate of traitors to his own cause or turncoats who abandoned enemy commanders in his favor. His generosity to brave foes was also legendary. The most famous of the latter, a man named Jebe, nicknamed "the arrow," won the khagan's affection and high posts in the Mongol armies by standing his ground after his troops had been routed and fearlessly shooting Chinggis Khan's horse out from under him.

A special unit supplied Mongol armies with excellent maps of the areas they were to invade, based largely on information supplied by Chinggis Khan's extensive network of spies and informers. New weapons, including a variety of flaming and exploding arrows, gunpowder projectiles, and later bronze cannons, were also devised for the Mongol forces. By the time Chinggis Khan's armies rode east and west in search of plunder and conquest in the second decade of the 13th century, they were among the best armed and trained and the most experienced, disciplined, and mobile soldiers in the world.

Conquest: The Mongol Empire Under Chinggis Khan

When he was proclaimed the khagan in 1206, Temujin was probably not yet 40 years old. At that point, he was the supreme ruler of nearly one-half million Mongol tribesmen and the overlord of 1 to 2 million more nomadic tribesmen who had been defeated by his armies or had voluntarily allied themselves with this promising young commander. But Chinggis Khan had much greater ambitions. He once remarked that his greatest pleasure in life was making war, defeating enemies, forcing "their beloved [to] weep, riding on their horses, embracing their wives and daughters." He came to see himself and his sons as men marked for a special destiny: warriors born to con-

This Chinese painting of a Mongol warrior clearly enjoying hunting small game suggests the well-deserved reputation the Mongols had earned for their skills as riders and archers.

A 14th-century miniature painting from Rashid al-Din's History of the World *depicts Mongol horsemen charging into battle against retreating Persian forces.*

quer the known world. In 1207, he set out to fulfill this ambition. His first campaigns humbled the *Tangut* kingdom of Xi-Xia in northwest China, whose ruler was forced to declare himself a vassal of the khagan and pay a hefty tribute. Next, the Mongol armies attacked the much more powerful Qin Empire, which the Manchu-related Jurchens had established a century earlier in north China.

In these campaigns, the Mongol armies were confronted for the first time with large, fortified cities that their inhabitants assumed could easily withstand the assaults of these uncouth tribesmen from the steppes. Indeed, the Mongol invaders were thwarted at first by the intricate defensive works that the Chinese had perfected over the centuries to deter nomadic incursions. But the adaptive Mongols, with the help of captured Chinese artisans and military commanders, soon devised a whole arsenal of siege weapons. They included battering rams, catapults that hurled rocks and explosive balls, and bamboo rockets that spread fire and fear in besieged towns.

Chinggis Khan and the early Mongol commanders had little regard for these towns, whose inhabitants they regarded as soft and effete. Therefore, when resistance was encountered, the Mongols adopted a policy of terrifying retribution. Though the Mongols often spared the lives of famed scholars—whom they employed as advisors—and artisans with particularly useful skills, towns that fought back were usually sacked once they had been taken. The townspeople were slaughtered or sold into slavery; their homes, palaces, mosques, and temples were reduced to rubble. Towns that surrendered without a fight were usually spared this fate, though they were required to pay tribute to their Mongol conquerors as the price of their deliverance.

First Assault on the Islamic World: Conquest in China

Once he had established a foothold in north China and solidified his empire in the steppes, Chinggis Khan sent his armies westward against the Kara-Khitai Empire established by a Mongolian-speaking people a century earlier. Having overwhelmed and annexed the Kara-Khitai, in 1219 Chinggis Khan sent envoys to demand the submission of *Muhammad Shah II,* the Turkic ruler of the Khwarazm Empire to the west. Outraged by the audacity of the still little-known Mongol commander, one of Muhammad's subordinates had some of Chinggis Khan's later envoys killed and sent the rest with shaved heads back to the khagan. These insults, of course, meant war—a war in which the Khwarazm were overwhelmed. Their great cities fell to the new siege weapons and tactics the Mongols had perfected in their north China campaigns. Their armies were repeatedly routed in battles with the Mongol cavalry. Again and again, the Mongols used their favorite battle tactic in these encounters. Cavalry were sent to attack the enemy's main force. Feigning defeat, the cavalry retreated, drawing the opposing forces out of formation in the hope of a chance to slaughter the fleeing Mongols. Once the enemy's pursuing horsemen had spread themselves over the countryside, the main force of Mongol heavy cavalry, until then concealed, attacked them in a devastating pincers formation.

Within two years, his once flourishing cities in ruin and his kingdom in Mongol hands, Muhammad Shah II, having retreated across his empire, died on a desolate island near the Caspian Sea. In addition to greatly enlarging his domains, Chinggis Khan's victories meant that he could incorporate tens of thousands of Turkic horsemen into his armies. With his forces greatly enlarged by these new recruits, he once again turned eastward, where in the last years of his life his armies destroyed the Xi-Xia kingdom and overran the Qin Empire of north China. By 1227, the year of his death, the Mongols ruled an empire that stretched from eastern Persia to the North China Sea.

Life Under the Mongol Yoke

Despite their fury as warriors and the horrible destruction they could unleash on those who resisted their demands for submission and tribute, the Mongols proved remarkably astute and tolerant rulers. Chinggis Khan himself set the standard in this enterprise. He was a complex man, capable, as we have seen, of gloating over the ruin of his enemies. But he was also open to new ideas and committed to building a world where the diverse peoples of his empire could live together in peace. Though illiterate, Chinggis Khan was neither the ignorant savage nor the cultureless vandal often depicted in the accounts of civilized writers—usually those who had never met him. Once the conquered peoples had been subdued, he took a keen interest in their arts and learning, though he refused to live in their cities. Instead he established a new capital at *Karakorum* on the steppes and summoned the wise and clever from all parts of the empire to the lavish palace of tents with gilded pillars where he lived with his wives and closest advisors.

At Karakorum, Chinggis Khan consulted with Confucian scholars about how to rule China, with Muslim engineers about how to build siege weapons and improve trade with the lands farther west, and with Daoist holy men, whom he hoped could provide him with an elixir that would make him immortal. Though he himself followed the shamanistic (focused on the propitiation of nature spirits) beliefs of his ancestors, all religions were tolerated in his empire. An administrative framework that drew on the advice and talents of both Muslim and Chinese bureaucrats was created. A script was devised for the Mongolian language in order to facilitate record keeping and the standardization of laws. Chinggis Khan promulgated a legal code that was enforced by a special police force. Much of the code was aimed at putting an end to the divisions and quarrels that had so long occupied the Mongols. Grazing lands were systematically allotted to different tribes, and harsh penalties were established for rustling livestock or stealing horses.

The Mongol conquests brought a peace to much of Asia that in some areas persisted for generations. In the towns of the empire, handicraft production and scholarship flourished and artistic creativity was allowed free expression. Chinggis Khan and his successors actively promoted the growth of trade and travelers by protecting the caravans that made their way across the ancient Asian silk routes and by establishing rest stations for weary merchants and fortified outposts for those harassed by bandits. One Muslim historian wrote of the peoples within the domains of the khagan that they "enjoyed such a peace that a man might have journeyed from the land of sunrise to the land of sunset with a golden platter upon his head without suffering the least violence from anyone."

Secure trade routes made for prosperous merchants and wealthy, cosmopolitan cities. They also facilitated the spread of foods such as sorghum, sugar, citrus fruits, and grapes; inventions such as firearms, printing, and windmills; and techniques ranging from papermaking to the improvement of irrigation, from one civilization to another. Paradoxically, Mongol expansion, which sedentary chroniclers condemned as a "barbarian" orgy of violence and destruction, became a major force for economic and social development and the enhancement of civilized life.

The Death of Chinggis Khan and the Division of the Empire

When the Mongols had moved west to attack Kara Khitai in 1219, support was demanded from the vassal king of Xi-Xia. The Tangut ruler had impudently responded that if the Mongols were not strong enough to win wars on their own, they were best advised to refrain from at-

This portrait of Ogedei Khan, who was elected to succeed Chinggis Khan as the grand khan of the Mongols, is from a 13th-century album of Chinese emperors.

tacking others. In 1226, his wars in the west won, Chinggis Khan turned east with an army of 180,000 warriors to punish the Tanguts and complete a conquest that he regretted having left unfinished over a decade earlier. After routing a much larger Tangut army in a battle fought on the frozen waters of the Yellow River, the Mongol armies overran Xi-Xia, plundering and burning and mercilessly hunting down any Tangut survivors. As his forces closed in on the Tangut capital and last refuge, Chinggis Khan, who had been injured in a skirmish some months earlier, fell grievously ill. After impressing upon his sons the dangers of quarreling among themselves for the spoils of the empire, the khagan died in August 1227.

With one last outburst of Mongol wrath, this time directed against death itself, his body was carried back to Mongolia for burial. The Mongol forces escorting the funeral procession hunted down and killed every human and animal in its path. As Chinggis Khan had instructed, his armies also treacherously slaughtered the unarmed inhabitants of the Tangut capital after a truce and surrender had been arranged.

The vast pasturelands the Mongols now controlled were divided between Chinggis Khan's three remaining sons and *Batu,* a grandson and heir of the khagan's recently deceased son Jochi. Towns and cultivated areas like those in north China and parts of Persia were considered the common property of the Mongol ruling family. A kuriltai was convened at Karakorum, the Mongol capital, to select a successor to the great conqueror. In accordance with Chinggis Khan's preference, *Ogedei,* his third son, was elected grand khan. Though not as capable a military leader as his brothers or nephews, Ogedei was a crafty diplomat and deft manipulator—skills much needed if the ambitious heads of the vast provinces of the empire were to be kept from each others' throats.

For nearly a decade, Ogedei directed Mongol energies into further campaigns and conquests. The areas that were targeted by this new round of Mongol expansion paid the price for peace within the Mongol Empire. The fate of the most important victims—Russia and eastern Europe, the Islamic heartlands, and China—will be the focus of much of the rest of this chapter.

The Mongol Drive to the West

While in pursuit of the Khwarazm ruler, Muhammad Shah II, the Mongols had made their first contacts with the rich kingdoms to the west of the steppe heartlands of Chinggis Khan's empire. Raids of reconnaissance into Georgia and across the Russian steppe convinced the Mongol commanders that the Christian lands to the west were theirs for the taking. Russia and Europe were added to their agenda for world conquest. The subjugation of these regions became the project of the armies of the *Golden Horde,* which was named after the golden tent of the early khans of the western sector of the Mongol Empire. The territories of the Golden Horde made up the four great khanates into which the Mongol Empire had been divided at the time of Chinggis Khan's death. The khanate to the south, called the *Ilkhan Empire,* claimed the task of completing the conquest of the Muslim world that had begun with the invasion of the Khwarazm domains. Though neither Europe nor the Islamic heartlands were ultimately subdued, Mongol successes on the battlefield and the fury of their assaults affected the history of the regions that came under attack, particularly Russia and the Islamic world.

In a very real sense, the Mongol assault on Russia was a side campaign, a chance to fine-tune the war machine and win a little booty while they were en route to the real prize: western Europe. In the first half of the 13th century when the Mongol warriors first descended, a more

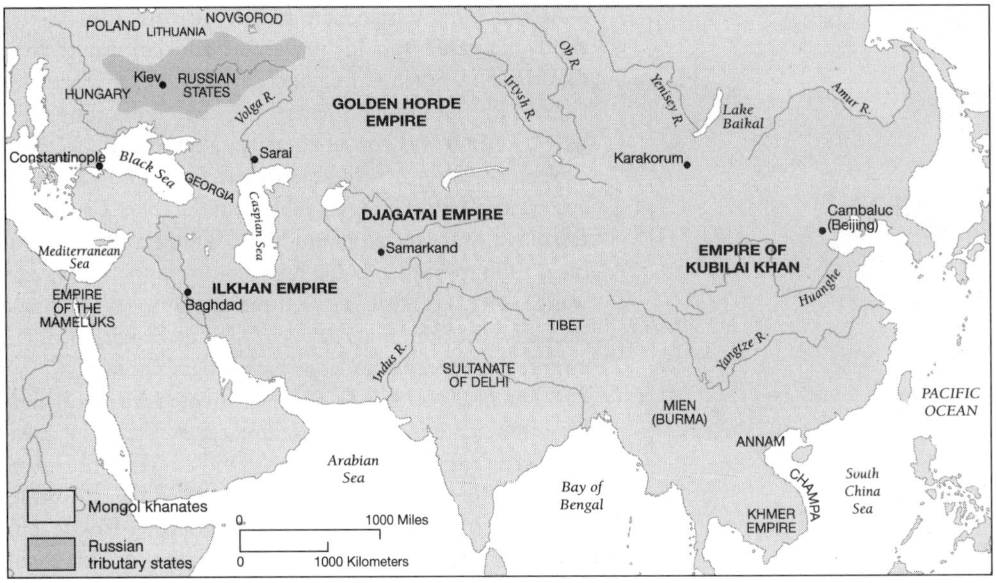

The Four Khanates of the Divided Mongol Empire, c. 1290

united Russia had been divided into numerous petty kingdoms, centered on trading cities such as Novgorod and Kiev. By this time Kiev, which had originally dominated much of central Russia, had been in decline for some time. As a result there was no paramount power to rally Russian forces against the invaders. Despite the dire warnings spread by those who had witnessed the crushing defeats suffered by the Georgians in the early 1220s, the princes of Russia refused to cooperate. They preferred to fight alone, and they were routed individually.

In 1236, Chinggis Khan's grandson Batu led a Mongol force of upwards of 120,000 cavalrymen into the Russian heartlands. From 1237 to 1238 and later in 1240, these "Tartars," as the Russian peoples called them, carried out the only successful winter invasions in Russian history. In fact, the Mongols preferred to fight in the winter. The frozen earth provided good footing for their horses, and frozen rivers gave them access rather than blocking the way to their enemies. One after another, the Mongol armies defeated the often much larger forces of local nomadic groups and Russian princes. Cities such as Ryazan, Moscow, and Vladimir, which resisted the Mongol command to surrender, were razed to the ground; their inhabitants were slaughtered or led into slavery. As a contemporary Russian chronicler observed, "no eye remained to weep for the dead." Just as it seemed that all of Russia would be ravaged by the Mongols, whom the Russians compared to locusts, Batu's armies withdrew. The largest cities, Novgorod and Kiev, appeared to have been spared. Russian priests thanked God; the Mongol commanders blamed the spring thaw, which slowed the Mongol horsemen and raised the risk of defeat in the treacherous mud.

Salvation yielded to further disasters when the Mongols returned in force in the winter of 1240. In this second campaign, even the great walled city of Kiev, which had reached a population of over 100,000 by the end of the 12th century, fell. Enraged by Kievan resistance—its ruler had ordered the Mongol envoys thrown from the city walls—the Mongols reduced the greatest city in Russia to a smoldering ruin. The cathedral of Saint Sophia was spared, but the rest of the city was systematically looted and destroyed, and its inhabitants were smoked out and slaughtered. Novgorod again braced itself for the Mongol onslaught. Again, according to the Russian chroniclers, it was "miraculously" spared. In fact, it was saved largely because of the willingness of its prince, Alexander Nevskii, to submit, at least temporarily, to Mongol demands. In addition, the Mongol armies were eager to move on to the main event: the invasion of western Europe.

Russia in Bondage

The crushing victories of Batu's armies initiated nearly two and a half centuries of Mongol dominance in Russia. Russian princes were forced to submit as vassals of the khan of the Golden Horde and to pay tribute or risk the ravages of Mongol raiders. Mongol exactions fell particularly heavily on the Russian peasantry, who had to yield up their crops and labor to both their own princes and

DOCUMENT

Marco Polo on Mongol Military Prowess

You see, when a Tartar prince goes forth to war, he takes with him, say, one hundred thousand horses. Well, he appoints an officer to every ten men, one to every hundred, one to every thousand, and one to every ten thousand, so that his own orders have to be given to ten persons only, and each of these ten persons has to pass the orders only to other ten, and so on; no one having to give orders to more than ten. And every one in turn is responsible only to the officer immediately over him; and the discipline and order that comes of this method is marvelous, for they are a people very obedient to their chiefs. Further, they call the corps of one hundred thousand men a *Tuc;* that of ten thousand they call a *Toman;* the thousand they call *Miny;* the hundred *Guz;* the ten *On*. And when the army is on the march they have always two hundred horsemen, very well mounted, who are sent a distance of two marches in advance to reconnoitre, and these always keep ahead. They have a similar party detached in the rear, and on either flank, so that there is a good lookout on all sides against a surprise. When they are going on a distant expedition they take no gear with them except two leather bottles for milk; a little earthenware pot to cook their meat in, and a little tent to shelter them from rain. And in case of great urgency they will ride ten days on end without lighting a fire or taking a meal. On such an occasion they will sustain themselves on the blood of their horses, opening a vein and letting the blood jet into their mouths, drinking till they have had enough, and then staunching it.

They also have milk dried into a kind of paste to carry with them; and when they need food they put this in water, and beat it up till it dissolves, and then drink it. It is prepared in this way: they boil the milk, and when the rich part floats on the top they skim it into another vessel, and of that they make butter; for the milk will not become solid till this is removed. Then they put the milk in the sun to dry. And when they go on an expedition, every man takes some ten pounds of this dried milk with him. And of a morning he will take a half pound of it and put it in his leather bottle, with as much water as he pleases. So, as he rides along, the milk paste and the water in the bottle get well churned together into a kind of pap, and that makes his dinner.

When they come to an engagement with the enemy, they will gain the victory in this fashion. They never let themselves get into a regular medley, but keep perpetually riding round and shooting into the enemy. And as they do not count it any shame to run away in battle, they will sometimes pretend to do so, and in running away they turn in the saddle and shoot hard and strong at the foe, and in this way make great havoc. Their horses are trained so perfectly that they will double hither and thither, just like a dog, in a way that is quite astonishing. Thus they fight to as good purpose in running away as if they stood and faced the enemy, because of the vast volleys of arrows that they shoot in this way, turning round upon their pursuers, who are fancying that they have won the battle. But when the Tartars see that they have killed and wounded a good many horses and men, they wheel round bodily, and return to the charge in perfect order and with loud cries: and in a very short time the enemy are routed. In truth they are stout and valiant soldiers, and inured to war. And you perceive that it is just when the enemy sees them run, and imagines that he has gained the battle, that he has in reality lost it; for the Tartars wheel round in a moment when they judge the right time has come. And after this fashion they have won many a fight.

From *The Travels of Marco Polo* (New York: Grosset & Dunlap, 1931), pp. 79–81.

the Mongol overlords. Impoverished and ever fearful of the lightning raids of Mongol marauders, the peasants fled to remote areas or became, in effect, the serfs of the Russian ruling class in return for protection.

The decision on the part of many peasants to become the lifetime laborers of the nobility resulted in a major change in the rural social structure of Russia. Until the mid-19th century, the great majority of the population of Russia would be tied to the lands they worked and bound to the tiny minority of nobles who owned these great estates. Some Russian towns made profits on the increased trade made possible by the Mongol links. Sometimes the gains exceeded the tribute they paid to the Golden Horde. No town benefited from the Mongol presence more than Moscow. Badly plundered and partially burned in the early Mongol assaults, the city was gradually rebuilt, and its ruling princes steadily swallowed up nearby towns and surrounding villages. After 1328, Moscow also profited from its status as the tribute collector for the Mongol khans. Its princes not only used their position to fill their own coffers but annexed further towns as punishment for falling behind on the payment of their tribute.

As Moscow grew in strength, the power of the Golden Horde declined. Mongol religious toleration benefited both the Orthodox church and Moscow. The *Metropolitan,* or head of the Orthodox church, was made the representative of all the clergy in Russia, which did much to enhance the church's standing. The choice of Moscow as the seat of the Orthodox leaders brought new sources of wealth to its princes and buttressed Muscovite claims to be Russia's leading city. In 1380, those claims received an additional boost when the princes of Moscow shifted from being tribute collectors to being the defenders of Russia. In alliance with other Russian vassals, they raised an army that defeated the forces of the Golden Horde at the battle of Kulikova. Their victory and the devastating blows Timur's attacks dealt the Golden Horde two decades later effectively broke the Mongol hold over Russia. Mongol forces raided as late as the 1450s, and the princes of Muscovy did not formally renounce their vassal status until 1480. But from the end of the 14th century onward, Moscow was the center of political power in Russia, and armies from Poland and Lithuania then posed the main threat to Russian peace and prosperity.

Though much of the Mongols' impact was negative, their conquest proved a decisive turning point in Russian history in several ways. In addition to their importance to Moscow and the Orthodox church, Mongol contacts led to changes in Russian military organization and tactics and in the political style of Russian rulers. Claims that the Tartars were responsible for Russian despotism, either Tsarist or Stalinist, are clearly overstated. Still, the Mongol example may have influenced the desire of Russian princes to centralize their control and minimize the limitations placed on their power by the landed nobility, the clergy, and wealthy merchants. By far the greatest effects of Mongol rule, however, were those resulting from Russia's relative isolation from Christian lands farther west. On one hand, the Mongols protected a divided and weak Russia from the attacks of much more powerful kingdoms such as Poland, Lithuania, and Hungary as well as the "crusades" of militant Christian orders like the Teutonic Knights, who were determined to stamp out the so-called Orthodox heresy. On the other hand, Mongol overlordship cut Russia off from key transformations in western Europe that were inspired by the Renaissance and led ultimately to the Reformation. The Orthodox clergy, of course, would have had little use for these influences, but their absence severely reduced the options available for Russian political, economic, and intellectual development.

Mongol Incursions and the Retreat from Europe

Until news of the Mongol campaigns in Russia reached European peoples such as the Germans and Hungarians farther west, Christian leaders had been quite pleased by the rise of a new military power in central Asia. Rumors and reports from Christians living in the area, chafing under what they perceived as the persecution of their Muslim overlords, convinced many in western Europe that the Mongol Khan was none other than *Prester John.* Prester John was the name given to a mythical rich and powerful Christian monarch whose kingdom had supposedly been cut off from Europe by the Muslim conquests of the 7th and 8th centuries. Sometimes located in Africa, sometimes in central Asia, Prester John loomed large in the European imagination as a potential ally who could strike the Muslim enemy from the rear and join up with European Christians to destroy their common adversary. The Mongol assault on the Muslim Khwarazm Empire appeared to confirm the speculation that Chinggis Khan was indeed Prester John.

The assault on Christian, though Orthodox, Russia made it clear that the Mongol armies were neither the legions of Prester John nor more partial to Christians than to any other people who stood in their way. The rulers of Europe were nevertheless slow to realize the magnitude of the threat the Mongols posed to western Christendom. When Mongol envoys, one of whom was an Englishman,

The Abbasid capital at Baghdad had long been in decline when the Mongols besieged it in 1258. The Mongols' capture and sack of the city put an end to all pretense that Baghdad was still the center of the Muslim world.

arrived at the court of King Bela of Hungary demanding that he surrender a group of nomads who had fled to his domains after being beaten by the Mongols in Russia, the king contemptuously dismissed them and Batu's demand that he submit to Mongol overlordship. Bela reasoned that he was the ruler of a powerful kingdom, whereas the Mongols were just another ragtag band of nomads in search of easy plunder. As had so often been the case in the past, his foolish refusal to negotiate provided the Mongols with a pretext to invade. Their ambition remained the conquest and pillage of all western Europe. That this goal was clearly attainable was demonstrated by the sound drubbing they gave to the Hungarians in 1240 and then to a mixed force of Christian knights led by the German ruler, King Henry of Silesia.

These victories left the Mongols free to raid and pillage from the Adriatic Sea region in the south to Poland and the German states of the north. It also left the rest of Europe open to Mongol conquest. Just as the kings and clergy of the western portions of Christendom were beginning to fear the worst, the Mongol forces disappeared. The death of the khagan Ogedei, in the distant Mongol capital at Karakorum, forced Batu to withdraw in preparation for the struggle for succession that was under way. The campaign for the conquest of Europe was never resumed. Perhaps Batu was satisfied with the huge empire of the Golden Horde that he ruled from his splendid new capital at Sarai; most certainly the Mongols had found richer lands to plunder in the following decades in the Muslim empires of the Middle East. Whatever the reason, Europe was spared the full fury of the Mongol assault. Of the civilizations that fringed the steppe homelands of the Mongols, only India would be as fortunate.

The Mongol Assault on the Islamic Heartlands

After the Mongol conquest of the Khwarazm Empire, it was only a matter of time before they struck westward against the far wealthier Muslim empires of Mesopotamia and North Africa. The conquest of these areas became the main project of *Hulegu,* another grandson of Chinggis Khan and the ruler of the Ilkhan portions of the Mongol Empire. One of the key results of Hulegu's assaults on the Muslim heartlands was the capture and destruction of Baghdad in 1258. The murder of the Abbasid caliph, one of some 800,000 people who were reported to have been killed in Mongol retribution for the city's resistance, brought an end to the dynasty that had ruled the core regions of the Islamic world since the middle of the 8th century. A major Mongol victory over the Seljuk Turks in 1243 also proved critical to the future history of the region. It opened up Asia Minor to conquest by a different Turkic people, the Ottomans, who would be the next great power in the Islamic heartlands.

Given the fate of Baghdad, it is understandable that Muslim historians treated the coming of the Mongols as one of the great catastrophes in the history of Islam. The murder of the caliph and his family left the faithful without a central authority. The sack of Baghdad and numerous other cities from central Asia to the shores of the Mediterranean devastated the focal points of Islamic civilization. The Mongols had also severely crippled Muslim military strength, much to the delight of the Christians, especially those like the *Nestorians* who lived in the Middle East. Some Christians offered assistance in the form of information; others, especially the Nestorians from inner Asia, served as commanders in Hulegu's armies. One contemporary Muslim chronicler, Ibn al-Athir, found the tribulations the Mongols had visited on his people so horrific that he apologized to his readers for recounting them and wished that he had not been born to witness them. He lamented that:

> **. . . in just one year they seized the most populous, the most beautiful, and the best cultivated part of the earth whose inhabitants excelled in character and urbanity. In the countries that have not yet been overrun by them, everyone spends the night afraid that they may yet appear there, too. . . . Thus, Islam and the Muslims were struck, at that time by a disaster such as no people had experienced before.**

Given these reverses, one can imagine the relief the peoples of the Muslim world felt when the Mongols were finally defeated in 1260 by the armies of the *Mamluk,* or slave, dynasty of Egypt at Ain Jalut. Ironically, *Baibars,* the commander of the Egyptian forces, and many of his lieutenants had been enslaved by the Mongols some years earlier and sold in Egypt, where they rose to power through military service. The Muslim victory was won with the rare cooperation of the Christians, who allowed Baibars's forces to cross unopposed through their much diminished Crusader territories in Palestine.

Hulegu was in central Asia, engaged in yet another succession struggle, when the battle occurred. Upon his return, he was forced to reconsider his plans for conquest of the entire Muslim world. The Mameluks were deeply entrenched and growing stronger; Hulegu was threatened by his cousin *Berke,* the new khan of the Golden Horde to the north, who had converted to Islam. After openly clashing with Berke and learning of Baibars's overtures for an alliance with the Golden Horde, Hulegu decided to settle for the sizable kingdom he already ruled, which stretched from the frontiers of Byzantium to the Oxus River in central Asia.

The Mongol Impact on Europe and the Islamic World

Though much of what the Mongols wrought on their westward march was destructive, some benefits were reaped from their forays into Europe and their conquests in Muslim areas. For example, they taught new ways of making war and impressed on their Turkic and European enemies the effectiveness of gunpowder. As we have seen, Mongol conquests facilitated trade between the civilizations at each end of Eurasia, making possible the exchange of foods, tools, and ideas on an unprecedented scale. The revived trade routes brought great wealth to traders, such as those from north Italy, who set up outposts in the eastern Mediterranean, along the Black Sea coast, and as far east as the Caspian Sea. Because the establishment of these trading empires by the Venetians and Genoese provided precedents for the later drives for overseas expansion by peoples such as the Portuguese and English, they are of special significance in global history.

Perhaps the greatest long-term impact of the Mongol drive to the west was indirect and unintended. In recent years, a growing number of historians have become convinced that the Mongol conquests played a key role in transmitting the fleas that carried bubonic plague from south China and central Asia to Europe and the Middle East. The fleas may have hitched a ride on the livestock the Mongols drove into the new pasturelands won by their conquests or on the rats that nibbled the grain transported by merchants along the trading routes the Mongol rulers fostered between east and west. Whatever the exact connection, the Mongol armies unknowingly paved the way for the spread of the dreaded Black Death across the steppes to much of China, to the Islamic heartlands, and from there to most of Europe in the mid-14th century. In so doing, they unleashed possibly the most fatal epidemic in all human history. From mortality rates higher than half the population in some areas of Europe and the Middle East to the economic and social adjustments that the plague forced wherever it spread, this accidental, but devastating, side effect of the

Mongol conquests influenced the course of civilized development in Eurasia for centuries to come.

The Mongol Interlude in Chinese History

Of all the areas the Mongols conquered, perhaps none was administered as closely as China. Following decades of hard campaigning in the middle of the 13th century, the Mongol interlude in Chinese history lasted only about a century. Though the age-old capacity of the Chinese to assimilate their nomadic conquerors was evident from the outset, the Mongols managed to retain a distinct culture and social separateness until they were driven back beyond the Great Wall in the late 1360s. They also opened China to influences from Arab and Persian lands, and even to contacts with Europe, which would come to full fruition in the following centuries of indigenous Chinese revival under the Ming dynasty.

Soon after Ogedei was elected as the great khan, the Mongol advance into China was resumed. Having conquered the Xi-Xia and Qin empires, the Mongol commanders turned to what remained of the Sung empire in south China. In the campaigns against the Sung, the Mongol forces were directed by *Kubilai Khan,* one of the grandsons of Chinggis Khan and a man who would play a pivotal role in Chinese history for the next half century. Even under a decadent dynasty that had long neglected its defenses, south China proved one of the toughest areas for the Mongols to conquer. From 1235 to 1279, the Mongols were continually on the march; they fought battle after battle and besieged seemingly innumerable, well-fortified Chinese cities. In 1260, Kubilai assumed the title of the great khan, much to the chagrin of his cousins who ruled other parts of the empire. A decade later in 1271, on the recommendation of Chinese advisors, he changed the name of the Mongol dynasty to the Sinicized Yuan. Though he was still nearly a decade away from fully defeating the last-ditch efforts of Confucian advisors and Chinese generals to save the Sung dynasty, Kubilai ruled most of China, and he now set about the task of establishing Mongol control on a more permanent basis.

As the different regions of China came under Mongol rule, Kubilai promulgated many laws to preserve the distinction between Mongol and Chinese. He forbade Chinese scholars to learn the Mongol script, which was used for records and correspondence at the upper levels of the imperial government. Mongols were forbidden to marry ethnic Chinese, and only women from nomadic families were selected for the imperial harem. Even friendships between the two peoples were discouraged. Mongol religious ceremonies and customs were retained, and a tent encampment in the traditional Mongol style was set up in the imperial city even though Kubilai usually resided in a Chinese-style palace. Kubilai and his successors continued to enjoy key Mongol pastimes such as the hunt, and Mongol military forces remained separate from Chinese.

In the Yuan era, a new social structure was established in China with the Mongols on top and their central Asian nomadic and Muslim allies right below them in the hierarchy. These two groups occupied most of the offices at the highest levels of the bureaucracy. Beneath them came the north Chinese; below them, the ethnic Chinese and the minority peoples of the south. Though ethnic Chinese from both north and south ran the Yuan bureaucracy at the regional and local levels, they could ordinarily exercise power at the top only as advisors to the Mongols or other nomadic officials. At all levels, their activities were scrutinized by Mongol functionaries from an enlarged and much-strengthened censors' bureau.

Mongol women in particular remained aloof from Chinese culture—at least Chinese culture in its Confucian guise. They refused to adopt the practice of footbinding, which so constricted the activities of Chinese women. They retained their rights to property and control within the household as well as the capacity to move freely about town and countryside. No more striking evidence of their independence can be found than contemporary accounts of Mongol women riding to the hunt, both with their husbands and at the head of their own hunting parties. The daughter of one of Kubilai's cousins even went to war, and she refused to marry until one of her many suitors proved able to throw her in a wrestling match. Unfortunately, the Mongol era was too brief to reverse the trends that were lowering the position of Chinese women. As neo-Confucianism gained ground under Kubilai's successors, the arguments for the confinement of women multiplied.

Mongol Tolerance and Foreign Cultural Influences

Like Chinggis Khan and other Mongol overlords, Kubilai and Chabi had unbounded curiosity and very cosmopolitan tastes. Their generous patronage drew scholars, artists, artisans, and office-seekers from many lands to the splendid Yuan court. Some of the most favored came from regional Muslim kingdoms to the east that had also come under Mongol rule. Muslims were included in the second highest social grouping, just beneath the Mongols themselves. Persians and Turks were admitted to the inner circle of Kubilai's administrators and advisors. Muslims designed and supervised the building of his Chinese-style imperial city and proposed new systems for the more efficient collection of taxes. Persian astronomers imported more advanced Middle Eastern instruments for celestial observations, corrected the Chinese calendar, and made some of the most accurate maps the Chinese had ever seen. Muslim doctors ran the imperial hospitals and added translations of 36 volumes on Muslim medicine to the imperial library. Though some of Kubilai's most powerful advisors were infamous for their corrupt ways, most served him well and did much to advance Chinese learning and technology through the transmission of texts, instruments, and weapons from throughout the Muslim world.

In addition to the Muslims, Kubilai welcomed travelers and emissaries from many foreign lands to his court. Like his grandfather, Kubilai displayed a strong interest in all religions and insisted on toleration in his domains. Buddhists, Nestorian Christians, Daoists, and Latin Christians made their way to his court. The most renowned of the latter were members of the Polo family from Venice in northern Italy, who traveled extensively in the Mongol Empire in the middle of the 13th century. Marco Polo's account of Kubilai Khan's court and empire is perhaps the most famous travel account written by a European. Marco accepted fantastic tales of grotesque and strange customs, and he may have cribbed parts of his account from other sources. Still, his descriptions of the palaces, cities, and wealth of Kubilai's empire enhanced European interest in the "Indies" and helped to inspire efforts by navigators like Columbus to find a water route to these fabled lands.

Social Policies and Scholar-Gentry Resistance

Kubilai's efforts to promote Mongol adaptation to Chinese culture were overshadowed in the long run by countervailing measures to preserve Mongol separateness. The ethnic Chinese who made up the vast majority of his subjects, particularly in the south, were never really reconciled to Mongol rule. Despite Kubilai's cultivation of Confucian rituals and his extensive employment of Chinese bureaucrats, most of the scholar-gentry regarded the Mongol overlord and his successors as uncouth barbarians whose policies endangered Chinese traditions. As it was intended to do, Kubilai's refusal to reinstate the examination route to administrative office prevented Confucian scholars from dominating politics. The favoritism he showed Mongol and other foreign officials further alienated the scholar-gentry.

To add insult to injury, Kubilai went to great lengths to bolster the position of the artisan classes, who had never enjoyed high standing, and the merchants, whom the Confucian thinkers had long dismissed as parasites. The Mongols had from the outset shown great regard for artisans and because of their useful skills had often spared them the slaughter meted out to their fellow city dwellers. During the Yuan period in China, merchants also prospered and commerce boomed, partly owing to Mongol efforts to improve transportation and expand the supply of paper money. The Mongols developed—with amazing speed for a people who had no prior experience with seafaring—a substantial navy, which played a major role in the conquest of the Sung Empire. After the conquest of China was completed, the great Mongol war fleets were used to put down pirates, who threatened river and overseas commerce, and, toward the end of Kubilai's reign, to conduct overseas expeditions of conquest and exploration. Thus, during the Yuan period, artisans and traders enjoyed a level of government backing and social status that was never again equaled in Chinese civilization.

Ironically, despite the Mongols' ingrained suspicion of cities and sedentary lifestyles, both flourished in the Yuan era. The urban expansion begun under the Tang and Sung dynasties continued, and the Mongol elite soon became addicted to the diversions of urban life. Though traditional Chinese artistic endeavors, such as poetry and essay writing, languished under the Mongols in comparison with their flowering in the Tang–Sung eras, popular entertainments, particularly musical dramas, flourished. Perhaps the most famous of Chinese dramatic works, *The Romance of the West Chamber*, was written in the Yuan period. Dozens of major playwrights wrote for the court, the rising merchant classes, and the well-heeled Mongol elite. Actors and actresses, who had long been relegated by the Confucian scholars to the despised status of "mean people," achieved celebrity and some measure of social esteem. All of this rankled the scholar-gentry, who bided their time, waiting for the chance to restore Confucian decorum and what they believed to be the proper social hierarchy for a civilized people like the Chinese.

Initially, at least, Kubilai Khan pursued policies toward one social group, the peasants, that the scholarly class would have heartily approved. He issued edicts forbidding Mongol cavalrymen from turning croplands into pasture and restored the granary system for famine relief that had been badly neglected in the late Sung. Kubilai also sought to reduce peasant tax and forced-labor burdens, partly by redirecting peasant payments from local nonofficial tax farmers directly to government officials. He and his advisors also formulated a revolutionary plan to establish elementary education at the village level. Though the level of learning they envisioned was rudimentary, such a project—*if* it had been enacted—would have provided a major challenge to the educational system centered on the elite that hitherto had dominated Chinese civilization.

The Fall of the House of Yuan

Historians often remark on the seeming contradiction between the military prowess of the Mongol conquerors and the short life of the dynasty they established in China. Kubilai Khan's long reign encompassed a good portion of the nine decades that the Mongols ruled all of China. Already by the end of his reign, the dynasty was showing signs of weakening. Sung loyalists raised the standard of revolt in the south, and popular hostility toward the foreign overlords was expressed more and more openly. The Mongol aura of military invincibility was badly tarnished by Kubilai's rebuffs at the hands of the military lords of Japan and the failure of the expeditions that he sent to punish them, first in 1274 and again in a much larger effort mounted in 1280. The defeats suffered by Mongol forces engaged in similar expeditions to Vietnam and Java during this same period further undermined the Mongols' standing.

Kubilai's dissolute lifestyle in his later years, partly brought on by the death of his most beloved wife, Chabi, and five years later the death of his favorite son, set the tone for a general softening of the Mongol ruling class as a whole. Kubilai's successors lacked his capacity for leadership and cared little for the tedium of day-to-day administrative tasks. Many of the Muslim and Chinese functionaries to whom they entrusted the finances of the empire enriched themselves through flagrant graft and corruption. This greatly angered the hard-pressed peasantry who had to bear the burden of rising taxes and demands for forced labor. The scholar-gentry played on this discontent by calling on the people to rise up and overthrow the "barbarian" usurpers.

By the 1350s, the signs of dynastic decline were apparent. Banditry and piracy were widespread, and the government's forces were too feeble to curb them. Famine hit many regions and spawned local uprisings, which grew to engulf large portions of the empire. Secret religious sects, such as the *White Lotus Society,* were formed and were dedicated to the overthrow of the dynasty. Their leaders' claims that they had magical powers to heal their followers and to confound their enemies helped encourage further peasant resistance against the Mongols. As had been the case in the past, rebel leaders quarreled and fought with each other. For a time, chaos reigned as the Yuan regime dissolved, and those Mongols who could escape the fury of the mob retreated back into central Asia. The restoration of peace and order came from an unexpected quarter. Rather than a regional military commander or an aristocratic lord, a man from an impoverished peasant family, *Ju Yuanzhang,* emerged to found the *Ming dynasty,* which would rule China for most of the next three centuries.

The Eclipse of the Nomadic War Machine

As the shock waves of the Mongol and Timurid explosions amply demonstrated, nomadic incursions into the civilized cores have had an impact on global history that far exceeds what one would expect, given the relatively small numbers of nomadic peoples and the limited resources of the regions they inhabited. From the time of the great Indo-European migrations in the formative epoch of civilized development in the 3rd and 2nd millennia B.C.E. through the classical and postclassical eras, nomadic peoples periodically emerged from their steppe, prairie, and desert fringe homelands to invade, often build empires, and settle in the sedentary zones of Eurasia, Africa, and the Americas. Their intrusions have significantly altered political history by destroying existing polities and even—as in the case of Assyria and Harappa—whole civilizations. They have also generated major population movements, sparked social upheavals, and facilitated critical cultural and economic exchanges across civilizations. As the Mongols' stunning successes in the 13th century illustrate, the capacity of nomadic peoples to break through the defenses of the much more populous civilized zones and to establish control over much richer and more sophisticated peoples arose primarily from the advantages the nomads possessed in waging war.

A reservoir of battle-ready warriors and mobility have from ancient times proved to be the key to success for expansion-minded nomads. Harsh environments and ongoing intertribal and interclan conflicts for survival within them produced tough, resourceful fighters who could live off the land on the march and who regarded combat as an integral part of their lives. The horses and camels on which pastoral peoples in Eurasia and Sudanic Africa relied gave them a degree of mobility that confounded the sedentary peoples who sought to ward off their incursions. The mounted warriors of nomadic armies possessed the advantages of speed, surprise, and superior intelligence, which was gathered by mounted reconnaissance patrols. The most successful nomadic invaders, such as the Mongols, also proved willing to experiment with and adapt to technological innovations with military applications. Some of these, such as the stirrup and various sorts of harnesses, were devised by the nomads themselves. Others, such as gunpowder and the siege engines—both Muslim and Chinese—that the Mongols used to smash the defenses of walled towns were borrowed from sedentary peoples and adapted to the nomads' fighting machines.

Aside from the considerable military advantages that accrued from the nomads' lifestyles and social organization, their successes in war owed much to the weaknesses of their adversaries in the sedentary, civilized zones. The great empires that provided the main defense for agricultural peoples against nomadic incursions were, even in the best circumstances, diverse and overextended polities. Imperial control—and protection—diminished steadily as one moved away from the capital and core provinces. Imperial boundaries were usually fluid, and the outer provinces were consistently vulnerable to nomadic raids if not conquest.

Classical and postclassical empires, such as the Egyptian and Han and the Abbasid, Byzantine, and Sung enjoyed great advantages over the nomads in terms of the populations and resources they controlled. But their armies, almost without exception, were too slow, too low on firepower, and too poorly trained to resist large and well-organized forces of nomadic intruders. In times of dynastic strength in the sedentary zones, well-defended fortress systems and ingenious weapons—such as the crossbow, which could be fairly easily mastered by the peasant conscripts—proved quite effective against nomadic incursions. Nonetheless, even the strongest dynasties depended heavily on "protection" payments to nomad leaders and the divisions between the nomadic peoples on their borders for their security. And even the strongest sedentary empires were periodically shaken by nomadic raids into the outer provinces. When the empires weakened or when large numbers of nomads were united under able leaders, such as Muhammad and his successors or Chinggis Khan, nomadic assaults made a shambles of sedentary armies and fortifications.

In many ways, the Mongol and Timurid explosions represented the apex of nomadic power and influence on world history. After these remarkable interludes, age-old patterns of interaction between nomads and farming town-dwelling peoples were fundamentally transformed. These transformations resulted in the growing ability of sedentary peoples to first resist and then dominate nomadic peoples, and they mark a major watershed in the history of the human community. Some of the causes of the shift were immediate and specific. The most critical of these was the devastation wrought by the Black Death on the nomads of Central Asia in the 14th century. Though the epidemic proved catastrophic for large portions of the civilized zones as well, it dealt the relatively sparse nomadic populations a blow from which they took centuries to recover. The more rapid demographic (relating to population trends) resurgence of the sedentary peoples greatly increased their already considerable numerical advantage over the nomadic peoples in the following centuries. The combination of this growing numerical advantage, which in earlier epochs the nomads had often been able to overcome, with key political and economic shifts and technological innovations proved critical in bringing about the decline of the nomadic war machine.

In the centuries after the Mongol conquests, the rulers of sedentary states found increasingly effective ways of centralizing their political power and mobilizing the manpower and resources of their domains for war. Some improvements in this regard were made by the rulers of China and the empires of the Islamic belt. But the sovereigns of the nascent states of western Europe surpassed all other potentates in advances in these spheres. Stronger control and better organization allowed a growing share of steadily increasing national wealth to be channeled toward military ends. The competing rulers of Europe also invested heavily in technological innovations with military applications, from improved metalworking techniques to the development of ever more potent gunpowder and firearms. From the 15th and 16th centuries, the discipline and training of European armies also improved markedly. With pikes, muskets, fire drill, and trained commanders, European armies were more than a match for the massed nomad cavalry that had so long terrorized sedentary peoples.

With the introduction early in the 17th century of light, mobile field artillery into European armies, the nomads' retreat began. States such as Russia, which had centralized power on the western European model, as well as the Ottoman Empire in the eastern Mediterranean and the Qing in China, which had shared many of the armament advances of the Europeans, moved steadily into the steppe and desert heartlands of the horse and camel nomads. Each followed a conscious policy of settling part of its rapidly growing peasant population in the areas taken from the nomads. Thus, nomadic populations not only were brought under the direct rule of sedentary empires but saw their pasturelands plowed and planted wherever the soil and water supply permitted.

These trends suggest that the nomadic war machine had been in decline long before the new wave of innovation that ushered in the Industrial Revolution in the 18th century. But that process sealed its fate. Railways and repeating rifles allowed sedentary peoples to penetrate even the most wild and remote of the nomadic refuges and subdue even the most determined and fierce of nomadic warriors, from the Plains Indians of North America to the bedouin of the Sahara and Arabia. The periodic nomadic incursions into the sedentary zones, which had recurred sporadically for millennia, had come to an end.

The Mongol Legacy

As we have seen, the Mongols' impact on the many areas where they raided and conquered varied considerably. The sedentary peoples on the farms and in the cities, who experienced the fury of their assaults and the burden of their tribute exactions, understandably emphasized the destructive side of the Mongol legacy. But the Mongol campaigns also decisively influenced the course of human history in the ways they altered warfare and the political repercussions they generated in invaded areas. Mongol armies, for example, provided openings for the rise of Moscow as the central force in the creation of a Russian state, they put an end to Abbasid and Seljuk power, and they opened the way for the Mamluks and the Ottomans. The Mongol empire promoted trade and important exchanges among civilizations, though, as the spread of the Black Death illustrates, the latter were not always beneficial. Mongol rule also brought stable, at times quite effective, government and religious toleration to peoples over much of Asia.

FURTHER READING

A substantial literature has developed on the Mongol interlude in global history. The most readable and reliable biography of Chinggis Khan is René Grousset's *Conqueror of the World* (1966). Grousset has also written a broader history of central Asia, entitled *The Empire of the Steppes* (1970). Peter Brent's more recent *The Mongol Empire* (1976) provides an updated overview and wonderful illustrations. Berthold Spuler's *The Mongols in History* (1971) makes some attempt to gauge their impact on world history, and his *History of the Mongols* (1968) supplies a wide variety of firsthand accounts of the Mongols from the founding of the empire to life in the successor states. T. Allsen's *Mongol Imperialism* provides the best account of the rise and structure of the empires built by Chinggis Khan and his successors.

For specific areas, George Vernadsky's *The Mongols in Russia* (1953) remains the standard, though some of its views are now contested. Morris Rossabi's recent *Kubilai Khan: His Life and Times* (1988) is by far the best work on the Mongols in China. James Chambers's *The Devil's Horsemen* (1979) and Denis Sinor's *History of Hungary* (1957) contain good accounts of the Mongol incursions into eastern and central Europe. The fullest and most accessible summary of the links between Mongol expansion and the spread of the Black Death can be found in William H. McNeill's *Plagues and Peoples* (1976).

CHAPTER 12

Byzantium and Orthodox Europe

KEY TERMS

Byzantine Empire
Eastern Orthodox
Justinian
Body of Civil Law
Bulgaria
iconoclasm
schism
Cyril and Methodius
Kievan Rus'
Vladimir I
Tartars

DISCUSSION QUESTIONS

What factors contributed to the decline of the Byzantine Empire?

Why did Eastern and Western European forms of Christianity split?

How was Russian society and government influenced by the Byzantine Empire?

During the postclassical period, in addition to the great civilizations of Asia and North Africa, two major, though related, civilizations took shape in Europe. One was anchored in the Byzantine Empire, which straddled western Asia and southeastern Europe but expanded with the spread of Orthodox Christianity to eastern Europe. The other was defined above all by the beliefs and institutions of Catholicism in western and central Europe. Both European civilizations were colored by Islamic dynamism, but they operated according to different principles. Comparable to African civilization in some ways—for example, in building political institutions in areas where formal states had not existed before—these civilizations carved out many distinctive features as well.

The Byzantine Empire maintained particularly high levels of political, economic, and cultural life during much of the period from 500 to 1450 C.E. It controlled an important, though somewhat fluctuating, swath of territory in the Balkans, the northern Middle East, and the eastern Mediterranean. The leaders of the empire regarded themselves as Roman emperors, and indeed their government was in many ways a direct continuation of the eastern portion of the late Roman Empire. This was not really Rome moved eastward, however, though the governmental structure built on traditions of late Roman emperors such as Diocletian and Constantine. The term *Byzantine*, though not used at the time, accurately suggests the distinction from Rome itself: This was a political heir to Rome, but with geography and focus of its own.

The real significance of the Byzantine Empire goes well beyond its ability to keep Rome's memory alive. The empire lasted for almost a thousand years, between Rome's collapse in the West and the final overthrow of the regime by Turkish invaders. The empire's capital, Constantinople, was one of the truly great cities of the world, certainly the most opulent and important city in Europe in this period. From Constantinople radiated one of the two major branches of Christianity: the Orthodox Christian churches that became dominant throughout most of eastern Europe.

Like the other great civilizations of the period, the Byzantine Empire spread its cultural and political influence to parts of the world that had not previously been controlled by any major civilization. Just as Muslim influence helped shape civilization in parts of Africa south of the Sahara, and Indian and Chinese dynamism helped define cultural zones in Southeast Asia, the Byzantines began to create a new civilization area in the Balkans and particularly in western Russia (present-day Ukraine and Belarus as well as western Russia proper). Here was a major case, indeed, of the remaking of the civilizational map that formed such an important characteristic of the early centuries of the postclassical millennium.

Ultimately, the empire's most important stepchild was Russia, whose rise as a civilized area relied heavily on influences from the Byzantines to the south. Russia took many initial cultural and political characteristics from the Byzantine Empire and would ultimately claim to inherit the mantle of the empire itself. However, the postclassical millennium formed a preliminary, somewhat tentative gestation period for civilization in Russia, and historians must be cautious in drawing too many parallels between the patterns displayed at this point and subsequent developments when Russia more fully hit its stride. A Byzantine or Byzantine-influenced heritage would remain, but it was highly selective.

The history of civilization in eastern Europe in this period involves one other interpretive issue in addition to the complexity of the relationship between Byzantine flourish and decline and the patterns to the north. This issue consists, quite simply, of how to frame the story of the spread of Christianity in Europe between the eastern and western portions of the continent. There were many

100 C.E.	600 C.E.	800 C.E.
1st century C.E.–**650** Slavic migrations into eastern Europe **527–565** Justinian **330s** Constantinople made capital of Eastern Roman Empire	**718** Defeat of Arab attack on Constantinople	**855** According to legend, Rurik king of Kievan Russia **864** Beginning of missionary work of brothers Cyril and Methodius in Slavic lands **896** Magyars settle in Hungary **870** First kingdom in what is now Czech and Slovak Republics **c. 960** Emergence of Polish state

commonalities between developments in eastern Europe and those of the Christian West. In both cases, civilization spread northward, because of the missionary appeal of the religion itself. In both cases, polytheism gave way to monotheism—though important compromises were made, particularly at the popular level. In both cases, more northerly political units, such as Russia, Poland, Germany, and France, struggled for political definition without as yet being able to rival the political sophistication of the more advanced civilization areas in Asia and North Africa—or in Byzantium itself. In both cases, new trading activities brought northern regions into contact with the major centers of world commerce, including Constantinople, with important long-range as well as short-term results. In both cases, newly civilized areas looked back to the Greco-Roman past, as well as to Christianity, for cultural inspiration, using as a result some of the same political myths and, with due modifications, artistic styles.

Yet, with all these shared ingredients, the civilizations that expanded in the East and developed in the West operated largely on separate tracks. They produced different versions of Christianity, which culturally as well as organizationally were rather separate—even hostile. The civilizations had little mutual contact, particularly in the formative centuries before western Europe became strong enough to trade significantly with Constantinople. Commercial patterns in both cases ran south–north, rather than east–west. Political evolution was also somewhat distinct. The fact was that during most of the postclassical millennium, major portions of eastern Europe were significantly more advanced than the West in political sophistication, cultural range, and economic vitality. Even the relationship with the classical Mediterranean past differed, as eastern Europe maintained important features of the late Roman Empire explicitly, whereas western leaders ultimately turned to a much more selective borrowing and imitation. Thus, eastern Europe worked directly from the classical architectural tradition, whereas western Europe, after a modest classicism, developed a much different dominant style.

By 1400, essentially two civilizations existed in Europe, with very few contacts and only a handful of basic similarities. This relationship would later change, with new contacts developing on the basis of contiguous geography, the common adherence to Christianity, and new commercial exchanges. In this formative period, however, the distinct paths must be emphasized along with the undeniably greater importance, in terms of larger world history before 1450, of the eastern European civilization. The boundary line between East and West was somewhat fuzzy, embracing important regions, such as Hungary, where overlapping and competing influences between western and eastern Europe helped define a special identity—where indeed a special identity exists to this day. In the major centers of the two European civilizations, however—in Byzantium and Russia, or France and the Low Countries—different paths were defined after the fall of Rome, marked by different cycles of dynamism and decline. When the two civilizations did meet, in this period as later, they met as distant cousins, related but not close kin.

The Byzantine Empire

The Byzantine Empire unfolded initially as part of the greater Roman Empire. Then, as this framework shattered with Roman decline, it took on a life of its own, particularly from the reign of the emperor Justinian onward. It centered on a territory both different from and smaller than the eastern Mediterranean as Rome had defined it. This was the result of new pressures, particularly the surge of Islam throughout North Africa and the bulk of the Middle East. Despite many attacks, the Empire largely flourished until the 11th century.

980–1015 Conversion of Vladimir I of Russia to Christianity
1018 Defeat of first Bulgarian Empire, taken over by Byzantines
1019–1054 Yaroslav king of Russia
1054 Schism between Eastern and Western Christianity
1100–1453 Byzantine decline; growing Turkish attack
1203–1204 Capture of Constantinople during the Fourth Crusade
1237–1241 Capture of Russia by Mongols (Tartars)
1453 Capture of Constantinople by Ottoman Turks; end of Byzantine Empire
1480 Expulsion of Tartars from Russia

1000 C.E. **1200** C.E. **1400** C.E.

Origins of the Empire

The *Byzantine Empire* in some senses began in the 4th century C.E., when the Romans set up their eastern capital in Constantinople. This city quickly became the most vigorous center of the otherwise fading imperial structure. The emperor Constantine constructed a host of elegant buildings, including Christian churches, in his new city, which was built on the foundations of a previously modest town called Byzantium. Soon, separate Eastern emperors ruled from the new metropolis, even before the western portion of the empire fell to the Germanic invaders. They warded off invading Huns and other intruders while enjoying a solid tax base in the peasant agriculture of the eastern Mediterranean. Constantinople was responsible for the Balkan peninsula, the northern Middle East, the Mediterranean coast, and North Africa. Although for several centuries Latin served as the court language of the eastern empire, Greek was the common tongue, and after the emperor Justinian in the 6th century, it became the official language as well. Indeed, in the eyes of the easterners, Latin became an inferior, barbaric means of communication. Knowledge of Greek enabled the scholars of the eastern empire to read freely in the ancient Athenian philosophical and literary classics and in the Hellenistic writings and scientific treatises.

The new empire benefited from the high levels of civilization long present in the eastern Mediterranean. Commerce continued at a considerable pace, though the merchant classes declined and state control of trade increased. New blood was drawn into administration and trade as Hellenized Egyptians and Syrians, long excluded from Roman administration, moved to Constantinople and entered the expanding bureaucracy of the Byzantine rulers. The empire faced many foreign enemies, though the pressure was less severe than that provided by the Germanic tribes in the West. It responded, however, by recruiting armies in the Middle East itself, not by relying on barbarian troops. And the empire increasingly turned from the emphasis on army power, so characteristic of Rome in its later phases, to add a growing, highly trained civilian bureaucracy. Tensions between strong generals and bureaucratic leaders remained, but the empire did not rely primarily on force for its internal rule. Complex administration around a remote emperor, who was surrounded by elaborate ceremonies, increasingly defined the empire's political style.

Eastern Orthodox Christianity

As an Eastern Empire took shape politically, Christianity also began to split between East and West. In the West, the pope, based in Rome, officially headed the framework of church organization. He claimed control over bishops, sent missionaries to the north, and tried to regulate doctrine. No comparable single leader developed in the Eastern church. For several centuries, the Eastern church acknowledged the pope's authority as first among equals, but in practice, papal directives had no hold over the Byzantine church. Rather, it was the emperors themselves who regulated church organization, creating a pattern of state control over church structure far different from the tradition that developed in the West, where the church insisted, though not always successfully, on its independence. Byzantine emperors used their claim to be God's representative on earth to cement their own power. Correspondingly, they kept a close eye on church affairs while trying to force non-Christians to convert. From the time of Justinian, the number of non-Christians allowed in Constantinople was carefully limited.

Furthermore, the Eastern church experienced several different influences from those prevalent in Western Christianity. Monasticism developed earlier in the East than in the West. Many individuals and groups of monks tried to follow Christ in a more complete way through special lives of fasting, celibacy, and prayer, staying apart from worldly concerns. Several leaders undertook to regulate this holy life, and a rule for monasteries developed by *Basil,* the patriarch of Constantinople in the mid-4th century, became particularly important in the East. Basil's rule helped formalize the separation between monasteries and ordinary people, pledging monks to lives of poverty, charity, and prayer. Unlike Western monastic orders, Eastern monks devoted little attention to scholarship. Their social role was great, however, for Eastern people venerated holy men and gave them considerable authority in the larger affairs of the church. Monasteries, along with traveling missionaries, provided food and medical care while seeking to drive away demons; they were far closer to popular Christianity than the official religion of the imperial court.

Orthodox Christianity, in sum, shared a host of features with its Western cousin, including intolerance for other beliefs. Different political organizations, however, launched a largely separate pattern of religious development in terms of specific church structures, monasticism, religious art, and theology. These differences, in turn, caused ongoing mutual suspicion and hostility. A late 12th-century church patriarch in Constantinople even argued that Muslim rule would be preferable to that of the pope: "For if I am subject to

Mosaics in Ravenna, Italy, from the early period of the Byzantine Empire, illustrate some of the highest achievements of Byzantine religious art and provide a dazzling, ornate environment for worship. This mosaic features a rather militant Christ the Redeemer.

the Muslim, at least he will not force me to share his faith. But if I have to be under the Frankish rule and united with the Roman Church, I may have to separate myself from God."

Justinian's Achievements

The early history of the Byzantine Empire was marked by a recurrent threat of invasion. Eastern emperors, relying on their local military base plus able generalship by upper-class Greeks, beat off attacks by the Sassanian Empire in Persia and by Germanic invaders.

Then, in 533 C.E., with the empire's borders reasonably well assured, a new emperor, Justinian, attempted to reconquer western territory in a last, futile effort to restore an empire like that of Rome. Ironically, Justinian's reign would confirm Byzantium's basis in the Greco-Roman heritage, through massive architectural and legal achievements in the classical mode, while also furthering the empire's relocation toward the *Balkans* and the western part of present-day Turkey, away from the Mediterranean coast.

Justinian himself, who faced and brutally suppressed serious social unrest, has been variously judged by contemporaries and later historians alike. He was a somber personality, autocratic, and prone to grandiose ideas. A contemporary historian named Procopius, no friend of the emperor, described him as "at once villainous and amenable; as people say colloquially, a moron. He was never truthful with anyone, but always guileful in what he said and did, yet easily hoodwinked by any who wanted to deceive him." The emperor was also heavily influenced by his wife Theodora, a courtesan connected with Constantinople's horse-racing world, who was eager for power. It was Theodora who stiffened Justinian's backbone in response to popular unrest and who prodded the plans for expansion.

Justinian's positive contributions to the Byzantine Empire lay in rebuilding Constantinople, ravaged by earlier riots against high taxes, and systematizing the Roman legal code. Extending later Roman architecture, with its addition of domes to earlier classical styles, Justinian's builders constructed many new structures—the most inspiring of which was the huge new church, the *Hagia Sophia,* long one of the wonders of the Christian world. This was an achievement in engineering as well as architecture, for no one had previously been able to construct the supports for a dome of comparable size. Justinian's codification of Roman law reached a goal earlier emperors had sought but not achieved. Unified law not only reduced confusion but also served to unite and organize the new empire itself, paralleling the state's bureaucracy. Justinian's code, called the *Body of Civil Law,* stands as one of the clearest and most comprehensive systems created by any culture. The code summed up and reconciled a host of Roman edicts and decisions, making Roman law a coherent basis for political and economic life throughout the empire. Recurrently updated by later emperors, the code would also ultimately help spread Roman legal principles in various parts of Europe.

Justinian's military exploits had more ambiguous results. The emperor wanted to recapture the old Roman Empire itself. With the aid of a brilliant general, *Belisarius,* new gains were made in North Africa and Italy. The Byzantines hoped to restore North Africa to its role as grain producer for the Mediterranean world, while Italy would be the symbol of past imperial glories. Unable to hold Rome against the Germans, Justinian's forces made their temporary capital, Ravenna, a key artistic center, embellished by some of the most beautiful Christian mosaics known anywhere in the world. But the major Italian holdings were short-lived, unable to withstand Germanic pressure, while North African territory was soon besieged as well.

Furthermore, Justinian's westward ambitions had weakened the empire in its own sphere. Persian forces attacked in the northern Middle East, while new Slavic groups, moving into the Balkans, pressed on another front. Justinian finally managed to create a new line of defense and even pushed Persian forces back again, but some Middle Eastern territory was irretrievably lost. Furthermore, all these wars, offensive and defensive alike, created new tax pressures on the government and forced Justinian to exertions that almost literally wore him to his death in 565 C.E.

Arab Pressure and the Empire's Defenses

Justinian's successors, after some renewed hesitations and setbacks, began to concentrate more fully on defending the Eastern Empire itself. Persian successes in the northern Middle East were reversed in the 7th century, and the population was forcibly reconverted to Christianity. The resultant empire, centered in the southern Balkans and the western and central portions of present-day Turkey, was a far cry from Rome's greatness—far even from the wealth of the Eastern Empire itself when it had a firmer hold on the fertile lands of the northern Middle East. It was sufficient, however, to amplify a rich Hellenistic culture and blend it more fully with Christianity while advancing Roman achievements in engineering and military tactics as well as law.

The Byzantine Empire was also sufficiently strong to withstand the great new threat of the 7th century, though not without massive loss: the surge of the Arab Muslims. The Arabs, by the mid-7th century, had built a fleet that challenged Byzantine naval supremacy in the eastern Mediterranean while repeatedly attacking Constantinople. They quickly swallowed the empire's remaining provinces along the eastern seaboard of the Mediterranean and soon cut into the northern Middle Eastern heartland as well. Considerable Arab cultural and commercial influence also affected patterns of life in Constantinople.

The Byzantine Empire, however reduced, held out nevertheless. A major siege of the capital in 717–718 C.E. was beaten back, partly owing to a new weapon called *Greek fire* (a petroleum, quicklime, and sulfur mixture) that devastated Arab ships. The Arab threat was never entirely removed. Furthermore, wars with the Muslims had added new economic burdens to the empire, as invasions and taxation, weakening the position of small farmers, resulted in greater aristocratic estates and new power for aristocratic generals. The free rural population that had served the empire during its early centuries—providing military recruits and paying the bulk of the taxes—was forced into greater dependence. Greater emphasis was given to careful organization of the army and navy. The history of the empire, after the greatest Arab onslaughts had been faced and their results assimilated, offered a dizzying series of weak and strong emperors. Periods of vigor alternated with seeming decay. Arab pressure continued. Conquest of the island of Crete in the 9th century allowed the Muslims to harass Byzantine shipping in the Mediterranean for several centuries. Slavic kingdoms, especially *Bulgaria,* periodically pressed Byzantine territory in the Balkans, though at times military success and marriage alliances

Imperial cavalry, detail from "Chronicle" of John Scylitzes, 14th century.

World Civilizations: The Global Experience, Second Edition
Chapter 15: Civilization in Eastern Europe: Byzantium and Orthodox Europe

brought Byzantine control over the feisty Bulgarian kingdom. Thus, while a Bulgarian king in the 10th century took the title of *tsar,* a Slavic version of the word *Caesar*, steady Byzantine pressure through war eroded the regional kingdom. In the 11th century, the Byzantine emperor Basil II, known appropriately enough as *Bulgaroktonos,* or slayer of the Bulgarians, used the empire's wealth to bribe many Bulgarian nobles and generals. He defeated the Bulgarian army in 1014, blinding as many as 15,000 captive soldiers—the sight of whom brought on the Bulgarian king's death. Bulgaria became part of the empire, its aristocracy settling in Constantinople and merging with the leading Greek families. Thus, despite all its problems, the imperial core displayed real strength, governing a territory about half the size of the previous eastern portion of the Roman Empire and withstanding a series of enemies. More than a long-standing barrier to the Arabs, the empire would soon make its greatest contributions to subsequent world history by reaching northward in trade and culture, creating a new zone of civilization precisely because so much of the Mediterranean had fallen to Arab hands.

The Empire's High Point

The Byzantine Empire entered a particularly stable period during the 9th and 10th centuries, when a new ruling dynasty managed to avoid the quarrels over succession to the imperial throne that had bedeviled many heirs before and after Justinian. The result was growing prosperity and solid political rule. The luxury of the court and its buildings steadily increased. Elaborate ceremonies and rich imperial processions created a magnificence designed to dazzle the empire's subjects. Briefly, at the end of the 10th century, the Byzantine emperor may have been the most powerful single monarch on earth, with a capital city whose rich buildings and abundant popular entertainments awed visitors from western Europe and elsewhere, while giving Eastern rulers a growing confidence in the validity of their own institutions and values.

Byzantine Society and Politics

The Byzantine political system bore unusual resemblance to the earlier patterns in China. The emperor was held to be ordained by God—head of church as well as state. He appointed church bishops and passed religious and secular laws. The elaborate court rituals symbolized the ideals of a divinely inspired, all-powerful ruler, though they also often immobilized rulers and inhibited innovative policy. At key points, women held the imperial throne, while maintaining the ceremonial power of the office.

Supplementing the centralized imperial authority was one of history's most elaborate bureaucracies. Trained in Greek classics, philosophy, and science in a secular school system that paralleled but contrasted with church education for the priesthood, Byzantine bureaucrats could be recruited from all social classes. As in China, aristocrats predominated, but there was some openness to talent among this elite of highly educated scholars. Bureaucrats were specialized into various offices, and officials close to the emperor were mainly eunuchs. Provincial governors were appointed from the center and were charged with keeping tabs on military authorities. An elaborate system of spies helped preserve loyalty while also creating intense distrust even among friends. It is small wonder that the word *Byzan-*

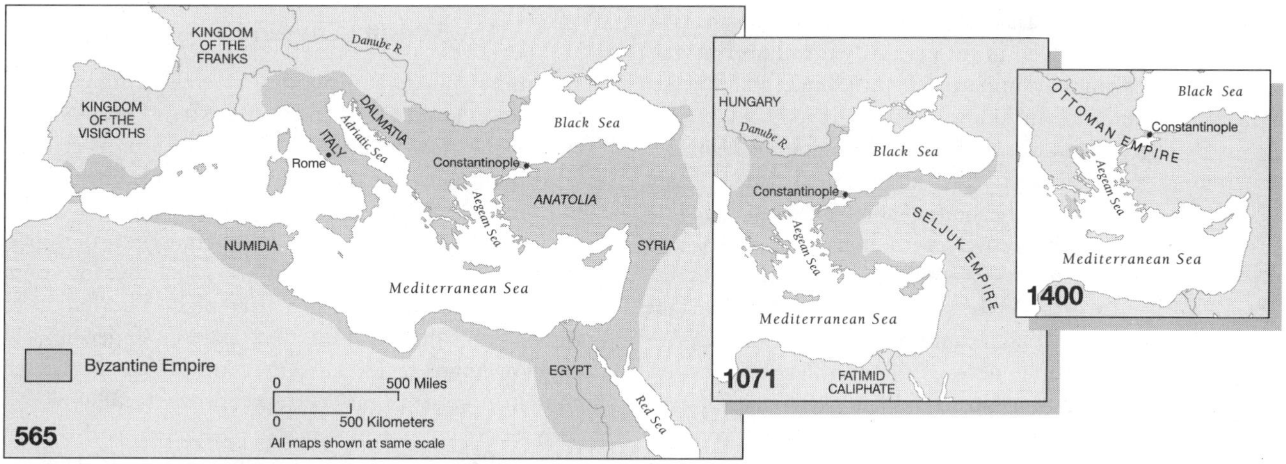

The Byzantine Empire, 565–1400 C.E.

tine came to refer to complex and convoluted institutional arrangements. At the same time, the system was sufficiently successful to constitute one of the cements that preserved the longest-lived single government structure the Mediterranean world has ever known.

Much of the empire's success depended on careful military organization. Byzantine rulers adapted the later Roman system by recruiting troops locally and rewarding them with grants of land in return for their military service. The land could not be sold, but sons inherited its administration in return for continued military responsibility. Many outsiders, particularly Slavs and Armenian Christians, were recruited for the army in this fashion. Increasingly, hereditary military leaders assumed considerable regional power, displacing more traditional and better-educated aristocrats. One emperor, Michael II, was a product of this system and was notorious for his hatred of Greek education and his overall personal ignorance. On the other hand, the military system had obvious advantages in protecting a state recurrently under attack from Muslims of various sorts—Persians, Arabs, and later Turks—as well as nomadic intruders from central Asia. Until the 15th century, the Byzantine Empire effectively blocked the path to Europe for most of these groups.

Socially and economically, the empire depended on Constantinople's control over the countryside, with the bureaucracy regulating trade and controlling food prices. The large peasant class was vital in supplying goods and also in providing the bulk of tax revenues. Food prices were kept artificially low, in order to content the numerous urban lower classes, in a system supported largely by taxes on the hard-pressed peasantry. Other cities were modest in size—Athens, for example, dwindled—as the focus was on the capital city and its food needs. The empire developed a far-flung trading network with Asia to the east and Russia and Scandinavia to the north. Silk production expanded in the empire, with silkworms and techniques initially imported from China, and various luxury products, including cloth, carpets, and spices, were sent northward. This gave the empire a favorable trading position with less sophisticated lands. Only China produced luxury goods of comparable quality. The empire also traded actively with India, the Arabs, and East Asia while receiving simpler products from western Europe and Africa. At the same time, the large merchant class never gained significant political power, in part because of the elaborate network of governmental controls. In this, Byzantium again resembled China and differed notably from the looser social and political networks of the West, where merchants were rising and gaining greater voice.

Byzantine cultural life centered on the secular traditions of Hellenism, so important in the education of bureaucrats, and on the evolving traditions of Eastern, or Orthodox, Christianity. While a host of literary and artistic creations resulted from this climate, there was little fundamental innovation except in art and architecture. The Byzantine strength lay in preserving and commenting on past forms more than in developing new ones. A distinct Byzantine style had developed fairly early in art and architecture. The adaptation of Roman domed buildings, the elaboration of powerful and richly colored religious mosaics, and a tradition of *icon* painting—paintings of saints and other religious figures, often richly ornamented—expressed this artistic impulse and its marriage with Christianity. The blue and gold backgrounds set with richly dressed religious figures were meant to display on earth the unchanging brilliance of heaven. The important controversy over religious art arose in the 8th century, when a new emperor attacked the use of religious images in worship (probably responding to Muslim claims that Christians were idol-worshippers). This attack, called *iconoclasm* because of the breaking of images, roused huge protest from Byzantine monks, which briefly threatened a split between church and state. After a long and complex battle, the use of icons was gradually restored, while the tradition of state control over church affairs was also reasserted. Cultural issues in Byzantium reflected strong feelings, in part the fruit of the great diversity of peoples and cultural habits under the empire's sway, even if major new intellectual principles did not result. A certain amount of diversity could be accepted because of common allegiance to Christianity and the military and administrative effectiveness of the empire at its best.

The Schism Between East and West

Byzantine culture and politics, as well as its economic orientation toward Asia and northeastern Europe, helped explain the growing break between its Eastern version of Christianity and the Western version headed by the pope in Rome. There were many milestones in this rift. Different rituals developed as the West translated the Greek Bible into Latin in the 4th century. Later, Byzantine emperors deeply resented papal attempts to interfere in the iconoclastic dispute, for the popes, understandably enough, hoped to loosen state control over the Eastern church in order to make it conform more fully to their own idea of church-state relations. There was also scornful hostility to efforts by a Frankish ruler, Charlemagne, to proclaim himself a Roman emperor in the 9th century.

In this mosaic of Christ, dating from about 1100 C.E., note the difference from the images of Christ common in Western Christianity, which place more emphasis on suffering and less on divine majesty.

Byzantine officials knew full well that they were the true heirs of Rome and that Western rulers were crude and unsophisticated. They did, however, extend some recognition to the "Emperor of the Franks."

Contact between the two branches of Christianity trailed off, though neither East nor West cared to make a definitive break. Then, in 1054, an ambitious church patriarch in Constantinople raised a host of old issues, including a quarrel over what kind of bread to use for the celebration of Christ's last supper in the church liturgy. He also attacked the Roman Catholic practice, developed some centuries earlier, of insisting on celibacy for its priests; Eastern Orthodox priests could marry. Delegations of the two churches discussed these disputes, but this led only to new bitterness. The Roman pope finally excommunicated the patriarch and his followers—that is, banished them from Christian fellowship and the sacraments. The patriarch, no slouch, responded by excommunicating all Roman Catholics. Thus the split between the Roman Catholic church and Eastern Orthodoxy—the Byzantine or Greek, as well as the Russian Orthodox, Serbian Orthodox, and others—became formal and has endured to this day.

The East–West split fell short of complete divorce. A common Christianity with many shared or revived classical traditions and frequent commercial and cultural contacts continued to enliven the relationship between the two European civilizations. The split also reflected significant distinctions in political systems, most obviously in the principles of church–state relations but also between an imperial administration and the more divided Western state system. And it reflected the different patterns of development followed by the two civilizations during the postclassical millennium. Byzantium, for all its ups and downs, was well aware of its advantages over the West during the early centuries following Rome's collapse. The East–West split occurred right at the end of Byzantium's period of greatest glory. By this point, however, the West was beginning to develop new strengths of its own, and over the next few centuries, its dynamism would eclipse that of most of eastern Europe.

The Empire's Decline

Shortly after the schism between East and West, the Byzantine Empire entered a long period of decline. Turkish invaders who had converted to Islam in central Asia began to press on its eastern borders, having already gained increasing influence in the Muslim caliphate. In the later 11th century, Turkish troops, the Seljuks, seized almost all the Asiatic provinces of the empire, thus cutting off the most prosperous sources of tax revenue as well as the territories that had supplied most of the empire's food. The Byzantine emperor lost the disastrous battle of Manzikert in 1071, his larger army was annihilated, and the empire never recovered. It staggered along for another four centuries, but its doom, at least as a significant power, was virtually sealed.

Eastern emperors appealed to Western leaders for help against the Turks, but their requests were largely ignored. The appeal helped motivate Western Crusades to the Holy Land, but this did not help the Byzantines. At the same time, Italian cities, blessed with powerful navies, gained in Constantinople increasing advantages, such as special trading privileges—a sign of the shift in power balance between East and West. One Western Crusade, in 1204, ostensibly set up to conquer the Holy Land from the Muslims, actually turned against Byzantium. Led by greedy Venetian merchants, the Crusade attacked and conquered Constantinople, briefly unseat-

The Byzantine Empire developed a distinctively stylized religious art, adapted from earlier Roman painting styles and conveying the solemnity of the holy figures of the faith. This 11th-century miniature features the holy women at the sepulchre of Christ.

ing the emperor altogether and weakening the whole imperial structure. But the West was not yet powerful enough to hold this ground, and a small Byzantine Empire was restored, able through careful diplomacy to survive for another two centuries. Not only Western and Turkish pressure but also the creation of new, independent Slavic kingdoms in the Balkans, such as Serbia, showed the empire's diminished power. Turkish settlements pressed ever closer to Constantinople in the northern Middle East—in the area that is now Turkey—and finally, in 1453, a Turkish sultan brought a powerful army, equipped by artillery purchased from the West, against the city, which fell after two months. By 1461, the Turks had conquered remaining pockets of Byzantine control, including most of the Balkans, bringing Islamic power farther into eastern Europe than ever before. The great Eastern Empire was no more.

The fall of Byzantium was one of the great events in world history, and we will deal with its impact in several later chapters. It was a great event because the Byzantine Empire had been so durable and important, anchoring a vital corner of the Mediterranean even amid the rapid surge of Islam. The empire's trading contacts and its ability to preserve and disseminate classical and Christian learning made it a vital unit during the whole postclassical period. After its demise, its influence would affect other societies, including the new Ottoman empire.

The Spread of Civilization in Eastern Europe

Missionary attempts to spread Christianity, new Byzantine conquests in the Balkans (particularly Bulgaria), and trade routes running north and south through western Russia and Ukraine created abundant contacts with key portions of eastern Europe. A number of regional states formed. Kievan Rus', in a territory including present-day Ukraine, Belarus, and western Russia, developed some of the formative features of Russian culture and politics. Mongol invasions ended this period of early Russian history, redividing parts of eastern Europe in the process.

Long before the Byzantinc decline after the 11th century, the empire had been the source of a new northward surge of Christianity. Orthodox missionaries sent from Constantinople busily converted most people in the Balkans—in what is now Bulgaria, Yugoslavia, and parts of Romania and Hungary—to their version of Christianity, and some other trappings of Byzantine culture came in their wake. In 864, the Byzantine government sent the missionaries *Cyril* and *Methodius* to the territory that is now the Czech and Slovak republics. Here the effort failed, in that Roman Catholic missionaries were more

East European Kingdoms in the 12th Century

successful. But Cyril and Methodius continued their efforts in the Balkans and in southern Russia, where their ability to speak the Slavic language greatly aided their efforts. One of the Catholic objections to Methodius was in fact his insistence on using Slavic rather than Latin in church services. The two missionaries devised a written script for this language, derived from Greek letters; to this day, the Slavic alphabet is known as Cyrillic. Thus, the possibility of literature and some literacy developed in eastern Europe along with Christianity, well beyond the political borders of Byzantium. Byzantine missionaries were quite willing to have local languages used in church services—another contrast with Western Catholicism.

Orthodox Missionaries and Other Influences

Eastern missionaries did not monopolize the borderlands of eastern Europe. Roman Catholicism and the Latin alphabet prevailed not only in the Czech area but also in most of Hungary (which was taken over in the 9th century by a Turkic people, the Magyars) and in Poland. Much of this region would long be an area of competition between Eastern and Western political and intellectual models. During the centuries after the conversion to Christianity, this stretch of eastern Europe north of the Balkans was organized in a series of regional monarchies, loosely governed amid a powerful, landowning aristocracy. The kingdoms of Poland, Bohemia (Czechoslovakia), and Lithuania easily surpassed most western kingdoms in territory. This was also a moderately active area for trade and industry. Ironworking, for example, was more developed than in the West until the 12th century. Eastern Europe during these centuries also received an important influx of Jews, who were migrating away from the Middle East but also fleeing intolerance in western Europe. Poland gained the largest single concentration of Jews. Eastern Europe's Jews, largely barred from agriculture and often resented by the Christian majority, gained strength in local commerce while maintaining their own religious and cultural traditions. A strong emphasis on extensive education and literacy, though primarily for males, distinguished Jewish culture not only in eastern Europe but also compared with most societies in the world at this time.

This was an early phase of the development of eastern Europe beyond the Byzantine heartland, for by Asian (or Byzantine) standards the region remained backward, lightly populated, and not yet able to produce a significant written or artistic culture beyond rudimentary church buildings and monkish chronicles of events. Many features of Byzantium, including its elaborate bureaucracy, were irrelevant to what was, like most of western Europe at the same time, a developing region.

The Emergence of Kievan Rus'

Russia shared many features with the rest of northeastern Europe before the 15th century, including rather hesitant advances in economy and politics. A full-fledged Russian civilization had yet to emerge. Yet, as with much of eastern Europe, the centuries of Byzantine influence were an important formative period that would influence later developments considerably.

Slavic peoples had moved into the sweeping plains of Russia and eastern Europe from an Asian homeland during the time of the Roman Empire. They mixed with and incorporated some earlier inhabitants and some additional invaders, such as the Bulgarians who adopted Slavic language and customs. The Slavs already knew the use of iron, and they extended agriculture in the rich soils of what is now Ukraine and western Russia, where no

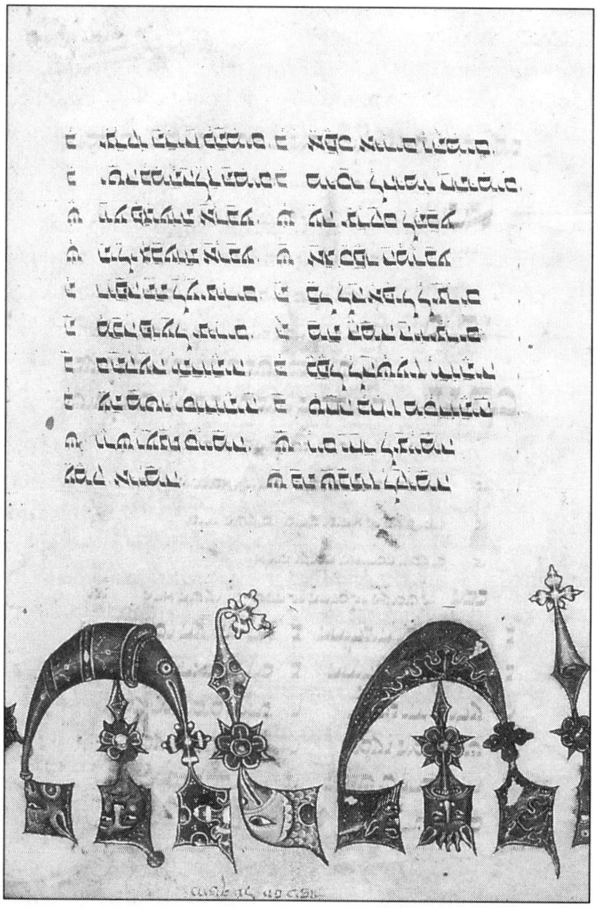

This 14th-century illustrated German-Jewish prayer book is a remnant from the spread of Jews and Jewish culture during the postclassical period.

durable civilization had previously taken root. Slavic political organization long rested in family tribes and villages. The Slavs maintained an animist religion with gods for the sun, thunder, wind, and fire. The early Russians also had a rich tradition of folk music and oral legends, and they developed some very loose regional kingdoms.

During the 6th and 7th centuries, traders from Scandinavia began to work through the Slavic lands, moving along the great rivers of western Russia, which run south to north—particularly the Dnieper. Through this route the Norse traders were able to reach the Byzantine Empire, and a regular, flourishing trade developed between Scandinavia and Constantinople. Luxury products from Byzantium and the Arab world traveled north in return for furs and other relatively crude products. The Scandinavian traders, militarily superior to the Slavs, gradually set up some governments along their trade route, particularly in the city of *Kiev*. A monarchy emerged, and according to legend a man named *Rurik*, a native of Denmark, became the first prince of Kievan Rus' about 855 C.E. The Kievan principality, though still loosely organized through alliances with regional, landed aristocrats, flourished until the 12th century. It was from the Scandinavians also that the word *Russia* was coined, possibly from a Greek word for "red," which applied to the hair color of many of the Norse traders. In turn, the Scandinavian minority gradually mingled with the Slavic population, particularly among the aristocracy.

Contacts between Kievan Rus' and Byzantium extended steadily. Kiev, centrally located, became a prosperous trading center, and from there many Russians visited Constantinople. These exchanges led to growing knowledge of Christianity. Prince *Vladimir I,* a Rurik descendant who ruled from 980 to 1015, finally took the step of converting to Christianity—not only in his own name but on behalf of all his people. He was eager to avoid the papal influence that came with Roman Catholicism, which he knew about through the experiences of the Polish kingdom. Orthodox Christianity gave a valid alternative that still provided a sophisticated replacement for the prevailing animism. Islam was rejected, according to one account, because Vladimir could not accept a religion that forbade alcoholic drink. Russian awe at the splendor of religious services in Constantinople also played a role. Having made his decision, Vladimir proceeded to organize mass baptisms for his subjects, forcing conversions by military pressure. Early church leaders were imported from Byzantium, and they helped train a literate Russian priesthood. As in Byzantium, the king characteristically controlled major appointments, and a separate *Russian Orthodox Church* soon developed.

As Kievan Rus' became Christian, it was the largest single state in Europe, though highly decentralized. Rurik's descendants managed for some time to avoid damaging battles over succession to the throne. Following Byzantine example, they issued a formal law code, which among other things reduced the severity of traditional punishments and replaced community vendettas with state run courts, at least in principle. The last of the great Kievan princes, *Yaroslav,* issued the legal codification while also building numerous churches and arranging the translation of religious literature from Greek to Slavic.

Institutions and Culture in Kievan Rus'

Kievan Rus' borrowed much from Byzantium, but it was in no position to replicate major institutions such as the

DOCUMENT

The Acceptance of Christianity

Russia's conversion to Orthodoxy was a fundamental step in the division of Europe between East and West. This excerpt from The Russian Primary Chronicle explains how the decision was made.

6494 (986). Vladimir was visited by Volga Bulgars of Mohammedan faith. . . . Then came the Germans, asserting that they came as emissaries of the Pope. . . . The Jewish Khazars heard of these missions, and came themselves. . . . Then the Greeks sent to Vladimir a scholar. . .

6495 (987). Vladimir summoned together his vassals and the city elders, and said to them, "Behold, the Volga Bulgars came before me urging me to accept their religion. Then came the Germans and praised their own faith; and after them came the Jews. Finally the Greeks appeared, criticizing all other faiths but commending their own, and they spoke at length, telling the history of the whole world from its beginning. . . .

. . . The Prince and all the people, chose good and wise men to the number of ten, and directed them to go first among the Volga Bulgars and inspect their faith. The emissaries went their way, and when they arrived at their destination they beheld the disgraceful actions of the Volga Bulgars and their worship in the mosque; then they returned to their own country. Vladimir then instructed them to go likewise among the Germans, and examine their faith, and finally to visit the Greeks. They thus went into Germany, and after viewing the German ceremonial, they proceeded to Tsargrad (Constantinople), where they appeared before the Emperor. . . .

Thus they returned to their own country, and the Prince called together his vassals and the elders. Vladimir then announced the return of the envoys who had been sent out, and suggested that their report be heard. He thus commanded them to speak out before his vassals. The envoys reported, "When we journeyed among the Volga Bulgars, we beheld how they worship in their temple, called a mosque, while they stand ungirt. The Volga Bulgars bows, sits down, looks hither and thither like one possessed, and there is no happiness among them, but instead only sorrow and a dreadful stench. Their religion is not good. Then we went among the Germans, and saw them performing many ceremonies in their temples; but we beheld no glory there. Then we went on to Greece, and the Greeks led us to the edifices where they worship their God, and we knew not whether we were in heaven or on earth. For on earth there is no such splendor or such beauty, and we are at a loss how to describe it. We only know that God dwells there among men, and their service is fairer than the ceremonies of other nations. . . . Then the vassals spoke and said, "If the Greek faith were evil, it would not have been adopted by your grandmother Olga, who was wiser than all other men." Vladimir then inquired where they should all accept baptism, and they replied that the decision rested with him. . . .

By divine agency, Vladimir was suffering at that moment from a disease of the eyes, and could see nothing, being in great distress. The Princess declared to him that if he desired to be relieved of this disease, he should be baptized with all speed, otherwise it could not be cured. . . . The Bishop of Kherson, together with the Princess's priests, after announcing the tidings, baptized Vladimir, and as the Bishop laid his hand upon him, he straightway received his sight. Upon experiencing this miraculous cure, Vladimir glorified God, saying, "I have now perceived the one true God." When his followers beheld this miracle, many of them were also baptized.

From *The Russian Primary Chronicle* by Samuel H. Cross in *Harvard Studies and Notes in Philology and Literature,* Vol. 12, pp. 183–184, 197–201, 204–205, 210–211, and 213 (Cambridge, MA: Harvard University Press). Reprinted by permission

This painting shows the Russian king, Vladimir, accepting Christianity.

bureaucracy or an elaborate educational system. Major princes were attracted to Byzantine ceremonials and luxury and to the concept (if not yet the reality) that a central ruler should have wide powers.

Many characteristics of Orthodox Christianity gradually penetrated Russian culture. Fervent devotion to the power of God and to many Eastern saints helped organize worship. Churches were relatively ornate, filled with icons and the sweet smell of incense. A monastic movement developed that stressed prayer and charity. Traditional practices, such as polygamy, gradually yielded to the Christian family ethic that insisted on only one wife. The emphasis on almsgiving as a manifestation of religious feeling long described the sense of obligation felt by wealthy Russians toward the poor, and it would actually delay the formation of more institutionalized welfare arrangements.

The Russian literature that developed, which used the Cyrillic alphabet, mainly summed up a mixture of religious and royal events and was filled with praises to the saints and invocations of the power of God. Disasters were seen as expressions of the just wrath of God against human wickedness, while success in war followed from the aid of God and the saints in the name jointly of Russia and the Orthodox faith. This tone also was common in Western Christian writing during these centuries, but in Kievan Rus' it monopolized formal culture more fully; a distinct, additional philosophical or scientific current did not emerge in the postclassical period.

Russian and Ukrainian art focused on the religious also, with icon painting and illuminated religious manuscripts becoming something of a Kievan specialty. Orthodox churches, built in the form of a cross surmounted by a dome, similarly aped Byzantine styles, though frequently the building materials were wood rather than stone. Religious art and music were rivaled by continued popular entertainments in the oral tradition, which combined music, street performances, and some theater. The Russian church tried to suppress these forms, regarding them as pagan, but with incomplete success.

Overall, this formative period in Russian society saw the development of a powerful religious sentiment, with particular cultural emphasis on art and music. This cultural development, although parallel to some features in emerging Western culture because of the common process of creating a new literary tradition from a polytheistic background and because of shared Christian beliefs, operated quite separately from specific patterns in the West. Russian–Western contacts, at this point and for several centuries to come, were virtually nonexistent, though Yaroslav, interestingly, married his daughter to a French king, indicating his awareness of possible beneficial interchange.

The same separate development marked Russian social and economic patterns. Russian peasants at this juncture were fairly free farmers, though an aristocratic landlord class existed. Russian aristocrats, called *boyars*, had less political power than their counterparts in western Europe, though the Kievan princes had to negotiate with them.

Kievan Decline

The Kievan principality began to fade in the 12th century. Rival princes set up regional governments, while the royal family frequently squabbled over succession to

St. Sophia in Kiev, though built after the postclassical period, utilized artistic themes developed earlier in Byzantium.

the throne. Invaders from Asia whittled at Russian territory. The rapid eclipse of Byzantium reduced Russian trade and wealth, for the kingdom had always depended heavily on the greater prosperity and sophisticated manufacturing of its southern neighbor. A new kingdom was briefly established around a city near what is now Moscow, but by 1200, Russia was weak and disunited. The final blow in this first chapter of Russian history came in 1237–1238 and 1240–1241, when two invasions by Mongols from central Asia moved through Russia and into other parts of eastern Europe. The initial Mongol intent was to add the whole of Europe to their growing empire. The Mongols, or *Tartars* as they are called in the Russian tradition, easily captured the major Russian cities, but they did not penetrate much farther west because of political difficulties in their Asian homeland. For over two centuries, however, much of Russia would remain under Tartar control.

This control, in turn, further separated the dynamic of Russian history from that of western Europe. Russian literature languished under Tartar supervision. Trade lapsed in western Russia, and indeed, the vigorous north–south commerce of the Kievan period never returned. At the same time, loose Tartar supervision did not destroy Russian Christianity or a native Russian aristocratic class. So long as tribute was paid, Tartar overlords left day-to-day Russian affairs alone. Thus, when Tartar control was finally forced out in the second half of the 15th century, a Russian cultural and political tradition could reemerge, serving as a partial basis for the further, fuller development of Russian society.

Russian leaders, moreover, retained during the period of eclipse an active memory of the glories of Byzantium. When Constantinople fell to the Turks in 1453, just as Russia was beginning to assert its independence from the Tartars, it was logical to claim that the mantle of east European leadership had fallen on Russia. A monk, currying favor, wrote the Russian king in 1511 that while heresy had destroyed the first Roman Empire, and the Turks had cut down the second, Byzantium—a "third, new Rome,"—under the king's "mighty rule" "sends out the Orthodox Christian faith to the ends of the earth and shines more brightly than the sun." "Two Romes have fallen, but the third stands, and there will be no fourth." This sense of an Eastern Christian mission, inspiring a Russian resurgence, was not the least of the products of this complicated formative period in the emergence of a separate European civilization in the Slavic lands.

The End of an Era in Eastern Europe

With Byzantium and Russia both under siege, east European civilization unquestionably fell on hard times at the end of the postclassical era. Brighter days were ahead, though the struggle to define anew a full civilization after 1453 would not prove easy. In the meantime, the connection of key border territories, such as Poland, to the west European cultural zone would deepen—another complication for the subsequent history of the region—while the Balkans lay under Turkish rule.

These difficulties confirmed the largely separate trajectories of West and East in Europe, for western Europe remained free from outside control and, despite some new problems, maintained a clearer vigor in politics, economy, and culture. When eastern Europe did reemerge, it would be at some disadvantage to the West, in terms of power and economic-cultural sophistication—a quite different balance from that which had prevailed during the glory days of Byzantium and the cruder vigor of Kievan Russia.

At the same time, the disruption caused by Tartar invasion and Byzantine collapse warns against projecting too much continuity between these early east European centuries and what would come later. Byzantine patterns were never recaptured. Key features of Kievan social structure would not characterize the later development of imperial Russia. Yet continuity was not entirely lost. Not only Christianity but the particular east European assumptions about political rulers and church-state relations as well as the pride in a lively artistic culture would serve as organizing threads when Russia and other Slavic societies turned to rebuilding.

The Byzantine Empire was one of the great centers of civilization during the postclassical period, though smaller than the other three centers in the Middle East (plus North Africa), India, and China. Alone of the great centers, it did not simply decline but disappeared, and this suggests some of the limitations of its final centuries of existence. Yet the empire was not simply a random feature of the postclassical period that must be inserted to keep the historical record straight. Its role in shaping one of the major versions of Christianity and its active effort in spreading religion, commerce, and the trappings of civilization northward helped prepare for later developments in the east European region. These developments, headed by the rise of Russia, began to take shape when the shock of Byzantium's fall and the Mongol invasions finally wore off.

FURTHER READING

J. M. Hussey's *The Byzantine World* (1982) provides a useful overview. Byzantine Christianity is studied in G. Every's *The Byzantine Patriarchate, 451–1204* (1978) and S. Runciman's *The Byzantine Theocracy* (1977); see also D. M. Nicol's *Church and Society in the Last Centuries of Byzantium* (1979). On culture, see E. Kitzinger's *Byzantine Art in the Making* (1977). Byzantine relations with the West form the main topic in H. J. Magoulias's *Byzantine Christianity: Emperor, Church and the West* (1982).

On Byzantine influence in eastern Europe, D. Obolensky's *The Byzantine Commonwealth: Eastern Europe, 500–1453* (1971) is an excellent analysis. See also S. Runciman's *A History of the First Bulgarian Empire* (1930).

On Russian history, the best survey is Nicholas Riasanovsky's *A History of Russia* (5th ed., 1992), which has a good bibliography. Three books deal with early Russian culture: N. P. Kondakov's *The Russian Icon* (1927), J. H. Billington's *The Icon and the Axe: An Interpretive History of Russian Culture* (1966), and Arthur Voyce's *The Art and Architecture of Medieval Russia* (1967).

Two source collections are also very helpful on early Russian history: T. Riha, ed., *Readings in Russian Civilization,* vol. 1, *Russia before Peter the Great, 900–1700* (1969); and especially S. A. Zenkovsky, ed. and trans., *Medieval Russia's Epics, Chronicles and Tales* (1963).

CHAPTER 13

Medieval Western Europe

KEY TERMS

Barbarian kingdoms	*investiture controversy*
Franks	*nation-state*
aristocracy	*Hundred Years' War*
Carolingians	*Joan of Arc*
Charlemagne	*Black Death*
serf	*Jacquerie*
vassals	*Great Schism*
feudalism	*John Wycliffe*
monastery	*Jan Hus*
Crusades	*William of Ockham*
Thomas Aquinas	*nominalism*

DISCUSSION QUESTIONS

In what ways did Roman and German traditions blend to produce the social and political order of medieval Europe?

What kinds of tensions developed between aristocrats and kings? Between kings and the Church?

Why were towns so important to the development of European culture?

The Making of the Barbarian Kingdoms

The existence of a united empire had long been only a dream. In the year 500, Emperor Anastasius I (491–518) could delude himself that, through appointed agents, he ruled the whole empire of Augustus, Diocletian, and Constantine, both east and west. This imperial unity was more apparent than real. The Italian governor was the Ostrogothic king Theodoric the Great (493–526), whose Roman title meant less than his Ostrogothic army. The imperial representative in the Rhone Valley was the Burgundian king Gondebaud (480–516). The Roman officer in Aquitaine and Spain was the Visigothic king Alaric II (485–507), and the Gallic consul was the Frankish king Clovis (482–511). Each of these rulers courted imperial titles and recognition, but none regarded Anastasius as his sovereign.

In the early sixth century all of the Germanic peoples within the old Roman Empire acknowledged the Goths as the most successful of the barbarian peoples. The Ostrogoths had created an Italian kingdom in which Romans and barbarians lived side by side. The Visigoths ruled Spain and southern Gaul by combining traditions of Roman law and barbarian military might. Yet neither Gothic kingdom endured more than two centuries.

The motley collection of Saxons, Angles, Jutes, Frisians, Suebians, and others who came to Britain as federated troops and stayed on as rulers did not coalesce into a united kingdom until almost the eleventh century. Instead, these Germanic warriors carved out small kingdoms for themselves, enslaving or absorbing most of the Romanized Britons and driving others into Wales. Unlike the Goths, none of these peoples had previously been integrated into the Roman world. Thus rather than fusing Roman and Germanic traditions, they largely eradicated the former. Urban life disappeared and with it the Roman traditions of administration, taxation, and culture.

The Franks: An Enduring Legacy

In the fourth century various small Germanic tribes along the Rhine coalesced into a loose confederation known as the Franks. A significant group of them, the Salians, made the mistake of attacking Roman garrisons and were totally defeated. The Romans resettled the Salians in a largely abandoned region of what is now Belgium and Holland. There they formed a buffer to protect Roman colonists from other Germanic tribes and provided a ready supply of recruits for the Roman army. During the fourth and fifth centuries, these Salian Franks and their neighbors assumed an increasingly important role in the military defense of Gaul and began to spread out of their "reservation" into more settled parts of the province. Although many high-ranking Roman officers of the fourth century were Franks, most were neither conquerors nor members of the military elite. They were rather soldier-farmers who settled beside the local Roman peoples they protected.

In 486 Clovis, leader of the Salian Franks and commander of the barbarized Roman army, staged a successful coup (possibly with the approval of the Byzantine emperor), defeating and killing Syagrius, the last Roman commander in the west. Although Clovis ruled the Franks as king, he worked closely with the existing Gallo-Roman aristocracy as he consolidated his control over various Frankish factions and over portions of Gaul and Germany held by other barbarian kingdoms. Clovis's early conversion to orthodox Christianity paved the way for assimilation of Franks and Romans into a new society.

The mix of Frankish warriors and Roman aristocrats spread rapidly across western Europe. Clovis and his successors absorbed the Visigothic kingdom of Toulouse, the Thuringians, and the kingdom of the Burgundians, and expanded Frankish hegemony through modern Bavaria and south of the Alps into northern Italy. Unlike other barbarian kingdoms such as those of the Huns or Ostrogoths, which evaporated almost as soon as their great founders died, the Frankish synthesis was enduring. Although the dynasty established by Clovis, called the Merovingian after a legendary ancestor, lasted only until the mid-eighth century, the Frankish kingdom was the direct ancestor of both France and Germany.

With the establishment of the barbarian kingdoms, the theoretical unity of the western empire was forever destroyed. Within each of these smaller polities, rulers and ruled began forging from their complex Roman and Germanic traditions a new cultural synthesis.

Europe Transformed

The substitution of Germanic kings for imperial officials made few obvious differences in the lives of most inhabitants of Italy, Gaul, and Spain. The vast majority of Europeans were poor farmers whose lives centered on their fields and villages. For them the seasons in the agricultural year, the burdens of rent and taxation, and the fre-

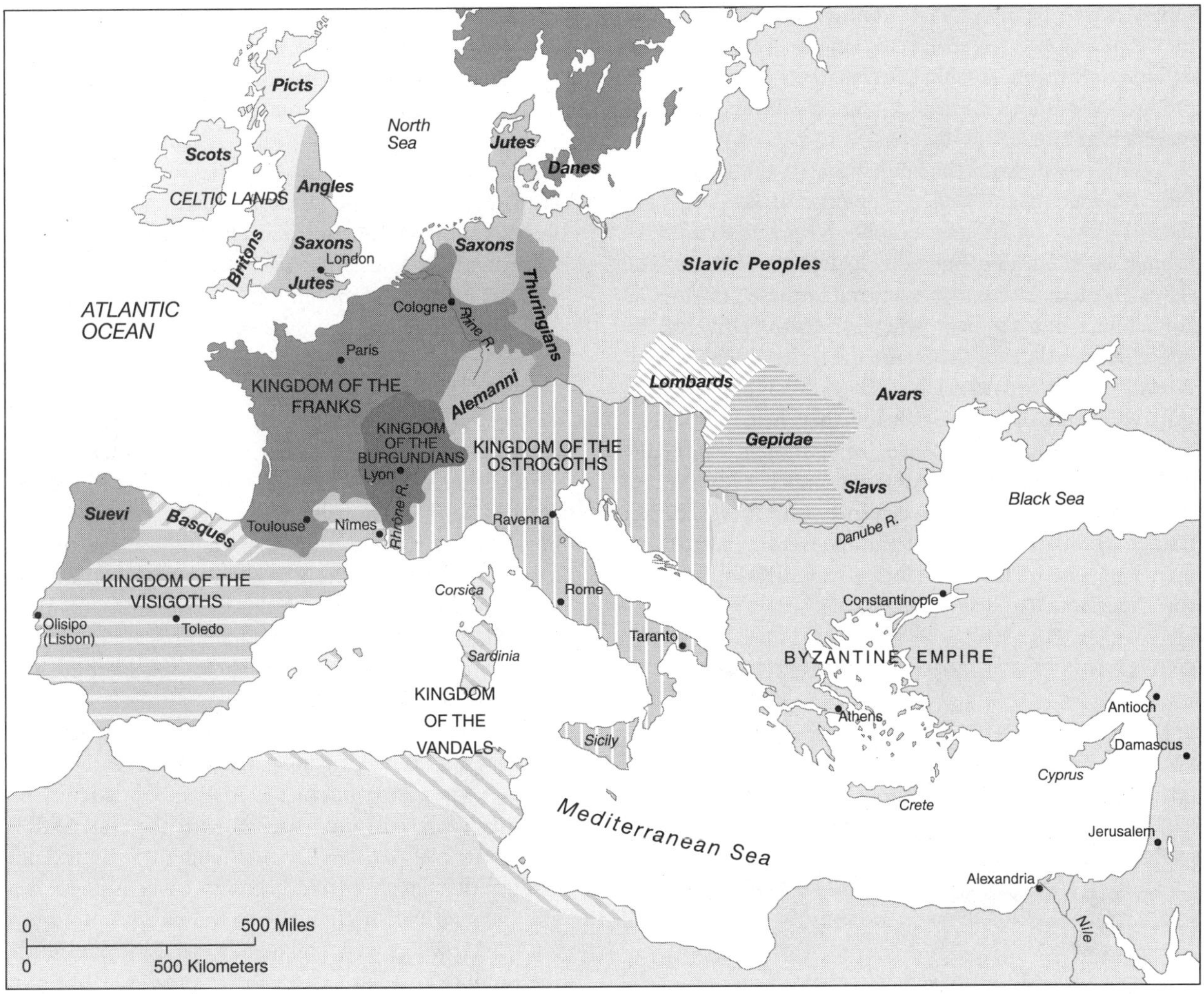

Barbarian Kingdoms

quent poor harvests, food shortages, famines, and epidemics were more important than empires and kingdoms. Nevertheless, fundamental if imperceptible changes were transforming ordinary life. These changes took place at every level of society. The slaves and semifree peasants of Rome gradually began to form new kinds of social groups and to practice new forms of agriculture as they merged with the Germanic warrior-peasants. Elite Gallo-Roman landowners came to terms with their Frankish conquerors, and these two groups began to coalesce into a single, unified aristocracy. In the same way that Germanic and Roman society began to merge, Germanic and Roman traditions of governance united between the sixth and eighth centuries to create a powerful new kind of medieval kingdom.

Creating the European Peasantry

Three fundamental changes transformed rural society during the early Middle Ages. First, Roman slavery virtually disappeared. Next, the household emerged as the primary unit of social and economic organization. Finally, Christianity spread throughout the rural world. Economics, not ethics, destroyed Roman slavery. In the kind of slavery typical of the Roman world, large gangs of slaves were housed in dormitories and directed in large-scale operations by overseers. This form of slavery demanded a highly organized form of estate management and could be quite costly, since slaves had to be fed and housed year-round. Since slaves did not always reproduce at a rate sufficient to replace themselves, the supply had to be replenished from without. However, as the empire ceased to expand, the supply of fresh captives dwindled. As cities shrank, many markets for agricultural produce disappeared, making market-oriented, large-scale agriculture less profitable.

As a result, from the sixth through the ninth centuries, owners abandoned the practice of keeping gang slaves in favor of the less complicated practice of establishing slave families on individual plots of land. The slaves and their descendants cultivated these plots, made annual payments to their owners, and also cultivated the undivided portions of the estate, the fruits of which went directly to the owner. Thus slaves became something akin to sharecroppers. Gradually they began to intermarry with colons and others who, though nominally free, faced an economic situation much like that of slaves. By the tenth and eleventh centuries, peasant farmers throughout much of Europe were subject to the private justice of their landlords, regardless of whether their ancestors had been slave or free.

The "labors of the months" was a popular motif in medieval art. This illustration from the Astronomical Notices *was found in Salzburg. The annual round of agricultural tasks, such as sowing, reaping, and threshing, vine dressing and grape picking, and the autumn slaughter of pigs are depicted along with scenes of hunting and hawking.*

The division of estates into separate peasant holdings contributed to the second fundamental transformation of European peasant society: the formation of the household. Neither the Roman tradition of slave agriculture nor the Germanic tradition of clan organization had fostered the household as the basic unit of society. Now individual slaves and their spouses were placed on manses, which they and their children were expected to cultivate. The household had become the basic unit of western European economy.

The household was, however, more than an economic unit. It was also the first level of government. The head of the household, whether slave or free, male or female—women, particularly widows, were often heads of households—exercised authority over its other members. This authority made the householder a link in the chain of the social order, which stretched from the peasant hovel to the royal court. Households became the basic form of peasant life, but not all peasants could expect to establish their own household. The number of manses was limited, a factor that condemned many men and women to life within the household of a more fortunate relative or neighbor.

Peasant culture, like peasant society, experienced a fundamental transformation during the early Middle Ages: the peasantry became Christian. Christianity penetrated deeply into rural society with the systematic establishment of parishes, or rural churches. By the ninth century this parish system began to cover Europe. Bishops founded parish churches in the villages of large estates, and owners were obligated to set aside one-tenth of the produce of their estates for the maintenance of the parish church. The priests who staffed these churches came from the local peasantry and received a basic education in Latin and in Christian ritual from their predecessors and from their bishops. Through the village priests and the parish system, European folklife began to take on Christian values and beliefs.

Creating the European Aristocracy

At the same time that a homogeneous peasantry was emerging from the blend of slaves and free farmers, a homogeneous aristocracy was evolving out of the mix of Germanic and Roman traditions. In Germanic society, the elite had owed its position to a combination of inherited status and wealth, perpetuated through military command. Families who produced great military commanders were thought to have a special war-luck granted by the gods. The war-luck bestowed on men and women of these families a near-sacred legitimacy. This legiti-

Societies and Cultures in World History
Chapter 9: Western European Culture and Society, 500–1300

macy made the aristocrats largely independent of their kings. In times of war kings might command, but otherwise the extent to which they could be said to govern aristocrats was minimal.

The Roman aristocracy was also based on inheritance, but of land rather than leadership. During the third and fourth centuries Roman aristocrats' control of land extended over the persons who worked that land. At the same time, great landowners were able to free themselves from provincial government. Like their Germanic counterparts, Roman aristocrats acquired a sacred legitimacy, but within the Christian tradition. They monopolized the office of bishop and became identified with the sacred and political traditions associated with the Church. Between the sixth and tenth centuries these two traditions merged.

The aristocratic lifestyle focused on feasting, on hospitality, and on the male activities of hunting and warfare. During the fall and winter, aristocratic men spent much of their time hunting deer and wild boar in their forests. In March, aristocrats gathered their retainers, who had enjoyed their winter hospitality, and marched to war. The enemy varied. It might be rival families with whom feuds were nursed for generations. It might be raiding parties from a neighboring region. Or the warriors might join a royal expedition led by the king and directed against a rival kingdom. Whoever the enemy, warfare brought the promise of booty and, equally important, glory.

Within this aristocratic society women played a wider and more active role than had been the case in either Roman or barbarian antiquity. In part women's new role was due to the influence of Christianity, which recognized the distinct—though always inferior—rights of women, fought against the barbarian tradition of allowing chieftains numerous wives, and recognized women's right to lead a cloistered religious life. In addition, the combination of Germanic and Roman familial traditions permitted women to participate in court proceedings, to inherit and dispose of property, and, if widowed, to serve as tutors and guardians for their minor children. Finally, the long absence of men at the hunt, at the royal court, or on military expeditions left wives in charge of the domestic scene for months or years at a time. The religious life in particular opened to aristocratic women possibilities of autonomy and authority previously unknown in Europe.

Governing Europe

The combination in the early Middle Ages of the extremes of centralized Roman power and fragmented barbarian organization produced a wide variety of governmental systems. At one end of the spectrum were the politically fragmented Celtic and Slavic societies. At the other end were the Frankish kingdoms, in which descendants of Clovis, drawing on the twin heritages of Roman institutions and Frankish tradition, attempted not simply to reign but to rule.

Rulers and aristocrats both needed and feared each other. Kings had emerged out of the Germanic aristocracy and could rule only in cooperation with aristocrats. Aristocrats were primarily concerned with maintaining and expanding their own spheres of control and independence. They perceived royal authority over them or their dependents as a threat. Still, they needed kings. Strong kings brought victory against external foes and thus maintained the flow of booty to the aristocracy. Aristocrats in turn redistributed the spoils of war among their followers to preserve the bonds of warrior society. Thus under capable kings aristocrats were ready to cooperate, not as subjects but as partners.

As heirs of Roman governmental tradition, kings sought to incorporate these traditions into their roles. By absorbing the remains of local administration and taxation, kings acquired nascent governmental systems. Through the use of written documents, Roman scribes expanded royal authority beyond the king's household and personal following. Tax collectors continued to fill royal coffers with duties collected in markets and ports.

Finally, by assuming the role of protector of the Church, kings acquired the support of educated and experienced ecclesiastical advisors and the right to intervene in disputes involving clergy and laity. Further, as defenders of the Church, kings could claim a responsibility for the preservation of peace and the administration of justice—two fundamental Christian (but also Roman) tasks.

Early medieval kings had no fixed capitals from which they governed. Instead they were constantly on the move, supervising their kingdoms and consuming the produce of their estates. Since kings could not be everywhere at once, they were represented locally by aristocrats who enjoyed royal favor. In the Frankish world these favorites were called *counts* and their districts *counties*. In England royal representatives were termed *ealdormen* and their regions were known as *shires*. Whether counts or ealdormen, these representatives were military commanders and judicial officers drawn from aristocratic families close to the king. Under competent and effective kings, partnership with these aristocratic families worked well. Under less competent rulers and during the reigns of minors, these families often managed to turn their districts into hereditary, almost autonomous regions.

Thus at both ends of the social spectrum, Germanic and Roman traditions and institutions were combining to create a new society, organized not by nationality or ethnicity but by status and united by shared religious values and political leadership.

The Carolingians and the New Europe

The Merovingian dynasty initiated by Clovis presided over the synthesis of Roman and Germanic society. It was left to the Carolingians who followed to forge a new Europe. In the seventh century, members of the new aristocracy were able to take advantage of royal minorities and dynastic rivalries to make themselves into virtual rulers of their small territories. By the end of the century the kings had become little more than symbolic figures in the Frankish kingdoms. The real power was held by regional strongmen called dukes. The most successful of these aristocratic factions was led by Charles Martel (ca. 688–741) and his heirs, known as the Carolingians.

Charles Martel was ruthless, ambitious, and successful. He crushed rivals in his own family, subdued competing dukes, and united the Frankish realm. He was successful in part because he molded the Frankish cavalry into the most effective military force of the time. His mounted, heavily armored warriors were extremely effective but extremely costly. He financed them with property confiscated from his enemies.

Charles Martel looked beyond military power to the control of religious and cultural institutions. He supported Anglo-Saxon missionaries such as Boniface (ca. 680–755), who were trying to introduce on the mainland the Roman form of Christianity they knew in England. This hierarchal style of Christianity served Carolingian interests in centralization, especially since Charles appointed his loyal supporters as bishops and abbots. Missionaries and Frankish armies worked hand in hand to consolidate Carolingian rule.

The ecclesiastical policy that proved most crucial to later Carolingians was Charles's support of the Roman papacy. Charles caught the attention of Pope Gregory III (731–41) in 732, when he defeated a Muslim raiding party near Tours, which had appeared to threaten the northward expansion of Islam. A few years later, when the pope needed protection from the Lombards to maintain his central Italian territories, he sought and obtained help from the Frankish leader.

The alliance with the papacy solidified during the lifetime of Charles's son Pippin (ca. 714–68). Pippin inherited his father's power. However, since he was not of the royal Merovingian family, he had no more right to supreme authority than any other powerful aristocrat. Pippin needed more than the power of a king: he needed the title. No Frankish tradition provided a precedent by which a rival family might displace the Merovingians. Pippin turned instead to the pope. With the cooperation of Pope Zacharias (741–52) Pippin deposed the last Merovingian and in 751 a representative of the pope anointed Pippin king of the Franks. The alliance between the new dynasty and the papacy marked the first union of royal legitimacy and ecclesiastical sanction in European history.

Charlemagne and the Renewal of the Western Empire

Pippin's son Charlemagne was the heir of the political, religious, and social revolutions begun by his grandfather and father. He was a conqueror, but he was also a religious reformer, a state builder, and a patron of the arts. As the leader of a powerful, united Frankish kingdom for over forty years, Charlemagne changed western Europe more profoundly than anyone since Augustus. He subdued the Aquitainians and Bavarians, conquered the kingdom of the Lombards and assumed the title of King of the Lombards, crushed the Saxons, annexed the Spanish region of Catalonia, and destroyed the vast Pannonian kingdom of the Avars. In wars of aggression, his armies were invincible. Not only were they better armed and mounted, but their ability to transport men and material great distances was unmatched.

War booty fueled Charlemagne's renewal of European culture. As a Christian king he considered it his duty to reform the spiritual life of his kingdom and to bring it into line with his concept of the divinely willed order. To achieve this goal, he needed a dedicated and educated clergy. Most of the native clergy were poorly educated and indifferent in their observance of the rules of religious life. Charlemagne recruited leading intellectuals from England, Spain, Ireland, and Italy to the royal court to lead a thorough educational program. He supported schools in great monasteries such as Fulda and St. Gall for the training of young clerics and laymen. Schools needed books, and Charlemagne's educational reformers scoured Italy for fading copies of works by Virgil, Horace, and Tacitus.

The reformers of this era laid the necessary foundation for what has been called the Carolingian renaissance. Their successors in the ninth century built on this foundation to make creative contributions in theology, philosophy, and historiography, and to some extent in literature. The pursuit of learning was not a purely clerical affair. In the later ninth century, great aristocrats both male and female were highly literate and collected their own personal libraries.

Carolingian Government

Charlemagne recognized that conquest alone could not unify his enormous kingdom with its vast differences in languages, laws, customs, and peoples. The glue that held it together was loyalty to him and to the Roman Church. He appointed as counts throughout Europe members of the great Frankish families who had been loyal to his family for generations. Thus he created what might be termed an "imperial aristocracy" truly international in scope. In addition to supervising the royal estates in their counties, each spring these counts led the local military contingent, which included all the free men of the county. Counts also presided over local courts, which exercised jurisdiction over the free persons of the county. The king maintained his control over the counts by sending teams of emissaries, or *missi dominici*, composed of bishops and counts to examine the state of each county.

Charlemagne recognized that while his representatives might be drawn from Frankish families, he could not impose Frankish legal and cultural traditions on all his subjects. The only universal system that might unify the kingdom was Roman Christianity. Unity of religious practices, directed by the reformed and educated clergy, would provide spiritual unity.

Carolingian government was no modern bureaucracy or state system. The laymen and clerics who served the king were tied to him by personal oaths of loyalty rather than by any sense of dedication to a state or nation. Still, the attempts at governmental organization were far more sophisticated than anything that western Europe had seen for four centuries or would see again for another four. The system of counts and missi provided the most effective system of government prior to the thirteenth century and served as the model for subsequent medieval rulers.

The size of Charlemagne's empire approached that of the old Roman Empire in the west. Only Britain, southern Italy, and parts of Spain remained outside Frankish control. With the reunification of most of western Europe and the creative adaptation of Roman traditions of culture and government, it is not surprising that Charlemagne's advisors began to compare his empire to that of Constantine. This comparison was accentuated by Charlemagne's conquest of Lombard Italy and his protection of Pope Leo III—a role traditionally played by the Byzantine emperors. By the end of the eighth century the throne in Constantinople was held by a woman. Irene (752–802) was powerful and capable, but male leaders in the Frankish kingdom considered her unfit for such an office by reason of her sex. All these factors finally converged in one of the most momentous events in Western political history: Charlemagne's imperial coronation on Christmas Day in the year 800.

Historians debate the precise meaning of this event, particularly since Charlemagne was said to have remarked

Carolingian Empire

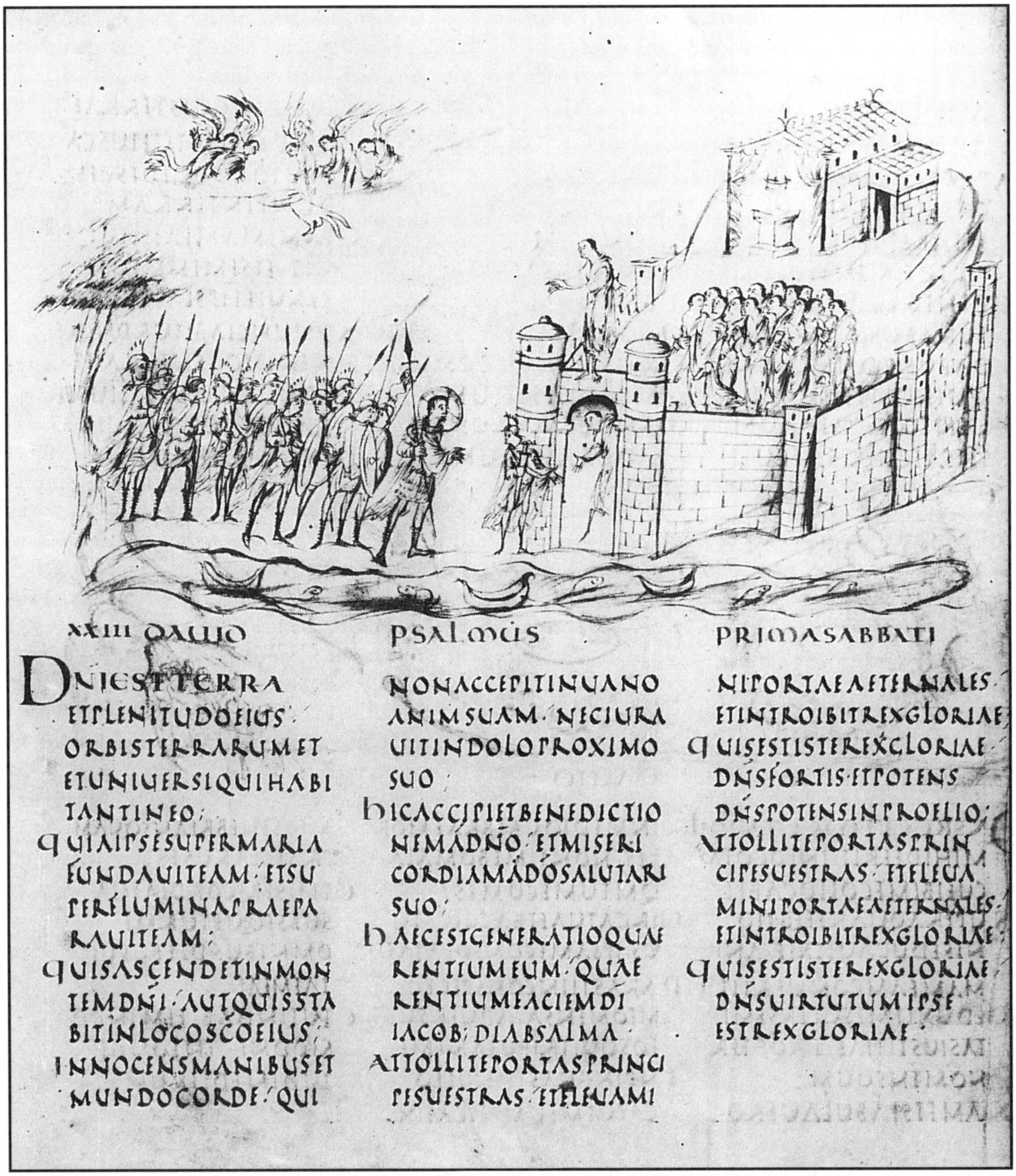

The Twenty-fourth Psalm (Twenty-third in the Vulgate), from the Utrecht Psalter, *Reims, made in about 820. The imagery of the drawings and the arrangement of the script on the page recall models from late antiquity.*

afterward that he would never have entered St. Peter's Basilica in Rome had he known what was going to happen. Presumably he meant that he wished to be proclaimed emperor by his Frankish people rather than by the pope, since this is how he had his son Louis the Pious acclaimed emperor in 813. Nevertheless, the imperial coronation of 800 subsequently took on great significance. Louis attempted to make his imperial title the sole basis for his rule, and for centuries Germanic kings traveled to Rome to receive the imperial diadem and title from the pope. In so doing they inadvertently strengthened papal claims to enthrone—and at times to dethrone—emperors.

After the Carolingians: From Empire to Lordships

Charlemagne, despite his imperial title, had remained dependent on his traditional power base, the Frankish aristocracy. For them, learned concepts of imperial renovation meant little. They wanted wealth and power. Under Charlemagne, the empire's prosperity and relative internal peace had resulted largely from continued, successful expansion at the expense of neighbors. Its economy had been based on the redistribution of war booty among the aristocracy and wealthy churches. But in the ninth and tenth centuries, new threats to the security of western Europe arose with the advent of the Vikings and the Magyars. The Vikings, or Northmen, burst out of Scandinavia to terrorize coastal areas all around the shores of Europe and the British Isles. They established settlements in Ireland, Britain, Normandy, and in what is today Russia and Ukraine. The Magyars, or Hungarians, came from the eastern steppes. They took over part of Pannonia and raided into the Carolingian empire, while Saracen Muslims from Spain and North Africa raided the northern Mediterranean coast. As wars of conquest under Charlemagne gave place to defensive actions against Magyars, Vikings, and Saracens, the supply of wealth dried up. Aristocratic supporters were rewarded with estates within the empire and thus became enormously wealthy and powerful.

Competition among Charlemagne's descendants as well as grants to the aristocracy weakened central authority. By fate rather than by design, Charlemagne had bequeathed a united empire to his son Louis the Pious (814–40). Charlemagne had intended to follow Frankish custom and divide his estate among all his sons but only Louis survived him. Louis's three sons, in contrast, fought one another over their inheritance, and in 843 they divided the empire among them. The eldest son, Lothair (840–55), who inherited his father's imperial title, received an unwieldy middle portion that stretched from the Rhine south through Italy. Louis the German (840–876) received the eastern portions of the empire. The youngest son, Charles the Bald (840–77), was allotted the western portions. In time this West Frankish kingdom became France, and the eastern Frankish kingdom became the core of Germany. The middle kingdom, which included modern Holland, Belgium, Luxembourg, Lorraine, Switzerland, and northern Italy, remained a disputed region into the twentieth century.

The disintegration of the empire meant much more than its division among Charlemagne's heirs. In no region were his successors able to provide the degree of peace and public control that he had established. The Frankish armies, designed for offensive wars, were too clumsy and slow to defend against the lightning raids of Northmen, Magyars, and Saracens. The constant need to please aristocratic supporters made it impossible for kings to prevent aristocrats from absorbing free peasants and churches into their economic and political spheres. Increasingly, these magnates were able to transform the offices of count and bishop into inherited familial positions. They also determined who would reign in their kingdoms and sought kings who posed no threat to themselves.

Most aristocrats saw this greater autonomy as their just due. Only dukes, counts, and other local lords could organize resistance to internal and external foes at the local level. They needed both economic means and political authority to provide protection and maintain peace. These resources could be acquired only at the expense of royal power. Thus during the late ninth and tenth centuries, much of Europe found its equilibrium at the local level as public powers, judicial courts, and military authority became the private possession of wealthy families.

Ultimately, new royal families emerged from among these local leaders. The family of the counts of Paris, for

Division of Charlemagne's Empire

example, gained enormous prestige from the fact that they had led the successful defense of the city against the Vikings in 885–86. For a time they alternated with Carolingians as kings of the West Franks. After the ascension of Hugh Capet in 987, they entirely replaced the Carolingians.

In a similar manner, the eastern Frankish kingdom, which was divided into five great duchies, began to elect non-Carolingians as kings. In 919 the dukes of this region elected as their king Duke Henry of Saxony (919–36), who had proven his abilities fighting the Danes and Magyars. Henry's son, Otto the Great (936–73), proved to be a strong ruler who subdued the other dukes and definitively crushed the Magyars. In 962 Otto was crowned emperor by Pope John XII (955–64), thus reviving the empire of Charlemagne, although only in its eastern half. However, the dukes of this eastern kingdom chafed constantly at the strong control the Ottonians attempted to exercise at their expense. Although the empire Otto reestablished endured until 1806 as the Holy Roman Empire, he and his successors never matched the political or cultural achievements of the Carolingians. It remained a loosely united amalgam of Germanic, Slavic, and Italian territories and principalities, and imperial authority seldom proved effective outside the power base of the current emperor's own family.

By the tenth century, the early medieval kingdoms, based on inherited Roman notions of universal states and barbarian traditions of charismatic military leadership, had all ended in failure. However, although western Europe was not united politically, the separate regions shared the cultural and institutional heritage of the Carolingians. After the demise of the Carolingian empire, western Europe began to develop this common heritage to create stability at a more local but also more permanent level.

Society and Culture in the High Middle Ages

The economic, social, and cultural transformations of Europe during the centuries that followed the collapse of the Carolingian empire were as profound as the political transformations of that period. The demographic upsurge of the tenth and eleventh centuries, the revolution redirecting agriculture toward markets rather than subsistence, the rebirth of towns and the development of complex commercial networks transformed the lives of Europeans everywhere. As peasants emerged from servitude and established autonomous social and cultural traditions, aristocrats wove together strands of Christianity and the warrior ethos to create an enduring social stratum whose values dominated elite ideology until the twentieth century. The increase in literacy and in the institutions of higher learning contributed to new visions of the relationship among people and between people and God.

The Peasantry: Serfs and Free

From the tenth through the thirteenth centuries enormous transformations re-created the rural landscape of Europe. The most significant of these changes concerned the peasantry, but they are difficult to chronicle since until the nineteenth century the majority of the common people left no record of their lives.

By the tenth century the population of Europe was growing, and with this population growth came new forms of social organization and economic activity. Between the years 1000 and 1300 Europe's population almost doubled, from approximately 38 million to 74 million. Various reasons have been proposed for this growth. Perhaps the end of the Viking, Magyar, and Saracen raids left rural society in relative peace to live and reproduce. The decline of slavery meant that individual peasant families could grow and reproduce themselves without constraints imposed by masters. Gradually improving agricultural techniques and equipment lessened somewhat the constant danger of famine. Possibly, too, a slowly improving climate increased agricultural yields. None of these explanations are entirely satisfactory. Whatever the cause of the population growth, it changed the face of Europe.

During the tenth century the great forests that had covered most of Europe began to be cut back as population spread out from the islands of cultivation. The peasants who engaged in the opening of this internal frontier were the descendants of the slaves, unfree farmers, and petty free persons of the early Middle Ages. In the east along the frontier of the Germanic empire, in the Slavic world, in Scandinavia, in southern Gaul, in northern Italy, and in the reconquered portions of Christian Spain, they were free persons who owned land, entered into contracts with magnates, and remained responsible for their own fates. Across much of northwestern Europe, and in particular in France in the course of the eleventh century, the various gradations in status disappeared, and the peasantry formed a homogeneous social category termed "serfs." Their degraded status, their limited or nonexistent access to public courts of law, and their enormous dependency on their lords left them in a situation similar to that of those Carolingian slaves settled on individual farmsteads in the ninth century. Each year, peasants had to hand over to their lords certain fixed portions of their meager harvests. In addition, they were obligated to work a certain number of days on the *demesne*, or reserve of the lord, the produce of which went directly to him for his use or sale. Finally, they were required to make ritual payments symbolizing their subordination.

The expansion of arable land offered new hope and opportunities to peasants. As rapid as it was, between the tenth and twelfth centuries population growth did not keep up with the demand for laborers in newly settled areas of Europe. Thus labor was increasingly in demand and lords were often willing to make special arrangements with groups of peasants to encourage them to bring new land under cultivation. From the beginning of the twelfth century peasant villages acquired from their lord the privilege to deal with him and his representatives collectively rather than individually. But gradually during the late twelfth and thirteenth centuries, the labor market stagnated. Europe's population, particularly in France, England, Italy, and western Germany, began to reach a saturation point. As a result, lay and ecclesiastical lords found that they could profit more by hiring cheap laborers than by demanding customary services and payments from their serfs. They also found that their serfs were willing to pay for increasing privileges.

Peasants could purchase the right to marry without the lord's consent, to move to neighboring manors or to nearby towns, and to inherit. They acquired personal freedom from their lord's jurisdiction, transformed their servile payments into payments of rent for their manses, purchased their own land, and commuted their labor services into annual or even one-time payments. In other words, they began to purchase their freedom. This free peasantry benefited the emerging states of western Europe, since kings and towns could extend their legal and fiscal jurisdictions over these persons and their lands at the expense of the nobility. Governments thus encouraged the extension of freedom and protected peasants from their former masters. By the fourteenth century, serfs were a rarity in many parts of western Europe.

Even as western serfs were acquiring a precious though fragile freedom, the free peasantry in much of eastern Europe and Spain were losing it. In much of the Slavic world, through the eleventh century, peasants lived in large, roughly territorial communes of free families. Gradually, however, princes, churches, and aristocrats began to build great landed estates. By the thirteenth century, under the influences of western and Byzantine models and of the Mongols, who dominated much of the Slavic world from 1240, lords began to acquire political and economic control over the peasantry. A similar process took place in parts of Spain. In all of these regions, the decline of the free peasantry accompanied the decline of public authority to the benefit of independent nobles. The aristocracy rose on the backs of the peasantry.

The Aristocracy: Fighters and Breeders

Beginning in the late tenth century, writers of legal documents began to employ an old term in a novel manner to designate certain powerful free persons who belonged neither to the old aristocracy nor to the peasantry. The term was *miles*. In classical Latin *miles* meant "soldier." As used in the Middle Ages, we would translate it as "knight."

The center of the knightly lifestyle was northern France. From there, the ideals of knighthood, or chivalry, spread out across Europe, influencing aristocrats as far east as Byzantium. The essence of this lifestyle was fighting. Through warfare this aristocracy had maintained or acquired its freedom and through warfare it justified its privileges. The origins of this small elite (probably nowhere more than 2 percent of the population) were diverse. Many were descended from the old aristocracy of the Carolingian age. They traced descent through the male line, inheritance was usually limited to the eldest sons, and daughters were given a dowry but did not share in inheritance. Younger sons had to find service with some great lord or live in the household of their older brothers.

Such noble families, proud of their independence and ancestry, maintained their position through complex kin networks, mutual defense pacts with other nobles, and control of castles, from which they could dominate the surrounding countryside. Safe behind the castle walls, they were by the twelfth century often independent even of the local counts, dukes, and kings. This lesser nobility absorbed control of such traditionally public powers as justice, peace, and taxation.

For the sons of such nobles preparation for a life of warfare began early, often in the entourage of a maternal uncle or a powerful lord. There boys learned to ride, to handle a heavy sword and shield, to manage a lance on horseback, to swing an axe with deadly accuracy. They also learned more subtle but equally important lessons about honor, pride, and family tradition. The feats of ancestors or heroes, sung by traveling minstrels at the banqueting table on long winter nights, provided models of knightly action. The culmination of this education for

English and French nobles came in a ceremony of knighting. An adolescent of age sixteen to eighteen received a sword from an older, experienced warrior. No longer a "boy," he now became a "youth," ready to enter the world of fighting for which he had trained.

A "youth" was a noble who had been knighted but who had not married or acquired land either through inheritance or as a reward from a lord for service, and thus had not yet established his own "house." During this time the knight led the life of a warrior, joining in promising military expeditions and amusing himself with tournaments—mock battles that often proved as deadly as the real thing—in which one could win an opponent's horses and armor as well as renown. Drinking, gambling, and lechery were other common activities. This was an extraordinarily dangerous lifestyle, and many youths did not survive to the next stage in a knight's life, that of acquiring land, wife, honor, and his own following of youths.

The period between childhood and maturity was no less dangerous for noblewomen than for men. Marriages were the primary forms of alliances between noble houses, and the production of children was essential to the continued prosperity of the family. Thus daughters were raised as breeders, married at around age sixteen to cement family alliances, and then expected to produce as many children as possible. Many noblewomen died in childbirth, often literally exhausted by frequent successive births. Although occasionally practiced, contraception was condemned both by the Church and by husbands eager for offspring.

In this martial society, the political and economic status of women declined considerably. Because they were considered unable to participate in warfare, in northern Europe women were also frequently excluded from inheritance, estate management, courts, and public deliberations. Although a growing tradition of "courtliness" glorified the status of aristocratic women in literature, women were actually losing ground in the real world. Some noblewomen did control property and manage estates, but usually such roles were possible only for widows who had borne sons and who could play a major part in raising them. Both secular tradition and Christian teaching portrayed women as devious, sexually demanding temptresses often responsible for the corruption and downfall of men. Many men felt threatened by this aggressive sexual stereotype. They resented the power wielded by wealthy widows and abbesses.

To maintain a lifestyle of conspicuous consumption required wealth, and wealth meant land. The nobility was essentially a society of heirs who had inherited not only land but also the serfs who worked their manors. Lesser nobles acquired additional property from great nobles and from ecclesiastical institutions in return for binding contracts of mutual assistance. This tradition was at least as old as the Carolingians, who granted their followers land in return for military service and demanded that free warriors swear oaths of fealty to them. In later centuries, counts and lesser lords continued this tradition, exchanging land for support. Individual knights became *vassals* of lay or ecclesiastical magnates, that is, they swore fealty or loyalty to the magnate and promised to defend and aid him. In return the magnate swore to protect his vassal and granted him a means of support by which the vassal could maintain himself while serving his lord. Usually this grant, termed a fief, was a

A knight and lady in a fifteenth-century garden. The ideals of chivalry and courtly love glorified women in literature and song, but in real life the subordinate status of women reflected the values of a martial society.

parcel of productive land and the serfs and privileges attached to it, over which the vassal exercised economic and judicial control. The vassal did not actually own the land but simply had the use of it as long as he and his descendants provided the service to his feudal lord (so called from the Latin word for fief) for which it has been granted. In addition the vassal owed his lord certain specific duties and payments and was subject to the lord's court in matters directly concerning his fief and his relationship with his lord.

Individual lords often had considerable numbers of vassals, who might also be the vassals of other lay and secular lords. The networks thus established formed vital social and political structures. However, these bonds were personal, not public. A feudal lord was a superior, a first among equals, but not a sovereign. In some unusual situations, such as in England immediately after the Norman Conquest and in the Latin Kingdom of Jerusalem founded following the First Crusade in 1099, these structures of lords and vassals constituted systems of hierarchical government culminating in the king. Elsewhere, while kings were feudal lords of many of the great aristocrats in their kingdoms, individuals often held fiefs from and owed service to more than one lord, and not all of the individuals in a given county or duchy owed their primary obligation to the count or duke. Likewise, often most of a noble's land was owned outright rather than held in fief, thus making the feudal bond less central to his status. As a result these bonds, anachronistically called *feudalism* by French lawyers of the sixteenth and seventeenth centuries, constituted just one more element of a social system tied together by kinship, regional alliances, personal bonds of fealty, and the surviving elements of Carolingian administration inherited by counts and dukes.

The Church: Saints and Monks

The religious needs of the peasantry remained those that their pre-Christian ancestors had known: fertility of land, animals, and women; protection from the ravages of climate and the warrior elite; supernatural cures for the ailments and disabilities of their harsh life. The cultural values of the nobility retained the essentials of the Germanic warrior ethos, including family honor, battle, and display of status. The rural Church of the High Middle Ages met the needs of both, although it subtly changed them in the process.

Most medieval people, whether peasants or lords, lived in a world of face-to-face encounters, a world in which abstract creeds counted for little and in which interior state and external appearance were rarely distinguished. In this world, religion meant primarily action, and the essential religious actions were the liturgical celebrations performed by the clergy, many of whom had received only rudimentary instruction from their predecessors and whose knowledge of Latin and theology was minimal. But these intellectual factors would become significant only centuries later. Ordinary lay people wanted priests who would not extort them by selling the sacraments and would not seduce their wives and daughters. They wanted priests who would not leave the village for months or years at a time to seek clerical advancement elsewhere rather than remaining in the village performing the rituals necessary to keep the supernatural powers well disposed toward men and women in the community.

The most important of these supernatural powers was not some distant divinity but the saints—local, personal, even idiosyncratic persons. During their lives saintly men and women had shown that they enjoyed special favor with God. After their deaths, they continued to be the link between the divine and the earthly spheres. Through their bodies, preserved as relics in the monasteries of Europe, they continued to live among mortals even while participating in the heavenly court. Thus they could be approached just like local earthly lords and like them be won over through offerings, bribes, oaths, and rituals of supplication and submission.

Monasteries did more than orchestrate the cult of the saints. They were also responsible for the cult of the ordinary dead, for praying for the souls of ordinary mortals. In particular, monastic communities commemorated and prayed for those members of noble families who, through donations of land, had become especially associated with the monastic community. Across Europe noble families founded monasteries on their own lands or invited famous abbots to reorganize existing monasteries. These monasteries continued the ritual remembrance of the family, providing it with a history and forming an important part of its material as well as spiritual prestige.

Although monks and bishops were spiritual warriors, most abhorred bloodshed among Christians and sought to limit the violence of aristocratic life. This attitude combined altruistic and selfish motives, since Church property was often the focus of aristocratic greed. The decline of public power and the rise of aristocratic autonomy and violence were particularly marked in southern France. There, beginning in the tenth century, churchmen organized the Peace of God and the Truce of God, movements that attempted to protect peasants, merchants, and clerics from aristocratic violence and to limit the times when warfare was allowed. During the eleventh century, the goals of warfare were shifted from attacks against other Christians to the defense of Christian society. This redirection produced the Crusades, those religious wars of conquest directed against Europe's non-Christian neighbors.

In order to direct noble violence away from Christendom, Pope Urban II (1088–99) in 1095 urged Western knights to use their arms to free the Holy Land from Muslim occupation. In return he promised to absolve them from all of the punishment due for their sins in this life or the next. The First Crusade was remarkably successful. The crusaders took Jerusalem in 1099 and established a Latin kingdom in Palestine. For over two centuries bands of Western warriors went on armed pilgrimage to defend this precarious kingdom and, after the reconquest of Jerusalem by the Muslim commander Salah ad-Din (known to the Latins as Saladin) in 1187, to attempt to recapture it. Other such holy wars were directed against the Muslims in Spain, the Slavs in eastern Europe, and even against heretics and political opponents in France and Italy. By the end of the thirteenth century the military failure of the Crusades, the immorality of many of the participants, and doubts about the spiritual significance of such wars contributed to their decline.

Until the twelfth century, peasants, lords, and monks made up the great majority of Europe's population and lived together in mutual dependence, sharing involvement with the rhythm of the agrarian life. From the later part of the twelfth century, however, this rural world became increasingly aware of a different society, that of the growing cities and towns of Europe, whose citizens moved to a different rhythm, that of commerce and manufacture.

Medieval Towns

Monastic preachers liked to remind their listeners that according to the Bible, Cain had founded the first town after killing his brother Abel. Towns seemed somehow immoral and perverse but at the same time fascinating. Still, as rude warriors were transformed into courtly nobles, these nobles were drawn to the luxuries provided by urban merchants and became indebted to urban moneylenders in order to maintain their "gracious" lifestyles. For many peasants, towns were refuges from the hopelessness of their normal lives. "Town air makes one free," they believed, and many serfs fled the land to try their fortunes in the nearby towns. Clearly, something was very different about the urban communities that emerged, first in Italy, then in the Low Countries and across Europe in the later eleventh and twelfth centuries. These were centers of manufacture, commerce, and administration, structured less by the traditional relationships of vassalage and lordship than by the more fluid possibilities of wealth and patronage.

Through the early Middle Ages the coastal cities of Amalfi, Bari, Genoa, and especially Venice had continued to play important roles in commerce both with the Byzantines and with the new Muslim societies. For Venice, this role was facilitated by its official status as a part of the Byzantine Empire, which gave it access to Byzantine markets. In order to protect their merchant ships, Italian coastal cities developed their own fleets, and by the eleventh century they were major military forces in the Mediterranean. Venice's fleet became the primary protector of the Byzantine Empire and Venice was thereby able to win more favorable commercial rights than those enjoyed by Greek merchants. As the merchants of the Italian towns penetrated the markets at the western end of the great overland spice routes connecting China, India, and central Asia with the Mediterranean, they established permanent merchant colonies in the East. They did not hesitate to use military force to win concessions.

Italian Towns and Cities

Societies and Cultures in World History
Chapter 9: Western European Culture and Society, 500–1300

An illustration from a fourteenth-century manuscript. The Venetian merchant Marco Polo (1254–1324), with his father and uncle, is seen departing from Venice for points east in 1271. Marco traveled as far as China and did not return home to Venice until twenty-four years later.

The Crusades, armed pilgrimages for pious northern nobles, were primarily economic opportunities for the Italians, who had no scruples about trading with Muslims. Furthermore, only the Italians had the ships and the expertise to transport the crusaders by sea, the only option that offered hope of success, since every Crusade but the first that had followed an overland route had ended in failure. Moreover, the ships of the Italian cities were the only means of supplying the crusading armies once they were in Palestine. Crusaders paid the Italian merchants handsomely for their assistance and also granted them economic and political rights in the Palestinian port cities such as Tyre and Acre. The culmination of this relationship between northern crusaders and Italians was the Fourth Crusade. In 1204 a renegade Crusade short on funds was sidetracked by the Venetians into capturing and sacking Constantinople.

By the thirteenth century, Italian merchants had spread far beyond the Mediterranean. The great merchant banking houses of Venice, Florence, and Genoa had established offices around the Mediterranean and Black seas; south along the Atlantic coast of Morocco; east into Armenia and Persia; west to London, Bruges, and Ghent; and north to Scandinavia. Some individual merchants, the Venetian Marco Polo (1254–1324) for example, traded as far east as China.

These international commercial operations required more sophisticated systems of commercial law and credit than Europe had ever known. Italian merchants developed the practices of double-entry bookkeeping, limited-liability partnership, commercial insurance, and international letters of exchange. Complex commercial affairs also required the development of a system of credit and interest-bearing loans, an idea abhorrent to traditional rural societies.

Urban Culture

In the late eleventh and early twelfth centuries, the pace of urban intellectual life quickened. The combination of population growth, improved agricultural productivity, political stability, and educational interest culminated in what has been called the "renaissance of the twelfth century." Bologna and Paris became the undisputed centers of the new educational movements. Bologna specialized in the study of law. There from the eleventh century a number of important teachers began to make detailed, authoritative commentaries on the Justinian Code *(Corpus iuris civilis)*, the sixth-century compilation of law prepared on the order of the Roman emperor Justinian. In the next century the same systematic study was applied to Church law, culminating in the *Decretum Gratiani*, or "Concord of Discordant Canons," prepared around 1140 in Bologna by the monk Gratian. The growing importance of legal knowledge in politics, international trade, and Church administration drew students from across Europe to Bologna, where they organized a *universitas*, or guild of students, the first true university. Professors and administrators were controlled by the guild and were fined if they broke any of the regulations.

North of the Alps, Paris became the center for study of the liberal arts and of theology during the twelfth century. The city's emergence as the leading educational center of Europe resulted from a convergence of factors. Paris was the center of an important cathedral school as well as of a monastic school. In the twelfth century it became the capital of the French kings, who needed educated clerics, or clerks, for their administration.

By 1200 education had become so important in the city that the universitas, or corporation of professors, was granted a charter by King Philip Augustus, who guaranteed its rights and immunities from the control of the city. Unlike that at Bologna, the University of Paris remained a corporation of masters rather than of students. It was organized like other guilds into masters; bachelors, who were similar to journeymen in other trades; and students, who were analogous to apprentices.

Students began their studies at around age fourteen or fifteen in the faculty of arts. After approximately six

Medieval Trade

years, they received a bachelor of arts degree, which was a prerequisite to enter the higher faculties of theology, medicine, or law. After additional years of reading and commenting on specific texts under the supervision of a master, they received the title of master of arts, which gave them the license to teach anywhere within Christian Europe.

Through the thirteenth and fourteenth centuries the intellectual life of the universities was dominated by a pagan philosopher already dead for a thousand years. The introduction of the works of Aristotle into western Europe between 1150 and 1250 created an intellectual crisis every bit as profound as that of the Newtonian revolution of the seventeenth or the Einsteinian revolution of the twentieth century. For centuries, European thinkers had depended on the Christianized Neoplatonic philosophy of Origen and Augustine. Aristotle was known in western Europe only through his basic logical treatises, which in the twelfth century had become the foundation of intellectual work. Logic, or dialectic, was seen as the universal key to knowledge, and the university system was based on its rigorous application to traditional texts of law, philosophy, and Scripture.

Beginning in the late twelfth century, Christian and Jewish scholars began translating into Latin Aristotle's treatises on natural philosophy, ethics, and metaphysics. Suddenly Christian intellectuals who had already accepted the Aristotelian method were brought face to face with Aristotle's conclusions: a world without an active, conscious God; a world in which everything from the functioning of the mind to the nature of matter could be understood without reference to a divine creator. Further complicating matters, the texts arrived not from the original Greek, but normally through Latin translations of Arabic translations accompanied by learned commentaries by Muslim and Jewish scholars, especially by Ibn Rushd (Averroës), the greatest Aristotelian philosopher of the twelfth century.

As the full impact of Aristotelian philosophy began to reach churchmen and scholars, reactions varied from condemnation to wholehearted acceptance. To many, it appeared that there were two irreconcilable kinds of truth, one knowable through divine revelation, the other through human reason.

One Parisian scholar who refused to accept this dichotomy was Thomas Aquinas (1225–74), a professor of theology and the most brilliant intellect of the High Middle Ages. Although an Aristotelian who recognized the genius of Averroës, Aquinas refused to accept the possibility that human reason, which was a gift from God, led necessarily to contradictions with divine revelation. Properly applied, the principles of Aristotelian philosophy

As towns grew, the numbers and types of jobs grew as well. In this fifteenth-century Flemish manuscript illumination, a guild master of the dyer's guild supervises as men of the guild dye cloth.

could not lead to error, he argued. However, human reason unaided by revelation could not always lead to certain conclusions. Questions about such matters as the nature of God, creation, and the human soul could not be resolved by reason alone. In developing his thesis, Aquinas recast Christian doctrine and philosophy, replacing their Neoplatonic foundation with an Aristotelian base. Although not universally accepted in the thirteenth century (in 1277 the bishop of Paris condemned many of Aquinas's teachings as heretical), his synthesis came to dominate Christian intellectual life for centuries.

The Romano-barbarian chieftains who inherited political power in the western Roman Empire experimented with a variety of ways to combine the political heritage of Rome and the military traditions of their peoples into enduring polities. The most successful were the Franks, whose early acceptance of orthodox Christianity made possible an amalgam of Roman and barbarian peoples. Under their kings, especially Charlemagne, they brought most of the old western empire under their control and introduced throughout it their synthesis of Frankish and Roman culture and institutions. The Frankish model proved enduring. The cultural renaissance laid the foundation of all subsequent European intellectual activities, and the alliance between Church and monarchy provided the formula for European kings for almost a thousand years. The idea of the Carolingian empire, the symbol of European unity, has never entirely disappeared from western Europe.

By 1300 Europe had achieved a level of population density, economic prosperity, cultural sophistication, and political organization greater than at any time since the Roman Empire. Across Europe, a largely free peasantry cultivated a wide variety of crops both for local consumption and for growing commercial markets, while landlords sought increasingly rational approaches to estate management and investment. In cities and ports, merchants, manufacturers, and bankers presided over an international commercial and manufacturing economy that connected Scandinavia to the Mediterranean Sea. In schools and universities, students learned the skills of logical thinking and disputation while absorbing the traditions of Greece and Rome to prepare themselves for careers in law, medicine, and government.

The Invention of the State

The disintegration of the Carolingian empire in the tenth century left political power fragmented among a wide variety of political entities. In general these were of two types. The first, the papacy and the empire, were elective, traditional structures that claimed universal sovereignty over the Christian world, based on a sacred view of political power. The universality of these two claims brought popes and emperors into direct confrontation, ultimately weakening both. The second, largely hereditary and less extravagant in their religious and political pretensions, were the limited kingdoms that arose within the old Carolingian world or on its borders. These kingdoms, especially France and England, built on less ambitious traditions of royal prerogative as well as on the feudal bonds of lord and vassal to create new and lasting forms of political organization.

The Universal States: Empire and Papacy

The Frankish world east of the Rhine had been less affected than the kingdom of the west Franks by the onslaught of Vikings, Magyars, and Saracens. The eastern Frankish kingdom, a loose confederacy of five great duchies—Saxony, Lorraine, Franconia, Swabia, and Bavaria—had preserved much of the Carolingian religious, cultural, and institutional traditions. In 919 Duke Henry I of Saxony (919–36) was elected king, and his son Otto I (936–73) laid the foundation for the revival of the empire. In 955 Otto inflicted a devastating defeat on the Magyars, subdued the other dukes, and tightened his control over the kingdom. He accomplished this largely through the extensive use of bishops and abbots, whom he appointed as his agents and sources of loyal support. In 951, in order to prevent a southern German prince from establishing himself in northern Italy, Otto invaded and conquered Lombardy. Eleven years later he entered Rome, where he was crowned emperor by the pope.

Otto, known to history as "the Great," had established the character and content of German imperial policy for the next three hundred years. It involved conflict with the German aristocracy, reliance on bishops and abbots as imperial agents, and preoccupation with Italy. His successors, both in his own Saxon dynasty (919–1024) and in the succeeding dynasties, the Salians (1024–1125) and the Staufens (1138–1254), continued this tradition. The German Dukes and other aristocrats or magnates elected the German kings who were then consecrated as emperors by the pope. Generally, kings were able to bring about the election of their sons, and in this manner they attempted to turn the kingship into a hereditary office. However, the royal families did not manage to produce male heirs in each generation, and thus the magnates continued to exercise real power in royal elections. The magnates' ability to expand their own power and autonomy at the expense of their Slavic neighbors to the east also contributed to the weakness of the German monarchy.

The second cornerstone of imperial power was the appointment of bishops and abbots. In order to counter aristocratic power, emperors looked to the Church both for the development of the religious cult of the emperor as "The Anointed of the Lord" and as a source of reliable military and political support. While the offices of count and duke had become hereditary within the great aristocracy, the offices of bishop and abbot remained public charges to which the emperor could appoint loyal supporters.

The early successes of this imperial program created the seeds of its own destruction. Imperial efforts to reform the Church resulted in a second, competing claimant to universal authority, the papacy. In the later tenth and early eleventh centuries, emperors had intervened in papal elections, deposed and replaced corrupt popes, and worked to ensure that bishops and abbots would be educated, competent churchmen. The most effective reformer was Emperor Henry III (1039–56), who took seriously his role as the anointed of the Lord to reform the Church both in Germany and in Rome. When three rivals claimed the papacy, Henry called a synod, or meeting of bishops, which deposed all three and installed the first of a series of German popes. The most effective was Henry's own cousin who, as Leo IX (1049–54), traveled widely in France, Germany, and Italy. He condemned simony, that is, the practice of buying Church offices, and fostered monastic reforms such as that of Cluny. He also encouraged the efforts of a group of young reformers drawn from across Europe.

In the next decades, these new, more radical reformers began to advocate a widespread renewal of the Christian world, led not by emperors but by popes. These reformers pursued an ambitious set of goals. They sought to reform the morals of the clergy and in particular to eliminate married priests. They tried to free churches and monasteries from lay control both by forbidding lay men and women from owning churches and monasteries

The Empire of Otto the Great

and by eliminating simony. They particularly condemned "lay investiture," that is, the practice by which kings and emperors appointed bishops and invested them with the symbols of their office. Finally, they insisted that the pope, not the emperor, was the supreme representative of God on earth and as such had the right to exercise a universal sovereignty.

Every aspect of the reform movement met with strong opposition throughout Europe. However, its effects were most dramatic in the empire because of the central importance there of the imperial church system. Henry III's son Henry IV (1056–1106) clashed head-on with the leading radical reformer and former protege of Leo IX, Pope Gregory VII (1073–85), over the emperor's right to appoint and to install or invest bishops in their offices. This investiture controversy changed the face of European political history. Legal scholars for both sides searched Roman and Church law for arguments to bolster their claims, thus encouraging the revival of legal studies at Bologna. For the first time, public opinion played a crucial role in politics, and both sides composed carefully worded propaganda tracts aimed at secular and religious audiences. Gradually, the idea of the separate spheres of church and state emerged for the first time in European political theory. The conflict ended only in 1122, when Emperor Henry V (1106–25) and Pope Calixtus II (1119–24) reached an agreement known as the Concordat of Worms, which differentiated between the royal and the spiritual spheres of authority and allowed the emperors a limited role in episcopal election and investiture. This compromise changed the nature of royal rule in the empire, weakening the emperors and contributing to the long-term decline of royal government in Germany.

The investiture controversy ultimately compromised the authority of the pope as well as that of the emperor. First, the series of compromises beginning with the Concordat of Worms established a novel and potent tradition in Western political thought: the definition of separate spheres of authority for secular and religious government. Secondly, while in the short run popes were able to exercise enormous political influence, after the thirteenth century they were increasingly unable to make good their claims to absolute authority.

During the thirteenth century the papacy continued to perfect its legal system and its control over clergy throughout Europe. However, politically the popes were unable to assert their claims to universal supremacy. This was true both in Italy, where the communes in the north and the kingdom of Naples in the south resisted direct papal control, and in the emerging kingdoms north of the Alps, where monarchs successfully intervened in Church affairs. The old claims of papal authority rang increasingly hollow. When Pope Boniface VIII (1294–1303) attempted to prevent the French king Philip IV (1285–1314) from taxing the French clergy, boasting that he could depose kings "like servants" if necessary, Philip proved him wrong. Philip's agents hired a gang of adventurers who kidnaped the pope, plundered his treasury, and released him a broken, humiliated wreck. The French king who had engineered Boniface's humiliation represented a new political tradition much more limited but ultimately more successful than either the empire or the papacy—the medieval nation-state.

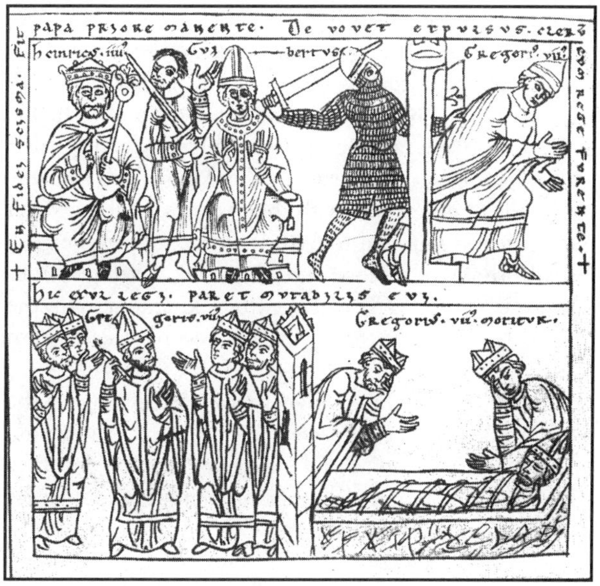

Scenes from the investiture controversy. In the top panel at right Pope Gregory VII is seen being expelled from his throne, while at the left, Henry IV sits with Bishop Guibert of Ravenna, his choice for pope. At the bottom, Gregory dies in exile.

The Nation-States: France and England

King was a less pretentious and more familiar office than that of emperor. As the Carolingian world disintegrated, a variety of kingdoms had appeared in France, Italy, Burgundy, and Provence. Beyond the confines of the old Carolingian world, kingship was well established in England and northern Spain. In Scandinavia, Poland, Bohemia, and Hungary powerful chieftains were consolidating royal power at the expense of their aristocracies. The claims of kings were much more modest than those

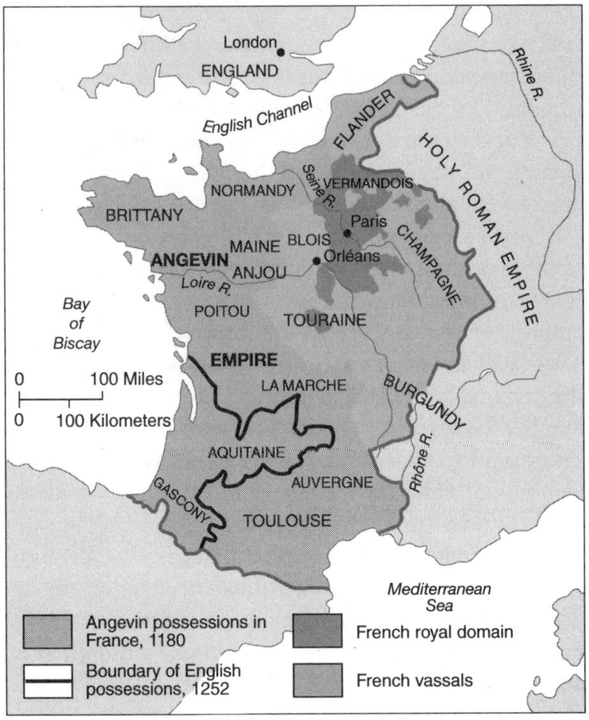

England and France in the Mid 1200s

of emperors or popes. Kings lay claim to a limited territory and, while the king was anointed, and thus a "Christus" (from the Greek word for sacred oil), kings were only one of many representatives of God on earth. Finally, kings were far from absolute rulers. Much of their real power derived, like that of other lords, from the feudal bonds uniting them with their vassals. Still, between the tenth and fourteenth centuries some monarchies, especially those of France and England, developed into powerful, centralized, and vigorous kingdoms. In the process they gave birth to what has become the modern state.

In 987, when Hugh Capet was elected king of the west Franks, no one suspected that his successors would become the most powerful rulers of Europe, for they were relatively weak magnates whose only real power lay in the region between Paris and Orléans.

Biology and bureaucracy created the medieval French monarchy. Between 987 and 1314, every royal descendant of Hugh Capet (after whom the dynasty was called the Capetian) left a male heir—an extraordinary record for a medieval family. During the same period, by comparison, the office of emperor was occupied by men from no less than nine families. By simply outlasting the families of their great barons, the Capetian kings were able to absorb lands when other families became extinct. This success was not just the result of luck. Kings risked excommunication in order to divorce wives who had not produced male heirs. The Capetians also wisely used their position as consecrated sovereign to build a power base in the Ile de France (the region around Paris) and among the bishops and abbots of the kingdom, and then to insist on their feudal rights as the lords of the great dukes and counts of France. It was this foundation that Louis VII's son Philip II (1180–1223) used to create the French monarchy.

Philip II was known to posterity as Augustus or the aggrandizer, because through his ruthless political intrigue and brilliant organizational sense he more than doubled the territory he controlled and more than quadrupled the revenue of the French crown. Philip's greatest coup was the confiscation of all the Continental possessions of the English king John (1199–1216). Although sovereign in England, as lord of Normandy, Anjou, Maine, and Touraine, John was technically a vassal of King Philip. When John married the fiancée of one of his Continental vassals, the outraged vassal appealed to Philip in his capacity as John's lord. Philip summoned John to appear before his court, and when he refused to do so, Philip ordered him to surrender all of his Continental fiefs. This meant war, and one by one John's Continental possessions fell to the French king. Philip's victory over John's ally the emperor Otto IV (1198–1215) at Bouvines in 1214 sealed the English loss of Normandy, Maine, Anjou, Poitou, and Touraine.

As important as the absorption of these vast regions was the administrative system Philip organized to govern them. Using members of families from the old royal demesne, he set up administrative officials called ***baillis*** and ***seneschals***, salaried agents who collected his revenues and represented his interests. The baillis in particular, who were drawn from nonnoble families and who often had received their education at the University of Paris, were the foundation of the French bureaucracy, which grew in strength and importance through the thirteenth century. By governing the regions of France according to local traditions but always with an eye to the king's interests, these bureaucrats did more than anyone else to create a stable, enduring political system.

By a quite different path the English monarchy reached a level of power similar to that of the French kings by the end of the thirteenth century. France was made by a family and its bureaucracy. The kingdom originally forged by Alfred and his descendants was transformed by the successors of William the Conqueror, using its judges and its people, often in spite of themselves.

In 1066 the Norman conquerors of England acquired a small insular kingdom that had been united by Viking raids little more than a century before. Hostile Celtic societies bordered it to the north and west. Still, it had important strengths. First, the king of the English was not simply a feudal lord—he was a sovereign. Secondly, Anglo-Saxon government had been participatory, with the free men of each shire taking part in court sessions and sharing the responsibilities of government. Finally, the king had agents, or *reeves*, in each shire (shire reeves, or sheriffs) who were responsible for representing the king's interests, presiding over the local court, and collecting royal taxes and incomes.

William preserved English government while replacing Anglo-Saxon officers with his Continental vassals, chiefly Normans and Flemings. He rewarded his supporters with land confiscated from the defeated Anglo-Saxons, but he was careful to give out land only in fief. In contrast to Continental practice, where many lords owned vast estates outright, in England all land was held directly or indirectly of the king. Because he wanted to know the extent of his new kingdom and its wealth, William ordered a comprehensive survey of all royal rights. The recorded account, known as the Domesday Book, was the most extensive investigation of economic rights since the late Roman tax rolls had been abandoned by the Merovingians.

Almost two decades of warfare over the succession in the first half of the twelfth century greatly weakened royal authority, but Henry II (1154–89), reestablished central power by reasserting his authority over the nobility and through his legal reforms. Using his Continental wealth and armies, he brought the English barons into line, destroyed private castles, and reasserted his rights to traditional royal incomes. He strengthened royal courts by expanding royal jurisdiction at the expense of Church tribunals and of the courts of feudal lords.

Henry's program to assert royal courts over local and feudal ones was even more successful, laying the foundation for a system of uniform judicial procedures through which royal justice reached throughout the kingdom—the common law. In France, royal agents observed local legal traditions but sought always to turn them to the king's advantage. In contrast, Henry's legal system simplified and cut through the complex tangle of local and feudal jurisdictions concerning land law. Any free person could purchase, for a modest price, a letter, or *writ*, from the king ordering the local sheriff to impanel a jury to determine if that person had been recently dispossessed of an estate, regardless of that person's legal right to the property. The procedure was swift and efficient. If the jury found for the plaintiff, the sheriff immediately restored the property, by force if necessary. While juries may not have meted out justice, they did resolve conflicts, and they did so in a way that protected landholders. These writs became enormously successful and expanded the jurisdiction of royal courts into areas previously outside royal jurisdiction.

Henry's son John may have made the greatest contribution to the development of the English state by losing Normandy and most of his other Continental lands. Loss of these territories forced English kings to concentrate on ruling England, not on their Continental territories. Moreover, John's financial difficulties, brought about by his unsuccessful wars to recover his Continental holdings, led him to such extremes of fiscal extortion that his barons, prelates, and the townspeople of London revolted. In June 1215 he was forced to accept the "great charter of liberties," or *Magna Carta*, a conservative, feudal document demanding that he respect the rights of his vassals and of the burghers of London. The great significance of the document was its acknowledgment that the king was not above the law.

Between the eleventh and the fourteenth centuries, western European societies experimented with a variety of forms in which political power was wielded. The Germanic emperors claimed the legacy of the Carolingians, but found it increasingly difficult to enforce any public authority over the great aristocrats and independent-minded towns of their empire. Likewise the popes, relying on a universal divine mandate, found it increasingly difficult to command obedience in areas increasingly seen as outside the religious sphere. At the same time, kings in France and England, by manipulating traditions of feudalism, justice, and personal allegiance, extended their authority over ever widening spheres of life in constantly expanding kingdoms.

War and Politics in the Later Middle Ages

In the fourteenth and fifteenth centuries, royal power continued to face challenges from traditions of private lordship and family ambitions which, for aristocrats across Europe, still took precedence over royal pretensions. Familial rivalries engulfed the feudal monarchies of France and England in the Hundred Years' War, which threatened to overwhelm them at the same time that weakening economic climates and demographic catastrophe exacerbated dynastic crises. In the empire, regionalism and dynastic concerns took precedence over

DOCUMENT

The Great Charter

Faced with defeat at the hands of the French King Philip Augustus abroad and baronial revolt at home, in 1215 King John was forced to sign *Magna Carta*, the "great charter" guaranteeing the traditional rights of the English nobility. Although a conservative document, in time it was interpreted as the guarantee of the fundamental rights of the English.

John, by the grace of God king of England, lord of Ireland, duke of Normandy and of Aquitainc, and count of Anjou, to his archbishops, bishops, abbots, earls, barons, justiciars, foresters, sheriffs, reeves, ministers, and all his bailiffs and faithful men, greeting. Know that, through the inspiration of God, for the health of our soul and [the souls] of all our ancestors and heirs, for the honour of God and the exaltation of Holy Church, and for the betterment of our realm, by the counsel of our venerable fathers . . . of our nobles . . . and of our other faithful men—

1. We have in the first place granted to God and by this our present charter have confirmed, for us and our heirs forever, that the English Church shall be free and shall have its rights entire and its liberties inviolate . . . We have also granted to all freemen of our kingdom, for us and our heirs forever, all the liberties hereinunder written, to be had and held by them and their heirs of us and our heirs.
2. If any one of our earls or barons or other men holding of us in chief dies, and if when he dies his heir is of full age and owes relief [that heir] shall have his inheritance for the ancient relief . . .
6. Heirs shall be married without disparagement.
7. A widow shall have her marriage portion and inheritance immediately after the death of her husband and without difficulty; nor shall she give anything for her dowry or for her marriage portion or for her inheritance—which inheritance she and her husband were holding on the day of that husband's death . . .
8. No widow shall be forced to marry so long as she wishes to live without a husband; yet so that she shall give security against marrying without our consent if she holds of us, or without the consent of her lord if she holds of another.
12. Scutage or aid shall be levied in our kingdom only by the common counsel of our kingdom, except for ransoming our body, for knighting our eldest son, and for once marrying our eldest daughter; and for these [purposes] only a reasonable aid shall be taken. The same provision shall hold with regard to the aids of the city of London.
17. Common pleas shall not follow our court, but shall be held in some definite place.
20. A freeman shall be amerced for a small offence only according to the degree of the offence; and for a grave offence he shall be amerced fined according to the gravity of the offence, saving his contenement [sufficient property to guarantee sustenance for himself and his family]. And a merchant shall be amerced in the same way, saving his merchandise; and a villein in the same way, saving his wainage [harvested crops necessary for seed and upkeep of his farm].
39. No freeman shall be captured or imprisoned or disseised [dispossessed of his estates] or outlawed or exiled or in any way destroyed, nor will we go against him or send against him, except by the lawful judgment of his peers or by the law or the land.
54. No one shall be seized or imprisoned on the appeal of a woman for the death of any one but her husband.

imperial tradition. At the same time, new directions in elite and popular culture encouraged a flowering of a fragmented but vibrant intellectual life.

One Hundred Years of War

Territorial and dynastic rivalry were the triggers that set off the Hundred Years' War between France and England. The English king Edward III (1327–77), a grandson of the French king Philip the Fair, claimed the throne that had passed to Philip VI (1328–50) after the death of the last Capetian. This question of succession, combined with disputes over the remaining possessions of the English king on the Continent, led Edward to declare war in 1337. But if these rivalries were the triggers, the deeper cause of the war was chivalry, a code of conduct that required the elites of Europe not only to maintain their honor by violence but also to cultivate violence to increase that honor.

In spite of chivalrous ideals, nobles no longer fought as vassals of the king but as highly paid mercenaries. The nature of this service differed greatly on the two sides of the Channel. In France, the tactics and personnel had changed little since the twelfth century. The core of any army was the body of heavily armored nobles who rode into battle with their lords, supported by lightly armored knights. Behind them marched infantrymen recruited

The battle of Agincourt (1415) was one of the great battles of the Hundred Years' War. The heavily armored French cavalry met defeat at the hands of a much smaller force of disciplined English pikemen and longbowmen.

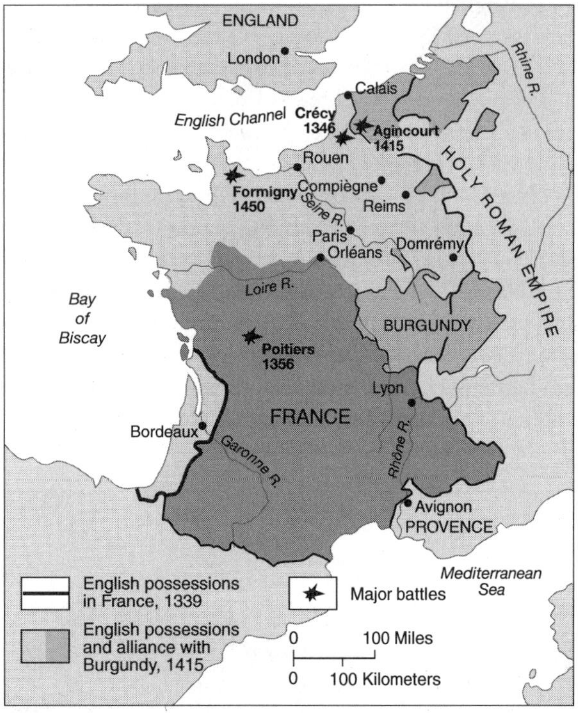

The Hundred Years' War

from towns and armed with pikes. Although the French also hired mercenary Italian crossbowmen, the nobles despised them and never used them effectively.

In contrast, centuries of fighting against Welsh and Scottish enemies had transformed and modernized the English armies and their tactics. The great nobles continued to serve as heavily armored horsemen, but professional companies of pikemen and longbowmen made up the bulk of the army. Time and again the antiquated French cavalry lost pitched battles against numerically inferior English armies. But pitched battles were not the worst defeats for the French. More devastating were the constant raiding and systematic destruction of the French countryside by the English companies. Raiding and pillaging continued for decades, even during long truces between the French and English kings. During periods of truce unemployed free companies of French and English mercenaries roamed the countryside, supporting themselves by banditry while awaiting the renewal of more-formal hostilities. Never had the ideals of chivalric conduct been so far distant from the brutal realities of warfare.

The French kings were powerless to prevent such destruction, just as they were unable to defeat the enemy in open battle. Since the kings were incapable of protecting their subjects or of leading their armies to victory, the "silken thread binding together the kingdom of France," as one observer put it, began to unravel, and the kingdom so painstakingly constructed by the Capetian monarchs began to fall apart. Not only did the English make significant territorial conquests, but the French nobles began carving out autonomous lordships. Private warfare and castle building, never entirely eradicated even by Louis IX and Philip IV, increased as royal government lost its ability to control the nobility. Whole regions of the kingdom slipped entirely from royal authority. Much of the so-called Hundred Years' War was actually a French civil war.

During this century of war the French economy suffered even more than the French state. Trade routes were broken and commerce declined as credit disappeared. French kings repeatedly seized the assets of Italian merchant bankers in order to finance the war. Such actions made the Italians, who had been the backbone of French commercial credit, extremely wary about extending loans in the kingdom. Politically and economically France seemed doomed.

The flower of French chivalry did not save France. Instead, at the darkest moment of the long and bloody struggle, salvation came at the hands of a simple peasant girl from the county of Champagne. By 1429 the English and their Burgundian allies held virtually all of northern France, including Paris. Now they were besieging Orléans, the key to the south. The heir to the French throne, the dauphin, was the weak-willed and uncrowned Charles VII (1422–61). To him came Joan of Arc (1412–31), a simple, illiterate but deeply religious girl who bore an incredible message of hope. She claimed to have heard the voices of saints ordering her to save Orléans and have the dauphin crowned according to tradition at Reims.

Charles and his advisers were more than skeptical about this brash peasant girl who announced her divinely ordained mission to save France. Finally convinced of her sincerity if not of her ability, Charles allowed her to accompany a relief force to Orléans. The French army, its spirit buoyed by the belief that Joan's simple faith was the work of God, defeated the English and ended the siege. This victory led to others, and on 16 July 1429 Charles was crowned king at Reims.

After the coronation, Joan's luck began to fade. She failed to take Paris, and in 1431 she was captured by the Burgundians, who sold her to the English. Eager to get rid of this troublesome peasant girl, the English had her tried as a heretic. Charles did nothing to save his savior. After all, the code of chivalry did not demand that a king intervene on behalf of a mere peasant girl, even if she had saved his kingdom. She was burned at the stake in Rouen on 30 May 1431.

Despite Joan's inglorious end, the tide had turned. The French pushed the English back toward the coast. In the final major battle of the war, fought at Formigny in 1450, the French used a new and telling weapon to defeat the English—gunpowder. Rather than charging the English directly as they had done so often before, they mounted cannon and pounded the English to bits. Gunpowder completed the destruction of the chivalric traditions of warfare begun by archers and pikemen. By 1452 English Continental holdings had been reduced to the town of Calais. The Continental warfare of more than a century was over.

Life and Death in the Later Middle Ages

The warfare and dynastic competition of the later Middle Ages took place against a backdrop of famine, disease, and popular revolt. Much of this misery was caused or at least intensified by political violence. Some appeared to the populace of western Europe to be caused by divine wrath.

Dancing With Death

By the end of the thirteenth century, population growth in Europe had strained available resources to the breaking point. At the same time, kings and nobles demanded ever higher taxes and rents to finance their wars and extravagant lifestyles. The result was a precarious balance in which a late frost, a bad harvest, or hungry mercenaries could mean disaster. Between 1315 and 1317 the first great famine of the fourteenth century struck Europe, triggered by crop failures and war. People died by the thousands. Urban workers, because they were chronically undernourished, were particularly hard hit. Disease accompanied famine. Crowded and filthy towns, opposing armies with their massed troops, and overpopulated countrysides provided fertile ground for the spread of infectious disease. Moreover, the greatly expanded trade routes of the thirteenth and fourteenth centuries that carried goods and grain between east and west also provided highways for deadly microbes.

This famine was but a prelude. Between 1347 and 1352 from one-half to one-third of Europe's population died from a virulent combination of bubonic, septicemic, and pneumonic plague known to history as the Black Death. The disease, carried by the fleas of infected rats, traveled the caravan routes from central Asia. It arrived in Messina, Sicily, aboard a merchant vessel in October 1347. From there the Black Death spread up the boot of Italy and then into southern France, England, and Spain. By 1349 it had reached northern Germany, Portugal, and Ireland. The following year the Low Countries, Scotland, Scandinavia, and Russia fell victim.

The plague was all the more terrifying because its cause, its manner of transmission, and its cure were totally unknown until the end of the nineteenth century. Preachers saw the plague as divine punishment for sin.

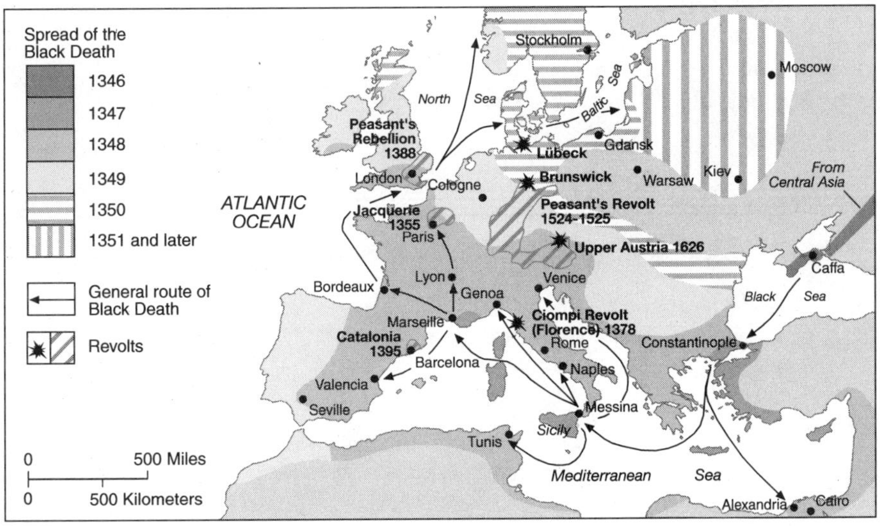

The Spread of the Black Death

DOCUMENT

The Black Death in Florence

Giovanni Boccaccio set his Decameron *in Florence at the height of the Black Death. His eyewitness description of the plague is the most graphic account of the disease and its effects on society.*

I say, then, that the sum of thirteen hundred and fifty-eight years had elapsed since the fruitful Incarnation of the Son of God, when the noble city of Florence, which for its great beauty excels all others in Italy, was visited by the deadly pestilencc. Some say that it descended upon the human race through the influence of the heavenly bodies, others that it was a punishment signifying God's righteous anger at our iniquitous way of life. But whatever its cause, it had originated some years earlier in the East, where it had claimed countless lives before it unhappily spread westward, growing in strength as it swept relentlessly on from one place to the next . . . Against these maladies, it seemed that all the advice of physicians and all the power of medicine were profitless and unavailing . . . Some people were of the opinion that a sober and abstemious mode of living considerably reduced the risk of infection. They therefore formed themselves into groups and lived in isolation from everyone else . . . Others took the opposite view, and maintained that an infallible way of warding off this appalling evil was to drink heavily, enjoy life to the full, go round singing and merrymaking, gratifying all of one's cravings whenever the opportunity offered, and shrug the whole thing off as one enormous joke . . . There were many other people who steered a middle course between the two already mentioned, neither restricting their diet to the same degree as the first group, nor indulging so freely as the second in drinking and other forms of wantonness, but simply doing no more than satisfy their appetite. Instead of incarcerating themselves, these people moved about freely, holding in their hands a posy of flowers, or fragrant herbs, or one of a wide range of spices, which they applied at frequent intervals to their nostrils, thinking it an excellent idea to fortify the brain with smells of that particular sort, for the stench of dead bodies, sickness, and medicines seemed to fill and pollute the whole of the atmosphere.

Some people pursuing what was possibly the safer alternative callously maintained that there was no better or more efficacious remedy against the plague than to run away from it . . .

Of the people who held these various opinions, not all of them died. Nor, however, did they all survive. On the contrary, many of each different persuasion fell ill here, there, and everywhere, and having themselves, when they were fit and well, set an example to those who were as yet unaffected, they languished away with virtually no one to nurse them. This scourge had implanted so great a terror in the hearts of men and women that brothers abandoned brothers, uncles their nephews, sisters their brothers, and in many cases wives deserted their husbands. But even worse, and almost incredible, was the fact that fathers and mothers refused to nurse and assist their own children, as though they did not belong to them.

From Giovanni Boccaccio, *The Decameron.*

Ordinary people frequently accused Jews of causing it by poisoning drinking water. The medical faculty of Paris announced that it was the result of the conjunction of the planets Saturn, Jupiter, and Mars, which caused a corruption of the surrounding air.

Responses to the plague were equally varied. In many German towns terrified Christian citizens looked for outside scapegoats and slaughtered the Jewish community. Cities, aware of the risk of infection although ignorant of its process, closed their gates and turned away outsiders. Individuals with means fled to country houses or locked themselves in their homes to avoid contact with others. Nothing worked. As devastating as the first outbreak of the plague was, its aftershocks were even more catastrophic. Once established in Europe, the disease continued to return roughly once each generation. The last outbreak of the plague in Europe was the 1771 epidemic in Moscow that killed 60,000.

The Black Death, along with other epidemics, famines, and war-induced shortages, affected western much more than eastern Europe. The culminating effect of these disasters was a darker, more somber vision of life than that of the previous centuries. This vision found its expression in the Dance of Death, an increasingly popular image in art. Naked, rotting corpses dance with great animation before the living. The latter, depicted in the dress of all social orders, are immobile, surprised by death, reluctant but resigned.

The Black Death was the greatest disaster ever to befall Europe. It touched every aspect of life, hastening a process of social, economic, and cultural transformation already under way. Nothing had prepared Europe for this catastrophe, no teaching of the Church or its leaders could adequately explain it, and in spite of desperate attempts to fix the blame on Jews or strangers, no one but God could be held responsible. Survivors stood alone and uncertain before a new world. Across Europe, moralists reported a general lapse in traditional ethics, a breakdown in the moral codes. The most troubling aspect of this breakdown was what one defender of the old order termed "the plague of insurrection" that spread across Europe.

The Plague of Insurrection

Initially, even this darkest cloud had a silver lining. Lucky survivors of the plague soon found other reasons to rejoice. Property owners, when they finished burying their dead, discovered that they were far richer in land and goods. At the other end of the social spectrum, the plague had eliminated the labor surplus. Peasants were

A page from the fourteenth-century psalter and prayer book of Bonne of Luxembourg, Duchess of Normandy. The three figures of the dead shown here contrast with three living figures on the facing page of the psalter to illustrate a moral fable.

suddenly in great demand. For a time at least, they were able to negotiate substantially higher wages and an improved relationship with landlords.

These hopes were short-lived. The rise in expectations produced by the redistribution of wealth and the labor shortage created new tensions. Landlords sought laws forcing peasants to accept preplague wages and tightened their control over serfs in order to prevent them from fleeing to cities or other lords. At the same time governments attempted to benefit from laborers' greater prosperity by imposing new taxes. In cities, where the plague had been particularly devastating, the demographic decline sharply lowered demand for goods and thus lowered the need for manufacturing and production of all kinds. Like rural landowners, master craftsmen sought legislation to protect their incomes. New laws reduced production by restricting access to trades and increased masters' control over the surviving urban laborers. Social mobility, once a characteristic of urban life, slowed to a halt. Membership in guilds became hereditary, and young apprentices or journeymen had little hope of ever rising to the level of independent master craftsmen.

These new tensions led to violence when kings added their demands for new war taxes to the landlords' and masters' attempts to erase the peasants' and workers' recent gains. The first revolts took place in France, where peasants and townspeople, disgusted with the incompetence of the nobility in their conduct of the war against England, feared that their new wealth would be stolen from them by corrupt and incompetent aristocrats.

In 1358 the French government attempted to increase taxes on the peasantry. Peasants in the north of France rebelled against their landlords. The revolt, known as the Jacquerie, was a spontaneous outburst directed against the nobility, whom the peasants saw as responsible for all their ills. Without real leadership or program, peasants attacked as many nobles as they could find, killing them along with their wives and children and burning their homes and castles. The peasants' brutality deeply shocked the upper classes, whose own violence was constrained within the bounds of the chivalric code. Because the Church largely supported the power structure, the uprising was also strongly anticlerical. Success bred further attacks, and the disorganized army of peasants began to march south toward Paris, killing, looting, and burning everything associated with the despised nobility.

In the midst of this peasant revolt, Etienne Marcel (ca. 1316–58), a wealthy Parisian cloth merchant, led an uprising of Parisian merchants, which sought to take control of royal finances and force fiscal reforms on the dauphin, the future Charles V. Although initially the rebels were primarily members of the merchant and guild elite, Marcel soon enlisted the support of the radical townspeople against the aristocracy. He even made overtures to the leaders of the Jacquerie to join forces. For a brief time it appeared that the aristocratic order in France might succumb. However, in the end peasant and merchant rebels were no match for professional armies. The Jacquerie met its end outside Paris, where an aristocratic force cut the peasants to pieces. The Parisian revolt met a similar fate. Aristocratic armies surrounded the city and cut off its food supply. Marcel was assassinated and the dauphin Charles regained the city.

The French revolts set the pattern for similar uprisings across Europe. Rebels were usually relatively prosperous peasants or townspeople whose economic situations were threatened by aristocratic attempts to turn back the clock to the period before the Black Death. In 1381 English peasants, reacting to new and hated taxes,

Jacquerie rebellion, from a fifteenth-century manuscript. The well-armed soldiers have won the day, and the unarmed rebels are consigned to the river to sink or swim. Such rebellions were put down with great ruthlessness.

PROMINENT FIGURES OF THE LATER MIDDLE AGES

1049–54	Pope Leo IX
1073–85	Pope Gregory VII
1088–99	Pope Urban II
1119–24	Pope Calixtus II
1170–1221	Saint Dominic
1182–1226	Saint Francis of Assisi
1198–1216	Pope Innocent III
1225–74	Saint Thomas Aquinas
1265–1321	Dante
1294–1303	Pope Boniface VIII
c. 1300–49	William of Ockham
1330–84	John Wycliffe
1364–c. 1430	Christine de Pisan
1343–1400	Geoffrey Chaucer
1412–31	Joan of Arc
1417–31	Pope Martin V

rose in a less violent but more coordinated revolt known as the Great Rebellion. Peasant revolts took place in the northern Spanish region of Catalonia in 1395 and in Germany throughout the fourteenth and fifteenth centuries. The largest was the great Peasant's Revolt of 1524. Although always ruthlessly suppressed, European peasant uprisings continued until the peasant rebellion of 1626 in upper Austria. These outbursts indicated not necessarily the desperation of Europe's peasantry, but the new belief that they could change their lives for the better through united action.

Urban Life in the Later Middle Ages

In France and the Low Countries, population decline, war, and class conflict fatally weakened the vitality of the commercial and manufacturing system. These same events reduced the market for Italian goods and undermined the economic strength of the great Italian cities. The Hundred Years' War bankrupted many of Florence's greatest banking houses who lent to both French and English kings. Commercial activity declined as well. While Italians did not disappear from northern cities, they no longer held a near monopoly on northern trade.

These setbacks for the Italians worked to the advantage of German towns. Along the Baltic Sea, in Scandinavia, and in northern Germany, towns such as Lübeck, Lüneburg, Visby, Bremen, and Cologne formed a commercial and political alliance to control northern trade. During the second half of the fourteenth century, this Hanseatic League—the word *Hansa* means "company"—monopolized the northern grain trade and forced Denmark to grant its members exclusive rights to export Scandinavian fish throughout Europe. Hanseatic merchants established colonies from Novgorod to London to Bruges and even in Venice. They carried dried and salted fish to Prague and supplied grain from Riga to England and France.

English towns also profited from the decline of Flanders and France. The population decline of the fourteenth century led many English landowners to switch from traditional farming to sheep raising, since pasturing sheep required few workers and promised cash profits. While surviving peasants were driven off the land and forced to beg for a living, lords produced more wool than ever before. However, because the Hundred Years' War hampered the exportation of wool to Flanders, the English began to make cloth themselves. Protected by high tariffs on imports and low duties on exports, by the middle of the fifteenth century, England became a major exporter of finished cloth.

Some made fortunes from the new circumstances, many others fell into hopeless poverty. Driven both by mounting compassion for the urban poor and by a growing fear of the violent potential of this ever increasing population, medieval towns developed novel systems to deal with poverty. The first was public assistance, the second social control and repression.

Traditionally, charity had been a religious act that focused more on the soul of the giver than on the effect on the life of the recipient. The same had been true of charitable organizations such as confraternities and hospitals. Confraternities were pious religious organizations of lay people and clergy who ministered to the poor and sick. Hospitals were all-purpose religious institutions providing lodging for pilgrims, the elderly, and the ill. By the fourteenth century, such pious institutions had become inadequate to deal with the growing numbers of poor and ill. Towns began to assume control over a centralized system of public assistance.

One consequence of poverty was increased crime. Fear of the poor led to repressive measures and harsh punishments. During the later Middle Ages, gruesome forms of mutilation and execution became common for a long list of offenses. Petty larceny was punished with whipping, cutting off ears or thumbs, branding, or expulsion. In some towns, robbery of an amount over three pence was punished with death.

The later Middle Ages was a time of stark contrasts, of famine, pestilence, and revolt as well as of aristocratic opulence and royal pageantry. The streets and markets of fifteenth-century towns bustled with the sights and sounds of rich Hanseatic merchants, Italian bankers, and prosperous local tradesmen. The back alleys on the edges of these towns teemed with a growing mass of desperate and despairing workers and their families.

The Spirit of the Later Middle Ages

The Dance of Death and the gallows were not the only images of later medieval life. The constant presence of death made life more precious. Europeans celebrated life with a vigor and creativity characterized by a growing sense of individuality, independence, and variety. During the fourteenth century, the Church failed to provide unified spiritual and cultural leadership to Europe. The institutional division of the Church was paralleled by divisions over how to lead the proper Christian life. Many devout Christians developed independent lifestyles intended to bring them closer to God without reliance on the Church hierarchy. They elaborated beliefs branded by the Church as heresy. Others called into question the philosophical bases of theological speculation developed since the time of Aquinas. Finally, the increasing pluralism of European culture gave rise to new literary traditions that both celebrated and criticized the medieval legacy of Christianity, chivalry, and social order.

Christendom Divided

The universal empire as well as its traditional competitor, the universal Church, declined in the later Middle Ages. The papacy never recovered from the humiliating defeat Pope Boniface VIII suffered at the hands of King Philip the Fair in 1303. The ecclesiastical edifice created by the thirteenth-century popes was shaken to its foundations, first by becoming a virtual appendage of the French monarchy, and then by a dispute that for over forty years gave European Christians a choice between two, and finally three, claimants to the chair of Saint Peter.

In 1305 the College of Cardinals elected as pope the bishop of Bordeaux. The pope took up residence not in Rome but in the papal city of Avignon on the east bank of the Rhone River. Technically, Avignon was a papal estate within the Holy Roman Empire. Actually, with France just across the river, the pope at Avignon was under French control. For the next seventy years French popes and French cardinals ruled the Church. The traditional enemies of France as well as religious reformers who expected leadership from the papacy looked on this situation with disgust.

In 1377 Pope Gregory XI (1370–78) returned from Avignon to Rome but died almost immediately upon arrival. Thousands of Italians, afraid that the cardinals would elect another Frenchman, surrounded the church where they were meeting and demanded an Italian pope. The terrified cardinals elected an Italian, who took the name of Urban VI (1378–89). Once elected, Urban attempted to reform the curia, but he did so in a most undiplomatic way, insulting the cardinals and threatening to appoint sufficient non-French bishops to their number to end French control of the curia. The cardinals soon left Rome and announced that because the election had been made under duress it was invalid and that Urban should resign. When he refused they held a second election and chose a Frenchman, Clement VII (1378–94), who took up residence in Avignon. The Church now had two heads, both with reasonable claims to the office.

The chaos created by this so-called Great Schism divided western Christendom. Nothing in Church law or tradition offered a solution to this crisis. Nor did unilateral efforts to settle the crisis succeed. Twice France invaded Italy in an attempt to eliminate Urban but failed

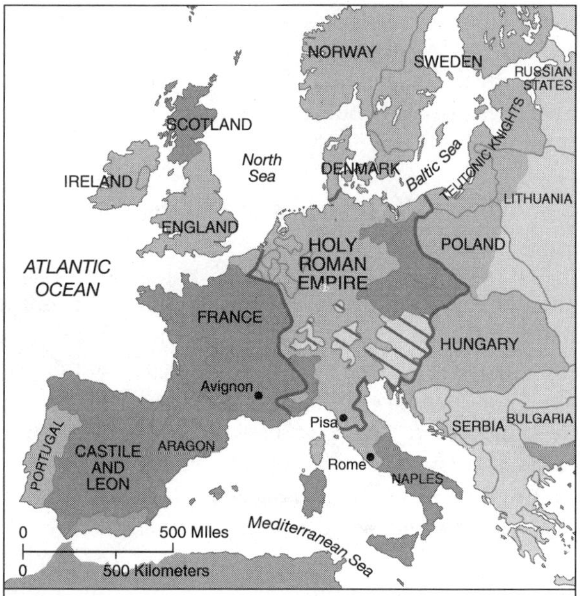

The Great Schism

THE LATER MIDDLE AGES, 1300-1500

1305–1377	Avignon papacy
1337–1452	Hundred Years' War
1347–1352	Black Death spreads through Europe
1358	Jacquerie revolt of French peasants; Etienne Marcel leads revolt of Parisian merchants
1378–1417	Great Schism divides Roman Christianity
1381	Great Rebellion of English peasants
1414–1417	Council of Constance ends Great Schism
1415	Jan Hus executed
1455–1485	English Wars of the Roses

both times. The situation perpetuated itself. When Urban and Clement died, cardinals on both sides elected successors. By the end of the fourteenth century, France and the empire were exasperated with their popes and even the cardinals were determined to end the stalemate.

Church lawyers argued that a general council alone could end the schism. Both popes opposed this "conciliarist" argument because it suggested that an assembly of the Church rather than the pope held supreme authority. However, in 1408 cardinals from both sides summoned a council in the Italian city of Pisa. The council deposed both rivals and elected a new pope. But this solution only made matters worse, since neither pope accepted the decision of the council. Europe now had to contend with not two but three popes, each claiming to be the true successor of Saint Peter.

Six years later the Council of Constance managed a final solution. There under the patronage of the emperor-elect Sigismund (1410–37), cardinals, bishops, abbots, and theologians from across Europe met to resolve the crisis. Their goal was not only to settle the schism but also to reform the Church to prevent a recurrence of such a scandal. The participants at Constance hoped to restructure the Church as a limited monarchy in which the powers of the pope would be controlled through frequent councils. The Pisan and Avignon popes were deposed. The Roman pope, abandoned by all of his supporters, abdicated. Before doing so, however, he formally convoked the council in order to preserve the tradition that a general council had to be called by the pope. Finally, the council elected as pope an Italian cardinal not aligned with any of the claimants. The election of the cardinal, who took the name Martin V (1417–31), ended the schism.

The relief at the end of the Great Schism could not hide the very real problems left by over a century of papal weakness. The prestige of the papacy had been permanently compromised. Everywhere the Church had become more national in character. The conciliarist demand for control of the Church, which had ended the schism, lessened the power of the pope. Finally, during the century between Boniface VIII and Martin V, new religious movements had taken root across Europe, movements that the political creatures who had occupied the papal office could neither understand nor control. The disintegration of the Church loomed ever closer as pious individuals turned away from the organized Church and sought divine help in personal piety, mysticism, or even magic.

Discerning the Spirit of God

Even as Europeans were losing respect for the institutional Church, people everywhere were seeking closer and more intimate relationships with God. Distrusting the formal institutions of the Church, lay persons and clerics turned to private devotions and to mysticism to achieve union with the divine. Most of these stayed within the Church. Others, among them many female mystics, maintained an ambiguous relationship with the traditional institutions of Christianity. A few broke sharply with it.

Christians of the later Middle Ages sought to imitate Christ and venerated the Eucharist, or communion wafer, which the Church taught was the actual body of Jesus. Male mystics focused on imitating Jesus in his poverty, suffering, and humility. Women developed their own form of piety, which focused not on wealth and power but on spiritual nourishment, particularly as provided by the Eucharist. For women mystics, radical fasting became preparation for the reception of the Eucharist, often described in highly emotional and erotic terms.

Only a thin line separated the saint's heroic search for union with God from the heretic's identification with God. The radical Brethren of the Free Spirit believed that God was all things and that all things would return to God. Such pantheism denied the possibility of sin, punishment, and the need for salvation. Members of the sect were hunted down and many were burned as heretics. The specter of the Inquisition, the ecclesiastical court system charged with ferreting out heretics, hung over all such communities.

When unorthodox Christians were protected by secular lords, the ecclesiastical courts were powerless. This was the case with John Wycliffe (ca. 1330–84), an Oxford theologian who attacked the doctrinal and political bases of the Church. He taught that the value of the sacraments depended on the worthiness of the priest administering them, that Jesus was present in the Eucharist only in spirit, that indulgences were useless, and that salvation depended on divine predestination rather than individual merit. Normally these teachings would have led him to the stake. But he had also attacked the Church's right to wealth and luxury, an idea whose political implications pleased the English monarchy and nobility. Thus he was allowed to live and teach in peace. Only under Henry V (1413–22) were Wycliffe's followers, known as Lollards, vigorously suppressed by the state. Before this condemnation took place, however, Wycliffe's teachings reached the kingdom of Bohemia through the marriage of Charles IV's daughter Anne of Bohemia to the English king Richard II. Anne took with her to England a number of Bohemian clerics, some of whom studied at Oxford and absorbed the political and religious teachings of Wycliffe, which they then took back to Bohemia.

In Prague some of Wycliffe's less radical teachings took root among the theology faculty of the new university, where the leading proponent of Wycliffe's teachings was Jan Hus (1373–1415), an immensely popular young master and preacher. Although Hus rejected Wycliffe's ideas about the priesthood and the sacraments, he and other Czech preachers attacked indulgences and demanded a reform of Church liturgy and morals. They grafted these religious demands onto an attack on German dominance of the Bohemian kingdom. These attacks outraged both the Pisan pope John XXIII (1410–15) and the Bohemian king Wenceslas IV (1378–1419), who favored the German faction. The pope excommunicated Hus, and the king expelled the Czech faculty from the university. Hus was convinced that he was no heretic and that a fair hearing would clear him. He therefore agreed to travel to the Council of Constance under promise of safe conduct from the emperor-elect Sigismund to defend his position. There he was tried on a charge of heresy, convicted, and burned at the stake.

News of Hus's execution touched off a revolt in Bohemia. Unlike the peasant revolts of the past, however, this revolt had broad popular support throughout all levels of Czech society. Peasants, nobles, and townspeople saw the attack on Hus and his followers as an attack on Czech independence and national interest by a Church and an empire controlled by Germans. Soon a radical faction known as the Taborites was demanding the abolition of private property and the institution of a communal state. Although moderate Hussites and Bohemian Catholics combined to defeat the radicals in 1434, most of Bohemia remained Hussite through the fifteenth century. The sixteenth-century reformer Martin Luther declared himself a follower of Jan Hus.

Illustration from the sixteenth-century Bohemian Gradual of Mala Strana. Jan Hus, wearing the traditional heretic's cap adorned with devils, is burned at the stake.

William of Ockham and the Spirit of Truth

The critical and individualistic approach that characterized religion during the later Middle Ages was also typical of the philosophical thought of the period. The delicate balance between faith and reason taught by Aquinas and other intellectuals in the thirteenth century disintegrated in the fourteenth. As in other areas of life, intellectuals questioned the basic suppositions of their predecessors, directing intellectual activity away from general speculations and toward particular, observable reality.

The person primarily responsible for this new intellectual climate was the English Franciscan William of Ockham (ca. 1300–49). Ockham developed a truly radical political philosophy. Imperial power, he argued, derived not from the pope but from the people. People are free to determine their own form of government and to elect rulers. They can make their choice directly, as in the election of the emperor by electors who represent the people, or implicitly, through continuing forms of government. In either case, government is entirely secular. He also denied the absolute authority of the pope, even in spiritual matters. Rather, Ockham argued, parishes, religious orders, and monasteries should send representatives to regional synods, which in turn would elect representatives to general councils.

As radical as Ockham's political ideas were, his philosophical outlook was even more extreme and exerted a more direct and lasting influence. The Christian Aristotelianism that developed in the thirteenth century had depended on the validity of general concepts called universals, which could be analyzed through the use of logic. Aquinas and others who studied the eternity of the world, the existence of God, the nature of the soul, and other philosophical questions believed that people could reach general truths by abstracting universals from particular, individual cases. Ockham argued that universals were merely names, no more than convenient tags for discussing individual things. Universals had no connection with reality and could not be used to reason from particular observations to general truths. This radical nominalism (from the Latin *nomen*, "name") thus denied that human reason could aspire to certain truth.

Ockham's ideas on Church governance by a general council representing the whole Christian community offered the one hope for a solution to the Great Schism that erupted shortly after his death. Conciliarists drew on Ockham's attack on papal absolutism to propose an alternative church. The Council of Constance, which ended the schism, was the fruit of Ockham's political theory.

Just as Ockham's political theory dominated the later fourteenth century, his nominalist philosophy won over the philosophical faculties of Europe. Since he had discredited the value of Aristotelian logic to increase knowledge, the result was, on the one hand, a decline in abstract speculation and on the other, a greater interest in scientific observation of individual phenomena. In the next generation Parisian professors, trained in the tradition of Ockham, laid the foundation for scientific studies of motion and the universe that led to the scientific discoveries of the sixteenth and seventeenth centuries.

Vernacular Literature and the Individual

Just as the religious and philosophical concerns of the later Middle Ages developed within national frameworks and criticized accepted authority from the perspective of individual experience, so too did the literature, increasingly written in the many languages spoken by Europeans rather than in learned Latin, begin to explore the place of the individual within an increasingly complex society. Poets used their native tongues to express a spectrum of sentiments and to describe a spectrum of emotions and values. The themes and ideas expressed ranged from the polished, traditional values of the aristocracy trying to maintain the ideals of chivalry in a new and changed world to the views of ordinary people, by turns reverent or sarcastic, joyful or despondent.

In Italy, a trio of Tuscan poets, Dante Alighieri (1265–1321), Petrarch (1304–74), and Boccaccio (1313–75), not only made Italian a literary language but composed in it some of the greatest literature of all time. Dante, the first and greatest of the three, wrote philosophical treatises and literary works, which culminated in his *Divine Comedy*, written during the last years of his life.

The Divine Comedy is a view of the whole Christian universe, populated with people from antiquity and from Dante's own day. The poem is both a sophisticated summary of philosophical and theological thought at the beginning of the fourteenth century and an astute political commentary on his times.

English literature emerged from over two centuries of French cultural domination with the writings of William Langland (ca. 1330–95) and Geoffrey Chaucer (ca. 1343–1400). Both presented images of contemporary society with a critical and often ironic view. In *Piers Plowman* Langland presents society from the perspective of the peasantry. In Chaucer's great poem, *Canterbury Tales*, pilgrims traveling together to Canterbury represent every walk of life and spectrum of society. Chaucer uses them and the stories they tell to comment in subtle and complex ways on the literary, religious, and cultural traditions of which they are a part.

Much of Italian and English literature drew material and inspiration from French, which into the fifteenth century was the language of courtly romance. In France, most literature continued to project an unreal world of allegory and nostalgia for a glorious if imaginary past. Popular literature, developed largely in the towns, often dealt with courtly themes, but with a critical and more realistic eye.

In this literary world appeared a new and extraordinary type of poet, a woman who earned her living with her pen, Christine de Pisan (1364–ca. 1430). As a professional woman of letters, de Pisan fought the stereotypical medieval image of women as weak, sexually aggressive temptresses. In her *Hymn to Joan of Arc*, she saluted her famous contemporary for her accomplishments, bringing dignity to women, striving for justice, and working for peace in France. De Pisan's life and writing epitomized the new possibilities and

Christine de Pisan presenting a manuscript of her poems to Isabeau of Bavaria, the wife of King Charles VI of France.

new interests of the fifteenth century. They included an acute sense of individuality, a willingness to look for truth not in the clichés of the past but in actual experience, and a readiness to defend one's views with tenacity.

The third literary tradition in fifteenth-century France was that of realist poetry. Around 1453, just as the English troops were enduring a final battering from the French artillery, Duke Charles of Orléans (1394–1465) organized a poetry contest. Each contestant was to write a ballad that began with the contradictory line, "I die of thirst beside the fountain." The duke, himself an outstanding poet, wrote an entry that embodied the traditional courtly themes of love and fortune:

> ***I die of thirst beside the fountain,***
> ***Shaking from cold and the fire of love;***
> ***I am blind and yet guide the others;***
> ***I am weak of mind, a man of wisdom;***
> ***Too negligent, often cautious in vain,***
> ***I have been made a spirit,***
> ***Led by fortune for better or for worse.***

An unexpected and very different entry came from the duke's prison. The prisoner-poet, François Villon (1432–ca. 1464), was a child of the Paris streets, an impoverished student, a barroom brawler, a killer, and a thief who spent much of his life trying to escape the gallows. He was also the greatest realist poet of the Middle Ages. His entry read:

> ***I die of thirst beside the fountain,***
> ***Hot as fire, my teeth clattering,***
> ***At home I am in an alien land;***
> ***I shudder beside a glowing brazier,***
> ***Naked as a worm, gloriously dressed,***
> ***I laugh and cry and wait without hope,***
> ***I take comfort and sad despair,***
> ***I rejoice and have no joy,***
> ***Powerful, I have no force and no strength,***
> ***Well received, I am expelled by all.***

The duke focused on the sufferings of love; the thief on the physical sufferings of the downtrodden. The two poets represent the contradictory tendencies of literature in the later Middle Ages.

In the centuries that followed the disintegration of the Carolingian empire, the eastern half of the Carolingian world continued the imperial universalist tradition of the Carolingians until its conflicts with the other universalist tradition, that of the papacy, contributed to its disintegration into small autonomous principalities. In western Europe, public order was for a time largely replaced by numerous individual principalities. Gradually, however, first in France and in England, and then in the Iberian Peninsula, a new type of kingship emerged. Less ambitious than that in the east, it proved more enduring, surviving the centrifugal forces of the fourteenth and fifteenth centuries to emerge as the foundation of the nation-state.

The fourteenth and fifteenth centuries, with their demographic collapse, warfare, and dissension, placed enormous strains on these emerging forms of social and cultural organization. Individuals sought their own answers to the problems of life and death, using the legacy of the past, but using it in novel and creative ways. Mystics and heretics sought God without benefit of traditional religious hierarchies, and poets and philosophers sought personal expression outside the confines of inherited tradition.

The legacy of the Middle Ages was a complex and ambiguous one. The thousand-year synthesis of classical, barbarian, and Christian traditions did not disappear. The bonds holding this world together were not yet broken, but the last centuries of the Middle Ages bequeathed a critical detachment from this heritage, expressed in the revolts of peasants and workers, the preaching of radical religious reformers, and the poems of mystics and visionaries.

FURTHER READING

General Reading

Daniel Waley, *Later Medieval Europe* (London: Longman, 1975). A brief introduction with a focus on Italy.

* Johan Huizinga, *The Waning of the Middle Ages* (New York: St. Martins Press, 1954). An old but still powerful interpretation of culture and society in the Burgundian court in the late Middle Ages.

The Invention of the State

* Joseph R. Strayer, *On the Medieval Origins of the Modern State* (Princeton, NJ: Princeton University Press, 1970). A very brief but imaginative account of medieval statecraft by a leading French institutional historian.

John W. Baldwin, *The Government of Philip Augustus: Foundations of French Royal Power in the Middle Ages* (Berkeley, CA: University of California Press, 1986). A detailed but important study of the crucial reign of Philip II.

* Horst Fuhrmann, *Germany in the High Middle Ages, c. 1050-1200* (New York: Cambridge University Press, 1986). A fresh synthesis of German history by a leading German historian.

M. T. Clanchy, *England and Its Rulers, 1066-1272* (New York: B & N Imports, 1983). A good, recent survey of English political history.

War and Politics in the Later Middle Ages

* C. T. Allmand, *The Hundred Years War: England and France at War c. 1300-c. 1450* (New York: Cambridge University Press, 1988). A recent, brief introduction to the Hundred Years' War by a British historian.

* Joachim Leuschner, *Germany in the Late Middle Ages* (Amsterdam: Elsevier, 1980). An introduction to late medieval German history.

Richard W. Kaeuper, *War, Justice and Public Order: England and France in the Later Middle Ages* (Oxford: Oxford University Press, 1988). A fine analysis of the effects of war on England and France.

Life and Death in the Later Middle Ages

* Philip Zieger, *The Black Death* (New York: Harper & Row, 1969). A reliable introduction to the plague in the fourteenth century.

H. A. Miskimin, *The Economy of Early Renaissance Europe, 1300-1460* (New York: Cambridge University Press, 1975). An accessible introduction to the economic history of the later Middle Ages.

* Edith Ennen, *The Medieval Town* (New York: North-Holland Publishing Co., 1979). A brief history of medieval cities by a German specialist.

Georges Duby, ed., *A History of Private Life Volume 2. Revelations of the Medieval World* (Cambridge, MA: Harvard University Press, 1988). A series of provocative essays on the origins of privacy and the individual.

Bronislaw Geremek, *Power or Pity: Europe and the Poor From the Middle Ages to the Present* (forthcoming). A history of the origins of public welfare, focusing on the late Middle Ages.

* Michel Mollat and Philippe Wolff, *The Popular Revolutions of the Late Middle Ages* (London: Allen and Unwin, 1973). An accessible history of late medieval revolts, focusing on those of medieval cities.

The Spirit of the Later Middle Ages

* Geoffrey Barraclough, *The Medieval Papacy* (New York: W. W. Norton, 1968). A brief overview of the papacy.

*Emmanuel Le Roy Ladurie, *Montaillou: the Promised Land of Error* (New York: G. Braziller, 1978). A brilliant if controversial view of a medieval village as revealed through testimony given the Inquisition.

* Heiko A. Oberman, *The Harvest of Medieval Theology* (Cambridge, MA: Labyrinth Press, 1963). A technical but rewarding account of late medieval theology.

Howard Kaminsky, *A History of the Hussite Revolution* (Berkeley, CA: University of California Press, 1967). The best account of the Hussite movement.

Gordon Leff, *Heresy in the Later Middle Ages* (Manchester: Manchester University Press, 1967). A survey of heretical movements in the fourteenth and fifteenth centuries.

* Caroline Walker Bynum, *Holy Feast and Holy Fast: The Religious Significance of Food to Medieval Women* (Berkeley, CA: University of California Press, 1987). An imaginative and scholarly examination of the role of food in the spirituality of medieval women.

E. F. Chaney, *Franáois Villon in His Environment* (Oxford: Oxford University Press, 1946). An old but still valuable study of Villon and his world.

H. S. Bennett, *Chaucer and the Fifteenth Century* (Oxford: Oxford University Press, 1961). An accessible historical introduction to Chaucer.

John Freccero, *Dante and the Poetics of Conversion* (Cambridge, MA: Harvard University Press, 1986). A serious and rewarding study of Dante by an acknowledged master.

* Indicates paperback edition available.

CHAPTER 14

The Americas on the Eve of Invasion

KEY TERMS

Mesoamerica	*calpulli*
Toltec	*pipiltin*
Aztec	*Inca*
Tenochtitlan	*Andes*
chinampas	*quipu*

DISCUSSION QUESTIONS

What role did religion play in Aztec government and society?

Compare and contrast Inca and Aztec motives for conquest and how they governed their empires.

During the postclassic period, societies in the Americas remained entirely separate from those of the Old World. Some displayed features similar to the great centers of Asia and the Mediterranean in that they were able to build on earlier precedents from the classic period. Thus, Mesoamerican civilizations formed large cities, based on elaborate political and economic organization, that would later dazzle European intruders much as Constantinople or the great cities of China did. But these similarities were accidental, and they were outweighed by the vast differences that resulted from American isolation.

As in the classical centuries, American societies continued to display extraordinary diversity. Other continuities marked the pre-Columbian experience up to the year of Columbus's arrival and indeed beyond. Great American civilizations were marked by elaborate cultural systems and a highly developed agriculture, yielding a distinctive array of foods. The postclassic period saw significant changes in the Americas also, particularly in the increasingly extensive organization of agriculture and in the people's ability to form larger political units.

By 1500, the Americas were densely populated in many places by Indian peoples long indigenous to the New World. The term *Indian* is, of course, a misnomer created by Columbus when he thought he had reached the Indies, but the label is also somewhat misleading because it implies a certain recognition of commonality among the peoples of the Americas that did not exist until after the arrival of Europeans. *Indian* as a term to describe all the peoples of the Americas could have a meaning only when there were non-Indians to apply it. Still, the term has been used for so long—and is still in use by many Native Americans today—that we will continue to use it.

As should already be clear, there were many Indian peoples with a vast array of cultural achievements. This variety of cultural patterns and ways of life of pre-Columbian civilizations prohibits a detailed discussion of each, but we can concentrate our attention on a few areas where major civilizations developed, based on earlier achievements. By concentrating on these regions we can demonstrate the continuity of civilization in the Americas. We shall examine in some detail Mesoamerica, especially central Mexico, and the Andean heartland. In both these areas great imperial states were in place when European expansion brought them into direct and continual contact with the Old World. We shall also discuss in less detail a few areas influenced by the centers of civilization—and some whose development seems to have been independent of them—in order to provide an overview of the Americas on the eve of invasion.

Postclassic Mesoamerica, 1000–1500 C.E.

Chief among the civilizations that followed the collapse of Teotihuacan and the abandonment of the classical Maya cities in the 8th century C.E. were the Toltecs and later the Aztecs, who built on the achievements of their classic predecessors but rarely surpassed them except in the areas of political and military organization. The Toltecs created a large empire whose influence extended far beyond central Mexico. In the 15th century, the Aztecs rose from humble beginnings to create an extensive empire organized for war, motivated by fervent religious zeal, and based on a firm agrarian base.

The collapse of Teotihuacan in central Mexico and the abandonment of the classical Maya cities in the 8th century C.E. signaled a significant political and cultural change in Mesoamerica.

MESOAMERICA	**1200–1500** Mississippian culture flourishes **1000** Toltec conquest of Chichén Itzá and influence in Yucatan **1150** Fall of Tula, disintegration of Toltec Empire **968** Tula established by Toltecs
ANDEAN WORLD	**900–1465** Chimor Empire based on Chan Chan on north coast **900** End of Intermediate Horizon and decline of Tihuanaco and Huari
	900 C.E. **1150** C.E.

In central Mexico, nomadic peoples from beyond the northern frontier of the sedentary agricultural area took advantage of the political vacuum to move into the richer lands. Among these peoples were the *Toltecs,* who established a capital at Tula in about 968. They adopted many cultural features from the sedentary peoples and added to them a strongly militaristic ethic. This included the cult of sacrifice and war that is often portrayed in Toltec art. Later Mesoamerican peoples, such as the *Aztecs,* had some historical memory of the Toltecs and thought of them as culture heroes, the givers of civilization. Thus, being able to trace one's lineage back to the Toltecs later became a highly prized pedigree. The archaeological record, however, indicates that Toltec accomplishments were often fused or confused with those of Teotihuacan in the memory of the Toltec's successors.

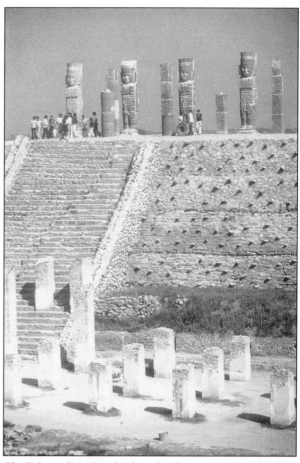

The Toltec political and cultural influence spread from its capital at Tula in northern Mexico (shown here) to places as far south as Chichén Itzá in Yucatan.

The Toltec Heritage

Among the legends that survived about the Toltecs were those of *Topiltzin,* a Toltec leader and apparently a priest dedicated to the god *Quetzalcoatl* (the Feathered Serpent), who later became confused with the god himself in the legends. Apparently, Topiltzin, a religious reformer, was involved in a struggle for priestly or political power with another faction. When he lost, Topiltzin and his followers went into exile, promising to return in the future to claim his throne on the same date according to the cyclical calendar system. Supposedly, Topiltzin and his followers sailed for Yucatan; there is considerable evidence of Toltec influence in that region. The legend of Topiltzin-Quetzalcoatl was well known to the Aztecs and may have influenced their response when the Europeans later arrived.

The Toltecs created an empire that extended over much of central Mexico, and their influence spread far beyond the region. About 1000 C.E., *Chichén Itzá* in Yucatan was conquered by Toltec warriors, and it and several other cities were then ruled for a long time by central Mexican dynasties or by Maya rulers under Toltec influ-

25 Aztecs established in central xico; Tenochtitlan founded

1434–1472 Rule of Nezhualcoyotl at Texcoco

1434 Creation of triple alliance

1440–1469 Moctezuma I

1502–1520 Moctezuma II

1350 Incas established in Cuzco area

1434–1471 Great expansion under Inca Pachacuti

1438 Incas dominate Cuzco and southern highlands

1471–1493 Inca Topac Yupanqui increases areas under control

1493–1527 Huayna Capac expands into Ecuador; his death results in civil war

.E.

1450 C.E.

ence. Some Maya states in Guatemala, such as the Quiché kingdom, also had Toltecized ruling families.

Toltec influence spread northward as well. Obsidian mines were exploited in northern Mexico, and the Toltecs may have traded for turquoise in the American Southwest. It has been suggested that the great Anasazi adobe town at Chaco Canyon in New Mexico was abandoned when the Toltec Empire fell and the trade in local turquoise ended.

The Aztec Rise to Power

The Toltec Empire lasted until about 1150, at which time it was apparently destroyed by nomadic invaders from the north, who also seem to have sacked Tula about that date. After the fall of Tula, the center of population and political power in central Mexico shifted to the valley of Mexico and especially to the shores of the large chain of lakes in that basin. The three largest lakes were connected by marshes; together they provided a rich aquatic environment. While the eastern lakes tended to be brackish from the minerals that emptied in them from the surrounding rivers, the southern and western portions contained fresh water. The shores of the lakes were dotted with settlements and towns. A dense population lived around the lakes to take advantage of their life-giving water for agriculture, the fish and aquatic plants and animals, and the advantages of transportation. Of the approximately 3000 square miles in the basin of the valley, about 400 square miles were under water.

The lakes became the cultural heartland and population center of Mexico in the postclassic period. In the unstable world of post-Toltec Mesoamerica, various peoples and cities jockeyed for supremacy of the lakes and the advantages they offered. The winners of this struggle, the Aztecs (or as they called themselves, the Mexica), eventually built a great empire, but when they emerged on the historical scene they were the most unlikely candidates for power.

From their obscure origins, the Aztec rise to power and their formation of an imperial state was as spectacular as it was rapid. According to some of their legends, the Mexica had once inhabited the central valley and had known agriculture and the "civilized" life but had lived in exile to the north in a place called Aztlan (from whence we get the name Aztec). This may be an exaggeration by people who wished to lay claim to a distinguished heritage. Other sources indicate that the Aztecs were simply one of the nomadic tribes that used the political anarchy, following the fall of the Toltecs, to penetrate into the area of sedentary agricultural peoples. Like the ancient Egyptians, the Aztecs rewrote history to suit their purposes.

What seems clear is that the Aztecs were a group of about 10,000 people who migrated to the shores of Lake Texcoco in the central valley of Mexico around the year 1325. After the fall of the Toltec Empire, the central valley was inhabited by a mixture of peoples—Chichimec migrants from the northwest and various groups of sedentary agriculturalists. These peoples were divided into small political units that claimed greater or lesser authority on the basis of their military power and their connections to Toltec culture or Toltec descendants. Many of these peoples spoke *Nahuatl,* the language the Toltecs had spoken. The Aztecs too spoke this language, a fact that made their rise to power and their eventual claims to legitimacy more acceptable.

In this period, the area around the lake was dominated by several tribes organized into city-states. The city of Azcapotzalco was the real power but was challenged by an alliance centered in the city of Texcoco. Another city, Culhuacan, which had been part of the Toltec Empire, used its position as legitimate heir to the Toltecs as a means of creating alliances by marrying its princes and princesses to more powerful but less distinguished states. This was a world of political maneuver and state marriages, competing powers and shifting alliances.

An intrusive and militant group, such as the Aztecs, were distrusted and disliked by the dominant powers of the area, but their fighting skills could be put to use, and this made them attractive as mercenaries or allies. For about a century the Aztecs wandered around the shores of the lake, being allowed to settle for a while and then driven out by more powerful neighbors.

In a period of militarism and warfare, the Aztecs had a reputation as tough warriors and fanatical followers of their gods, to whom they offered continual human sacrifices. This reputation made them both valued and feared. Their own legends foretold that their wanderings would end when they saw an eagle perched on a cactus with a serpent in its beak. Supposedly, this sign was seen on a marshy island in Lake Texcoco, and there, on that island and one nearby, the Aztecs settled. The city of *Tenochtitlan* was founded about 1325, and on the neighboring island the city of *Tlatelolco* was established shortly thereafter. The two cities eventually grew together, although they maintained separate administrations.

From this secure base the Aztecs began to take a more active role in regional politics. Azcapotzalco and Texcoco, two powerful city-states, were locked in a struggle, and the Aztecs now began to serve Azcapotzalco as mercenaries. This alliance brought pros-

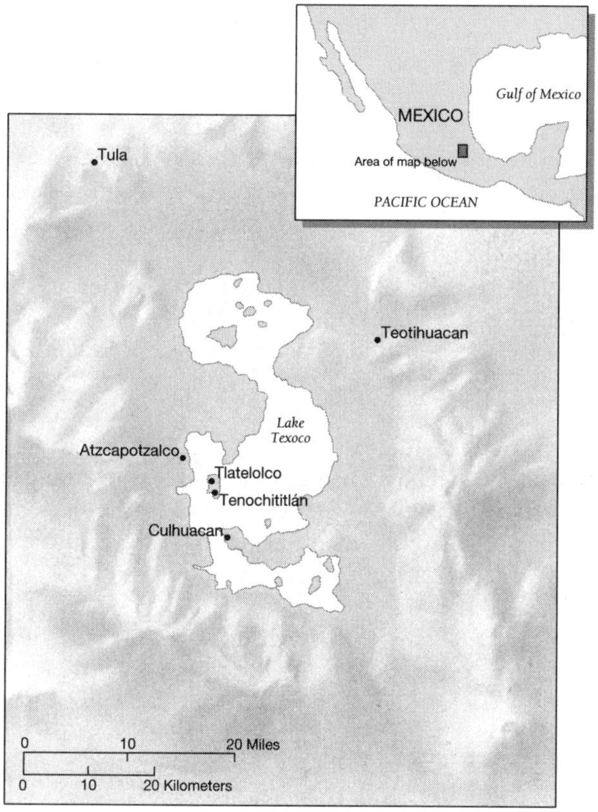

Central Mexico and Lake Texcoco

perity to the Aztecs, especially to their ruler and the warrior nobility, which was now acquiring lands and tribute from conquered towns. By 1428, however, the Aztecs had rebelled against Azcapotzalco and had joined with Texcoco in destroying it. From that victory the Aztecs emerged as an independent power. In 1434, Tenochtitlan, Texcoco, and a smaller city, Tlacopan, joined together in a triple alliance that exercised control over much of the central plateau. In reality, Tenochtitlan and the Aztecs dominated their allies and controlled the major share of the tribute and lands taken.

The Aztec Social Contract

According to the Aztec accounts of this history, a social and political transformation had also taken place. The conquest of Azcapotzalco assured the position of the nobility. Moreover, the ruler of Tenochtitlan emerged from this process no longer as a spokesman for a general council but as a supreme ruler with wide powers. Succeeding rulers expanded that power and the boundaries of Aztec control, although a few independent states remained within central Mexico. Aztec domination extended from the Tarascan frontier southward to the Maya area. Subject peoples were forced to pay tribute, surrender lands, and sometimes do military service for the growing Aztec Empire.

Aztec society had been transformed in the process of expansion and conquest. From a loose association of clans, the Mexica had become a stratified society under the authority of a supreme ruler of great power. A central figure in these changes was *Tlacaelel,* a man who served as a sort of prime minister and advisor under three rulers from 1427 to his death around 1480. Under his direction, the histories were rewritten and the Mexica were given a self-image as a people chosen to serve the gods. Human sacrifice, long a part of Mesoamerican religion, was greatly expanded under his direction into a cult of enormous proportions in which the military class played a central role as suppliers of war captives to be used as sacrificial victims. It was also a policy of Tlacaelel to leave a few territories unconquered so that periodic "flower wars" could be staged in which both sides could obtain captives for sacrifice. Whatever the religious motivations of this cult, Tlacaelel and the Aztec rulers manipulated it as an effective means of political terror. By the time of Moctezuma II, the Aztec state was dominated by a king who represented civil power and served as a representative of the gods on earth. The cult of human sacrifice and conquest was united with the political power of the ruler and the nobility.

Religion and the Ideology of Conquest

Aztec religion incorporated many features that had long been part of the Mesoamerican system of beliefs. Religion was a vast, uniting, and sometimes oppressive force in which little distinction was made between the world of the gods and the natural world. The traditional deities of Mesoamerica—the gods of rain, fire, water, corn, the sky, and the sun, many of whom had been worshiped as far back as the time of Teotihuacan—were known and venerated among the Aztecs. There were at least 128 major deities, but the number of gods, in fact, seemed innumerable, for often each deity had a female consort or feminine form, because a basic duality was recognized in all things. Moreover, gods might have different forms or manifestations, somewhat like the avatars of the Hindu deities. Often each god had at least five aspects, each associated with one of the cardinal directions and the center. Certain gods were thought to be the patrons of specific cities, ethnic groups, or occupations. This extensive pantheon was supported by a round of yearly festivals and a highly complex ceremonialism that involved various forms of feasting and dancing along with penance and sacrifice.

This bewildering array of gods can be organized into three major themes or cults. The first were the gods of fertility and the agricultural cycle, such as *Tlaloc,* or the god of rain (called Chac by the Maya), and the gods and goddesses of water, maize, and fertility. A second theme centered on the creator deities, the great gods and goddesses who had brought the universe into being. The story of their actions played a central role in Aztec cosmography. Tonatiuh, the warrior god of the sun, and Tezcatlipoca, the god of the night sky, were among the most powerful and respected gods among the peoples of central Mexico. Much of Aztec abstract and philosophical thought was devoted to the theme of creation. Finally, the cult of warfare and sacrifice built on the preexisting Mesoamerican traditions that had been expanding since Toltec times but which, under the militaristic Aztec state, became the cult of the state. *Huitzilopochtli,* the Aztec tribal patron, became the central figure of this cult, but it included Tezcatlipoca, Tonatiuh, and other gods as well.

The Aztecs revered the great traditional deities—such as Tlaloc and Quetzalcoatl, the ancient god of civilization—so holy to the Toltecs, but their own tribal deity, Huitzilopochtli, became paramount. The Aztecs identified him with the old sun god, and they saw him as a warrior in the daytime sky fighting to give life and warmth to the world against the forces of the night. In order to carry out that struggle, the sun needed strength—and just as the gods had sacrificed themselves for humankind, the nourishment the gods needed most was that which was most precious: human life in the form of hearts and blood. The great temple of Tenochtitlan was dedicated to both Huitzilopochtli and Tlaloc. The tribal deity of the Aztecs and the ancient agricultural god of the sedentary peoples of Mesoamerica were thus united.

In fact, while human sacrifice had long been a part of Mesoamerican religion, it had expanded considerably in the postclassic period of militarism. Warrior cults and the militaristic images of jaguars and eagles devouring human hearts were characteristic of Toltec art. The Aztecs simply took an existing tendency and carried it to an unprecedented scale. Both the types and frequency of sacrifice increased, and a whole symbolism and ritual, which included ritual cannibalism, developed as part of the cult. How much of Aztec sacrifice was the result of religious conviction and how much was imposed as a tac-

Human sacrifice existed among many Mesoamerican peoples, but the Aztecs apparently expanded its practice for political reasons and religious beliefs.

tic of terror and political control by the rulers and the priest class is a question still open to debate. Beneath the surface of this polytheism, there was, however, also a sense of spiritual unity. *Nezhualcoyotl,* the king of Texcoco, composed hymns to the "lord of the close vicinity," an invisible creative force that supported all the gods. Yet, his conception of a kind of monotheism, much like that of Pharaoh Akhenaten in Egypt, was too abstract and never gained great popularity.

While the bloody aspects of Aztec religion have gained much attention, we must also realize that the Aztecs concerned themselves with many of the great religious and spiritual questions that have preoccupied other civilizations: Is there life after death? What is the meaning of life? What does it mean to live a good life? Do the gods really exist?

Nezhualcoyotl, whose poetry survived in oral form and was written down in the 16th century, wondered about life after death:

Do flowers go to the land of the dead?
In the Beyond, are we dead or do we still live?
Where is the source of light, since that which gives life hides itself?

He also wondered about the existence of the gods:

Are you real, are you fixed?
Only You dominate all things
The Giver of Life.
Is this true?
Perhaps, as they say, it is not true.

Aztec religious art and poetry is filled with images of flowers, birds, and song—all of which the Aztecs greatly admired—as well as human hearts and blood: the "precious water" needed to sustain the gods. It is this mixture of images that makes the symbolism of Aztec religion so difficult for modern observers to understand.

Aztec religion depended on a complex mythology that explained the birth and history of the gods and their relation to peoples and on a religious symbolism that infused all aspects of life. As we have seen, the Mesoamerican calendar system was a religious one, and many ceremonies coincided with particular points in the calendar cycle. Moreover, the Aztecs also believed in a cyclical view of history and believed that the world had been destroyed four times before and would be destroyed again. Thus, there was a certain fatalism in Aztec thought and a premonition that eventually the sacrifices would be insufficient and the gods would again bring catastrophe.

Feeding the People: The Economy of the Empire

Feeding the great population of Tenochtitlan and the Aztec confederation in general depended on traditional forms of agriculture and on innovations developed by the Aztecs. Lands of conquered peoples were often appropriated, and food was sometimes demanded as tribute. In fact, the quantities of maize, beans, and other foods brought into Tenochtitlan annually were staggering. In and around the lake, however, the Aztecs adopted an ingenious system of irrigated agriculture by constructing *chinampas* for agriculture. These were beds of aquatic weeds, mud, and earth that had been placed in frames made of cane and rooted to the lake floor. They formed artificial floating islands about 5 meters long and 30 to 100 meters wide. This narrow, striplike construction allowed the water to reach all the plants, and willow trees were also planted at intervals to give shade and help fix the roots. Much of the land of Tenochtitlan itself was chinampa in origin, and in the southern end of the lake, over 20,000 acres of chinampas were constructed.

The yield from chinampa agriculture was high: four corn crops a year were possible. Apparently, this system of irrigated agriculture had been used in preclassic days, but a rise in the level of the lakes had made it impossible to continue. After 1200, however, lowering of the lake levels once again stimulated chinampa construction, which the Aztecs carried out on a grand scale. They also constructed dikes to close off the fresh waters in the southern and western parts of the lake from the brackish waters elsewhere. Today, the floating gardens of Xochimilco represent the remnants of the lake agriculture.

Production by the Aztec peasantry, and tribute, provided the basic foods. In each Aztec community, the local clan apportioned the lands, some of which were also set aside for support of the temples and the state. In addition, individual nobles might also have private estates, which were worked by servants or slaves from conquered peoples. Each community had periodic markets—according to various cycles in the calendar system, such as every 5 and 13 days—in which a wide variety of goods were exchanged. Cacao beans and gold dust were sometimes used as currency, but much trade was done as barter. The great market at Tlatelolco operated daily and was controlled by the special merchant class, or *pochteca,* which specialized in long-distance trade in luxury items

Agriculture was the basis of Aztec society, and a diet centered on maize sustained the dense populations of the Valley of Mexico.

such as plumes of tropical birds and cacao. The markets were highly regulated and under the control of inspectors and special judges. Despite the existence and importance of markets, this was not a market economy as we usually understand it.

The state controlled the use and distribution of many commodities and served to redistribute the vast levies of tribute received from subordinate peoples. Tribute levels were assigned according to whether the subject peoples had accepted Aztec rule or had fought against it. Those who surrendered paid less. Tribute payments, such as food, slaves, and sacrificial victims, served political and economic ends and provided a wide variety of commodities. Over 120,000 mantles of cotton cloth alone were collected as tribute each year and sent to Tenochtitlan. The Aztec state redistributed these goods. After the original conquests, it rewarded its nobility richly, but the commoners received far less. Still, the redistribution of many goods by the state interfered with the normal functioning of the market and created a peculiar state-controlled mixed economy.

Aztec Society in Transition

Aztec society became increasingly hierarchical as the empire grew and social classes with different functions developed, although the older organization based on calpullis never disappeared. Tribute was drawn from subject peoples, but Aztec society confronted technological constraints that made it difficult to maintain the extensive population of central Mexico.

Widening Social Gulf

During their wanderings, the Aztecs had been divided into seven calpulli, or clans—a form of organization that they would later expand and adapt to their imperial position. By the 16th century there were about 20 major calpulli; 40 associated ones were in Tenochtitlan alone. The calpulli were no longer only kinship groups but also residential groupings, which might include neighbors, allies, and dependents. Much of Aztec local life remained based on the calpulli, which performed important functions such as distributing land to heads of households, organizing labor gangs and military units in times of war, and maintaining a temple and school. Calpulli were governed by councils of family heads, but not all families were equal, nor were all calpulli of equal status.

The calpulli had obviously been the ancient and basic building block of Aztec society. In the origins of Aztec

CLOSEUP

Tenochtitlan, the Foundation of Heaven

The city-state with its ruler-spokesman was a key central Mexican concept, and it applied to Tenochtitlan, the Aztec capital. Tenochtitlan became a great metropolis, with a central zone of palaces and white-washed temples surrounded by adobe brick residential districts, smaller palaces, and markets. The craftsmanship and architecture were outstanding. Hernán Cortés, the Spanish conqueror who viewed the city, personally reported, "The stone masonry and the woodwork are equally good; they could not be bettered anywhere." There were gardens, and a zoo was kept for the ruler. The nobility had houses two stories high, sometimes with gardens on the roofs.

Tlatelolco, at first a separate island city, was eventually incorporated as part of Tenochtitlan. It too had impressive temples and palaces, and its large market remained the most important place of trade and exchange. By 1519, the city covered about five square miles. It had a population of 150,000, larger than contemporary European cities such as Seville or Paris.

Its island location gave Tenochtitlan a peculiar character. Set in the midst of a lake, the city was connected to the shores by four broad causeways and was crisscrossed by canals that allowed the constant canoe traffic on the lake access to the city. Each city ward, controlled by a *calpulli*, or kin group, maintained its neighborhood temples and civic buildings. The structural achievement was impressive. A Spanish foot soldier who saw it in 1519 wrote:

> Gazing on such wonderful sights, we did not know what to say, or whether what appeared before us was real, for on one side, on the land, there were great cities, and in the lake ever many more, and the lake was crowded with canoes, and in the cause-way were many bridges at intervals, and in front of us stood the great city of Mexico. . . .

Tenochtitlan was the heart of an empire and drew tribute and support from its allies and dependents, but in theory it was still just a city-state ruled by a headman, just like the other 50 or more city-states that dotted the central plateau. Even so, the Aztecs called it the "foundation of heaven," the basis of their might. Present-day Mexico City rises on the site of the former Aztec capital.

The great Aztec capital of Tenochtitlan was dominated by the pyramid and twin temples of Huitzilopochtli shown here in a modern miniature reconstruction.

society every person—noble and commoner—had belonged to a calpulli, but Aztec power increased and the rule of the empire expanded. The calpulli had been transformed, and other forms of social stratification had emerged. Legends of the Aztecs' origins emphasized that at one time they had all been peasants and had worked for others. As Aztec power expanded, a class of nobility, the *pipiltin*, emerged, based on certain privileged families in the most distinguished calpulli. Originating from the lineages that headed calpulli—especially those that had married into non-Mexica families or could claim Toltec background—and by marriages, military achievements, or service to the state, this group of nobility accumulated high office, private lands, and other advantages. The most prominent families in the calpulli, those who had dominated leadership roles and formed a kind of local nobility, were eventually overshadowed by the military and administrative nobility of the Aztec state.

While some commoners might receive promotion to noble status, most nobles were born into the class—although birth merely qualified an individual for high position, which ultimately depended on performance and ability. Nobles controlled the priesthood and the military leadership. The military, in fact, was organized into various ranks based on experience and success in taking captives. Military virtues were linked to the cult of sacrifice and infused the whole society; they became the justification for the nobility's predominance and the ideology of the nobility's identity. The "flowery death," or death while taking prisoners for the sacrificial knife, was the fitting end to a noble life and assured eternity in the highest heaven—a reward also promised to women who died in childbirth. The military was highly ritualized. There were orders of warriors: the jaguar, eagle, and other groups each had a distinctive uniform and ritual and fought together as units. Distinctive banners, cloaks, and other insignia marked off the military ranks.

The social gulf that separated the nobility from the commoners was widening as the empire grew and the pipiltin accumulated the lands and tribute that the expansion implied. Egalitarian principles that may have once existed in Aztec life disappeared—a situation similar to what happened among the warring German tribes of early medieval Europe. Social distinctions were made apparent by the use of, and restrictions on, clothing, hairstyles, uniforms, and other outward symbols of rank. The imperial family became the most distinguished of the pipiltin families.

As the nobility broke free from their old calpulli and acquired private lands, a new class of workers was created to serve as laborers on these lands. These

In the militarized society of the Aztec Empire, warriors were organized into regiments and groups distinguished by their distinctive uniforms. They gained rank and respect by capturing enemies for sacrifice.

mayeques, or serfs, were sometimes from dependent clans or more often from conquered peoples. Unlike the commoners attached to the land-controlling calpulli, the mayeques did not control land and worked at the will of others. Their status was low, but it was still above that of the slaves, who might have been war captives, persons punished for crimes, or those who had sold themselves into bondage to escape hunger. The mayeques often did domestic work, and while they could buy their freedom, they could also be offered as sacrifices by their owner. Together, the mayeques and the slaves formed a growing sector of the population, whose situation was directly tied to the fortunes of the nobility and the strength of the Aztec Empire and who had little to gain from its success. Finally, there were other social groups. The scribes, artisans, and healers all constituted part of a kind of intermediate group, especially important in the larger cities. The long-distance merchants formed a sort of calpulli with their own patron gods, privileges, and internal divisions. They sometimes served as spies or agents for the Aztec military, but despite this role and their wealth, they were subject to restrictions that hindered their entry into or rivalry with the nobility.

It is possible to see an emerging conflict between the nobility and the commoners and to interpret this as a class struggle, but some specialists emphasize that to interpret Aztec society on that basis is to impose Western concepts on a different reality. Corporate bodies, such as the calpulli, temple maintenance associations, and occupational groups, cut across class and remained important in Aztec life. Competition between corporate groups was often more apparent and more violent than competition between social classes.

Overcoming Technological Constraints

Membership in society was defined by participation in various wider groups, such as the calpulli or a specific social class, and by gender roles and definitions. Aztec women assumed a variety of roles. Peasant women helped in the fields, but their primary domain was the household, where child-rearing and cooking took up much time. Above all, skill at weaving was highly regarded. The responsibility for training young girls fell on the mature and elderly women of the calpulli. Marriages were often arranged between lineages, and virginity at marriage was highly regarded for young women. Polygamy existed among the nobility, but the peasants were monogamous. Aztec women could inherit property and pass it to their heirs. The rights of Aztec women seem to have been fully recognized, but in political and social life their role, while complementary to that of men, remained subordinate.

The technology of the Americas limited social development in a variety of ways. Here we can note a significant difference between the lives of women in Mesoamerica and in the Mediterranean world. In the maize-based economies of Mesoamerica, women spent six hours a day grinding corn by hand on stone boards, or metates, to prepare the household's food. Although similar hand techniques were used in ancient Egypt, they were eventually replaced by animal- or water-powered mills that turned wheat into flour. The miller or baker of Rome or medieval Europe could do the work of hundreds of women. Maize was among the simplest and most productive cereals to grow but among the most time-consuming to prepare. Without the wheel or suitable animals for power, the Indian civilizations were unable to free women from the 30 to 40 hours a week that went into the preparation of the basic food.

Finally, we must consider the size of the population of the Aztec state. Estimates have varied widely from as little as 1.5 million to over 25 million, but there is now considerable evidence that population density was high, resulting in a total population that was far greater than previously suspected. Historical demographers now estimate that the population of central Mexico under Aztec control reached over 20 million, excluding the Maya areas. This underlines the extraordinary ability of the Aztec state to intimidate and control such vast numbers of people.

A Tribute Empire

Each of the city-states was ruled by a speaker chosen from the nobility. The Great Speaker, the ruler of Tenochtitlan, became first among supposed equals. He was in effect the emperor, with great private wealth and public power, and was increasingly attributed with the symbols and status of a living god. His court was magnificent and surrounded with elaborate rituals. Those who approached him could not look him in the eye and were required to throw dirt upon their heads as a sign of humility. In theory he was elected, but his election was really a choice between siblings of the same royal family. The prime minister held a position of tremendous power and was usually a close relative of the ruler. There was a governing council; in theory, the rulers of the other cities of the triple alliance also had a say in government, but in reality most power was in the hands of the Aztec ruler and his chief advisor.

Over the course of a century of Aztec expansion, a social and political transformation had taken place. The position and nature of the old calpulli clans had changed radically, and a newly powerful nobility with a deified and virtually absolute ruler had emerged. Under the sponsorship of the prime minister, Tlacaelel, the ancient cult of military virtues had been elevated to a supreme position as the religion of the state, and the double purpose of securing increasing tribute for the state and obtaining more victims for Huitzilopochtli combined to drive further Aztec conquests.

The empire was never integrated, and local rulers often stayed in place to act as surrogates and tribute collectors for the Aztec overlords. In many ways the Aztec Empire was simply an expansion of long-existing

DOCUMENT

Aztec Women and Men

In the mid-16th century, Bernardino de Sahagún, a Spanish missionary, prepared an extraordinary encyclopedia of Aztec culture. His purpose was to gather this information to learn the customs and beliefs of the Indians and their language in order to better convert them. While Sahagún hated the Indian religion, he came to admire many aspects of their culture. His work, *The General History of the Things of New Spain,* is one of the first ethnographies and a remarkable compendium of Aztec culture. Sahagún used numerous Indian informants to tell him about the days before the European arrival, and so, even though this work dates from the postconquest era, it contains much useful information about earlier Aztec life.

In the following excerpts, the proper behavior for different roles of both women and men in Aztec society are described by the Aztecs themselves.

Father

One's father is the source of lineage. He is the sincere one. One's father is diligent, solicitous, compassionate, sympathetic, a careful administrator of his household. He rears, he teaches others, he advises, he admonishes one. He is exemplary; he leads a model life. He stores up for himself; he stores up for others. He cares for his assets; he saves for others. He is thrifty; he saves for the future, teaches thrift. He regulates, distributes with care, establishes order.

The bad father is incompassionate, negligent, unreliable. He is unfeeling . . . a shirker, a loafer, a sullen worker.

Mother

One's mother has children; she suckles them. Sincere, vigilant, agile, she is an energetic worker—diligent, watchful, solicitous, full of anxiety. She teaches people; she is attentive to them. She caresses, she serves others; she is apprehensive for their welfare; she is careful, thrifty—constantly at work.

The bad mother is evil, dull, stupid, sleepy, lazy. She is a squanderer, a petty thief, a deceiver, a fraud. Unreliable, she is one who loses things through neglect or anger, who heeds no one. She is disrespectful, inconsiderate, disregarding, careless. She shows the way to disobedience; she expounds nonconformity.

The Ruler

The ruler is a shelter—fierce, revered, famous, esteemed, well-reputed, renowned.

The good ruler is a protector: one who carries his subjects in his arms, who unites them, who brings them together. He rules, he takes responsibilities, assumes burdens. He carries his subjects in his cape; he bears them in his arms. He governs; he is obeyed. To him as a shelter, as refuge, there is recourse. . . .

The bad ruler is a wild beast, a demon of the air, an ocelot, a wolf—infamous, avoided, detested as a respecter of nothing. He terrifies with his gaze; he makes the earth rumble; he implants; he spreads fear. He is wished dead.

The Noble

The noble has a mother, a father. He resembles his parents. The good noble is obedient, cooperative, a follower of his parents' ways, a discreet worker; attentive, willing. He follows the ways of his parents; he resembles his father; he becomes his father's successor; he assumes his lot.

Mesoamerican concepts and institutions of government, and it was not unlike the subject city-states over which it gained control. These city-states, in turn, were often left relatively unchanged, provided they recognized Aztec supremacy and met their obligations of labor and tribute. Tribute payments served both an economic and a political function, concentrating power and wealth in the Aztec capital. Archeologists at the recent excavations of the Great Temple beneath the center of Mexico City have been impressed by the large number of offerings and objects that came from the farthest ends of the empire and beyond. At the frontiers, neighboring states, such as Michoacan, preserved their freedom; while within the empire, independent kingdoms, such as Tlax-

One of noble lineage is a follower of the exemplary life, a taker of the good example of others, a seeker, a follower of the exemplary life. He speaks eloquently; he is soft-spoken, virtuous, deserving of gratitude. He is noble of heart, gentle of word, discreet, well-reared, well-taught. He is moderate, energetic, inquiring, inquisitive. He scratches the earth with a thorn. He is one who fasts, who starves his entrails, who parches his lips. He provides nourishment to others. He sustains one, he serves food, he provides comfort. He is a concealer [of himself], a belittler of himself. He magnifies and praises others. He is a mourner for the dead, a doer of penances, a gracious speaker, devout, godly, desirable, wanted, memorable.

The bad noble is ungrateful and forgetful, a debaser, a disparager of things, contemptuous of others, arrogant, bragging. He creates disorder, glories over his lineage, extols his own virtues.

The Mature Common Woman

The good mature woman is candid. She is resolute, firm of heart, constant—not to be dismayed; brave like a man; vigorous, resolute, persevering—not one to falter. She is long-suffering; she accepts reprimands calmly—endures things like a man. She becomes firm—takes courage. She is intent. She gives of herself. She goes in humility. She exerts herself.

The bad woman is thin, tottering, weak—an inconstant companion, unfriendly. She annoys others, chagrins them, shames, oppresses one. She becomes impatient; she loses hope, becomes embarrassed—chagrined. Evil is her life; she lives in shame.

The Weaver of Designs

She concerns herself with using thread, works with thread. The good weaver of designs is skilled—a maker of varicolored capes, an outliner of designs, a blender of colors, a joiner of pieces, a matcher of pieces, a person of good memory. She does things dexterously. She weaves designs. She selects. She weaves tightly. She forms borders. She forms the neck. . . .

The bad weaver of designs is untrained—silly, foolish, unobservant, unskilled of hand, ignorant, stupid. She tangles the thread, she harms her work—she spoils it.

The Physician

The physician is a knower of herbs, of roots, of trees, of stones; she is experienced in these. She is one who conducts examinations; she is a woman of experience, of trust, of professional skill: a counselor.

The good physician is a restorer, a provider of health, a relaxer—one who makes people feel well, who envelops one in ashes. She cures people; she provides them health; she lances them; she bleeds them . . . pierces them with an obsidian lancet.

Questions: In what ways do the expectations for men and women differ in Aztec society? To what extent do the roles for men and women in Aztec society differ from our own? Did the Aztecs value the same characteristics as our own and other historical societies?

cala, maintained a fierce opposition to the Aztecs. There were many revolts against Aztec rule or a particular tribute burden, which the Aztecs often put down ruthlessly.

In general, the Aztec system was a success because it aimed at exerting political domination and not necessarily direct administrative or territorial control. In the long run, however, the increasing social stresses created by the rise of the pipiltin and the system of terror and tribute imposed over subject peoples were internal weaknesses that ultimately contributed to the Aztec Empire's collapse.

The Aztecs, then, represented a continuation of the long process of civilization in Mesoamerica. The civilizations of the classic era did not simply disappear in central Mexico or among the Maya in Yucatan and

Central America, but they were reinterpreted and adapted to new political and social realities. When Europeans arrived in Mexico, they assumed that what they found was the culmination of Indian civilization, when in fact it was the militarized afterglow of earlier achievements.

Twantinsuyu: World of the Incas

After about 1300 C.E. in the Andean cultural hearth, a new civilization emerged and eventually spread its control over the whole region. The *Inca* empire, or *Twantinsuyu,* was a highly centralized system, which integrated various ethnic groups into an imperial state. Extensive irrigated agriculture supported a state religion and a royal ancestor cult. With notable achievements in architecture and metallurgy, the Incas, like the Aztecs, incorporated many elements of the civilizations that preceded them.

Almost at the same time that the Aztecs extended their control over much of Mesoamerica, a great imperial state was rising in the Andean highlands, and it eventually held sway over an empire some 3000 miles in extent. The Inca Empire incorporated many aspects of previous Andean cultures but fused them together in new ways—and with a genius for state organization and bureaucratic control over peoples of different cultures and languages, it achieved a level of integration and domination previously unknown in the Americas.

Throughout the Andean cultural hearth, during the period following the breakup or disintegration of the large "horizon" states of Tihuanaco and Huari (ca. 550–1000 C.E.), several smaller regional states continued to exercise some power. Rather than the breakdown of power that took place in postclassic Mesoamerica, in the Andean zone many relatively large states continued to be important. Some states in the Andean highlands on the broad open areas near Lake Titicaca, and those states along rivers on the north coast, such as in the Moche valley, remained centers of agricultural activity and population density. This time in the ultimate development of the Andean imperial state was a period of considerable warring between rival local chiefdoms and small states and in some ways was an Andean parallel to the post-Toltec militaristic era in Mesoamerica. Of these states, the coastal kingdom of Chimor, centered on its capital of Chan Chan, emerged as the most powerful. Between 900 and its conquest by the Incas in 1465, it gained control of most of the north coast of Peru.

The Inca Rise to Power

While Chimor spread its control over 600 miles of the coast, in the southern Andean highlands, where there were few large urban areas, ethnic groups and politics struggled over the legacy of Tihuanaco. Among these groups were several related Quechua-speaking clans, or ayllus, living near Cuzco, an area that had been under the influence of Huari but had not been particularly important. Their own legends stated that ten related clans emerged from caves in the region and were taken to Cuzco by a mythical leader. Wherever their origins, by about 1350 C.E. they resided in and around Cuzco, and by 1438 they had defeated their hostile neighbors in the area. At this point under their ruler, or Inca, *Pachacuti* (1438–1471), they launched a series of military alliances and campaigns that brought them control of the whole area from Cuzco to the shores of Lake Titicaca.

Over the next 60 years, Inca armies were constantly on the march, extending control over a vast territory. Pachacuti's son and successor, *Topac Yupanqui* (1471–1493) conquered the northern coastal kingdom of Chimor by seizing its irrigation system, and he extended Inca control into the southern area of what is now Ecuador. At the other end of the empire, Inca armies reached the Maule River in Chile against stiff resistance from the Araucanian Indians. The next ruler, Huayna Capac (1493–1527) consolidated these conquests and suppressed rebellions on the frontiers. By the time of his death, the Inca Empire—or, as they called it, Twantinsuyu—stretched from what is now Colombia to Chile and eastward across Lake Titicaca and Bolivia to northern Argentina. Between 9 million and 13 million people of different ethnic backgrounds and languages came under Inca rule, a remarkable feat given the extent of the empire and the technology available for transportation and communication.

Conquest and Religion

What impelled the Inca conquest and expansion? The usual desire for economic gain and political power that we have seen in other empires provides one suitable explanation, but there may be others more in keeping with Inca culture and ideology. The cult of the ancestors was extremely important in Inca belief. Deceased rulers were

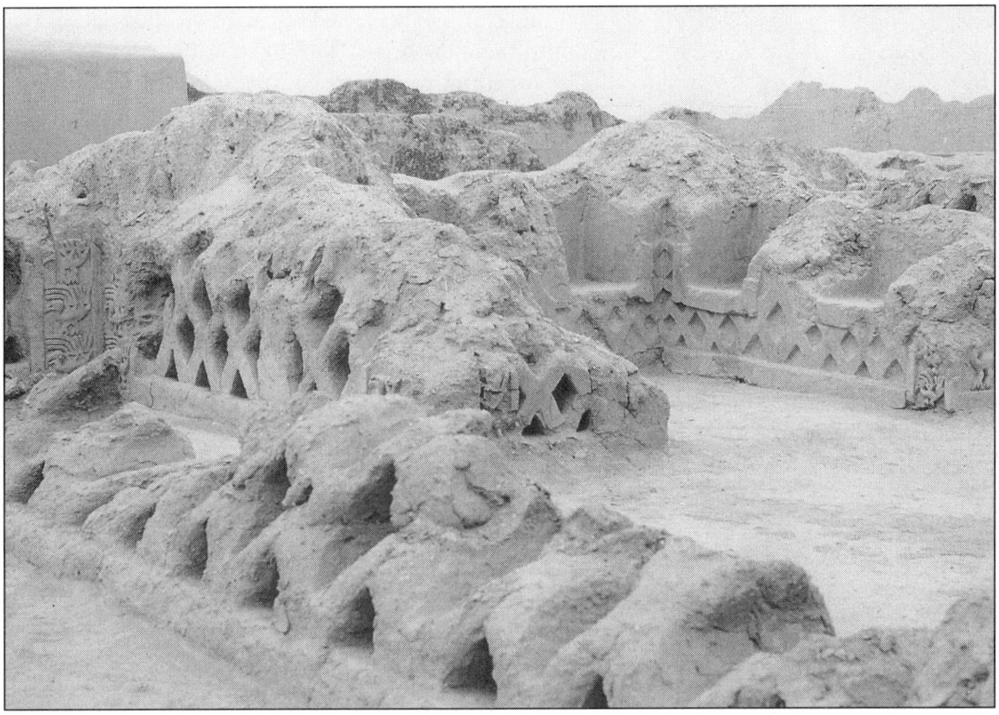

The great mud-walled city of Chan Chan in northern Peru, capital of the Chimu state, covered an area of six square kilometers. The Chimu Empire dominated the region prior to the rise of the Incas.

mummified and then treated as intermediaries with the gods, paraded in public during festivals, offered food and gifts, and consulted on important matters by special oracles. From the Chimor kingdom the Incas adopted the practice of royal *split inheritance* whereby all the political power and titles of the ruler went to his successor, but all his palaces, wealth, land, and possessions remained in the hands of his male descendants, who used them to support the cult of the dead Inca's mummy for eternity. Each new Inca, then, in order to ensure his own cult and place for eternity, needed to secure land and wealth, and these normally came as part of new conquests. In effect, the greater the number of past Inca rulers, the greater the number of royal courts to support and the greater the demand for labor, lands, and tribute. This system created a self-perpetuating need for expansion, tied directly to ancestor worship and the cult of the royal mummies, as well as tensions between the various royal lineages. In a way, the cult of the dead weighed increasingly heavily on the living.

Inca political and social life was infused with religious meaning. Like the Aztecs, the Incas held the sun to be the highest deity and considered the Inca to be the sun's representative on earth. The magnificent *Temple of the Sun* in Cuzco was the center of the state religion, and in its confines the mummies of the past Incas resided. The cult of the sun was spread throughout the empire, but the Inca did not prohibit the worship of local gods.

Other deities were also worshiped as part of the state religion. Viracocha, a creator god, was a favorite of Inca Pachacuti and remained important. Popular belief was based on a profound animism that endowed many natural phenomena with spiritual power. Mountains, stones, rivers, caves, or tombs and temples were considered to be huacas, or holy shrines. At these places, prayers were offered and sacrifices of animals, goods, and humans were made. In the Cuzco area, imaginary lines running from the Temple of the Sun organized the huacas into groups for which certain ayllus took responsibility. The temples were served by many priests and women dedicated to the preparation of cloth and food for sacrifice. The temple priests were mainly responsible for the great festivals and celebrations and for the divinations upon which state actions often depended.

The Techniques of Inca Imperial Rule

The Inca were able to keep control over their vast empire by using techniques and practices that assured either cooperation or subordination. The empire was

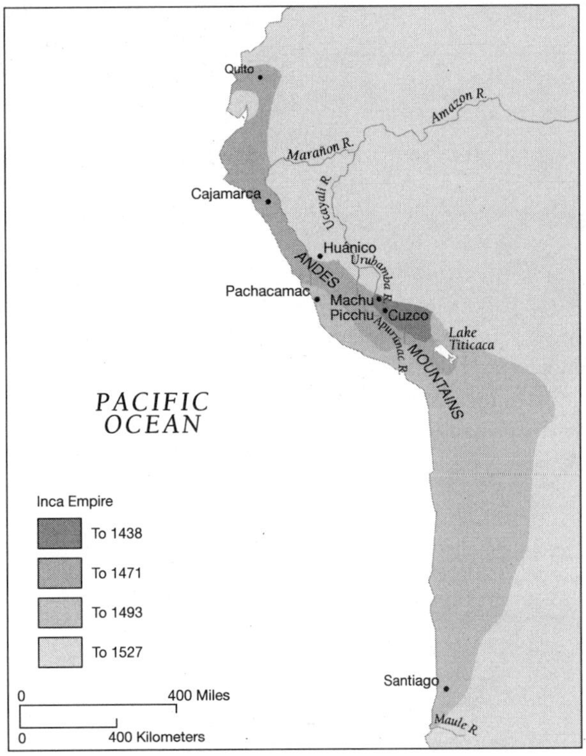

Inca Expansion

ruled by the Inca, who was considered virtually a god. He ruled from his court at Cuzco, which was also the site of the major temple; the high priest was usually a close relative. Twantinsuyu was divided into four great provinces, each under a governor, and then divided again. The Incas developed a state bureaucracy in which almost all the nobility played a role. While some chroniclers spoke of a state organization based on decimal units of 10,000, 1,000, 100, and smaller numbers of households to mobilize taxes and labor, recent research reveals that many local practices and variations were allowed to continue under Inca rule. Local rulers, or curacas, were allowed to maintain their position and were given privileges by the Inca in return for their loyalty. The curacas were exempt from tribute obligations and usually received labor or produce from those under their control. For insurance, the sons of conquered chieftains were taken to Cuzco for their education.

The Incas intentionally spread the Quechua language as a means of integrating the empire. The Incas also made extensive use of *mitmaq,* or colonists. Sometimes Quechua-speakers from Cuzco might be settled in a newly won area to provide an example and a garrison. On other occasions, a restive conquered population was moved to a new home. Throughout the empire, a complex system of roads was constructed, with bridges and causeways when needed. Along these roads, way stations, or *tambos,* were placed about a day's walk apart to serve as inns, storehouses, and supply centers for Inca armies on the move. Tambos also served as relay points for the system of runners who carried messages throughout the empire. The Inca probably maintained over 10,000 tambos.

The Inca Empire functioned to extract land and labor from subject populations. Conquered peoples were enlisted in the Inca armies under Inca officers and were rewarded with goods from new conquests. Subject peoples received access to goods not previously available to them, and the Inca state undertook large projects of building and irrigation that formerly would have been impossible. In return, the Incas demanded loyalty and tribute. The state claimed all resources and redistributed them. The Incas divided conquered areas into lands for the people, lands for the state, and lands for the sun—that is, for religion and the support of priests. There were also private estates held by some nobles.

With few exceptions the Incas, unlike the Aztecs, did not demand tribute in kind, but rather exacted labor on the lands assigned to the state and the religion. Communities were expected to take turns working on state and church lands and sometimes on building projects or in mining. These labor turns, or *mita,* were an essential aspect of Inca control. In addition, the Inca required women to weave high-quality cloth for the court and for religious purposes. The Incas provided the wool, but each household was required to produce cloth. Woven cloth, a great Andean art form, had political and religious significance. Some women were taken as concubines for the Inca; others were selected as servants at the temples, the so-called Virgins of the Sun. In all this, the Inca had an overall imperial system but remained sensitive to local variations, so that its application accommodated regional and ethnic differences.

In theory, each community aimed at self-sufficiency and depended on the state for goods difficult to acquire. The ayllus of each community controlled the land, and the vast majority of the male population were peasants and herdsmen. Women aided in the fields, wove cloth, and cared for the household. Roles and obligations were gender specific and theoretically equal and interdependent. Andean peoples recognized parallel descent, so that property rights within the ayllus and among the nobility passed in both the male and female lines. Women passed rights and property to daughters, men to sons. Whether

The role of women in Inca agriculture is emphasized in this 16th-century drawing of the symbolic irrigation of the fields. Complex Inca irrigation systems permitted the farming of steep hillsides and marginal lands.

in pre-Inca times women may have served as leaders of ayllus is open to question, but under the Incas this seems to have been uncommon. The Inca emphasis on military virtues reinforced the inequality of men and women, even though an ideology of complementarity of the sexes was very strong.

The concept of close cooperation of men and women was also reflected in the Inca view of the cosmos. Gods and goddesses were worshiped by men and women, but women felt a particular affinity for the moon and the goddesses of the earth and corn—the fertility deities. The Inca queen, the Inca's senior wife (who was usually also a sister of the Inca), was viewed as a link to the moon. Queen and sister of the sun, she represented imperial authority to all women. But despite an ideology of gender equality, Inca practice created a hierarchy of gender relationships that meshed with the dominance of the Inca state over subject peoples. This fact is supported, and the power of the empire over local ethnic groups is demonstrated, by the Incas' ability to select the most beautiful young women to serve the temples or be given to the Inca.

The integration of imperial policy with regional and ethnic diversity was a political achievement. Ethnic headmen were left in place, but over them were Inca administrators drawn from the Inca nobility in Cuzco. Reciprocity and verticality continued to characterize Andean groups as they came under Inca rule; reciprocity between the state and the local community was simply an added level. The Inca state could provide roads, irrigation projects, and hard-to-get goods. Maize, for example, was usually grown on irrigated land and was particularly important as a ritual crop. State-sponsored irrigation added to its cultivation. The Inca state manipulated the idea of reciprocity to extract labor power, and it dealt harshly with resistance and revolt. In addition to the ayllu peasantry, there was also a class of people, the *yanas,* who were removed from their ayllus and served permanently as servants, artisans, or workers for the Inca or the Inca nobility.

Members of the Inca nobility were greatly privileged, and those related to the Inca himself held the highest positions. The nobility were all drawn from the ten royal ayllus. In addition, the residents of Cuzco were given noble status to enable them to serve in high bureaucratic posts. The nobles were distinguished by dress and custom. Only they were entitled to wear the large ear spools that enlarged the ears and caused the Spaniards to later call them *orejones,* or "big ears." Noticeably absent in most of the Inca Empire was a distinct merchant class. Unlike Mesoamerica, where long-distance trade was so important, the Incas' emphasis on self-sufficiency and state regulation of production and surplus limited trade. Only in the northern areas of the empire, in the chiefdoms of Ecuador, the last region brought under Inca control, did a specialized class of traders exist.

The Inca imperial system, which controlled an area almost 3000 miles in extent, was a stunning achievement of statecraft, but like all empires it lasted only as long as it could control its subject populations and its own mechanisms of government. A system of royal multiple marriages as a way of forging alliances created rival claimants for power and the possibility of civil war. That is exactly what happened in the 1520s, just before the arrival of the Europeans. When the Spanish first arrived in Peru, they saw an empire weakened and wasted by civil strife.

Inca Cultural Achievements

The Incas drew on the artistic traditions of their Andean predecessors and the skills of subject peoples. Beautiful pottery and cloth were produced in specialized workshops. Inca metallurgy was among the most advanced in the Americas, and Inca artisans worked gold and silver with great technical skill. The Incas also used copper and some bronze for weapons and tools. Like the Mesoamerican peoples, the Incas made no practical use of the wheel, but unlike them, they had no system of writing. The Incas, however, did make use of a system of knotted strings, or *quipu,* with which numerical and perhaps other information could be recorded. It functioned something like an abacus, and with it the Incas took censuses and kept financial records. The Incas had a passion for numerical order, and the population was divided into decimal units from which population, military enlistment, and work details could be calculated. The existence of so many traits associated with civilization in the Old World and yet the absence of a system of writing among the Incas should make us realize the variations of human development and the dangers of becoming too attached to certain characteristics or cultural features in defining civilizations.

The Incas' genius was best displayed in their statecraft and in their architecture and public buildings. Inca stonecutting was remarkably accurate; the best buildings were constructed of large fitted stones without the use of masonry. Some of these buildings were immense. These constructions, the large agricultural terraces and irrigation projects, and the extensive system of roads were among the Incas' greatest achievements, displaying their technical ability and workmanship as well as their ability to mobilize large amounts of manpower.

Comparing Incas and Aztecs

Both the Inca and the Aztec empires were based on a long development of civilization that preceded them; and while in some areas of artistic and intellectual achievement, earlier peoples had surpassed their accomplishments, both represented the success of imperial and military organization. Both empires were based on intensive agriculture organized by a state that accumulated surplus production and then controlled the circulation of goods and their redistribution to groups or social classes. In both states, older semikinship-based institutions, the ayllu and the calpulli, were being transformed by the emergence of a social hierarchy in which the nobility was increasingly predominant. In both areas, this nobility was also the personnel of the state, so that the state organization was almost an image of society.

Table 14.1
A Population Estimate for the Western Hemisphere, 1492

Area	*Population in thousands*
North America	4,400
Mexico	21,400
Central America	5,650
Caribbean	5,850
Andes	11,500
Lowland South America	8,500
Total	57,300

Sources: William M. Deneven, *The Native Population of the Americas in 1492* (1976), 289–292; John D. Durand, "Historical Estimates of World Population," *Population and Development Review,* 3 (1957), 253–296; Russell Thornton, *American Indian Holocaust and Survival* (1987).

While the Incas attempted to create an overarching political state and made conscious attempts to integrate their empire as a unit (the Aztecs did less in this regard), both empires recognized local ethnic groups and political leaders and were willing to allow considerable variation from one group or region to another—that is, provided that Inca or Aztec sovereignty was recognized and tribute paid. Both the Aztecs and the Incas, like the Spaniards who followed them, found that their military power was less effective against nomadic peoples who lived on their frontiers. Essentially, the empires were created by the conquest of sedentary agricultural peoples and the extraction of tribute and labor from them.

We cannot overlook the considerable differences between Mesoamerica and the Andean region in terms of climate and geography nor ignore the differences between the Inca and Aztec civilizations. Trade and markets, for example, were far more developed in the Aztec Empire and earlier in Mesoamerica in general than in the Andean world. There were considerable differences in metallurgy, in writing systems, and in social definition and hierarchy. But within the context of world civilizations, it is probably best to view these two empires and the cultural areas they represent as variations of similar patterns and processes, of which sedentary agriculture is the most important. Basic similarities underlying the variations can also be seen in systems of belief and cos-

Table 14.2
World Population c. 1500

Area	*Population in thousands*
China	100,000–150,000
Indian subcontinent	75,000–150,000
Southwest Asia	20,000–30,000
Japan	15,000–20,000
Rest of Asia (except Russia)	15,000–30,000
Europe (except Russia)	60,000–70,000
Russia (USSR)	10,000–18,000
Northern Africa	6,000–12,000
Remainder of Africa	30,000–60,000
Oceania	1,000–2,000
Americas	57,000–72,000
Total	389,000–614,000

Sources: William M. Deneven, *The Native Population of the Americas in 1492* (1976), 289–292; John D. Durand, "Historical Estimates of World Population," *Population and Development Review,* 3 (1957), 253–296; Russell Thornton, *American Indian Holocaust and Survival* (1987).

mology and in social structure. Whether similar origins, direct or indirect contact between the areas, or parallel development in Mesoamerica and the Andean area explains the similarity remains to be explored. But the American Indian civilizations shared much with each other, and that factor plus their relative isolation from external cultural and biological influences gave them their peculiar character and ultimately their vulnerability. At the same time, their ability to survive the shock of conquest and to contribute to the formation of societies after conquest demonstrates much of their strength and resiliency. Long after the Aztec and Inca empires had ceased to exist, the peoples of the Andes and Mexico continue to draw on these cultural traditions.

The Other Indians

The civilizations of Mesoamerica and the Andes, and the imperial states in place at the moment of contact with the wider world, were high points of an Indian cultural achievement cut short by subsequent contact and conquest. The Americas, however, continued to be occupied by a wide variety of peoples who lived in different ways, ranging from highly complex sedentary agricultural empires to simple kin-based bands of hunters and gatherers.

Rather than a division between "primitive" and "civilized" Indians, it is more useful to consider series of gradations according to material culture and social complexity that also recognize similarities. Groups like the Incas had many things in common with the tribal peoples of the Amazon basin, such as the division into clans or into halves—that is, a division of villages or communities into two major groupings with mutually agreed-upon roles and obligations. Moreover, as we have seen, the diversity of ancient America forces a reconsideration of ideas of human development based on Old World examples. If social complexity is supposedly dependent on an agricultural base for society, that theory is not supported by the existence in the Americas of some groups of fishermen and hunters and gatherers, such as the Indians of the northwest coast of the United States and British Columbia, who developed hierarchical societies. For those who see control of water for agriculture as the starting point for political authority and the state, exceptions are provided by such societies as the Pimas of Colorado and some of the chiefdoms of South America, who practiced irrigated agriculture but did not develop states.

How Many Indians?

A major issue that has fascinated students of the Americas for centuries is the question of population size. For many years after the European conquests, many people discounted the early descriptions of large and dense Indian populations as the exaggeration of the conquerors and missionaries who wished to make their own exploits seem more impressive. In the early 20th century, the most repeated estimate of Indian population about 1492 was 8.4 million (4 million in Mexico, 2 million in Peru, and 2.4 million in the rest of the hemisphere). Since that time, new archaeological discoveries, a better understanding of the impact of disease on indigenous populations, new historical and demographic studies, and improved estimates of agricultural techniques and productivity have led to major revisions. Estimates still vary widely, and some have gone as high as 112 million at the time of contact. Despite disagreements, most scholars agree that Mesoamerica and the Andes supported the largest populations. Table 14.1 summarizes one of the most careful estimates, which places the total figure at over 57 million, although an American Indian demographer has adjusted this figure upward to 72 million.

These figures should be set in a global context. About 1500, the population of the rest of the world was probably about 500 million, of which China and India each had 75 to 100 million people and Europe had 60 to 70 million, a figure roughly equivalent to the Americas. The peoples of the Americas clearly made up a major segment of humanity.

Differing Cultural Patterns

While it is impossible to summarize the variety of cultural patterns and lifeways that existed in the Americas on the eve of contact, we can mention the major patterns outside the main civilizational areas. The area of northern South America and part of Central America was an intermediate area, which shared many features with the Andes and some with Mesoamerica and perhaps served at times as a point of cultural and material exchange between the two regions. In the mountain valleys of central Colombia large chiefdoms of the Muisca and Tairona peoples, based on sedentary agriculture, mobilized large numbers of peasant agriculturalists for building projects and extracted surpluses from them. Warfare seems to have been endemic in these societies, and there was a strong religious cult associated with political authority. In fact, with the exception of monumental architecture, the intermediate-zone chieftainships resemble the sedentary agriculture states in many ways.

Similar kinds of chieftainships based on sedentary agriculture were found elsewhere in the Americas. There is strong evidence of large and populous chieftainships along the Amazon, where the rich aquatic environment supported complex and perhaps hierarchical societies. The island Arawaks that Columbus first encountered in the Caribbean on the island of Hispaniola were agriculturalists organized in a hierarchical society and divided into chiefdoms. These Indian chiefdom-level societies bear a strong resemblance to the societies of Polynesia. On the bigger Caribbean islands, such as Hispaniola and Puerto Rico, chieftainships ruled over dense populations, which lived primarily from the production of manioc.

Agriculture was widely diffused throughout the Americas by 1500. Some peoples, like those of the eastern North American woodlands and the coast of Brazil, combined agriculture with hunting and fishing. Techniques such as slash-and-burn farming led to the periodic movement of villages when production declined. Social organization in these societies often remained without strong class divisions, craft specializations, or the demographic density of people who practiced permanent, intensive agriculture. Unlike Europe, Asia, and Africa, nomadic herdsmen were lacking in the Americas. However, throughout the Americas from Tierra del Fuego to the Canadian forests, peoples remained who lived in small, mobile, kin-based groups of hunters and gatherers. Their material culture was simple and their societies were more egalitarian.

Nowhere is the problem of American Indian diversity more apparent than in North America. In that vast continent perhaps as many as 200 languages were spoken by 1500, and a variety of cultures reflected Indian adaptation to different ecological situations. By that time, the concentrated towns of the Mississippian Mound Builder cultures had mostly been abandoned, and only a few groups in southeastern North America still maintained the social hierarchy and religious ideas of those earlier cultures. In the Southwest, the descendants of the Anasazi and other cliff dwellers had taken up residence in the adobe pueblos along the Rio Grande, where they practiced various forms of terracing and irrigation to support their agriculture. Their rich religious life, their artistic ceramic and weaving traditions, and their agricultural base reflected their own historical traditions.

Elsewhere in North America, most groups were hunters and gatherers or combined those activities with some agriculture. Sometimes an environment was so rich that complex social organization and artistic specialization could develop without an agricultural base. This was the case among the Indians of the northwest coast, who depended on the rich resources of the sea. In other cases, technology was a limiting factor. The tough grasses of the prairies could not be easily farmed without the use of metal plows, nor could the buffalo be effectively hunted prior to the European introduction of the horse. Thus, the Great Plains were only sparsely occupied.

Finally, we should note that while there was great variation among the Indian cultures, some aspects stood in marked contrast to contemporary societies in Europe and Asia. With the exception of the state systems of Mesoamerica and the Andes, most Indian societies were strongly kin-based. Communal action and ownership of resources, such as land or hunting grounds, were emphasized, and material wealth was often disregarded or placed in a ritual or religious context. It was not that these societies were necessarily egalitarian but rather that ranking was usually not based on wealth. Women, although often subordinate, in some societies held important political and social roles and usually played a central role in crop production. Indians tended to view themselves as part of the ecological system and not in control of it. These attitudes stood in marked contrast to those of the contemporary Eurasian civilizations.

American Indian Diversity in World Context

By the end of the 15th century, two great imperial systems had risen to dominate the two major centers of civilization in Mesoamerica and the Andes. Both of these empires were built on the achievements of their predecessors, and both reflected a militaristic phase in their area's development. These empires proved to be fragile—weakened by their own internal strains and the conflicts that any imperial system creates, but also limited by their technological inferiority when challenged by Eurasian civilization.

The Aztec and Inca empires were one end of a continuum of cultures that went from the most simple to the most complex. The Americas contained a broad range of societies, from great civilizations with millions of people to small bands of hunters. In many of these societies, religion played a dominant role in defining the relationship between people and their environment and between the individual and society. How these societies would have developed and what course the American civilizations might have taken in continued isolation remains an interesting and unanswerable question. The first European observers were simultaneously shocked by the "primitive" tribesmen and astounded by the wealth and accomplishments of civilizations like that of the Aztecs. Europeans generally saw the Indians as curiously anachronistic. In comparison with Europe and Asia, the Americas did seem strange—more like ancient Babylon or Egypt than contemporary China or Europe—except that without the wheel, large domesticated animals, the plow, and to a large extent metal tools and written languages, even that comparison is misleading. The relative isolation of the Americas had remained important in physical and cultural terms, but that isolation came to an end in 1492—often with disastrous results.

FURTHER READING

Alvin M. Josephy, Jr.'s *The Indian Heritage of America* (1968) is a broad, comprehensive history that deals with North and South America and provides much detail without being tedious. It is a logical starting point for further study. Frederick Katz's *The Ancient Civilizations of the Americas* (1972) is now somewhat out of date, but it still provides the best overall survey that compares Mesoamerica and Peru. It traces the rise of civilization in both areas.

The literature on the Aztecs is growing rapidly. Sahagún's Florentine Codex: *The General History of the Things of New Spain,* Charles Dibble and Arthur J. O. Anderson, eds. and trans., II vols. (1950–1968) is a fundamental source. A good overview is Jacques Soustelle's *Daily Life of the Aztecs* (1961), but more recent is Frances Berdan's *The Aztecs of Central Mexico: An Imperial Society* (1982). Miguel Leon-Portilla's *Aztec Thought and Culture* (1963) deals with religion and philosophy in a sympathetic way. Burr Cartwright Brundage has traced the history of the Aztec rise in several books such as *A Rain of Darts* (1972); his *The Jade Steps* (1985) provides a good analysis of religion. Nigel Davies's *The Aztec Empire* (1987) is a political and social analysis. Susan D. Gillespie's *The Aztec Kings* (1989) views Aztec history in terms of myth.

On Peru, a good overview through solid scholarly articles is provided in Richard W. Keatinge, ed., *Peruvian Prehistory* (1988). The article on Inca archaeology by Craig Morris is especially useful. Alfred Metraux's *The History of the Incas* (1970) is an older but still useful and very readable book. John Murra's *The Economic Organization of the Inca State* (1980) is a classic that has influenced much thinking about the Incas. J. Hyslop's *The Inka Road System* (1984) examines the building and function of the road network. The series of essays in John V. Murra, Nathan Wachtel, and Jacques Revel, eds., *Anthropological History of Andean Polities* (1986) shows how new approaches in ethnohistory are deepening our understanding of Inca society. Interesting social history is now being done. Irene Silverblatt's *Moon, Sun, and Witches: Gender Ideologies and Class in Inca and Colonial Peru* (1987) is a controversial book on the position of women before, during, and after the Inca rise to power.

From a comparative perspective is Geoffrey W. Conrad's and Arthur A. Demerest's *Religion and Empire: The Dynamics of Aztec and Inca Expansionism* (1984). These two archaeologists compare the political systems of the two empires and the motivations for expansion. The authors find more similarities than differences. Excellent studies on specific themes on Mexico and Peru are found in George A. Collier, et al., eds., *The Inca and Aztec States, 1400–1800* (1982).

Credits

Page 4 Reprinted from *Life: Introduction to Biology*, 3rd ed., by Beck, Liem & Simpson © 1991/Reprinted by permission HarperCollins Publishers, Inc.; **5** Musée de L'Homme, Paris; **9** British Crown Copyright, reproduced by permission of The Department of Environment; **11** Encyclopaedia Universalis; **19** Kazuyoshi Nomachi/Pacific Press Service; **20** Federal Department of Antiquities, Nigeria; **26** Hirmer Fotoarchiv, Munich; **29** Hirmer Fotoarchiv, Munich; **34** George Holton/Photo Researchers; **35** The Metropolitan Museum of Art, Rogers Fund, 1931 (31.3.157); **45** Borroemo/Art Resource, NY; **46** Archaeological Museum, Mohenjo Daro; **49** Courtesy of The Cultural Relics Bureau, Beijing and The Metropolitan Museum of Art; **55** D. Donne Bryant Stock/Art Resource, NY; **61** The Cleveland Museum of Art, Purchase from the J. H. Wade Fund, 30.331; **64** From Percy Brown's *Indian Architecture: Buddhist and Hindu Period.* Published by D. B. Taraporevala Sons & Co., Ltd., Bombay; **67** Copyright British Museum; **74** Government of India Tourist Office; **78** Eliot Elisofon, *Life* Magazine ©Time Inc.; **79** Jehangir Gazdar/Woodfin Camp & Associates; **90** Seth Joel/Laurie Platt Winfrey, Inc.; **93** The Granger Collection, New York; **101** Hirmer Fotoarchiv, Munich; **103** Copyright British Museum; **105** Scala/Art Resource, NY; **108** Copyright British Museum; **114** © bpk, Antikensammlung, Berlin; **115** The Metropolitan Museum of Art, Fletcher Fund, 1931 (31.11.10); **119** The Metropolitan Museum of Art, Rogers Fund, 1952 (52.11.4); **121** Hirmer Fotoarchiv, Munich; **126** The Metropolitan Museum of Art, Rogers Fund, 1911 (11.90); **135** Bibliothèque Nationale, Paris; **137** Shell Photographic Unit, London; **140** Giraudon/Art Resource, NY; **141** Carbone & Danno, Naples; **142** Alinari/Art Resource, NY; **143** Romische-Germanisches Zentralmuseum Mainz; **150** Erich Lessing/Art Resource, NY; **152** Alinari/Art Resource, NY; **156** Alinari/Art Resource, NY; **157** Alinari/Art Resource, NY; **159** Werner Forman Archive; **163** ©Photo RMN; **169** The British Library; **172** Spencer Collection/New York Public Library, Astor, Lenox and Tilden Foundations; **173** Courtesy of the Freer Gallery of Art, Smithsonian Institution, Washington, D.C.; **180** The British Library; **183** YAN; **189** The Granger Collection, New York; **199** Floyd Norgaard/Ric Ergenbright Photography; **202** SuperStock, Inc.; **203** The British Library; **209** Lent by the Guennol Collection, Courtesy The Brooklyn Museum; **211** Authenticated News International; **221** British Library, London/Art Resource, NY; **228** The Granger Collection, New York; **233** Tokyo National Museum; **236** Werner Forman Archive; **239** Courtesy of the Freer Gallery of Art, Smithsonian Institution, Washington, D.C.; **240** National Museum of Korea, Seoul; **243** Tony Stone Images; **253** Corbis-Bettmann Archive; **254** Wan-go Weng Archive; **255** Bibliothèque Nationale, Paris; **257** The Metropolitan Museum of Art, Gift of Mrs. Edward S. Harkness, 1947 (47.81.1x); **261** The Granger Collection, New York; **273** Alinari/Art Resource, NY; **274** Biblioteca Nacional, Madrid; **277** Erich Lessing/Art Resource, NY; **278** From *Miniatures Armeniennes*, ©1960 Editions Cercle d'Art, Paris; **280** © bpk, Staatsbibliothek, Berlin; **282** Biblioteca Nacional, Madrid; **283** Novosti Press Agency; **288** Österreichische Nationalbibliothek, Vienna; **292** Bibliotheek der Rijksuniversiteit, Utrecht; **296** The British Library; **299** Bodleian Library, Oxford MS Bodl. 264, fol. 218r; **301** The British Library; **303** Larousse; **307** Lambeth Palace Library; **311** The Metropolitan Museum of Art, The Cloister Collection, 1969 (69.86); **312** Bibliothèque Nationale, Paris; **316** National Library of the Czech Republic, Prague: University Library; **318** The British Library; **323** Peter Menzel; **326** Scala/Art Resource, NY; **328** Biblioteca Medicea Laurenziana, Florence; **329** Instituto Nacional de Antropologia e Historia; **330** Courtesy of the Newberry Library, Chicago; **335** Ric Ergenbright Photography; **337** American History Division/New York Public Library, Astor, Lenox and Tilden Foundations.

Index

A

K

L

M

N

O

S